D0872370

THE
AFRICAN QUEST
FOR FREEDOM
AND
IDENTITY

CAMEROONIAN WRITING
AND THE NATIONAL
EXPERIENCE

RICHARD BJORNSON

INDIANA UNIVERSITY PRESS
Bloomington and Indianapolis

The paper used in this publication meets the minimum requirements
of American National Standard for Information Sciences—Perma-
nence of Paper for Printed Library Materials, ANSI Z39.48–1984.
∞™

Manufactured in the United States of America

Library of Congress Cataloging-in-Publication Data

Bjornson, Richard.
The African quest for freedom and identity : Cameroonian writing
and the national experience / Richard Bjornson.
p.   cm.
Includes index.
ISBN 0–253–31194–2 (cloth : alk. paper)
1. Cameroon literature (French)—History and criticism.
2. National liberation movements in literature.   3. Cameroon
literature—History and criticism.   4. National liberation
movements—Cameroon.   5. Cameroon—Politics and government.
6. Nationalism in literature.   7. Nationalism—Cameroon.   I. Title.
PQ3988.5.C27B55   1991
840.9′96711—dc20   90–39423
CIP

1   2   3   4   5   95   94   93   92   91

CONTENTS

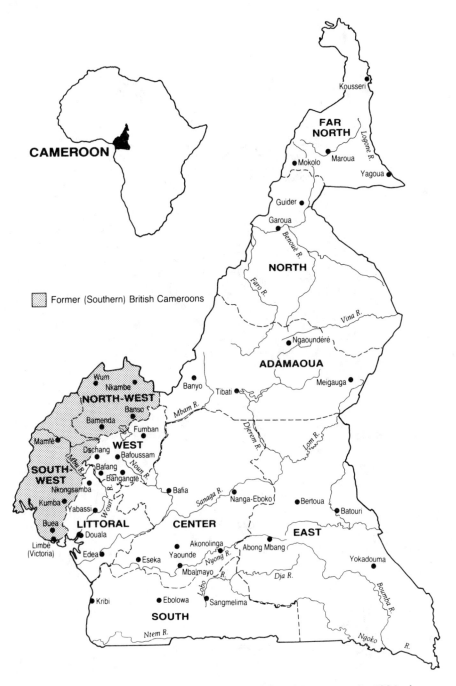

Map 1. Major cities and administrative divisions of Cameroon. In 1984, the former Center-South was divided into two provinces, and the former Northern province was divided into three provinces. (Map by Yvonne Holsinger)

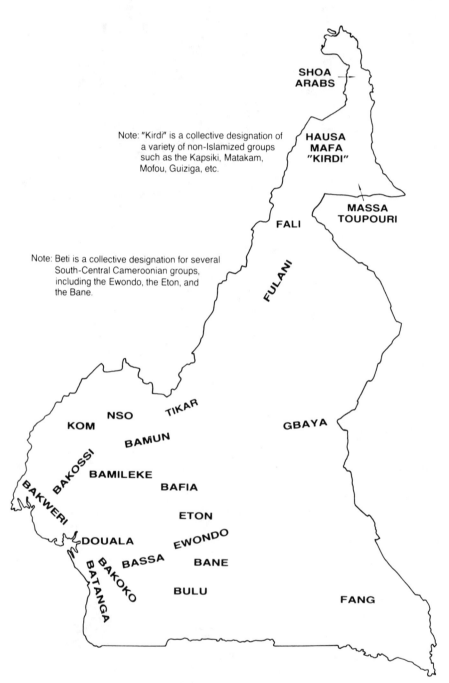

Map 2. Principal ethnic groups in Cameroon.

PREFACE

The African Quest for Freedom and Identity has taken shape over a number of years. It is essentially an attempt to comprehend the birth and early evolution of a literate national culture in one African country—Cameroon. Such an enterprise would hardly have been possible without the generosity of many Cameroonians who shared with me their perspectives on the literature and society of their country. I regard this book as part of an ongoing dialogue with them, and if it stimulates others to write about the sorts of problems I have raised, I shall feel that my own efforts have been richly rewarded.

No book is without its biases, and I must admit that my own sympathies lie with Cameroonians who have courageously pursued the quest for freedom and identity in the face of pressures for conformity to some official version of the truth, whether proclaimed by colonial administrations or by the Cameroonian governments that succeeded them. If I condemn the repressive measures that have been imposed on such people, I do so in the belief that freedom of expression is a fundamental human right. *The African Quest for Freedom and Identity* is the history of one people's attempt to exercise that right.

It would be impossible to mention everyone who has helped me during the course of my work on Cameroon, but I would like to thank some of them by name. In particular, I have benefited from conversations and interviews with René Philombe, Bernard Fonlon, Marcien Towa, William Etekiia Mbumua, Joseph Charles Doumba, Samuel-Martin Eno Belinga, François Sengat-Kuo, Patrice Ndedi Penda, Alexandre Kum'a Ndumbe III, Guillaume Oyono-Mbia, Hubert Mono Ndjana, Jeanne Ngo Mai, Adamou Ndam Njoya, Rabiatou Njoya, Rémy Medou Mvomo, Bassek ba Kobhio, Charles Henry Bebbe, Buma Kor, Paul Dakeyo, Fernando D'Almeida, Jean Dihang, René Douala Bell, Elolongue Epanya Yondo, Jacques Fame Ndongo, Valère Epée, Simon Mpondo, François-Borgia Marie Evembe, Basile-Juléat Fouda, Patrice Kayo, Henry de Julliot, François de Gastines, Patrick Sam-Kubam, David Kemzeu, Thérèse Kuoh-Moukouri, Jacques Kuoh-Moukouri, Werewere Liking, Sankie Maimo, Marie-Charlotte Mbarga, Jean Mfoulou, Bidoung Mkpatt, Pabe Mongo, Isaac Monthé, Léopold Moumé Etia, Albert Mukong, Engelbert Mveng, Marcel Mvondo II, Désiré Naha, Bernard Nanga, Timothée Ndzagaap, Joseph Ngongwikuo, Christophe Nguedam, Ebenezer Njoh-Mouelle, Jean-Paul Nyunaï, Jean-Baptiste Obama, James Oto, Louis-Marie Pouka M'Bague, Simon Rifoé, René Simo, Kume Tale, Vroumsia Tchinaye, Jean Zoa, and Abel Zomo Bem.

I would also like to express my appreciation to scholars who have generously shared their insights and research materials with me: Steve Arnold, Ken Harrow, Karen Keim, Lilyan Kesteloot, Claire Dehon, Eloise Brière, Fred Michelman, Richard Joseph, David Gardinier, Wolfgang Zimmer, Betty Taska, Curtis Schade, Phil Noss, and Milt Krieger. In this regard, I owe a special debt of gratitude to Victor LeVine, whose friendship, encouragement, and advice have helped me in countless ways. My friend and colleague Abiola Irele has also provided me with invaluable counsel. To both of them as well as to Valentin Mudimbe, Mary Wolf, Gene Holland, Marilyn Waldman, János Riesz, Hans-Jürgen Lüsebrink, and Josef Gugler, I am grateful for constructive criticisms on earlier manuscript versions of the book or parts of it. Librarians Mette Shayne, Ulla Schild, Peter Chateh, and Eleanor Daniel facilitated my search for hard-to-find materials. Gisela Tschoungi, Thérèse Sita Bella, Gerard Markoff, David Weir, James DeCou, Jerry Prillaman, John Lambo, Simon-Pierre Issock, Christine Djockua, Kitts Mbeboh, Josaphat Kubayanda, Bernth Lindfors, John Sekora, Bob Rehder, Germaine Brée, Isaac Mowoe, Charles Long, James Olney, G. Micheal Riley, and Aija Bjornson also contributed in a variety of ways.

A Fulbright Special Research Award enabled me to collect materials in Cameroon, and a grant from the National Humanities Center gave me the opportunity to reflect on the broader issues of literate culture and the national experience in Africa. Generous support from the College of Humanities at The Ohio State University has made it possible for me to complete many stages of my work on Cameroon, including the publication of this book in its present form.

Earlier versions of materials contained in *The African Quest for Freedom and Identity* have been published in *Komparatistische Hefte*, *Festschrift Karl Hoffmanns*, *African Literature: Retrospectives and Perspectives*, and *Semper Aliquid Novi: Littérature comparée et littératures d'Afrique*. They are published here with the kind permission of the editors of those publications.

INTRODUCTION

Africa has experienced profound changes since the Second World War. European colonial empires have collapsed, and a welter of nation-states has arisen in their place. Ethnically diverse rural societies with complex oral traditions have been transformed by the spread of formal schooling, the introduction of advanced technologies, and the rapid growth of cities. Substantial segments of the population have adopted nontraditional outlooks and aspirations. One of the most far-reaching results of the modernization process has been the emergence of literate cultures in the recently independent countries of Africa. As in other parts of the world, literate culture has played a crucial role in fostering a heightened sense of national consciousness because it has helped establish the shared references by means of which people recognize their participation in a specific universe of discourse. At the same time, the works of individual writers and the mosaic of world views they express mirror the specific social and cultural realities that characterize the countries in which they originated.

The Republic of Cameroon provides an excellent example of this process. Although its history during the colonial and postcolonial periods parallels that of other African countries, the circumstances under which its institutions came into being and the uniqueness of its ethnic composition have produced a society with its own distinctive set of cultural references. Confronted by a particular set of historical circumstances, several generations of Cameroonian writers have created a detailed record of issues that have preoccupied the country's literate population. Among the most important of these issues are the desire for freedom from various forms of oppression and the need to forge a viable sense of individual and collective identity. *The African Quest for Freedom and Identity* surveys the way in which these issues have been treated in a broad spectrum of works by Cameroonian writers. At the same time, it seeks to define the universe of discourse in which a sense of Cameroonian national consciousness has gradually taken shape.

The term *universe of discourse* refers to the rules, procedures, assumptions, and conventional meanings that permit verbal communication among individuals from the same community of language users. Several discourse communities may exist in the same country, and a single individual may belong to more than one of them, as in the case of Africans who speak to other members of their ethnic group in an African language but conduct formal transactions in a European tongue. Discourse communities can also extend across national frontiers. If common interests, aspirations, and cultural affinities are sufficiently strong, they may even develop among speakers of different languages, as has occurred with regard to the concept of an African identity that transcends regional differences. The fact that a universe of discourse exists within a particular community of language users does not imply uniformity of opinion. On the contrary, it provides people with the verbal tools they need in order to articulate their differences. A background of generally accepted meanings and meaning-producing techniques allows them to agree or disagree with one another.

In this sense, discourse is a cultural practice that constantly interacts with the nondiscursive (or nonverbal) cultural practices that constitute social, economic, and political life within the community. Discourse draws its significance from these other spheres of human activity while at the same time determining much of the significance that is attached to them. As a part of the culture-specific apparatus for making sense of the world, it enables people to conceptualize goals and ways of pursuing them, although the goals themselves may well have originated as a result of political or economic motives. For example, the stereotyped images of Africa that served to justify European exploitation of the continent during the colonial era belonged to a European universe of discourse that facilitated countless individual projects designed to enrich Europeans and enhance their power over others. However, once this universe of discourse was assimilated by Africans, it became the ground upon which they formulated their own aspirations for freedom and a viable sense of identity.

To comprehend the functioning of concepts such as freedom and identity within any universe of discourse, one must relate them to the historical context in which they interact with a variety of nonverbal cultural practices. In communities with literate cultures, the availability of written texts offers the scholar an opportunity to examine how these concepts have impinged on the world views of many different individuals. Like archeologists, scholars can probe the fragmentary evidence at their disposal to decipher its meaning and to reconstruct a composite image of the society from which it came. In the case of Cameroon, a substantial corpus of writings has been published during the past half-century. When placed in relationship to the country's institutions, its social and political history, and its economic development, these writings cast considerable light upon the nature of the emerging Cameroonian national community.

In Africa, as elsewhere, people do not identify only with national communities. Many regard themselves primarily as members of ethnic groups, whereas others insist that all Africans belong to the same community. The written literatures that have evolved in Africa during the past fifty years can certainly be analyzed within the context of these implicit reading communities. Studies of Yoruba, Swahili, Shona, Hausa, Xhosa, Zulu, Gikuyu, and other African-language literatures reveal the way in which networks of shared references link together members of linguistic communities whose frontiers transcend contemporary political boundaries. Illuminating research has also been done on the elements of discourse that characterize European-language works written by people from a single ethnic group such as the Igbo in Nigeria, the Wolof in Senegal, and the Beti in Cameroon.

At the same time, African literary scholarship has, until recently, tended to treat writing from the entire continent as part of a single tradition. Negritude and other authenticity movements provided a rationale for this tendency, which was reinforced by the recognition of common features in the belief systems of different ethnic groups, parallels in the history of colonization throughout the continent, and similarities in the sorts of societies that emerged in different parts of Africa after independence. Another factor that encourages a global approach to African literature is the existence of multinational publishing firms that distribute the same books to many different countries. Formal and informal networks link writers and scholars from across the continent, and school reading lists in Africa generally include works by authors from a variety of national backgrounds. Under such circumstances, it is not surprising that the most widely read books about African literature are general introductions that discuss a diverse collection of works from different countries. Just as studies of ethnic particularity have produced valuable insights into the nature of African writing, these general studies of African literature have identified common characteristics in works from across the continent and drawn attention to the explosion of literary creativity that has been taking place there since the early 1950s.

Focusing on the national community as a locus of literate activity in Africa is not an alternative to ethnically based or global approaches. On the contrary, such an orientation complements them by providing a sociopolitical context for the universes of discourse that have made possible the emergence of many African literatures in their present forms. The evolution of independent countries in Africa has followed patterns that can also be discerned in other parts of the world. Among these patterns is a growing popular awareness of the need to address the concrete problems of development within the boundaries of existing nation-states. As institutional structures become established in many of these countries, a national discourse begins to take shape, and the people of one country come to share with each other a set of reference points unfamiliar to people from other countries. A detailed record of these reference points exists in the writings of individuals from these countries, and an incipient sense of national consciousness is clearly apparent in this record.

Within the African context, national consciousness nearly always involves some attempt to reconcile the demands of modernization with the cultural and sociopolitical realities of people living within a specific geographically defined area. Paradoxically, modernization has produced both a heightened awareness of individual identity and a growth in the power of the state to control the activities of individuals. In fact, contemporary African literature is often marked by a tension between these two tendencies. This tension derives in part from the acceptance of a concept of the state that has been evolving in the Western world since the sixteenth century—a concept inherited by African countries at the moment of independence. In theory, this concept assumes that the success of a state is contingent upon the capacity of its citizens to realize their potential as individuals. In practice, the modern state has often restricted the individual's right to self-realization on the pretext of pursuing a greater social good. In reality, such restrictions usually serve the interests of a small privileged class.

In any case, concepts of individual identity are central to the discourse that has evolved in most African countries, and the practice of writing has helped transform these concepts into models for the definition of selfhood in contemporary African society. The fact that authors sign their work reinforces the assumption that individuals have the right to take credit for the words they commit to writing. By the same token, authors must also assume responsibility for the ideas they express—a grave responsibility in countries where the state does not tolerate dissenting opinions. By recording a variety of real and imaginary attempts to define the individual self, writers in a country such as Cameroon also bear witness to the ways in which conventional concepts like identity have become part of that country's discourse.

As the works of these writers demonstrate, however, individualism has both positive and negative connotations in the contemporary African context. One of the most common themes in Cameroonian written literature is the individual's quest for freedom to develop a personally satisfying identity in the face of outmoded traditional practices or corrupt modern institutions that erect barriers to the realization of his or her aspirations. At the same time, Cameroonian writers have usually blamed acquisitive individualism (and the moral blindness it engenders) for the malaise that afflicts their society. The spiritual deadness and isolation depicted in many recent works by Cameroonian authors also characterizes modern literatures from other parts of the world. But in an African setting, such qualities are thrust into stark contrast with the communal solidarity and sense of harmony with nature that these authors tend to associate with traditional ethnic practices. In fact, they often cultivate idealized images of traditional society as a means of criticizing the corrupt nature of the modern world. Reflecting a profound ambivalence toward the rise of individualism, Cameroonian writers have frequently opted for a hybrid definition of the self. The resultant syntheses of modern and traditional values suggest that the claims of competing identity concepts are capable of being reconciled for individuals as well as for the nation.

In Cameroon, as elsewhere in Africa, the quest for a viable identity has unquestionably been a dominant concern for writers and intellectuals. Inextricably linked with this concern is their preoccupation with freedom. The most acculturated writers of the colonial period espoused European values as a means of escaping from traditional customs that they had come to regard as ignorant and barbarous. Others proclaimed the need for Cameroonians to liberate themselves from a European dominance that prevented them from living according to their own conceptions of themselves. Since independence, the desire to be free from social, cultural, economic, and political constraints has been expressed in many ways. The nature of this desire varies widely from writer to writer, but it is nearly always present in one form or another. In the chapters that follow, I propose to examine how the concept of freedom functions in the universe of discourse upon which these writers drew.

Each of their works is but a partial realization of the Cameroonian universe of discourse, but when viewed within the context of a national literate culture, it helps illustrate how concepts such as freedom and individual identity come to be shared by large numbers of people. Such concepts obviously do not have the same semantic content whenever they appear in written texts. On the contrary, the universe of discourse in which these texts participate is characterized by a perpetual conflict among competing interpretations of such concepts. During the colonial period in Cameroon, for example, the overwhelming majority of people who learned to read and write had been educated in Christian mission schools. The moral idealism they absorbed in these schools often remained an integral part of their attitudes toward life, even if they themselves had ceased to be practicing Christians. However, this moral idealism found expression in a variety of different world views, ranging from those based upon an unquestioning acceptance of Eurocentric cultural assumptions, through those that sought to reconcile opposing ideologies, to those that repudiated the entire colonialist enterprise as inherently unjust.

Although a broad spectrum of world views is present in writings by individual Cameroonians, the writings themselves tend to address the same sets of problems and possibilities. In fact, the political history of the country might well be explained in terms of a dialectic between conflicting visions of national destiny. The Cameroonian situation was complicated by the fact that the area had originally been claimed as a protectorate by the Germans in the 1880s and then divided into French and British mandate territories under a League of Nations dispensation after the First World War. Resistance to the French colonial presence coalesced around a radical nationalist movement and its charismatic leader, Ruben Um Nyobé, during the late 1940s and early 1950s, by which time the two Cameroons had become United Nations trust territories. According to United Nations policy, trusteeship status implied an evolution toward eventual self-government. In conjunction with the rise of anticolonial sentiment throughout the world, the possibility of self-governance stimulated the emergence of a new political discourse in both territories. For example, the vision of national destiny popularized by Um Nyobé included independence and a democratic, socialist form of government for a reunified Cameroon. Adamantly opposed to this vision were the colonial administration and the conservative Cameroonian politicians who held out the promise of progress and prosperity within an enlightened French empire.

The conservative forces eventually triumphed. Um Nyobé was killed by French troops after the radical nationalist movement he headed had been declared illegal, and the country achieved independence under the French-supported government of Ahmadou Ahidjo. Nevertheless, Um Nyobé established the terms in which competing visions of Cameroonian national destiny would be framed by future generations. Suppressed by the colonial authorities and later by the Ahidjo government, his ideas were ultimately coopted by Ahidjo in formulating the "great idea" of national unity that served as the cornerstone of his own nation-building ideology.

By calling into question the rationale behind the entire colonialist project in Africa, Um Nyobé's vision of Cameroonian destiny was actually a plea for freedom from oppression and an attempt to define an identity concept that would reaffirm a Cameroonian sense of self-worth. At the same time that the

French were seeking to suppress the radical nationalist movement, the colonial administration was offering enhanced educational opportunities to young Cameroonians, many of whom became outspoken proponents of the nationalist position. Among them were the country's first major writers—writers who applied what they had learned in the French school system to discredit the stereotyped image of Africa so often cited by Europeans to justify their presence on the continent. These writers depicted the consequences of colonialist oppression from an African point of view. In doing so, they raised questions that constantly resurfaced in Cameroonian writings: How can traditional African values such as communal solidarity and harmony with nature be reconciled with European ideals of freedom and justice? What can be done to liberate people from an oppression they do not even recognize? Yet, although Cameroonian writers unequivocally condemned the practice of colonialism, they could not completely escape the ambiguities of their own situation, for they were, in a very real sense, products of the system they were attacking.

Shortly after the French trust territory became independent in 1960, the southern portion of the British Cameroons voted to federate with it, bringing into being the only African country that employs two European languages for official purposes. Although French-English bilingualism constitutes a unique dimension of the Cameroonian experience, it has also created serious problems of national integration. In particular, it has fostered a sense of resentment among anglophone Cameroonians who insist upon preserving a regional identity that they feel is being menaced by pressures exerted on them by the francophone majority. Ahidjo sought to capitalize on popular enthusiasm for independence and reunification by promoting the "great idea" of national construction, but his government's conception of national unity implied a rigorous centralization of power and the imposition of a new social order from above. In his view, for example, the government needed to shape a new national culture as a means of consolidating support for its political and economic goals.

The utopian vision implicit in the Ahidjo government's nation-building rhetoric became part of the country's universe of discourse during the early postcolonial period. Echoed in the writings of some Cameroonian authors, it serves as a dialectical counterpoint to the competing visions present in the works of others. Although the radical nationalist movement was silenced inside Cameroon after a long and bitter guerilla struggle, its vision of national independence remained alive in the writings of individuals disillusioned with the society that had come into being under Ahidjo. This vision competed with the one implicit in Ahidjo's "great idea," and the conflict between them played a dominant role in the evolution of the country's literate culture.

By the late 1960s, the Cameroonian government had embraced a Negritude-inspired cultural nationalism. For the politically conservative, predominantly Christian proponents of Negritude, such an ideological position offered Cameroonians the opportunity to integrate a spiritual dimension into the national consciousness while synthesizing a new identity from traditional and modern values. Opponents of Negritude viewed it as an obfuscation that distracted people from the need to address urgent practical problems in a rational, socially just manner. The Negritude debates that preoccupied the Cameroonian intellectual community during the late 1960s and early 1970s thus provided an arena for the clash of opposing views about the most appropriate way to define freedom and identity within the national context.

Against the background of such debates, a majority of the country's writers focused upon what they perceived as the social and psychological realities of Cameroonian society. Their interpretations of this society became a major component of the national universe of discourse. Convinced that a government should express the will of all the people, some of these writers attacked Ahidjo's nation-building rhetoric as a hypocritical sham that camouflaged the acquisition of wealth and power by members of a privileged class much like those in the process of consolidating their positions throughout Africa. The disparity between this rhetoric and the visibly corrupt behavior of the Cameroonian privileged class was exacerbated by the government's refusal to tolerate dissent. The perception of this disparity resulted in a widespread cynicism toward corruption, injustice, and the unfulfilled promise of independence.

Yet Cameroonians continued to believe in a better future, and those who expressed themselves in writing lent a variety of shapes to this belief. Christian humanists distanced themselves from the repressive policies of the government. They and others often proclaimed the need for a return to the moral and spiritual values they associated with traditional African society. Radical social critics, many of whom lived and published in exile, exposed the hypocrisy of the nation-building rhetoric and sought to raise people's consciousness by persuading them that they were being subjected to a neocolonialist system just as oppressive as the colonialist one that had preceded it.

In the discussion that follows, I propose to demonstrate how these interpretations of Cameroonian reality both drew upon an emergent national discourse and contributed to its evolution. To accomplish this goal, I have sought to examine the individual writings of Cameroonians within two contexts: the world views of the writers themselves and the constellation of cultural, political, and economic factors that govern relations of dominance and power in the Cameroonian state. I chose to focus upon the key concepts of freedom and identity because an understanding of how they function in the Cameroonian universe of discourse and an appreciation for the diversity of viewpoints projected into them can help decipher the complex written evidence of one African country's experience of nationhood. Such an enterprise will also, I hope, shed light upon the role of literate culture in the formation of other national societies in contemporary Africa and clarify the meaning of such terms as *national literature* and *national identity* in the African context.

THE_____
AFRICAN QUEST
FOR FREEDOM
AND
IDENTITY

CHAPTER

1

NATIONAL IDENTITY AND NATIONAL LITERATURES IN AFRICA

In the modern era it seems natural for the world to be divided into nations with sharply defined geographical boundaries. Everyone is presumed to be the citizen of some nation, and allegiance to the nation is often so strong that people are willing to die for its sake. Yet nationhood and nationalism as we understand them today are relatively recent phenomena, reflecting historical currents that initially surfaced in Europe and the Americas. Because these currents became intimately linked with a number of culture-specific assumptions about the nature and purpose of human social organization, the application of the nation-building model to non-Western societies has often produced a conflict between traditional belief systems in those societies and the contingencies of national development as prescribed by the model. Nowhere has this conflict been more apparent than in Africa. Thus, before examining the literature of Cameroon in relation to its sociopolitical context, we must reflect seriously upon the concept of nationhood and the extent to which it is legitimate for us to speak of nations in Africa.

The word *nation* derives from the Latin *nasci* (to be born) and originally designated people who were born in the same place. At medieval European universities, for example, it was used in reference to students from a particular region. With the breakup of the feudal order and a rapid expansion of trade, the national states that emerged in Renaissance Europe provided a mechanism for protecting the capital investments of the rising middle classes while preserving the social and legal prerogatives of the aristocracy. Machiavelli speculated brilliantly on the governance of what might be regarded as a national state, but it was not until the late eighteenth century that the word *nation* acquired the meaning generally associated with it today. Although Voltaire persisted in defining the nation only in terms of a self-conscious elite capable of influencing the intellectual and political movements that determine a people's destiny, other eighteenth-century thinkers and Rousseau in particular popularized the idea that a nation should express the collective will of all people living within its borders.

This conviction was based on the assumption that the universe is rationally organized and can be accurately apprehended by human beings who are free to act as they choose. By defining their own enlightened self-interest and acting according to it, the citizens of a community could presumably establish a harmonious social order capable of satisfying all their needs. This utopian ideal found expression in the American and French revolutions, which linked nationhood with progress and the collective will of populations living in a geographically bounded space. In both cases, people justified the overthrow of an existing political order on the basis of claims that they were defending basic human rights and seeking to implement universally valid laws of social organization. Although such claims actually reflected a specific set of historical circumstances, they came to be regarded as eternal verities that continue to sanction feelings of loyalty to the nations that emerged from this process. They also provided a model for other communities that desired to assert their independence from regimes that they felt were depriving them of their right to act in accordance with their own true identities as free peoples.

When the Napoleonic wars subordinated much of Europe to a unified system of administration and justice, the principles behind this system inspired many conquered cultural communities to proclaim their own national identities in opposition to French hegemony. By the mid-nineteenth century, these principles had become fairly widespread in Europe, and John Stuart Mill could declare that national identity corresponds to a people's consciousness that its citizens are bound together by shared sympathies that do not exist between themselves and any other people—sympathies that motivate their desire to live under the same government while encouraging them to work together for the common welfare. As industrialization spread through Europe, the idea of the nation became even more strongly identified with progress because the bureaucratic organization of the nation-state facilitated the building of transportation and communication networks, the enactment of uniform laws, and the establishment of broad-based educational systems, all of which created favorable conditions for further industrialization. As political leaders and commercial entrepreneurs recognized the advantages of this situation for themselves, nationalism (which had generally been a popular, progressive movement for independence from "foreign" dominance during the early nineteenth century) often evolved into a conservative ideology that supported the unequal distribution of wealth while appealing to feelings of national pride as a means of maintaining the status quo.[1]

By the middle of the twentieth century, as most African countries acceded to independence, the idea of the nation had become generally accepted as a universal form of sociopolitical organization. The League of Nations and the United Nations had given juridical status to the assumption that the world should be apportioned into discrete political units that reflect the aspirations of the people living within their borders. This concept of nationhood had evolved in Europe and the Americas during the previous century and a half, and although it was not designed for the ethnically pluralistic societies that became independent within the boundaries of former colonial territories, most African leaders quickly espoused the principal tenets associated with it—political autonomy, national unity, economic development, modernization, mass education, and an ideology that conflates government policy with the will and welfare of the people. The promulgation of this concept unquestionably influenced the way Africans define themselves, for despite worsening economic conditions and widespread scepticism about the rhetoric of nation building, the people in most African countries have acquired the consciousness of belonging to a particular nation.[2]

However, African countries achieved their independence under different circumstances from those that prevailed in eighteenth- and nineteenth-century Europe, and the nature of an individual African's allegiance to them reflects these differences. In most cases, European nationalism crystallized around an existing cultural or linguistic community that desired to free itself from foreign domination so that it could fulfill what it perceived to be its unique historic destiny. The shared language or culture became a central reference point in the definition of individual identity because it assured people of their inclusion in the national group. In contrast, nearly all African states inherited a multiplicity of linguistic and ethnic communities. When the appeal for a new sense of national identity was made, it was usually couched in the language of the former colonizer and explained in terms that would have been equally applicable in most other parts of the continent. As a result, many Africans did not have a strong sense of attachment to the emergent nation in which they had been born. Most continued to identify primarily with their own ethnic groups, whereas an influential minority were committed to the ideal of pan-African unity. The initial cohesiveness that sustained national identity in Europe was thus absent in many African countries at the moment of independence.

Nevertheless, a sense of national identity is evolving in many of these countries, and the reasons behind this development reflect the same conditions that fostered the rise of nations and nationalisms in other parts of the world. The discovery of printing played a crucial role in preparing the way for nationalistic movements in Europe. In conjunction with Bible translations into vernacular languages and a marked increase in literacy, the proliferation of printing firms intent upon exploiting new markets helped to create coherent linguistic communities with shared points of reference. Under these circumstances, printing standardized vernacular languages by privileging some dialectal variants and relegating others to oblivion. By implicitly challenging the myth of an elite language that gave scribes and priests special access to the truth, it also promoted a new faith in the capacity of individuals to make their own judgments. By giving permanent form to folk materials, by recording history from a culture-specific perspective, by reproducing the works of local writers, and by promoting newspapers, journals, and almanacs, the vernacular print culture of Europe created reading audiences that formed the basis for the cultural communities that later insisted upon becoming independent nations.³ In other words, printing enabled a national literate discourse to come into being.

The wave of nationalist movements in the Americas during the late eighteenth and early nineteenth centuries took a somewhat different form, but they too were linked with communities that came into being when local print cultures established the shared vocabulary that enabled people to conceive of themselves as a group with common interests and values. Such groups did not question the use of Spanish or English, and they often retained the cultural values of their European forebears; in fact, the revolt against imperial authority was generally led by the literate elites who felt they had been excluded from the full exercise of rights and privileges they would have enjoyed if they had been living in the mother country. But the nations that emerged from these movements gradually acquired their own myths, their own histories, their own sets of shared reference points.

With increasing industrialization, however, the role of print culture began to play a quite different role with regard to nationalist sentiment in Europe and the Americas. By the late nineteenth century, nationalism had become the rallying cry of politically conservative forces in many countries of the Western world. It served as a justification for maintaining the existing relations of wealth and power. It idealized values that the privileged classes attributed to themselves. And for a handful of European nations, it provided a convenient rationale for the colonization of Africa and Asia. If a nation's culture is truly superior, they argued, that nation has a moral right to occupy underutilized portions of the world and to bring civilization to the people living there. In addition, colonies were viewed as a source of wealth and prestige at a time when European nations conceived of themselves as being in a state of relentless competition with each other; thus, the scramble for Africa that intensified during the last few decades of the nineteenth century was in large part an expression of the nationalistic mood that prevailed in Europe. To popularize this enterprise in the colonizing countries themselves, print culture was exploited to reinforce stereotyped notions about the inherent superiority of European civilization and the unregenerate primitiveness of Africans.

The absence of print cultures in Africa and the illiteracy of Africans lent support to such notions. However, the colonial administration, private trading firms, and Christian missions all needed at least some Africans who could use European languages so they might serve as auxiliaries and as intermediaries with the local populations. As literate Africans became more numerous, they grew increasingly aware of their ambiguous social status, which in some ways resembled that of the early nineteenth-century colonial elites in the Americas. Whatever their abilities and accomplishments might have been, they were denied the rights and privileges accorded to citizens of the mother country. At the same time, their situation was quite different from that of Latin Americans who prided themselves on their European backgrounds and cultivated few ties with indigenous languages and cultures. Educated Africans generally retained contact with their own ethnic communities, and as black people, they were subjected to the racial stereotyping that pervaded the culture they were in the process of assimilating.

As these educated Africans developed networks of communication among themselves, they gradually realized that European-language print culture could be adapted for their own purposes. On the one hand, they employed it to counter European denigrations of African culture and to assert the dignity of black humanity, thereby reinforcing the idea of an incipient pan-African community. In fact, personal and political links that extended across colonial boundaries proved to be a significant factor in the movement toward independence, particularly in francophone Africa. On the other hand, educated Africans exploited the colonizer's print culture to forge alliances with other educated Africans in the same colonies. By doing so, they helped create some of the historical, political, and cultural referents that would later serve as the basis for a sense of national identity. In both cases, Africans skilled in the use of written language were clearly demonstrating the falsity of myths about African primitivism. They were also doing what earlier nationalists had done: they were using the written word to proclaim their freedom and assert their right to a collective identity in accordance with their own system of values.

Yet when independence did come to most African states after 1956, it seldom fulfilled the high expectations that had been aroused by its proponents. There are a variety of reasons for the widespread disillusionment that ensued, but although the postcolonial situation differs from one part of Africa to another, most African countries were obliged to confront a similar set of problems. They tended to be ethnically pluralistic societies that were further fragmented by religious, political, and regional differences.[4] Drawing upon Western models of nationhood, the first governments in these countries generally addressed this situation by espousing an ideology of national unity and economic development. In conjunction with radio and later television, print culture enabled them to promote this ideology by identifying it with the pursuit of utopian ideals, the rewriting of history, the preservation of traditional values, and the success of sporting teams in international competitions. Even writers and intellectuals who criticized the regimes in power contributed to the reservoir of allusions that ultimately came to be shared by the population at large.

For those who live in these countries, one of the most obvious facts is often a glaring disparity between the official nation-building rhetoric and the reality of political practice. Rather than diminishing ethnic rivalry, many African governments exacerbated it through favoritism and the cultivation of ethnically based patronage systems. Rather than fostering African languages and cultural values, they brought into being a system that perpetuated the language and cultural values of the former colonizer. Rather than contributing to the common welfare, ruling elites often collaborated with foreign interests to exploit local resources, enriching themselves at the same time that living conditions deteriorated for a majority of the country's population. The social and financial costs of corruption, coups, inefficient management, and internecine struggles have been enormous. Yet even under such circumstances a sense of national identity has begun to evolve in most African countries, and print culture has been a crucial enabling factor in this development.

The written word is essential to this process in two ways. First, it allows people to store and disseminate vast amounts of information in standardized form. Even illiterate individuals gain access to this information by talking with others or by listening to radio and television broadcasts that are dependent upon scripts. Merely being subject to the legal, political, and fiscal institutions of the state entails a rudimentary awareness of the government's rationale for decisions it takes in the name of the people. Some of this information is official rhetoric—the idealized image of a head of state, highly selective accounts of the country's history, utopian projections of the future, exhortations to support national construction. But the publication of newspapers, folk materials, imaginative literature, academic discourse, and even oppositional political tracts also contributes to the storehouse of reference points that, shared by many people throughout the country, constitute a universe of discourse that makes a sense of national identity possible.[5]

Second, nearly all African countries have proclaimed their commitment to modernization, which assumes widespread literacy and specialization. In contrast to the social organization of traditional ethnic groups, this specialization implies an indifference to the personal identity of the individual who holds any given position. Jobholders in modern nations are at least theoretically interchangeable as long as they possess the necessary competence to perform the tasks assigned to them. In practice, of course, this principle is often ignored, but to the extent that people exploit personal relationships to acquire positions for which they lack qualifications, the country will jeopardize the modernization necessary to satisfy the needs of a population whose expectations have been raised by the nation-building rhetoric.

To acquire a pool of individuals with the bureaucratic and technical skills to make a modern society function efficiently, most African countries have expanded their school systems and standardized the curricula. As literacy increases, more and more people are exposed to a set of cultural references that they share with others who have attended school and who may well not be members of the same ethnic group. Together, these individuals constitute a potential reading audience for anything that is published by their fellow countrymen, and mass media disseminate the products of literate culture to an even wider audience. Although people never encounter most other members of the potential reading audience in their countries, an implicit awareness of their existence heightens the conviction that one belongs to a larger national community that transcends ethnic, regional, or political differences. In the schools and elsewhere, this conviction is reinforced by appeals to traditional values and historical precedents that are often unrelated to the modernization process. Such values and precedents might become part of the country's collective memory,[6] but they are always assembled in retrospect. The national identity they sustain is thus an artificial construction, and the community that it defines has invented itself during the course of its own historical evolution.[7] This is precisely what is happening in many African countries today.

Literary works are never the unmediated expressions of a national sentiment. They are always filtered through the consciousness of individual writers whose views of the world, although similar in their general outlines, have been influenced by idiosyncratic experiences. If the collective memory of a nation is a discursive space containing points of reference that are shared in varying degrees by members of an "imagined community," writers can draw upon these "reference points" in a multitude of oblique and veiled ways. After the works of these authors are published, they in turn become part of an ongoing dialectic that is continually taking place in the collective memory. Before speaking about national literatures, then, we must examine the mechanisms by means of which writers and intellectuals transform the raw materials suggested by their environments into fictional worlds that reflect the content of a people's collective memory, influence the course of its evolution, and extend its imaginative grasp of its own situatedness in the world.

The term *collective memory* is misleading insofar as it implies an amorphous body of information that exists independently of individual human consciousness. In reality, the collective memory of any group must perpetually be reconstituted by individuals as they mature into full-fledged members of the group. As the result of constant negotiations with their physical and cultural environments, these individuals develop relatively uniform conceptions about the nature of the world, but because each of them undergoes a slightly different set of experiences, no two views of the world will be absolutely identical; in fact, each individual has only a partial and often quite idiosyncratic awareness of what has been called the collective consciousness. Attitudes toward shared points of reference and interpretations of their meanings vary greatly. When we employ the term *collective memory*, therefore, we are referring to a broad spectrum of individual world views, beliefs, and assumptions.

All members of a national community are born with similar means of processing the information they receive through their senses, and they are confronted with the same basic problem of organizing and storing this information so they can subsequently draw upon it in making plans and setting goals. Like people everywhere, they have an urge to know, and the information they acquire in responding to this urge enables them to map their environment in a functional manner.[8] The mapping process continues throughout each person's life and contributes to the elaboration of a relatively stable but flexible image of the world, an image that defines, among other things, what a particular person regards as true or meaningful. This overall image of the world consists in part of schemas that can be applied to a variety of specific situations, allowing people to interpret their surroundings by filling in gaps left by fragmentary perceptions. These schemas can be expanded through the assimilation of new information, and they are often modified to accommodate perceptions or insights that invalidate previously held assumptions. The salient fact about any individual's overall image of the world is that it will always remain incomplete and schematic, no matter how elaborate it eventually becomes. Because there is no way to compare such images directly with the world itself, one cannot say that they are true in the sense that they correspond to what exists outside the human mind, although they may be more or less effective in permitting people to attain goals they set for themselves.

Within a given community, individual images of the world tend to be structurally similar because social interaction produces consensus about the structural properties of schemas and the inference procedures according to which schemas can be applied in the interpretation of sensory data.[9] In fact, the culture of such a community can be defined in terms of this consensus, which often maintains its stability over many generations. The conventionality of the schemas embedded in individual images of the world facilitates communication among members of the community and heightens their sense of a common identity, but it also predisposes them to accept without question many assumptions that they themselves have never verified. In everyday discourse, individuals assume they have understood an event when they have selected a schema with which to model it and formulated a set of propositions that would be regarded as adequate and acceptable to the community. What they have actually done is to regularize the event by bringing it into harmony with their own system of references. Their truth is thus not a function of objective reality, as they often claim, but rather a proposition that has been constructed and validated on the basis of largely conventional expectations.

Some notion of individual identity is central to any overall image of the world. This notion too is constructed as the result of ongoing interactions with the cultural and physical environment, and many of the schemas associated with it are highly conventional. A sense of national identity ultimately depends upon this notion and its relationship to other points of shared reference in the universe of discourse that is actualized in slightly different ways within the broad spectrum of world images held by actual members of a national community. In modern societies, written literature provides a remarkably accessible record of attempts to define the individual self. Within the African context, a careful examination of this record reveals the tensions and conflicts that have accompanied individual self-definition at a time when most countries were in a state of transition between ethnically based oral cultures and literate mass societies, between the overt oppression of colonialism and the disappointed expectations of independence. To address the full significance of the national literature question in Africa, we must therefore examine the spectrum of individual self-concepts that have been projected into works written by people from the same country.

When confronted by otherness, people are obliged to reflect upon their own identity, and nineteenth-century European imperialism thrust Africans into just such a confrontation. In traditional African societies, there were differences in the way individuals defined themselves, but all members of a given ethnic group tended to accept their places in a society they viewed as part of a larger cosmic order. However, the European intrusion superimposed a set of demeaning stereotypes upon Africans. In reality, Europeans were often projecting their own otherness, their own fears and fantasies, into their images of Africans as childlike innocents or savage barbarians. The technological superiority of Europeans and their organizational efficiency enabled them to dominate most of Africa, thereby calling into question the cosmic order upon which identity had been based in traditional society. European assumptions about the inherent intellectual inferiority of black people also served to sanction the blatant exploitation of Africans and the denigration of their value systems. Because the vast majority of Africans continued to live in rural areas during the colonial era, they continued to define themselves largely in traditional terms. Even the small number of educated elites who became literate in European languages and worked in the cities tended to maintain strong ties with their own ethnic groups. Yet it was among these elites that a self-conscious sense of identity began to emerge as early as the mid-nineteenth century. Edward Wilmot Blyden played a major role in this movement, which was also influenced by the awakening of black consciousness in America.

The response of these elites to the colonialist humiliation took two forms. Some educated Africans appropriated identity schemas from Europe and regarded themselves as individual human beings who deserved the right to realize themselves in the modern world. Others borrowed European modes of thought and categorization to construct new identity schemas based upon traditional African values and customs.[10] These schemas helped rehabilitate a menaced sense of African dignity and nurtured feelings of pan-African solidarity. They also established an additional reference point with which Africans could identify in defining themselves. With increasing modernization, the growth of literacy, and the advent of political independence, Africans encountered a hierarchy of such reference points: the autonomous self, the ethnic group, the emergent state, and all of Africa. Many individuals were intensely loyal to an identity concept associated with a single level of the hierarchy, but most felt some allegiance to the other levels of identity as well. The consequence of this situation was a broad range of hybrid self-concepts that included elements of European and traditional African identity schemas in varying combinations. The hybridization of world views is not unusual. It has taken place in every part of the world. But it can create serious problems if components of the new world view remain in obvious conflict with each other, as has been the case in many parts of Africa.

For example, the modernization process that helped spawn the concept of nationhood also brings with it a cluster of assumptions that profoundly affect the way individuals conceive of themselves. But these assumptions have often been assimilated with considerable ambivalence by educated Africans. Although modernization is routinely advocated as a means of improving the conditions of people's lives and freeing them from economic dependency, it is also distrusted as a process that engenders vast disparities of wealth and subverts the cherished values of traditional societies. No aspect of modernization is more deeply implicated in this ambivalence than the doctrine of individualism.

When African states adopted models of social, political, and economic organization from the former colonizing powers, they were implicitly accepting a view of human nature that had gained currency in eighteenth- and nineteenth-century Europe. According to this view, each citizen has a set of motivations that are distinctively organized around an individual self. By acting rationally in pursuit of their own self-interest, such citizens are assumed to be promoting their individual and collective well-being. As rationality became linked with print culture and as the need for a literate work force grew, the idea that the evolution of every individual self should be channeled through a system of universal schooling achieved widespread acceptance.[11] In fact, people in Western society came to regard formal education as a prerequisite to individual success and the solution to most social problems. This faith in mass education and an underlying belief in the autonomous, rational self gradually permeated the societies of many African countries as they pursued the goal of modernization.

Individualism appealed to Africans on many counts. It was liberating in the sense that it offered them a new freedom of choice in areas that had in the past been governed by traditional customs or reserved for decisions by the elders. Younger educated Africans were particularly attracted to the prospect of choosing their own careers, selecting their own marriage partners, and enjoying the material benefits of modern technology. On the social level, the doctrine of individualism held out the promise of a guaranteed respect for human rights, the possibility for everyone to participate in the political decision-making process, and the hope for economic progress based on the rational behavior of citizens as workers and as consumers. In conjunction with the increased use of writing, individualism also fostered the emergence of a literature that reflects a new preoccupation with the self and its place in history. Authors asserted the uniqueness of their identities by signing their work; poetry and prose fiction focused upon problems of self-definition; histories reinforced the notion that individuals do participate in shaping their own destiny. In short, many Africans began to perceive themselves in terms of an identity schema that presupposes every person's right to self-realization. As an alternative to the restrictiveness of traditional society, this schema offered people a chance to emancipate themselves from the weight of the past, and by calling certain aspects of ethnic allegiance into question, it at least theoretically opened the way for individuals to identify more closely with the new states of Africa.

Yet individualism also has a darker side. Even in the Western world where it originated, people have associated it with alienation, vulgar materialism, and the spoliation of nature. Within the African context, individualism and its corollary, schooling in European languages, provide the impetus for the formation of a privileged class that increasingly enjoys the wealth, power, and status separating it from the majority of the population.[12] Many members of this class have adopted European lifestyles, and through corruption or collusion with foreign interests, they often reap financial benefits totally out of proportion with their contributions to society. Such a situation is demoralizing for large numbers of Africans who remain blocked in their aspirations for social advancement. The spiritual malaise that results from this debilitating cleavage of society is commonly attributed to the spread of a Western-style individualism that many people contrast unfavorably with traditional African values.

These values exist on two different planes. In actual ethnic communities, they continue to be lived unselfconsciously in a variety of ways. At the same time, proponents of authenticity movements such as Negritude have synthesized ideal sets of African values—emotivity, rhythm, a heightened sense of community, the primacy of force over matter, etc. In either case, traditional values can be regarded as responding to important human needs that would remain unsatisfied if the doctrine of individualism were to prevail throughout society.

The common factors in nearly all African discourse on this subject have been a preoccupation with identity and a desire for freedom from oppressive conditions or false constructions of reality. Frequently these concerns have coalesced with the urge to synthesize conflicting assumptions about human existence into new identity schemas that will, it is hoped, be simultaneously African and modern. For example, the Christian message brought to Africa by the early missionaries was one part of a European power-knowledge system that sanctioned the colonial occupation of Africa. At the same time, it introduced literacy, a universalistic conception of divine purpose, and elements of individualism into oral societies that tended to be communally oriented and ethnically particularistic in their religious practices. Although missionary discourse interacted in many different ways with local institutions in Africa, converts were often attracted to Christianity by the promise of a more satisfying self-image and by the hope of liberation from what they had been conditioned to regard as ignorance and superstition. During the history of Christian proselytism in Africa, there have been repeated attempts to reconcile these impulses with a reaffirmation of African values.

The acculturated Africans of the colonial period, the founders of the Negritude movement, the leaders of the anticolonialist struggle, the proponents of nation building, and the Marxist-influenced new philosophers have all been engaged in similar enterprises. Although reacting against different sorts of restraint and pursuing divergent goals, they have sought to satisfy their desire for freedom and a viable sense of identity within contexts profoundly influenced by the modernization process.

A revealing record of such projects is contained in the written literature that has been produced by African authors during the past fifty years. Some have described the quest for freedom and identity in a straightforward, expository manner. Others have projected it into the imagined worlds they have depicted in affective or figurative language. But in one form or another it is nearly always present in their works. The very act of writing implies an individual's assertion of the right to conceptualize goals of particular psychic significance and to seek their realization by adopting strategies drawn from his or her own image of the world. In the process of pursuing these strategies, writers leave traces of the identity schemas by means of which they situate themselves in the world.[13] Since many elements of these schemas are conventions shared with other members of the cultural and linguistic community to which individual writers belong, one index of the community's collective memory can be found in its written literature. As in the community at large, however, the overall images in which these schemas are embedded will vary considerably from one writer to another, obliging us to consider a spectrum of constantly evolving world views rather than a static set of beliefs, assumptions, and symbolic references that could be associated with a specific national identity.

If an urge to freedom and a concern for identity are implicit in the act of writing, they were greatly intensified in the African context by the historical circumstances under which print culture was introduced to the continent. During the colonial period, traditional customs were thought to be incompatible with modern civilization, and black people were, in general, regarded as intellectually backward. The language of high culture was the language of the European colonizer, and those who employed it for their own writing encountered two major obstacles. First, they had to overcome a gap between the expressive possibilities of their own languages and those of European languages that had evolved in response to a physically and culturally foreign environment. Second, they had to reconcile themselves with the fact that most people from their own part of the world were incapable of reading their works or even understanding the language in which they had been written; in fact, such works were generally more accessible to European reading audiences than to African ones. As a result of this situation, African writers who used European languages often found themselves in a state of intellectual exile, and it is in exile that one is continually challenged to define one's self in the face of an omnipresent otherness. By articulating a sense of their own identity, these writers were also expressing a desire to free themselves from the racial and cultural stereotypes that had been applied to their people.

After independence, the situation changed somewhat. Literacy in European languages increased to the point where there were sizeable potential reading audiences in many African countries. The publication of literature in African languages became more widespread.[14] Direct colonialist oppression had ceased, and the case for the dignity of black humanity had largely been made. Yet the language of the former colonizer tended to remain the vehicle of high culture in most African countries. With the rise of authoritarian governments, the institutionalization of neocolonialist practices, and increased poverty in many parts of Africa, blatant disparities continued to exist between the rhetoric of those in power and the reality perceived by the majority of their countrymen. Although most writers accepted the necessity of forging new identity concepts that would reconcile traditional values with the exigencies of modernization, there has been little consensus about the manner in which such a project might be realized. As a result, the identity question remains central in postcolonial

African literature, and the urge to freedom continues to be a dominant concern for contemporary African writers—freedom from economic necessity, freedom from oppressive political systems, freedom from outmoded stereotypes, and freedom to pursue goals of one's own choosing.

The texts produced by these writers contain a variety of materials culled from memories of real-life situations, fantasies, and readings of existing texts by other writers. Polyphonic in the sense that they embrace voices ranging from those found in African oral cultures to those characteristic of European written literatures, these texts generally conform to European genre expectations, but not always and not in all respects. Insofar as their meaning depends upon the same schemas that are used to model the real world, they embody a type of knowledge about that world. For all these reasons, such texts offer us a remarkable insight into the spectrum of hybrid world views that have been elaborated by literate Africans in response to the ambiguity of their historical situation. What gives specific form to their works, however, is the motivations that impelled them to write in the first place. In the case of many African writers, these motivations include the urge to be free and the desire to define who they are and what they might become if accorded the opportunity to realize themselves. When they create fictional worlds in their poetry, drama, and prose fiction, these worlds are frequently structured around such a quest for freedom and identity.

The conditions of this quest differ from one African country to another, and authors from any given country tend to draw upon the same materials and reference points. Thus, despite the proliferation of individual world views, the ensemble of texts from a single country is likely to share a common ground that is not present in the literary corpus of other African countries. Of course there are thematic and stylistic parallels that link literary works from different parts of the African continent, but as educational institutions and informal intellectual networks increasingly focus on what has been written by and about the citizens of a specific country, the awareness of a national literary culture begins to emerge, stimulating others to write texts that will also become part of that culture.

Popular consciousness of a national literary heritage is created only retrospectively as the schools teach a set body of works by the country's authors to successive generations of students.[15] The rise of a national literature is also generally accompanied by the rewriting of history to focus on the destiny of the national community. Reflecting the emergence of implicit reading alliances as the basis for a sense of national identity, both developments are part of the larger modernization process that fosters individualism and favors the nation-state as the most efficient form of political organization. Within this context, literary works are important, for by integrating the fragmentary, disjointed events of the phenomenal world into coherent texts, they become interpreters of that world, facilitating our comprehension of the human realities behind historical processes and preserving the spectrum of world views that are often obscured beneath the official rhetoric of nation building.

A sense of national identity is obviously related to the emergence of a national literature, but a national literature is never the direct expression of a national character or essence. On the contrary, it is always a disparate body of texts that reflect a variety of individual world views. Just as national identity depends upon the shared reference points and schemas that have been assimilated into these world views, the texts that make up a national literature draw upon them in diverse and often indirect ways.[16] Viewed from this perspective, the history of literary production in many African countries bears a distinct resemblance to the evolution of national literatures in Europe.

There the use of writing was generally restricted to a small group of literate elites who were concentrated in the courts and in the larger urban centers. Adopting one form of the current language and identifying it with high culture, they established implicit standards of taste, linguistic usage, and political morality. The language they used gradually became a norm that served to marginalize dialect and minority literatures, which often disappeared entirely. Retrospectively, national epics such as *El Cid*, the *Nibelungenlied*, the *Divine Comedy*, *Os Lusíades*, or the *Chanson de Roland* came to be regarded as expressions of idealized national values, and authors such as Petrarch, Cervantes, Molière, Goethe, and Shakespeare acquired status as representatives of the national consciousness, although they themselves had frequently borrowed from foreign sources or focused primarily on a small segment of the total population.

The rise of Protestantism accelerated the growth of national literatures by encouraging Bible translations into the languages actually spoken by the people. This enterprise was accompanied by the relatively rapid spread of print culture, which in turn fostered the publication of language-instruction manuals, almanacs, local histories, collections of folktales and proverbs, and works of imaginative literature. By the eighteenth century, the newspaper and the novel had emerged in many European countries, and they helped consolidate the implicit reading audiences that identified with specific nations and their literatures. Later, as national identity came to be taken for granted, the spectrum of individual world views expressed in European national literatures expanded considerably, and the linkage between literary expression and national sentiment became extremely diffuse.

Despite similarities between these developments in Europe and the emergence of literate traditions in African countries, however, there remains one significant difference. The emergence of national literatures in Europe was intimately linked with the rise of national languages, whereas much of modern African literature continues to be written in European languages. The reasons for this are obvious. During the colonial era, people soon realized that it was in their interest to learn the language of the colonizer, for a knowledge of French or English or Portuguese granted them access to the knowledge-power systems that had been imposed upon them. Those who became literate in these languages were well positioned to take advantage of the social and political institutions that evolved as African countries achieved independence, and since their privileged status depended in part on their mastery of a European language, they tended to favor its continued use for official purposes and in the schools.

Furthermore, there were practical reasons for continuing to use European languages in Africa. Because of the ethnic diversity that characterizes most African countries, the language of the former colonizer is often the only one that individuals from different areas have in common with each other. Also, European languages are world languages that enable people to enjoy the benefits of foreign trade, technological knowledge, and modern culture. The use of these languages is further reinforced by the aid policies of developed countries that provide Africa with schoolteachers, printed materials, cultural exchange programs, and technical assistance. But the major reason for the persistence of European languages in Africa has been the perception that anyone who desires to succeed in society must acquire them. As long as this assumption maintains its hold over people, parents will continue to insist upon sending their children to schools where European languages are taught.

With regard to the production of literature, those who attend these schools are far more likely to become writers than those who do not, and although many educated people speak an African language fluently, their entire experience with literate culture has often been in a European language, the only language in which they feel comfortable when they write. As in Europe, Protestant missionaries and Bible translators played an important role in giving written form to African languages, but because there were few publishing opportunities for works in these languages, they seldom generated either a substantial literary corpus or an implicit reading audience that might prefigure the emergence of a national community.[17]

In fact, when Africans did write literary works in European languages, particularly during the colonial period, their real audience was not a national one at all. Generally published by European firms, their manuscripts were evaluated and edited on the basis of European tastes and generic expectations. In many cases, more copies of their books were sold in Europe than in Africa. After independence, the situation changed in response to the rise of local publishing and substantial increases in the potential reading audiences of most African countries; however, many authors continued to seek the cachet of publishing their work in Europe or receiving a foreign literary prize.

In terms of the national literature question, the use of European languages had several important consequences that prevented the modern literatures of Africa from following the path traced by their European predecessors. The sorts of legendary figures who inspired the European epics were present in the rich oral traditions of Africa, but with a few notable exceptions they did not become the subjects of European-language literary works capable of transforming them from ethnic leaders into heroes who embody the ideal virtues with which an entire nation could identify. Furthermore, the most well known European-language authors from Africa attained reputations as African writers, and only secondarily as writers from a specific African country. And many of them encouraged this identification by addressing their works to a pan-

African audience rather than to a specifically national one. As a result of such tendencies, the literary corpus of most African countries lacks the constitutive epic or the classic authorial voice around which European national literatures tended to coalesce.

In light of the fact that most Africans have only limited access to texts in European languages, many people have argued that national literatures in Africa must be based on African languages. Ngugi wa Thiong'o is the most well known proponent of this position, and he declares unequivocally that "African literature can only be written in African languages."[18] According to him, African writing in European languages is an epiphenomenon of European literature, and those who cultivate it remain imprisoned in the universe of discourse articulated by their former colonial masters. African writers who publish their works in European languages are, he contends, depriving their own people of a broader intellectual vision and refusing to participate with them in building a community that could sustain a genuine national literature. Acting upon his convictions, Ngugi himself has begun to publish his works in Gikuyu. Others would go even further and impose a single African language on the entire population of ethnically pluralistic countries in Africa.[19] Although there are enormous obstacles to the realization of such plans, they draw attention to the paradoxical fact that the most important writers and thinkers in many African countries publish their works in languages that the majority of their countrymen are incapable of reading.

However, the language issue can also be viewed from a different perspective. The growth of national literatures in the Americas demonstrates that European languages can serve as the principal medium of expression for writers from multilingual communities in which most citizens can neither read nor write. Mass education is a relatively recent phenomenon even in Europe, where a majority of the people remained illiterate well into the nineteenth century. As in Africa, national literary traditions in Europe and the Americas originated among small minorities. Furthermore, the initial stimulus for the emergence of a national literature has often been a revolt against some form of oppression.

In medieval Europe, the Catholic church had a vested interest in maintaining a monopoly over schooling and the use of written language. It frequently eradicated the cultural heritage of entire populations when it attacked their allegedly heathen customs and beliefs. Martin Luther and others like him effectively challenged the church's dominance in this area, but when national literatures later coalesced around vernacular languages, the defense of a specific language was only part of a larger demand for cultural and political freedom.

In Africa and the Americas, the earliest texts that displayed an awareness of potential national audiences were written by colonial elites who enjoyed European-language literacy. Although the authors of these texts clearly modeled their work on European notions of style and genre, those who followed them diverged from European precedents, particularly after independence when implicit national reading audiences developed in response to political debate, the availability of local newspapers, the publication of school texts designed for specific countries, and the emergence of printing firms that catered to local needs.

Within this context, not all African writers agree that the use of European languages alienates them from their national constituencies. As Bernard Dadié from the Ivory Coast points out, if he wrote in an African language, the vast majority of his countrymen would have to read him in translation or not at all. Desiring to avoid being imprisoned in this language, he is convinced that "the use of the French language is not an obstacle to the full realization of [him]self."[20] The Nigerian novelist Chinua Achebe has also argued that African writers can mold a language such as English to their own purposes.

In fact, as European languages change under local circumstances and become adapted to African-language speech patterns, they gradually become African-ized in ways that influence a country's print culture, as can be seen in the market literature that has surfaced in many parts of the continent but also in works such as Amos Tutuola's *The Palm-Wine Drinkard* and Ahmadou Kourouma's *Les Soleils des indépendances*. In time, African forms of English, French, and Portuguese might well become independent languages, just as individual Romance languages evolved from local variations of Latin.[21] Such languages might even prove to be appropriate vehicles for the further develop-ment of national literary traditions in many parts of Africa. In any case, African writers have grown less dependent upon the imitation of European literary models and more confident in the existence of an audience for European-language writings in their own countries. Such tendencies are clearly propitious for the emergence of national literatures in Africa.

In other parts of the world, national literatures have often passed through a cycle leading from the imitation of foreign models and the struggle for collec-tive self-definition to a diffuse heterogeneity in which no writer can be regarded as speaking for the nation as a whole. In most African countries, anticolonialist sentiment and the later nation-building ethos provided considerable impetus for writers to repudiate European literary stereotypes while giving voice to a newfound sense of identity. Of course many of these efforts were pan-African in scope, and some dealt specifically with ethnic identity, but the nature of the decolonization process increasingly obliged Africans to conceive of them-selves in terms of collective destinies that would unfold within the boundaries of the former colonial territories, no matter how arbitrary these boundaries might have been at the outset. Yet developments that had taken place over long periods of time in Europe and the Americas were being telescoped into several decades in Africa, and the third stage in the national literature cycle—the proliferation of literary voices—began before the second stage had run its full course. This fragmentation of purpose in the literature of many African coun-tries was exacerbated by the individualism characteristic of modern society and by the conflictual, often chaotic conditions in the countries themselves.

Like national literatures everywhere, then, the nascent literatures of African countries will be recognized by the shared reference points in the spectrum of world views that individual writers project into their works. These reference points result from experiences with the same milieu, memories of the same events, readings of the same texts, familiarity with the same cultural symbol systems, and relationships with the same sorts of people. Different literary accents and affective styles achieve dominance in some countries, and they too become reference points.[22] An awareness of these reference points is reinforced when a country's writers develop formal and informal networks of communication, when discussions of their work appear in local publications, when critics point out similarities among them, and when their writings are included in the school reading lists.

All these developments have begun to occur in African countries, suggesting that the term *national literature* might well provide a legitimate framework for understanding the diversity of literary production in Africa.[23] If we expect to understand this diversity, we must undertake detailed studies of the literatures that have actually emerged in African countries. Because everything written by individuals from a particular country participates in the evolution of that country's field of shared symbolic references, we should not confine these studies to a limited selection of canonical texts. On the contrary, we should examine the broadest possible spectrum of texts in relation to the overlapping systems of historical, cultural, and political activity in that country.

The following chapters represent an attempt to comprehend the literature of Cameroon along these lines. There are obvious similarities between this literature and literatures from other African countries, but there are also differences, whose significance can be gauged only when we are in a position to make detailed comparisons among them. If every country's literature is a function of its intellectual life, we need to determine how individuals from that country orient themselves with regard to the universe of discourse they share with each other. This study seeks to explain this situation in terms of the Cameroonian experience. Although conclusions based on a single example may not be valid for all African countries, they can help define the terms of the debate and suggest the fruitfulness of carrying out similar investigations in other African countries.

CHAPTER

2

THE AMBIGUOUS BLESSING
European Culture in Cameroon

Within the African context, "assimilation" meant the adoption of European tastes, languages, customs, and colonial government policies by Africans.[1] During the colonial period, individuals had many incentives to assimilate the culture of those who claimed sovereignty over them: social and material advancement, access to the modern world, liberation from ignorance and superstition, a relaxation of the harsh measures routinely applied to "native populations." Yet the process of assimilation was filled with latent contradictions. Viewed from the European perspective, the colonization of Africa represented the arrival of a morally and technologically superior civilization in an area inhabited by a race of people who had presumably been living in a state of primitive savagery for thousands of years. Even the most well intentioned missionaries and colonial administrators perceived their efforts as part of a larger enterprise that would eventually bring "civilization" to the continent.

As Africans adopted various aspects of this civilization, they soon discovered the anomaly of their own situation in the new order. The assimilation of European culture implied a renunciation of traditional African values, but many of these values continued to serve educated Africans as primary points of reference in their universe of discourse. For them, the abandonment of all such values would be tantamount to relinquishing a distinctive part of their own identity, and because the color of their skin prevented them from passing as Europeans, no attempt to identify with the culture of their colonizers could ever completely compensate them for this loss.

However, European culture presented itself as the guardian of a universally valid conception of human nature. Moral standards and legal rights were presumably based upon a rational understanding of it. When Africans extended this conception of human nature to themselves and demanded to be treated accordingly, they encountered unyielding resistance on the part of the very people who claimed to be civilizing them. At this point, the disparity between the benevolent rhetoric of the colonialist myth and the harsh reality of colonialist self-interest became apparent. The victims of this disparity were Africans, for it placed them in an untenable situation. They were obliged to assimilate some European values to survive in the modern world, but when they acted in conformity with these values, they were forcibly reminded that they could not escape the African identity they had been encouraged to abandon. Despite the ambiguity of this situation, European culture left an indelible imprint on the African mentality, and many Africans developed a strong sense of allegiance to it.

The most common response to this dilemma was an attempt to seek freedom and a viable sense of identity by means of a synthesis between modern and traditional values, although such approaches did not always produce satisfactory solutions, as can be seen in the case of Cameroon. Characterized by marked cleavages between a heavily Christianized South and a Moslem-dominated North as well as between an anglophone West and a francophone East, Cameroon is an ethnically and geographically diverse country with over two hundred ethnic groups and a complex history of colonial rule by three different European powers. From 1884 until World War I, it was a German protectorate. After Versailles, it was divided into French and English mandates under League of Nations supervision, a situation that continued (with several important modifications) after World War II within the framework of the United Nations trusteeship system. The British governed their part of Cameroon through the colonial administration in Nigeria and treated the people there with relatively benign neglect, whereas the French incorporated the eastern region into their existing colonial empire and introduced a more repressive system of social control, including forced labor and the head tax. Already under the Germans serious conflicts had arisen between the colonial administration and Cameroonians who had assimilated aspects of European culture.

As in other parts of Africa, the ethnic groups that lived along the coast of Cameroon were the first to interact with European explorers and traders. Serving as intermediaries between the Europeans and the hinterland, the Douala in particular profited initially from a lucrative trade in slaves and, later, from the sale of ivory and palm oil. During the early nineteenth century, their contacts were largely with the British, and by the 1840s, Baptist missionaries had introduced print culture in both English and Douala to the area.[2] With the British, the Douala skillfully negotiated formal agreements governing trade and jurisdictional disputes. Several of them traveled to England, and at least one, Manga Bell, completed his education there. Thus, when the Douala kings Dika Mpondo Akwa and Ndoumb'a Lob'a Bell signed the 1884 treaty establishing a German protectorate over the entire territory that subsequently became known as Cameroon, a cadre of literate Doualas already existed.

Their numbers grew during the following thirty years as the Germans incorporated large numbers of them into subordinate civil-service positions. The educational system expanded under the auspices of the Basel Mission, which had replaced the Baptists, and the creation of a civil-service training center in Buea enabled many Doualas to obtain a relatively high level of education. Sons and daughters of the royal families studied in Germany, and others made the trip under church sponsorship. One of them, the future pastor Josef Ekolo, recorded his impressions in Douala and later published them in German translation as *Wie ein Schwarzer das Land der Weiszen ansieht* (1908). By the early twentieth century, then, Doualas had begun to develop a literate culture with a sizeable potential reading audience.

One of the most brilliant products of this culture was Rudolph Douala Manga Bell, who became paramount chief of the Douala in 1910 after having earned a law degree in Europe. The most difficult issue he had to confront was the colonial administration's plan to expand the European settlement on the banks of the Wouri River by expropriating lands that had been allocated to the Douala by the 1884 treaty. Such a proposal could be justified neither in terms of traditional Douala concepts of justice nor on the basis of German law. Despite the protests that Douala Manga Bell lodged with parliamentary representatives and colonial authorities in Berlin, the German governor ordered the forcible evacuation of Doualas from the contested area in 1913. Accused of treason, Douala Manga Bell refused to flee and was summarily executed the following year.

The life of Douala Manga Bell symbolically recapitulates the contradictions experienced by many Cameroonians who maintained roots in their own ethnic communities while assimilating the knowledge and values of a colonizing power that denied them the fully human status on which its own moral and legal systems were based. With a profound sense of justice and humanity, he sought to reconcile the demands of traditional society with German law, but he could not survive in a system that preached civilization while pursuing the self-interest of the colonizing power in a brutal and arbitrary fashion. For later generations of Cameroonians, Douala Manga Bell became a heroic example of resistance to unjust authority, inspiring not only Douala protest actions against French colonial rule during the 1920s and 1930s but also the larger independence movement they helped spawn.[3] Like him, many Doualas assimilated Western culture and then used its modes of thought to defend their own interests against abuses of power by the colonial authorities. Although repeatedly prevented from realizing such aspirations, they were the first group in Cameroon to acquire the widespread literacy associated with national identity in the modern world.

During the German colonial period, individuals from other Cameroonian ethnic groups also experienced the difficulty of forging a new intellectual universe from the elements of two disparate cultures, and their struggles earned them a similar legendary status to that enjoyed by Douala Manga Bell. For example, Martin-Paul Samba spent many years in Berlin as an officer in the Imperial Army before returning to his native Bulu country in south-central Cameroon, where he participated in numerous campaigns against rebellious local populations and became a wealthy merchant before undergoing a change of heart and orchestrating a network of resistance to the colonial authorities. Like Douala Manga Bell, he was executed by the Germans shortly after the outbreak of World War I.

Among the Bamun farther to the west, Sultan Ibrahim Njoya ruled for over forty years and proved to be one of the most brilliant intellectuals in the country's history. Njoya possessed a remarkable ability to transform the essential elements of what he saw in other cultures into useful innovations in his own society. When he solicited Fulani aid to curb internal opposition early in his reign, for example, he became aware of their Koranic texts and decided to invent a written script for his own language. As early as 1895 he developed a five hundred-character alphabet that he later reduced to the seventy-three characters and ten numbers he used in writing a tract on herbal medicines, a history of Bamun laws and customs, and a philosophical volume that synthesizes Islam, Christianity, and traditional Bamun beliefs into a new religion. Schools were established throughout his realm, and instruction was given in the new script. But during the 1920s, French colonial officials grew increasingly insistent upon imposing their own political and educational models. They destroyed the printing press Njoya had designed, closed the Bamun schools, and eventually exiled him to Yaounde, where he spent the last two years of his life in disillusioned isolation from his people.[4]

Like Douala Manga Bell and Samba, Njoya was an extraordinarily talented individual who fell victim to the colonial paradox according to which Africans were invited to adopt modern ways of looking at the world and then punished for exploiting them to defend a new hybrid identity they had articulated for themselves and their people. Many Cameroonians would later experience some variation of this paradox, but the stories of these three men are particularly significant because they ultimately became shared reference points for a constituency that transcended the boundaries of their own ethnic groups. Although they were martyred by the colonialist system, their images continued to embody notions of freedom and identity long after the men themselves had died.

Most of those who learned to read and write in European languages during the colonial period did not suffer the dramatic fate of these three men, but in their own ways they all confronted the same paradoxical situation. Under the Germans a literate elite had come into being because the colonial administration and the Christian missions needed African auxiliaries and intermediaries who could function in both cultures. Civil servants, catechists, teachers, Protestant pastors, and later Catholic priests all served in this capacity. They too occupied an ambiguous position between the Europeans, who treated them with condescension and dismissed their traditional values as primitive, and their fellow Africans, who often distrusted them or regarded them as turncoats.

Among the most influential of these intermediaries were the secretary-interpreters. The position they held was initially created by the Germans and later retained in a modified form by the French and the British; for many years, it represented the highest civil-service rank to which Africans could aspire. Because secretary-interpreters had to explain local customs to their European superiors while communicating the demands of the colonial authorities to the people, they gained a good understanding of both cultures. And because they accompanied these superiors to areas where their own languages were not spoken, they often learned several Cameroonian languages as well as a European one. Some of them, such as Isaac Moumé Etia and R. Jabea K. Dibongué, even mastered a second European language and successfully moved from the German colonial administration into the civil-service systems established by the French and by the British after the First World War. In 1926, there were approximately three hundred secretary-interpreters in the French mandate territory; they constituted a literate group of individuals who formed friendships across ethnic boundaries and provided enhanced educational opportunities for their own children.[5]

In eastern Cameroon during the 1920s and 1930s, these secretary-interpreters formed the nucleus of an intellectual elite, and it is not surprising that they began to write. Their travels within the country enabled them to develop a comparative perspective on ethnic practices, and their access to French publications offered them models for their own efforts. Jacques Kuoh-Moukouri composed a monograph on Douala dress and culinary practices for his reception into the French Académie d'Outre Mer. Moumé Etia translated selections from the *Thousand and One Nights* into Douala, published a collection of Douala folktales in a bilingual Douala-French edition, and compiled several Douala dictionaries and grammars. Both of them, as well as Louis-Marie Pouka M'Bague, Henri Essomba-Atangana, Frédéric-Richard Manga, Theodore Sengat, and Paul Monthé, contributed ethnographic descriptions, folk materials, and commentaries on proverbs to the colonial administration's official monthly publication *La Gazette du Cameroun*.

Some of the earliest creative writing in Cameroon also emerged from this group. When the French colonial administrator Leon Salasc published his "Chants du Logone" in the magazine *Togo-Cameroun*, his sentimentalized impressions of northern Cameroon provoked a rash of imitations by aspiring poets from different parts of the territory.[6] The most successful of them was Pouka, who later became the first Cameroonian to publish a poetry volume and to achieve some recognition for his work. He eventually distanced himself from the French Romantic models that dominated his early verse, but he never relinquished the political and ethical idealism he had assimilated during the years he spent at a Catholic seminary and in the colonial service. His image of the world was influenced by the mysticism of his father, a traditional Bassa seer, but no matter how deeply attached Pouka was to traditional culture, he always depicted it in his writings from the vantage point of a man who had transcended it by identifying with French civilization and the Catholic religion. His own study of the Bible had convinced him that Christian love was a force for good in the universe; it also reaffirmed his faith in the existence of God and his disdain for the vanity of earthly things. In conjunction with his advocacy of orderly change and the rule of law, these themes remain constant throughout his work.[7]

The poems Pouka wrote during the 1930s are couched in an idiom that echoes the work of such French Romantic poets as Hugo and Lamartine. These early poems contain allusions to winter and summer rather than to the rainy and dry seasons of his native Cameroon, and they are filled with images drawn from the Bible and Greek mythology. Their regular Alexandrine lines are obvious imitations of French originals. For example, his "Souvenir d'enfance" (Memory of Childhood) is a short lyric that nostalgically recreates his early childhood and fondly evokes the solicitousness of a mother who raised him as her only child.[8] Published in a government-sponsored magazine, this poem conformed to a stereotyped European notion about the simplicity of African rural life, and like the prize-winning piece he wrote on the hunting practices of the Bassa for the *Gazette du Cameroun*'s 1935 essay contest, it presupposes a readership that views traditional customs from the enlightened perspective of a superior civilization. The underlying assumption in all Pouka's writing at this time was that European literature provided the only available model for his work. He generally focused on local subject matter, but his manner of presenting it betrays his conviction that European values and literary conventions reflect a higher culture that will enable his people to escape their backwardness.

This assumption was central to the expansion of formal schooling that took place during the 1920s and 1930s, particularly in the south-central and coastal regions of the French mandate. The uneven growth of literacy in other parts of Cameroon was largely determined by diverse administrative policies and by the varying accessibility of mission schools. In the Moslem-dominated North, for example, both the British and the French adopted a policy of indirect rule that allowed local Fulani aristocracies to retain their prerogatives in return for maintaining order and collecting taxes. One reason for the low reported literacy rates in these areas was the resistance of Fulani royal families to the establishment of European-style schools. However, such statistics are deceptive because they fail to take into account literacy in non-European languages. Numerous Koranic schools existed at the time, and more than twenty percent of Fulani men were capable of reading a text in *ajami*.[9] In the South, the situation differed in the French and British mandate territories.

In the eastern part of Cameroon, the French colonial administration intruded far more directly into the lives of the people. They named administrative chiefs in many areas to facilitate the governance of what they regarded as primitive tribes, although their refusal to respect ethnic protocols and hierarchies often engendered tensions and hastened a breakdown of the social fabric in traditional societies. In 1924 the French promulgated the *indigénat*, a system of summary justice according to which most Africans were defined as "subjects" who could be arbitrarily punished for a long list of crimes that ranged from circulating rumors and aiding vagabonds to practicing traditional medicine and failing to display proper deference toward a colonial official.

To create an infrastructure of roads, railroads, and large plantations without making major capital investments, the French resorted to forced labor and to a form of statutory labor that required each "subject" to donate ten days of unremunerated work to the state each year.[10] Thousands of Cameroonians perished under the brutally oppressive conditions in the work camps that were organized when the French extended the existing German-built railroad from Makak to Yaounde; the situation was so bad at Ndjock that the site of the camp there became synonymous in the popular imagination with slavery and death. The costs of such projects as constructing the Douala-Yaounde road, exploiting the mines at Betaré-Oyo, and clearing the plantations at Dizangué were also high in human suffering.

For the relatively small cadre of literate elites, this situation was highly ambiguous. As "citizens" rather than "subjects," they were exempt from forced labor and the *indigénat*. They enjoyed a privileged status to which others aspired, and because schooling offered the surest means of access to such status, parents in many parts of the territory were anxious to enroll their children in the new schools. The French assumed that the graduates of these schools would assimilate civilized European values and become the backbone of a permanent French presence in the colonized areas, but their expectations were fulfilled only in part. As educated black Africans observed the cruelties of the system and experienced the daily humiliation of not being accepted into the white power structure, they could not completely ignore the injustice of colonialist domination. Ironically, the education that justified their privileges also made them capable of understanding the latent contradictions behind the assimilationist ideal that many of them were pursuing.

The impressive growth of schooling in the south-central and coastal regions was largely the result of missionary activity. American Presbyterians had established missions in the Bulu-Bassa country south of Yaounde before the First World War, and the provisions of the League of Nations mandate allowed them to remain, although the French generally allowed only Catholic missions to operate in their African colonies. The importance of the Protestant contribution in Cameroon can be gauged by the fact that until 1930 nearly half of all pupils in the French mandate were enrolled in schools they had established in a relatively small area. The rapid expansion of Catholic schools among the Ewondo-speaking people around Yaounde during the 1930s did redress the balance, but the crucial fact is that Christian missions played the decisive role in creating a community of literate individuals in the area. As enrollments in government-supported eastern Cameroonian schools were increasing from 3,122 in 1921 to 10,310 in 1938, enrollments in mission schools expanded from 3,000 to 92,491 during the same period.[11]

The French authorities accepted this situation because the missions were more than willing to finance schools, and they themselves were reluctant to spend money on public education in areas where revenues were uncertain. They nevertheless exercised considerable control over the mission schools and insisted that all instruction be given in French as opposed to the local languages. The standard curriculum in the colonial schools had been designed during the late nineteenth century by Jules Ferry; it stressed mathematics and a proper use of the French language. Little attempt was made to foster an interest in traditional ethnic cultures, and students learned nothing about their own history or geography. An emphasis on high standards was premised on the assumption that Africans should become as much like educated Frenchmen as possible, and because few Africans were considered capable of attaining this goal, a rigorous selection process prevented more than a small number from ever going beyond the primary grades. The colonial authorities discouraged the missions from creating secondary schools, preferring them to restrict postprimary education to the seminaries.[12] For many years the only secondary school in eastern Cameroon was the Ecole Primaire Supérieure in Yaounde, and its graduates were mainly destined for coveted civil-service positions.

As it turned out, the Catholic seminaries around Yaounde proved to be a major breeding ground for future intellectuals. As early as 1906 German Pallotines had founded a school for catechists and teachers at Einsiedeln near Buea. They were also active in the area near Kribi, and when the Ewondo paramount chief Charles Atangana invited them to Yaounde, they founded an important school at the Mvolye Mission, a forerunner of the major seminary that was later moved to Otélé. A minor seminary was also established at Akono. These institutions demanded rigorous preparation and admitted only the best students. Because future priests would be serving as intermediaries between two cultures, some of the seminary students began to reflect seriously upon their own ethnic cultures while assimilating French civilization and Catholic dogma. Among the first eight Cameroonians to receive ordination into the priesthood in 1935, for example, was Theodore Tsala, whose *Moeurs et coutumes des Ewondo* and collections of folk materials qualify him as one of the first scholars from the territory.

The missions also made other important contributions to the emergence of print culture in Cameroon. By 1916, the American Presbyterians had begun to operate a printing press at Elat in Yaounde. They used it to publish not only Bulu and Bassa translations of the Bible, but also a Bulu newspaper, *Kalate Mefoe* (Book of News), with a circulation of over three thousand copies. It included ethnographic descriptions, proverbs, sermons, testimonials, travel accounts, anecdotes, and autobiographical success stories by local members of the church. In 1939, the press at Elat also printed the first Cameroonian work of prose fiction, Jean-Louis Njemba Medou's *Nnanga kôn* (The White Ghost), which depicts Bulu life at the time when the first white man arrived in the area. Drawing upon oral stories told by his mother and his uncle, Njemba Medou created characters who became so popular they later entered local folk traditions.[13] Nine years later, the press brought out Ondoua Engutu's *Bulu bon be Afri kari* (The Journey of the Children of Afri kari). A narrative account of the origins and migrations of the Fang, it proved so popular that it went through three editions in eight years. Both Engutu and Njemba Medou were schoolteachers whose local success testified to the emergence of a sizeable reading community among the Bulu. Although the press at Elat was used primarily as an instrument of evangelization, it played a significant role in the creation of this community.

A similar reading community also developed among the Ewondo as the result of Catholic publishing efforts in the Yaounde area. During the 1930s, the diocese there introduced an Ewondo newspaper, *Nleb Bkristen* (The Christian Adviser), which eventually attained a circulation of over six thousand copies. One of the first creative literary publications for this audience was the Ewondo epic poem *Nkat Zamba* (Judgment of God). Written by the priest Tobi Atangana in the mid-1930s and modeled on the local *mvet* tradition,[14] it portrays the torments of a Hell to which all earthly sinners will ultimately be committed. *Nkat Zamba* was adopted as part of the standard curriculum for all Catholic schools in the area and thus became a shared reference point for an entire generation of students.[15] Within the context of the later nation-building process, these ethnically based reading communities received little encouragement from the government, but their existence paved the way for a high rate of European-language literacy in south-central Cameroon and for the subsequent emergence of a reading public that transcended ethnic boundaries.

In the British Cameroons, the colonial presence was neither as harshly felt nor as effective in introducing literacy. Like the French, the British hesitated to invest in a territory that might not remain under their control, but their approach to the situation was different. They more or less ignored the local population and allowed German entrepreneurs to buy back the large landholdings they had exploited before World War I. In fact, until the outbreak of the Second World War, Germans outnumbered Englishmen in the territory, and they were responsible for most of the road, railroad, and port construction undertaken at the time. They even built schools and hospitals. As the largest employers of salaried labor in all of Cameroon, the predominantly German plantations near the coast attracted workers from many different regions, including the grasslands to the north, the French mandate, and Nigeria. Conditions on these plantations may have been harsh, but they were never resented in the same way as forced labor in eastern Cameroon. And although workers tended to remain among members of their own ethnic groups, communication began to take place across ethnic lines, and pidgin English became a lingua franca in the area. For workers from West Cameroons, this experience raised their level of awareness about concerns they shared with people from other ethnic groups.

The rest of the British mandate territory languished between the two world wars, and many villages never even experienced the visit of a colonial administrator. Unlike the French, the British did not insist upon standardizing school curricula or enforcing the proper use of their own language. In eighty percent of the primary schools, the first years of instruction were offered in the local languages. There was also a greater emphasis on practical skills and technical subjects. For both reasons, schools in the British Cameroons proved less disruptive of the social fabric than those in the French territory. Yet they were also less widespread. Total school enrollments rose from only 9,391 in 1927 to 11,179 in 1937; among a population of over 800,000 in 1938, only 66 people obtained the first school-leaving certificate, usually obtained in Great Britain at about the age of fifteen.[16]

The schools that were created at this time resulted almost entirely from the initiative of Christian missionaries, who were teaching more than ninety percent of the territory's students as late as 1947. There was not a single secondary school in the British zone until 1938, when the Catholic church established a boys' school at Sasse. A large percentage of the territory's early literate elite graduated from St. Joseph's-Sasse. Others studied at the teacher training institute that had been established at Kumba in the mid-1930s, and a few managed to attend secondary schools in Nigeria. Under these circumstances, the implicit reading community grew slowly, and because the territory was governed through Nigeria, its members often found civil-service positions and settled in Lagos rather than remaining in the Cameroons.

The fact that Christian missions were chiefly responsible for heightened literacy in both mandate territories helped determine the nature of the intellectual climate that emerged after World War II and culminated in independence. For the churches, schooling was part of a larger proselytizing effort, and instruction at the missions tended to be accompanied by a moral idealism that later found expression in the political and imaginative writings of individuals who had received their educations at that time; however, this moral idealism did not always retain the form in which it was initially preached by European missionaries.

The very presence of Christian missions in Africa was premised on the conviction that Western culture is superior to local ethnic cultures. Even the most well intentioned missionaries implicitly collaborated with colonial authorities by conditioning Africans to regard European modes of thought and behavior as superior to their own. In many instances, they prohibited practices that fulfilled important social functions they themselves did not understand, and because they offered no alternative way of performing these functions, the result was often the dislocation of communal value systems and the decline of traditional forms of artistic expression. Furthermore, because many Africans viewed the mission schools as an avenue to social and economic advancement, the practical advantages of a Christian education were often more fully assimilated than the religious message. In conjunction with the breakdown of traditional ethnic value systems, this tendency contributed to the secularization of many deeply religious societies. Under such circumstances, the moral idealism of the churches was often transmuted into a demand for political and social justice.

In fact, the essential message of Christianity is itself incompatible with colonialist exploitation, and the education provided by mission schools offered Cameroonians a frame of reference for condemning the injustices that had been inflicted upon them. The American Presbyterian mission in the French mandate territory played a particularly significant role in this regard. Its emphasis on self-reliance and independent thinking profoundly influenced a number of leaders in the later national independence movement and stimulated a popular desire for freedom from the colonial yoke. As a later student explained, the atmosphere in these schools allowed individuals to "feel free and equal in a different way than in the French administrative system."[17] The Catholic seminaries near Yaounde also contributed to this awakening, in the sense that they produced a group of highly educated individuals who recognized the contradictions between colonialist rhetoric and colonialist practice. Many of them never entered the priesthood, and some became outspoken critics of the church, but nearly all of them retained the moral idealism that had been inculcated in them as part of their Christian education. If the missions were the primary vehicles in the assimilation process, they also helped cultivate the consciousness that would call the validity of that process into question.

By the early 1940s there were three sizeable literate communities in the French mandate—among the Douala along the coast,[18] among the Bulu and Bassa farther inland, and among the Ewondo and other Beti peoples in the region around Yaounde. The Second World War set in motion a series of forces that helped coalesce these and other ethnically based communities into a potential national reading audience. The war itself stimulated the Cameroonian economy, but most of the profits accrued to the white settler population that exploited the crisis to expand its landholdings (particularly those seized from the Germans in the western part of the territory) and to justify the increased use of forced labor. For most Cameroonians, the war was a disaster: inflation wiped out all salary increases received by civil servants and reduced the real wages of unskilled laborers to half of what they had been in 1937.[19] Forced labor caused many young men to seek refuge in the British Cameroons or in the cities; in the Bafang subdivision alone, eighty-six percent of all workers designated for forced labor either left the territory or deserted the camps.[20] The population of Douala doubled during the war, and most of this increase resulted from the influx of young men with little hope of ever finding jobs. The war thus hastened the urbanization process that has generally accompanied the rise of nationalism, and it exacerbated the contradictions inherent in the colonialist enterprise.

Among literate elites, an awareness of this situation was heightened by exposure to new perspectives and by increased opportunities to form alliances across ethnic boundaries. One of the first groups to formalize these tendencies was Jeucafra (Jeunesse Camerounaise Française), an organization composed largely of civil servants from various ethnic groups and supported by the French as a means of countering German propaganda in the territory. As early as 1933, a group of civil servants led by Paul Soppo Priso and including Jean-Faustin Betayéné, Charles Okala, André Fouda, Paul Monthé, and Ruben Um

Nyobé had formed a cultural and social improvement society called Jeunesse Camerounaise. Although the society was avowedly apolitical, its members did discuss the possibility of reunification with the West Cameroons because they felt that an appeal to British judicial procedures might help end the *indigénat* and forced labor.[21] All members of this society joined Jeucafra when the French encouraged Soppo Priso to create it in 1938. Seeking to generate support for the war effort, the colonial authorities allowed many of them to travel throughout the territory and to speak with representatives from different ethnic groups.

Although originally conceived as an expression of French-Cameroonian solidarity in the face of German aggression, Jeucafra gradually evolved into an instrument for the articulation of a nascent political consciousness. The contacts established by the members of Jeucafra convinced them that all Cameroonians were confronted by similar problems in the existing colonial framework, and as the war drew to a close, they publicly demanded the suppression of the *indigénat*, the Cameroonization of the territorial administration, guarantees of free speech and legislative representation, and the elimination of all preferential treatment for white Europeans.[22] Furthermore, parallels between the occupation of France and the colonialist domination of Africa did not escape the attention of literate young people, whose opinions were often influenced by their contacts with French Communists and socialists who had entered the colonial service or become teachers in the colonies when the Popular Front came to power during the late 1930s in France. French unionists such as Gaston Donnat helped form reading groups in which Um Nyobé, Charles Assalé, Léopold Moumé Etia, Jacques N'Gom, and many others, including students, were exposed to a radical analysis of the colonial situation. After the war, Jeucafra transformed itself into the short-lived Unicafra (Union Camerounaise Française), and although its members later adopted a wide variety of political positions, the French-sponsored organization and the more radical reading-discussion groups contributed significantly to the awareness that Cameroonians from different ethnic groups had common interests and confronted similar problems.

This heightened political consciousness emerged at a time when developments triggered by the Second World War were already generating intellectual currents that would change the face of colonialism on a global scale. As the end of the war approached, colonized peoples in many parts of the world began to proclaim their right to self-determination. Both the United States and the Soviet Union opposed the continuation of colonial rule in Asia and Africa. As a means of countering these pressures and formulating French policy for postwar Africa, Charles de Gaulle's commissioner of the colonies, René Pléven, convened a conference of territorial administrators at Brazzaville in early 1944. A black man, Felix Eboué from Guyana, was governor of French Equatorial Africa at the time, and he played a crucial role in drafting the agreements that emerged from the conference. Many of the administrators at the Brazzaville meeting had been appointed to their positions under the Popular Front government, and they tended to be more liberal than the colonies' white settler populations. Yet even they could envisage the future of French Africa only in terms of an associationist policy that would link the colonies more closely than ever to France.

In his opening remarks at the conference, de Gaulle referred to "our African possessions" and eulogized the colonialist military forces that had brought peace and civilization to a continent that, he contended, had been "miserable and impenetrable" since the dawn of history.[23] As for Pléven, he blandly asserted that "in greater France, there are neither people to be freed, nor racial discriminations to be abolished. There are people who feel themselves to be French . . . [and] who expect no other independence than the independence of France."[24] The paternalistic assumptions behind such statements governed much of French policy toward Africa for the next fourteen years, and they were clearly reflected in the document that was published at the end of the conference. In it the goals of the French colonial administration are defined in terms of facilitating the assimilation of French civilization by Africans while assuring a place for the economic activities of Europeans. The preamble explicitly excludes the possibility of independence or any future development outside the political structure of greater France.

For African elites such as those involved with Jeucafra, the Brazzaville agreement was greeted as a first step toward the attainment of greater freedoms because it gave voice to many of their own demands. It sanctioned the abolition of the *indigénat*, forced labor, and travel restrictions; it guaranteed unions the right to organize; it provided for the establishment of territorial assemblies and for African representation at the constituent assembly of the French Republic; it advocated public investment in health and agricultural services. In conformity with the assimilationist philosophy of most delegates at the conference, it placed renewed emphasis on the use of French in the schools and even prohibited instruction in African languages. In other words, it held out the promise of liberation from an unjust colonial system and the hope of genuine integration into a larger community of French-speaking peoples.

For the white settler populations in the colonies, however, the Brazzaville declaration and the constitution later drafted by the first constituent assembly threatened a way of life they had created for themselves. In Cameroon they banded together in Ascocam (Association des Colons du Cameroun) and supported the Douala Chamber of Commerce in calling a meeting of white settlers and businessmen from throughout the French African empire to protest the elimination of forced labor, the establishment of a minimum wage, and the legalization of unions. This meeting resulted in the formation of the Etats Généraux de la Colonisation Française, a well-financed pressure group that proved instrumental in defeating the first proposed constitution when the French voted on it in 1946. The Etats Généraux also influenced the far more conservative version that was approved later that year. In the meantime, serious outbreaks of violence in Indochina, Madagascar, and North Africa had alarmed the French middle classes and provoked considerable sympathy for the adoption of a hard-line policy in all the colonies. Under these circumstances, independence movements everywhere were accused of being linked with the "Communist menace," and many of them were suppressed with great violence.

In Cameroon, the first step in this direction occurred when the railroad engineers from Douala went on strike for better wages and working conditions. Ascocam and the Douala Chamber of Commerce organized vigilante patrols to provoke the strikers into violence, and partly in response to their actions, the people from the slum areas in the New Bell section of the city began to riot, giving vent to their own vaguely defined grievances but also providing the vigilante patrols and local police with a pretext for firing into the crowds.[25] Although the white settlers failed to destroy the union, they did gain a strategic advantage because they could subsequently defend their conservative political stance by depicting all African protest movements as purveyors of violence.

During the decade after the war, the European population in eastern Cameroon increased more than fivefold to over seventeen thousand, and French government investments in ports, roads, bridges, airports, and communication facilities helped them maintain their dominance in the economic sphere. For many white settlers, Africans were primitives who had to be kept in their places so that Europeans could develop the territory's unrealized potential. During the immediate postwar years, then, Cameroonians encountered two conflicting tendencies in French colonial policy: first, the assimilationist thrust that gained added momentum from the Brazzaville Conference, and second, the racist authoritarianism promoted by the white settlers and their conservative allies in France. Both tendencies shaped the intellectual climate in the territory, and individual responses to them became a principal theme in the later writings that record the Cameroonian quest for freedom and identity.

This quest was intensified by the fact that both parts of Cameroon became United Nations trust territories after the end of the war. There was considerable anticolonialist sentiment in this organization from the beginning, and according to its charter, trusteeship status meant that a territory was moving toward independence or self-government. Because such objectives conflicted with France's plan to administer Cameroon as an integral part of its own empire, the willingness of the UN's Committee on Trusteeship and Self-Governing Territories to hear direct appeals from the territories opened the possibility for Cameroonians to oppose French colonial policies by appealing to a higher authority. In formulating their memoranda to the Trusteeship Committee and their testimony in the local hearings conducted by UN visiting missions, they often presented themselves as an incipient nation struggling to free itself from French oppression. Such presentations exerted pressure on the French to respect internationally recognized standards of justice. They also captured the popular imagination in Cameroon, stimulating intense political activity among intellectual elites and producing a widespread public identification with the idea of a Cameroonian identity.

The first attempt to create an interethnic association of literate individuals from the British territory was the short-lived Cameroons Welfare Union that was founded at Victoria in 1939 and had branches in various Cameroonian and Nigerian cities. The following year the Lagos branch of the CWU was succeeded by the Cameroons Youth League, which in turn established branches in Bamenda, Kumba, and several Nigerian cities. The CYL was organized for the express purpose of promoting the interests of Cameroonians, fostering concord among the territory's ethnic groups, preserving their cultural heritage, and creating a general sense of Cameroonian solidarity.[26] Its membership included teachers, students, and civil servants such as Dr. Emmanuel Endeley, Paul M. Kale, Nerius N. Mbile, and John Ngu Foncha. The organization's publication of a monthly newsletter reinforced the awareness of a transethnic intellectual community from the area. At this time there was no serious discussion of a possible merger with eastern Cameroon, and nearly all the members of the CYL joined the largely Igbo NCNC (National Council of Nigeria and the Cameroons) after it formed in 1944. In fact, most literate individuals from the area continued to assume that their future would lie with Nigeria.

The overall literacy rate was low in the British Cameroons, and there was only one printing press in the entire territory. As a result, political and intellectual activity remained restricted to a small group of individuals, and the flurry of ephemeral publications that occurred in eastern Cameroon never had its analog in the western trust territory. However, popular conceptions about a Cameroonian identity were affected by two developments that occurred in the late 1940s: the government consolidation of the large ex-German plantations into the state-owned CDC (Cameroons Development Corporation) and the completion of an all-weather road from Kumba to Mamfe.

At one point, the CDC employed more than half the salaried work force in the territory and produced more than two-thirds of its exports.[27] It operated the only railroad in West Cameroons, built roads and port facilities, established schools and adult education programs, collected taxes, provided medical care, organized sporting events, and awarded scholarships to children of employees; in short, the CDC created a modern infrastructure by means of which large numbers of people were drawn into the political arena and exposed to European cultural models.

The Kumba-Mamfe road opened the hinterland for development. Before it was built, the only way to travel from the Bamenda area to the coastal plantations was by foot; the same was true for overland travel to Nigeria. Yet, if the road facilitated transportation within the territory, it also produced a gradual influx of Igbos, whose presence provoked a hostility that in 1961 decisively influenced the western Cameroonians' vote to federate with eastern Cameroon rather than become a province of Nigeria.

By this time, some West Cameroonians had begun to argue that a sense of common identity existed in the territory and that it justified their appeals for internal autonomy. One of the first to realize that the right of appeal to the United Nations gave Cameroonians added leverage in the debate over this question was Endeley. In 1949 the Cameroons Provincial Council, the CYL, and several ethnic improvement associations in Lagos demanded separate regional status for the trust territory, and when Endeley brought together a number of diverse organizations to form the CNF (Cameroon National Federation), he advocated regional status as a step toward separation from Nigeria and eventual reunification with eastern Cameroon.[28] After the 1950 elections, most members of the CNF retained their affiliation with the NCNC, but four years later the British Cameroons was accorded the status of a quasi-federal state, and those who maintained their allegiance to the NCNC were soundly defeated in elections to the new state parliament because the majority of Cameroonians had become convinced that their interests were not identical with those of Nigeria on a number of economic and political issues. Despite shifting political alliances, a heightened sense of collective identity was gradually emerging in the British Cameroons, particularly among the literate elites.

For francophone Cameroonians during the 1950s, the question of collective identity was couched in terms of an ongoing debate over the territory's future: should it become an independent nation with its own institutions, or should it continue to pursue the assimilationist ideal by remaining part of a larger French community? The colonial administration and many enlightened Frenchmen supported the assimilationist course, which also appealed to a large number of literate Cameroonians and profoundly influenced the way they thought of themselves. In Cameroon, the primary spokesman for this position was the Algerian-born French doctor Louis-Paul Aujoulat, who was well known as a builder of hospitals and as the founder of an important charitable organization, Ad Lucem. Generally distrusted by the white settler population because of his support for liberal policies toward Cameroonian civil-service employees, education for Africans, and labor regulations, Aujoulat was a devout Catholic who, like Léopold Sédar Senghor in Senegal, was committed to the idea of a Franco-African confederation. Elected to both the territorial assembly and the French national assembly from his district in south-central Cameroon, he used his position to create the BDC (Bloc Démocratique Camerounais), which drew its support largely from the Catholic Ewondo area around Yaounde. He also became a powerful figure on the French political scene, and as the patron of numerous Cameroonians, he inculcated in them the belief that they could realize themselves only by adopting the civilized world view that was being offered to them by a benevolent France.

This line of argument was reiterated in many different guises by Frenchmen who contributed to the burgeoning print culture in eastern Cameroon. In the early 1950s, the Paris-based De Breteuil consortium purchased the territory's principal newspaper and renamed it *La Presse du Cameroun*. Addressed largely to the expatriate community, *La Presse* took most of its copy directly from the parent organization's wire service. Although occasional articles and letters by Cameroonians were accepted for publication, the editors never opened their columns to commentaries that were critical of French colonial policy. For example, they published an open letter to the opposition leader Ruben Um Nyobé, recommending that he follow the lead of the Ivoirian Houphouët-Boigny in seeking reconciliation with the French, but they refused to print his reply; in fact, their editorial policy was clearly reflected in a feature article by a Frenchman who believed that an African's reference to himself as French was sufficient justification for concluding that, "everything considered, our method is the best."[29]

The paternalistic assumptions behind such statements are reflected in the ethnographic study of African customs from a European perspective that reduces ethnic practices to exotic encyclopedia items and refuses to grant them any truth or moral value of their own. The implicit corollary of such an enterprise is the need to abandon traditional values in favor of European ones. In eastern Cameroon, the colonial administration had a vested interest in assuring that ethnographic work was conducted in this spirit, and when the territorial governor J. Repiquet founded the Société des Etudes Camerounaises in 1935, he regarded it and its journal, *Etudes Camerounaises*, as instruments of France's civilizing mission in Africa. In a later essay, he praised colonial administrators and missionaries in Cameroon for having eliminated customs "contrary to the principles of civilization" and for having raised black people "above their moral and material condition."[30]

The wartime governor Cornarie revived the society eight years later and praised its efforts to forge a body of informed opinion about Cameroon as a contribution to the war effort. After the war, the society became a branch of the Dakar-based IFAN (Institut Français d'Afrique Noire) and acquired considerable discretionary authority over the kind of research that could be carried out in the territory. Cameroonians themselves were virtually excluded from membership, and only one of them ever published a full-length article in *Etudes Camerounaises* during its more than twenty years of publication. As a consequence, the image of traditional cultures that reached print in the territory's only scholarly journal was entirely dominated by Europeans.

But even the most generous-spirited Europeans could not help but project their own preoccupations and desires into their images of African reality. Men such as Roger Lagrave and the Catholic priests Jean-Marie Carret and Henry de Julliot contributed a good deal to the emergence of francophone literature in Cameroon by offering encouragement and advice to aspiring writers. Lagrave founded the Club du Livre Camerounais, a series that published books by several Cameroonians, and he helped many others revise their manuscripts. Carret devoted thirty years of his life to missionary work among the Bassa and in the coastal town of Kribi. He built countless schools and always encouraged young people in their attempts to write. De Julliot taught literature to several generations of students at the elite Collège Libermann in Douala, and he created the Frères Réunis, for many years the only well-stocked bookstore in the French trust territory.

De Julliot also wrote a regular literary column in *La Presse du Cameroun* and scrupulously commented upon the manuscripts that were submitted to him by his readers. He delivered public lectures on literature and helped many young writers to publish their works in Europe. However, the literary and ethical norms that all three men applied to Cameroonian writing were those of a high French culture that did not always respond to the expressive possibilities of an African reality as perceived by Africans. For example, de Julliot's own poetry is frequently set in Cameroon, but it is rigidly patterned on French classical models and tends to exalt a simple life in which the bounty of God's creation becomes apparent. When judging the work of others, he looked for stylistic purity and a morally uplifting view of the world.

Carret too wrote about Cameroon, and his novel *Kel'lam, fils d'Afrique* provides an excellent example of how a fictional world can be structured to support an ideological position, in this case the belief that Africans cannot achieve their potential without adopting European culture and accepting the patronage of Europeans. In the Cameroonian context, *Kel'lam* serves as a defense of French colonialism and a plea for maintaining the territory as part of the French Union. It is also a narrative justification of Carret's own life, for he projects himself into the figure of a white priest who notices the young Kel'lam in his village, changes the boy's life by bringing him to a mission school, and later awakens him to the moral responsibilities he must accept if he hopes to become a leader of his people. Kel'lam's ultimate success and happiness are depicted as rewards for his willingness to pursue the assimilationist ideal, but his success would have been impossible without the help of the white priest. Carret and his fictive narrator do espouse the cause of African liberation, but only at a future time when Africans will have become like them.

To reinforce this message, Carret depicts African society before the arrival of Europeans as the "quasi-vegetative life" of "neolithic savages" who had wallowed in superstition, fear, poverty, slavery, and cannibalism during a "millenary torpor." The people of Kel'lam's village can neither provide themselves with meat on a regular basis nor cope rationally with the illnesses that plague them, and they know nothing about the outside world. As the colonial presence spreads irresistibly across Africa, the priest argues, the people of the continent will have to "adapt themselves or perish"; thus, when he offers to enroll Kel'lam at the mission school, he proclaims, "I am bringing you freedom," because he is convinced that European-style schooling is the only way to liberate Africans from a backward way of life that is dooming them to extinction.[31]

But education alone is not enough, for after graduating and becoming a secretary-interpreter, Kel'lam remains susceptible to the temptations of materialism and sensual pleasure. The only way he can shield himself against them is by internalizing a higher ideal capable of inspiring him to help his people overcome their backwardness, and he accomplishes this feat after a trip to France and conversations with Senator André (Aujoulat), a black intellectual (Senghor), and the priest. The name Kel'lam means "happy day" in Bassa, suggesting that his successful internalization of European values represents a model that could assure happiness for those who emulate it. Viewed in these terms, Carret's novel is essentially an argument in favor of the assimilationist ideology and the Franco-African community it implies.

Despite his thirty years in Cameroon, Carret remained an outsider who never personally experienced the contradictions of attempting to live an identity prescribed for him by a foreign culture. Alexandre Douala Manga Bell, the son of Rudolph, the legendary paramount chief of the Doualas, knew the drama of this situation from the inside, and although he published virtually nothing, he was one of the most brilliant men of letters in the history of Cameroon. When he returned to his homeland in 1919 after having spent fifteen years in Germany, he was a stranger to his own people. His possessions and his throne had been taken from him by the French, but he sued in the courts and eventually recovered them by virtue of his eloquence and persistence. His letter to the Versailles Conference in 1919 is a profoundly humanistic appeal for the recognition of Cameroonians' rights to self-determination, due process under the law, and opportunities for advanced education.[32]

Fluent in ten languages and a charismatic orator, the flamboyant Alexandre was the only Cameroonian elected to the first French national assembly after the Second World War. Although initially opposed by the colonial authorities, who resented his earlier legal suits against them, he later became the leading Cameroonian spokesman for the French assimilationist position in their struggle against radical nationalist leaders such as Um Nyobé. De Julliot was convinced that his friend Alexandre could have become the greatest of all Cameroonian writers, but like Sultan Njoya, the Douala king spent his final years in silence and solitude, the victim of irreconcilable contradictions in the colonialist situation.[33] He had mastered European culture to the point where he understood its ideals better than did the colonial authorities who sought to impose their version of it on him, but when confronted by a popular nationalist movement that had adapted many of these same ideals to Cameroonian circumstances, he allied himself with the very system that had victimized him for so many years. Alexandre could not fully adopt the identity of a Westernized African, but he could not fully repudiate it either.

The assimilationist thrust of colonial administration policy found clearest expression in the rapid growth of schooling in the French territory during the 1950s. Primary school enrollments soared from 119,000 in 1947 to 330,988 in 1959, and with the construction of nine new secondary schools, the number of students registered at the more advanced level jumped from 926 to 7,148 in the same period.[34] Large increases in French government spending on education were partly responsible for this growth, but the Catholic educational system was also expanding rapidly, although the relative importance of Protestant schools declined, even in the Bulu and Bassa areas where the colonial administration actively encouraged the establishment of Catholic missions. The required curriculum was revised to reflect the assimilationist sentiments proclaimed at the Brazzaville Conference, and Cameroonian examination schedules became the same as those of France, partly in response to the demands of parents who did not want their children to be denied the opportunity of a higher education. As a result, Cameroonian students spent at least half their time studying the literature and culture of France, while learning virtually nothing about the African context in which they were living.

Despite the absence of African materials in the official curriculum, however, the students who attended secondary school in the postwar period were soon applying modern modes of analysis to their own situation. In fact, the outburst of literary activity that occurred in the 1950s was largely the product of their attempts to redefine themselves in terms that reflected the specifically African dimension of their existence. Efforts to reconcile modern European and traditional African culture were being made at nearly every center of literate activity in eastern Cameroon and with particular intensity in the Catholic seminaries near Yaounde, where intelligent and highly motivated students often found themselves in opposition to a Eurocentric church hierarchy.

A variety of reading materials was available at the major seminary in Otélé; reading, discussion, and individual reflection were encouraged, and students there developed the disciplined habits necessary for extended intellectual undertakings. By the mid-1950s, seminary authorities had become more tolerant toward the study of traditional culture, and in this atmosphere, a study group, Rencontre de Deux Mondes, was formed in 1957. Motivated by the desire to be fully African and fully Christian, the members of this group proposed to collect and inventory the cultural patrimony of their respective ethnic groups. They then undertook to analyze these materials in the hope of discovering ways of linking the philosophical insights they contained with Catholic doctrine. The underlying assumption was that such a project would enable them to become more effective priests and better mediators between the two cultures.[35]

Much of their work appeared in the review *Lumina*, of which twenty-one issues were published in the late 1950s and early 1960s. Transcriptions of oral literature, commentaries on traditional ethnic practices, essays on the compatibility of traditional customs and Catholic belief, attacks on racism and colonialism, and poems reaffirming the dignity of black Africans appeared in the pages of *Lumina*. Although those who contributed to the review encountered resistance on the part of some European priests, they persevered in the attempt to comprehend the nature of their world, and whether or not they ever entered the priesthood, their own subsequent writings were marked by the desire to synthesize a world view capable of reflecting the moral idealism and intellectual rigor of the seminary while responding to real sociocultural conditions rather than to the image of Africa that had been defined for them by others.

During the 1950s, all Cameroonian writers confronted this desire in some form, although many of them identified strongly with European civilization and the idea of a French Union that would include francophonic peoples from around the world under the leadership of France. The writings of these individuals stress the benefits enjoyed by Africans as the result of colonialism and present the assimilation of European culture as a liberation from primitive customs and beliefs. However, such a stance placed them in an ambiguous situation, as their own works testify.

After the Second World War, the most well known literary proponent of assimilation was the poet and former secretary-interpreter Louis-Marie

Pouka. So strong was his identification with France that he wrote an entire volume of poetry, *Pleurs sincères* (1943), to lament the suffering of Frenchmen during the German occupation while ignoring the rigors imposed on his fellow Cameroonians by the *indigénat* and forced labor. In "France Immortelle," for example, he eulogizes the mother country as the cradle of freedom and the sensitive heart of Europe. But despite bowed head and legs shackled in irons, the poet assures his readers, she will survive and remain the "salvation" of black people.

The same naive optimism characterizes his 1943 one-act verse drama *Hitler ou la chute de l'hydre*, in which he prophetically imagines the German dictator committing suicide, although for rather implausible reasons. Overcome with remorse for the crimes he has committed, Pouka's Hitler recognizes the folly of his grandiose plans and acknowledges the omnipotence of God before killing himself. As the oppressor of the poet's beloved France, Hitler deserves to die, but in Pouka's eyes, the dictator's real punishment lies in his consciousness of having committed a crime, for evil destroys itself. At the heart of Pouka's world view is a moral idealism that divides the universe into good and evil, then assumes that the good will triumph because it is in harmony with the will of God. According to him, the fatal flaw of evil individuals is their capacity to realize that their actions place them in conflict with a divinely sanctioned order in the world. Weakened by this awareness, they become incapable of sustaining their resolve to pursue evil goals.

By regarding the French colonialist enterprise as part of God's plan, Pouka was able to justify his belief that it had been providential for Africans. The future of Cameroon would, he was convinced, be assured by a mutually beneficial cooperation with the mother country. In "La Main dans la main," written shortly after the end of the war, he celebrates their eternal friendship and imagines them marching forward like twin suns, shedding peace and light on the rest of the world. As the metaphor suggests, he believes that Cameroon will be able to realize its destiny only in conjunction with the benevolent support of the French colonizer.

However, Pouka's stay in France during the late 1940s and early 1950s obliged him to reexamine his assimilationist assumptions. These were lonely years for him. As he reflected from a distance on the situation in Cameroon and became familiar with a real France that didn't correspond to his idealized image of it, he redefined his attitude toward colonialism and rethought his relationship to French culture. The poems he wrote during this period were melancholy contemplations on the deceptiveness of earthly love or angry denunciations of French policies that prevented Africans from leading free and dignified lives in their homelands. His reaction against colonialism betrays the resentment of a man who realizes he has been duped by an idealistic rhetoric that he cannot relinquish because it expresses beliefs that have become central to his conception of himself. His solution was to reaffirm his faith in the ideals of French culture while condemning abuses in colonialist practice as aberrations in a divine plan that would eventually culminate in the civilizing of Africa. In his verse, the drama of confronting this dilemma takes place in the consciousness of the lyric "I" that he models on the sensitive self of the French Romantic poets he had read so avidly as a young seminarian.

This poetic "I" was not uncommon in the Cameroonian poetry of the period. Louis-Marie Ongoum adopts a similar one in his unpublished volume *Sentiers, sentes et laïes*, an intimate journal in regular rhymed couplets that record another former seminarian's spiritual evolution and eventual disillusionment. The poetic "I" in *Sentiers* is that of a self-pitying idealist who bemoans his melancholy destiny in a world that holds out false promises and then crushes those sufficiently naive to believe in them. Despite Ongoum's recourse to a stereotypical European poetic persona, his autobiographical cycle is noteworthy because it illustrates a growing preoccupation with the self and an increasingly widespread assumption that the unique experiences of any sensitive person merit literary treatment. Both notions reflect the impact of individualism and print culture on Africans' attempts to redefine themselves within the context of the modern world.

Pouka's lyric "I" exemplifies the same tendencies, and he employs many of the sentimental clichés that also appear in *Sentiers*, but the thrust of his poetry differs from that of Ongoum insofar as Pouka never lost the moral idealism that allowed him to interpret human foibles against the backdrop of divine purpose. In his poems, he repeatedly alludes to death as the unavoidable destiny that awaits everyone and renders absurd all earthly vanities. Although many of his works deal with sensuous pleasure and the love of women, he realizes that earthly love offers only the illusion of happiness, a necessary illusion perhaps and one he is unwilling to abandon, but in retrospect he invariably regards it as a pale reflection of the higher and more permanent love of God. Similarly, his volume *L'Innombrable Symphonie* revolves around the conceit that the world is a divinely composed symphony with countless parts; by attending to the sights and sounds of nature, the poet gains insight into the harmony of God's plan. For Pouka, this detached observation leads to wisdom, and poetry becomes the vehicle by means of which his voice conveys this wisdom to the people and preserves his own unique identity for posterity.

After his return to Cameroon in 1951, there is a considerable ambivalence in Pouka's poetic voice, for if God is good and French ideals are benevolent, the persistence of injustice and suffering in the territory is difficult to explain. Yet he does find an explanation for it in the bad faith of Europeans who claimed to be guiding Africans toward a higher level of civilization while actually exploiting them for their own profit. He refers to their strategy as "la grande Ruse" [the big Lie]. Within this context, he presents the voice of wisdom in his poetry as an instrument in the struggle for liberation. It can mitigate the people's fear by showing them the pettiness of the colonialists' duplicity when viewed against the background of divine love and the vanity of earthly things. It can also make the false colonialists aware of the suffering they have caused, obliging them, like Hitler in the *Hydra* play, to feel remorse and to recognize the disjunction between their actions and God's plan for a peaceful, harmonious universe. Their own demoralization would then, he contends, cause them to modify their behavior or to leave the colonies entirely. At that point, the true ideals of French culture could finally be put into practice, enabling Africans for the first time to realize their full human potential under the benign guidance of the mother country.

Pouka's works reflect his belief in a form of poetic justice that stems from the underlying goodness of the universe and ultimately punishes those who do evil. Within the Cameroonian political context, this naive optimism implied that concrete action was unnecessary to rectify an unjust colonial situation because the world evolves in such a way that it would be eliminated during the normal course of events. Another corollary of Pouka's faith in the divine plan was his willingness to accept the colonizer's image of what he and his fellow Cameroonians should become. In an imagined conversation with a white European, he even admits, "I acknowledge that you are my master."[36] What he means is that Africans were liberated from the tyranny of ignorance by the arrival of Europeans and still have a great deal to learn from them.

Yet Africans do not need to become like Europeans in every respect, as many of his poems suggest. Pouka himself repeatedly proclaims that all human beings are equal in their vulnerability to suffering and death, in their capacity for love, and in their urge to be free. After his sojourn in France, he suspected that French colonialism was incompatible with his idea of equality, but he could not abandon his commitment to either of them because both were crucial to his own self-image. The result was a vague uneasiness that pervades the poetry he wrote throughout the 1950s. He sought to suppress this malaise by drawing attention to the advantages of adopting European culture and by holding out the promise of a mutually beneficial cooperation in the future, but he could not escape the intimation that his pursuit of the assimilationist ideal was based on a series of false premises.

During the same period, many other educated francophone Cameroonians felt a strong sense of attachment to European culture, and when they wrote in a biographical or autobiographical vein, their stories emphasized how Africans had benefited from French colonialism. Even the sense of self they had acquired through contact with colonial institutions became an implicit argument in favor of the French presence in Cameroon. Portrayed as a liberation from ignorance and superstition, their awareness of themselves as individuals is depicted as a step toward the reconceptualization of group identity they regard as necessary in the modernization of African society. The most well known example of such writing is Joseph Owono's novel *Tante Bella*, which is essentially a polemic in support of his campaign for the emancipation of Cameroonian women. Owono's 1953 essay about problems created by the dowry system in eastern Cameroon was the only full-length article by a Cameroonian ever to appear in *Etudes Camerounaises*, and in it he praises the French for reforming outmoded traditional customs. Shortly after writing this essay, Owono founded the charitable organization Evocam (Evolution et Affranchissement de la Femme Camerounaise) to combat the oppression of women. In the hope of reaching a larger audience for his ideas, he cloaked them in narrative form and produced *Tante Bella*.

The novel is divided into two sections. The first records several conversations among educated Cameroonians and enlightened Frenchmen who discuss the status of women in the territory. The second contains the title character's story, which is read aloud during one of these conversations to illustrate the injustice inflicted upon women by the dowry system. The central character in the first section is the Europeanized Cameroonian Jean ("Grospieds"), whose mission-educated wife, Rosie, had persuaded him by her intelligence and kindliness that married life is most satisfying when it is based on monogamous fidelity and mutual respect, as it presumably was in Europe. From this perspective, Grospieds becomes convinced that African women must be freed from a dowry system that allows them to be bought and sold as if they were objects.

The Frenchmen and Europeanized Africans who gather at a Corsican restaurant to enjoy a social evening together represent in microcosm the elite community that Carret envisioned as the basis for an ideal French Union in his novel *Kel'lam*. Because they all agree on the civilized standards that should be applied to people everywhere, they have no trouble reaching consensus on a condemnation of Cameroonian marriage practices, which they feel prevent women from realizing their human potential and impede the modernization of Africa. Introduced by Grospieds as a manuscript written by a Garoua schoolteacher, Bella's story corroborates the world view already adopted by those present and justifies the lifestyle they have chosen for themselves.

There are two foci of interest in the schoolteacher's account of Bella's life: the tribulations she suffered as a consequence of the dowry system and the impact of her example upon his consciousness. Taken from her family at the age of six and later subjected to a series of brutal, unloving husbands, she never rebelled against the dowry system because she accepted it as part of the natural order. She did find brief happiness in her secret marriage to a German officer, but he was killed at the outbreak of World War I, and she was obliged to marry several more husbands before retiring to her village, where she raised the young boy who later became the Garoua schoolteacher.

At first, he knew her only as a kindly, generous woman, but after her death, he stumbles upon the German officer's strongbox and discovers that she and her mulatto daughter Olga were heirs to a substantial fortune. In reflecting upon Bella's fate, he realizes that her life had been a preventable tragedy, for the oppressive conditions imposed on her are actually unjust cultural practices that can be changed. This insight motivates the schoolteacher to collaborate with Olga in founding a charitable organization that buys widows out of "dowry-slavery." For him, Bella becomes a symbol of the unnecessary suffering inflicted on Cameroonian women, and he dedicates himself to the elimination of such suffering in the future. By recounting her story, he defends his new perspective, which is essentially the product of his exposure to European-style schooling and social institutions. Rhetorically, this story within a story functions as a concluding argument in support of the author's attack on one traditional custom as judged from an assimilationist point of view.

Both Grospieds and the Garoua schoolteacher are thinly veiled projections of Owono himself. By affirming the validity of a world view that sets him apart from the majority of Cameroonians, he is implying that Africans must become like Europeans if they hope to achieve full humanity. Much autobiographical writing of the preindependence period is based on the same assimilationist assumption. For example, Marie-Claire Matip's autobiographical novella *Ngonda* and Jacques Kuoh-Moukouri's autobiography *Doigts noirs* both trace the way in which individual Cameroonians acquired the Europeanized mentalities that emancipated them from the backwardness of traditional society and enabled them to participate in the civilizing process.

Published in Lagrave's Club du Livre Camerounais series, *Ngonda* is a success story that relates a young woman's maturation from a happy but naive village girl into a self-confident adult who contributes to the modernization of her world along lines suggested by European models. *Doigts noirs* is also a success story, for the former secretary-interpreter Kuoh-Moukouri was the highest-ranking Cameroonian civil servant at the time of independence, and he presents himself as a forerunner who helped "pave the way" to civilization for subsequent generations of his people. He prides himself on his assimilation of European virtues such as personal ambition, a thirst for knowledge, and an unwavering allegiance to the service ideal. In fact, the sense of individual identity that emerges in his book and in *Ngonda* reinforces their implicit contention that the French colonial presence which fostered it was essentially benevolent.

A few West Cameroonians identified with British culture in the same way that Pouka, Kuoh-Moukouri, and Owono identified with French culture, but their numbers were much smaller, and they seldom perceived a contradiction between the assimilation of European modes of thought and their images of themselves as Africans. Unlike the French, the British never held out the promise that black people from the colonies could fully assimilate their culture. Furthermore, literacy rates remained low in the British Cameroons, and those who contributed to its intellectual life were often living in Nigeria. Largely through the efforts of Christian missionaries, school enrollments did rise from 25,200 in 1947 to 50,618 in 1957, but even after the establishment of a Baptist secondary school at Bali in 1948, it and St. Joseph's-Sasse were still the only two such institutions in the entire territory until 1963.[37] Some Cameroonians pursued their educations in Nigeria, but relatively few people in the territory had sufficient training in English to become writers or perceptive readers of literary texts in that language. Those who did write had no outlets for their work in the Cameroons, although several brought out works with Nigerian publishers or managed to have them broadcast on Nigerian radio. As early as 1949, for example, Vincent Nchami began selling his stories to the BBC in Lagos, but in general anglophone Cameroonians published relatively little in the years before independence.

What was written at this time tended to be inspirational or morally didactic, reflecting the missionary influence on the schooling that most literate anglophone Cameroonians had received. While studying at a seminary in Nigeria, for example, Bernard Fonlon composed a number of highly crafted poems in an archaic diction that echoed his extensive readings in the Bible, the Latin classics, and nineteenth-century English writers such as Scott and Tennyson. His frequently reprinted "The Fear of Future Years" and "Nightmare" dramatize the momentary despair of a man haunted by his own mortality and by the possibility of failure but buoyed by his faith in the divine plan of a Christian God. Both poems illustrate how an attachment to the good, the true, and the beautiful can sustain an individual even in a morally corrupt environment. Although there is little in Fonlon's early poetry that would identify its author as an African, the defensive tone that frequently surfaces in francophone Cameroonian assimilationist writing is absent from his work.

One of the most active anglophone writers from the British Cameroons was Sankie Maimo, who founded an ephemeral journal, *Cameroons Voice*, at Ibadan in 1955. His play *I Am Vindicated* and his children's book *Adventuring with Jaja* deal specifically with the identity question and its relationship to European cultural norms. In the former, an educated young man unmasks a sorcerer, whose death symbolizes the overcoming of superstition. At the end of the play, the villagers rejoice at their liberation from evil forces, and the young people are promised the schooling that will enable them to cope with life in a rational manner. The underlying assumption is of course that Africans must, for their own good, adopt European ways of looking at the world.

The identity question is posed somewhat differently in Maimo's book for children. At the time he wrote it, he was a secondary-school teacher in Lagos, and he conceived of it as a text for his students. By adapting the adventure-story format of *Tom Sawyer* and *Don Quixote* to a typically Nigerian setting, Maimo offered his students the opportunity to empathize with characters like themselves and to recognize how the actions of those characters might be relevant to their own situations. The central dilemma in *Adventuring with Jaja* is a choice between conformity to mundane social norms in a corrupt, materialistic world and the excitement of pursuing a Romantic dream.

The choice that confronts the youthful narrator, Kayode, is a typically Western one. A materialistic society molds people into well-behaved but unimaginative drudges who never experience life with intensity. Yet they also have access to books that offer them Romantic models of behavior. If they conform to conventional social norms, they might well assure their material well-being while suffering a death of the spirit. However, if they pursue a Romantic dream, they might live with intensity but suffer repeated setbacks in the physical world, as Kayode's flamboyant friend Jaja does. By dramatizing this dilemma for young readers, Maimo invites them to conceive of themselves as individuals who must make similar choices in articulating their own sense of identity. *Adventuring with Jaja* thus reinforces the individuality concept that is so closely linked with modernization and the emergence of nations in Europe.

Within the Cameroonian context, the introduction of European culture was indeed an ambiguous blessing. Literacy was largely the result of Christian missionary activity. Schooling and print culture fostered the emergence of new identity concepts based on individualistic premises. The very fact that writers signed their works drew attention to the individuality that was being preserved in them. Rational modes of thought made technological progress possible and called outmoded social practices into question. European political and moral ideals appealed to many Cameroonians, although European colonial practice often failed to respect these ideals, and culturally based European definitions of human nature often seemed inadequate to encompass the complexity of life as perceived by Africans.

Literate Cameroonians responded to this situation in a broad spectrum of ways that ranged from an enthusiastic embrace of European culture through attempts to synthesize hybrid world views to a violent rejection of European cultural dominance in Africa. Particularly in the French trust territory, advocates of the assimilationist position often found themselves imprisoned in the paradoxical dilemma of trying to acquire an identity that could never be fully their own. Yet even the most outspoken opponents of the European presence in Africa drew inspiration from European cultural models, which served as a portal through which they passed on the way to independence and modern African systems of thought.

CHAPTER

3

ANTICOLONIALISM
AND REVOLUTION

As latent contradictions in the assimilationist position became increasingly apparent, Cameroonian opposition to the colonial presence grew, especially in the eastern trust territory. Precedent for this movement can be found in the writings and demonstrations of the Doualas, who continued, throughout the 1920s and 1930s, to protest against the expropriation of their lands, but it was also inspired by ideals that Cameroonians had assimilated as a result of their contact with European culture. These ideals had achieved their clearest formulation in post-Enlightenment European thought and included concepts of social justice, human rights, modernization, individualism, and national identity. Thus, although advocates of the anticolonialist position defined themselves primarily in terms of their opposition to European oppression and cultural dominance, their demands for national liberation and the right to articulate their own cultural identity can also be regarded as an application of Western political values to the African situation.

Ironically, the Brazzaville agreements and the 1946 French constitutional reforms provoked the very developments its organizers had hoped to forestall. Rather than binding the colonial territories closer to France, they heightened African expectations of further concessions and created the institutional mechanisms that provided a platform for the expression of anticolonialist sentiments. In 1946, representatives of territorially based parties from many of the French colonies met in Bamako (Mali) and formed the RDA (Rassemblement Démocratique Africain), a political coalition that pursued some of the same reformist goals that had been outlined at Brazzaville.

The organization that catalyzed the anticolonialist movement in Cameroon was the UPC (Union des Populations du Cameroun). It received much of its initial support from the trade unions that had been legalized after the Brazzaville conference, and although their leadership had been influenced by the Marxist discussion groups organized during the Second World War, it was not a particularly radical party at the time of its founding in 1948, when it declared its intention to pursue its political objectives within the framework of the French Union. Supported by politically moderate cultural associations such as the Douala Ngondo and the Bamileke Kumszé, its program demanded that the territory be governed according to democratic principles and that European business interests no longer be granted unfair advantages in the local economy. Nevertheless, the UPC was regarded with suspicion by the colonial administration, which offered various inducements for moderate supporters to sever their ties with it. The white settler population was also violently opposed to the UPC and broke up several of its early meetings.

The UPC initially allied itself with the RDA, but when Houphouët-Boigny convinced most members of the RDA to split with the French Communist party, which had supported it in the legislative assembly, and to join forces with the IOM (Indépendents d'Outre Mer—the party of Senghor and Aujoulat), the UPC refused to cooperate. The ensuing break with the RDA had serious consequences for the UPC. It maintained close ties with the Communist party, which continued to serve as its spokesman during parliamentary debates in France.

However, at a time when French Marxists were being repatriated from the colonies and Communists were being blamed for the turmoil that had emerged throughout the French colonial empire, the UPC's linkage with the French Communist party provided the colonial administration with a pretext for labeling the Cameroonian movement subversive and seeking to suppress its activities. To counter the appeal of the UPC, the French authorities also encouraged alternative loyalties—to French civilization, to the Catholic church, to regional and ethnic associations. In the face of continued support for the French Union by both the RDA and supporters of the assimilationist position in Cameroon, the UPC became the territory's principal advocate for a national identity concept based on independence, democracy, and transethnic solidarity —a concept that would decisively influence the shape of the country's future.

The spiritual and intellectual leader of the UPC was the union organizer and former civil servant Ruben Um Nyobé. Revered by large numbers of Cameroonians for his integrity, his charisma, and his breadth of vision, Um Nyobé forged his image of the world from four principal sources. An important part of his personal heritage, the cultural and religious values of the Bassa imbued him with a respect for the wisdom of traditional society. The American Presbyterian schools near his village of Boumnyébél inculcated in him a spirit of self-reliance, independence, and democratic participation that inspired much of his thought. The Marxist reading groups he attended during the war provided him with an understanding of the historical and economic forces behind the French presence in Africa. Finally, his experiences as a magistrate's clerk and as a union organizer had given him a profound insight into the practical realities of colonialist oppression: its human dimensions and its points of vulnerability.

Scattered through ephemeral publications, pamphlets, personal communications, and diaries, the writings of Um Nyobé reveal him to be a man whose compassion and sense of fairness impelled him to fight against a colonialist system that had inflicted forced labor, the *indigénat*, and countless other indignities on people who deserved to enjoy the same rights as those who were imposing this system on them.[1] According to him, the UPC had become the "soul of the Cameroonian people" in the sense that it expressed their desire to live in freedom. By frustrating this desire, the colonial authorities were, he argued, condemning Cameroonians to live in a state of slavery. To counter the false constructions of reality by means of which the French justified this inequitable situation, Um Nyobé sought to awaken his fellow Cameroonians to the true nature of a system that disenfranchised them and robbed them of resources that rightfully belonged to them. Because he was convinced that no force could destroy the solidarity of a people determined to liberate itself and establish a socially just national community, he urged Cameroonians to develop a unity of purpose based on the reconciliation of ethnic rivalries and the abandonment of assimilationist aspirations. Um Nyobé himself was appalled by the prospect of violence and repeatedly declared that a policy based on physical force was a sign of weakness, not strength. At the same time, he was fully aware that sacrifice would be necessary for Cameroonians to free themselves from colonialist rule.

By 1951, Um Nyobé realized that Cameroon's status as a UN trust territory offered the UPC a unique opportunity to present its case for national independence. When he appeared before the trusteeship committee the following year, his attack upon French colonial policy and his defense of Cameroonian aspirations for nationhood were warmly received. Published in pamphlet form as *Ce que veut le peuple camerounais*, this UN speech gained wide circulation within the territory, despite efforts by the colonial authorities to confiscate all copies of it. In fact, the UPC's use of printed and mimeographed materials was a significant part of its campaign to gain popular support for its anticolonialist, nationalist agenda. For example, Léopold Moumé Etia wrote a tract to demythify the figure of Alexandre Douala Manga Bell, who had been flown to New York by the French to serve as one of their spokesmen in UN debates over the territory's future, and Um Nyobé used this pamphlet in attempting to convince Cameroonians that their interests had often been betrayed by their own representatives working in conjunction with the colonial administration. The use of print culture in this form and participation in the UN hearings lent legitimacy to Um Nyobé's position at home and reinforced the credibility of UPC demands for Cameroonian independence.

Dr. Felix-Roland Moumié was a more radical UPC leader, but his tract *Religion ou colonialisme* served a similar demythifying function by demonstrating the incompatibility between Christian teachings and colonialist practices. In this pamphlet, Moumié accuses French priests of condoning racism and of collaborating with the organizers of forced-labor camps. He attacks the clergy for blinding people to the fraud being perpetrated against them by the colonialist system. If all people were created in God's image, he argues, God would hardly be content to see his image reduced to slavery. Moumié's arguments exercised a strong appeal over young people, and years after his pamphlet first appeared, copies of it were still circulating clandestinely in Cameroonian schools. Addressed to a transethnic reading audience, UPC publications such as those of Um Nyobé, Moumé Etia, and Moumié helped consolidate the idea of a Cameroonian national identity while at the same time popularizing the anticolonialist sentiment that inspired much of the territory's literature during the 1950s.

Yet the success of the UPC depended even more upon its ability to transform the political awareness of a literate elite into a popular nationalist movement. Um Nyobé constantly emphasized the need to reach all Cameroonians, and he himself traveled by foot through the countryside to speak with groups of workers and peasants. By dressing in a modest fashion and refusing the privileges of rank, he demonstrated his identification with the common people, and by offering them the vision of a just, self-respecting society as an alternative to colonial domination, he gave them renewed confidence in their ability to determine their own future. Between 1952 and 1955, UPC membership grew from thirty thousand to over one hundred thousand, and many more people sympathized with its objectives. It was the largest single party in eastern Cameroon, although fraudulent election procedures prevented it from being represented in either the territorial assembly or the French national assembly. Because the UPC was denied a voice in French-dominated political institutions, Um Nyobé devoted his efforts to the organization and education of common people. At least 450 local UPC committees were formed at this time to promote discussion and to coordinate the struggle against colonialist oppression.[2] By 1955, Um Nyobé and the UPC had generated widespread enthusiasm for the idea of an independent Cameroonian nation.

Much of French policy in the territory during the 1950s can be understood as an attempt to stem the growing popularity of the UPC. Within the context of their collapsing empire in Indochina and North Africa, colonial authorities had been encouraged by the success of compromise solutions with leaders such as Houphouët-Boigny, whose earlier anticolonialism had been tempered into an advocacy of institutional reforms with guarantees for the security of French investment capital. The French government hoped to bring about a similar compromise in Cameroon when it appointed Roland Pré as the territory's high commissioner in 1955. Embarrassed by Um Nyobé's appearances at the UN and placed on the defensive by the UPC challenge to fundamental assumptions behind the assimilationist doctrine, the colonial administration under Pré's leadership intensified its campaign against the radical nationalist movement. At the same time, it implemented liberal reforms and cultivated support among civil servants and moderate political leaders for the idea of a more autonomous Cameroon within the French Union.

In May 1955, riots erupted in Douala, and they were suppressed with a show of violence by the French authorities. Blaming the unrest on the UPC, they used the situation as a pretext for banning the movement and carrying out a series of armed reprisals against its supporters. Moumié and the Bamileke UPC leaders Abel Kingué and Ernest Ouandié fled to the British Cameroons, leaving Um Nyobé isolated from his principal lieutenants when he retreated into the Bassa country and began to transform the UPC there into an underground organization. For a year and a half, Um Nyobé continued to plead for reconciliation and the reinstatement of the UPC as a legal political party, but with the implementation of Gaston Deferre's *Loi cadre* (enabling act) in 1956, he realized that the enhanced power of elected representatives in the territorial assembly would eliminate the UPC from any meaningful role in determining the future of the territory because its members were prohibited from participating in elections. Cameroonian leaders from other parties found this situation to their advantage, for it allowed them to fill the void left by the absence of the territory's largest and most influential political movement. By the time of the December 1956 elections, the colonial administration had placed the UPC in an impossible dilemma: it could either allow the French to stifle the popular nationalist sentiment it represented, or it could take up arms against a colonial regime that persisted in imposing its own assimilationist vision upon the territory.

Um Nyobé never believed in a purely military solution to the colonialist situation, and the UPC was not well prepared to wage war against the government in power, but he reluctantly acquiesced in a guerilla campaign to disrupt the elections. Electric power lines were cut, road and railroad traffic was halted, and several moderate candidates were killed. This outburst of violence profoundly altered the psychological climate in eastern Cameroon. If it heightened the resolve of committed UPC adherents, it also alienated a broad spectrum of more conservative nationalists who might otherwise have supported the movement.

At the time, the UPC enjoyed its strongest support in Douala and in two adjacent areas—among the Bassa to the southeast and among the Bamileke to the north. The most disciplined wing of the party was in the Bassa area, where Um Nyobé and his adjunct Theodore Mayi Matip had established a network of local committees that often functioned as alternative administrations, performing routine police duties and even issuing birth, death, and marriage certificates.[3] The idea was of course to convince people that they could participate in their own governance and ultimately liberate themselves from foreign domination. For two years, Um Nyobé and Mayi Matip relied upon this network of committees as they directed an underground struggle against the increasingly brutal "pacification" program of the French security forces. But Um Nyobé was captured and executed in October 1958; shortly afterward, Mayi Matip emerged from hiding and claimed to be acting upon the dead UPC leader's final wishes when he asked his followers to lay down their arms. Almost at once, the troubles in the Bassa area ceased, although they were just beginning to gather momentum in the Bamileke region, where they would continue until the 1970s.

The death of Um Nyobé had important consequences for the eventual shape of Cameroonian independence. By provoking the one truly nationalist party in the territory into armed revolt, the colonial administration had already isolated the UPC from potential supporters who were repulsed by the violence of the Bassa uprising. Because Um Nyobé was the only UPC leader to have enjoyed virtually universal respect among Cameroonians, the loss of his conciliatory, unifying presence assured the further erosion of UPC support and the marginalization of the movement under the more radical leadership of the party's Bamileke wing. Under such circumstances, the French were able to legitimize a conservative form of government that has maintained itself in power for thirty years. Rather than the socialist participatory democracy that Um Nyobé envisioned for the country, Cameroon became an authoritarian state that, like the colonialist regime, benefited the few at the expense of the many.

Recognizing the enormous popularity of Um Nyobé, both the colonial administration and its Cameroonian successor government sought to minimize his legacy by refusing him proper burial and by excising his name from official accounts of the country's history. Yet their efforts were not entirely successful. The memory of Um Nyobé remained alive, not only in the Bassa oral tradition that transformed him into an epic hero, but also in the dream of a socially just society—a dream that even today animates an undercurrent of opposition to the conservative forces that filled the "national vacuum" created by the French suppression of the UPC. In this way, Um Nyobé has become a major reference point in the universe of discourse that defines a sense of collective consciousness in Cameroon.

By the mid-1950s, leading political moderates in eastern Cameroon realized that the only platform capable of generating widespread popular support was one that included the UPC demands for national independence, reunification with the British Cameroons, and the elimination of preferential treatment for expatriate Europeans. These were among the objectives of the National Union movement that Soppo Priso organized shortly before the 1956 elections, and most moderate leaders quickly adhered to it. Yet their own parties, like those of the more conservative forces in the territorial assembly, were built upon ethnic rather than national constituencies. By encouraging traditional Fulani rulers from the North to join in an alliance against the more radical forces that had begun to emerge in that region, French colonial authorities laid the groundwork for a parliamentary coalition that elected the conservative Catholic André-Marie Mbida from Aujoulat's BDC to serve as the territory's first prime minister in 1957.

Because the autocratic Mbida thought his future lay with the French Union, he attacked moderate nationalists such as Soppo Priso and popular causes such as independence and reunification. This stance and his identification with the violent suppression of the Bassa uprising cost him any support he may have had among the people. Exasperated by Mbida's erratic behavior, the French high commissioner ultimately engineered his replacement by Ahmadou Ahidjo, the leader of the coalition from the North. Ahidjo's dependency upon French advisers and his continuing need for French economic and military assistance assured that French interests in Cameroon would be respected even after independence. In fact, the economic infrastructure created by French colonial rule would remain largely in place during the entire twenty-five years that Ahidjo stayed in power, and the social inequities it engendered would continue to fuel the widespread discontent upon which the UPC had always drawn for support of its socialist and nationalist platform.

But this scenario could not have been foreseen at the time, and as popular support for national independence grew, increasing numbers of Cameroonians participated in the debate over what shape it should take. Journalistic activity flourished between 1955 and 1960. Political parties, religious groups, trade unions, ethnic associations, and even private individuals began to publish newspapers in French as well as in several Cameroonian languages.[4] Aujoulat's *Cameroun de Demain* and Soppo Priso's *Cameroun Espoir* provided their owners with vehicles for the expression of their own political views. Marcel Bebey-Eyidi's *L'Opinion au Cameroun* opened its columns to a broad spectrum of contributors, including Um Nyobé and others who attacked the colonial system. The UPC newspaper *Cameroun mon pays* and its various successors enjoyed great popularity, particularly in the Douala area, although they, like *L'Opinion*, were repeatedly seized by the colonial administration under authorization provided by a 1939 press law that forbade the publication of any materials regarded as "foreign" or capable of harming the national interest. Originally promulgated to prevent the dissemination of German propaganda, this law was, ironically, used to restrict the expression of Cameroonian national sentiment in Cameroon itself. Nevertheless, the explosion of journalistic writing during the last five years of the colonial era did reinforce an awareness of the implicit reading community upon which a modern sense of national identity has generally been based.

Among the most active participants in this flurry of publishing activity was the Catholic church, which initially opposed national independence. However, as indigenous Cameroonian priests became increasingly influential in the ecclesiastical hierarchy during the 1950s, the church's official position on colonialism began to change.[5] Christianity was no longer regarded as incompatible with independence, and new theological doctrines were formulated to eliminate the Eurocentric bias of earlier missionary teachings. Although the church continued to condemn the UPC as an atheistic party that sowed hatred, fear, and violence among the people, it eventually appropriated many of the UPC's causes as its own.

For example, the longest-lived newspaper to emerge from the journalistic effervescence of the middle and late 1950s was the Catholic weekly *L'Effort Camerounais*.[6] Its relatively independent character was shaped by its first director, the French priest Pierre Fertin. Although Fertin was a fervently anti-Communist proponent of obedience to hierarchical authority in the church, he was also deeply committed to humanitarian ideals. He believed that Catholics should be well-informed citizens who concerned themselves with morality in public life. He empathized with Cameroonian aspirations for freedom and the right to define a collective identity in harmony with their own cultural heritage. In contrast with *La Presse du Cameroun*, his *L'Effort* carried articles on Cameroonian history and ethnic practices, poems and essays by Cameroonians, and editorials in support of Cameroonian independence. A regular "Dialogue" column contained discussions of national liberation movements in other parts of Africa.

One of the regular contributors to *L'Effort* was the Douala journalist Iwiyé Kala Lobé, whose articles on pan-African solidarity, the abuses of the colonialist system, and the advantages of working with well-intentioned Frenchmen such as Pré and Aujoulat exercised considerable influence over the newspaper's readership. As violence in the Bassa and Bamileke areas intensified, *L'Effort* grew more antagonistic toward the UPC. Nevertheless, it did consolidate support for Cameroonian independence by popularizing the idea that good Catholics could also be good nationalists and by demonstrating that the church itself was capable of applying Christian moral principles to the colonial system. Coupled with the newspaper's anti-UPC tendencies, its moderate nationalist position helped shape the climate of opinion in which many Cameroonians, particularly in the heavily Catholic areas around Yaounde, proved willing to accept the conservative coalition that came to power under Ahidjo.

Similar views were expressed in two widely disseminated pamphlets by the territory's first African bishops—Jean Zoa's *Pour un nationalisme chrétien* and Thomas Mongo's *Principes pour le pays*. In contrast to the Catholic hierarchy's earlier opposition to Cameroonian independence, Zoa acknowledged that nationalism represents a healthy movement toward unity and human dignity, but because nationalism by itself is a blind force, he contended that it should be guided by the principles of Christian humanism and regarded as a first step toward universal brotherhood. When he asserted that the nationalist movement must be inspired by people who recognize the spiritual dimension of human existence and accept moral responsibility for their actions, he was implicitly exhorting Catholics to assume leadership roles in the struggle for independence and warning them against allowing the atheistic UPC to dominate it.

Like Zoa, Mongo believed that the Cameroonian nation should be founded on Christian principles, but he argued that Christianity is actually the universalization of moral and spiritual insights that are also present in traditional Cameroonian religions. In *Principes pour le pays*, he cautioned his readers against embracing socioeconomic systems, such as Communism or liberal capitalism, that repudiate these principles in practice. Both Mongo and Zoa were espousing the cause of national independence and redefining it in Christian terms. The moral idealism of the church thus inserted itself into the dialogue about national identity at a moment when conservative political forces were seeking new content for a concept that had initially been advanced by their opponents.

As the debate over the territory's future grew more intense, a major center of Cameroonian intellectual activity emerged in France, where students from different ethnic backgrounds developed a heightened sense of their identity as Cameroonians at the same time that they were becoming aware of revolutionary cultural and political forces that were reshaping black consciousness in other parts of the world. Throughout the 1950s, the colonial administration sought to consolidate support for the idea of a francophone community by offering more and more young Africans the opportunity to study in France. The number of Cameroonians studying there soared from 24 in 1947 to 1,127 in 1958.[7] Contrary to official expectations, however, many of these students adopted a highly critical stance toward the colonialist enterprise by applying the analytical tools and political ideals they had learned in French schools to the existing situation in their own areas of the world.

In France, contact with other Africans and distance from their homelands allowed them to gain perspective on this situation, and they realized more clearly than before that colonialist rhetoric was based upon an image of Africa that conflicted with their own experiences. In seeking to demonstrate the falsity of stereotyped European notions about Africa, Cameroonian students living in France during the 1950s produced the territory's first major outburst of literary publication. The poets François Sengat-Kuo, Elolongue Epanya Yondo, and Jean-Paul Nyunaï as well as the novelists Ferdinand Oyono, Mongo Beti, Benjamin Matip, and Jean Ikelle-Matiba all belong to this generation, and the unifying strand that runs through their work is an opposition to colonialism. These young people rejected the assimilationist assumptions behind books such as Carret's *Kel'lam*. They found it insulting to their sense of themselves and false in the sense that it ignored the crimes and humiliations that had been inflicted on Africans by European colonialism. Their writing reflects the passion with which they pursued the quest for freedom and identity at the very moment when a wave of French popular interest in the colonies opened publishing possibilities that had never before existed for Africans.

The intellectual climate in which much of this writing took place was intense. Within the student organizations that emerged at this time, there was considerable optimism about the future. There was also a general feeling of solidarity in the struggle against colonialism. Yet the opinions of these students were by no means uniform, for a broad spectrum of individual world views found expression in the newsletters, journals, and other ephemeral publications that proliferated among them at the time. As early as 1951, Bebey-Eyidi's support made possible the founding of the AECF (Association des Etudiants Camerounais en France), and its long-time president Bala Benoit increased its membership by recruiting students at universities and secondary schools throughout France. Many of these students also belonged to FEANF (Fédération des Etudiants d'Afrique Noire en France), which had been created the previous year to provide francophone African students with an opportunity to meet and discuss matters of common concern.

At first, neither the AECF nor FEANF was overtly political, but many of the students who arrived from Cameroon in 1952 had been influenced by UPC activities in their secondary schools at home. The presence of these students inspired support for a more militantly nationalist stance, a sentiment reinforced by Um Nyobé's discussions with members of the AECF when he

stopped in Paris on the way back from his 1952 appearance at the UN. Although both Soppo Priso and Aujoulat sought to exert a moderating influence on Cameroonian students in France, a group favorable to the UPC gained control of the AECF in 1956 when Sengat-Kuo was elected president and the organization's name was changed to UNEK (Union Nationale des Etudiants Kamerunais), adopting the UPC's practice of spelling the territory's name in German to emphasize a commitment to national independence and reunification with the British Cameroons.

Some of the more moderate students dropped their affiliations with UNEK in protest against its new political orientation, but the majority remained, and the organization's intellectual life grew increasingly intense. Animated meetings and informal discussions took place at its headquarters in the Foyer des Etudiants Camerounais on the Rue Montmartre in Paris. Reading groups were formed, and several Cameroonian students joined amateur theatrical troupes. Others were writing polemical essays, poems, short stories, and novels. For three years Sengat-Kuo and several of his friends brought out *Kasó*, a nationalist journal devoted to commentary upon Cameroonian social, economic, and political problems as seen from a global perspective. Contributors to *Kasó* and the *Bulletin de l'UNEK* (a mimeographed newsletter that succeeded the earlier *L'Etudiant du Cameroun*) criticized liberal Frenchmen such as Aujoulat and the older generation of Cameroonian politicians for their assimilationist views. These student journals also attacked colonialism and advocated Cameroonian independence outside the French Union. Among them and their fellow students at the Foyer, a self-confident sense of national identity was clearly being articulated.

Many of these same students had also become involved with the journal *Présence Africaine*, which was intimately linked with the Negritude movement and committed to both pan-African solidarity and the rehabilitation of black culture throughout the world. Its editor, Alioune Diop, was married to a woman from Cameroon, and the two of them frequently welcomed Cameroonian students into their home. Epanya Yondo had spent much of his childhood with them, and nearly all the Cameroonian students who later became known as writers were influenced by Diop, whose reaffirmation of black culture inspired many of them to regard their own ethnic heritage in a new light. But the common motivation behind their commitment to UNEK and *Présence Africaine* was the anticolonialism that characterized both institutions.

Like the Cameroonian student organization, FEANF became increasingly politicized and eventually affiliated with the Prague-based International Union of Students. In 1956, participants in FEANF's annual congress passed a resolution demanding complete independence for all African peoples. Two years later they attacked Mbida and Ahidjo as counterrevolutionaries, publicly supported the UPC, and condemned France for conducting a "barbarous war" against the Cameroonian people.[8] During this time, Cameroonian students were frequent contributors to FEANF's official publication *L'Etudiant Noir*. However, if nearly all Cameroonian students supported national independence by 1958, many of them felt uncomfortable with the radical orientation of UNEK and FEANF. As in Cameroon, a moderate nationalism gained ground among them, and they expressed their support for it in a variety of ways. At the urging of Mbida and Aujoulat, Adalbert Owona helped organize a splinter group of Catholic Ewondo students. With the support of Bebey-Eyidi and several Protestant groups, Abel Eyinga organized the Cercle Culturel Camerounais, which condemned the repressive policies of Mbida and advocated open discussion as the best way of resolving the problems that confronted the territory.

Also with the support of Bebey-Eyidi, Eyinga helped bring out *La Revue Camerounaise*, which appeared irregularly during the late 1950s. In it, essays on Cameroonian culture were interspersed with liberal commentaries on the abuses of colonialism and appeals to the Cameroonian intellectual's sense of civic responsibility. Similar articles by Cameroonians appeared in journals sponsored by religious groups—*L'Etudiant Africain Protestant*, which was edited for several years by Marie-Claire Matip, the author of *Ngondo*, and *Tam-Tam*, a Catholic publication supported by the Upper Volta intellectual Joseph Ki-Zerbo and containing frequent discussions of the need for national independence and cultural emancipation.

UNEK itself became more moderate when William Eteki and Omar Senzé engineered the election of Vroumsia Tchinaye to the presidency of the organization. Tchinaye was a Massa from northern Cameroon, and he had the support of Ahidjo.[9] Nevertheless, some members of UNEK remained severely critical of Ahidjo's government and of the role played by the French in bringing it to power. For this reason, French authorities closed the Foyer in 1960, ordered UNEK to disband, and withdrew scholarship support from five of its most outspoken members.

The intellectual currents that affected Cameroonian students in France paralleled those that were shaping the climate of opinion in Cameroon itself. The concept of national independence initially advocated by radical groups was appropriated by more moderate ones and given a meaning that could be reconciled with many elements of the existing colonialist system. Those who persisted in opposing this solution were either marginalized or excluded from participating in its implementation. Even Tchinaye's election as president of UNEK helped prepare the way for the transition between colonial rule and a highly conservative Cameroonian government that was to maintain close ties with the former colonizing power.

What did emerge from the intellectually charged atmosphere of the Cameroonian student community in France was a remarkable flowering of anticolonialist literature. The poetry of young men such as Sengat-Kuo, Epanya Yondo, and Nyunaï is forged from the synthesis of Negritude and an ardent nationalism. The consciousness they project into their writing reflects a dynamic tension between passionate engagement and rational contemplation. Their world views are characterized by a tendency to perceive historical time as the movement from a peaceful traditional past through the suffering and injustice of the colonialist present to a utopian future in which their people will be free to live the identity they define for themselves. Drawing attention to the hope that sustains their sense of themselves and the memory that nourishes it, the poetic "I" at the core of their work fuses the intensely personal with an allegiance to the anticolonialist cause. Like Pouka, they expressed themselves in a print medium that reinforced the influence of modern individualism on their conceptions of themselves, but unlike him, they refused to model their self-images upon European assimilationist assumptions.

In fact, Pouka served the younger generation of Cameroonian writers as a foil against which they reacted in formulating their own theories of literary practice. He was the territory's most widely recognized author in 1954 when he wrote to Sengat-Kuo and asked him how he conceived the future of Cameroonian poetry. Sengat-Kuo's response became the outline of a new poetic credo. It did not circulate widely in the territory itself because it was intercepted by French censors, but when it was published as "Lettre à un Camerounais" in the *Bulletin de l'AECF*, it exercised considerable influence among Cameroonian students living in France.[10]

Although Pouka claimed to be speaking on behalf of the people, Sengat-Kuo accused him of having betrayed them on two counts. First, by indulging himself in gratuitous outpourings of sentimentality for the entertainment of a small leisure class, he was promoting religious and political ideas based on colonialist stereotypes that imprisoned his own people in a slave mentality. A true Cameroonian poet would, Sengat-Kuo argued, enlighten the masses about the nature of their enslavement and exhort them to fight for their own liberation. Second, by cloaking his verse in French Alexandrines and nineteenth-century Romantic conventions, Pouka was being inauthentic in the sense that his image of the world and its rhythms did not reflect the way Africans related to reality. According to Sengat-Kuo, a true poet of the people would interrogate traditional culture in an attempt to reappropriate a genuine African identity that had been submerged beneath an overlay of European customs and modes of thought. Furthermore, he concludes, most Cameroonians will never be moved by poetry written from a European perspective because they cannot identify with its exclusion of the cultural values according to which they define themselves.

Sengat-Kuo does not advocate the indiscriminate resurrection of African traditions or the wholesale repudiation of European precedents. Traditions evolve and must be adapted to the modern world, and foreign models might be useful in this process, but he insists that borrowing from others without being firmly grounded in one's own identity can only lead to alienation. Playing upon a Douala proverb that resurfaces in his own poetry, Sengat-Kuo reminds Pouka that "a tree can only grow by sinking its roots as deeply as possible into the nourishing earth."[11] Like the tree that reaches toward the sun, poets who aspire to the truth can move toward it only by anchoring themselves in an awareness of their own identity and of the origins from which it springs.

Within the Cameroonian context, such an awareness implied, for Sengat-Kuo, an allegiance to Um Nyobé's national independence movement. In the

essays he wrote for *Présence Africaine* during the mid-1950s, he repeatedly attacked the French Union as a pretext for reinstalling colonialism under a more
benevolent-sounding name. He was convinced that the first priority for Africa
must be economic development, but progress toward this goal was, he felt,
being blocked by an educational system that blinded Africans to their enslavement and produced a privileged elite that remained tied to the interests of
the colonizing powers. According to him, the only way to break out of this
vicious circle would be for Africans to assert their independence from paternalistic European experts and to formulate their own development goals. Sengat-
Kuo's poetry and politics thus spring from the same idealistic conviction that
every human community has the right to shape its destiny in conformity with
its own authentic identity. As a poet, he regards himself as the instrument
through which this conviction can be proclaimed and made comprehensible
to his people. His conception of Cameroonian poetry differs markedly from
that of Pouka, and it was the one that prevailed among the younger generation
of Cameroonians.

The same year that Sengat-Kuo replied to Pouka's inquiry, he also published a collection of verse, *Fleurs de latérite*, and a long poem, *Heures rouges*.
Both exemplify the kind of poetry he was advocating in "Lettre à un camerounais." In contrast to Baudelaire's "flowers of evil," his "flowers of laterite" are
lyrics that, he says, emerged from the red laterite soil of his native Cameroon,
raised their petals toward the sun, and released their liberating pollen to insemi-
nate other nearby flowers. The form-giving impulse behind this bouquet of
revolutionary verse is the individual consciousness of a poet who laments his
people's pain, reasserts their cultural values, and demands that they be treated
with justice and dignity. From the perspective of this consciousness, *Fleurs
de latérite* is an accusation of Europeans who profited from the ruthless exploitation of Africans while hypocritically claiming to be concerned for their welfare.
It is also a profession of faith in the poet's own identity as a black man proud
of his traditional African heritage.

In this collection of poems, Sengat-Kuo's attack upon colonialism takes
three forms: a graphic depiction of the suffering and humiliation imposed on
Africans, an unmasking of the dishonest slogans adduced to justify this oppression, and an appeal for Africans to unite and liberate themselves from the
colonialist yoke. In "Préjugé," he recalls the image of Cameroonians sweating
and dying as they built the white man's road near Edea. In "Ils m'ont dit,"
he catalogues the white men's commands for the African to dance, to abandon
his religions, and to fight their wars for them; each time the African obeys,
and each time the white colonialists, confident in the superiority of their civilization, laugh derisively at the docility of their subject. In "Mystification" and
"Ils sont venus," Sengat-Kuo shows how this civilization preaches liberty, equality, and fraternity but relies on force in reducing black people to slavery, for
if Europeans arrived in Africa with "Bibles under their arms," they were invariably carrying "guns in their hands."[12]

Yet Sengat-Kuo knows that Africans were not completely cowed by the threat of force, and his poetry celebrates their resilience. The workers of the forced-labor gang in "Préjugé" continue to sing "the joy of living" and "the sweetness of loving." At the end of "Ils m'ont dit," the terrified white men command the African to die for having declared his solidarity with all the pariahs of the universe, but he refuses and announces that he is a thousand-headed hydra. No matter how many of his heads are cut off, others will always remain to haunt his oppressors. Strengthened by this spirit of revolutionary optimism, the poet concludes "Mystification" with a plea for Africans to cast off the burden of past defeats and assert their right to freedom and independence. In all these poems, the poetic narrator presents himself as the spokesman for black humanity, making clear to the people what they already know in a vague and nebulous fashion. The assumption is that, if such poetry fulfills its intended function, it will move the people to act on the basis of the insight it offers them into the nature of their own oppression. Unlike Pouka, Sengat-Kuo believes that Cameroonians have the capacity to determine their own fate and that poetry can help them do it.

Another dimension of *Fleurs de latérite* derives from the poet's determination to recreate an authentically African identity in a milieu dominated by European customs and modes of thought. As he gazes around his Paris room in "Fidélité," for example, he reflects that, although Europe may have altered his consciousness, it could never tame his soul that "pulses to the warm rhythm of the drum" and to the "living rhythm of the world."[13] Something inside him responds to the image of peace, harmony, and vitality that he associates with precolonial Africa. In "Ils sont venus" and "Nostalgie," he describes how Europeans had systematically destroyed these qualities and replaced them with its own "metallic soul." To halt this process, he seeks to reawaken memories of the drums, dances, oral tales, and masks he had experienced as a child in Cameroon. Like a proud warrior from the tribal past, he imagines himself as an instrument of war that can help preserve his people's right to live without constraint in a culture that corresponds to the identity they feel inside themselves. Even his punctuationless free verse echoes a desire to liberate himself from regular French prosody and to find a medium capable of echoing the rhythms of his own thought processes, of following the birth of an idea into consciousness and tracing its movement into the realm of action.

Like Senghor, Sengat-Kuo envisions African authenticity as the first step toward a worldwide civilization in which every culture will be respected and allowed to contribute the wisdom it has acquired during the course of its history.[14] In the concluding poem of *Fleurs de latérite*, he invites all humanity to participate in an African dance. This dance symbolizes humanity's capacity to celebrate its harmony with the natural rhythms of the world—a capacity that white colonialists mistakenly dismissed as pagan, thereby preventing themselves from experiencing an insight that is essential for their own spiritual health. In this poem, the poet's nostalgia for a repressed childhood merges with an idealized image of the African past to yield a vision of future peace and harmony. Only in such a vision can he fully reconcile the European and

African influences that have shaped his image of himself. Until this vision becomes a reality, however, he must continue to struggle with the injustices of a corrupt world. *Fleurs de latérite* is the record of his struggle.

Similarly, *Heures rouges* relives the poet's childhood memories of the 1945 general strike in Douala, although the significance of his perceptions becomes clear only in the retrospective interpretation of the adult poet who sees in them a key to understanding the colonial situation and the possibilities for overcoming it. The poem itself is divided into three parts. In the first part, "Une voix d'homme," he recalls how a simple railroad worker entered his father's house and explained the rationale behind the strike. The voice of this uneducated but righteous man reverberates with indignation at the sufferings of Africans and at the hypocrisy of Europeans who exploit the misery of others for their own gain. It also pulses with a self-confident determination to recover the freedom and joyful attachment to life that find expression in African laughter and dancing.

In the second part, "Flaques de sang," Sengat-Kuo turns the colonialist rhetoric on its head by demonstrating that the true barbarians are the white colonialists who indiscriminately kill Africans in an effort to preserve their unjustified wealth and power. False pretexts are invented to justify firing upon the unarmed masses; a drunken African (a product of "their" civilization) is killed because he ventured into "their" street; a white priest shoots people in the back when they seek refuge in his church. When challenged, the mask of colonialist benevolence falls, revealing the greed, inhumanity, and cowardice of those who support a system that oppresses Africans and then blinds them to their oppression.

The final section of the poem, "Silence peuplé de voix," describes how the events of 1945 were buried in an official silence while the "pools of blood" on the streets and in the hearts of survivors bore testimony to the tragedy that had taken place. As the voices of the living and the dead join those from all over Africa to demand justice, it becomes clear that the single voice of the honest worker has swelled to a deafening chorus. The age of a new political consciousness has dawned. By transforming childhood memories of a specific historical event into a symbol capable of reinforcing revolutionary passion in the present, Sengat-Kuo helped establish one of the shared reference points that were gradually coalescing into a sense of Cameroonian national identity.

Epanya Yondo shared his cousin's commitment to African authenticity and Cameroonian independence. He too created a new poetic idiom by fracturing the regularities of French prosody and reconfiguring it into an appropriate vehicle for expressing a modern African consciousness. The anticolonialist thrust of his poetry also originated in the dialectic between memory and hope. His "Souviens-toi" provides a good example of how he, like Sengat-Kuo, could elevate an intensely personal experience into a symbol of colonialist injustice. When he returned to Cameroon during the school holidays in 1949, he was arrested and thrown into jail. While there, he witnessed the execution of a young protester: "He had only fifteen years / Fifteen years of age, of hope and of courage / They killed him. . . ."¹⁵ Yet the boy did not die in vain. The image of his death remained etched in the poet's memory, and when he wrote about it, he realized that the boy's executioners had become prisoners of their own crime. Unlike him, they would never experience the liberating hope of a new age. Reversing the stereotyped notion that European knowledge is superior to the knowledge of Africans, the poet claims that the victims of colonialism knew more about the human condition than did those who were oppressing them. In his eyes, the first duty of the poet is to articulate what the people had experienced and to present it in such a way that they could understand its full significance. The image of the young boy's execution represents one of his attempts to impress upon his readers the ugly reality of colonialism.

According to Epanya Yondo, Africans must choose between a false consciousness promoted by colonialists in an effort to obscure the causes of oppression and a true consciousness of the need for solidarity in the struggle to achieve a utopian future that respects the traditional past. Many of the poems in his collection *Kamerun! Kamerun!* are structured around his desire to discredit this false consciousness while demonstrating how the spirit of solidarity survives despite brutal attempts to suppress it. In "L'Homme de main," for example, he portrays a black soldier who tortures and kills his fellow Africans at the behest of his white superiors. Such a person is a traitor imprisoned in his own false consciousness; he may benefit materially from his obedience, but he denies his own humanity in the process because he is implicitly accepting the white colonialists' assumption that all black men are content to be what someone else has defined them as being. In "Nation camerounaise," Epanya Yondo presents the Cameroonian nation as a future possibility, an ideal that can inspire individuals to band together for the purpose of shaping their own destiny. Faith in such an ideal represents true consciousness for him, and anyone who seeks to prevent Cameroonians from acting upon it should be opposed by force. In this sense, *Kamerun! Kamerun!* is an exhortation to revolution.

Nyunaï's poetry also embraces the anticolonialist struggle, but almost reluctantly, as if the glaring injustice of the European presence in Africa had momentarily distracted him from his vision of the poet's true vocation—a highly personal quest for truth, beauty, and love. Influenced by the surrealistic qualities of earlier Negritude writers, his poems evoke a series of images that, taken together, recreate an emotion—a state of being within the poetic "I." In *La Nuit de ma vie*, for example, he records the solitude and despair of a young African who seeks to overcome the anguish of having lost the woman he loved. From memories of past happiness, he eventually distills a rationale for living in the present; the very process of writing poetry allows him to achieve self-definition in the modern world.

In his other collections of poetry, *Piments sang* and *Chansons pour Ngo Lima*, Nyunaï reasserts the dignity of the African past, laments the effacement of that past during a period of enslavement, and holds out the promise of future liberation. Ngo Lima is the Bassa god of hope, and just as the poet in *La Nuit de ma vie* forges a new hope from images of lost love and unity, the poet in these more polemical works conceives a new hope by resurrecting the authentic meaning behind African traditions that the white colonialists had reduced to the status of museum pieces. Not only does this hope enable the people to withstand the burden of present suffering, it also motivates them to fight for a better future. Their spirit of resistance in turn evokes fear in the hearts of their oppressors. Within this context, Nyunaï believes it is the poet's duty to make people aware of their own enslavement while strengthening their resolve to liberate themselves.

But in declaring his allegiance to revolutionary goals, he never completely abandons the voice of a solitary individual yearning to discover the truth about himself. The ironic "Teledict" is presented in the form of a mock telegram instructing local colonial administrators to establish a more just society in the face of widespread rebellions, but even it culminates in the image of a lone figure slumping, exhausted, over his writing table. Like Sengat-Kuo and Epanya Yondo, Nyunaï was committed to collective solidarity in the fight against colonialism, but also like them, he chose to express himself in a medium that reinforces modern self-concepts by preserving the record of an individual consciousness struggling to make sense of the world.

The anticolonialist novels written by Cameroonian students who lived in France during the 1950s also reflect a heightened preoccupation with individual consciousness. They too emphasize the need to define a new sense of identity capable of embracing both traditional values and the modern perspectives that would enable Africans to overthrow the tyranny of European colonialism. Like the poets of this period, they were intent upon rectifying the false images that Europeans had propagated as a means of justifying their own presence in Africa, but the medium of prose fiction provided them with a broader canvas on which to depict the complex sociohistorical dimensions of the colonialist situation.

By drawing upon French moral values and literary techniques to portray Cameroonians as fully rounded human beings victimized by an unjust system, writers such as Ferdinand Oyono, Mongo Beti, Benjamin Matip, and Jean Ikelle-Matiba attacked the colonialist mentality by applying European standards of value to the system that Europeans themselves had created in Africa. By focusing on real-seeming events, these writers presented a counterversion of colonialist history that had until then been told only from a European perspective. In effect, they were recuperating a usable past and mapping it with reference points that would eventually become part of a shared national consciousness in Cameroon.

With the exception of the Oyono and Beti novels that will be discussed in the next two chapters, the most important works of prose fiction written by Cameroonians during the preindependence period were Matip's *Afrique, nous t'ignorons* and Ikelle-Matiba's *Cette Afrique-là*. Both depict the reality of colonialism as seen from an African point of view, revealing how injustice was perpetrated in the name of civilization and calling European accounts of the process into question. The narrator in *Cette Afrique-là* recognizes the need to reexamine stereotyped European notions about Africa when he declares that "international opinion has been too manipulated since the beginning of colonization because the colonizer alone had access to the news media. To transform his mode of life into a fixed and permanent universal system, he invented a literature, a style, and even a morality, and it is by means of such clichés that we are judged."[16] By offering an alternative view of colonial history, Matip and Ikelle-Matiba reaffirmed an African sense of dignity and discredited the clichés upon which European justifications of the colonialist enterprise had often been based.

The narrative structure of *Afrique, nous t'ignorons* provides an effective vehicle for this message because Matip's narrative is presented as a letter from an anonymous Cameroonian to a French friend who has expressed interest in learning the truth about Africa. In the hope of communicating the essential character of a continent that disturbs him by its silence, the narrator records a series of episodes that occurred in his village when news about the outbreak of World War II affected different groups of people in different ways. By revealing the conflicts that separate these groups, the narrator offers his correspondent a remarkable insight into the complexity of a situation that Europeans had usually portrayed in biased and overly simplistic terms. An awareness of this complexity enables the actual readers of the novel to repudiate stereotyped views of Africa and to grasp the true nature of colonialism.

The story told by Matip's narrator is a simple one: having heard rumors about the impending war, elders in the Bassa village of Bidoé send emissaries to an American missionary, a European merchant, and a traditional sorcerer to gather information about the situation and its implications for their village; a decision about the community's response to this situation will be made during the council meeting that is taking place at the end of the novel. The drama in this situation arises from the fact that traditional wisdom remains a way of life for the elders, whereas the world views of the young men reflect their exposure to European-style schools. Further conflict is injected into this situation by the attitudes of the expatriate Europeans who profit in various ways from the colonialist system and are intent upon retaining their privileged positions vis-à-vis the Africans in the village.

Guimous exemplifies the wisdom of the older generation, but because he understands the need for technological progress, he willingly sends his son Sam to the local mission school. Nevertheless, he fears that the school and its analytical approach to knowledge will blind his son to the "essential truth" embedded in the traditional way of life. This essential truth involves the forces that govern the interconnectedness of all things, and by placing himself in harmony with them, Guimous himself becomes capable of insights that remain inaccessible to the pragmatic, materialistic mentality of Europeans. For Guimous, the spirit behind the traditional way of life aspires toward wisdom, dignity, integrity, and a harmonious participation in the totality of life. It is symbolically present in the formal codes that govern Bassa social life and in the giant baobab tree beneath the branches of which important village councils are held.

Sam does feel attracted to the traditional belief system, for he has experienced the harmony with nature and the sense of community it fosters among his people, but he cannot uncritically accept it because the mission school has conditioned him to regard the codes and the veneration of a baobab tree as superstitions. The school also reduced African history before the white man's arrival to a void that his father's stories of traditional society cannot entirely fill. Because Sam sees the colonial presence in Africa as a humiliating injustice, he is impatient with the older generation's lethargy and ineffectualness in opposing it. Besides, modern civilization appeals to him, and he wants to be part of it, although he has repeatedly encountered the stereotyped notions of the area's expatriate white men who regard all Africans as inherently inferior to themselves and therefore incapable of becoming full participants in the contemporary world. Sam is thus caught between two worlds—drawn to both but incapable of integrating himself into either of them.

When he encounters a classmate who suggests that the outbreak of war in Europe offers the young people of the area an excellent opportunity to attack the nearby town of Kézzaé (Eseka) and raze its white-owned businesses, he immediately identifies with the plan, but upon returning to his father's compound, he realizes that he and his father inhabit different mental worlds. Guimous is preoccupied with the past and the orderliness of his traditions; Sam can think only about revolting against oppression and injustice. The codes and the baobab tree appear irrelevant to him in light of the fraud that has been perpetrated upon his people by the colonialist system. If he is in rebellion against this system and its chief representatives, the European businessman Robert and the Protestant pastor William, he is also in rebellion against the passivity of the elders, and once he has adopted this attitude, he can no longer sustain a belief in the "essential truth" that is so important to Guimous.

Just as news of the war brings the latent conflict between Guimous and Sam to the surface, it reveals the anxiety and poverty of imagination behind the white colonialists' masks of superiority. The central chapter of *Afrique, nous t'ignorons* is entitled "L'Enfer" (Hell). It is the section in which Guimous visits his old friend Robert and the lay preacher Zachée visits William to gather information about the war. The implication is that the world shaped by the colonialist presence is a hell not only for Africans but also for the Europeans who have become entrapped in their own egocentric pursuit of wealth and power. When compared with the quiet wisdom of Guimous, the pretentiousness of Robert and William seems hypocritical and self-destructive.

Although Robert appears to be in control, he is actually a broken man who believes in nothing other than himself and suffers constant humiliation as the result of his wife's infidelities. News of the war frightens him: he might be drafted, and a threatened general uprising could deprive him of everything he values most. Aware of this possibility, he transfers all his goods to Guimous's compound, where he himself intends to take refuge, but he never arrives because, when he leaves home, he loses his way in the forest and presumably dies. Long before his disappearance, however, the true nature of his mentality had become apparent during his conversation with Guimous. Admitting that "I am my politics," Robert boasts that he doesn't believe in any God and that he would willingly accept Nazi rule if he could keep his privileged position in society.[17] According to him, every individual is a potential enemy. Guimous is appalled by these revelations, but they do give him insight into the European mentality that also produced colonialism and world wars. At this point, he asks Robert why Europeans, who are so strong, have never discovered the secret of peace, justice, and harmony. The question reverberates through the book.

The answer to it lies in the mentality of men such as Robert, whose materialistic individualism isolates him from everyone else and prevents him from recognizing the mysterious interconnectedness of all things in the world. Such an attitude breeds insecurity, and by the end of his conversation with Robert, Guimous feels pity for the man because he realizes that Robert, like the society he represents, is imprisoned in a psychological hell of his own making. Guimous's own "essential truth" contrasts sharply with the mentality behind this "hell" and undermines all European claims to moral superiority.

Similarly, Pastor William's Christianity proves inadequate when the faithful Zachée queries him about the war, for William reminds himself that "there are souls who should be kept in ignorance" and then says aloud, "there is no war."[18] His lie is rationalized in his own mind as a benevolent concern for his parishioners' peace of mind. In reality, he disdains their capacity to deal with the truth and fears that news of the war might trigger a general revolt capable of calling his own privileged position into question. Although Christian missionaries were supposedly helping to civilize Africans by showing them the way to the truth, Guimous realizes that their religion is no more true than the Bassa worship of Lô-Lômb, the Great Ancestor who had created the world. In fact, his own sense of the sacred is obviously stronger than the routinized faith of William, who, like Robert, is revealed to be a selfish and hypocritical individual.

At the end of the novel, the entire clan gathers by the baobab tree, where the eight eldest patriarchs will weigh the evidence gathered by their emissaries and determine the group's response to the rumored outbreak of war in Europe. They must choose between the revolutionary fervor of the younger generation and the older generation's desire for peace and harmony. Guimous knows that the colonizers' prosperity was built on stolen land and broken promises. He also knows that their power depends on the submissiveness of his people, and he is appalled by the vacuity of Robert's godlessness, but he sees the situation as part of a larger whole that is tending toward reconciliation.

In contrast, Sam no longer believes in the assumptions behind his father's view of the world. As the council discussions proceed, he concludes that traditional wisdom is outmoded and that the huge baobab should be cut down. His inclination is to blow up the whole colonialist system, but to do so, he would have to overcome the opposition of the elders as well as that of the white men. The conflicts that separate the younger generation from the older one and both of them from the European colonizer are left unresolved in the letter-writer's narrative, but the readers of Matip's novel have been given the opportunity to appreciate the complexity of an African reality that conflicts with European notions about it and provides a basis for judging the true nature of European colonialism.

Like *Afrique, nous t'ignorons*, Ikelle-Matiba's *Cette Afrique-là* is a rewriting of colonial history from an African point of view. It too involves a story within a story, for the narrator in *Cette Afrique-là* is an actual historical personage, Franz Mômha, who recounts his life on two successive nights during the rainy season in his Bassa village of Bitutuk II. His oral autobiography is embedded in the author's written record of it, which in turn is addressed to an implied audience of educated Europeans. Mômha's detailed explanations of Bassa customs and French colonial practices are superfluous within the context of his oral narration, but they make sense in light of this larger audience.

If one of Ikelle-Matiba's goals is to rebut stereotyped images of Africa for the benefit of such an audience, his portrayal of Mômha's character serves as one of his most persuasive arguments. Already well known in the community as a man of integrity and courage in the face of unjust suffering, the sixty-year-old Mômha makes his fellow villagers aware of a past that has been greatly distorted in European accounts of it, and he passes on to them the wisdom he has extracted from his own experience of life. Despite the excesses of the German and French colonial administrations under which he has lived, Mômha preaches reconciliation with Europeans, for he believes in the possibility of synthesizing a new African identity from the positive elements of every culture he has experienced—the Bassa moral codes, the traditional sense of harmony with the world, the German ideal of civic responsibility, French humanitarianism, modern technology, and Christian respect for the sanctity of the person. By successfuly integrating such influences into his own personality, Mômha becomes an implicit spokesman for Senghorian Negritude, arguing that Africans are as human as any other people and should be allowed to make their own distinctive contribution to the "civilization of the universal."

The story he tells is both a justification for this position and an explanation of how he came to hold it. Before the arrival of the Germans, the young Mômha had grown up in a peaceful and harmonious society, where he was destined to become a leader. The German occupation put a brutal end to this paradisaical era, but it also enabled Mômha to acquire some of his most important traits—a Romantic belief in a higher ideal, personal discipline, and a strong sense of civic duty. Realizing that the world was changing, his parents enrolled him in the new German school at Die Ngombé (Edea), where he became aware of the larger world beyond Bitutuk and committed himself to the German conception of a higher civilization in Africa. For him and his comrades, the years they spent in a series of German schools represented "the most beautiful moments of [their] lives."[19] Employment in the German civil service gave concrete form to the ideals he had imbibed at school and imbued him with the sense of belonging to a community larger than his own ethnic group. When he was posted to the German colonial office in Yaounde, he himself admitted: "I felt myself more and more Cameroonian. I was completely detribalized."[20] The German colonial experience had altered Mômha's sense of identity and transformed him into the potential citizen of a modern state.

However, when the French assumed control over the territory after the First World War, Mômha retired to Bitutuk, married a young woman in a Christian ceremony, and began to farm his lands with the discipline and techno- logical efficiency he had learned from the Germans. But he could not simply retreat into the idyllic life he had known as a child, because the French colonial system introduced a new form of corruption into village life. An administrative chief of Bitutuk had been appointed by the colonial authorities, and he vented his resentment against the respected Mômha by having him impressed into a forced-labor gang. Sustained by a conviction of his own righteousness and a faith in Christianity, Mômha survives and maintains a sense of inner nobility, but when he returns to Bitutuk, he discovers that the chief's men had pillaged his home and his farm. The point of this episode is to illustrate the injustice of the French system and its debilitating effect on the people.

At the moment when Mômha is telling his story, the *indigénat* has been abolished as a result of the Brazzaville agreements, and the Second World War is receding into the background of people's memories. The French have intro- duced political reforms that allow the people of a reconstructed Bitutuk to elect their own chief, and Mômha is serving as his principal adviser. In fact, his story is one of the ways he contributes his wisdom and moral idealism to the rest of the community. He himself exemplifies the hybrid modern identity he advocates, and as long as his story remains etched in the hearts of his listen- ers, he will continue to inspire them with the desire to realize their full human potential. By allowing Mômha's voice to reach a larger reading audience, Ikelle- Matiba's *Cette Afrique-là* demands that European accounts of the colonial pe- riod be reexamined and implicitly advocates a Negritude-influenced reconcilia- tion of European and African values.

As Cameroonian students in France were giving eloquent expression to their anticolonialist sentiments, eastern Cameroon itself had begun moving toward independence. With the death of Um Nyobé, there was no truly na- tional hero around whom a feeling of collective identity might have coalesced. Nevertheless, Ahidjo gradually consolidated his control over the territory, and by the time independence was declared on January 1, 1960, he had positioned himself to remain in power indefinitely. His original coalition with Aujoulat and Mbida's BDC had been directed against the UPC, but it also enabled conservative forces from the North and Center-South to prevent moderate na- tionalists such as those in Soppo Priso's Movement of National Union from participating in the government that would take control of the country after independence. Yet Ahidjo remained wary of the Catholic church's influence in the BDC because he and the Fulani aristocracy regarded its proseletyzing activities as potentially dangerous to the existing social order in the North. When he founded the UC (Union Camerounaise) in 1958, it was a largely

Islamic, regional party, although it expanded after independence and eventually became the country's only legal political organization.

By the time he became prime minister in 1958, Ahidjo had already adopted many of the popular goals initially advanced by the UPC, but he still faced considerable opposition from radical and moderate nationalists who regarded his administration as an instrument of French interests, not an expression of the people's will. Although the UPC uprising among the Bassa had come to an end by early 1959, UPC activities in the Bamileke country were growing increasingly violent, and the French had already committed troops to the area. Lacking the heroic stature that many African leaders enjoyed at the moment of independence, Ahidjo was not a popular figure, and because he relied heavily on French support, he failed to receive the backing of third-world and Soviet-bloc countries in the international arena. This situation made him even more dependent on the French and on conservative African leaders such as Houphouët-Boigny and Senghor, both of whom publicly defended the legitimacy of his government.

Under these circumstances, Ahidjo's administration became increasingly intolerant of dissent, inhibiting the free flow of ideas and stifling the lively intellectual climate that had emerged in the territory during the mid-1950s. Open hostilities in the Bamileke country offered Ahidjo a pretext to request the territorial assembly for the right to rule by decree during the first six months of independence. Vehemently opposed by Soppo Priso and several Bamileke leaders, the measure eventually passed. This emergency powers law became the model for Ahidjo's style of governance, and it was subsequently employed to suppress a broad range of socially and politically critical writings. Having appropriated the idea of national independence for themselves, Ahidjo and his conservative supporters gave it a practical meaning that its original proponents would hardly have recognized.

In any case, the UPC position had been greatly weakened by 1959. A refusal to participate in elections had deprived it of any legal representation in the government, and its terrorist activities in the Bamileke country had resulted in a loss of public sympathy. The suppression of liberal newspapers such as Bebey-Eyidi's *L'Opinion au Cameroun* made it difficult for its spokesmen to reach a larger audience, and Ahidjo managed to split the movement by incorporating some former members of the UPC into his government while branding others, including Moumié, Ouandié, and Kingué, as extremists. Those who had taken asylum in Conakry and Accra became increasingly isolated from the situation in Cameroon, and internecine squabbling among guerilla leaders in the Bamileke area prevented them from coordinating their efforts.

When the territorial assembly voted to seek independence in late 1958, the UPC was constrained to argue at the UN that independence should be deferred until new elections could be held. Ahidjo contended that the existing parliament was sufficiently representative and that elections should be held after independence; with the support of de Gaulle and most of the Western nations, his position prevailed, and the last serious challenge to the sovereignty of his government had been repulsed. Thus, by 1960 when Moumié, Um Nyobé's successor as the head of the UPC, was assassinated in Geneva, his party had ceased to be an effective threat to Ahidjo's exercise of power.

One question remained to be answered: would the two trust territories be reunited, or would the British Cameroons become part of Nigeria? The idea of reunification was based in part on a romanticized conception of the German protectorate, but until 1949 it had not enjoyed much popular support, except among the Douala and Bamileke living in the western territory.[21] At that time both Um Nyobé and Endeley realized that the question of reunification constituted an issue that could be raised at the UN, and they exploited it as a means of consolidating support among their respective constituencies. The UPC held several joint meetings with various West Cameroonian political factions, and they adopted a common position on the question. Um Nyobé's speeches popularized the idea in the French trust territory, while a growing resentment against the Igbos who had flooded into the area after the completion of the Kumba-Mamfe road contributed to its popularity in the British trust territory. As the idea became more closely linked with the goals of independence and modernization, it captured the popular imagination in both territories, and by 1955 it had been adopted by nearly all the major political parties.

By seizing upon this idea as an alternative to further domination by Nigeria and by cultivating the support of traditional rulers in the grassfields area around Bamenda, John Ngu Foncha gained sufficient support to be elected prime minister in 1959, thereby inheriting political power during the crucial period before the territory's future would be decided in a UN-sponsored plebiscite. At about this time, Foncha made an informal trip to eastern Cameroon and met Soppo Priso, who provided him with the financial backing to establish the first anglophone newspaper in the British trust territory, *The Cameroon Times*.

With the creation of a newspaper and the intensification of public debate over the territory's future, polemical writing increased. S. A. George and Paul M. Kale published pamphlets in which they defined a specifically Cameroonian identity in terms of ethnic affinities and a common history of German colonialism. Aloys Tellen brought out a *Kamerunian's Bedside Catechism* to address questions that Catholics might have about national independence. Students at Lagos and Ibadan publicly supported reunification, as did those in England, although their numbers were small and they were never as politically or literarily active as their counterparts in France. The One Kamerun Party had been founded earlier as an offshoot of the UPC, and its president, Ndeh Ntumazah, authored a number of pamphlets attacking the colonialist system and advocating reunification. The student wing of the One Kamerun Party in Ibadan defended a similar position in their modest newspaper, *The Patriot*. This ephemeral literature bears witness to the emergence of a print culture that helped define the sense of national identity taking root in the British Cameroons.

Exactly what reunification might mean in practical terms was not always clear in either trust territory. Support for the idea came from individuals with a broad range of political ideologies, and anglophone Cameroonians were perhaps more attached to their territory and its independence from Nigeria than they were to the goal of a reunified Cameroon in which they would be a minority enclave. Nevertheless, an idea that had taken shape among a small literate elite articulating its grievances before the UN trusteeship committee gradually developed a life of its own, acquiring powerful symbolic significance for many people in both territories and enabling them to identify with the idea of a greater Cameroon.

But this idea was inherited and redefined by the same conservative forces that were in the process of giving their own meaning to the concept of national independence. Both Ahidjo and Foncha were from the less-developed hinterland, and they distrusted an idea that had initially been advanced by intellectuals from the areas closer to the coast. When they met for the first time in 1959, they discussed the matter privately, but by then they had already become captives of an idea that had gained enough momentum to overcome their own reservations about it. In the UN plebiscite that was held two years later, West Cameroonians from the northern parts of the trust territory voted to become part of Nigeria, but those from the southern part opted for federation with the Republic of Cameroon, and much of the credit for their decision must be attributed to Foncha's support for it.

Thus, although the agenda for national independence and reunification had originally been supported by a popular anticolonialist movement that found powerful literary expression in the works of young Cameroonians living in France, the political power that presided over the attainment of these goals remained in the hands of a conservative coalition headed by Ahidjo, whose political dominance in an independent Cameroon remained contingent upon the backing of the former colonialist power. However, one of the major legacies of the immediate preindependence period in Cameroon was a body of anticolonialist writing that gave voice to a revolutionary yearning for freedom and a viable sense of collective identity. The two most influential contributors to this dynamic literate culture were Ferdinand Oyono and Mongo Beti, whose novels have become classic statements of the African dilemma under colonial rule.

CHAPTER
4

DREAM AND DISILLUSIONMENT IN THE NOVELS OF FERDINAND OYONO

Although frequently paired together as comic satirists with strong anticolonialist sentiments, Ferdinand Oyono and Mongo Beti actually represent two fundamentally different ways of looking at the world. As a politically engaged social critic who believes in the efficacy of revolutionary struggle, Beti wrote his early novels to provoke readers into opposing the colonialist system and supporting the right of Africans to determine their own destiny. In contrast, Oyono is a detached humanist who believes that all people live in a harsh, unfair world where artificial social distinctions often distort their perceptions of themselves and their relations with others; his attack on colonialism is based upon its refusal to respect the fact that Africans are just as human as Europeans.[1]

All three of Oyono's novels—*Une Vie de boy*, *Le Vieux Nègre et la médaille*, and *Chemin d'Europe*—focus upon the dilemma encountered by Africans who choose to pursue the assimilationist dream of "becoming somebody" in the colonial context. As Oyono clearly demonstrates, this dilemma derives from inherent contradictions in the colonialist situation and from Africans' blindness to what is most valuable in themselves. The contradictions are obscured by the use of a benevolent language that does not correspond with the reality to which it is being applied. For example, most European colonialists in Oyono's novels regard themselves as superior beings who are bringing civilization to a dark continent. They hold out the promise of friendship, knowledge, and material prosperity to Africans who adopt European ways of looking at the world. In reality, these Europeans are insecure individuals who insist upon maintaining the myth of their own superiority to justify their exploitation of Africa and to avoid seeing themselves as they truly are. Because their own conception of themselves is based on the assumption that Africans are inherently inferior to them, their promises to Africans are ultimately hollow, and they deal harshly with any African who even unwittingly challenges this assumption.

For the African protagonists in Oyono's novels, there are two ways of pursuing these false promises. The young Toundi in *Une Vie de boy* and the old man Meka in *Le Vieux Nègre* accept the assimilationist dream at face value and suffer as a result of their naiveté. Both are eventually obliged to acknowledge the folly of believing they could "become somebody" by trusting in the friendship of white men. In contrast, Barnabas, the autobiographical narrator in *Chemin d'Europe*, recognizes the duplicity behind colonialist rhetoric, but he cynically resolves to manipulate it for his own benefit. The irony is that he succeeds where Toundi and Meka fail, although he pays for his success by becoming as hypocritical and alienated as the Europeans he emulates. Pride motivates each of these three characters to seek self-realization through identification with the colonialist system. The same pride blinds them to the fact that the nature of their enterprise renders them vulnerable to European denials of their humanity and isolates them from their fellow Africans. Like Europeans in colonial Africa, all three characters pretend to be other than what they really are, and whether they embrace the assimilationist dream or merely exploit it for their own purposes, they must play psychological tricks on themselves to avoid realizing that they are living a lie.

In all of Oyono's novels, the artificial distinctions introduced by the colonialist mentality are implicitly contrasted with the humanistic assumptions of an underlying world view that recognizes the basic similarity of all people, whatever their race or cultural heritage might be. Everyone must confront solitude, suffering, and death. Like animals compelled to satisfy common physical needs, people can be ludicrous and ugly. They also have a capacity for compassion, love, and integrity. But whether they are well intentioned or malicious, the world in which they live does not necessarily reward them according to their merits, for it is, in Oyono's eyes, a harsh world where survival depends upon physical force or the ability to outwit others.[2] For him, the colonialist presence in Africa had blurred an awareness of these fundamental truths by superimposing its falsely benevolent "civilizing" rhetoric upon them.

The traditional way of life may have generated a strong sense of communal solidarity, a capacity for joy, and a respect for the interconnectedness of all things, but it had proved incapable of sustaining itself in the face of European technological superiority, and in a world governed by relationships of power, Oyono was convinced that Africans could not simply retreat into their own past. As one of his characters asserts in citing a Bulu proverb to explain his renunciation of traditional religious beliefs: "the river doesn't flow back to its source."[3] In the novels themselves, characters who cling to traditional values often do so in an attempt to justify unjust social hierarchies and outmoded superstitions. Their behavior can be just as ridiculous as that of their fellow Africans who blindly pursue the assimilationist dream. Like the false promises of colonialism, the allure of traditional values is deceptive, for they too can beguile people into misinterpreting the true nature of a harsh world. Faced with two equally untenable alternatives, Oyono does not offer a solution to the problem of African self-definition in a rapidly changing world, but he does intimate that the quality people need most is intellectual penetration—an ability to discern the human truth beneath the illusory appearances that are maintained by social convention.

This is precisely the quality he seeks to elicit from his readers in his first two novels, *Une Vie de boy* and *Le Vieux Nègre*. Both are clearly set in the Bulu country of south-central Cameroon, and shortly after having published them, he asserted that "Cameroon was a country over which a phantasmagorical curtain had been drawn. Thus, the Cameroonian writer should above all seek to raise this curtain. . . ."[4] What he means is that stereotyped thinking about traditional society and about the civilizing mission of French colonialism prevented people from recognizing what was actually happening in countries such as Cameroon, and he defined the writer's task in terms of recovering the truth about them. One of the ways he accomplishes this goal is to portray his protagonists as fully rounded human beings whose capacity for joy and suffering refutes stereotyped colonialist notions about African simple-mindedness or barbarity.

The principle behind this technique becomes apparent in the relationship between the narrator and the text in *Une Vie de boy*. The story of Toundi was contained in two school notebooks that the dying young man had brought with him when he fled from Cameroon to Spanish Guinea; these notebooks were subsequently translated from Ewondo into French and published by an anonymous Cameroonian who had been vacationing in Spanish Guinea when Toundi arrived there. If the translator of Toundi's notebooks had been in Cameroon and heard the same news that was initially brought to him by the talking drums in Spanish Guinea, he might have felt an impersonal pity for the battered young man, but he would not, he admits, have been deeply affected by the event. Conventional ways of interpreting reality would have predisposed him to regard Toundi's fate as a normal event in the day-to-day life of the country. However, in Spanish Guinea he has acquired a certain distance from the colonialist system in Cameroon, and he sees its dehumanization of Africans in a new light.

After Toundi dies, his belongings are entrusted to the anonymous Cameroonian, who is fascinated by the diary entries in the notebooks because they awaken him to the reality of his own situation. Like Toundi, he is a black African whose humanity has been systematically denied within the colonialist context. He is vulnerable to the same arbitrary injustices that were inflicted on Toundi. That is why he is struck by the dying man's questions: What are we? What are all the black men who are called French? By translating Toundi's notebooks and making them available to others, he is presenting materials that can be used to answer such questions. He is also acknowledging his affinity with Toundi. The narrative situation in *Une Vie de boy* thus exemplifies the very response Oyono is seeking to evoke in his readers—an insight into the humanity they share with an individual whom the colonialist system has dismissed as not fully human.

A similar goal is achieved in Oyono's first two novels by the narrative structure of the stories being told. In this sense, they resemble the "ritual process" described by the anthropologist Victor Turner.[5] According to him, traditional rituals that mark life crises or the passage from one social status to another can serve to reinforce the generic human bond that is often obscured in everyday life beneath distinctions of rank and power. Such distinctions are necessary for the practical organization of society, but they dissolve into meaninglessness in the face of such universally human experiences as suffering and death. The ritual process obliges people to recognize the artificiality of social distinctions, often by transforming marginal or socially inferior individuals into symbolic bearers of a common humanity.

Une Vie de boy and *Le Vieux Nègre* function like the ritual process by stripping away artificial social distinctions and by presenting Africans, who have been relegated to an inferior status in colonial society, as representatives of that which all human beings share with each other. By placing Toundi and Meka into a harsh world where neither traditional customs nor colonialist stereotypes provide adequate models for self-definition, Oyono is suggesting that they, like everyone else, are alone and fated to die. The drama in his first two novels revolves around a conflict between colonialism's reductionist view of Africans and a series of events that demonstrate their full humanity. Despite the humiliation and suffering of Toundi and Meka, their stories do not culminate in despair but, like Turner's ritual process, in a reaffirmation of the common humanity that readers share with the supposedly inferior people of their own artificially structured social world. The two novels enable them to vicariously experience the literary equivalent of a ritual process that reveals the falsity and unjustifiable cruelty of the colonialist mentality.

Both novels depict a naive protagonist's attachment to the assimilationist dream of being accepted into the European-dominated colonialist power structure. In actuality, this dream is unrealizable because Europeans are unwilling to accept the idea that an African is a human being like themselves. Nevertheless, they encourage him to continue pursuing the dream because his faith in it allows them to control and exploit him. Under such circumstances, Toundi and Meka commit themselves to the assimilationist ideal in the belief that it offers them an opportunity to improve their status in society. For a while, a self-satisfied pride in their own vision of future happiness blinds them to repeated indications that Europeans regard them as objects to be manipulated rather than as people to be treated with respect and compassion.

However, increasingly harsh contacts with the disdain behind Europeans' pretensions of friendship oblige Toundi and Meka to realize that they have been duped by the false promises of the colonialist system. In their pain and humiliation, they eventually relinquish their illusions, although it is too late for them to do anything other than recognize their own folly and accept their solitude in a world that does not operate according to human conceptions of justice and fairness.[6] But readers perceive that Toundi and Meka are not objects, as the Europeans in Oyono's first two novels assume. On the contrary, both characters are human beings whose sorrows and joys implicitly refute stereotyped colonialist notions about them.

The first stage on their path to disillusionment involves a decision to identify with the assimilationist dream as a means of "becoming somebody" in colonialist society. For both Toundi and Meka, this decision takes shape during a relatively long period of time. When the young Toundi quarrels with another boy over the sugar cubes that the white missionary Father Gilbert has tossed to the children of his village, he receives a beating from his father, who also deprives him of his dinner. At this point, Toundi runs away to the priest, who gives him the remains of his dinner and some clothes before taking him to the mission at Dangan and making him into his own houseboy. Because Father Gilbert teaches him not only to read and write but also to regard Africans as primitives, he becomes convinced that his own future happiness depends on his ability to imitate white men and "to live like them." The rationale for Toundi's decision is clear. Given the alternative between unjustly harsh treatment at home and the benevolence of Father Gilbert, he opts for what appears to be the most pleasant way of life for himself. By defining himself in terms of the white men's values, he believes he is assuring himself a more comfortable way of life and, at the same time, acquiring superiority over his fellow Africans.

As he gradually realizes that he can never accede to the white man's way of life, Toundi modifies his dream so that even a subordinate relationship to individual white people can enhance his stature in his own eyes. For example, when Father Gilbert dies, Toundi happily agrees to become the houseboy of the local commandant Décazy because "the dog of the king is the king of dogs."[7] In other words, he assumes that Africans are inferior to Europeans and can improve their standing in society by serving the most prestigious among them. Initially he admires Décazy as a man of superior power and knowledge. He also idealizes the commandant's wife as a paragon of feminine perfection. But his respect for them is self-serving in the sense that he can believe in his own superiority over other Africans only as long as he believes in his masters' superiority over him.

Meka's commitment to the assimilationist dream has also evolved through time. Long before the events described in *Le Vieux Nègre* take place, he had renounced his adherence to many traditional values and become a model citizen of the colonial empire. When he discarded the white man's skull that had been given to him after he killed his first panther, he was symbolically abjuring African superstitions in favor of a Europeanized world view that would motivate him to work diligently in his cocoa fields, to donate his ancestral lands to the local Catholic mission, and to feel proud that both his sons had died while fighting for France in the Second World War. As a means of reinforcing the exemplary attitude of "good niggers" such as Meka, the white commandant in the town of Doum decides to award him a friendship medal at the annual Bastille Day celebrations.[8] In real terms, such medals were not valueless. They exempted Africans from the *indigénat* and forced labor, and they enabled people to obtain certain privileges, including the right to own a gun. However, Meka sees the anticipated medal as much more. For him, it is both a justification for all the sacrifices he has made and the fulfillment of his dream to become like a white man.

Meka's dream, like Toundi's, is difficult to sustain because it is based on a set of false premises. Both characters exert considerable effort to ignore anything that might contradict these premises and menace their visions of future happiness. For example, Europeans are not what Meka and Toundi would like to think they are. In *Une Vie de boy*, neither the commandant nor his wife actually epitomizes the power, knowledge, beauty, or kindness that Toundi initially associated with them. Décazy is a petty individual who has been repeatedly humiliated by his wife's infidelities. She is a shallow woman consumed with sexual desire and a passion for respectability. When Europeans like them speak to Toundi of friendship, they mean that he must humbly acknowledge his inferior place in society; if he does not, of course, he will be obliged to do so by force.

Similarly, the white commandant in *Le Vieux Nègre* explains the promised medal to Meka in terms of the friendship that supposedly unites them. In reality, it is a reward for the old man's "healthy" attitude toward the colonialist system and an announcement to other Africans that rewards are reserved for those who conform to European standards of African behavior. Despite numerous indications of the true motivations behind the benevolent rhetoric of these Europeans, Meka and Toundi persist in overlooking what they should be able to perceive. The reason for this self-imposed blindness is their attachment to an assimilationist vision of future happiness. If they cannot believe in the friendship of Europeans, they cannot believe in the positive self-images they have created for themselves.

The Europeans in these two novels also have false conceptions about Africans, and both major characters partially accept these false notions to heighten their chances of realizing their own dreams. Toundi readily admits that he is "the thing that obeys," and Meka could be described in the same terms when he docilely stands at attention in the hot sun for an hour and a half on the parade ground where he is to receive his medal. The commandant has positioned him there in the middle of a chalk circle to make certain that the African will be in the proper place as soon as the high commissioner arrives to present the medals. The other medal recipient is a Greek merchant, and he remains comfortably seated on the veranda of the commandant's residence as everyone awaits the delayed opening of the ceremonies. Different standards are obviously being applied to the two men, and the commandant's indifference to Meka's suffering reflects the white man's inability to recognize the full humanity of the African, but because such distinctions are routinely made in colonial society, Meka regards them as normal, repressing the suspicion that they contradict the assumptions on which his dream rests.

Both Toundi and Meka momentarily lose contact with important dimensions of their own personalities as they pursue their visions of future happiness.

In dealing with Europeans, for example, Meka must always appear to be other than he really is. They insist upon a certain decorum and divide the world into artificial constructs such as kilometers and hours, whereas he feels most comfortable when he can share his feelings openly with others or when he is in harmony with the organic impulses of nature. He never laughs in the company of Europeans, and their straight gravel roads are painful to him in a way the sinuous forest paths are not. Thus, when he stands on the parade ground and sweats profusely in his European-style suit and tight-fitting leather shoes, he yearns simply to be himself—to remove his shoes and to urinate freely on the ground. But he resists such temptations, partly because he is proud of his manliness in withstanding pain, but mainly because he does not want to risk losing the medal that he needs to reaffirm his image of himself. The assimilationist dream thus imposes constraints upon a more genuine identity that lies beneath the false mask he adopts to meet European expectations of him.

Toundi too loses a part of his true identity when he distances himself from his own people. Unlike his fellow servants at the commandant's residence, he cannot laugh spontaneously at his masters' foibles, and he is cut off from the sense of community that sustains the people in his village. He also lacks a healthy relationship to his own awakening sexuality. Because he had left his father's compound shortly before the initiation rite in which he would have been circumcised, he feels incapable of making love to the African women who hint of their interest in him; he is afraid to face their scorn when they discover that he is not yet a full-fledged man. At the same time, he is obsessed with an impossible passion for Madame Décazy, the unattainable white woman who denies his humanity for other reasons. Without a legitimate outlet for his own sexuality, Toundi overcompensates by developing a morbid curiosity about the affairs of his masters. For him as for Meka, the Europeanized identity he invents for himself becomes a prison for the natural impulses that surge up within him.

If Meka and Toundi deny the truth about these impulses, they also refuse to recognize the meaning of incidents that should have convinced them that their dreams were unrealizable within the colonialist system. Even Toundi's beloved Father Gilbert treats him like a pet dog, pulling his ears, kicking him, and training him to work from before sunrise until long after sunset. No such regimen would be imposed upon European children, but Toundi naively accepts his condition as normal. He himself recognizes the falsity of Father Gilbert's belief that the Holy Spirit guided the boy to him, for he knows he had actually been attracted to the priest by the sugar cubes that symbolize the promise of a sweet and comfortable life. When he records the episode in his diary, he explicitly compares the boys fighting over sugar cubes to wild parrots lured into the village with grains of maize. If he had carried this metaphor to its logical conclusion, he would have understood how Europeans hold out illusions of future happiness to Africans, entrap them, and then exploit them for their own purposes.[9] But Toundi avoids drawing this conclusion because it would invalidate the major premise on which his concept of himself is based.

For the same reason, he persists in ignoring the meaning behind his perceptions of European cruelty and hypocrisy during the time he serves the white commandant. He witnesses two Africans being beaten into unconsciousness by the prison director, Moreau, and he himself suffers numerous kicks and other painful indignities. Yet he refuses to realize that Europeans who treat Africans in this way will not hesitate to destroy him if he stands in the way of something they desire. Similarly, he seeks to repress his awareness of Madame Décazy's lust and her adulterous liaison with Moreau because he has a psychological investment in the perfection of both his masters; if they are less than he thought they were, he cannot for long sustain his belief in himself.

Even when he begins to perceive the fallibility of his masters, Toundi misinterprets its significance. For example, he glimpses Décazy taking a shower and realizes that his master is uncircumcised, just like himself. Rather than diminishing his fears about his own lack of manliness, the sight of the naked commandant kills his respect for the supposedly superior being with whom he had wanted to identify. He is of course justified in recognizing the white man's vulnerability, but he is tragically wrong in supposing that he need no longer fear him. Whether or not Décazy is fully a man in African eyes, he has the power of the colonial system behind him. Despite warnings from others and his own insight into the hypocrisy of his masters, Toundi remains in their service because his curiosity about them and his fascination with the unattainable Madame Décazy overcome his rational awareness of the danger they represent to him.

Meka also refuses to comprehend the signs that should have alerted him to the duplicity of the colonialist system that is making a fool of him. True friendship would not tolerate the unnecessary suffering imposed on him at the parade ground or the priest's waving him away from a group of white men with the back of his hand or the high commissioner's diplomatic refusal to share the meal of goat meat he offers him. The priest's gesture is particularly galling to Meka because the priest had always insisted he was a friend of the old man who had led such an exemplary Christian life and donated his lands to the church. Meka literally closes his eyes to the meaning of such slights. The friendship medal enables him to overcome any doubts they evoke in him because he sees it as a concrete symbol of his success in attaining his dream. Actually the medal represents Meka's humiliation in the sense that it rewards him for acquiescing in a system that denies his full humanity, but he, like Toundi, is so attached to the idea of "becoming somebody" that his pride continues to prevent him from recognizing his folly.

Only after they have been unjustly arrested and beaten do they comprehend the fraud that has been perpetrated upon them by Europeans who held out the false promise of friendship with Africans. In *Une Vie de boy*, Toundi is accused of having helped the agricultural engineer's black mistress, Sophie, steal a cash box. There is no evidence that he was involved in the crime, but each of the Europeans in the room at that time has a reason for wanting to eliminate Toundi. The agricultural engineer has hated him ever since the time Toundi slept in the same room with Sophie during an official tour of the back country. Although Toundi's reticence prevented him from making love to her, Magnol's exaggerated jealousy reflects the anxiety he feels about his own sexual potency. By discharging his anger on the innocent houseboy, he can evade the truth about his own fears and ignore his own responsibility for the loss of the cash box.

The commandant and his wife are also willing to make Toundi a scapegoat for their own inadequacies. By the time the accusation is made against him, they have reconciled the differences that arose as the result of her affair with Moreau. As long as Toundi remains at the Residence, Madame Décazy cannot completely deny her unfaithfulness, and her husband cannot completely forget his pusillanimity in returning to her and pretending that nothing had happened. All three Europeans want to regard the houseboy as a "thing that obeys," but his potential for unmasking their pretentions makes them fear that he is actually a "person who sees." Under such circumstances, they welcome the pretext to remove him from the scene in the same way they might discard a troublesome object, for by denying his full humanity, they need feel no compunction about having him arrested to avoid looking into themselves. Ironically, Toundi's initial decision to identify with Europeans as a means of escaping his father's brutality culminates in a far more brutal beating at the hands of the Europeans with whom he identified.

Like him, Meka undergoes a traumatic revelation of European indifference to him as a human being. Falling into a drunken stupor at the celebration that follows the awarding of the medals, he awakens to the first storm of the rainy season and barely escapes from the Foyer Africain before it collapses, leaving him utterly alone in a dark, flooded area where all the usual landmarks have been obliterated. At first, he thinks he might be experiencing the end of the world, and when he discovers that his medal is no longer on his jacket, he laments that he has lost everything. The Biblical flood was supposed to purge the world of sinfulness, and in the sense that the flooding of Doum strips Meka of the false identity symbolized by his friendship medal, it serves a similar function in *Le Vieux Nègre*.[10]

Having inadvertently wandered into the European section of town, Meka is then arrested and held in jail overnight. The next morning, contrary to his expectations, the police chief, Gosier d'Oiseau, fails to recognize him as the recipient of the friendship medal, strikes him ten times, and spits in his face. The shock of this reception causes Meka to understand what he should have understood from the beginning—friendship is impossible with people who do not regard him as a full human being, and Europeans use false promises of future happiness as a means of persuading Africans to give more than they receive in return, just as Meka gave his two sons and his land to the French in return for a single medal. Gosier d'Oiseau's blows awaken him to the folly of his mistake.

Just as Toundi was lured into the assimilationist trap by Father Gilbert's sugar cubes, Meka was beguiled into it by the promise of the medal. By the end of *Une Vie de boy* and *Le Vieux Nègre*, both of them gain insight into the true nature of the colonialist system and renounce the illusions that had bound them to it. Toundi's insight is symbolically encapsulated in a nightmare vision that he experiences at the hospital shortly after having received a particularly sadistic beating from one of the guards: perched among the highest branches of an enormous tree, he gazes down upon an ocean of lepers, cripples, women with ripped-open stomachs, and slimy old men. Keeping order over them with whips are millions of Gosiers d'Oiseau, who are seated on giant termite hills.[11] In his dream, Toundi imagines himself diving into this sordid world, where his head explodes like a bomb, leaving behind nothing but darkness and a wisp of cloud.

Embedded in this vision is the recognition that his original situation in his father's compound was but one small part of the misery from which all Africans were suffering. Represented by the proliferation of Gosier d'Oiseau, the presence of Europeans had intensified this misery while brutally imposing their own conceptions of order upon it. Toundi's plunge into this world recalls his earlier decision to identify with Europeans, and his annihilation suggests that he at least subconsciously recognizes the death that awaits him as the result of this decision. The pride that had sustained his dream of becoming somebody in colonial society is gone, and in its place is a clear-sighted understanding of the harsh world in which he is obliged to live. On the basis of this understanding, he decides for the first time to take his fate into his own hands by fleeing to Spanish Guinea, where even if he dies, he will have the satisfaction of knowing that he escaped from the hypocritical Europeans of Dangan. Although his initiative occurs too late to save his life, it is significant because it reflects the intellectual penetration that Oyono regards as essential in coping with a world of illusory appearances.

Meka acquires this quality in response to the humiliation inflicted on him by Gosier d'Oiseau. At that moment he realizes for the first time that, when he threw the white man's skull into the river as a token of his willingness to accept a European definition of African identity, he was agreeing to become a slave. From his new perspective, he understands that the medal and the beating are complementary expressions of the same colonialist mentality that refuses to acknowledge his humanity; both are simply tools employed by Europeans to manipulate Africans into behaving in prescribed ways. When the disillusioned Meka returns to his compound, he communicates this insight in the cryptic announcement that, having died in Gosier d'Oiseau's jail, he is now returning from the "path that leads to the ghosts."[12] In south-central Cameroon, the word *ghosts* has a double significance: it refers to the dead, but it was also used to designate Europeans, who were initially thought to be from the realm of the dead on account of their white skins. By claiming to have returned from the path that leads to the ghosts, Meka is admitting that he has abandoned his pursuit of the assimilationist dream because he realizes that his attempt to become like a white man was tantamount to dying.

When Meka and Toundi chose to define themselves in terms of European expectations of them, they risked losing touch with two human qualities that have been preserved in traditional African society—communal solidarity and harmony with the natural world. While seeking to become somebody in colonial society, both characters are curiously alone because they have repudiated the traditional community but remain incapable of integrating themselves into the European-dominated modern world. Yet they can always recover the neglected human qualities by renouncing their assimilationist aspirations. For example, Meka feels rejuvenated as he walks through the forest after his encounter with Gosier d'Oiseau. He is no longer pretending to be an important person. In contrast with his agony on the parade ground, he walks barefoot and urinates unconstrainedly on the wet grass. He baptizes his surroundings the "forest of return," for by renewing his contact with the natural world, he is returning to his true self.

The communal solidarity he experiences after reaching his compound is something the Europeans could never have given him. If he suffers, his clansmen suffer with him, and their shared laughter momentarily frees him from the solitude in which his false identity had imprisoned him. In *Une Vie de boy*, Toundi's isolation becomes apparent in his inability to join in the laughter of his fellow servants, but when he is unjustly imprisoned, other Africans commiserate with him and come to his aid. Unlike the Europeans who remain indifferent to Toundi's suffering, they recognize him as a human being who feels what they themselves would feel under similar circumstances. After listening to the story of Meka's humiliation, one of his clansmen defines the nature of this group solidarity when he says, "what happened to the man named Meka has happened to all of us through him."[13] In a larger sense, Oyono's first two novels seek to evoke a similar response among readers. Like the ritual process, they strip away artificial social distinctions and reveal the genuine humanity, indeed the tragic nobility, of individuals who have been seduced by false promises while being relegated to a less-than-human status by the colonialist system.

Une Vie de boy and *Le Vieux Nègre* draw attention to the cruelty, hypocrisy, and injustice of this system. They also demonstrate the inherent contradictions of the assimilationist ideal. But they offer no hope for an escape from the harsh, arbitrary world in which all people must live. Although traditional African communities preserve human values that are largely absent from colonial society, they cannot defend themselves against the encroachments of European power, and their spokesmen are often ignorant and ineffectual. But if the old ways fail to provide adequate guidance in the modern world, the new ones lead to unnecessary suffering and humiliation.

Although Toundi and Meka eventually abandon their false identities, they remain painfully aware of their solitude. Meka does participate in the outburst of shared laughter that momentarily unites the people gathered at his compound, and laughter does offer solace in the face of absurd conditions that one cannot change, but laughter is not a solution to the problem of colonialism. What ultimately allows both Meka and Toundi to confront their fates with dignity is the intellectual penetration that enables them to accept the truth about themselves. Thus, if there is a cardinal virtue in Oyono's first two novels, it is the ability to perceive reality behind deceptive appearances.

The narrative techniques and rhetorical strategies in Oyono's *Chemin d'Europe* differ from those he employed in *Une Vie de boy* and *Le Vieux Nègre*, but the underlying world view remains the same. Rather than focusing on a naive central character whose illusions of future happiness shatter upon the harsh realities of the colonialist system, his third novel lays bare the complex mentality of an autobiographical narrator who unwittingly reveals his weakness and shame while telling the story of how he succeeded in realizing the assimilationist dream of going to France. Like Toundi and Meka, Aki Barnabas wants to become somebody in colonial society, but unlike them, he does not accept the false promises of Europeans at face value.[14] On the contrary, he internalizes the cynical, exploitative attitude beneath the benevolent colonialist rhetoric and calculatedly seeks to assure his own advantage in the same way that Europeans do.

In an interview several years after the publication of the novel, Oyono admitted that Barnabas's culture "permits him to become a man like everyone else."[15] But not everyone else is particularly admirable. In fact, Barnabas is far more pathetic than either Toundi or Meka because he consciously repudiates his most human qualities and never realizes how the colonialist system has distorted his mentality. Yet the character of the narrating Barnabas is part of Oyono's rhetorical strategy because the very existence of his mentality is an implicit condemnation of the colonial society that engendered it.

Barnabas is telling his story more than a year after leaving Cameroon and taking up residence in France. His motivation in recording it is twofold: he hopes to project a favorable image of himself as a man who overcame great obstacles to achieve his goal in a hostile world, and he wants to avenge himself upon all those who stood in his way. To underscore the credit he believes he deserves for what he presents as his success in life, he even overstates the difficulties he encountered. "Poor, without relatives, without friends, and scorned for my hopes, I nevertheless refused to be discouraged," he boasts at one point, adding that he was "a prodigious optimist in a country where the lust for wealth and power, the cult of self-interest, had dehumanized man."[16] In reality, he did have friends and relatives, and his education at the seminary allowed him to obtain several positions while most young men in the area remained unemployed. Furthermore, the traits he ascribes to his social environment also characterize his own corrupt mentality. Those who opposed him or scorned his aspirations are turned to ridicule in his portrayals of them. In other words, the narrating Barnabas uses his autobiography as an instrument to achieve goals that are of great psychological importance to him.

The model for his enterprise is the spur-of-the-moment account he gave of his life at a revivalist meeting where European missionaries, impressed with his display of faith, selected him for a trip to Europe.[17] Near the end of the novel, Barnabas relates how he stumbled upon the meeting and listened to several people confessing their sins. Knowing that he could fabulate a better story than those he had just heard, he approached one of the white organizers of the meeting, and the first sentence of his confession occurred to him—the sentence that would open the "road to Europe" for him. Like the novel itself, the story he told in front of the missionaries was intended not primarily as a communication of the truth but as an instrument to obtain what he desired.

Despite distortions and self-serving commentaries, however, Barnabas's auto-biography details the evolution of his Europeanized consciousness so clearly that readers can easily understand how he became what he is. His concept of himself is initially forged in a rebellion against his overbearing but simple-minded father, a "vieux nègre" who, like Meka, has been duped by the assimila-tionist myth into identifying with the culture of the colonizers. Having become a gardener for the priests at the local mission, the hunchbacked old man en-rolls his son at their school in the hope that the boy will someday become a priest. But Barnabas resents his father's desire to enhance his own stature by taking credit for the accomplishments of a talented son, so he mocks the old man's physical deformity and religious piety. The split between them becomes definitive when Barnabas leaves the seminary and dashes his father's cherished dream of having a son among the clergy.

Barnabas's attitude toward his father is apparent at the old man's funeral, for rather than mourning the death of a parent, he resents the "slap in the face" he receives when a spurt of water strikes him as the coffin sinks into a flooded grave. His interpretation of this accidental occurrence reveals the shame he feels at being associated with a man whom he cannot respect. Because of this shame, he seeks to distance himself from his father and to avoid resem-bling him in any way. Even at the moment of telling his story, Barnabas still desires to show that he is not like him. By depicting the old man as a grotesque buffoon, he tries to avenge the shame he continues to feel at the thought of being related to such a person. What most galls Barnabas about his father is the way the old man naively accepts the Europeans' false promises and allows himself to be exploited by them. Believing that this attitude makes his father a fool, Barnabas decides that he himself will never be duped by the colonialist rhetoric. For this reason, he determines to act as Europeans do—out of self-interest—and not according to their stereotyped notions about how Africans should act.

But Barnabas is not a strong-willed man who can take what he wants. The success of his various schemes depends on his ability to convince others to do for him what he cannot do for himself. The impetus for this sort of behavior can be found in his relationship with his mother. Like many of the other women in Oyono's novels, she possesses an inner strength and resource-fulness that most of the male characters lack. Young and beautiful, she sustains him in his moments of weakness. He in turn wants to make her happy and to draw her away from his father. Even as a full-grown man, he remains so attached to her that he feels incapable of loving any other woman. However, his attachment to her harms him in two ways: it renders him dependent on her for emotional support, and it prevents him from developing normal relationships with other women. Whenever he feels sorry for himself, he cries on her shoulder. Whenever he needs to be reassured about his own self-worth, he turns to her. She is the one who seizes upon his fantasy of going to France and makes it seem realizable. For him, the idea was originally nothing more than a daydream; for her, it is a goal to be achieved by practical efforts. If Barnabas lacks resolve and relies more upon cajolery than upon hard work, he is acting as he learned to act in eliciting his mother's support.

The first three positions he occupies after leaving home expose Barnabas to major aspects of European culture: Christianity, commerce, and romantic love. Each of them is based on illusory appearances, but rather than falling victim to the false promises they hold out to him, he appropriates the cynical attitude behind these promises. From the beginning, he is sceptical about the white man's religion, but he agrees to enter the seminary because he wants to acquire the knowledge he needs to obtain a civil-service appointment that would exempt him from the *indigénat*. He himself refers to his decision as the "Trojan horse of a religious vocation." During his seven years at the seminary, he becomes accustomed to the comforts of a European lifestyle, but he is eventually expelled on suspicion of having engaged in a homosexual relationship. In response, he becomes obsessed with a desire to avenge himself upon the seminary director, although he maintains a façade of injured innocence in front of the townspeople.

Barnabas's experiences at the seminary give concrete form to his dream—he wants to enjoy the same lifestyle as Europeans do. These experiences also establish a narrative pattern that recurs throughout the novel: after donning a false mask to deceive others into giving him what he wants, he either loses patience with his role or fails to carry it out resolutely. To avoid blaming himself for the ensuing failure, he directs his resentment against others and presents himself as the victim of their malice. His brief stint as a solicitor for the Greek merchant Kriminopoulos reinforces the cynical attitude he had already developed by this time. Kriminopoulos's dishonesty is that of a typical colonialist entrepreneur: he buys agricultural produce as cheaply as possible from the local farmers and sells manufactured goods back to them at exorbitant prices. Like the Catholic church, his business succeeds because he convinces gullible people to believe in false appearances. Barnabas himself cannot believe in them, but he recognizes the advantage of being on the side of the deceivers rather than among the deceived.

His third situation in colonial society teaches him a different sort of lesson. When he accepts a position as private tutor to the eight-year-old daughter of an expatriate Frenchman, he is hoping that his employer will help him find a way of obtaining the lifestyle he desires. But once he enters the Gruchet household, he becomes obsessed with the man's wife and begins to see himself as the hero of a French Romantic novel.[18] She is both the unattainable white woman and the symbolic incarnation of the country he had been taught to revere. Although he never communicates his sentiments to her, he incorporates her words and actions into an imagined affair between them.

The entire romance exists only in his mind, yet it does serve as a catalyst to reveal the profound insecurity that haunts him as a consequence of his attempt to become like a Frenchman. At one point he thinks Madame Gruchet might help him forget the "terrifying sensation of emptiness" he feels inside, and when he momentarily mistakes her despair over her daughter's illness for a romantic interest in him, he desires to take her in his arms, but he is prevented from doing so by "a feeling of impurity that made me disgusted with myself."[19] Beneath Barnabas's forced self-confidence lurk anxiety and shame; the romantic role he imagines for himself is merely one of the many psychological ploys he adopts in attempting to suppress an awareness of them.

In three subsequent episodes, he distances himself from people who remind him of this shame. He cannot take his own dream seriously in their presence, and rather than admitting how his pursuit of this dream has warped his own mentality, he reaffirms his commitment to the dream and attributes the cause of his shame to them. By fleeing from them he can avoid looking into himself. First, his mother takes him to the traditional chief, Fimtsen Vavap, in the hope that he and the elders will finance her son's study in Europe so that the young man can later return home and become somebody in whom the entire group might take pride. However, Barnabas is so disgusted with the degeneracy of Vavap and the elders that he refuses to humble himself in front of them, and his lack of respect dooms in advance any chance of obtaining the desired support. Like his father, they represent a link with the part of himself he is attempting to repress, and he renounces any aid they might have offered because he does not want to be identified with them in any way.

His affair with the prostitute Anatatchia and his employment with the French anthropologist Cimetierre are intertwined in such a way that they too threaten to expose the truth about what Barnabas has become in pursuing his dream. In return for a small salary, he dutifully feigns childlike simplicity as he provides Cimetierre with opportunities to photograph "authentic" exotica, and he praises the Frenchman's fanciful interpretations of African culture.[20] With Anatatchia, he suffers the humiliation of having his pants thrown into the courtyard when he resists her attempt to initiate him into the bizarre lovemaking techniques of her favorite white lover. When she appears during one of his nocturnal sessions with Cimetierre, Barnabas develops such a "violent disgust with everything" that he rushes madly into the darkness. What he vaguely realizes is that he and Anatatchia are in the man's room for the same reason: they are both prostitutes who take money for finding ways of pleasing a white man.

Later, when he overhears her mocking him and his dreams in a conversation with other women, he slinks from the scene and decides to leave town because he cannot bear the thought that others are ridiculing him behind his back. His response to the incident is the same as his response to Anatatchia's presence in Cimetierre's room. Less concerned with learning the truth about himself than with repressing the sense of shame that undermines his European-ized self-image, he once again flees from others to avoid recognizing what he has become. As the narrator, he gains a measure of revenge on them by reducing them to caricatures, but in doing so, he is still repressing an awareness of the shame and anxiety they evoke in him.

The final scenes in the novel reveal the cynical opportunism with which he can mask such feelings and conform to the expectations of those who are in a position to give him what he desires. On the bus to Yaounde, where he hopes to obtain a government scholarship that will enable him to study in France, his fellow passengers learn of his projected journey and shower him with money because they naively assume he will return to Cameroon and become their savior. Although Barnabas has no assurance he will ever actually go to France, he cynically pockets their contributions, for he knows that, if the world is composed of deceivers and deceived, it behooves him to be among the deceivers.

He tries to operate according to this principle when he pleads with a colonial administrator to grant him a scholarship. In fact, his praise of French civilization is so extravagant that he himself fears the administrator will notice his calculated use of colonialist clichés and have him jailed for his effrontery. The Frenchman accepts the young man's chauvinism at face value but still re-fuses him the desired scholarship. In this instance, Barnabas fails to achieve his objective, although he demonstrates his willingness to adopt even the most hypocritical role in the hope that it will persuade others to give him what he wants.

After suffering disappointment in his quest for a scholarship, Barnabas is close to despair because it appears that he will be unable to realize the dream in which he has invested his entire personality. At this point, he is obliged to confront his anxiety and shame once again, for when he accompanies the middle-aged shrimp salesman Bendjanga Boy into a European nightclub, he cannot ignore the white men's hostile stares and their outburst of rage at Bend-janga Boy's desire to pay for the services of a white prostitute. The two Africans are dumped on the garbage cans behind the establishment and chased by a mob intent upon lynching them. As in his encounter with Madame Gruchet, this experience makes Barnabas intensely aware of the void inside himself, and it should have taught him the folly of trying to model his concept of himself upon those of people who refuse to recognize that he is as human as they are. But such insights are uncomfortable, and when he arrives at the revivalist meeting, he readily catches his breath, composes himself, and tells the story that will procure him a ticket to France. His chameleonlike change of counte-nance and his ability to disregard disturbing insights are possible only because he has completely internalized the mentality behind the colonialist enterprise. Like the white men he is emulating, Barnabas represses all evidence that sug-gests he has purchased his success at the price of his humanity.

Taken together, Oyono's novels constitute a remarkable anatomy of the assimilationist dream. Toundi, Meka, and Barnabas are all attracted to the enhanced status they would enjoy if they could become like Frenchmen, and they become so attached to a Europeanized image of themselves that they fail to perceive how it alienates them from humanly important dimensions of their own existence. Toundi and Meka are duped by the benevolent-sounding rhetoric of French colonialism, but they eventually realize that its false promises are merely a means of exploiting them. In practice, the European colonialists in *Une Vie de boy* and *Le Vieux Nègre* do not accept the full humanity of Africans, but the stories of Toundi and Meka clearly refute this reductionist stereotype. In contrast, Barnabas consciously appropriates the cynical mentality behind the colonialist rhetoric; however, by doing so, he becomes just as anxiety-ridden and hypocritical as the Europeans he aspires to resemble.

The French doctrine of assimilation thus appears to offer Africans a set of equally untenable alternatives: if they accept its promises at face value, they will be exploited and eventually confronted by its denial of their humanity; if they adopt the self-serving attitudes behind the colonialist rhetoric, they will lose touch with what is most valuable in themselves. From Oyono's perspective, intellectual penetration and a recognition of the common humanity beneath artificial social distinctions are the two cardinal virtues in a chaotic world where neither traditional African values nor colonialist myths provide a viable basis for forging a stable sense of identity. When judged according to this standard of value, European colonialism stands condemned.

CHAPTER

5

MONGO BETI
Counterhistory and
Critical Consciousness

Mongo Beti's literary career falls into two distinct periods. The first spanned the last decade of the colonial era and spawned the four anticolonialist novels for which he has become known throughout Africa. The second began after a fourteen-year hiatus, and because it includes works that focus on postcolonial African society, it will be discussed in a later chapter. If Oyono viewed colonial Cameroon as the scene of a universally comprehensible drama in which artificial social roles obscure the basic humanity of the actors and permit privileged individuals to treat others with great cruelty, Beti regarded it during his early period as an example of the colonial institutions that oppress Africans and condition them to accept their degradation as normal. According to him, people must take the initiative for changing these institutions, and he thought of his own writing as a means of discrediting the false images that supporters of European colonialism employ to justify them. In the four novels he wrote before 1960, he created alternative images that contest the validity of stereotyped notions about Africa and demand a critical reexamination of the assumptions behind the colonialist enterprise.

Despite a flurry of European interest in works by and about Africans during the 1950s, Beti was convinced that journalists, anthropologists, and even novelists were continuing to propagate the false images that reinforce a corrupt status quo. In his eyes, writing is by its nature a political act, and writers necessarily adopt ideological positions when they choose to describe some aspects of the African environment while ignoring others. Because he believed that "the present reality of black Africa, its only profound reality, is colonization and its crimes,"[1] he felt that anyone who wrote about Africa was implicitly taking a stand for or against colonialism. Authors such as Camara Laye who focus on traditional African society while overlooking the distortions that had been imposed on it by the European presence were, he argued, as guilty of disseminating colonialist stereotypes as were reporters who described Africa in terms that assumed the Europeans' right to control the continent.

By placing primary emphasis on initiation rites, snake fetishes, and picturesque village scenes, for example, Laye deflects attention from the dehumanizing consequences of a colonialism that had profoundly marked the lives of all Africans. When a situation is of such overriding importance, Beti concluded, writers who fail to include it in their portrayal of African society are actually obscuring the relations of power that govern the historical evolution of that society. In doing so, they implicitly sanction a common European assumption that the colonialist system is in the best interest of Africans themselves.

Similarly, Beti attacked European anthropologists for reducing Africans to an abstract "otherness" that confined them in a state of unchanging traditions and immutable laws. By implying that all outside influences distort genuine traditions, the perspective behind this approach assumes that Africans must either preserve their traditions intact or abandon them altogether. For Beti, however, these are not the only alternatives; traditions have always changed as the result of contact with other cultures, and tradition itself is merely one aspect of modern African society. When anthropologists isolate a single stage in a long historical evolution and establish it as a norm, Beti feels they are denying Africans the option of defining their collective identity in terms of their own present needs.

In the face of false images and reifying abstractions of Africa, Beti responded like Banda, the hero of his first novel, *Ville cruelle*. When Banda overhears people recounting events in which he has just participated, he can barely restrain himself from shouting, "no, no, that's wrong! It didn't happen that way; you're misinformed; they lied to you. That's not true. Listen, I know the story very well."[2] Like Banda, Beti wanted to correct the record, to establish the truth about a situation he knows intimately. Drawing inspiration from the real experiences of people whom he remembered from the south-central region of Cameroon, Beti wrote novels that depict a reality quite different from the one described by journalists, anthropologists, and authors of escapist fiction.

Because he felt that colonialism and its crimes should be the primary subject of a morally responsible African literature, he developed a rhetorical strategy that emphasizes the two primary obstacles to African liberation from the colonialist system: an oppressive institutional context and the colonized mentality that accepts this context as a given in the modern world. For this reason, his first four novels all have a dual focus. They reveal the mechanisms that perpetuate the corrupt institutions of colonial society, and they describe a crisis of consciousness experienced by young men seeking to define themselves in this environment, to make sense of it, and to free themselves from the restraints they feel have been arbitrarily imposed upon them. In other words, narrative fiction serves Beti as a vehicle for reasserting the right of Africans to control the image of Africa that had been usurped by Europeans and their assimilationist protégés.

By focusing on the actual life processes of the people, Beti hoped to foster a critical understanding of the forces that impinge on them and shape their destinies in colonial society.[3] His four early novels implicitly challenge stereotyped preconceptions about Africa and prod readers to ask what he regards as the basic question: who controls the destiny of Africans, and for what purpose? In the fictional worlds of these novels, Beti allows the self-contradictions of colonialism to play themselves out, revealing the way Europeans manipulate false images of reality to exploit Africans for their own profit. Rather than bringing civilization to benighted savages, European colonialists in these works are primarily interested in reaffirming their conception of themselves through the exercise of power over others.

But if their dominance in Africa is based upon a fundamental injustice, traditional society as Beti portrays it fails to offer a viable alternative. Many traditional practices are themselves unjust and prevent Africans from coping with the modern world and its relations of power; others have been distorted by the introduction of a money economy and an administrative system that makes local chiefs dependent upon white colonial officials; still others allow corrupt elders to wield unjust authority over women and younger men. Against a background of irreversible change in Beti's novels, colonialist institutions and traditional hierarchies contribute to the oppression under which the majority of Africans are obliged to live. Brief episodes of love, friendship, and insight suggest that this oppression is not preordained. On the contrary, it results from a form of social organization that can be changed to assure Africans the opportunity to enjoy honest human relationships, material well-being, and a sense of self-worth.

According to Beti, such change is prevented from taking place by the false images that blind Africans and well-intentioned Europeans to the truth about colonial society. By drawing attention to the disparity between these false images and the dehumanizing consequences of the colonialist presence in Africa, Beti is exhorting readers to renounce false images and to recognize the need for revolutionary change. The principal strand of action in his fourth novel, *Le Roi miraculé*, illustrates the rhetorical strategy he adopts in pursuing this objective. Near the end of the novel, the colonial administrator Lequeux has the white priest Le Guen removed from the mission at Essazam for having encouraged the local chief Essomba Mendouga to repudiate all but one of his twenty-three wives.[4] Le Guen had desired to effect the chief's dramatic conversion to Christianity, but his meddling in the affairs of Essazam actually provoked a pitched battle among the various clans that had assembled there to protest Essomba's treatment of the spurned wives. Le Guen himself was slightly injured in the melee, and Lequeux had led troops into the area when he heard about the violence. Lequeux's case against Le Guen is based partly on the argument that the priest should never have tried to eliminate polygamy because it is a traditional African custom.

The false images that Beti attacks in this sequence of events exist on four levels. First, Lequeux adopts an anthropological approach that permits him to overlook the fact that the introduction of a money economy had enabled chiefs and other older men to exploit the traditional dowry system by purchasing more wives than they could otherwise have obtained. In reality, the French colonial administrator is concerned not with the preservation of traditional customs but with maintaining the peaceful lethargy of the people in an area that falls under his jurisdiction. Anthropological pseudoknowledge serves him as an instrument for perpetrating the conditions of dependency on which the entire colonialist enterprise is based.

Second, Le Guen's missionary activity would be regarded as altruistic and benevolent according to conventional European norms of judgment, but Beti reveals it as being motivated by the priest's selfish desire to receive credit for making African society conform to his idea of what it should be. Third, Essomba wants to believe that he is a legitimate chief, and he justifies his rule over the Essazam on the basis of tradition, but his claim to the throne is tenuous, and he owes his power at least in part to the support of French colonial authorities. Instead of promoting communal well-being in Essazam, his reign imprisons his people in a state of ignorance and dependency.

Finally, if the events described in *Le Roi miraculé* were reported by French journalists, they would undoubtedly emphasize that French soldiers had quelled a native uprising during which a white priest had been injured. Such an account would create the erroneous impression that Le Guen had been the innocent victim of savages who could be subordinated to civilized order only by a show of military force. Beti's description of these events demonstrates the inadequacy of such reporting by disclosing Le Guen's role in the affair and by showing how the corrupt social milieu introduced by European colonialism demeans Africans rather than bringing them the blessings of European civilization. In this sense, Beti's novel is a counterhistory that rebuts the false images promulgated by people who wittingly or unwittingly support the European colonialist presence in Africa.

In the corrupt social environment that characterizes each of his first four novels, Beti places young men who experience the contradictions of colonialism while attempting to forge a viable sense of identity. Most of them rebel against unjust authority, and all achieve some degree of insight into the oppressive forces that shape their destinies, but none discovers a way to liberate himself or his people from such forces. In the end, they all remain mired in an ambivalence that reflects their unresolved quest for freedom and identity. Conscious of their individuality, they are modern Africans whose personalities have been formed in the interaction between their aspirations for self-realization and the resistance of a society hostile to those aspirations. Neither traditional nor European values offer them adequate behavioral models for coping with a complex, rapidly changing world without adequate channels for the expression of their talents and energies.

Within the context of Beti's world view, they could escape the limbo of indecisiveness by engaging themselves in the revolutionary struggle for a just society. In such a society, they would be able to define themselves by establishing decent human relationships with others, but until they choose to engage themselves, they will be condemned to an ambiguous state of mind that parallels the malaise afflicting colonial society as a whole. In this way, Beti illustrates the pressures to which Africans are subjected by the contradictory demands of the colonialist system.

What these young men lack is the critical consciousness that Beti seeks to foster among his readers by presenting them with a real-seeming counterhistory of colonial society. Unlike Oyono, who thought literature should be unequivocally universal in its appeal, Beti wrote for two audiences. The vast majority of Africans could not read, and there were neither publishing houses nor substantial markets for literature in Africa during the 1950s; therefore, if francophone African writers wanted their works to be published, reviewed, and read, they had to create texts capable of interesting a French middle-class reading public. In general, Beti argued, this public expected its fundamental assumptions about the world to be reaffirmed in the literature it read, and when writers such as Laye focus on the folkloric aspects of African life, they are pandering to such readers by assuring them that their stereotyped notions about Africa are correct.

Realizing that an open attack on the colonial system would hardly please the French audience for whom, under existing circumstances, he was obliged to write, he followed the example of writers such as Voltaire, Montesquieu, and Mark Twain, who showed him how he might appeal to European readers while calling some of their most cherished ideological assumptions into question.[5] By adopting an ironic perspective on fictional events that, when viewed more closely, reveal the hypocrisies and cruelties of colonialism, he could satisfy the minimum requirements for being published in France without reaffirming the false images that had been popularized by journalists, anthropologists, and authors of escapist fiction.

At the same time, Beti was convinced that African writers would ultimately be judged on how well they had written for African audiences. The primary criteria for success in this area would be, he thought, the accuracy with which they depicted African reality and the extent to which they contributed to the emancipation of mentalities that had been enslaved by the colonialist system.[6] On one level, Beti's early novels are addressed to Europeans. In a humorously ironic fashion, he informs them about the harsh reality behind stereotypically benevolent images of colonial society, and he appeals to their sense of truth and justice. On another level, these works speak to and for Africans, revealing the mechanisms of a system that distorts their lives and drawing attention to the conditioning process that predisposes them to regard such distortions as normal. On both levels, he is prodding readers into a critical consciousness that would enable them to comprehend colonialist oppression as it occurs in the real world beyond the pages of his novels.

A genuine comprehension of this situation would, he believed, culminate in the desire to change it. He himself participated in UPC activities and in the Cameroonian student movement. His first published fiction, the short story

"Sans Haine, sans amour," revolves around the thoughts of a young Kenyan who, having found meaning in life by committing himself to the Mau-Mau struggle for independence, undertakes a mission from which he will probably not return. The passionate repudiation of unjust authority that motivates the central character in "Sans Haine, sans amour" remains at the center of Beti's early novels, but rather than depicting the revolutionary act itself, these novels focus on the conditions that make such acts necessary.

As Beti himself implies in all these works, the lethargy of the people and the indecisiveness of the younger generation are major impediments to revolutionary change. In *Le Roi miraculé*, for example, the secondary-school student Kris empathizes with the humiliation of his aunt Makrita, Essomba's first wife and one of those who have been ordered to leave his compound. Sitting down next to her, Kris asks himself, "why do people always allow others to trample on them this way?"[7] One reason for their resignation in the face of injustice is the fact that they have been conditioned to accept existing authority as part of a world they believe they cannot change. By demonstrating the falsity of the assumptions behind this process and by revealing the arbitrariness of commonly accepted authority systems in colonial society, Beti challenges the rationale for refusing to oppose the existing situation, for if people can grasp the truth about the forces that enslave them, they can also take the initiative to liberate themselves from those forces. The first step toward revolutionary change is the same critical consciousness that Beti seeks to elicit from his readers.

When he portrays the dehumanizing context of the colonialist system, Beti himself calls upon readers to exercise this critical consciousness to comprehend the mechanisms that enable Europeans to exploit Africans. *Ville cruelle* provides an excellent example of his rhetorical strategy in this respect because Tanga, the "cruel city" that emerged as the result of the colonialist intrusion, is a dominant presence in the novel. An extended metaphor illustrates the effect of this city on its black inhabitants: the logs that feed its lumber industry are like the rural people who have been drawn to Tanga in search of employment. Floated down the river that flows through the city, the logs are lifted from the water by giant cranes, and after they have been "squared, rounded off, reduced to the proper proportions for factory and civilization" by axes, they are "bleached, numbered, and soberly placed to rest on long railway cars."[8] Similarly, masses of people flood to Tanga, where they are molded into suitable identities and given menial tasks to perform; like the logs, they are exploited for the profit of Europeans.

Viewed from Beti's perspective, all white-dominated institutions in Tanga—the Catholic mission, the colonial administration, the police, the schools—support this exploitative enterprise. But if the origins of Tanga's cruelty lie in the Europeans' pursuit of wealth and power, the corrupt mentality they engendered among Africans spread through the city like a contagious disease. Although a frenetic social life develops around the bars and dance halls in the African section of Tanga, traditional social sanctions break down, and as Africans emulate the acquisitive individualism of their European masters, a harsh atmosphere emerges among them. People develop "a certain propensity for petty calculation, irritability, alcoholism, and everything that excites disdain for human life."⁹ They begin to regard themselves as isolated individuals rather than as members of a community; they forget their origins and have no idea of where they are headed. With indifference they watch others being beaten and murdered, and they dance while neighbors are burying their dead. Their spontaneity is the "only remnant of their lost innocence." Ironically, by adopting the corrupt mentality of the cruel city, they themselves are prolonging their imprisonment in the colonialist system that exploits them.

This mentality is fostered by the division of the city into European and African sections, for the assumption behind a rigorous separation of the races is that black people are inherently inferior to white people and should be kept in their proper place. A corollary of this assumption is that any European mistreatment of Africans is acceptable, whereas the slightest African offense against a European must be severely punished. To sustain such practices in good conscience, Europeans often completely disregard the truth.

For example, when a French businessman refuses to pay his workers for several weeks, they start to carry him to the police station and demand their rights, but they drop him when they are attacked by a group of guards, and he dies of a skull fracture. The young mechanic Koumé is regarded as a ringleader of the rebellious workers, and he is obliged to flee from the police. In his weekly sermon, the local white priest eulogizes the French businessman and excoriates Koumé as a criminal, although unbeknownst to him the young man has already died of a skull fracture after falling into the river bed as Banda tried to lead him to safety. The colonial administration, the police, and the church claim to be defending truth and justice, but because the real crime was committed by the French businessman, they are actually supporting the white man's right to profit in any way he can by exploiting the labor of his black workers.

Insofar as Africans accept this distortion of the truth, they are acknowledging their own inferiority. Many of them even internalize it to the extent that they treat their fellow Africans in the same way the Europeans treat them. The cocoa control officers who confiscate Banda's cocoa beans on a spurious pretext and later sell them for their own profit are perfect illustrations of this assimilationist mentality. Such attitudes contribute greatly to the malaise that afflicts colonial society, yet by depicting the city's attraction for young people such as Banda and Koumé, Beti is also suggesting that colonialism set in motion an irreversible historical trend. Tanga may well be a cruel city, but urbanization is part of the modern world, and Africans must learn to cope with it, even if they succeed in freeing themselves from colonialist oppression.

Although Christian proselytism has usually been regarded as an altruistic activity that benefits Africans, Beti is convinced that it is an integral part of this oppression. His portrayals of Catholic priests in Le Pauvre Christ de Bomba and Le Roi miraculé even suggest that the motivation of missionaries is far less generous than most people assume. Both Drumont in *Le Pauvre Christ* and Le Guen in *Le Roi miraculé* formulate grandiose plans for the Christianization of Africans and assign themselves a heroic role in realizing these plans. Their reward is the psychological gratification of believing they can shape an alien reality into their image of what it should be. However, they become so attached to their heroic self-images that they blind themselves to reality and act in ways that ultimately prevent them from achieving their goals. Both priests fail to understand African society, but their greatest sin is the pride that impels them to live out their fantasies at the expense of others. The irony of Beti's critique resides in the fact that he allows the priests to condemn themselves by the very nature of the projects they undertake.

Drumont's heroic dream can be traced back nearly twenty years to the early 1920s when he first discovered his missionary vocation. Disgusted with the materialism and rationalism of contemporary Europe, he imagined that Africans, uncorrupted by modern civilization, were so close to paradise that it would require little to assure their salvation. In his own mind, he saw himself as a redeemer who would create in Africa the Christian community that was no longer possible in Europe. The initial response to his mission confirmed this fantasy and convinced him that he could reach his goal if he pursued it vigorously. People listened to him; they obeyed his every command, and he exploited their labor to construct houses and churches on a grand scale. By inculcating in them an attitude compounded of obedience, humility, and resignation in the face of suffering, he thought he could orchestrate all their activities. He envisioned himself as godlike in his power over them, and the preservation of this self-image ultimately became his primary goal in life.

After his initial success, however, Drumont noticed a turning away from the church, particularly among the people of Tala. Three years before the events described in the novel, he decided to punish the Talans by withdrawing from their region. His expectation was that they would recognize the error of their ways and welcome him back with open arms. This scheme filled him with visions of grandeur, as he later confides to the colonial administrator Vidal: "in my mind's eye I raised myself to the level of Napoleon tracing on a map the famous plan that was to assure him the victory of Austerlitz."[10] Drumont's choice of a metaphor for his stratagem is revealing because he sees himself as a military leader plotting the conquest of the Talans, whom he clearly wants to subordinate to his will.

The authoritarian potential of this attitude becomes evident during his long-anticipated return to the country of the Tala, a journey that occupies nearly two-thirds of the novel. Wherever he goes, Drumont wants to regulate the minutest details of his parishioners' lives, and when they don't conform to his image of what they should be, he becomes angry and seeks to force them into obedience. His summary punishment of the sorcerer Sanga Boto is justified in his eyes because "I had prohibited [people] from having recourse to the services of sorcerers."[11] The crucial word in this passage is *I*. Sanga Boto is condemned not for any specific crime he may have committed but because his presence in the village contravenes the will of a priest who wants to exercise a godlike control over the people; therefore, the priest humiliates the sorcerer to preserve the illusion of his own omnipotence. Whether he compares himself to Christ or to Napoleon, the point is the same: Drumont is an egocentric individual with delusions of grandeur.

As in *Le Pauvre Christ*, much of the action in *Le Roi miraculé* revolves around a priest's arrogant desire to reshape African reality according to his image of what it should be. Le Guen had been Drumont's adjunct at the time of the events portrayed in *Le Pauvre Christ*, and for ten years after the collapse of Drumont's mission, he has directed the mission at Essazam. Although he distances himself from Drumont's grandiose projects and considers himself a modern clergyman who identifies with the people he serves, he is plagued by doubts and would like to effect at least one dramatic conversion to justify his presence in Africa.

The opportunity for such a conversion presents itself when Essomba falls gravely ill and his half-demented aunt Yosifa performs a farcical pseudobaptism over him. Le Guen had already fantasized about converting the chief to Christianity after the slumbering Essomba had reached out and requested one of the rosaries he was carrying on his arm. That gesture had convinced him that his dream was on the verge of realization and that he was about to become a religious hero who brings truth and light to a benighted people. Thus, when he learns of Yosifa's baptism, he immediately declares it a valid sacrament, although he fully realizes that Yosifa has neither the right to baptize nor the knowledge to carry out the ceremony properly. Once he has imagined himself as the agent of a miracle, he tries to make all subsequent events conform with his desire, for if his dream is realized, he can believe in the heroic self-image he has created for himself.

When Essomba's condition worsens, Le Guen performs extreme unction over him; however, the chief regains his strength, and many people attribute his recovery to the "magic" that the priest practiced at his bedside. Le Guen does not contradict them. The conversion is too important to him. But before receiving Essomba into the church, he insists that the chief renounce all except one of his wives, and for his own reasons, Essomba agrees to this proviso. Le Guen's strategy is similar to Drumont's project in the sense that both priests desire to reaffirm their conceptions of themselves by manipulating Africans to play supporting parts in dramas that reserve the hero's roles for them.

Yet both priests misunderstand the situations in which they find themselves, and their dreams of glory eventually shatter on the disparity between reality and their skewed interpretations of it. Apparent throughout the two novels, this disparity serves a twofold rhetorical purpose. It reveals the hypocrisy of the priests' motivations, and it explains why the consequences of their actions are so disastrous for Africans. Shortly before Drumont's journey to the land of the Tala, his faith in his vision of reality begins to waver. He suspects that the Bantu sensibility is more complex than he originally thought, and he fears that people had turned to his religion for quite pragmatic reasons rather than from sincere religious conviction. Although he represses such thoughts, they sap the energy he needs to sustain his heroic self-image, and when his experiences among the people of Tala demonstrate the folly of his grandiose plan, he almost succumbs to despair. "I'm useless here," he admits during the final stage of his journey, "nobody needs me."[12] If no one needs him, he is obviously not the hero he has imagined himself to be, and his only recourse is to leave the scene of his failure.

But if he leaves without accepting responsibility for the collapse of his mission, he will still be avoiding the truth about himself. His manner of dealing with the scandal of the sixa at the Bomba mission clearly shows that he is unprepared to relinquish his heroic self-image and to admit his guilt in bringing about the suffering of others.[13] When he returns from the Tala country, Drumont discovers that the catechist in charge of the sixa has exploited his position to sell the sexual favors of the young women under his supervision to men from inside and outside the mission; as a result, the vast majority of these women have contracted syphilis. Desiring to regard himself as a man who insists upon knowing the whole truth, he interrogates every woman from the sixa. However, his a priori assumption is that they are all guilty. Each of them is greeted with fifteen blows and obliged to confess under the threat of further beatings. "The Devil is in you," he tells the first woman to appear before him, "you spoiled the sixa."[14] Later, he ascribes the women's conduct to the inherent sensuality of the black race. His authoritarian posture in this situation is the same as it has always been, for he is relying on force to impose his vision of reality on others.

In reality, Drumont is blaming the women to avoid recognizing his own culpability. The syphilis-infested sixa is actually a symbol for the moral corruption he had introduced into the area, and he himself must bear responsibility for the fiasco because he never inspected the sixa after having established it twenty years previously. If he had, he would have noticed the deplorable sanitary conditions and the promiscuity that reigned there. Rather than consider the real causes of the situation, he admonishes the women: "You make me ashamed. You dishonor my house. I don't want to see you anymore."[15] His emphasis is still on the "I" whom they have supposedly wronged by their lascivious behavior.

But Drumont is obviously not concerned with their welfare. He sends them away without having had them treated for their infection. He even picks up a stick to chase off a few stragglers who are reluctant to leave because they have been at the mission so long they no longer have a home to which they can return. The urgency with which he wants them out of his sight reflects his preoccupation with maintaining a positive self-image, for if he does not have to confront the living evidence of the scandal, he can continue to regard himself as a martyr who fought for a heroic cause. Even his melodramatic claim that the memory of the sixa will remain with him like a "cancer of the stomach" serves to bolster this image of injured innocence. But unlike the people of Bomba, he will not have to live with the consequences of a situation he helped create. When he retires to a life of philosophical contemplation in Europe, he can keep alive his positive self-image because no one there will be able to contradict it.

Le Guen too mastered the art of sustaining his heroic self-image by re-pressing any evidence that might call it into question. For example, when he thought Essomba was reaching out for the Christian truth symbolized by the rosaries on his arm, the chief was actually groping for what he regarded as a fetish to reassure himself that he was descended from Akomo, the common ancestor of the Essazam. He desperately wanted this assurance to assuage the bad conscience he felt for having collaborated with the French in raising forced-labor gangs among his own people. Similarly, he is dreaming of Akomo when Yosifa performs her mock baptism over him. But Le Guen is unconcerned with Essomba's real state of mind. He is even willing to take credit for a miraculous cure that he would have condemned if it had been attributed to a traditional sorcerer. Ironically, the people assume that the last rites he pronounced at Essomba's bedside brought the dying man back to life, but such an interpretation is in blatant contradiction with Catholic doctrine, which defines extreme unc-tion as a preparation for physical death and spiritual life. Le Guen overlooks such contradictions because a recognition of them would oblige him to aban-don the heroic dream in which he has vested so much of his own identity.

Like Drumont, Le Guen fails to comprehend the complexity of a society in which he has been living for many years, and in his ignorance, he sets in motion a chain of events that culminate in the complete collapse of his missionary enterprise. His demand that Essomba renounce all but one of his wives is both unjust and unwise. It is unjust because the spurned wives would be arbitrarily deprived of everything that was of any importance to them—their children, their friends, their status, their houses, their gardens. It is unwise because the political stability of the Essazam people was based upon alliances that had been consummated by the chief's marriages with women from different clans. In fact, at the announcement of Essomba's intention to repudiate his wives, the various clans gather at Essazam to defend the rights of their "daugh-ters." Despite this potentially explosive situation, Le Guen holds a mass during which he gives the chief the name "Lazarus," thereby assuming credit for the miraculous cure and formally acknowledging the chief's marriage to a single wife. Convinced he has won a great victory, Le Guen is oblivious to the artifici-ality of his accomplishment, but when an interclanic battle breaks out and brings Lequeux to the town, the priest is removed from his parish, and his dream of effecting a dramatic conversion is dashed forever. Both Drumont and Le Guen fail, and their failures reflect the inadequacy of the stereotyped images of Africa on which they built their heroic conceptions of themselves.

Beti's first point about missionary activity in Africa is to question the motivation of its practitioners. In contrast to commonly accepted European notions, missionaries such as Drumont and Le Guen are concerned less with truth and charity than with the gratification of their own selfish desires to affirm their imagined heroism by exercising power over others. His second point involves the effects of missionary proselytism upon the way Africans perceive themselves. As he demonstrates in *Le Pauvre Christ*, mission Christianity influenced African mentalities in two ways.

First, by preaching obedience to existing authority and by holding out the promise of happiness in the afterlife, missionaries conditioned Africans to accept the misery and humiliation that was being imposed on them in this world. Although Drumont denies his complicity in preparing Africans to become docile subjects in a system that exploits them, his conversation with Vidal reveals a dawning awareness of how the activities of the church and those of the colonial administration reinforce each other. From Beti's perspective, authentic Christian doctrine was more harmful to Africans than Drumont's unchristian example because it prevented them from achieving the critical consciousness necessary to comprehend the nature of their own oppression.[16]

Second, Drumont's mission is like a successful business, and those who imitate the priest's example instead of following his precepts become as materialistic and individualistic as the Europeans from whom he had fled twenty years earlier. As an educated Frenchman, he adopts a cost-effective approach to the administration of his enterprise. Unpaid African labor allows him to increase its net worth, and he provides services only for those who have acquitted themselves of the mandatory tithe. Baptisms and marriages bring in additional revenue, and at every stop on his journey through Tala, he receives substantial gifts of food that are carefully transported back to the mission at Bomba.

Realizing that the physically comfortable life of the priest depends less on religious faith than on the accumulation of material possessions, perceptive Africans like the cynical cook Zacharie devote themselves to the acquisition of wealth. If it is necessary to wear a mask of Christian piety to succeed in this endeavor, he is perfectly willing to play the role that is expected of him. But whether enterprising individuals ally themselves with the mission, as Zacharie does, or set themselves up in competition with it, like the sorcerer Sanga Boto, they are committing themselves to the pursuit of material wealth. And they have customers, whose gullibility they exploit for their own profit. In short, they have internalized the implicit ethic behind all colonialist institutions, including the mission churches. Ironically, Drumont has helped to recreate in Africa the same mentality he had sought to escape by leaving Europe.

Whether Africans accept the Christian message of humility in the face of oppression or emulate the mercantile mentality of European Christians, they are blinding themselves to the truth about their own situation, and their blindness causes them to act in ways that perpetuate the corrupt colonial system. For example, when Vidal announces that a road will be constructed in the land of the Tala, many people become afraid because they know that French roads are built with forced labor, and forced labor means untold suffering for the people of the area. Nevertheless, some individuals rejoice. Zacharie knows that a road will be profitable for the mission business. An African schoolteacher defends the use of forced labor because there is no other way to build a road that will enhance the region's prestige and provide easier access to markets. But both Zacharie and the schoolteacher are exempt from forced labor, and their willingness to benefit from the suffering of others reflects the same cynicism that characterizes the European exploitation of Africans in the colonialist system at large.

In *Le Roi miraculé*, Christianity is portrayed as being in collusion with the colonial administration and the chieftaincy from the beginning. The relationship among them is symbolized in an early scene when Le Guen and the tax collector Mekanda follow the same zigzag path from house to house on their way to pay homage to Essomba. The fact that only the Christians conscientiously pay their taxes illustrates how the church prepares its adherents to accept the rules of the colonial administration, and the deference accorded Essomba by both men suggests that the three institutions they represent share a vested interest in maintaining their control over a docile population.

Although Le Guen's plan for a dramatic conversion threatens to disrupt the general lethargy, Lequeux restores it by having the priest removed from his parish. Worried about his chances of reaching heaven, Essomba periodically calls his wives together, banishes them, and takes communion, but the women never leave, and he always comes back to them with renewed gusto. This ritualization of a crisis in the history of the Essazam shows that even Le Guen's challenge to the group's political stability can be safely integrated into the corrupt fabric of a stagnant society. As portrayed by Beti, the Christianity of the missions played a crucial role in discouraging the emergence of a critical consciousness that might have enabled people to understand their victimization and to devise practical ways of overcoming it.

Within the context of an unjust colonial society that justifies its existence on the basis of a hypocritically benevolent rhetoric, the young men on whom Beti focuses attention in his first four novels are groping their way toward self-definition. Although none of them attain the critical consciousness that could liberate them from indecisiveness and anxiety, their lives do illustrate the identity crisis that many young Cameroonians faced during the 1950s. Vaguely dissatisfied with the identities that others want to impose on them, these young men have a penchant for reverie and often harbor suspicions of their own inadequacy. They are restless but have not yet discovered the specific direction in which they desire to move.

Banda in *Ville cruelle* is Beti's first variation on this sort of character. Neither the traditional hierarchy in his village nor the colonial establishment that sanctions the confiscation of his cocoa beans can offer him a viable sense of identity. He repudiates them both and seeks to define himself in terms of an individual freedom that would permit him to discover the truth on his own terms. Although he loves his mother deeply, he even resists her plans to shape his destiny by choosing a wife for him.[17] His own desires are embodied in two recurrent fantasies that suggest a tendency to avoid reality by retreating into an imaginary world.

Subconsciously aware of his mother's mortality, he wants a younger woman to love him as unconditionally as she does; for this reason, he fantasizes about having a little sister who would not, like a wife, restrict his movements. He also dreams of going to Fort-Nègre (Douala), where he believes he would be free to realize the destiny that awaits him if he can only grasp hold of it. Both fantasies are escapist illusions: as an adult man, he cannot hope to find a reincarnation of maternal love in an imagined sister, and Fort-Nègre is merely a larger version of Tanga. Nevertheless, these fantasies reveal what he most desires: a selfless love and the freedom to be himself.

When he meets Odilia and agrees to help her brother Koumé escape from the police, he believes he has found "the little sister about whom he had been dreaming all his life."[18] His mother accepts Odilia as the wife she had wanted for him, and after Banda stumbles across the money Koumé had appropriated from his dead employer and finds a lost suitcase for which he receives a substantial reward, the two young people marry and settle temporarily in her village. But despite his happiness, Banda has not found a permanent solution to the problem of defining his own identity.

The money does reaffirm a sense of self-worth that had been called into question by earlier setbacks: his failed attempt to learn something at the mission school, his failed attempt to sell his cocoa, his failed attempt to guide Koumé to safety. However, the money was unearned. It came to him through accidental circumstances that offer him no guarantee of being able to sustain himself in the future. By linking his manhood to the money, he is making the same mistake that distorted the lives of the Europeans in Tanga. Furthermore, he senses that his stay in Odilia's village is merely a stage in his life and that he will soon have to launch himself upon the "conquest of Fort-Nègre," an individualistic project that may well cause him to leave his wife just as he had sought to break away from the influence of his mother. At the end of *Ville cruelle*, it is unclear whether Banda will ever succeed in reconciling his desire for freedom with his yearning for love, but by portraying his confusion against the background of the cruel city, Beti added the complex psychological dimension that was missing from stereotyped European notions about Africans living under colonial rule.

This dimension becomes an even more central concern in *Le Pauvre Christ* and in Beti's third novel, *Mission terminée*. Both are fictional autobiographies in which young men recount crucial episodes from their own lives as part of an effort to understand who they are and what their experiences mean. Denis in *Le Pauvre Christ* and Medza in *Mission terminée* lack the critical consciousness to interpret the full significance of what they are reporting, and Beti expects readers to recognize that the mentalities of these narrators constitute one aspect of his critique of colonialist society. For example, Denis exemplifies the gullibility of a colonized subject who willingly acquiesces in his own subjugation. As a young choirboy who accompanies Drumont on his trip through the land of the Tala, Denis accepts the priest's distorted image of

Africa and identifies with his heroic conception of himself. In fact, his own sense of self-worth is completely invested in the man whom he regards as a surrogate father.

As long as Drumont remains strong, the boy, who considers himself weak, can participate in this strength by defining himself in terms of his relationship to it. He exults when Drumont acts decisively, as he does in humiliating Sanga Boto or in attacking the drums and balafons at a village ceremony, but when Drumont wavers, Denis becomes anxious because he fears that the whole glorious enterprise, including his own positive self-image, will collapse if the priest abandons his forceful approach. On the surface, Denis adopts the benevolent-sounding rhetoric of the church and sees Drumont as the priest wants himself to be seen. In reality, the boy is responding to what Drumont actually does rather than to what he claims he is doing.

For him, Drumont is like a powerful sorcerer who can control his environment, and the wealth of the mission bears testimony to his strength. Denis cannot understand why the priest would even consider abandoning his efforts in the Tala country when the construction of a road promises to guarantee the prosperity of the church in an area where Christians are generally exempted from forced labor. In other words, he is really identifying with Drumont's physical wealth and power, not with the spiritual qualities that he praises in the rhetoric he has borrowed from the church. The irony is that Denis attaches himself to the very person who has enslaved his mind and robbed him of his ability to judge the world objectively.

However, the self-concept he has forged as a result of his relationship with Drumont is an artificial one. To sustain his belief in it, he must continually repress the natural impulses that well up within him. At one of the villages where the priest's party spend the night during their journey through Tala, Zacharie's mistress, Catherine, seduces the adolescent Denis, and the experience thrusts him into a state of confusion. His sexual initiation gives him a pleasure he wants to repeat, but his internalization of the priest's Christian morality obliges him to feel guilty for having committed a sin. The dilemma haunts him for days, and he feels cleansed only after he has broken down and related the story to Drumont.

Actually, Denis's sexual impulses are natural; only an unnatural mindset prevents him from accepting them as part of his own psyche. He himself senses that his night with Catherine changed something inside him. "It is as if a stranger entered into me," he laments upon his return to the mission, "and is slowly taking up residence there, gradually substituting himself for me."[19] What Denis regards as a stranger is his true self invading the psychological space occupied by the artificial self he had created by identifying with Drumont.

By the end of his story and even at the moment of telling it, Denis has not fully overcome the conflict between these two selves. He does not want to relinquish the sense of importance he felt as a participant in Drumont's heroic enterprise, but he finds it increasingly difficult to repress his natural inclinations, especially after the scandal of the sixa and the collapse of the mission that followed Drumont's departure for Europe. Yet when he reflects on the appropriateness of Christianity for Africans, he still cautions himself, "I mustn't abandon myself to such thoughts: they might cause me to lose my faith!"[20] Even with the crumbling mission before his eyes, Denis resists the necessity of critically examining his presuppositions. Yet in the absence of Drumont, he no longer has a tangible means of reinforcing his assimilationist self-concept, and the pressure of reality is eroding the certainty with which he had previously judged the world. Like Banda in *Ville cruelle*, Denis fails to define a set of values that might allow him to escape his perplexity and indecisiveness, although the telling of his story might well be a first step toward critical consciousness.

In *Mission terminée*, the narrating Medza explicitly states that he is telling his story in an attempt to comprehend its significance. The story itself is relatively simple. After having failed the oral part of his baccalauréat examination, the young Medza returned to his village and somewhat reluctantly undertook the mission of bringing back his cousin Niam's errant wife from the forest community of Kala. There he encountered the vestiges of a more peaceful traditional society, engaged in his first sexual experience with the fifteen-year-old Edima, and gained sufficient self-confidence to liberate himself from an authoritarian father. By this time he has effectively repudiated the false identities that traditional and modern societies had sought to inculcate in him, but he has not yet found anything to put in their place.

After years of aimless wandering in the company of his cousin Zambo, he still returns obsessively to the memory of his journey to Kala because he suspects that it contains the key to an understanding of himself and his world. For this reason, he addresses his narrative to an anonymous group of fellow Cameroonians who had known him during his school days and who had undergone experiences similar to his own.[21] In the implicit dialogue between himself and them, he hopes to formulate general conclusions about the dilemma that confronts their generation. If he can discover the meaning behind his own experiences, he will have acquired the critical consciousness he needs to transcend the puzzlement and anxiety that continue to plague him.

The salient characteristic of Medza's mentality is the cerebral attitude he assimilated in the European-style schools that his father forced him to attend.[22] He interprets his own experiences by relating them to European literary precedents, and rather than experiencing reality directly, he tends to perceive it in terms of abstract categories or idealized concepts. Having seen through the hypocrisy of the colonialist rhetoric, he cannot adopt an assimilationist stance, but he is also prevented from identifying with the remnant of traditional society that still exists in villages such as Kala because the analytical faculties he developed at school oblige him to recognize its arbitrariness and ultimate futility. In a sense, Medza is a captive of his own Westernized mentality, for even if he repudiates the racist, materialistic values of colonial society, his only vocabulary is the one he learned in the colonial schools, and it is linked with modes of thought that are incapable of defining the meaning he seeks. Until he discovers new ways of looking at himself and at the world around him, he will remain imprisoned in this falsely abstract vocabulary.

Telling the story of his journey to Kala is part of his quest for new ways of understanding. Two episodes in this story have particular symbolic significance for him: his affair with Edima and his break with his father. They seem to offer the clues he is seeking. In Edima's presence, he experienced a simple, honest love that filled him with a sense of peace and harmony, but like Banda, he thought of the young woman as a stage on his path toward some better fate that was awaiting him. In retrospect, however, he transforms her into a symbolic embodiment of the ideal he claims to be pursuing still. He can believe in this ideal only as long as he remains physically distant from her and is not obliged to confront the reality of what she has become—the wife of his brother and the mother of three children. Viewing a woman as an idealized image capable of sustaining a belief in imaginary perfection reflects a characteristically European concept of romantic love. As readers of Medza's story realize, his encounter with Edima represented the possibility of decent human relationships, but unless Medza can find a nonescapist way of defining it, its relevance to his present situation will remain unclear to him.

The other event to which the narrating Medza attaches great importance is his repudiation of his father near the end of his story. The older man was a prime example of how a shrewd, ambitious African could profit by internalizing the materialistic principles of the colonialist value system. Before traveling to Kala, Medza had never defied the authority of this "domestic dictator," but his relationship with Edima has given him a new confidence in his own manhood, and he publicly asserts his independence upon his return home. What Medza desires at this point is the freedom to make his own decisions and to realize the potential he feels within himself.

Although he rejects the acquisitive individualism of his father, his own dream of individual freedom and self-actualization is equally based on European cultural models. Paradoxically, Medza's conception of himself makes it impossible for him to return home while at the same time preventing him from embracing either the modern world as defined by the colonialist presence or the traditional world as it has survived in places such as Kala. As a result, he is condemned to wander in search of a vaguely defined ideal that he suspects he will never find. The narrating Medza has proclaimed his freedom, but he does not yet know how to define it in terms that would guarantee him a stable sense of identity.

However, he does recognize the representative nature of his own dilemma, and his insight could point the way to the clarity for which he yearns. When he broke with his father, his cousin Zambo from Kala sided with him and later accompanied him on his wanderings. The narrator's friendship with Zambo remains one of the few stable points in his existence, and it reveals how the younger generation of Africans confront a common problem, whether they were educated in European-style schools or grew up without access to literacy.

Medza seeks to define this problem when he declares that his experiences in Kala had enabled him to understand that

> the drama our people are suffering is that of a man left to himself in a world that doesn't belong to him, a world he did not make, a world in which he understands nothing. It's the drama of a man without intellectual direction, of a man walking blindly at night in some hostile New York City. Who will teach him to cross Fifth Avenue only at the crosswalks? Who will teach him to unriddle the "wait" signs? Who will teach him to read a subway map, to make the connections?[23]

In creating this extended metaphor, Medza is generalizing on the *basis* of his personal experiences and inviting the imagined readers of his generation to corroborate his conclusion. Untutored in the complex conventions of urban life, his representative African does not know where to turn for the instruction he needs to survive in a baffling environment that he must confront, even though he never chose to be a part of it. Under such circumstances, freedom from the inequities of traditional society or parental authority may lead only to the anguish of exile, as Medza and Zambo have discovered. Beti's point is that Africans will never enjoy true freedom until they learn how to interpret the modern world and take the initiative for making it their own.

The narrating Medza has not yet attained this stage of critical consciousness, but his story reveals how he moved toward the partial awareness that is encapsulated in his portrait of the representative African. It also suggests that the meaning he seeks is implicit in his experiences if he can only decipher it. For example, after arriving in Kala, he spends many evenings trying to explain the secrets of European learning to the villagers, who regard him as a prodigy and vie with each other to host his presentations, but he soon discovers that his book knowledge reduces the world to a series of abstractions that are irrelevant to the lives of most Africans.

He could enlighten the Kalans about colonialist exploitation, but he chooses to conceal from them the very facts that might accord them some insight into the white man's power—the lynchings in America and the absence of black men among the producers of airplanes. Properly understood, these two facts symbolize how white men impose their will on others primarily through the threat of force and the monopoly control of modern technology. Medza himself fails to draw this conclusion because his teachers never taught him to apply his critical faculties to real-world situations. His education was primarily oriented toward preparing him to take abstruse examinations so he could obtain diplomas that would enhance his status in society. As his avoidance of the crucial facts indicates, his experience in the schools has conditioned him to ignore the causes of oppression in Africa. Medza's education is ineradicable in the sense that he is obliged to think in the only terms he knows, but if he hopes to discover the true meaning of his own life, he will have to unlearn many of the stereotypes he internalized as the result of attending colonial schools.[24]

One way his education distorted his mentality was by inculcating in him the idea that he should pursue socially respectable goals and govern his behavior according to abstract rules rather than by acting upon spontaneous impulses. As long as he clings to this self-conception, he will remain susceptible to the manipulations of others who know how to activate the automatic responses that are built into the role he has been trained to play. His contact with the joyful insouciance of the young Kalans convinced him that "if I continued along the path I had taken in spite of myself, I would never be myself."[25] More than anything else, his encounter with Edima allows him to abandon the path that is leading him away from his true self, but once he conceives of her as an obstacle to his self-realization, he sets in motion a process that culminates in his idealization of her as a symbol of unattainable purity. By fleeing from his relationship with the real Edima, he readopts the European habit of mind that imposes falsely abstract categories upon experience.

Yet despite the appeal of life in Kala, Medza realizes that it does not represent a viable alternative for him in his quest for freedom and identity. The hedonism of the young Kalans results in an enormous waste of talent and energy. Having glimpsed the possibilities of the larger world during his schooling, Medza cannot squander the rest of his life in this way, and he soon tires of it. Besides, a preoccupation with pleasure allows the youth of Kala to tolerate the oppression that the corrupt elders and the colonial administration exercise over them. For example, the chief had collaborated with the French in raising forced-labor gangs and collecting taxes; the people know he enjoys the support of the colonial authorities, and although they resent his exactions, they docilely accept his demand for contributions to the ceremonies that mark his marriage to a seventh wife.

The elders of Kala had lost much of their real power under colonial rule, but their monopoly of local wealth enabled them to increase their dominance over women and younger men. Medza himself experiences the effects of this system when his uncle Mama exploits his presence in the village to benefit from the gifts of people who want to host one of the nightly sessions with the young man from the city. Even his affair with Edima had been manipulated by the chief and his wife in an attempt to entrap Medza in a marriage they thought would be profitable to them. Realizing that he was as much a prisoner of other people's schemes in Kala as he had been at home under his father's authority, Medza feels he must escape from another false identity if he wants to become fully himself.

His experiences in Kala are crucial in shaping the mentality he reveals as the narrator of his own story, for they demonstrate how he has repudiated some of the false images associated with Western schooling and with the idealization of traditional culture. At the same time, these experiences illustrate the possibility of honest human relationships and the need for critical consciousness—values that can help Medza transcend the ambivalence of his situation if he integrates them into his view of the world.

Beti's final two variations on this sort of character appear on the margins of the action in *Le Roi miraculé*. Kris and Bitama bear the imprint of European-style schooling. Both recognize the perversity of the colonialist system and the decadence of traditional society. Both are seeking freedom and a viable sense of identity in the modern world. Yet they interpret events from different ideological perspectives. Kris's experiences have convinced him that he is living in a harsh world where he must take care of himself. Acting on this principle, he succeeds in outwitting others, but his cynical individualism ultimately leads to a dead end. He must flee from Essazam when one of his victims informs the French authorities about his illegal dealings in home-brewed alcohol. Neither he nor any profit he might obtain from his various ruses will ever be secure as long as the colonialist system remains in place.

Bitama realizes the shortsightedness of Kris's attitude, and his insight into the fraud being perpetrated upon Africans by the colonialist system prompts him to consider joining the revolutionary Parti Progressiste Populaire. But Bitama lacks the self-assurance to act upon his convictions. And when he inadvertently glimpses Kris making love to a beautiful young woman, his disgust purges him of his tendency to idealize. He even becomes close friends with the new colonial administrator. Years later, as a university student in a small French town, he reflects on the events he had witnessed in Essazam and concludes that the hypocrisy of the people there is as spiritually dead as it is in Europe. His insight is valid, but unless it moves him to action, he too will continue to be a victim of the colonialist system.

In *Le Roi miraculé*, as in all of Beti's early novels, the young men who possess the energy and intelligence to change this system remain entrapped in shortsighted individualism or intellectual immobility. By focusing on their dilemma and by situating it within the corrupt colonialist context, Beti created a critical counterdiscourse to discredit the false images that were being used to justify the continued exploitation of Africans.

The implicit message of his early novels is twofold. To Europeans, for whom he was obliged to write at the time, Beti was addressing a plea to acknowledge the hypocrisy and injustice of the colonialist enterprise in which their countries were engaged. To Africans, whom he considered the real audience for his work, he was directing an exhortation to recognize the mechanisms behind their oppression and to seize the historical initiative that would allow them to become masters of their own destiny. The humor and irony with which he cloaked such messages contributed to the enduring appeal of these novels, but the real line of continuity between them and the writings he began to publish in the early 1970s is his desire to create a counterhistory capable of revealing the falsity of commonly accepted stereotypes about Africa and promoting a critical examination of the situation that exists in Cameroon and elsewhere on the continent.

CHAPTER

6

INDEPENDENCE AND
THE MYTH OF
NATIONAL UNITY

When the United Nations agreed to terminate the trusteeship status in eastern Cameroon without holding new elections, as the UPC had demanded, Ahidjo and his advisers became free to shape the government of the new state. However, the task of forging a new sense of national identity was a daunting one. Ahidjo had never been strongly identified with the national independence movement, and he lacked popular support in most parts of the country. He encountered widespread opposition from moderate nationalists in the highly literate south-central and coastal regions, while an armed UPC revolt was gathering momentum in the Bamileke territory, and a majority of socialist and third-world countries were refusing to recognize his government. The terrorist attacks that marred independence celebrations in Yaounde and Douala on January 1, 1960, bore eloquent testimony to the tensions that would continue to wrack the country during its first three decades.

Nevertheless, the Ahidjo government was not without resources. People took pride in the new state and expected conditions to improve as Europeans lost their privileged status in society. Millions participated enthusiastically in the independence celebrations. On a quite practical level, the French continued to support the Ahidjo government, and the new president himself proved extremely adroit in negotiating compromises, coopting former opponents into his government, and brutally suppressing dissent when he could not stifle it in other ways. By the time the Federated Republic of Cameroon was transformed into a unitary state in 1972, it had actually become a relatively stable, economically viable country.

On the surface, Ahidjo appeared to have overcome most of the obstacles that had confronted his government twelve years earlier. Cameroon was self-sufficient in food production, and the economy was expanding at one of the most rapid rates in Africa. Peace had been restored to the Bamileke territory, and West Cameroon had been successfully incorporated into the country. Beneath the surface, however, there was considerable disaffection with the Ahidjo government and its attempt to centralize control over all aspects of the country's sociopolitical life. By concentrating ultimate decision-making power in the hands of a few individuals, this government, like many others in postcolonial Africa, gave the majority of its citizens the impression that they could exercise little influence over their own destinies. And by fostering the emergence of an ethnically based patronage system, it convinced people that rewards would be distributed on the basis of personal relationships, not according to merit.

As in other recently independent African countries, vast disparities of wealth, bureaucratic inefficiency, and the misappropriation of public funds made people sceptical toward the Ahidjo government's slogans about nation building and the need for individual sacrifice. Many were afraid to speak freely for fear of falling victim to the police-state tactics that the government did not hesitate to employ. Under such circumstances, a two-tiered sense of reality emerged. Most Cameroonians paid lip service to the official rhetoric that portrayed the country as a just and equitable society moving toward a utopian future. Yet their experience of everyday life showed them a far less idealistic picture of Cameroonian reality.

Ahidjo's approach to ideology was similar to that adopted by many heads of state throughout the continent. His official rhetoric revolved around the "great idea" of a nation that would be unified, productive, and confident of its own identity. Slogans varied from year to year as economic and cultural policies changed, but their basic purpose remained the same—to inculcate this "great idea" in the minds of the people so they would work toward the construction of the nation and support the government that claimed to represent their interests. During his first address at Douala, Ahidjo declared that this ideal could be realized if Cameroonians set aside their regional and ethnic differences, cooperated with the French to raise the country's standard of living, and strove to achieve a new synthesis between modern technology and traditional African values. The dominant theme in all his early speeches was the contention that national unity was necessary if Cameroonians hoped to achieve their "historic destiny." Rhetoric of this nature is a commonplace in the history of imagined communities that have evolved into nations, but when it is manipulated by a government that exercises arbitrary authority over its citizens, it contains an implicit threat against anyone who questions the official truth.

Throughout the 1960s, African governments became increasingly concerned with the formulation of cultural policies that could sustain the idea of national unity and help project a favorable image of their countries to the rest of the world. Cameroon was no exception. Ahidjo himself often referred to the country's national culture as its "identity card." Culture in this sense is not a system of traditional beliefs, social forms, and material practices, but a set of attitudes and behaviors that acknowledge the historical past while fostering participation in the modernization process. In contrast to ethnic culture that people accept as a given of their day-to-day lives, the new national culture must be consciously constructed; individuals must be persuaded to adopt its premises and to act in accordance with them. By defining and promoting such a culture, the Ahidjo government hoped to consolidate the feelings of national identity that had been awakened during the movement toward independence.

There were, however, major obstacles to the implementation of this approach to cultural politics. In the first place, traditional culture was profoundly rooted in ethnicity, and the sort of heroic accomplishments that inspire popular identification with a national culture were either ethnically based (as in the case of Rudolph Douala Manga Bell, Martin-Paul Samba, and Sultan Njoya), or they were related to the UPC struggle against French colonialism, as in the case of Ruben Um Nyobé. To avoid the resentments that would have arisen if some ethnic cultures were privileged over others, the Ahidjo government emphasized a vaguely defined, romanticized African culture as the traditional component of national identity, and because Ahidjo had come to power as a French-sponsored opponent of the UPC, a veil of silence was draped over its role in the independence movement. As a result, the cultural policies of the Cameroonian government never achieved their goal of synthesizing a national myth in which a majority of the people could believe.

In the second place, nationalism in the modern nations of Europe and the Americas had arisen partly in response to the need for a new form of social organization appropriate to the industrialization that was taking place there. The rise of literacy and the individualism that accompanied industrialization in these countries also occurred in Cameroon, but like most African countries, Cameroon had an insufficient economic base to provide adequate employment opportunities for those who had adopted the assumptions behind the modernization process. Furthermore, the ethnically based patronage system that emerged in Cameroon discouraged the respect for competence, the sense of civic responsibility, and the work ethic that had enabled European and American nations to attain a materially comfortable way of life. At the very moment when the Ahidjo government was heralding the promise of a better life as a part of its national identity concept, it was also undermining the attitudes that might have made that better life possible.

Yet the major reason for the failure of the Ahidjo government to inculcate its "great idea" in the minds of most Cameroonians was the same as it was in other parts of Africa—a glaring disparity between the idealism of its official rhetoric and the actual motivations of the people who acceded to power in the postcolonial era. In many ways, pronouncements about national unity and national identity served as instruments that allowed a small minority of the population to maintain its own wealth, power, and status by offering the rest of the people symbolic gratification for their real needs and by distracting their attention from the true causes of their misery. The system perpetuated itself largely because the privileged class expanded to incorporate a relatively large number of educated individuals, who then had a vested interest in preserving the existing social order.

For example, government bureaucracy grew rapidly during the 1960s, and talented younger people, particularly from the south-central and coastal regions, were quickly integrated into the civil service. Although they seldom entered the inner circle of Ahidjo's closest advisers, these technocratic and intellectual elites did share in the material benefits controlled by the government. Eventually, they formed an implicit coalition with the Fulani privileged classes from the North, an arrangement that permitted each group to protect its dominance in its own part of the country. As these groups consolidated their positions, a social stratification similar to that of the colonialist period began to reassert itself under a new guise.

In a process that was repeated throughout Africa, the privileged class in Cameroon appropriated a disproportionate share of the country's wealth. By the early 1970s, less than two percent of the total population received a third of the national income; the next ten percent also received a third, leaving the final third to be distributed among more than eighty-eight percent of the population.[1] This gap in income distribution becomes even wider when one considers the other perquisites reserved for the privileged class—subsidized housing, access to better medical care, admission to elite public schools for their children, and the expediting of administrative decisions. During the colonial period, there had been a sharp division between European and "native" residential areas in the cities; this division continued to exist, although Cameroonian members of the privileged class were now occupying many of the expensive villas in the formerly white neighborhoods. Under such circumstances, the official rhetoric of the Ahidjo government served to camouflage social inequities in much the same way colonialist rhetoric had obscured the true relationships of power under French rule.

In practical terms, Ahidjo and his supporters acted like the ruling elites in most other African countries as they consolidated their hold on power. For example, they moved quickly to dominate the institutional structure of the new country and to gain control over most sources of wealth and status. The rationale for this centralization of authority was the desire to achieve national unity by coordinating the country's productive efforts for the well-being of the society as a whole; the real reasons behind it often had more to do with personal ambition and the urge to exercise power over others. In any case, Ahidjo was largely successful in this endeavor. One knowledgeable commentator insisted that, by the early 1970s, nearly all political power and personal wealth in the country depended directly on the discretionary authority of the president.[2]

Two of the instruments employed in this consolidation of power were the constitution and the single-party system. Drafted by French technical advisers and modeled on the constitution of de Gaulle's Fifth Republic, the 1960 Cameroonian constitution accorded autocratic powers to the president. Although the south-central and coastal regions voted against this document, it was adopted on the basis of overwhelming support from the North. From this point forward, Ahidjo had legal sanction for his control of the government. When the constitution was revised the following year to accommodate federation with western Cameroon, the president officially acquired the characteristically Gaullist prerogative to rule by decree whenever the life, the independence, or the institutions of the nation were considered to be in danger. This rather vague wording permitted considerable latitude for interpretation, and it was later used to justify many of the arbitrary constraints imposed upon freedom of speech and action in Cameroon. In contrast to Ahidjo's "great idea" that defined the new nation as an expression of the people's will, the new constitutional framework assured that the will of the governing elites could be imposed upon the people.

In any case, Ahidjo's party had never been a spokesman for the desires of the people. During the first legislative session after independence, his Union Camerounaise controlled a bare majority, and most of its representatives had been elected without opposition from safe districts in the North, but moderate politicians from the south-central and coastal regions were soon incorporated into the UC, and plans were already being made to transform it into the country's only legal party. From the beginning, party ideologues had envisaged it as a tool for manipulating public opinion and for achieving goals defined by the leadership. For example, in addressing the third party congress in 1961, Samuel Kamé declared that the party should adopt "fascist methods" in suppressing all ideas that did not emanate from the party. According to him, the masses should be conditioned to accept unquestioningly whatever they are told by the party, and the most effective way of inculcating such a mentality in them is through the dissemination of easily remembered slogans. As a means of enforcing conformity to party directives, he even suggested the organization of vigilante groups.[3] Such totalitarian methods were often adopted by the Ahidjo government, and Kamé's advocacy of them clearly reveals his identification of the party with the government.

As early as 1961, Ahidjo himself stated that the UC was the only party that could lend unity and coherence of purpose to the political process in Cameroon. The following year he declared that the "era of micro-parties" was over because "oneness of view on the burning issues of the day" had become a vital necessity.[4] By mid-1962, the UC controlled eighty-six of the ninety-nine seats in the national assembly. Four years later, it was renamed the Union Nationale Camerounaise (UNC) and declared the single legal party in the country. In theory, the single party would eliminate the divisive squabbling of politicians from different ethnic groups and promote popular support for the government's conception of socioeconomic development.

Proclaimed a historic occasion by party leaders, the creation of the UNC was presented as an expression of the people's will. The government published a collection of patriotic poems that had been written to commemorate the event, and the editor of this volume exulted that Cameroonians in general and its poets in particular were reverberating to the appeals of the same myth and enthusiastically embracing "the Cameroonian humanism" that had motivated the founding of the UNC.[5] This idea was elaborated further by Sengat-Kuo after he became a principal architect of party ideology in the late 1960s, for he envisioned the party as an embodiment of the "fundamental idea" of a people who occupy a specific place in the "civilization of the universal." In many of the speeches he wrote for Ahidjo, the party is depicted as the organization that helps the people realize the dream of national unity by holding up the image of a just and humane future society and by making them aware of the cultural assumptions they already share.

In practice, the UNC remained peripheral to the lives of most Cameroonians. Its weekly newspaper, *L'Unité*, was largely unread, even by party militants, and the party itself functioned primarily as a means of exercising power from the top. Although it did play an important role in the patronage system and in the recruitment of political cadres, its real strength derived not from widespread popular support but from the government's control over the privileges and perquisites that people desired to obtain. Rather than transcending ethnic tensions, the party exacerbated them because favors were distributed according to a system of ethnic equilibration; in other words, what Ahidjo gave to one ethnic group was generally balanced by what he gave to others, and the competition for available resources became increasingly based on ethnic rivalries.

Within ethnic groups, Ahidjo gave some control over patronage and enrichment opportunities to individuals who in return were expected to maintain peace among their own people. Realizing that political and social advancement was contingent upon the good will of party members from one's own ethnic group, individuals became less concerned with demonstrating competency than with cultivating the favor of their ethnic patrons, and because rewards seldom correspond with merit under such circumstances, the idealistic pronouncements of the UNC were increasingly viewed with scepticism. Rather than minimizing the importance of ethnic origins and stressing the role of individual qualifications, as a modern state might be expected to do, the Ahidjo government and the single party jeopardized their avowed nation-building project by implementing a system that placed primary emphasis on ethnic affiliation.

In the sense that the UNC formed a coalition of privileged individuals from various ethnic groups, it did consolidate an interethnic support network for Ahidjo's policies. Because the status and wealth of these individuals depended on the existing social order, they owed a debt of loyalty to the Ahidjo regime, and public support of its programs was a partial repayment of that debt. If they failed to abide by the will of Ahidjo and his inner circle, the consequences could be serious. Corruption was tolerated, but not a lack of loyalty. For example, after the reputedly corrupt Victor Kanga was removed from his post as minister of finance, he and several others received long prison sentences for having been implicated in the publication of a pamphlet against corruption in government.

The demand for absolute loyalty was also apparent at the National Institute of Public Administration, where the entire curriculum was posited on the assumption that civil servants should unquestioningly carry out government policy. The party made its standpoint clear when it announced that no one would be elected to public office on the basis of competence or popularity but solely "as a function of their fidelity to the party, that is to say to the regime, [and] of their capacity to serve as loyal and effective pawns on the party's chess board."[6] The implicit corollary of this metaphor is that people who refuse to make the moves assigned to them can simply be removed from the board.

Institutions such as the army and the trade unions might have circumvented the ethnic brokerage system that emerged in the party and in the government, but the army became a reflection of the same social stratification that characterized the society at large, and the trade union movement was consolidated into a single national union during the late 1960s. No longer chosen by the membership, its officials were nominated by the leadership of the UNC. By the early 1970s, then, the government and the party effectively controlled the country's major social and political institutions, and because it also controlled the media, it could guarantee at least a superficial adherence to its conception of national unity.

One of the principal reasons for Ahidjo's success in this regard was the support he received from the French. Even before eastern Cameroon achieved independence, secret agreements governing cultural, military, and economic assistance had already been signed with France. The persistence of the UPC rebellion in the Bamileke territory rendered the Ahidjo government particularly dependent upon the French, who supplied over two thousand troops to help restore peace in the area. Also, support for the UPC from the Soviet bloc and from many newly independent African states isolated Cameroon from alternative influences and other sources of development capital. During the country's first year of independence, nearly eighty percent of its budget was provided by France. For more than ten years, the majority of commanding officers in the army were French. Key positions in every ministry and at the president's office were also occupied by French technical advisers. Most of the instructors at the newly created university were Frenchmen, and the government's feared secret police was created by the French.

The Ahidjo government could never have survived without massive French support, but the French also benefited from an arrangement that for many years enabled their firms to maintain a virtual monopoly over trade with Cameroon. From a cultural perspective, the French presence in Cameroon fostered an increased use of the French language and assured the continued influence of French tastes and modes of thought. Besides, the net cost of French aid was not as high as it might appear because a large proportion of it was paid directly to French technical advisers, teachers, workers, and businessmen who repatriated their earnings to France. The relationship between the Ahidjo government and the former colonizing power was thus a mutually beneficial one.

During the first ten years of Cameroonian independence, the French exercised a particularly strong influence over the government's economic policies. They drafted the first two five-year plans, which emphasized the improvement of communication and transportation networks, and they determined the administrative procedures that governed the budgetary process. In the early 1960s, the Ahidjo government had espoused a vaguely defined African social-ism that was ostensibly rooted in traditional practices such as communal land ownership and cooperative labor; however, by 1965, Ahidjo's advisers recog-nized that such an ideology had neither mobilized the support of the people nor attracted sufficient foreign capital to meet development needs. As a result, the government announced its new policy of "planned liberalism" the following year. Presented as a way of combining individual initiative and self-realization with communal well-being and social harmony, "planned liberalism" established highly favorable conditions for the investment of foreign capital and triggered a rapid growth in the overall economy.

In the business climate created by the new economic doctrine, many Came-roonians prospered, and some even became enormously wealthy. The num-ber of firms owned by Cameroonians multiplied, and Cameroonians increas-ingly occupied managerial positions in the large state-run corporations. But the success of such individuals in the commercial sector was not matched by a commensurate improvement in the country's general standard of living. To-gether with upper-level civil servants and professionals in various fields, these businessmen and managers enjoyed a lifestyle that contrasted sharply with the conditions under which the majority of their fellow countrymen were obliged to exist. In a few months, a member of this privileged class earned more than most farmers received during a lifetime of toil on the land.[7] The economic expansion that followed the implementation of the Ahidjo government's new policies did accelerate the modernization process, but the increased wealth it produced tended to accentuate the class distinctions that had already begun to emerge before independence.

Against this background, Ahidjo himself amassed a considerable fortune, and although he did not indulge in an ostentatious show of personal vanity, his wealth obviously placed him at the top of the privileged class in Cameroon. However, to obtain the support of the common people, he needed to project an image with which they could identify. As in many African countries, efforts were made to popularize the idea that the Cameroonian leader was a wise and benevolent man who always acted decisively for the common good, but only after Sengat-Kuo entered the cabinet in 1967 were the president's posi-tions synthesized into a coherent body of thought.[8] At the same time, Ahidjo himself was increasingly portrayed as a personification of the national ideal.

These initiatives were given concrete form in two government-subventioned books that were published in 1968 to mark the tenth anniversary of Ahidjo's accession to power under colonial rule. The first of these books, *The Political Philosophy of Ahmadou Ahidjo*, presented the president's world view as a moderate humanism and revealed the influence of Senghor and de Gaulle on his thinking. The second was *Ahmadou Ahidjo, pionnier de l'Afrique moderne*, a laudatory biography that the government commissioned the Swiss journalist Béat Christophe Baeschlin-Raspail to write. Because Ahidjo had not been a leader in the anticolonialist struggle, Baeschlin-Raspail was obliged to rewrite history in such a way that the president's "heroic role" in his country's movement toward independence might appear plausible.

In Baeschlin-Raspail's account, Ahidjo becomes an iron-willed, charismatic leader whose "realistic spirit" enabled him to overcome seemingly insurmountable obstacles and to fashion a prosperous, unified state from the chaos that prevailed when he assumed the reins of government in 1958. His penetrating intelligence supposedly permitted him to take in all of world history at a glance and to resolve difficult problems that baffled others. In the book, he is credited with orchestrating the defeat of the UPC rebels in the Bassa country, skillfully negotiating the terms of independence, crushing the UPC terrorists in the Bamileke territory, bringing about reunification with West Cameroon, creating a unified party that reflects the aspirations of the people, and forging a sense of national identity that transcends religious and ethnic differences. In short, he allegedly brought peace, unity, and prosperity to the country and therefore deserved the praise titles that had been bestowed upon him—Father of Independence, Hero of the Nation, Infallible Leader, Great Guide, Beacon of the Great National Party, Pioneer of Modern Africa, the First Cameroonian. Baeschlin-Raspail concludes that Ahidjo's remarkable accomplishments make him one of the twentieth century's outstanding statesmen and that "we ought to bow down before him."[9]

In the everyday lives of Cameroonians, this exaggeratedly heroic image of the president was constantly reinforced by allusions to his role as a traditional chief, by newspaper accounts of his activities, omnipresent photographs, posters, songs, streets named in his honor, and, more ominously, by a police surveillance that enforced public respect for his reputation. In all these ways, the government and the party sought to institutionalize a myth of Ahidjo as the heroic symbol of Cameroonian unity. The people may not have accepted this myth at face value, but its repetition in the media implanted the idea that Ahidjo's rise to power was historically inevitable. From schoolbooks and the official propaganda, the younger generation imbibed a misleading picture of what had actually taken place during the colonial period, and the villainy of the UPC appeared credible to many of them, especially in light of the terrorist activities that were still taking place in the Bamileke area. Although Ahidjo was not revered by the people, the 1960s did witness a growing acceptance of his regime.

Other African heads of state were exalted in a similar manner, and just as the resigned acceptance of their regimes was accompanied by a growing resentment against them, Cameroonians remained cynical about the heroic qualities ascribed to Ahidjo in the official myth. When he visited a city, streets that had not been repaired for years were suddenly resurfaced. Prisoners and soldiers decorated the streets with palm fronds and flags. Civil servants were obliged to contribute as much as a month's salary to stage lavish receptions in his honor and to purchase expensive gifts for him. Such fleeting and superficial shows of respect eroded confidence in the "great idea" that Ahidjo supposedly represented, but as political power became increasingly concentrated in his hands and in those of his close collaborators, he grew less receptive to opinions that diverged from official versions of the truth.

He himself may have ignored the profound scepticism with which he and his nation-building ideology were viewed by the majority of the population. Even his supporters recognized that he was an uninspiring public speaker whose political success depended primarily upon French support, patient deliberation, and a willingness to be absolutely ruthless in putting down dissent. The disparity between the myth of Ahidjo and the actual person who occupied the presidency was widely recognized, and it serves as an appropriate symbol for the growing malaise that afflicted Cameroonian society in the late 1960s and early 1970s because people throughout the country identified him not with the idealistic goals of national unity but with the unbridled desire for wealth and power.

The party, the government, and the privileged elites who benefited from the existing situation thus confronted a serious credibility gap that undermined efforts to mobilize the people for the attainment of national development goals. Because Ahidjo and his close collaborators controlled the media and most social institutions, they could oblige people to pay lip service to the official rhetoric, but they could not force people to believe in it. Having perceived the discrepancy between idealistic nation-building myths and reality, many people concluded that those in power were exploiting such myths for their own profit. Furthermore, Ahidjo's centralization of power and the rapid expansion of an arbitrary, often corrupt bureaucracy convinced most people that they had been excluded from any meaningful participation in the decision-making process.

This feeling of powerlessness was reinforced each time someone had to maneuver a dossier through various government offices in the hope of obtaining a job or a necessary document. People frequently learned of their promotions or demotions when they heard them being announced over the radio; even government ministers often lost their posts without warning. Many individuals were arrested and interrogated by the police for vaguely defined offenses. For most Cameroonians, such a system was demoralizing because it made them subject at any moment to the arbitrary exercise of power from above. The anxiety generated by a widespread feeling of powerlessness permitted the government to enforce a superficial allegiance to its official version of the truth, but obedience under such circumstances did not mean that the people actually identified with a national unity concept linked with the heroic image of Ahidjo. In fact, they often emulated the behavior of the privileged class, seeking to contribute as little as possible to the system while extracting as much as they could from it.

Furthermore, as in the rest of Africa, economic exploitation did not cease with the passing of the colonial era. Contrary to the expectations of many Cameroonians, the commercial sector continued to be dominated by European interests, and trading structures established under colonial rule remained largely in place throughout the 1960s. Investment decisions were still made from abroad, and they seldom responded to the country's long-term needs for jobs and domestic production. The implementation of Ahidjo's "planned liberalism" and the budgetary drain occasioned by a rapid expansion of the civil-service bureaucracy actually increased Cameroon's dependency on foreign management and capital.

Two examples suffice to illustrate the persistence of colonialist economic structures in independent Cameroon. First, although French export-import firms experienced some difficulty in the early 1960s, they flourished as a result of Ahidjo's liberalized investment policies, maintaining a virtual monopoly over the cocoa and coffee purchases that accounted for more than half the country's export income and increasing their profits from a lucrative import business in French consumer goods. From the farmers' point of view, independence benefited European traders more than it benefited them. Significant funding was designated for agricultural research, and advertising campaigns urged farmers to expand production, but their income stagnated or declined as they remained subject to the same trading structures that had existed during colonial times. The result was a growing resentment among small farmers and a loss of credibility for the government's pronouncements of support for rural development. Under such circumstances, many people left the countryside and joined the urban migrations that were gathering momentum during the late 1960s and early 1970s.

Second, the Péchiney-Ugine aluminum smelter near Edea profited enormously during the 1960s from a highly favorable arrangement with the Cameroonian government. Until 1969, the French conglomerate paid no taxes, and even then it became subject to only a 1 percent turnover tax. The high dam at Edea had been built during the 1950s with French government funds, but after independence, Péchiney-Ugine continued to buy 96 percent of the electric power it produced for only 4.5 percent of what it actually cost to produce that power. The management of the plant remained almost entirely in French hands during the 1960s, and very few jobs were created for Cameroonians. The totality of the aluminum production at Edea was exported to France, and all investment decisions were made from abroad without regard for the development needs of Cameroon.[10] The benefits of this arrangement for Péchiney-Ugine were obvious; the advantages for the average Cameroonian were less so. By one standard measure of economic prosperity, Cameroon appeared to be flourishing, for its per capita consumption of electricity was among the highest in Africa throughout the 1960s, but in light of the amount consumed by the foreign-owned aluminum smelter, it is clear that Cameroonians fared little better than their neighbors in this respect.

The society that emerged during the first decade of Cameroonian independence in many ways resembled the colonialist one it replaced. A privileged class continued to enjoy a standard of living that separated it from the vast majority of the population. The government proclaimed its dedication to the general welfare, but its idealistic rhetoric actually served as a hypocritical justification for maintaining the status quo. Most people felt they had little control over decisions that affected their destinies, and extensive police surveillance made them uneasy about expressing their opinions freely. Under such circumstances, the Ahidjo government could promote its conception of national identity, but it could not force people to internalize it. In fact, the dominant mood in the country during the late 1960s and early 1970s was one of disillusionment. Independence had generated expectations of a better life, and these expectations had not been fulfilled for most Cameroonians. The sense of commitment associated with the anticolonialist struggle had never translated into support for the Ahidjo regime, and as ethnic and regional rivalries proliferated, a pervasive cynicism prevented people from identifying with Ahidjo's "great idea" of national unity.

In practical terms, Ahidjo confronted two major obstacles to the consolidation of his power—virulent opposition from the UPC and the problem of integrating anglophone West Cameroon into the new nation after the 1961 UN plebiscite. Although he succeeded in overcoming both obstacles by the time the Cameroon Federation was transformed into a unitary republic in 1972, the issues raised by them left an enduring mark on the intellectual life of the country.

Because the radical nationalist movement had fought to eliminate the exploitative structures of French colonialism, many of its adherents opposed the perpetuation of these structures under the Ahidjo regime. Just as they had attacked the hypocrisy of colonialist rhetoric, they sought to raise the general level of consciousness about the disparity between reality and Ahidjo's nation-building rhetoric. However, under pressure from the Ahidjo government and its French supporters, the UPC itself became fragmented and ineffectual during the first decade of independence.

Throughout the 1960s, there were actually two wings of the UPC. The first was located primarily in the Bamileke territory, and it consisted of semiautonomous guerilla bands under the leadership of Ernest Ouandié. The second was composed of UPC militants living in exile. Both represented a serious challenge to the credibility of the Ahidjo government's concept of national identity. Unlike Um Nyobé's underground organization in the Bassa country during the 1950s, the Bamileke wing of the UPC had never been integrated into an existing framework of traditional institutions; in fact, its appeal was due largely to younger people who resented the inflexible authority structures of such institutions.

Operating on an ad hoc basis, small groups of UPC guerillas frequently carried out terrorist attacks on civilians. The Bamileke themselves were deeply divided in their attitudes toward the UPC, but the indiscriminate brutality of French troops under the command of General Briand tended to polarize opinion against the government in Yaounde. The result was an extended period of devastation in an area occupied by the largest and most enterprising ethnic group in the country. The mutual distrust that characterized relations between the Ahidjo government and the Bamileke also prevented the full integration of the Bamileke into the country's political patronage system. This state of affairs in turn reinforced Bamileke convictions that their interests were not being served by the existing system.

The event that marked the end of the UPC rebellion in the Bamileke territory was the capture of Ouandié in 1970. Shortly afterwards, the bishop of Nkongsamba, Albert Ndongmo, was also arrested. Together with more than a hundred codefendants, the two men were accused of fomenting a rebellion against the legitimate government of Cameroon and plotting to assassinate the president. In the ensuing show trial before a military tribunal in Yaounde, the prosecution established Ouandié's responsibility for a number of terrorist raids, but its case against Ndongmo and the "Mouvement de Sainte-Croix" was highly circumstantial. There had been intermittent contacts between Ouandié and Ndongmo as early as 1962, and Ndongmo frequently questioned the direction his country was taking. His sponsorship of the often-critical newspaper *L'Essor des Jeunes* and his support for independent cooperative enterprises had troubled the authorities in Yaounde, for they feared an alliance between the UPC and socially conscious Catholics in the Bamileke territory. In fact, the popular Ndongmo may have been linked with Ouandié as a means of discrediting him and forestalling such an alliance.

When both men were sentenced to death, there was considerable international pressure for Ahidjo to grant them clemency, and after Ndongmo requested a pardon, his punishment was commuted to life imprisonment, but Ouandié and two other UPC members were flown to Bafoussam and publicly executed. Throughout the trial, Ouandié refused to testify on his own behalf because his lawyers had not been allowed into the country, and he insisted upon not being blindfolded in front of the firing squad.

In one sense, the Ndongmo-Ouandié trial was a victory for the Ahidjo government. The party newspaper *L'Unité* portrayed it as a vindication of Cameroonian democracy and proof of national unity; the enemies of the state had been appropriately punished, for, as the lead editorial announced, "truth always triumphs in the end."[11] UPC terrorist activities in the Bamileke area virtually ceased after the trial, and with the support of Jean Zoa, the bishop of Yaounde, the government managed to separate Ndongmo's position from that of the Catholic church. Yet *L'Unité*'s official version of the truth was not universally accepted. Ndongmo's guilt was never convincingly established, and the image of Ouandié valiantly staring down his enemies remained etched in people's minds. Another martyr had been created, and the credibility of Ahidjo's idealistic nation-building rhetoric had been severely strained.

Rigorous police measures made it increasingly difficult to circulate radical nationalist literature in Cameroon, but members of the exile UPC continued to challenge the Ahidjo government's version of the truth in pamphlets, at international conferences, and on the radio, although they were increasingly hard pressed after de Gaulle declared the UPC illegal in France and when Cameroon itself established diplomatic relations with Ghana, Egypt, Guinea, and other African nations that had offered them asylum. By 1971 even Russia and China no longer supported the UPC cause. Nevertheless, writers such as Abel Kingué, Ndeh Ntumazah, the former student leader Woungly-Massaga, and the brilliant economist Osendé Afana continued to portray Ahidjo as the usurper of an authentically nationalist tradition in Cameroon. According to their writings, his government was not an expression of the people's will but a fascist dictatorship that served as a tool of French interests and subjected people to an exploitative system as invidious as the one imposed on them during the colonial era. In general, UPC writers emphasized the continuity between colonial rule and the existing situation in Cameroon, implying that the need to fight against oppression remained the same as before.

These writers detailed the repressiveness of the Ahidjo regime and drew attention to aspects of Cameroonian life that were never mentioned in the government's pronouncements: concentration camps, military atrocities, public executions, corruption, human rights violations, French influence over major policy decisions, suppression of a free press, and a general atmosphere of intimidation. In short, they argued that Ahidjo had destroyed any sense of responsible public opinion and made a mockery of the terms he used to justify his own exercise of power—independence, national unity, and democracy. "The country is in chains," declared one UPC writer. "Fascism has, inevitably, come of age in Kamerun."[12] The implicit thesis behind all the radical nationalist literature of the 1960s was that the society brought into being by Ahidjo's fascist regime was so riddled with contradictions that it would crumble of its own accord if only the truth could be made clear to people in Cameroon and elsewhere in the world. Their own writings represent an attempt to keep alive this truth and to undermine the idealistic myths that the Ahidjo government was using to obscure its own venality.

In an ill-fated effort to put radical nationalist theory into practice, Osendé Afana tried to establish a new front of UPC guerilla activity in the tropical forests of eastern Cameroon. In contrast to the exile leaders in Ghana, he had been deeply influenced by the example of Mao Tse-tung. His own *L'Economie de l'ouest africain* attacks African socialisms which, like Ahidjo's "planned liberalism," promulgate myths of national development and heroic leadership to camouflage the exploitation of the people by private investors and state-run corporations.

Osendé Afana's writing as well as his guerilla activity was premised on the assumption that committed individuals like himself could convince rural people that their poverty resulted from a system designed to benefit foreigners and a small class of privileged Africans at their expense. By urging people to rely on their own perceptions rather than on the official rhetoric of the Ahidjo government, he hoped to create groups of enlightened individuals who would gradually raise the general level of consciousness in the countryside. This heightened consciousness would, he thought, serve as the basis for genuinely revolutionary activity in Cameroon and throughout Africa. But like Ché Guévara in Bolivia, Osendé Afana was unprepared for the rigors of guerilla warfare and the mistrust of the people he had come to liberate. Betrayed by local villagers, he was captured by government forces and summarily executed.

There was a quixotic element in Osendé Afana's crusade, but his example and his ideas survived as an inspiration to others who were disillusioned with Ahidjo's definition of national identity.

By the early 1970s, the UPC no longer represented a political or military threat to the Ahidjo regime, although it continued to play a significant role in the country's intellectual life by providing an alternative interpretation of contemporary reality, a countertruth that challenged the government's contention that it was engaged in the noble task of constructing a nation and imbuing its people with a sense of collective identity. For example, Ouandié's death triggered the publication of numerous articles, pamphlets, and books that interpreted the event as part of an ongoing struggle between the people and their oppressors.

From this perspective, Ahidjo was not a great statesman but a bloodthirsty tyrant who ruled by intimidating the people and maintaining them in chronic poverty, whereas the UPC was the "immortal soul of the Kamerunian people," and its martyred leaders Um Nyobé, Moumié, Osendé Afana, and Ouandié were the true national heroes. As Woungly-Massaga wrote in his *L'Afrique bloquée: L'Exemple du Kamerun*, the national unity proclaimed by Ahidjo was a false unity because it was based on police terror, forced adhesion to the UNC, and the exploitation of a majority for the benefit of a privileged few. Although the publications of exile UPC writers could circulate only clandestinely within the country, their view of Cameroonian independence ultimately became widespread even among those who disavowed the violent methods of the UPC.

In addition to combating the UPC, Ahidjo and his close collaborators confronted the problem of integrating West Cameroon into the centralized system of governance they were gradually implementing in the eastern part of the country. West Cameroonians themselves had only vague notions about what to expect from federation with the former French trust territory. Most of them would undoubtedly have preferred to constitute an independent country of their own, but opposition in the UN to the further balkanization of Africa caused the 1961 plebiscite issue to be couched in terms of a choice between union with Nigeria and union with eastern Cameroon.

By this time, Endeley had reversed his initial support for a reunified Cameroon and was advocating union with Nigeria. Foncha adduced a shared colonial past and common ethnic backgrounds to persuade voters that they should join with eastern Cameroon, and he contended that West Cameroonians would be less likely to lose control over their own destiny among four million Cameroonians than among thirty-five million Nigerians. On the day of the plebiscite, West Cameroonians opted for union with eastern Cameroon.[13] Endeley and Foncha supporters voted largely along ethnic lines, and although the decisive factor was resentment against Igbo domination, Foncha and his followers were influenced in their choice by the expectation that West Cameroon would become a semiautonomous state in the new federation. However, when the new constitution was ratified, it was largely the product of Ahidjo's advisers, and they already had a clear idea of the centralized, unitary state they hoped to create.[14] As a result, West Cameroonians received considerably less autonomy than they had anticipated before the plebiscite.

The birth of the bilingual Republic of Cameroon was greeted with optimism in the former British trust territory, but the transition to subordinate status in a predominantly francophone country proved difficult for the anglophone westerners. The relative isolation of the region was intensified by the abrupt severance of ties with Nigeria and by an initial failure to establish new communication links with the rest of Cameroon. Roads in West Cameroon deteriorated. Public and private investment dropped to less than half of what it had been during the final years of the colonial period. Export earnings declined precipitously with the fall in banana prices and the loss of privileged access to commonwealth markets in 1963. The cost of living increased. Profoundly affected by the general depression, the CDC ceased to be the dominant social and economic force in the region, although it remained the largest single employer.[15]

On a significant symbolic level, West Cameroonians were obliged to adopt a new system of weights and measures, a new currency based on the French franc rather than on the pound sterling, a new form of government that lacked the characteristically British respect for civil liberties and parliamentary democracy, and an educational system that was restructured in conformity with French models. Even tastes in consumer goods had to be modified as English products became unavailable. And at a time when French political and cultural influence was growing in the country at large, West Cameroon became increasingly isolated from the English-speaking world as the British withdrew from the area. Tensions also mounted when eastern Cameroonian gendarmes treated West Cameroonians in the same harsh manner they habitually employed in dealing with UPC sympathizers in the East, or when federal authorities sought to impose French-inspired administrative structures on West Cameroonians.

Adjustments were inevitable under the circumstances, but coupled with a loss of the limited autonomy West Cameroonians had enjoyed during the last years of colonial rule, such sweeping changes caused them to fear that reunification would deprive them of the regional identity they had sought to preserve in voting as they did. Ahidjo's gradual centralization of power did nothing to allay this fear. By the early 1970s roads, railroads, and several small airports had been built, linking the area with Douala and integrating it into the Cameroonian economy. One consequence of this integration was to accelerate the emergence of a privileged class similar to the one in the eastern part of the country. For example, when the CDC became a state-owned corporation, the managerial staff was Cameroonized, but its members were as far removed from the underpaid, poorly housed workers as their European predecessors had been.

The formation of the UNC as the country's only legal party eliminated independent political activity in West Cameroon and fostered the emergence of a clientelistic patronage system much like the one that already existed in the East. The eclipse of Foncha and the rise of Solomon T. Muna, who eventually became prime minister and vice-president, illustrate how Ahidjo marginalized people who cultivated their own constituencies at the same time that he rewarded those who offered him their unqualified support. For Foncha sought to maintain his power base in West Cameroon, whereas Muna frequently quoted the president's speeches and refrained from appealing to symbols of regional identity. He was the one who transformed West Cameroonian administrative structures in accordance with Ahidjo's desire for a unified system.

The major impediment to any kind of autonomy for the region was a lack of financial resources. According to the 1961 constitution, the West Cameroonian state retained responsibility for most public expenditures, but it was accorded no substantial source of revenue. The income of both former trust territories derived principally from import duties, and these were specifically reserved for the federal government. This paradoxical situation made the West Cameroonian government perpetually dependent on federal subsidies and eventually provided the rationale for amalgamating the two parts of the federation into a unitary republic.[16] When this step was actually taken in 1972, it had great symbolic significance, for it signaled the political absorption of West Cameroon into the centrally administered system that Ahidjo and his collaborators had brought into being.

But political absorption was not the same as full integration into a unified nation. As West Cameroonians experienced the loss of decision-making power and the disappearance of social institutions to which they had become accustomed, they became disenchanted with Ahidjo's "great idea" and began to regard themselves as an oppressed minority. Much of their discontent stemmed from the fact that they had failed to receive what they expected from reunification. Shortly before the plebiscite, Ahidjo had visited the region and described a future united Cameroon as a "paradise in Africa."[17] By the time the unitary state was declared in 1972, West Cameroonians had become convinced that they were not moving in the direction of paradise. With twenty-two percent of the total population, they received only nine percent of the country's salaried income.[18] And this was long after the region had passed through the painful transition that accompanied reunification. Improved communications with the East made them even more intensely aware of the depressed economic conditions in their part of the country. In short, West Cameroonians tended to believe that their interests were being neglected by the Ahidjo government.

In response to what they perceived as a French and francophone Cameroonian attempt to suppress their regional identity, they clung to the idea of a distinctive anglophone culture, and the struggle to maintain parity for the use of English became a major issue for them. Yet precisely in this domain they felt increasingly slighted by the government in Yaounde. Many official documents were issued only in French. French-speaking administrators were often given responsible posts in West Cameroon, but anglophones were seldom entrusted with similar positions in the East. Fluency in French was required for many civil-service appointments, but competency in English was not. The university that was founded in Yaounde during the early 1960s remained an overwhelmingly French institution. And the Ahidjo government maintained strong ties with France but failed to supplement them in any meaningful way by establishing closer relationships with English-speaking countries.

During the mid-1960s the leading spokesman for French-English bilingualism as a distinguishing feature of Cameroonian national identity was Bernard Fonlon, who held several ministerial posts and enjoyed a reputation for absolute integrity. With the rise of Sengat-Kuo as presidential adviser and speechwriter in the late 1960s, Fonlon's influence waned, and the Ahidjo government backed away from its earlier support for bilingualism. When Fonlon lost his ministerial position shortly before the declaration of the unitary state, many anglophone Cameroonians interpreted his fall from power as a disavowal of the policies that he represented. In fact, by dismissing Fonlon and allowing Nzo Ekah Nghaky to become secretary-general at the Organization of African Unity (OAU), Ahidjo eliminated the two most articulate anglophone intellectuals from his entourage and opened the way for an even greater dominance of government policy by French-speaking Cameroonians. For West Cameroonians who regarded the English language as an important symbol of their cultural identity, the Ahidjo government's deemphasis of it was an affront to their dignity.

On May 20, 1972, mammoth celebrations were held thoughout Cameroon to commemorate the creation of the unitary republic. On the surface, Ahidjo had succeeded in forging a unified nation in spite of the enormous difficulties he had faced from the beginning. The economy was improving. The UPC was no longer a threat. West Cameroon had been peacefully absorbed into his system of government. Yet the public festivities that inaugurated the practice of celebrating May 20 as a national holiday could not disguise the fact that the majority of Cameroonians had become disillusioned with Ahidjo's nation-building rhetoric. Constructed around the implicit notion of an ideal Cameroonian personality, his ideology had been transformed into slogans that were repeated endlessly at schools, in the media, and during a variety of political and social functions. For most people, these slogans were hollow. Like the government's professed commitment to bilingualism, they were not backed by concrete actions. And like the government's supposed concern for the common welfare, they seemed hypocritical in a system that accorded a disproportionate share of the national wealth to a relatively small privileged class.

National identity in Cameroon obviously did not conform to Ahidjo's "great idea." Nevertheless, the events of the 1960s and early 1970s did bring about a heightened awareness that the people of Cameroon would have to solve their political, social, and economic problems within the context of the existing nation. As the Ahidjo government gained centralized control over most of the country's political institutions, two conflicting impulses seemed to govern Cameroonian public life: the ruling elite's desire to control the nation's destiny from the top and the people's skepticism about the rhetoric employed to justify this control. In the clash of these two impulses, Cameroonians developed a sense of being implicated in a common destiny.

Although Ahidjo's dominance of the political scene could not guarantee acceptance for his version of the national myth, the political slogans promoted by his government became shared reference points, even when the principles behind such slogans stood in blatant contradiction to perceived reality. Moreover, Ahidjo's regime was a central fact of existence in Cameroon. All citizens were subjected to the institutional structures it had introduced. Whether Cameroonians supported Ahidjo or reviled him, they defined themselves at least partly in response to his government and its conception of national identity.

With increased literacy and improved communication networks, Cameroonians also acquired shared references to historical events and to ethnic heroes such as Douala Manga Bell, Martin-Paul Samba, and Sultan Njoya. As these and many other shared references spread through Cameroonian society, they became integrated into a wide variety of individual world views and provided the basis for nationalistic sentiments that clearly find expression during international sporting competitions and conflicts with neighboring countries. Thus, despite widespread disaffection with the Ahidjo government and its official rhetoric, and despite the harsh reality of corruption and underdevelopment in an ethnically pluralistic society, Cameroonians developed a sense of national identity that reflects an awareness of the common destiny they share.

CHAPTER

7

CULTURAL POLITICS AND
THE NEW NATION

Although the slogans and myths of the Ahidjo government were greeted with skepticism by the people, the country's print culture emerged in an environment profoundly influenced by government policies. For example, a central feature of Cameroonian intellectual life during the 1960s was the institutionalization of French language and culture, a development encouraged by the strong ties that the Ahidjo government maintained with France. The schools and the churches played a significant role in this process. Even the collection of folk materials and the compilation of ethnic histories resulted in French-language publications. In a linguistically pluralistic society such as Cameroon, the language of the former colonizing power serves two important functions: it enables communication among people from a variety of ethnic backgrounds, and it provides access to the modern world. However, it also facilitates the government's attempt to control the flow of information within the country, and Cameroonian literature is in many ways a response to the suppression of opinion that accompanied Ahidjo's centralization of power.

All Cameroonian agreements with France accorded a privileged position to the French language, which was regarded as a vehicle of social and economic development. Yet French policies toward Cameroon were only part of de Gaulle's larger plan to preserve a francophonic community that would be based on the acceptance of cultural conventions and modes of thought associated with the French language. His assumption was that the political, military, and economic interests of France would be well served if there continued to be a large number of French-speaking people throughout the world. To foster linkages among such people, the French government liberally supported the creation of associations for French-speaking writers, journalists, historians, sociologists, and other professionals.

One of the most influential of these organizations was the Association des universités partiellement ou entièrement de langue française (AUPELF), which was founded in 1961. The role of the French language in its conceptualization becomes evident in the words of its president, Robert Gallet, who explained that AUPELF consisted of a network of universities "linked to each other by the French language that, above and beyond its practical significance, carries with it the virtues of a certain conception of humanity and offers the advantage of a subtlety with which an uncompromising rationality can serve all the needs of the emotions."[1] Implicit in Gallet's statement is the assumption that French is superior to African languages as a vehicle of communication because it is more universal in its range of expressive possibilities. At the same time, he acknowledges that this universality is posited on a particular conception of what it means to be human. French motivation for sponsoring such organizations thus reflects a desire to ensure that their view of the world would be shared by others. The irony is of course that many different conceptions of humanity can be expressed in the French language, and some of them are antagonistic to the assumptions behind such a motivation.

Throughout the 1960s the French government spent considerable amounts of money to reinforce the French cultural presence in Cameroon. During the first year of independence, French cultural centers opened in Yaounde and Douala. A few years later smaller centers were operating at Buea in the anglophone West and at Garoua in the Muslim-dominated North. The auditoriums in the Yaounde and Douala centers were for many years the only sites capable of accommodating larger audiences for public lectures or theatrical productions, and they were reserved for events conducted in French. All these centers regularly provided the government-controlled radio stations with pre-recorded materials that presented French culture in a highly favorable light.

Furthermore, the French cultural center in Yaounde boasted the largest public library and the largest collection of films in the country. By the early 1970s there were over five thousand registered readers at this center, and countless more visited it periodically to consult French newspapers, journals, and reference books. Fourteen large boxes with twenty-six hundred books also circulated through the center-south region, making French culture available even in many small villages. The center in Buea was particularly active in promoting the use of French by West Cameroonians. It not only offered courses in French but supplied materials for a daily "French by Radio" program and donated thousands of French-language texts to West Cameroonian schools.

The penetration of French culture in Cameroon was actually more extensive after independence than it had been before. For example, French theatrical practice profoundly influenced the emergence of Cameroonian drama, and this influence is at least partly attributable to the numerous French troupes that toured the country. In 1963 the French government created the Association française d'échanges artistiques et culturelles (ADEAC), which underwrote more than five hundred African tours for French theatrical groups and organized numerous workshops for African actors during the first four years of its existence.[2] When these groups performed at the French cultural centers, they generally attracted large crowds, and Cameroonian troupes often sought to emulate their success.

The idea of a Franco-African community was not only the product of

French desires for political and cultural domination. It was also supported by such African heads of state as Senghor, Diori Hamani, and the Tunisian president Habib Bourguiba. Senghor in particular exhorted Africans to embrace Negritude and francophony in a new hybrid culture that would permit them to comprehend each other on the basis of a shared verbal and mental universe. In 1970 this movement culminated in the creation of the Agence de coopération culturelles et techniques des pays francophones ("Francophony"). Generously funded by the French cultural minister André Malraux, this organization established a school in Bordeaux for the administration of cultural exchange programs and provided subventions for the publication of books written in French by Africans.

Like the drama and short-story contests conducted by the French national radio and the Senghor prizes awarded by the Union culturelle et technique de langue française, the African book exhibits sponsored by "Francophony" helped gain acceptance for the idea of a francophone community spanning the former colonial empire and uniting its members on the basis of a shared language and the cultural assumptions embedded in it. To avoid offending the anglophone minority in Cameroon, Ahidjo neither attended the summit meetings of francophone African heads of state nor signed the agreements that created "Francophony," but he did collaborate informally with both groups. The French government and the international francophone community thus established the framework within which French language and culture became increasingly accessible to Cameroonians.

The French cultural presence was also reinforced in less formal ways. For example, *La Presse du Cameroun* remained the country's only daily newspaper during the first fourteen years of independence, and it continued to reflect a decidedly French perspective on the world. Regular features such as "Langage et actualité: Connaissance du français" and "Francophonie-documents" were primarily concerned with the teaching of French, and the feuilleton page was dominated by accounts of works published in Paris. Few books about Africa were discussed in these columns, and they were generally by Frenchmen. Works by Africans were largely ignored, although Senghor's speeches were reported, especially when they involved his conception of Franco-African cooperation. Parisian theatrical productions, lectures, and thesis defenses were discussed far more frequently than were similar events taking place in Cameroon. A colloquium devoted to Africa and held in Paris invariably received more coverage than a comparable colloquium held in Cameroon. Although there was a regular column on the cinema, it focused almost entirely on films showing in France and seldom even mentioned the Indian and Egyptian films that were so popular in Cameroon during the mid-1960s. In short, there was little reporting of local cultural events or Cameroonian intellectual concerns in *La Presse*, which essentially reinforced French tastes and modes of thought in the country.

Many individual Frenchmen also supported the emergence of a literate francophonic culture in Cameroon. Among the most prominent of them were the Spiritain priest Henry de Julliot and the educational administrator Roger

Lagrave. In 1961 the two of them collaborated with Basile-Juléat Fouda in bringing out *Littérature camerounaise*, the first comprehensive discussion and anthology of Cameroonian literature. Both de Julliot and Lagrave encouraged younger Cameroonian writers by reading their manuscripts and by helping them publish their works. In addition, de Julliot, who wrote a column on French grammar and usage for *La Presse*, corresponded with numerous aspiring writers, and his Douala bookstore carried the largest stock of French-language books in Cameroon. Yet de Julliot's efforts were not always appreciated. Several Cameroonian writers reacted angrily to his reviews of their work, and it is true that his standards of judgment, based on classical French style and a strict Catholic sense of morality, were incapable of doing justice to the full range of Cameroonian world views. With good will and the utmost generosity, men such as Lagrave and de Julliot helped establish a francophonic literary tradition in Cameroon, but they also contributed to the retention of French high culture as a normative principle within this tradition.

In contrast to the French, the British played a relatively minor role in Cameroon during the first ten years of independence. Neither they nor the Americans were allowed to maintain cultural centers in the western part of the country, and the British Council did not open its small office in Yaounde until 1970. The United States Information Service (USIS) operated reading rooms in Yaounde and Douala, and its English courses enabled some francophone Cameroonians to acquire a working knowledge of the language, but even its efforts often reinforced the use of French in the country. For example, USIS subventions for the publication of French-language translations of American books under the Nouveaux Horizons imprint allowed such books to be sold for far less than books by Cameroonian writers. This policy was successful in disseminating American culture throughout francophone Africa, but it also made French-language texts available to large numbers of people who would not otherwise have been able to purchase them. In any case, the anglophone minority in Cameroon was isolated from the international support network that drew the country as a whole more deeply into the French sphere of cultural influence.

The most concerted effort to expand this sphere of influence occurred in the field of education. Between 1960 and 1974, the French provided nearly 50 billion CFA francs (approximately $200 million) worth of funding to support teaching personnel and capital improvements related to education. As late as 1969, the French government was still supplying half the country's educational budget.[3] One consequence of this massive aid was the assurance that the French language and French institutional models would continue to dominate the country's schools. In addition to the hundreds of teachers sent to Cameroon by the French Ministry of Education, at least three-fourths of the approximately fifteen hundred French "coopérants" in the country were assigned positions in educational fields.[4] Because the majority of eastern Cameroonian teachers and administrators had also been educated in the French system, there was a strong tendency for French tastes and habits of thought to be inculcated in the minds of students who had never directly experienced the French colonial presence. In this way, French language and culture continued to exercise a preponderant influence over the institutions around which a Cameroonian national consciousness was beginning to coalesce.

By the time the federal republic became a unitary state in 1972, however, primary and secondary education in Cameroon had undergone three major changes since the colonial era: schooling had been expanded to include a far larger percentage of the total population, the role of the mission schools had diminished, and modest steps had been taken to Africanize the curriculum. In eastern Cameroon, enrollment in public primary schools jumped from 112,562 to 434,101 during this period, while Catholic enrollments went from 159,510 to 213,660. The relative importance of Protestant schools again declined, although enrollments in them increased slightly from 75,737 to 90,512. Secondary-school enrollments also grew from 7,187 to 47,961, but even in 1972 the missions continued to enroll more than half the students at this level.[5] Yet school attendance varied widely in the East; it approached one hundred percent in the already literate areas in the center-south and along the coast, but as late as 1970, only twenty-two percent of school-age children in the North were actually enrolled in school.[6] In western Cameroon, primary-school enrollments jumped from 64,000 to 210,000 in this period, rising from twenty-seven percent of all school-age children to over seventy percent. At the same time, there was a tenfold increase in the number of West Cameroonians attending secondary school.[7] In contrast to the eastern part of the country, the vast majority of students in the West still attended confessional or private schools during the early 1970s.

The religious denominations found it difficult to meet the escalating costs of maintaining schools, and as their teachers' salaries fell below those in the public schools, the elite quality of confessional education suffered serious erosion, although some Catholic and Protestant secondary schools remained among the best in the country. Fearing the eventual demise of the religious schools that had been largely responsible for the creation of a literate elite in preindependence Cameroon, some people began to demand parity for the public funding of these schools, and there was a flurry of debate on the question in newspaper articles and pamphlets during the mid-1960s. Yet if the state paid as much for religious education as it did for public education, government authorities would press for a greater secularization of the system, thereby threatening the very distinctiveness that was adduced to justify support for the confessional schools in the first place.

In fact, beginning in 1968, all schools in eastern Cameroon were obliged to follow a standard curriculum that increasingly emphasized African history, geography, and literature. After a UNESCO-sponsored center for the production of school manuals was established at Yaounde in 1962, revised textbooks gradually became available, but the French influence on the school system remained strong. Between 1964 and 1966 alone, the French government donated over 5.1 million texts for use in African schools, and the Lagarde-Michard anthology of French literature remained a standard text in Cameroon until the mid-1970s.[8] Throughout the 1960s, French educational inspectors retained control over general examinations, academic competitions, and the awarding of degrees. Even when the content of the curriculum changed, French remained the language of instruction, and French institutional structures continued to serve as models for the Cameroonian educational system.

Participants at the first Pan-African Cultural Festival at Algiers in 1969 recommended that school curricula be reformed to embrace African cultural values, and when ministers of education from francophone African countries met the following year, they adopted a series of proposals that would result in the publication of Africa-centered texts by the "Francophony" agency. In response to such initiatives, the school curriculum in eastern Cameroon underwent some change, although it remained firmly linked with French-dominated organizations and continued to reflect French assumptions about the nature of formal education. In West Cameroon, the British-inspired educational system was gradually homologized with the prevailing system in the eastern part of the country, although English did remain the principal language of instruction.

Despite 1963 legislation that required French and English instruction at every school in the country, the attempt to introduce effective French-English bilingualism through the schools met with relatively little success. Four elite bilingual secondary schools were established, but they enrolled only a small fraction of the total school population, and elsewhere there was considerable resistance to learning a second European language. The strong French cultural influence in eastern Cameroon predisposed francophones to regard the learning of English as superfluous, and in West Cameroon, many parents objected to introducing French before their children had acquired sufficient grounding in English.

United States aid to the Cameroon College of Arts, Sciences, and Technology at Bambili helped establish the first preparatory center for university-level work in western Cameroon, where the proliferation of new schools expanded the number of people capable of using standard English, as opposed to pidgin, and heightened their attachment to a regional identity based on the language. Similarly, when the French continued to fund several secondary schools that awarded French degrees after the Cameroonization of the baccalauréat in the early 1970s, these schools increasingly enrolled the children of Cameroonian elites, who regard them as a more certain avenue to social advancement. In both parts of the country, there were incentives to retain the language of the former colonizing power in the school system, a situation that militated against the national unity concept that the Ahidjo government was promulgating.

Nevertheless, the rapid increase in school enrollments, the gradual secularization of the educational system, and the modest attempts to place greater emphasis on African materials in the curriculum did have important consequences for a sense of national identity. With increased literacy, the implicit community of readers grew substantially, and an awareness of the overall political situation in the country spread through the population in ways that would have been impossible during the colonial period. The characteristic individualism of modern states accompanied the growth of this literate community and constituted a foundation for the emergence of a nation in the contemporary sense of the word. The secularization of the schools and the standardization of the curriculum helped establish shared reference points in the world views of many hundreds of thousands of students and reinforced their consciousness of belonging to a society that defined itself in national terms. The content of these world views continued to be profoundly influenced by European languages and modes of thought, although the introduction of African materials did suggest the possibility of using those languages and modes of thought in new ways.

As in many other recently independent African countries, the Ahidjo government in Cameroon desired to create a university, which it viewed not only as a source of national pride but also as a means of training the individuals needed for the social and economic development of the country. The dependency on foreign universities for such training was unreliable in the sense that Cameroonians who studied abroad often remained there or returned home with radical, socially disruptive ideas. Although there was considerable sentiment for designing a form of higher education specifically suited to Cameroonian circumstances, the university that came into existence during the 1960s in Yaounde was actually conceived by the French in accordance with their own institutional models.

The projected French contribution to higher education in Cameroon was outlined in the 1960 cultural exchange agreements between the two countries. The following year the Institut National d'Etudes Universitaires was founded in Yaounde, and UNESCO sponsored the creation of the Ecole Normale Supérieure for the advanced training of teachers. When the decision to create a full-fledged university was reached in 1962, the original agreements with France were modified, and the Fondation Française de l'Enseignement Supérieure was created to oversee the implementation of the new plans. Integrating the institute and the Ecole Normale into the same administrative structure, Ahidjo officially created the new university a few days after signing the revised accords.

At the UC party congress in Ebolowa later that year, the president urged young people to pursue their studies at the new university rather than attempt to go abroad. However, the French culture they might have absorbed abroad was actually coming to them, for the teachers, books, and curricula at the University of Yaounde were largely drawn from the existing French system. During its first full year of operation in 1963, more than eighty percent of the new university's operating budget was supplied by France. Nearly all the instructors were French, and the entire collection in the university library had been donated by the French government.[9] The only legally recognized diplomas were French ones, and those from any other system could be accepted as equivalents only upon petition.

The French imprint upon the University of Yaounde was hardly an accident. On the contrary, it was part of France's overall cultural policy toward its former colonies. During its first ten years, the University of Yaounde was administered by a French vice-chancellor who exercised full budgetary control over all funds contributed by his government. Because he regarded the university as a regional institution with the mission of becoming the francophone intellectual center of equatorial Africa, he was not interested in promoting bilingualism. Canadian, United States, and German offers of assistance to the fledgling university were even refused on several occasions because the French insisted upon maintaining control over its orientation. Through the Fondation Française de l'Enseignement Supérieure, they prescribed the curriculum and determined what sort of research could be conducted at the university. By the time the administration passed into Cameroonian hands in 1973, the majority of the faculty members were Cameroonians, but the tone had been set, and they themselves had acquired a strong allegiance to French educational methods and degrees. Rather than becoming a specifically Cameroonian institution, the University of Yaounde served as an instrument for perpetuating the French language and French cultural assumptions.

Cameroonians themselves remained skeptical of the new university. Throughout the 1960s, there were still as many Cameroonian students in France as there had been before independence.[10] But if francophone Cameroonians persisted in seeking more prestigious academic credentials abroad, anglophone Cameroonians became openly resentful about the direction the new university was taking. According to them, the highest educational institution in the country should constitute a bilingual community where every student can follow any course in either English or French, yet until 1970 virtually all courses were taught solely in French. For this reason, less than 100 of the 1,899 students enrolled at the university that year were from West Cameroon.[11] Anglophones therefore perceived the university as a symbol of francophone dominance in their own country, and this impression was heightened in 1968 when it became mandatory for all lawyers and magistrates to attend courses at the French-language Ecole Nationale d'Administration. Feeling excluded from this system of higher education, increasing numbers of West Cameroonians pursued their studies in Nigeria, Great Britain, Canada, and the United States.

Despite overwhelming French influence upon the university and considerable skepticism about its seriousness of purpose, it was already beginning to create a new breed of intellectuals by the early 1970s. Similar to the Cameroonian students who had studied in France during colonial times, they were often critical of the official rhetoric. When they began to write, their works reflected a deep-lying dissatisfaction with the society in which they were living. In a larger sense, the university helped create an intellectual community that would later articulate many of the preoccupations lying at the center of the young nation's attempt to define itself.

In addition to the Ahidjo government's official projects in educational and cultural fields, the churches and individual clergymen often undertook initiatives aimed at increasing literacy and motivating people to realize themselves without losing touch with their African heritage. For example, the Cameroonian priest Jean Zoa had created a cultural center, Nova et Vetera, in 1956 before he was named archbishop of Yaounde. In late 1960 and with the support of many local Catholic intellectuals, he transformed the cultural center into a free university with a primary focus on adult literacy and vocational skills. The sponsoring organization for this educational project was the Association Nova et Vetera, and its primary goals were to rediscover authentic Cameroonian customs, to study them and learn their true significance, to evaluate them in light of contemporary knowledge and Christian belief, and to distinguish between relevant cultural traditions and parasitical or outdated ones. The results of these studies were to be disseminated through lectures, discussion groups, and articles in the association's newsletter.

As its name implies, Nova et Vetera was part of a larger movement among Catholic intellectuals who desired to synthesize a new Cameroonian culture from the best of the new and the best of the old. Zoa himself declared that the intention of the association was to help Cameroon "be itself without being the slave of parasitical forms from its past and without being the slave of peripheral forms that others may have contributed to it."[12] A library of several thousand volumes was donated by various individuals, and by 1965 there were over eight thousand people enrolled in courses at the free university. However, the main building was destroyed by fire in 1968, and although classes continued to meet in a local girls' school, the enterprise became increasingly difficult to coordinate, and it ceased to exist in 1974.

Among the Bamileke, the young priests Tchanda and Tchuen devised a system for teaching adult literacy in the Fé'Fé dialect and baptized it Nufi ("new thing" or "renewal"). In addition to inspiring their students with the desire to realize their own potential, the organizers of the highly successful Nufi method also strove to preserve a knowledge of Bamileke history, social mores, and traditional medicine. Similarly, the former seminarian Jean-Baptiste Obama founded the Foyer d'Education et d'Union (FEU) in 1964 to provide out-of-school adults with instruction in languages and vocational skills. Seeking to inculcate in his students a respect for traditional culture, he collected photographs and artifacts for his small Afri-Cam museum; he also wrote plays for his students about the clash between traditional and modern values as well as about historical figures such as Douala Manga Bell, Martin-Paul Samba, and Sultan Njoya.

Nova et Vetera, Nufi, and Obama's FEU were all founded by young Catholic intellectuals imbued with the desire to create a morally sound Cameroonian culture based on a synthesis of authentic African values and modern knowledge. They all sought to increase literacy among young adults who suffer from chronic unemployment, and their efforts were premised on the conviction that lasting development would occur only in a country where individuals accepted responsibility for their actions and worked to improve themselves. The success of such programs depended less on the assimilation of European culture than on the heightened self-esteem that resulted from older students' perceptions that they have reasons to be proud of their cultural heritage and can acquire the capacity to shape their own destiny. The young Catholic priests behind these educational undertakings owed a good deal to the elite educations they had received during the colonial era, but their attitudes also reflected the changed mood in the Catholic church after the first Vatican Council in 1960. In any case, organizations such as Nova et Vetera, Nufi, and FEU contributed significantly to the emergence of a reading public that addressed the problems of cultural identity in straightforward terms that the Ahidjo government itself avoided.

The churches also played a crucial role in making it possible for Cameroonians to publish their writings. The most important event in this respect was the founding of a Protestant-sponsored publishing house, Editions CLE, in 1963, although other organizations, including the Saint Paul bookstore in Yaounde, also began publishing books in the early 1960s. CLE in particular fostered an explosion of literary creativity in Cameroon by bringing out a wide range of fiction, poetry, drama, history, folktales, autobiographies, self-help manuals, and religious books.[13] Saint Paul tended to focus more exclusively on religious texts. The proliferation of Cameroonian writing on religious topics during the 1960s and early 1970s was in many ways an outgrowth of the mission school network that had educated the authors of such works and created a reading audience for them, but if the existence of CLE and Saint Paul reflected a continuation of the missionary presence in Cameroon, it was posited on a different set of assumptions than it had been during the colonial period. The capacity of Africans to participate in intellectual debates over the nature of religious belief was now taken for granted, and the publication of their works represented part of an ongoing dialogue that focused on issues relating to national identity, even though it took place outside official government channels.

A recurrent theme in the religious books published by CLE was the attempt to reconcile traditional African beliefs with Christianity. During the 1960s, CLE launched two series of such books. The first was avowedly inspirational and directed toward a popular audience; the second was more scholarly and included important works in African theology. Among the selections in the first series were Francis Grob's *Témoins de l'Evangile*, which recounts the stories of three Cameroonians who suffered martyrdom for their Christian faith, and Eleih-Ellé Etian's *Qui es-tu Jésus?*, a fictionalized account of Christ's final days as told by an African father to his son. Enveloping the Christian message of love in the form of an African oral tale, Etian seeks to demonstrate that the same kinds of political forces that led to the crucifixion of Christ also brought about the deaths of African patriotic heroes. In both books, the authors seek to integrate Christian faith into a genuinely African context. The Jesuit priest Meinrad Hebga's *Croyance et guérison* is a good example of the books in CLE's second religious series; it deals with the relationship between spiritual forces and illness within the framework of traditional healing practices.

The assumption behind it is that the knowledge of such forces is compatible with Christian belief.

Both CLE and Saint Paul also published sermons by Cameroonian ecclesiastics. The Protestant *Sermons de chez nous* by Eugene Mallo emphasizes such themes as self-reliance and individual responsibility; in contrast, the Catholic sermons of the 1960s were often overtly political, for Catholic priests had been the targets of terrorist attacks in the Bamileke territory, and they frequently preached against the UPC. The very title of Frédéric Njougla's *La Parole de Dieu au pays du terrorisme* reveals the author's premise that the Bible offers a way of confronting the evil represented by UPC terrorist bands. In fact, a major portion of his book is devoted to glossing Biblical passages as a means of demonstrating their relevance to contemporary Cameroon. Also, several biographies were dedicated to Cameroonian victims of UPC violence in the attempt to have them declared martyrs of the church. Such literature helped articulate the rationale for a Catholic humanist position that repudiated the revolutionary goals of the UPC while distancing itself from the corruption and hypocritical rhetoric of the Ahidjo government.

As evidenced by initiatives such as Nova et Vetera, Nufi, and FEU, this Catholic humanism also encouraged a revival of interest in traditional African values as an integral part of a viable modern identity in Cameroon. One way of preserving these values is to collect the folk materials in which they are embedded. By publishing French or English translations of traditional epics, tales, songs, and proverbs, individuals from specific ethnic groups were also making a part of that group's cultural identity accessible to a national audience. In written form, these materials retain neither the immediacy of impact nor the social function they possessed in the original oral context, but many Cameroonian intellectuals were convinced that the wisdom and morality implicit in them remained valid in the modern world. Furthermore, they argued that Africans could forge an adequate self-concept only if they maintained contact with their roots in traditional culture.

The availability of tape recorders, support from the national research institute, and a renewed interest in folk narrative among Bible translators, schoolteachers, and linguists resulted in the collection of vast amounts of material. Only a small portion of it has ever been published, but what did appear in print was substantial. CLE was particularly active in this field, but many folktale collections were also printed privately by individuals who hoped to preserve the cultural heritage of their own ethnic groups. Gradually, elements from these tales entered the national consciousness and became accessible to Cameroonians from other parts of the country.

The tendency to expand ethnically specific references into generically African ones is apparent in many of the early Cameroonian short stories that echoed oral tales or story-telling techniques. Benjamin Matip's *A la belle étoile*, Jacques Bengono's *La Perdrix blanche*, Jacques-Mariel Nzouankeu's *Le Souffle des ancêtres*, René Philombe's *Lettres de ma cambuse*, and Nkulngui Mefana's *Le Secret de la source* all contain stories with ethnically identifiable settings; however, these stories are couched in sufficiently general terms that the events depicted in them can be imagined as occurring elsewhere than in the author's own region.

For example, the stories in *Le Souffle des ancêtres* take place largely in the high plateaus of the Bamileke country, but the central conflict in each of them would be comprehensible anywhere in Cameroon because it invariably revolves around the disparity between human perceptions and the nature of existence as defined by the gods. No matter what human beings desire, believe, or seem to deserve, they remain subject to implacable forces that lie beyond their power to predict or control. This ultimate powerlessness in the face of existence is underscored by the fact that Nzouankeu's stories always culminate in death.

Such stories remain susceptible to a variety of interpretations, but it is precisely this ambiguity that Nzouankeu desires to preserve, for he sees in it the quintessential wisdom of a traditional oral culture that openly acknowledges the harsh and often unjust nature of the world. He is attempting not to communicate a particular truth but to convey an attitude toward life, and that attitude is as comprehensible to a Beti or a Bulu as it would be to another Bamileke. The dissemination of books such as *Le Souffle des ancêtres* to various parts of the country reinforced the idea that a Cameroonian national identity could be based on a generic conception of African culture.

In theory, the Ahidjo government promoted this idea because it offered support for the national unity concept. In practice, the ethnically based patronage system strengthened feelings of ethnic particularism, and the fear of triggering overt ethnic rivalries prevented the government from focusing special attention on the language or culture of any particular group. Nevertheless, the government did make some attempt to Cameroonize the study and promotion of traditional culture. The Centre Fédéral Linguistique et Culturel (CFLC) was established by presidential decree in 1962. Although its mandate included the preparation of future French and English teachers and the development of instructional methods for these languages, the CFLC was also assigned the task of collecting folk materials, photographs, and tape recordings for the national library and for a proposed national museum. The national research institute also sponsored work in this area. It assumed control over the old *Etudes Camerounaises*, but despite a change of name, most of the articles in it continued to be written by European scholars, and the journal itself ceased publication after a few years. In actuality, neither the CFLC nor the national research institute played a particularly visible role in rehabilitating traditional cultures and liberating them from European value judgments.

One of the government's strongest motivations for supporting the display of traditional culture was the desire to impress audiences both inside and outside the country with the dynamism of a specifically Cameroonian culture. One of the first initiatives of this kind was the formation of a national dance company in 1962 to represent Cameroon at an international drama festival in Paris. With the help of a UNESCO adviser and a former director of the

French cultural center in Douala, Obama and Michel Dooh Kingue were so successful in assembling a troupe of dancers from all over the country and in choreographing a composite performance that they won first prize in the competition.[14] Unfortunately, the ensemble was disbanded upon its return to Cameroon, but a precedent had been established, and for the next fifteen years the government sporadically organized dance troupes, theatrical groups, and musical ensembles that could represent the uniqueness of Cameroonian culture to the rest of the world.

To coordinate such efforts and to supervise the preservation of Cameroon's cultural heritage, a Service des Affaires Culturelles was created at the Ministry of Education in 1965. Its first director was the Jesuit priest Engelbert Mveng, who began by inventorying the country's museum artifacts, library holdings, archival resources, and artisanal capacities. He also surveyed Cameroonians' attitudes toward their own customs and discovered a deeply rooted attachment to specific ethnic practices. Ultimately, he saw these efforts as part of a larger plan to "create a Cameroonian soul, a soul nourished by the same cultural ideal, the same aspirations, and conscious of traditional values."[15] In this spirit, he oversaw preparations for a Cameroonian delegation to the 1966 Festival des Arts Nègres in Dakar, but although three of the four directors of the 1962 dance troupe worked on the project, it was not nearly as successful as the earlier effort, and plans for a permanent troupe were abandoned after the festival.

During Mveng's tenure as the head of the cultural affairs bureau, he did succeed in renovating a small auditorium and transforming it into a Cameroonian cultural center that was, ironically, dwarfed by the French cultural center. He also put together one of the country's first major expositions of African books. By awarding literary and artistic prizes, by organizing cultural events for major political celebrations, by laying the groundwork for a national museum, and by drawing attention to the enduring values of traditional culture, Mveng provided a small counterthrust to French cultural dominance in the country, although the government itself never adopted a consistent policy toward the role that specific Cameroonian languages and cultures might play in defining the national unity it proclaimed.

In addition to traditional culture, the interpretation of contemporary history constitutes a crucial dimension in the elaboration of a national identity. However, the Ahidjo government was unwilling to tolerate the open discussion that might have allowed the Cameroonian people to reach a credible consensus about the meaning of recent events in their own country. As part of the government's attempt to consolidate political and economic power, it strove to create the impression that everyone unquestioningly accepted its version of the truth. In the name of national unity, it systematically suppressed alternative accounts presented by journalists, writers, and others concerned with disparities between the official rhetoric and perceived reality. As early as 1961, Gabriel Mballa, the head of the government press office, explained the rationale behind this policy when he stated that censorship was indispensable in Cameroon because an unsupervised freedom of expression would spread disinformation and threaten the unified public opinion necessary for national construction.[16]

The laws that the Ahidjo government used to enforce this policy were largely derived from the French legal code of the colonial period. In fact, the press law passed by the territorial assembly seven months before independence was more restrictive than preceding legislation insofar as it reintroduced prior censorship and accorded greater discretionary authority to local police officials. It also granted the minister of the interior the right to accredit journalists, to seize whole issues of periodical publications, and to prohibit the distribution of printed material from abroad. This law remained in effect after independence, and it was arbitrarily used to imprison several journalists in 1960. Although newspapermen from all over the country gathered in Yaounde early the following year to demand the release of their jailed colleagues, the men remained in custody. From then on it was clear that the government intended to impose an orthodoxy of opinion on the print media in Cameroon.

Such a policy had important consequences for the shape of the written culture that emerged during the first dozen years of Cameroonian independence. Restrictions on freedom of expression hobbled the lively intellectual climate that had existed during the final years of the colonial period. They also placed Cameroonians before a difficult set of alternatives. Political rhetoric had diverged into two opposing streams, that of the Ahidjo government and that of the UPC. The world views of most people lay somewhere between these two extremes, for if the self-serving hypocrisy behind the official propaganda was generally recognized, the terrorist activities of the UPC had also alienated a large portion of the Cameroonian populace. However, in its zeal to suppress subversive literature and to create the appearance of national unity, the government refused to tolerate even moderate criticisms of the existing system.

Under these circumstances, many former students, among them William Eteki, Ferdinand Oyono, François Sengat-Kuo, Vroumsia Tchinaye, and Bernard Fonlon, accepted positions in the new government and at least implicitly supported its idealistic nation-building goals. Others, including Woungly-Massaga, Mongo Beti, Osendé Afana, and later Abel Eyinga, became outspoken opponents of the Ahidjo regime. But their works were published outside the country. For intellectuals who remained in Cameroon, it soon became apparent that social advancement was contingent upon loyalty to the government, not upon merit, and although they resented being subordinated to politicians they regarded as corrupt and incompetent, they realized that their own survival depended on remaining silent or paying lip service to the "glorious achievements" of Ahidjo.

There was considerable sympathy in Cameroon for the idealistic goals of nation building, but there was also a good deal of discontent with the authoritarianism that accompanied Ahidjo's centralization of power. Because possibilities for expressing this discontent became increasingly circumscribed during the 1960s and early 1970s, Cameroonians were largely prevented from participating in an honest dialogue about the nature of their collective existence as citizens of the same nation. Realizing that most of their fellow countrymen were losing rather than gaining control over their destinies, Cameroonian writers and intellectuals often transformed their disillusionment with independence into the concealed subject matter of their works. The lack of adequate communication systems and the inability of francophone authorities to read English did permit West Cameroonians to enjoy a greater freedom of expression than was possible in other parts of the country, but the malaise that resulted from the Ahidjo government's suppression of dissenting opinion was evident everywhere.

The fate of newspaper publishing in Cameroon bears eloquent testimony to the effectiveness of this policy, for by 1963 the flourishing press activity of the late 1950s had ceased to exist. Government harassment closed down the small-circulation independent newspapers, including all those that had been published in Cameroonian languages.[17] Only the church-sponsored newspapers continued to appear with any regularity, although they too were forced to terminate publication in the early 1970s. Throughout this period, Pierre Fertin's Catholic weekly *L'Effort camerounais*, the Protestant *La Semaine camerounaise*, and *L'Essor des jeunes*, founded by Bishop Ndongmo, drew attention to facts that were never reported in the European-controlled *La Presse du Cameroun* or in the UC party newspaper *L'Unité*. These were not virulent attacks on the government, but they did reflect a widespread critical attitude toward the course being followed by the new state, and the government imposed an increasingly rigorous censorship on them. Sometimes whole issues of newspapers were confiscated, and after a new press law was adopted in 1967, galleys were submitted to government authorities prior to publication; if individual articles were found to be objectionable, they were removed, and blank columns announced the absence of the suppressed news.

The most important of these newspapers was *L'Effort*, which at one point reached a circulation of over ten thousand and was far more widely read than either *La Presse* or *L'Unité*. But all three church-sponsored newspapers had substantial readerships, and particularly before the 1967 press law, they managed to publish occasional articles that expressed an awareness of the harsh reality beneath the government's optimistic nation-building rhetoric. For example, the following commentary appeared in a 1961 issue of *La Semaine camerounaise*:

> When the economy of a country falls into ruin, when misery and physical or psychological insecurity, accompanied by a long train of evil, become endemic among the people, when the national wealth is dispersed in insolent and gratuitous ostentation, or channeled into foreign hands, or siphoned off as graft, no flowering of culture is possible. People become mired in a brutish existence. Despite shining automobiles and fine-sounding speeches.[18]

Intellectuals such as the author of this column could visualize the possibility of a vigorous and just society capable of elaborating its own culture in the process of meeting the real needs of the people, but they also knew that, no matter what the Ahidjo government claimed to be doing, it was not creating such a society in Cameroon. And they were convinced that all the cultural initiatives of such a government would remain artificial as long as they failed to reflect the truth about contemporary Cameroonian society.

In early 1962, two events occurred that signaled the government's unwillingness to entertain such a notion. The first resulted from the deaths of twenty-eight political prisoners in a closed boxcar while they were being transported from Douala to Yaounde. Desiring to avoid a scandal, the government silently buried the victims in a mass grave, but Fertin learned about the tragedy in speaking with survivors during his regular rounds at the Yaounde General Hospital. After he printed an account of it in *L'Effort*, he was immediately expelled from the country. Within a month, the government had promulgated a new decree according to which it became illegal to disseminate rumors or interpretations of facts susceptible of harming the authorities in power. Presented as a means of eliminating subversion, this decree was employed primarily to imprison the government's political opponents, and it proved particularly effective because those accused under its provisions had no right of appeal.

The second event occurred a few months later and provided the first significant test of the new decree. After Theodore Mayi Matip's legal branch of the UPC and André-Marie Mbida's Ewondo-based BDC had been subjected to repressive measures by the government in early 1962, the two men joined with Marcel Bebey-Eyidi and Charles Okala to form a United National Front. All four of them signed an open letter to the UC, claiming that Ahidjo's plan to impose a single-party system on Cameroon would reduce people to inert bits of wood or robots that respond automatically to the commands of a dictator. They argued that true national unity can never be imposed by force but must arise from the unconstrained choices of free individuals who desire to work together for the pursuit of a common goal. In the process of national construction, they continued, the truth is never held by a single person or party; on the contrary, it can emerge only from a dialogue that includes all the people and their various points of view. The four men concluded by openly asking a question that preoccupied many Cameroonians at the time: "What good is national independence if it fosters neo-totalitarianism in the intention of replacing foreign colonialism with internal colonialism?"[19]

A week later, the four men circulated an even more strongly worded manifesto in which they accused Ahidjo of trying to impose the authoritarian Fulani social structure from the Islamicized North on all Cameroonians, transforming them into slaves and creating an atmosphere of lies, hatred, coercion, and blackmail. They specifically criticized the government's censorship policies and contended that genuine Cameroonian unity could be built only upon a foundation of mutual comprehension and respect. "Life is worth living only when one can live it as a free man," they declared. "If that is not possible, it would be better to die standing up than to live on one's knees."[20] Within a week all four men were in prison. Three weeks later they received long prison sentences for inciting hatred against the country's leaders, promoting religious conflict, and propagating rumors prejudicial to the authority of the government. Their trial and sentencing had a chilling effect on freedom of expression in Cameroon, for it signaled the government's intention to prevent open public discussion of political issues, even when the country's most prominent figures were involved. From this time forward, people realized that the most prudent course of action would be to accept the UC and to remain silent about any dissident sentiments they might harbor in their own minds. In fact, most of the legislative representatives who had been resisting the single party before the trial soon declared their allegiance to the UC.

Another important dimension of the national identity question in Africa and its relation to freedom of expression involves the rewriting of history to establish a national perspective on a past that had been severely distorted in European accounts of it. Although the Ahidjo government was intent upon suppressing a large part of the country's most recent history and particularly the role of the UPC, it did not discourage historical writing compatible with its official conception of an emerging national unity. Mveng's 1963 *Histoire du Cameroun* represented the first attempt to provide a comprehensive overview of the country's history, and although it is a rather hastily compiled compendium, it does contain a body of facts that could be organized into a unified image of the national past.

Mveng himself saw history as part of a liberating process during which a people proclaims "who it was, who it is, and who it wants to become."[21] As an enlightened Catholic moralist and a proponent of Negritude, he saw Cameroonian identity in terms of an evolution that commenced in the authentic traditions of a precolonial past and was moving toward a new unity based on the synthesis of African values and Christian ideals. Such a conception of Cameroonian history was misleading from a radical nationalist point of view, but it was in harmony with the official rhetoric of the Ahidjo government, which appointed Mveng to head the country's cultural affairs bureau shortly after the publication of his book.

The founding of Editions CLE opened new possibilities for the dissemination of historical writing, although its potential in this area remained largely unrealized. The editors of CLE did inaugurate a historical series with Eldridge Mohammadou's *L'Histoire de Tibati*, but despite the originality of this book, no immediate successors were forthcoming, and the series languished. *L'Histoire de Tibati* diverges from European-style documentary history in both style and substance. Lacking the footnotes of a scholarly monograph, it draws upon oral traditions as well as written documents to reconstruct an elusive past.

Mohammadou chose to write about Tibati for two reasons. As the Fulani lamidate closest to the southern forest peoples, Tibati had established trading and diplomatic relations with them in precolonial times; in this sense, it offers an excellent example of the unifying tendencies that existed in the area before the arrival of Europeans. Also, Mohammadou was convinced that the political organization of Tibati suggested social ideals that were more appropriate than European ones for determining how contemporary Cameroon should be governed, and his book seeks to demonstrate the validity of this belief. In both respects, *L'Histoire de Tibati* forges a genuinely Cameroonian perspective on the historical past. By making this perspective accessible to the general reading public, Mohammadou was promoting the idea that Cameroonian history was not primarily the story of European conquest but rather a function of what Cameroonians themselves had done. According to him, the recognition of this fact was a prerequisite for the emergence of any viable sense of national identity.

CLE did not publish any other Cameroonian histories, but it did occasionally bring out fictionalized accounts of events that had marked the lives of Cameroonians during the colonial period. Like the anticolonial novels of the 1950s, these narratives portrayed the fundamental injustice of the colonialist system from a Cameroonian point of view. For example, Henri-Richard Manga Mado's *Complaintes d'un forçat* recounts the experiences of three Cameroonians who had been obliged to work in forced-labor camps. The first was at Ndjock during the construction of the Douala-Yaounde railroad; the second was in the gold mines at Betaré-Oyo; and the third was on the rubber plantations near Dizangué. Each of these sites was notorious for the suffering inflicted on those who had been sent there, but by the late 1960s the memory of forced labor was no longer real for the majority of Cameroonians, and Manga Mado's book sought to reinsert it into their awareness of a common past. Such an enterprise could be reconciled with the government's official rhetoric because the oppressiveness of colonial rule represented the evil from which Ahidjo had supposedly saved the people of Cameroon. In this sense, the sufferings described by Manga Mado became part of the national mythology about the country's pre-independence history.

Although the Ahidjo government carefully monitored publications within the country, it could not prevent Cameroonians living abroad from writing about contemporary history in ways that contradicted its version of the truth. Disappointed with the sort of independence that was emerging in their own country, increasing numbers of them took up residence in France and, to a lesser extent, in England, Germany, Nigeria, Gabon, the United States, and Canada. The exile wing of the UPC of course publicized the abuses that the Ahidjo government refused to admit publicly: arbitrary arrests, political prisons, police torture, widespread corruption, censorship. But even those who did not belong to the UPC contributed to the current of critical thinking that the Ahidjo government was intent upon suppressing in Cameroon.

For example, in 1961, the politically moderate journalist Iwiyé Kala Lobé published an allegorical short story, "Grandeur et décadence de Mun'a moto, cultivateur camerounais," in *Présence Africaine*. The story is told by an old Douala man who recalls how French colonialism had transformed a harmonious agricultural community into a desolate jungle where charlatans preyed upon the superstitions of people who were increasingly abandoning the land and fleeing to the city. In this decadent society, Ngum (Ruben Um Nyobé) appeared and generated a new sense of community among the remaining farmers, but after he had organized a successful banana cooperative (the UPC) and earned the respect of the local population, he fell victim to bad advice. Discouraged by the pervasive corruption around him, Ngum was betrayed and arrested, and the narrator adopted a hermitlike existence on the site of the formerly prosperous community. Kala Lobé's story culminates in an apocalyptic final scene that prophesies the triumph of those who cultivate the land, but although he distances himself from the hard-line UPC position, he is also repudiating the Ahidjo government's official myth by linking the country's future promise with the aspirations of Um Nyobé, whom the Cameroonian government was seeking to eradicate from the memory of the people.

Throughout the 1960s and early 1970s, publications critical of the Ahidjo government continued to appear abroad. Even moderate organizations such as the Cercle Culturel Camerounais severed all ties with the Ahidjo goverment, and when writers such as Elolongue Epanya Yondo and Abel Eyinga left Cameroun to live in exile, they began writing about the oppressiveness of the regime in Yaounde. Books such as Daniel Ewandé's political satire *Vive le Président, la fête africaine,* David Kom's economic analysis *Le Cameroun,* and Mongo Beti's documentary exposé *Main basse sur le Cameroun* presented Ahidjo not as a national hero but as a straw man installed by the French to protect their interests in the area. In return for his cooperation, they contended, he received French support to govern the country in an arbitrary and totalitarian manner. Kom, for example, referred to Ahidjo as a "docile instrument of colonialism," a man whose single-party rule prevented the people from achieving their political aspirations and from fulfilling their desire for genuine economic independence. According to him, slogans such as "national unity" and "national construction" merely camouflaged a "growth without development" that benefited a small privileged elite while relegating the majority of Cameroonians to poverty and despair.[22]

Although opposition literature of this kind was banned in Cameroon, it did circulate clandestinely through informal networks of friends and acquaintances. For many people, it represented a forbidden source of information that corroborated their own perceptions of the harsh reality behind the hypocritical rhetoric of the regime in power. Such literature upheld political and social ideals according to which the actual performance of the Ahidjo government could be judged, and despite police attempts to control the flow of printed material into the country, it played a significant role in reinforcing a widespread disillusionment with Cameroonian independence.

The government's nation-building propaganda was merely one factor in the complex cultural politics that helped create the intellectual environment in which Cameroonian print culture evolved during the first dozen years of independence. French support for the Ahidjo government and rapid increases in schooling heightened the importance of French language and culture within the country. Christian churches continued to exercise considerable influence over intellectual life in Cameroon, often promoting an awareness of ethnic cultures and implicitly condemning the government's restrictions on freedom of expression. The Ahidjo administration was largely unsuccessful in its attempt to foster a sense of national unity by imposing political orthodoxy on the people and by preventing them from participating in the public interpretation of their own reality. Yet interpretation was continually taking place in a variety of ways that were never sanctioned by the government, and in the interplay of these interpretations, a sense of national identity began to emerge as Cameroonians with highly diverse views of the world accepted the assumption that they were facing a common destiny and would have to resolve their social and political problems in the context of the existing state.

CHAPTER

8

IN SEARCH OF
A POPULAR IDIOM

During the colonial period, the most significant literary works by Cameroonians were written and published abroad, but forces set in motion by independence gradually changed this situation. The Ahidjo government desired to promote a literature that would support its ideology and express the new nation's cultural identity. Aspiring writers hoped to find an audience for their works within the country, a possibility that seemed plausible in light of the journalistic and pamphleteering activity that had flourished during the 1950s. Also, the founding of Editions CLE in 1962 and the emergence of a few small printing establishments created the opportunity for increasing numbers of Cameroonians to publish their writings for local or African markets as opposed to European ones.

A major turning point in the evolution toward a literature produced by and for the people of the country occurred with the formation of the Association des Poètes et Ecrivains Camerounais (APEC) shortly after independence. For over twenty years, the driving force behind this national writers' union was the self-taught poet-novelist-journalist-playwright René Philombe. Having become involved with UPC union-organizing efforts while working in the colonial police service, Philombe had been obliged to withdraw from all public activities in the mid-1950s when he was struck by a crippling illness that reduced him to an invalid for three years and left him incapable of walking without the aid of crutches. Overcoming the despondency into which his affliction had thrust him, he founded and edited two newspapers—*La Voix du citoyen* in French and *Bebelu Ebug* (The Voice of Truth) in Ewondo. They soon attained a circulation of over five thousand and enabled him to become self-supporting, but like nearly all the other local publications that proliferated during the final years of the colonial period, Philombe's two newspapers eventually fell victim to censorship and police harassment.

The verse and mildly satirical essays that he published in his newspapers were the first pieces he signed with the pseudonym René Philombe.[1] His populist revolutionary leanings are apparent in these writings and can be clearly seen in the opening lines of a poem that first appeared in *La Voix du citoyen*: "We are the chosen of a salutary dawn. / The people are drumming their songs in our hearts."[2] The idea that the voice of the people speaks through the revolutionary is central to Philombe's conception of literature, for he has always been convinced that a writer can best address problems of universal human concern by speaking to his own people and on their behalf.

In 1959, two young schoolteachers began to visit Philombe for regular discussions of literary and cultural topics. During the independence day celebrations in Yaounde, the three of them set up a booth where they met a number of other aspiring writers. A short while later, eight of them gathered at Philombe's house and founded APEC. Louis-Marie Pouka was elected president, a largely honorary post he held for seven years, and Philombe became executive secretary.

Although the founding members of the organization held a variety of political opinions, they unanimously agreed that writers should play an important role in articulating a genuinely Cameroonian culture and, by extension, in defining a viable national identity. In concrete terms, they supported the revitalization of Cameroonian oral traditions and proposed to find ways of encouraging talented but unrecognized writers. They also planned to preserve important documents in the history of Cameroonian letters and to promote a general awareness of what had been written by their fellow countrymen. Such goals were not incompatible with official government policy, and when APEC was legally incorporated in 1961, it was placed under the jurisdiction of the Ministry of Education. Although the organization never received the public funding it needed to carry out its projects, Ahidjo personally gave its officers a substantial contribution.

One of the primary reasons for the creation of APEC was the desire to provide a mutual support network for Cameroonian writers who had previously been working in isolation. Their greatest difficulty was a dearth of publishing opportunities. Pouka had sold mimeographed copies of his poetry in local bookstores, but until CLE began to produce larger numbers of books in the late 1960s and early 1970s, local writers had little hope of seeing their works printed and distributed in a professional manner. With the support of Roger Lagrave and Lilyan Kesteloot, however, APEC inaugurated a literary magazine, *Cameroun Littéraire*, which appeared briefly in 1964 and again in 1971, and it sponsored the publication of three Cameroonian poetry anthologies.

The relationship between these efforts and the desire to forge a new national culture is apparent in Kesteloot's preface to the 1962 anthology. After applauding the Cameroonian poets included in the volume for their profound attachment to their country, she points out that many of them continue to imitate the French rhythms and techniques they learned in the colonialist school system rather than seeking new modes of expression more congenial to their own perceptions of reality. In conclusion, she urges them to build upon the promise of their collected work and to transmute their undeniably authentic sentiments into a truly "national literature."[3] Such publications reinforced the idea that writers from different ethnic groups were involved in a common project and that their works would ultimately form part of the national culture that Ahidjo was propounding as a symbol of unity.

The impression that APEC's goals were in harmony with those of the government was strengthened by the patriotic writings of its first president. According to Pouka, all people are created in the image of God, and they become free by loving others as much as they love themselves. When viewed from this perspective, true national independence depends upon people's willingness to forgive their former enemies and to work together with them. Therefore, Pouka exhorts his fellow countrymen to unite under the wise leadership of Ahidjo. In his long poem *Entrevue d'outre-tombe ou message de Ruben Um Nyobé*, for example, he depicts an imaginary encounter between himself (as the country's poet-prophet) and the spirit of the dead UPC leader. After describing his vision of a free and peaceful Cameroon, the apparition claims never to have ordered terrorist attacks against the people, and he praises Ahidjo as a "magnanimous ruler." The poet-prophet then eulogizes Um Nyobé and concludes by insisting that the "Great Leader from the North is guiding the country well."[4] By seeking to establish a continuity between Um Nyobé's anticolonialist struggle and the present government in Yaounde, Pouka hoped to persuade readers that Ahidjo, not the UPC guerillas, was the legitimate inheritor of the national independence movement.

In a number of other poems and essays, Pouka elaborated upon the idea that Ahidjo's rule was an expression of divine will. The implication was of course that the people of the country have a moral obligation to obey the commands of the "indefatigable navigator" who guides the ship of state safely to port, the founding father whose spirit gave birth to a new nation, the national hero whose head is crowned with an "immortal diadem."[5] If Ahidjo's power was divinely inspired, as the poet-prophet claimed, those who fought against it were sullying God's promise for a reign of peace, harmony, and justice in Cameroon. In one poem, they are even portrayed as a gangrene that is eating away at the people and killing them. By this time, Pouka thought of himself as a poet laureate who was transmuting Ahidjo's idealistic rhetoric about national unity into literature and bringing wisdom to the people.

But others saw him in a different light. His chauvinistic verse excited little response in the general public and met with open hostility on the part of many younger writers associated with APEC. In any case, the tone of the national writers' union was set less by its president than by its executive secretary. Philombe was the animating presence behind most of the organization's publications. He read and critiqued the work of younger writers. He helped create theater troupes to stage the plays of Cameroonian dramatists. He collected information on over a thousand Cameroonian writers and later published the results of his research in the first reliable history of his country's literature, *Le Livre camerounais et ses auteurs*.

Philombe also coined the slogan that would later be printed on the masthead of most APEC publications: "The best revolution that one can carry out for one's country is a cultural revolution."[6] According to him, a true cultural revolution must emanate from the people and speak directly to them. Because he believed that literature represents a crucial dimension of national identity in the modern world, he felt that writers could contribute significantly to the cultural revolution by expressing the inchoate desires of the people in a truthful, aesthetically coherent manner and by heightening people's awareness of the forces that shape their existence. Philombe's ideas were not necessarily in conflict with the idealistic nation-building goals of the Ahidjo government, but they obliged him to oppose the sort of society that was emerging in Cameroon—a society where a small privileged class lived in luxury while most people wallowed in poverty, a society dominated by superstition, greed, and a widespread lack of concern for the suffering of others. Such a stance placed Philombe and like-minded members of APEC in an ambiguous position between the indifference of the masses and the hostility of a privileged class that did not want the existing situation called into question.

The populist leanings of APEC's core group limited the participation of highly educated, materially comfortable writers in the activities of the organization. After a flurry of initiatives during the early and mid-1960s, internal dissension and a lack of financial resources reduced its membership to a small group intensely loyal to Philombe. In fact, his commitment kept alive the idea of a national writers' union when nearly everyone else had abandoned it. Perhaps the most important consequence of his work on behalf of the association was the emergence of informal networks among Cameroonian writers whose contact with each other reinforced the conviction that they were engaged in a common endeavor. Philombe's efforts also maintained an organizational framework that would serve as the foundation for a renewed outburst of literary undertakings in the early 1970s.

The tenth anniversary of Cameroonian independence provided the impetus for Philombe to relaunch *Cameroun Littéraire*. Although the modestly produced journal lasted for only eleven issues and ceased publication again by the end of 1971, it served briefly as a platform for Philombe's conception of a national literary culture. Along with poems and short stories, the *Cameroun Littéraire* of the early 1970s included interviews with people from the nonelite classes, essays on traditional customs, sociological studies, transcriptions of oral epics, theater reviews, and popular accounts of Cameroonian history. The eclecticism of these materials illustrates Philombe's contention that a national culture must be firmly rooted in the real concerns of the people. Introducing the first issue of the new series, he argued that writers can help define these concerns and establish a perspective from which to understand them. Because Cameroonians live in a society where "everyone seems to be obeying the laws of a vulgar materialism," he emphasized that APEC and *Cameroun Littéraire* are vital safeguards of the national destiny inasmuch as they preserve an appreciation for the country's authentic cultural presence and promote the humanistic values that literary creativity implies.[7]

In many issues of the journal, Philombe editorialized against two tendencies that he felt were jeopardizing the healthy evolution of Cameroonian literate culture. The first involved the rapid growth of a foreign-dominated print and media culture that trivialized human life or presented it in an ideologically biased manner. For example, French corporations monopolized commercial film distribution in the country, and they flooded the market with second-rate movies that glorified crime and pandered to the most prurient desires. The slick formats of illustrated European magazines and photo-novels attracted Cameroonian readers and conditioned them to disdain the less attractively packaged work of local writers. And books that were generously subsidized by foreign cultural services often sold in the country for a fraction of what it cost to produce works by Cameroonian authors. For the nation to sustain a viable literate culture, he concluded, some means must be found to make such works available to the people at affordable prices.[8]

The second trend that Philombe deplored was a growing tendency to define the nation's literate culture almost solely in terms of writings by socially privileged individuals who emulated European cultural models and addressed a small elitist readership. Because Philombe believed that a true national culture should be accessible to the majority of a country's citizens, he urged Cameroonian writers to eschew esoteric formulations and to develop an easily comprehensible style, for he viewed their common task as the depiction of Cameroonian reality in such a way that people could understand it better. On the surface, such a position complemented the Ahidjo government's attempt to promote national unity by cultivating a distinctively Cameroonian culture; however, Philombe's insistence upon examining contemporary society in light of his ideals actually drew attention to the disparity between the government's official rhetoric and reality. As a result, Philombe incurred the animosity of the authorities, and despite his infirmities, he was arrested and imprisoned at least seven times during Ahidjo's twenty-five-year presidency.

Another initiative on which Philombe collaborated at this time was the publication of *Ozila*, an innovative journal that encouraged both literary creativity and critical thinking by publishing poems, plays, and short stories as well as evaluative interpretations of them. The idea for the review emerged during a Yaounde colloquium attended by the German scholar-journalist Janheinz Jahn, and it brought together intellectuals from the university with many of the populist writers associated with APEC. The name *Ozila* was taken from a Bulu fertility dance that was part of an initiatory rite during which young people learned the traditions that enabled them to participate fully in adult society. In colonial times the Catholic missionaries had banned the ozila for its supposedly obscene character. By choosing this name, the editors of the new journal defined its purpose in terms of helping young writers acquire the tools and techniques they needed to participate in a genuinely Cameroonian tradition that had been stifled during the colonial period.

Ozila remained alive for a year and a half until differences among members of the editorial board resulted in its demise, but during that brief period, it proved extremely popular, particularly among secondary-school students, and it provided a model for the sort of intellectual dialogue that could help create an educated public for a national literature in Cameroon. The journal was avowedly apolitical, but numerous favorable allusions to Ahidjo and his cultural policies suggested that the editors envisioned their efforts as a contribution to the national cultural identity being promoted by the government. Like APEC and *Cameroun Littéraire*, *Ozila* was part of a self-conscious movement within the country to foster the development of a literature that would be accessible and relevant to the people.

Although most of the country's literary activity was centered in Yaounde during the 1960s, small clusters of writers also formed in other parts of the country. Timothée Ndzagaap founded a literary and drama group in Bafoussam, and Ekéké Moukoury started a literary circle in Douala. In anglophone Cameroon, there was little organized activity until 1970 when Buma Kor, the Irishman Michael Kelly, and several others created the Drama and Speech Performers' Society in Victoria. At the same time Sona Elonge organized a writers' and artists' workshop that met twice monthly to discuss manuscripts submitted by its members. As the director of English-language programming for the government's radio station in the area, Paul Kode wrote and produced over thirty half-hour radio dramas in English. He also supported the creation of "Young Writers' Forum," a popular local program in which Buma Kor and later Awah Dzeyenaga introduced the work of aspiring writers.

A bridge between this nascent literary activity in the western part of the country and APEC was established in 1971 when the enterprising Buma Kor traveled to Yaounde and made contact with Philombe and his friends. After returning to Victoria, Buma Kor became the organization's ambassador to West Cameroon, soliciting new members and enthusiastically promoting literary activity in the English-speaking provinces. Visiting more than twenty schools in the area, he constantly encouraged young people to write in English, or as he himself said, "to untie the knot that has bounded [*sic*] our literature from head to toe."[9] According to him, the knot that inhibited the development of anglophone Cameroonian literature was a psychological one. He therefore exhorted young people to overcome their self-doubt and contribute to the emergence of a new literature by giving free rein to their creative impulses. In 1973, Buma Kor also organized the first exhibit of anglophone Cameroonian literary texts at the national Agricultural Fair in Buea. Over a hundred manuscripts and mimeographed fascicles were on display at the fair, and although most of them had circulated only among small groups of the author's friends, the fact of bringing them together helped raise the general level of awareness about the existence of a budding literature in anglophone Cameroon. Buma Kor's promotional efforts also helped make APEC a truly national organization.

But even more than the existence of a national writers' union, the choice of Yaounde as the site of Editions CLE, francophone Africa's first major publishing house, resulted in a proliferation of literary works written primarily for African audiences by Cameroonians. After independence, the principal obstacle facing African writers was the difficulty of finding ways to disseminate their work. French publishing firms brought out fewer books by Africans as the esoteric appeal of Africa diminished and the excitement of the anticolonialist struggle receded into the past. Présence Africaine became the major producer of francophone African books in the early 1960s, but its publications tended to be written by highly educated individuals and addressed to an intellectual elite, not to the increasingly literate common people in countries such as Cameroon.[10] Some French presses, including Pierre Jean Oswald, printed modest editions of African literary works, but they required sizeable subventions from authors, and they lacked the resources to promote and distribute their books in Africa. Under these circumstances, most aspiring Cameroonian writers felt frustrated and did not know where to turn with their completed manuscripts.

The founding of CLE was a boon for them, although the new publishing firm was sponsored by a consortium of Protestant churches that conceived of it as an extension of their earlier missionary activities. The decision to establish a center in Africa for the publication of French-language books was taken during a meeting of Evangelical churches at Kampala, Uganda, in 1962. The motivation behind this initiative was to promote the spread of Christianity by making the written word more accessible to the people of francophone Africa. For this reason, the new religious publishing company was specifically charged to encourage the growth of a Christian literature written by and for Africans, to collect documents on Christianity in Africa, to translate relevant religious works into French, and to hold workshops for writers.[11] From the beginning, CLE shared facilities with the church's society for Bible distribution.

The first director of the firm was the Protestant pastor P. Feuter, and he interpreted his mandate in a narrowly Christian sense. In the regular column he contributed to *La Semaine Camerounaise* and in his own bimonthly review of books, *Dialogue*, he invariably related his comments on literature to Christian doctrine and morality. After a year of operation, he was convinced that CLE "is increasingly becoming an effective instrument of the churches. . . . There is no longer any doubt that Cameroon is playing a pioneering role in the work being done to support Christian literature in francophone Africa."[12] However, when Claude Molla took over the directorship of CLE in 1965, he broadened the scope of the center's publishing activities.

Such a step was implicit in the discussions at Kampala, where European participants reasoned that, since the church was largely responsible for introducing literacy into Africa, it had a moral obligation to help Africans master the use of print culture for their own purposes. The establishment of another publishing house in Europe would not, they felt, satisfactorily address this problem because a distant editorial staff would be less capable of offering guidance to writers and less responsive to the needs of a growing African reading public. In a very real sense, CLE was created to help writers improve the quality of their work. It was also envisioned as a way of popularizing written culture by making it available to large numbers of people in a more relevant form than works imported from abroad. Part of the new publishing center's goal was to foster an intellectual climate in which the reading and writing of French would flourish.[13]

Molla seized upon this conception of CLE's mission and expanded it to include the idea that the church-sponsored center should be concerned with the global education of people who needed to acquire the independence of judgment that would enable them to cope with the problems besetting contemporary Africa. He reduced the firm's emphasis on religious publishing and announced that it would focus more on general literature, on works about the African cultural heritage, and on self-help manuals for the common people.[14] Molla also traveled extensively throughout francophone Africa in search of publishable manuscripts. He hired the Congolese artist Ouassa to create the colorful book jackets that became a hallmark of CLE publications. He collaborated with a private entrepreneur to open a CLE bookstore in Yaounde, and he began to publicize writers by holding receptions and press conferences for them. In short, Molla transformed a religious publishing house into a general publisher that played a major role in the evolution of French-language African literature.

Because CLE was located in Yaounde, it developed strong ties with the local intellectual community, and the vast majority of manuscripts submitted to its editors were written by Cameroonians. Under these circumstances, it is hardly surprising that two-thirds of the 149 titles published by CLE during its first ten years of operation were authored by Cameroonian writers. No other francophone African country enjoyed such an extraordinary stimulus for the growth of literary activity until Nouvelles Editions Africaines (NEA) began operations in Dakar and Abidjan during the early 1970s. For this reason, the presence of CLE was undoubtedly the single most important influence on the development of a flourishing literature in Cameroon, and CLE was committed to the search for a popular idiom.

Unlike commercial European publishers, the editors at CLE regarded their task as an educational one. Throughout the 1960s they employed a unique method for the consideration of manuscript submissions. Most of the texts received at this time were handwritten, and the editors had them typed before sending them to consultant readers, who tended to be local university professors or professional journalists. Taking into consideration the comments of these readers, the editorial staff would reread each manuscript and decide whether or not to publish it. If they rejected it, they composed a letter to the author and always included suggestions for improvement. If they accepted it, they began a long copyediting process that often resulted in extensive revisions.[15] The popular idiom that resulted from this process was still the product of European standards of taste, in the sense that the editors and consultant readers were almost exclusively Europeans and Cameroonians who had received elite French educations. Their conceptions of style and content reinforced the influence of the French cultural presence in the country and implicitly supported the Ahidjo government's deemphasis of African languages.

In fact, the relationship between CLE and the government was an ambivalent one that influenced the kind of books published by the Yaounde firm. On the one hand, the existence of a publishing house in Cameroon was a matter of pride to the Ahidjo regime, which regarded it as an instrument for promoting a literate culture capable of strengthening a sense of national unity. For this reason, the president himself bestowed the country's highest cultural award upon CLE. On the other hand, the Protestant-sponsored firm consistently refused to publish works that might offend the authorities. The consequence of such a policy was to discourage the sort of socially critical writing that had characterized the most powerful works of the preindependence period, even though many writers and intellectuals were convinced that the abuses of the colonial era had survived under different guises in contemporary Cameroon. In conjunction with the limitations placed on any Christian publishing firm, CLE's sensitivity to the government's censorship policies ensured that a large part of the country's literature would be morally uplifting and generally supportive of the nation-building ethic.

Nevertheless, CLE experienced serious difficulties in its attempt to promote a francophone literary tradition that would appeal to common people while addressing problems of crucial concern to them. High import taxes on printing presses, ink, and paper made it necessary for CLE to produce books in Europe and ship them to Cameroon, where printed materials were not subject to customs duties. Coupled with the lack of preferential mailing rates for educational materials, the small number of libraries that purchased African books, the Ministry of Education's reluctance to include the works of Cameroonian authors on school reading lists (by far the country's largest market for books), and the absence of government subsidies, this situation guaranteed that CLE would remain financially dependent on church subventions from abroad, even though it had originally been projected as a self-supporting enterprise. Furthermore, CLE failed to develop the promotion and distribution networks capable of reaching larger audiences in Cameroon. The country's only daily newspaper, *La Presse du Cameroun*, virtually ignored its publications. CLE's precarious financial situation worsened as a result of the international monetary crisis in the early 1970s, and after 1973 its fortunes declined precipitously.

Despite the difficulties encountered by CLE, the firm played a major role in the evolution of Cameroonian literature. For more than ten years, it brought out a majority of all works published by Cameroonian writers, and it popularized the idea that African authors could reach substantial reading publics in their own countries without conforming to the demands of European publishers. Although CLE's implicit ideology decisively shaped Cameroonian literature during the 1960s and early 1970s, its promotion of print culture had effects that could hardly have been anticipated by its founders. Just as the French expansion of educational opportunities for Africans in the 1950s helped catalyze anticolonialist sentiment in Cameroon, the Christian and politically conservative impulses behind the founding of CLE helped create a climate in which people began to recognize the need for a literature that would deal honestly with the very institutions that had brought the new publishing firm into being. Hints of this attitude are even evident in some of the books published by CLE.

West Cameroonians did not enjoy the same access to publishing opportunities as did their francophone countrymen. During the 1960s and early 1970s, they occasionally published poems, short stories, and essays in reviews or in local newspapers such as the *Cameroon Times* and the *Cameroon Outlook*. At least two Cameroonians wrote Eastern Nigerian market novels, and many others were engaged in writing, although their work nearly always remained in manuscript form and circulated only among small groups of friends.[16] Interest in literature was widespread in the area partly because books were available at a relatively large number of places. During the colonial era, Igbo traders had established a precedent for selling books in local markets, and the Presbyterian church displayed a variety of English-language books in the shops it maintained at missions throughout the western part of the country. However, unless anglophone Cameroonian writers could find ways to publish their works, they would never reach a sizeable public and develop a popular idiom in which the people of the region might recognize themselves.

Two strategies that Cameroonian writers did adopt in seeking to reach larger audiences were the use of traditional oral techniques and the exploitation of autobiographical materials. Both strategies surfaced to some degree in most Cameroonian literary works of the period, and a few authors focused specifically on them. After independence, ethnically based folklore materials acquired a new significance as the country sought to define its cultural identity. Thousands of folktales were recorded and preserved at the national research institute. School and university students were encouraged to collect folk materials in their villages. Bible-translating societies published folktale collections as part of an effort to familiarize people with the written form of their own languages.

There was even a certain urgency in these activities because not many young people were learning the repertoire of tales and epics that story-tellers of previous generations had mastered, and if such materials were not recorded, they were likely to expire with their tellers. As they were translated into European languages and made accessible to a national audience, these tales came to resemble European prose narratives in many ways. Their general significance overshadowed their ethnically specific meanings, and they invited the rereadings that facilitate critical analysis. Such a form could obviously be modified by writers who wished to maintain continuity with their cultural heritage while addressing contemporary African problems.

The Cameroonian master of this technique was Benjamin Matip, whose collection of three stories, *A la belle étoile*, appeared two years after independence. In contrast to actual folktales, Matip's stories are not addressed to a specific ethnic audience, and although the moral precepts they illustrate are rooted in traditional Bassa wisdom, they have an obvious relevance to the contemporary political situation as well. In many ways these stories function like oral tales. For example, Matip's narrator establishes an ironic, conversational tone in the questions and comments he directs to his readers, giving them the impression that they are participating in the telling of a story that concerns them.

The three principal virtues in Matip's stories are intellectual penetration, awareness that the greatest force prevails in a harsh world, and faith in the possibility of a just society. The need for these virtues is apparent in the first story, "Adieu la guerre, adieu le paradis," in which a hunter transports a boa and her nine children from a landlocked pool to the middle of a large river in the hope of obtaining a talisman that will guarantee his success as a hunter. The man objects when the boa announces her intention to eat him because the law of existence is "to eat in order not to be eaten" and because good actions are always requited by evil ones, but the validity of these assertions is corroborated by a cow and a horse, who testify that their good services to human masters were followed by bad treatment. However, the tortoise calls the boa a liar, arguing that no hunter could carry her and her nine children in a sack. To prove her story, she and her brood crawl back into the sack, where they all perish at the hand of the hunter.

The moral of the story is that force always determines the outcome of any conflict—not mere physical force but a combination of physical strength and intelligence. When the hunter first encountered the boa, he could have killed her because he was in a position of superiority, but he renounced his advantage because he was blinded by desire for the talisman and pride in his own valor. This blindness placed him in a position of weakness, and only the tortoise's ruse enabled the man to regain a position of strength. Yet he is not wrong when he claims that promises are sacred and that good deeds should be repaid with good deeds. From Matip's perspective, such principles are necessary for ordered social intercourse, but unless they are proclaimed from a position of superior force, they risk being ignored. However, when they are ignored, as they were by the human beings who mistreated the cow and the horse, those who ignored them cannot expect to be treated otherwise. Within the contemporary political context, Matip is implying that the oppressed people of Africa may demand justice, but until they acquire the power to control their own destiny, they will continue to be exploited by those who are stronger than they are.

The social ramifications of this perspective and its relevance to contemporary Cameroon become evident in Matip's final two stories, "Drapeau du sourire" and "Le Vieil Homme et le singe." In the former, a frog refuses to accept its humble condition and the deterministic religious principles that prevent people from changing the existing system. His strength lies in his ability to penetrate deceptive appearances such as mock friendship ("the flag of smiles") and to act decisively. In the end, he marries the king's daughter and rules the kingdom with justice and compassion. The relationship between this story and the Cameroonian situation is obvious, for Matip is suggesting that the people of the country could also forge a just society by recognizing their own strength and by working for the common welfare rather than expecting to receive it from God.

Unfortunately, the rightful place of those who dedicate themselves to such goals is sometimes usurped by social parasites who live extravagantly at the people's expense and rule in a highly arbitrary fashion. Matip's third story illustrates this situation by recounting how a lonely old man becomes the rejuvenated young king of a forest community after his monkey makes him wealthy, enables him to marry the king's daughter, and kills the monster that has been terrorizing the local population. The man abandons himself to a life of luxury, forgetting the monkey and having its corpse thrown into an anonymous hole when it dies. The people of the community are scandalized by such behavior because they regard the monkey and not the man as their savior, although justice is served when the man awakens to find himself once again old and alone in the miserable hut where he had been living before he encountered the monkey.

This story contains an allegorical account of recent Cameroonian history. The monkey is like Ruben Um Nyobé, whom many people credited with their liberation from colonial rule and whose independence movement made possible Ahidjo's accession to power. The man resembles the president and the privileged elites who forgot their ties with the people and merely pay lip service to the hope of creating a better society. Like the man, Ahidjo had the body of his benefactor dumped in an unmarked forest grave, and like the monkey, Um Nyobé continued to inspire the people's dream of a just and equitable social order. The contrast between this dream and the actual situation in Cameroon during the early 1960s served as an implicit commentary on the Ahidjo government.

A la belle étoile was published in Paris and did not suffer the censorship to which it might have been subjected if the Cameroonian authorities had understood its socially critical message. Although the book did not reach a large audience in the country, it was a remarkable accomplishment in the sense that it fused traditional oral techniques and folklore materials into a contemporary idiom with which the common people could identify. Matip employed this popular idiom to address a fundamental question confronting nearly all African states at the time: how can a just and equitable national society be brought into being? By posing this question within the context of postcolonial Cameroonian society, he developed one possible strategy for reaching a larger reading public without betraying his perception of the truth.

For obvious reasons, such a strategy was seldom adopted in the country itself, although there were occasional allegorical allusions to the existing social situation in folklore-influenced narratives published by CLE. For example, Penda's *La Corbeille d'ignames* appears to be the innocent story of a Bamileke king who conceals himself in a basket of yams. From this hiding place, he eavesdrops on conversations and discovers that many of his most trusted advisers have been deceiving him and enriching themselves at the people's expense. When he reassumes his position of authority, he reforms his corrupt administration and spares the lives of those who have betrayed his trust because he does not believe he has the right to take away what he cannot give. In other words, he imposes justice tempered with mercy. As a result, his reign becomes "one of the most brilliant, prosperous, and flourishing in central Africa."[17] Within the Cameroonian context, this pseudofolktale drew upon the fairly widespread notion that Ahidjo was an honest man surrounded by evil counselors. If he could unmask them, Penda intimates, he might be able to transform a corrupt Cameroonian society into a happy and prosperous one. *La Corbeille d'ignames* is not a literary masterpiece, but it clearly illustrates the role folklore can play in the ongoing search for a popular idiom.

Like traditional oral themes and techniques, autobiographical elements frequently surfaced in the Cameroonian literature of the 1960s and early 1970s, although few actual autobiographies were published at this time. CLE was particularly receptive to morally instructive autobiographical narratives containing the kinds of places and events that would seem familiar to the average reader. Characteristic of this genre are three naive memoirs that appeared at this time: Simon Rifoé's *Le Tour du Cameroun en 59 jours*, Lazare Sanduo's *Une Dure Vie scolaire*, and Pabe Mongo's *Un Enfant comme les autres*. All three were the first publications of inexperienced writers whose work was heavily edited by Europeans or educated Africans. Rifoé recounted an adventurous six-thousand-kilometer bicycle trip that he undertook as a publicity stunt in 1964. Mongo nostalgically portrayed his childhood in an eastern Cameroonian village, and Sanduo described the difficulties he encountered in pursuing the education that would eventually lead him into the Protestant ministry.

All three authors were practicing Christians whose faith sustained them as they overcame a series of obstacles before reaching goals they had set for themselves. Their religious view of the world is encapsulated in the consolation Sanduo finds in the belief that "if men are evil, God is good and never forgets any person in distress."[18] This uncritical acceptance of divine benevolence is the opposite of Matip's demand for intellectual penetration, but it reinforces the self-help ethic that both the church and the Ahidjo government were seeking to instill in the minds of the people.

The most entertaining of these little books is Rifoé's *Tour*. His well-publicized bicycle trip had earned him a certain notoriety, and by promoting it as a feat that no white man had ever accomplished, he captured the public imagination and demonstrated how a single individual could, by an exercise of will, transcend the conflicts that divided the nation. When he approached the editors at CLE with his story, they saw the opportunity to create a popular book, so they asked him to relate his adventures into a tape recorder. They themselves polished the prose transcript of the recording and published it under his name. From one point of view, they were enabling a Cameroonian to communicate his story in written form. From another, they were collaborating with a self-aggrandizing individual who wanted to project himself as a romantic national hero.

Mixing fact with fantasy, Rifoé tells how, armed with a sword, a dagger, a copy of the New Testament, and boundless confidence in himself, he left Douala and fought his way past highwaymen, wild animals, and almost impassable stretches of road to complete his solo trip around the country. The heroic posturing that characterizes his attitude in the book reemerged in his subsequent avatars as a sideshow strong man, a flamboyant boxer, an organizer of gladiatorlike spectacles for paying customers, a would-be filmmaker, and a pinball machine entrepreneur. Rifoé's grandiose plans invariably failed, and he himself died a ragged, impoverished beggar in a village near Bafia. A journalist who reported on one of Rifoé's boxing matches once commented that, in the presence of his grandiloquent boasting, "one is certainly not far removed from our confused, ambiguous, disturbing daily reality."[19] Beneath the heroic pose he adopted in the *Tour*, Rifoé was a pathetically tragic figure; in fact, the disparity between his public persona and his inner anxieties symbolically mirrored the ambivalent social situation that resulted from the unfulfilled promise of independence.

Philombe was profoundly conscious of this ambivalence; in fact, he dedicated himself to the search for a popular idiom that could transmute it into a literature capable of expressing the concerns of the people and enlightening them about their own situation in the contemporary world. Drawing upon folklore materials, autobiographical snippets, and his familiarity with French-language literature, he developed a clear, unaffected style that fused elements of European and African literary traditions. The emergence of a literate culture in Cameroon was especially important to Philombe because he viewed the written word as an instrument for bringing about a more just and humane society.

According to him, development along these lines requires a stable sense of collective identity, and literature helps people define such an identity. He himself insisted that "the only true story of a people is the one they themselves tell."[20] As a writer, he believes he has a moral obligation to serve as a vehicle for telling the true story of the Cameroonian people. In a sense, he is allowing them to speak through him. "We find our principal source of inspiration at the heart of the daily lives of the people," he claimed. "A man of letters betrays his historical mission if he fails to draw his creative vigor from the human realities of our own age."[21] His own elaboration of a popular idiom is both a statement on behalf of the people and an attempt to articulate the collective identity that they themselves recognize only in a vague and nebulous way.

If Philombe identifies with the people, he also wants to enlighten them, to liberate them from the false notions that hold them in bondage. In fact, the metaphor of enslavement is the dominant trope in all his work. Africans had been physically enslaved during the colonial era, but even after independence they often remained trapped in a false consciousness that prevented them from realizing their potential for a fully human existence. False consciousness is a form of slavery, and some people allow themselves to be trapped in it by greed or ambition; others are blinded by ignorance and superstition, still others by their willingness to accept oppression as normal.

By portraying the mundane events of everyday life from the perspective of a wise, compassionate observer, Philombe hoped to show people how various kinds of false consciousness reduced them to slavery. For him, the opposite of a slave is a man, and as he declared in one of his early poems, his intention was to sing ". . . a song of man / to create man / in the heart of man."[22] Philombe's writing thus constitutes an attempt to liberate people from the false consciousness that prevents them from becoming what they are capable of becoming—fully aware human beings who deal honestly with each other.

To experience this sort of freedom, people must commit themselves to the pursuit of truth, and Philombe believes that literature can generate such commitment by presenting false consciousness in a light that enables readers to perceive how it distorts individual lives and sanctions the excesses of a cruel, hypocritical society. By provoking readers to reflect on the consequences of false consciousness in the imagined worlds he creates for them, Philombe cultivates a mode of seeing that can also be applied to the society in which they are living. To the extent that his works inspire a commitment to truth, they have a revolutionary significance because they invite readers to free themselves from all forms of blindness, including an uncritical acceptance of the government's official rhetoric.

Philombe's world view is clearly embedded in the short prose pieces that constitute *Lettres de ma cambuse* and *Histoires queue-de-chat*, two of his four books published by CLE during the 1960s and early 1970s. Modeled on Alphonse Daudet's *Lettres de mon moulin*, Philombe's "letters" were initially written while he was convalescing from the first attack of the illness that crippled him. In them, he recorded the trivial events he observed in his Yaounde neighborhood and transformed folklore materials into parables of modern African life. Enlivened by Philombe's sharp eye for significant detail, by his wry sense of humor, and by his commitment to social justice, these letters captured the unique traits of individual characters while revealing the universally human dimensions of the dilemmas they confront. The editors at CLE found them singularly appropriate to its vocation as center for the promotion of a literate culture in francophone Africa and elected to launch its literature series by publishing them.

Each section of *Lettres de ma cambuse* consists of an event that triggers reflection on the part of the narrator and culminates in an implicit moral that readers are expected to draw from the encounter between the event and the narrator's consciousness. The initial scene usually involves a minor incident that arises from some form of ignorance compounded by pretentiousness. Often linked with a proverb or proverblike statement, the incident could easily be dismissed as a normal, everyday occurrence, but because the narrator's inquiring temperament prompts him to scrutinize it more closely, he succeeds in stripping away the veil of conventionality that obscures its more profound implications. If the incident results in suffering or humiliation, the narrator sympathizes with the victim, a response that contrasts sharply with a wide- spread indifference to the tragedies of daily life in countries such as Cameroon. His attitude toward the situation prods readers to ask why such incidents occur and whether they might have been prevented if they had been handled differ- ently. These are precisely the sorts of questions that Philombe thought needed to be raised about analogous situations in the real world, and he envisaged his "letters" as a means of evoking them in the minds of his readers.

Both the animal parables and the anecdotes in *Lettres de ma cambuse* oper- ate according to the same consciousness-raising principle. For example, in "Le Bouc sanguinaire de Papa Mboya," the little goat Moambu joins a pack of hyenas and lures his former master's sheep into ambushes. As long as the ruse continues to work, Moambu is treated well and even accorded a privileged position in hyena society, but when Papa Mboya learns the truth and takes steps to protect the rest of his flock, the hyenas' hunting expeditions begin to fail, and they decide to eat the little goat they had formerly covered with honors. On an allegorical level, this story reveals the blindness of Cameroonians who assured themselves of wealth and status by collaborating in the European exploitation of Africa during the colonial period. The implication is that such individuals would enjoy their privileged status only as long as they continued to serve the interests of their colonial masters. Furthermore, by adopting Euro- pean cultural values and by deceiving their fellow Cameroonians, they were abandoning their own true identity.

Implicit in this story is a general moral principle that readers are expected to recognize: when people, pretending to be other than they are, profit from the misery of their fellow creatures, they are actually betraying themselves. Although Philombe never specifically states this principle, its relevance to a multitude of real-world situations becomes apparent once it has been formu- lated. Readers who discover such principles for themselves are already demon- strating the mental attitude that, according to Philombe, they will need if they hope to free themselves from the various forms of enslavement that still afflict so many of them. "Le Bouc sanguinaire de Papa Mboya" thus functions like a folktale in the sense that it invites the participation of the audience and rein- forces habits of mind that are useful in dealing with the real world. Like Matip, Philombe is drawing upon folklore themes and techniques to develop a popular idiom capable of treating contemporary problems in a morally serious fashion.

Although the five stories in *Histoires queue-de-chat* involve realistic portray- als of human situations, they resemble Philombe's animal parables in that they engage readers in the interpretation of familiar-seeming fictional events as a means of encouraging these readers to discern analogous situations in their own society. The term *histoires queue-de-chat* is a local expression that can be roughly translated as "cock-and-bull stories." It refers to the elaborate ruses that sorcerers and confidence men employ to profit from the gullibility of super- stitious Africans. Each story focuses on one such ruse and reveals, ironically, that the victimizer in these situations is as blind as his victim because both live according to principles that prevent them from realizing their human potential and participating in a genuine community of self-respecting individuals.

In "Le Petit Serpent du docteur Tchumba," for example, the hard-working villager Ndoumna Cyriac allows himself to be duped by an itinerant sorcerer who convinces him that he will become wealthy if he swallows a little magical snake, waits three months, and places nine eggs under his bed on the evening of the first full moon. Because Ndoumna is jealous of a former classmate who returns periodically from the city and parades his wealth before the admiring villagers, he willingly hands over his mother's life savings to the sorcerer and undergoes a sham ritual during which he believes he has actually swallowed the snake. The sorcerer of course disappears long before the three months have elapsed, and when the promised money fails to appear, Ndoumna becomes haggard and loses a considerable amount of weight. At this point, he travels to the city and visits the kindly Dr. Tchumba, who can find no physical cause for the young man's alarming symptoms, but after listening to the story of the sorcerer's ruse, he blindfolds Ndoumna, gives him a purgative, and releases a small snake into the sink where his patient has just vomited. When the blindfold is removed, Ndoumna glimpses the snake and immediately feels cured.

Both Ndoumna and the sorcerer in this story are slaves to a false conception of reality. The jealousy that motivated Ndoumna to enlist the aid of a sorcerer also blinds him to the fact that anyone capable of producing unlimited amounts of money would hardly need to be paid for his services. Within the narrative context provided by Philombe, the folly of lending credence to such a "cock-and-bull story" is obvious, but the superstitious cast of mind that predisposed Ndoumna to accept the sorcerer's words at face value remains widespread in Africa, where it impedes the rational solution of urgent social and economic problems. By offering readers an opportunity to grasp the absurdity of a fictional character's blindness to the truth, Philombe is hoping they will apply the same standards of judgment to the behavior of real people. Similarly, he is attempting to show that social parasites like the sorcerer are even more pitiful than their victims. Because they possess no real power over the events they claim to control, they must constantly fear exposure, and because they abuse the trust of others, they themselves can never experience the satisfaction of belonging to a community based on mutual trust. Despite any profits they might make, they remain isolated and alienated individuals.

The opposite of such sorcerers is Dr. Tchumba, who successfully diagnoses the psychosomatic nature of Ndoumna's illness and prescribes an appropriate cure for it. Although he recognizes the young villager's blindness, he refrains from mocking him and, in fact, treats him with compassion. As a rational approach to a problem in human psychology, his cure suggests the possibility of a society where people contribute to the general welfare rather than selfishly pursue their own short-term materialistic goals. By engaging readers in a critical reflection that culminates in utopian speculation, Philombe was implicitly commenting on the society that was emerging in Cameroon during the 1960s and early 1970s, for the Ahidjo government had created a climate in which the mentalities of Ndoumna and the sorcerer were far more common than the enlightened attitude of Dr. Tchumba. The popular idiom that Philombe cultivated in stories such as "Le Petit Serpent du docteur Tchumba" thus served as a vehicle for raising people's consciousness about the social malaise in their own country.

This same consciousness-raising intention is apparent in the two Philombe novels published by CLE at this time—*Sola ma chérie* and *Un Sorcier blanc à Zangali*. Both deal with forms of blindness that can be overcome only by articulating a viable sense of identity in the modern world and by liberating people from the false notions that enslave them. In *Sola ma chérie*, the central theme is the most common one in contemporary Cameroonian fiction—the generational conflict that arises with regard to the marriage of young women. For the older generation, the bride-price was a traditional custom that assured the orderly arrangement of marriages; however, young men and women who had received European-style educations regarded themselves as independent individuals with the right to choose their own marriage partners. In their eyes, the bride-price was an outmoded institution that had become corrupted in a money economy, allowing older men to purchase young wives and permitting fathers to enrich themselves by selling their daughters. Philombe depicts this situation as a case in which all parties to abusive bride-price practices are victims of a system that imprisons them in a kind of slavery.

Sola ma chérie recounts the story of the old man Nkonda, who regarded himself as superior to his fellow villagers because he worked hard, saved his money, and adopted European ways of looking at the world. After glimpsing the beautiful young Sola in the streets of Yaounde, he offers her parents a substantial bride-price, and they accept it, despite the fact that she loves the young student Tsango. For Nkonda, she is the symbol of his success, not a human being with feelings and desires of her own. He treats her as if she were a slave until she runs away with Tsango three years after the marriage. Nkonda then abandons his hard-earned possessions and is last seen wandering forlornly through the streets of Douala in search of Sola.

The most obvious victim in Philombe's first novel is Sola. Although reduced to the status of an object that can be bought and sold, she remains a human being who desires to love and to be loved. Her own emotional responses prove that she is far more than an object. When Tsango sees her weeping, the sentiments that had originally brought them together are reawakened in him, and he agrees to take her away with him. The story thus culminates in another person's reaffirmation of Sola's humanity, effectively repudiating the false identity that others had sought to impose on her.

But Sola's escape from Nkonda does not resolve the problem. She and Tsango must live far from the people they know, and they remain subject to laws that protect Nkonda's right to retrieve her. As long as people accept the institution of the bride-price in its present form, other young women will suffer the same oppression that Sola has been obliged to face. At one point, she herself defends a high dowry payment as the pledge of a man's esteem for his future wife. Her blindness to the real cause of her own enslavement suggests that the only permanent solution to her dilemma is a revolution in people's attitudes toward the institutions that victimize them.

Even more than Sola, Nkonda is the slave of a false self-image. Whereas she is painfully human in her misery, he represses an awareness of what he shares with other people. Having assimilated certain aspects of a European lifestyle, he feels superior to his fellow Africans, and his possession of Sola vindicates the self-image he has forged for himself. But in his failure to recognize that love and mutual respect provide the only viable basis for a lasting relationship between two people, he is imprisoning himself in a tragic solitude that becomes obvious after she leaves him. His forlorn search for her in the final scene reveals that he was more dependent on her than she had ever been on him, for without her, he can no longer believe in himself. Once readers perceive how Nkonda is victimized by a self-inflicted blindness, they become capable of recognizing similar behavior in real life, and that is precisely what Philombe intends them to do.

His use of a popular idiom to provoke reflection on contemporary social problems is also apparent in *Un Sorcier blanc à Zangali*, which is a rewriting of Mongo Beti's *Le Pauvre Christ de Bomba* to demonstrate the positive contribution of missionary Christianity within the larger context of colonialist oppression.[23] Set in 1915 when the French were replacing the Germans in eastern Cameroon, *Un Sorcier blanc* traces a white priest's journey into an area reputed to be hostile toward Christian missionaries. This priest, Father Marius, is accompanied by Azombo, a naive young boy who adores him, and by an attractive young woman from a neighboring village. Having left Europe to escape the memory of his wife's death, Marius had enthusiastically devoted himself to the eradication of heathen practices, and he saw his mission to Zangali as an opportunity to become a hero in the annals of church history. Like Drumont in *Le Pauvre Christ*, Marius encounters a widespread skepticism that calls into question the assumptions behind his campaign against African cultural values. During a conversation with the local French commandant, he, like Drumont, denies that colonialism and Christianity are pursuing the same goals in Africa. In the end, however, he too recognizes how the missionary presence complements the colonial administration's attempt to impose its conception of civilization on the area.

In *Un Sorcier blanc*, this civilization often proves more barbarous than the African one that is supposedly inferior to it. Two incidents of European cruelty frame the action in the novel and underscore its anticolonialist orientation. At the beginning, a commandant orders the beating of a wise old man from Azombo's village and halts the punishment only when the victim's bizarre dance makes him laugh uproariously. At the end of the novel, another commandant executes the chief of Zangali for not having prevented an attack on Marius after the priest had thoughtlessly disrupted a local religious ceremony. In both instances the authorities are satisfied that their actions have impressed the villagers with white superiority and convinced them to accord blind obedience to the implicit rules of the colonialist system. In reality, the two Cameroonians have demonstrated a nobility that the people perceive as a defiance of European oppression and as a condemnation of the white men who are persecuting them. The bizarre dance was the old man's way of declaring that, in beating him, the white men were committing a crime equivalent to the beating of their own fathers, and the chief faced death, rather than accept the commandant's offer to flee, because he refused to be chased from his own land. Viewed from this perspective, the colonialist enterprise was a crime against Africans.

Such a message had lost much of its relevance by the late 1960s when *Un Sorcier blanc* was published, except insofar as it corrected the historical record and sanctioned the retrieval of cultural values that could help Africans articulate a viable sense of identity in the modern world. But unlike *Le Pauvre Christ*, the principal focus of *Un Sorcier blanc* is not on the abuses of colonialism; it is on the transformation in Marius's attitude toward missionary Christianity and on the possibility of exploiting the positive contributions of the church for the future well-being of Africans.

Marius's conception of his task had originally been similar to that of Drumont. Fleeing from unpleasant memories in Europe, he found a new rationale for his own life. Regarding himself as an apostle of civilization in Africa, he built a network of mission churches. And acting upon the stereotyped assumption that Africans were like children in need of discipline, he adopted an authoritarian stance that expressed itself in the destruction of fetishes, the disruption of traditional rituals, and even the administration of corporal punishment. When he leaves for Zangali, he believes he can overcome the recalcitrance of the local people by adopting the same strict methods that had earned him his previous successes.

However, on his way to Zangali, he spends a night in the village of Pala, where he is confronted by a major moral dilemma. The people of Pala are militantly anti-Christian, and if he acknowledges his vocation they are likely to assassinate him. Azombo adroitly convinces them that his master is a powerful commandant, and Marius does not contradict him; in order not to destroy the credibility of this charade, Marius even accepts the chief's gift of his daughter Andela and takes her with him to Zangali. Before he arrives at his destination, the priest has already demonstrated that he is not the strong-willed hero he had imagined himself as being. Rather than imposing his image of reality on Africans, he is reduced to disguising his true identity and acting out a scenario that demeans his calling.

Chastened by this experience, Marius insists upon telling the people of Zangali that he is a priest who has come to establish a mission. Although the elders of the village are in favor of killing the intruder, the chief realizes that it would be foolhardy to provoke the newly installed French authorities, and he suggests that they assign the missionary and his two companions to an ill-omened plot of land where a former settlement had been surrendered to the forest after having been decimated by a malaria epidemic. The people of Zangali believe the site is cursed, and they abandon victims of the disease in the surrounding forest. Ironically, this overgrown cemetery accords Marius an ideal opportunity to demonstrate the most important contribution he can make in Africa, and his experiences there trigger the insight that liberates him from the blindness that had previously afflicted him.

The genuine contribution he makes at Zangali has nothing to do with his religious convictions. It derives solely from his technical expertise and his willingness to work hard. Confounding the expectations of the superstitious Zangalians, he clears the forest, erects buildings, and cures the malaria victims who had been left to die on the land that was ceded to him. He himself unwittingly acknowledges the irrelevance of Christian belief in this endeavor when he admonishes his two followers not to be afraid of the skeletons they discover there because "the dead are the dead."[24] In terms of Catholic dogma, Marius has just uttered a blasphemy. The entire teaching of Christ revolves around the idea of everlasting life. Yet if human beings desire to improve the quality of their lives on this earth, they must accept the finality of death and work productively within the limitations imposed on them by the nature of existence.

The insight that frees Marius from his false conception of the world occurs as the result of his audacity in spying on a ritual organized by the people of Zangali in an attempt to exorcise the malaria epidemic that is raging among them. When he raises his voice to condemn what he decries as the work of Satan, the villagers are incensed and want to put him to death, but Andela claims him as her husband and reminds them that they are forbidden to kill anyone who is related to them by marriage. One of the abandoned malaria victims also relates how the priest nursed him back to health. Ironically, the very rituals Marius has just been condemning are structurally similar to communion, confession, absolution, priestly intercession, sacred symbology, and communal singing in the Catholic church.

Philombe's point is that neither traditional religious ceremonies nor Christian rituals can check the spread of malaria. The only way to do it is to mount a rational assault upon the causes of the disease, and this is what Marius does through the resourceful use of his small stock of quinine. Readers of *Un Sorcier blanc* are expected to draw two conclusions from this situation: the religious rites of Europeans are not superior to those of Africans, and insofar as both are based on irrational beliefs, they cannot provide adequate solutions to the practical problems that Africans must confront in the contemporary world.

For Marius, his brush with death transforms his attitude toward his work. Until then, he had treated Africans in a paternalistic fashion because he believed they were racially and culturally inferior to Europeans. After his experience at the traditional religious ceremony, he realizes that what he shares with the people of Zangali is more important than what separates them. He becomes tolerant of their cultural values and places greater emphasis on teaching them practical lessons than on instructing them in Christian dogma. As he explains in a letter to his superior, he no longer talks to people first about Christ:

It seemed to me urgent and more important to save their lives. As I lavish care on them, I merely request that they commend themselves to Zamba, the Uncreated. I try to get them to trust me, and I speak to them about the natural religion that embraces all men as brothers who are condemned to live together on this earth. Every day I prove to them by my actions that "white sorcerers" desire the happiness of black men.[25]

In this letter, Marius is outlining a new missionary practice based on mutual respect and on the conviction that helping people escape from their misery is more important than obliging them to adopt foreign cultual values.

The final episode in the novel suggests that this new missionary practice will never be completely successful as long as the area remains under colonial rule. Despite Marius's pleas, the French commandant executes the chief of Zangali to impress upon the local villagers that they must never show a lack of respect for white men, as they had done in menacing the priest after his intrusion into their religious ceremony. At the very moment when Marius is praying that the commandant will remand his unjust decision, a shot rings out, signaling the death of the chief and the failure of the priest's attempt to save him. Prayer cannot prevent injustice. But as Marius realizes at the end of the novel, the colonialist system that perpetuates injustice can be changed if people approach the organization of society in the same pragmatic fashion that enabled him to rehabilitate a desolate plot of land and to cure people who had been dying of malaria.

Like the corrupt institution of the bride-price in *Sola ma chérie*, the entire colonialist enterprise has to be dismantled before the oppressors and the oppressed will be able to liberate themselves from the enslavement it imposes on them. To accomplish this goal, Philombe implies, Africans should repudiate the irrational beliefs that prevent them from taking destiny into their own hands and shaping it according to the best available knowledge about the workings of nature. The real subject of Philombe's novel is the mental attitude that frees people from the various forms of slavery to which they have been subjected. This attitude is a humanistic one that both reaffirms the dignity of African cultural values and appropriates the new knowledge introduced to Africa during the colonial period. *Un Sorcier blanc* thus culminates in an act of consciousness, and for Philombe, consciousness is the first step toward freedom.

A comparison with *Le Pauvre Christ de Bomba* reveals that, although Philombe drew inspiration from Beti's novel, he reworked his materials in such a way that he transformed a bitterly ironic anticolonialist story into an optimistic work that contains a relevant message for Africans in the postcolonial era. Whereas Drumont's project is a hypocritically self-serving business enterprise that collapses in a scandal symbolizing the rottenness of Catholic missionary activity, Marius's well-intentioned endeavor brings new knowledge to the area and culminates in the prospect that local villagers will learn from him how to improve the quality of their own lives. Drumont renounces his ministry and returns to Europe without accepting responsibility for the harm he has inflicted on Africans; in contrast, Marius discovers a new meaning in his ministry when he recognizes the legitimacy of African cultural values, the injustice of the colonial system, and the real contribution he can make to the welfare of the people. By showing that Marius is capable of intellectual growth in a way that Drumont was not, Philombe prods readers to scrutininze Marius's insights for clues to the solution of contemporary problems in countries such as Cameroon.

Throughout the 1960s and early 1970s, Philombe was at the center of the Cameroonian search for a popular idiom. He was largely responsible for keeping alive the national writers' union, and during this period CLE, a publishing house established to foster popular writing, brought out more books by him than by any other single author. Philombe himself was committed to developing a literary medium capable of encompassing reality as experienced by common people while at the same time teaching them to comprehend their own condition. As he sought to perfect this style, he projected much of his own sensibility into the narrative voice that is recognizable in all his works.

Like the whitmanesque "I," this voice is unmistakably rooted in a concrete national setting, but it also swells to embrace all humanity. "My own name is *Man!*" is a refrain that reverberates through all his early poetry.[26] Born in suffering and adversity, tempered by compassion, and inspired by an unswerving dedication to truth, Philombe's voice synthesizes folklore and autobiographical elements into a literary medium that engages the active participation of readers in the interpretive process. In the name of the people, it condemns hypocrisy, cruelty, and injustice. It upholds the ideal of a better society than the one that exists in contemporary Cameroon. It also promotes the consciousness that frees people from their blindness and permits them to be fully themselves. In this sense, the narrative voice in Philombe's works became a voice of the Cameroonian people, a voice that spoke to them while inviting dialogue with others.

CHAPTER

9

CAMEROONIAN REFLECTIONS ON NEGRITUDE AND AUTHENTICITY

During the 1960s and early 1970s, francophone African intellectuals became increasingly involved in an ongoing debate over the relevance of Negritude to the postcolonial situation.[1] The central issue in this controversy was the question of identity: is there an authentically African identity, and can it be reconciled with technological progress? In Cameroon, the Negritude conflict aroused passionate engagement on both sides of the question. Many Cameroonians had become familiar with Negritude while studying in France, and some of them became its principal advocates when they returned home.

Initially the proponents of Negritude encountered little resistance in Cameroon. Ahidjo had always promoted an ideology of cultural authenticity, and Cameroonian advocates of the Negritude position were generally inclined to support his cultural politics. In the mid-1960s his government established closer ties with Senegal, and under the influence of François Sengat-Kuo, elements of Senghorian Negritude became an increasingly prominent part of its official rhetoric. By this time, however, Negritude had already acquired many different and often contradictory connotations.

Coined by Aimé Césaire in the late 1930s to designate a proud acceptance of blackness and the cultural values of black people throughout the world, the term achieved widespread currency after the 1947 founding of *Présence Africaine* and the Société Africaine de Culture in Paris. Alioune Diop was the director of both enterprises, and he inspired countless individuals to work toward the rehabilitation of black culture and to help promote knowledge about the black world. Many of these people took part in the Congresses of Black Writers and Artists that Diop organized in 1956 and 1959. Although the participants in these conferences professed a wide variety of opinions on cultural and ideological matters, the general idea of Negritude gradually came to be identified with *Présence Africaine*.

The most prominent francophone African intellectual of his generation, the Senegalese president Léopold Senghor became the primary spokesman for Negritude as an economic and cultural development strategy, but the term is also linked for him with a characteristically African way of looking at the world. In "Orphée noir," the preface to Senghor's 1948 anthology of black poetry, Jean-Paul Sartre described Negritude as a form of negative consciousness that could liberate black people from the mental prison of European stereotypes. In Placide Tempels's book on Bantu philosophy, the Belgian Jesuit argued that the African world view is based on a spiritual understanding of the forces that underlie all existence. The Rwandan priest Alexis Kagame modified aspects of Tempels's system, but the basic concept of a unified African world view remained the same in a series of books and articles he wrote on the topic. Influenced by all three men, the German scholar Janheinz Jahn borrowed the word *muntu* (man) from Tempels and used it as the title of a book that claims to discover this world view in examples of black culture from various parts of the world. Such intellectual endeavors popularized the assumption that African belief systems are latent philosophies, and this perspective encouraged Africans to quarry the myths, folktales, and customs of their own ethnic groups in an effort to reconstruct the ideas behind them.

Throughout his writings, Senghor defended Negritude as a mode of being that offers Africans the only viable basis for defining their collective identity. He assumed that this mode of being is inscribed in traditional cultural practices that reveal an African aptitude for intuitively grasping the inner reality or essence of things. According to him, this kind of perception is linked with an intense emotivity, a mystically unified image of the world, a highly developed sense of rhythm, a propensity for analogical reasoning, and a capacity to appreciate asymmetrical parallelisms. Senghor realized that linear, analytical thinking had made scientific progress possible, but no matter how successful such an approach to reality might be, he was convinced it would remain incomplete without the wisdom embedded in traditional African culture. For this reason, he proposed a "cultural cross-fertilization" of African and European values that would benefit everyone while enabling Africans to recover their pride in an authentic identity they had been in danger of losing during the colonial period.

Even before most African countries achieved independence around 1960, there was considerable opposition to Senghor's brand of Negritude. Marxists objected that differences between Africans and Europeans reflect economic conditions, not racial characteristics. Others complained that Senghor's identification with French colonial policies and his allegiance to French literary culture prevented him from empathizing with the real concerns of most Africans. In general, those involved in the anticolonialist struggle faulted both Senghor and Diop for failing to support the cause of political independence. At the Second Congress of Black Writers and Artists in 1959, for example, Frantz Fanon attacked Negritude as an elite concept and argued that African peoples needed to forge their own cultural identities in a concrete struggle with the material conditions of existence. A few years later, Sembene Ousmane openly accused Negritude writers such as Senghor of allying themselves with reactionary forces that were intent upon keeping Africa in a perpetual state of backwardness.

At the same time, Negritude was largely rejected by anglophone African intellectuals. As early as 1959, Ezekiel Mphahlele characterized it as a reverse racism that could be misused to keep Africans in their places. According to him, the cultural traits idealized by Negritude writers could simply be taken for granted, and their preoccupation with the past was, he felt, an overcompensation for the void experienced by highly educated individuals who had become alienated from their own people. Wole Soyinka regarded Negritude as the intellectual luxury of a small francophone elite, and when he remarked that an African has as little need to proclaim his Negritude as a tiger to announce its "tigritude," he coined a slogan that has repeatedly been used to ridicule the movement. In any case, most anglophone African writers of the immediate postcolonial period saw their principal task neither as the celebration of the past nor as the reaffirmation of their own authenticity, but rather as the attempt to comprehend their world in the hope of ameliorating it.

By the late 1960s, the anti-Negritude movement had gathered considerable momentum among younger intellectuals in francophone Africa. Sekou Touré publicly denounced Negritude as an inadequate basis for development policy in Africa. Novelists such as Yambo Ouologueum and Ahmadou Kourouma depicted Africa in a way that contradicts the principal tenets of Senghorian Negritude. Philosophers and cultural critics such as Stanislas Adotevi, Paulin Hountondji, and Ferdinand Agblemagnon argued that Negritude perpetuates European stereotypes of Africans, distracts attention from the real causes of economic underdevelopment, and blocks the evolution of African states toward more equitable forms of government. By this time, Senghor had become a symbol of political conservatism for the younger generation of francophone Africans, and although he continued to elaborate his conception of Negritude, it was increasingly viewed as a questionable basis on which to construct a viable sense of collective identity in Africa.

The same conflict of ideas occurred in Cameroon, where it was particularly intense because the issues at stake were clearly related to the cultural politics of the Ahidjo government. Senghor himself was a major participant in the Cameroonian version of the Negritude debate. He visited the country on three occasions between 1966 and 1973, and each time he publicly defended his ideas, claiming that his critics had willfully distorted them and were fleeing from themselves when they refused to acknowledge their own Negritude. "An African who doesn't believe in Negritude is really a suicide victim," he told a University of Yaounde audience in 1969. "Let him be carried off to the grave."[2] Such an attitude proved popular among two frequently overlapping groups of Cameroonian intellectuals: those who identified with the government's attempt to forge a national cultural identity and those who embraced Negritude as an authentically African form of religious sentiment.

As minister of education between 1962 and 1974, William Etekia Mbumua played a key role in implementing the cultural policies that shaped the intellectual environment in which the Cameroonian Negritude debate took place. During his student days in Paris, Eteki had been profoundly influenced by Alioune Diop, and the "humanism" he later championed was essentially a modified form of Negritude. He believed in an African cultural unity based on the assumption that traditional customs and modes of thought express a characteristically African world view. His goal was to reconcile this world view and scientific knowledge in a new African philosophy capable of sustaining technological progress without succumbing to the acquisitive individualism so characteristic of the Western world. By adopting such a philosophy, he argued, Africans could liberate themselves and forge a dynamically creative culture that would be in harmony with their sense of themselves.

Within the Cameroonian context, Eteki's program implied that the people need to recognize and accept their African cultural identity. "In his desire to develop and flourish, the Cameroonian man must first of all take possession of his own cultural values," he declared, "and Negritude is simply the defining of one's cultural identity."[3] To facilitate this reacquisition of authentic Cameroonian values, Eteki proposed a cultural decolonization. The first step in this process would entail a survey of traditional beliefs. On the basis of this survey, he argued, one could eliminate attitudes that inhibit progress. One could also identify the essence of a heritage that could serve as a reservoir of inspiration for Cameroonians who desire to understand their place in the world.

The "new Cameroonian man" Eteki envisioned would not be imprisoned in a sterile return to the past because the second step in this process involves an acceptance of the modern scientific attitudes that would allow him to shape his own destiny by domesticating the forces of nature. Because these attitudes would be integrated into a world view that respected his own cultural identity, Eteki's new Cameroonian man could adopt them without subordinating his perceptions of reality to the European cultural assumptions with which they were generally associated. If Cameroonians embraced such a world view, Eteki concluded, they would encounter people from other cultures on an equal footing and help generate the international dialogue that he hoped would someday culminate in peace, reconciliation, and universal brotherhood.

In concrete terms, Eteki's cultural decolonization required a vast educational effort that could motivate Cameroonians to reevaluate their own traditions and to participate actively in the construction of the nation. Rather than emulating European educational models and relying on foreign "coopérants" as teachers, Eteki insisted that Cameroonian schools and adult education programs should be governed by traditional principles: a respect for the unity of all knowledge, a commitment to initiation as a recognition of maturity, an orientation toward collective enterprise, and an awareness that all members of the community have a right to be educated. By combining these principles with support for French-English bilingualism and modern scientific training,

Eteki hoped to foster the emergence of a national cultural identity that would embody Negritude ideals while responding to the aspirations of Ahidjo's nation-building rhetoric.

One result of Eteki's cultural policy was the founding of *Abbia* in 1962. Modeled on *Présence Africaine*, *Abbia* soon became the country's most important cultural journal. Eteki and Alioune Diop convinced Bernard Fonlon to assume the editorship of the new publication and to take responsibility for achieving the goals that had been set for it: promoting a Cameroonian cultural renaissance that would contribute to a sense of national unity and increasing the visibility of Cameroonian literate culture in other parts of the world. Initially, Fonlon produced the journal in collaboration with a group of young intellectuals including Marcien Towa, Eldridge Mohammadou, Lilyan Kesteloot, Engelbert Mveng, Sankie Maimo, Gaspard Towa-Atangana, and Françoise Towa-Atangana. Philombe and several other self-taught writers from APEC also participated in the editing of *Abbia* during its early years.

The people brought together by *Abbia* saw their efforts as a contribution to the creation of a literate national culture in Cameroon. They worked together with the editorial staff at CLE, evaluating manuscripts and advising inexperienced writers. They also produced a number of books that were published by CLE. In return, the Protestant publishing house served as the primary distributor for their journal and provided them with space for their editorial offices. The informal *Abbia* club met regularly in these offices to read and discuss the essays, poems, and short stories that were submitted to them. At one point, the group planned to sponsor a series of public discussions on the books published by CLE, but the idea was later abandoned, and as the principal collaborators moved away from Yaounde or became involved in other activities, the editorial work fell more and more exclusively on Fonlon's shoulders. His persistence kept the journal alive for more than twenty years, and when influential political enemies made it difficult for him to collect promised government subsidies, he successfully solicited funds from Senghor, Houphouët-Boigny, UNESCO, and other donors. Under such circumstances, *Abbia* increasingly bore the imprint of his personality.

The general thrust of Fonlon's thought was similar to that of Eteki. He too preached the need for a cultural decolonization that would liberate Cameroonians to pursue their own image of an "ideal man"—a man who proudly retained his authentic African nature while adopting the scientific attitudes necessary for progress in the modern world. Like Eteki, Fonlon believed in the power of education and committed himself to the task of creating a national cultural identity. On both counts, he felt that literature could play a decisive role in Cameroon because "literature is the voice and the true record of a people, a living influence which, by infusing the same spirit into each passing generation, preserves a people's identity against the ravages of time."[4] Through his work on *Abbia*, Fonlon sought to nurture a Cameroonian voice capable of performing this function.

His position seemed to support many of the principal tenets of Negritude.

In fact, Alioune Diop had been one of the major influences on his intellectual development, and having written one of the first European dissertations on black poetry from Africa and the New World, he was convinced that a unitary thread existed in black cultures wherever they might be found. After independence, Fonlon represented Cameroon at several international conferences of African writers and intellectuals. His experiences at these conferences remained etched in his mind and convinced him that Cameroonian problems had to be seen within the broader context of African unity and that Cameroonians, like Africans everywhere, had to become producers of their own culture. The first premise of his cultural politics was therefore the assumption that the Cameroonian nation must become an expression of authentic African values, understood and reappropriated in light of the contemporary world-historical situation.

A number of articles on Negritude appeared in the early issues of *Abbia*, and the approach of the 1966 Festival of Black Arts in Dakar stimulated considerable interest in the subject. However, several considerations prevented Fonlon from becoming an orthodox proponent of Negritude. As an anglophone from the western part of the country, he regarded the dominant French cultural presence in Cameroon as an impediment to national unity. Insofar as Senghor and other Negritude writers espoused the ideal of a francophonic community, he felt compelled to reject their internalization of typically French habits of mind.

Furthermore, his attendance at international conferences had made him aware of anglophone Africans' objections to the Negritude concept, and when he reported on these conferences in *Abbia*, he attributed the conflict to differences in terminology and emphasized the common denominator that united all the various approaches to African authenticity. Yet even when he was writing his dissertation in the late 1950s, Fonlon was primarily concerned not with resurrecting the past but with examining the black man's growing awareness of his own oppression. Already at that time he was convinced that "the life of every black man who encounters negrophobic hostility completely sums up the history of this race writhing in anguish across the centuries."[5] In other words, Fonlon was sympathetic to the arguments of Negritude critics such as Mphalele and Soyinka, who complained that an idealization of African traditions can obscure the historical realities that produced the oppression of black people.

Finally, Fonlon viewed human life in terms of perennial questions that are raised by great thinkers and artists from cultures throughout the world. He himself admitted to having found inspiration in Gandhi, Plato, Tennyson, Flaubert, Beethoven, Lincoln, Cardinal Newman, and many other non-Africans. As a result, he believed that the new nations of Africa could enrich themselves by encouraging the free circulation of ideas from other cultures. According to him, intellectuals and writers in a country such as Cameroon should winnow these ideas and relate them to their own historical situation, for in this way they keep alive the ideals of goodness, truth, and beauty that have always motivated people to imagine suitable destinies for themselves and to pursue the realization of their dreams. Fonlon regarded Negritude as a small portion of the total reality that Cameroonians needed to comprehend if they hoped to create a viable national identity.

For him, national identity is essentially a cultural phenomenon because "culture is to a nation like a soul to a man, that is, the principle of unity, of life and continuity."[6] But unlike many Negritude writers, Fonlon did not regard culture as a given that must be rediscovered; on the contrary, he saw it as a constantly evolving response to the needs and desires of the people. Every element of culture, he argued, originates in some need or desire. These needs and desires are universal, but different peoples have devised infinitely varied ways of satisfying them. Although a nation's cultural particularity resides in traditions that determine the contours of its "soul," Fonlon believed that the people of that nation can retain their vitality only if they are willing to be eclectic. "We have no choice but to borrow," he asserted, for every society evolves by drawing upon foreign ideas and adapting them to its own purposes.[7] The measure of any society's success is not the extent of its borrowings but the judiciousness and dignity with which it integrates these borrowings into its own ways of satisfying universal human needs and desires.

The ultimate goal of Fonlon's "cultural integration" is the full development of human potential. As a former seminarian, he was a profoundly religious man, and he believed that this development should occur in harmony with a divine will that gives meaning to human life. "The man who rejects God rejects the only hope of man," he wrote, "for without Him, our lot here below is but misery and despair."[8] This unshakable faith in God unifies Fonlon's thought and explains his conviction that human beings have the moral obligation to work together for the betterment of the world.

Because literature records the best that has been thought and said by people of insight and sensitivity, Fonlon regarded it as an invaluable guide in preparing Cameroonians to perform this task on the national level. According to him, education should be character formation, and literature forms character in the sense that it structures internal speech into aesthetically pleasing patterns while accustoming people to distinguish between the significant and the trivial. Seen in this light, literature is a pathway to wisdom, and as Cameroonians draw inspiration from a variety of sources to create their own literature, they are, he felt, contributing to a literate culture that will aid their fellow countrymen to realize their own potential. In this way, writers also help construct the nation in harmony with the supernatural forces that Fonlon regarded as the basis of all existence.

In practical terms, Fonlon was convinced that nation-building goals could be attained in Cameroon only under a democratic, socialistic form of government. If all people have a right to seek the fulfillment of their potential, he believed that the purpose of civil government is to guarantee all citizens equal access to the exercise of that right. And if culture reflects the ways people meet their needs and desires, the goal of a national culture should be the spiritual and material well-being of its citizens. As editor of the country's leading cultural journal, he considered it his moral obligation to defend such ideas in public, for they represented his contribution to the nation-building process. The epigraph he placed on the title page of *Abbia* reflects his conception of the journal's role in this regard:

> Not merely to recount
> what has been,
> but to share in moulding
> what should be.

By preserving a knowledge of the country's past and giving form to its dreams of the future, *Abbia* could, he felt, help nurture a literate culture that would become the "soul" of the Cameroonian nation.

Despite his support for the nation-building ethos, Fonlon's moral idealism was not always viewed favorably by the small group of Ahidjo's trusted advisers. Because he was committed to the belief that "truth is the basis of liberty," he championed the free circulation of ideas and insisted upon dealing honestly with the failures of the government in power.[9] According to him, a viable national culture requires an intellectual climate in which people can examine all sorts of ideas, drawing inspiration from those suitable for their purposes and rejecting the rest. Such tolerance was noticeably absent from contemporary Cameroonian society, and Fonlon's advocacy of it constituted an implicit criticism of the existing system.

He was more direct in his indictment of the social inequities that had arisen in the country since independence. As early as the mid-1960s, he declared: "At this stage, when the dawn of African independence is just breaking, evils which would normally come with decline and exhaustion have already overtaken us and are eating their way deep into the vitals of the body politic—corruption, embezzlement, nepotism, grasping individualism, cynical indifference to the general welfare. . . . There must be a radical reversal. Nothing short of a complete mental and moral revolution will do."[10] In his eyes, literature could help bring about this revolution, for it enabled people of good will to perform their moral duty by waging "relentless war on falsehood and wickedness, on stupidity and ineptitude sitting in high places."[11] Such socially critical comments were anathema to the authoritarian power structure that was emerging in Yaounde, and if Fonlon had not been protected by his personal friendship with Ahidjo, he would certainly have suffered for his outspokenness; in fact, he was officially reprimanded on two occasions about the supposedly subversive tenor of his essays. Yet he continued to proclaim the truth as he saw it, and his intellectual honesty contributed significantly to his legendary reputation for incorruptibility.

Fonlon was also the primary spokesman for anglophone literate culture in the bilingual republic. As a West Cameroonian who spoke fluent French, he promoted French-English bilingualism as a symbol of Cameroonian unity and as a distinctive feature of the country's national identity. Convinced that both languages should be vehicles for the expression of an authentically Cameroonian culture, he often attacked the chauvinism of the French, who offered economic assistance on the assumption that its recipients would adopt French cultural values. He also castigated the shortsightedness of his francophone compatriots who identified so intensely with these values that they lost sight of their African identity.

His own attitude is reflected in a short poem he wrote in the mid-1970s:

> I am no crusader for things English.
> I do not worship English.
> I worship Lamnso,
> But I am a plain, blunt, practical man.[12]

The poem appears in an essay that defends the use of English as a world language, a language that gives Cameroonians access to the modern world of science and commerce. Elsewhere, he had developed the argument that the mastery of two European languages could make Cameroon into a model of cultural integration in Africa and allow it to mediate between the continent's anglophone and francophone countries. When he disclaims an allegiance to English and admits his worship of Lamnso, the language of his ethnic group in the Northwest Province, he is reaffirming his belief that all people must retain a self-confident awareness of who they are, but by calling himself a plain, blunt, practical man, he is proclaiming his willingness to use English or French or any other language to express this sense of identity and to obtain what he needs in order to realize his potential.

During the years he served as government minister, editor of *Abbia*, and professor of African literature at the university, Fonlon did more than anyone else to foster the growth of an anglophone Cameroonian literary tradition. Although his own eloquent but archaic style was hardly a model that aspiring young writers could emulate, Fonlon's intellectual rigor and uncompromising pursuit of excellence inspired countless anglophone Cameroonians with a respect for literate culture. By publishing anglophone essays, short stories, and poems in *Abbia*, he encouraged his English-speaking countrymen to view their writing as an integral part of the national culture. His lectures at the university and his radio program, "University Quarter Hour," stimulated considerable interest in English-language literary activities, and he founded the English Club to promote creative writing among students. The writers' contest sponsored by this organization revealed a remarkable enthusiasm for literary creativity among anglophone Cameroonians, and Fonlon was principally responsible for drawing national attention to it.

For a few years in the mid-1960s, Fonlon played an important mediator's role in resolving conflicts between the eastern and western parts of the country, and his concept of cultural integration became a key component of Ahidjo's nation-building rhetoric. The essays Fonlon wrote at this time on national cultural policy even earned him a sizeable popular following when they were published in *Abbia* and reprinted in the *Cameroon Times*. In the public mind, Fonlon became the embodiment of Socratic wisdom in a country plagued by violent divisions, hypocrisy, greed, and social injustice. By truthfully addressing the question of national purpose and by advancing a morally honest vision of the future, he struck a responsive chord in those who wanted to believe in a national unity that transcends the cynical, self-serving attitudes of the privileged class. His advocacy of a government based on democratic socialism, bilingualism, cultural authenticity, and moral integrity made him the country's most respected commentator on cultural politics, and although his approach was eventually supplanted by the more orthodox Negritude ideology of Sengat-Kuo, Fonlon's ideas entered the public domain and contributed greatly to a popular image of what Cameroon could become if it were governed by people of integrity.

Although neither a promoter nor a detractor of Negritude, Fonlon laid the groundwork for the Negritude debates in Cameroon by drawing attention to the issues at stake in the larger conflict over African authenticity and by relating these issues to the national identity question. One of the people most responsible for familiarizing the Cameroonian public with the Negritude concept was Lilyan Kesteloot, who taught African literature for nearly a decade at the Ecole Normale. Her *Ecrivains noirs de langue française* was published in 1963 and soon became the authoritative work on the subject. She herself was personally acquainted with most of the Negritude writers, and when she presented them in her lectures and publications, her primary goal was to place them in their historical context. She also sought to demonstrate how their exposure to French culture made them aware of contradictions in the colonialist system and awakened in them the desire to reassert the dignity of black humanity.

By the time her *Negritude et situation coloniale* was published by CLE in 1970, writers such as Senghor had already come under attack, and she defends them against their critics. She points out that none of the early Negritude writers ever advocated a simple return to the past or excluded the possibility of scientific thinking; on the contrary, they had wanted to retain specific cultural values from the past to counter the overly materialistic attitudes that characterized the Western world and its impulse to colonial domination. According to her, their pride in their blackness was not a reverse racism but the prerequisite for a dialogue of reconciliation with white people who had always taken pride in their whiteness. Her concept of African authenticity was similar to that of Fonlon, and she invariably emphasized it in discussing contemporary Cameroonian writing, for she was convinced that a genuine national literature could emerge only when Cameroonians ceased imitating European models and began to forge new modes of expression from "the authentic roots of their own personality."[13]

Kesteloot's influence in Cameroon was magnified by the fact that her former students became teachers at schools throughout the country and themselves introduced younger generations to the Negritude works she had taught them. Her weekly radio program on literature and her role in having African works placed on school and university reading lists also helped disseminate information about the Negritude movement.

Actual Cameroonian disciples of the movement were invariably Christian intellectuals who embraced Negritude as a unified, essentially religious world view that could serve as the philosophical basis for a new national culture. Several of them held important government posts, and their reaffirmation of traditional values was incorporated into the official ideology at a time when the country was preparing to send academics, actors, dancers, and other representatives of Cameroonian culture to the 1966 Dakar Festival. As director of the cultural affairs bureau, Engelbert Mveng was at the forefront of this movement. His view of the world had been decisively marked by Senghor and Alioune Diop during his student days in Europe, and he remained convinced that Negritude had created an intellectual climate in which an authentic African literature could flourish for the first time.

Mveng was also a Jesuit priest, and all his writings are premised on the assumption that Christianity and Negritude are mutually reinforcing belief systems that can be integrated into a modern world view capable of sustaining a viable sense of African identity. He assumes a spiritual reality beneath the world of appearances and suggests that traditional culture gave Africans a privileged access to that reality. Christianity has the same goal, he argues, and for this reason it can supplement African religious thought by relating it to a larger context of universal love and salvation. But Mveng knows that Africans will comprehend this message only if it is communicated to them in a language they are capable of understanding. To forge such a language, he first seeks to discover the seminal genius of African culture in its history, art, music, and traditional customs. He then identifies the symbolic vocabulary in which this genius is preserved. By investing this vocabulary with a Christian message, he hopes to create an appropriate vehicle for communicating it to Africans. At the same time, he hopes to revivify an African sense of self-worth that was lost when people renounced their own forms of spirituality in favor of European ones.

To persuade Africans that Christianity is compatible with their own cultural heritage, Mveng attempts to demonstrate that the Christian message has always been latent in the African experience. In one of his poems, for example, he addresses God and claims:

> Everything told us of Your face:
> The cry of the baby in his bamboo cradle,
> The nocturnal paean of Initiates who've conquered the spirits of Death,
> And the song of nursing women, and the cry of warriors,
> And the voice of mourners by the houses, by the cradles, by the graves. . . .[14]

All the voices catalogued in this poem arise from the human soul and announce the same spiritual truth that was proclaimed by Christ. In particular,

Mveng draws attention to the sorrow of Africans mourning their dead, for he views their sorrow as an unrequited yearning to participate in the victory of life over death—the victory that, according to him, Christ made possible by his suffering on the cross. Throughout Mveng's poetry and essayistic writing, he presents monotheism, love, forgiveness, and a religious sense of life as characteristically African habits of mind. Repeatedly he cites them as evidence for the unity of African thought and its receptiveness to the Christian message.

But Mveng knows that, if this message is to reach Africans, it must be detached from the European cultural assumptions that accompanied it when it was first introduced to Africa during the colonial era. His Negritude-inspired theory of history enables him to do this by allowing him to present human experience as an ongoing conflict between good and evil. According to him, secular materialism in Europe was a corrupt influence that distorted the Christian message and supported the colonialist enterprise, but it was providential for Africans because it brought them into contact with a universal religion that overcomes the incompleteness of traditional belief systems. He therefore exhorts Africans to accept the essence of Christianity while eschewing the evil that had become associated with it in Europe. As he writes in another of his poems, "sin is more oppressive than the slave-owner on the island plantations ever was."[15] What he means is that people can be alienated from themselves more effectively by their own states of mind than by the material conditions to which they are subjected. In his eyes, the choice they have to make is whether to place themselves in harmony with the historical force of goodness or to allow the opposing force of evil to dominate them.

For him, Negritude or the characteristically African way of looking at the world offers them the best possible model for making this choice. As he points out in his *Les Sources grecques de l'histoire négro-africaine*, even the ancient Greeks acknowledged that Africans have an aptitude for the expression of religious sentiments, and throughout his writings, he identifies such sentiments with the underlying unity of African culture. He argues that African belief systems originated in the respect for life and in the desire for the triumph of life over death. As an expression of this respect, initiation rites became a crucial part of African religious practice because they introduced young people to the mystery of life and taught them to participate in the vital force that animates all things.

A knowledge of this force made Africans intensely aware of the difference between the world of reality and the world of appearances in which they were obliged to live. For this reason, they relied upon rhythm and symbols to express an awareness that could not be translated into words. In light of the perpetual struggle between life and death, good and evil, Mveng contends that Africans intuitively comprehend the appearance-reality split and the dialectic of history as givens of their destiny. Therefore, when they address the divine, they do so in a sacred language that is liturgical by its very nature.

Mveng believes this language is still admirably suited to the expression of African religious sentiments, although in his opinion it suffers from a lack that can be overcome only by an acceptance of the Christian God Who freely and lovingly assumed human form to reveal the mystery of eternal life. That Africans can know this God is, for Mveng, the beneficent result of an intercommunicating world where any culture can draw upon the wisdom of other cultures and contribute its own accomplishments to "the civilization of the universal." Like Senghor, Mveng insists that no group can participate fully in this "great fraternal dance" unless it proudly accepts its own cultural identity. If there is a single truth, he says, there are countless ways of expressing that truth in the world of appearances. Each culture has its own ways, and the inheritors of that culture will feel at home only in the symbolic language it has bequeathed to them. Mveng's literary project is thus similar to that of Senghor, for he too writes poetry in an attempt to revitalize African culture and to foster an appreciation for the riches it contains.

Mveng's poetry is often accompanied by his own drawings, and both forms of expression are modeled on his conception of African artistic creativity. According to him, traditional African artists first intuit the essential quality of the object to be portrayed; that is, they transform it into an abstraction. With the materials at their disposal, they then synthesize an aesthetically pleasing object that embodies the abstraction in symbolic form. Their work celebrates the human capacity for creative activity, but it also expresses a totalizing vision of the universe. This vision is inherently religious because it reflects an internalization of the struggle between life and death as well as the yearning toward a harmonious unity that can never be fully attained on earth. Like the Dogon fabrics into which the mysteries of life and joy are woven, his poems and drawings reenact this creative process.

The drama that pervades all of Mveng's work arises from his conviction that Africans, having lost their traditional sense of being in harmony with the universe, yearn to regain it. His poems and drawings are conceived as liturgical objects that reevoke the lost religious sentiments. Like the traditional African artist, he refuses to accept the death of the spirit and interprets the succession of generations as an example of life's victory over death. But he goes beyond the traditional artist's view of the world by suggesting that the dialectic of life and death can ultimately be transcended in a mystical union with the Christian God of love. At the heart of the new sacred language that he devises to communicate this message is the rhythm that he regards as a characteristically African response to the struggle between life and death. According to him, this rhythm defies the determinisms of the material world and clears the participant-observer's mental space for an acceptance of the divine. In conjunction with his use of symmetry and color symbolism, Mveng's emphasis on rhythm and emotivity identifies him as a disciple of Senghor.

When applied to the Cameroonian situation, Mveng's brand of Negritude leads to a utopian vision based on a religious faith in African authenticity. Defining the sense of national identity implicit in this vision entails, first of all, a detailed survey of Cameroonian history and culture to determine the essential traits of the Cameroonian personality. Mveng's own writings and his cataloguing of Cameroonian cultural artifacts during his tenure as director of cultural affairs were significant contributions in this endeavor. The second stage in this process involves the creation of a symbolic language capable of expressing this personality in conformity with its own principles of coherence. Mveng himself was pursuing this goal in his literary and artistic creations.

If such creations could reach the general public, he assumed they would trigger an awareness of the spiritual reality that lies beneath the world of appearances and unites all Cameroonians into a single community. This awareness would then presumably find expression in literary works and other artifacts that would become the foundation of a new national culture. Mveng's vision of Cameroonian unity was an extension of his Christian Negritude view of the world, and although he did not condone the totalitarian tendencies or the social inequities of the Ahidjo regime, his cultural politics proved highly compatible with the official rhetoric.

So did those of his fellow Jesuit and Negritude writer Meinrad Hebga. Like Mveng, Hebga believed that the Christian ethic of love and forgiveness remained the best foundation for creating a morally decent society in Africa, despite the fact that Africans had initially adopted Christianity in a European cultural guise that distanced them from their traditional spirituality. Also like Mveng, Hebga was convinced that Africans needed to reaffirm an identity that preserved a sense of continuity with the past, for only on this basis could they borrow intelligently from other cultures without losing their authentic nature, and only on this basis could they translate Christian principles into forms that would be truly meaningful to them.

His contribution to the definition of this authentic identity was a series of books and articles on sorcery and traditional healing practices in Cameroon. By showing how some medicine men had acquired a remarkable knowledge of curative herbs and human anatomy, Hebga established the empirical validity of their practices. He also examined their parapsychological powers and their symbolic representations of how good and evil forces influence the events of the world. His conclusion was that the close observation of nature had granted many Africans insight into spiritual phenomena that European Christians had described in different terms. For example, he explains the Ewondo concept of "evu" and argues that it expresses a profound understanding of the way evil originates in the human psyche.

He also discusses superstitions, curses, evil spells, and corrupt sorcerers because he desires to establish criteria for distinguishing between harmful cultural practices and those that should be retained because they are consistent with what is known about the world from other sources. His ultimate goal is to translate the essential message of Christianity into a system of authentically African symbols, customs, and modes of perception, for he is convinced that a genuine African Christianity could help people integrate the fragmentary experiences of modern life into a unified world view capable of reinvigorating African spirituality and channeling it into the construction of a society in which they would feel at home.

One of the most talented of Cameroon's Negritude poets was another priest, Charles Ngandé, who also believed that national identity and national culture should be expressions of the national soul. Influenced by Sengat-Kuo's "Lettre à un Camerounais," Ngandé returned home in the early 1960s after having studied at a seminary in France, and when he discovered that no one was writing the sort of poetry advocated by Sengat-Kuo, he published a programmatic essay, "La Poésie camerounaise," in the newly founded *Abbia*. In this piece, he argues that a genuine Cameroonian poet must be willing to embrace the mystic vitality of the people. Because this vitality manifests itself in history and in dimly perceived collective aspirations, he concludes that the poet's mission is to perpetuate a living memory of the past while giving concrete form to the people's dreams of the future. In other words, Ngandé's genuine poet discovers the reality of the people's soul and presents it to them in a form that enables them to comprehend themselves and to begin working toward their own liberation.

This theory of Cameroonian poetry finds expression in Ngandé's own most well known poem, "Indépendance," in which the birth of the nation is depicted in terms of the traditional ceremonies associated with the birth of a child. The period just before the birth had not been easy. In the darkness of the night, the people had lost hope and did not know where to find the grave of the Ancestor. The bird that sang the hopeful promise of life had been devoured by a python. "Where is the grave of the Ancestor to be found again," laments the poet, "in what spring can we season our blood again?"[16] His questions suggest that the people are disoriented because they have lost touch with themselves during the long night of colonial rule.

After the agonies of childbirth, however, their despair is broken by the crowing of a cock who announces the dawn of independence. Perched on the Ancestor's grave, the cock indicates the site where the people can reestablish their links with the past. The first rays of the sun reveal the spring where they can replenish their authenticity. In this new atmosphere, the poet predicts: "And in the evening we will dance around the same fire / Because together we will have brought forth / A great City above the grave of the Ancestor."[17] The poet's initial questions have been answered in a reaffirmation of traditional cultural values, and the joyful celebrations that take place at the end of the poem express the people's faith in their own ability to create a flourishing national community in the future. By fusing traditional customs with contemporary political concerns, Ngandé synthesized a symbolic language that illustrates how the Negritude theory he espoused in "La Poésie camerounaise" could be put into practice. In the process, he was reinforcing the cultural nationalism that eventually became an important part of the Ahidjo government's official ideology.

This ideology was sympathetically described in the pamphlet that Jean Calvin Bahoken was commissioned by UNESCO to write about cultural politics in Cameroon. Bahoken's approach to the task was premised on his own Negritude belief in a characteristically African way of looking at the world. When he wrote *Clairières métaphysiques africaines*, he sought to demonstrate that an intuitive knowledge of the Supreme Being forms the basis of all ontological reflection in traditional African society. Modeling his discussion of the subject on the work of Tempels and Kagame, he draws on Banen and Douala cultural practices to support his thesis. In both ethnic groups, he finds a belief in Nyambe, a benevolently omnipresent force that creates order in the universe. According to their image of the world, man or "muntu" is a subordinate force. The purpose of his existence is to penetrate as far as possible into the mystery of life and to place himself in conformity with the will of Nyambe, Who can never be approached directly but only through the symbolic mediation of prayer, divination, and a lifestyle harmoniously attuned to the social and natural environment. For believers, Bahoken explains, this mediated contact with the Supreme Being is experienced as an influx of force that fulfills their existence and transforms it into a joyful celebration of life.

Although Bahoken draws attention to parallels between Nyambeism and Christianity, he does not view African spirituality as the steppingstone to a more universal religion. On the contrary, he argues that African religion has an independent identity that permits it to enter into dialogue with other religions and, ultimately, to contribute its share of wisdom to a universal religion of peace and brotherhood. Although Bahoken was one of the few Protestant supporters of Negritude in Cameroon, the linkage of cultural authenticity and national destiny in his pamphlet on cultural politics reflects the same mystical faith in a latent Cameroonian community as that expressed by Mveng, Hebga, and Ngandé.

After 1965 the most vocal Cameroonian proponent of Negritude was the literary critic and university professor Thomas Melone. Although he was not a priest, Melone had attended the major seminary before studying in France and coming into contact with the *Présence Africaine* group. In any case, he retained an essentially mystical understanding of the world, and Senghorian Negritude became a surrogate religion for him. As a proselytizer for this religion, he exercised considerable influence over students who later rose to prominence in the country's literary and intellectual life, and he consistently promoted a cultural nationalism that reinforced the basic thrust of the Ahidjo government's official rhetoric.

Melone's real contribution to the Negritude debate was his attempt to transform Senghor's epistemology into a critical methodology capable of generating new insights into literary texts and other cultural artifacts. His early book *De La Négritude* laid the groundwork for this enterprise. Essentially a commentary on Senghor's conception of black consciousness, it defines what Melone regards as characteristically African modes of thought and perception. Even Negritude itself, he argues, must be approached in its own terms and not through the distorting lens of European rationality. What he means is that black consciousness can be understood only by those who project themselves into it and intuitively grasp its essence.

According to Melone, this process begins when black people abandon themselves to the object of their perceptions in an act of spontaneous enthusiasm. Having momentarily become one with the object, they seek to preserve the fleeting insight they have achieved into its inner reality, but they can do so only by silencing their rational faculties and by relying on a flight of imagination. When critical intelligence intrudes on the vision produced in this way, they are menaced with a despair that they habitually counter with instinct. Their Negritude emerges in the emotions they feel in the dialectic between enthusiasm and despair, vision and rationality. This process culminates in a new understanding of the self and in a sense of solidarity with others who can perceive reality in the same fashion. During the first stage of the Negritude movement, this mode of perception resulted in anxiety because, Melone argues, colonialism systematically suppressed black consciousness. However, once Africans had attained independence, he believes this consciousness could provide them with the basis for a national society in which they could assume their Negritude without contradiction.

But not without duality, for Melone realizes that Africans must also employ linear, analytical modes of thought to cope with the practical problems confronting them. He cites Senghor's Chaka as an illustration of the dilemma posed by this situation because "for Chaka the West represents the source of the principles that inspired his protest but also the obstacle he must destroy to achieve happiness."[18] Senghor had transformed the historical Chaka into a Negritude hero whose aspirations for the freedom and material well-being of his people originated in his awareness of European models. However, as Melone points out, the only way Senghor's Chaka can preserve the essence of his people's authentic identity is by opposing the physical intrusion of Europeans and the dominance of their dehumanizing approach to life. Melone contends that the solution to this dilemma is a willingness to embrace duality, as the early Negritude writers did when they appropriated the term *nègre* with all its connotations of ugliness and transformed it into a vision of beauty and poetic intensity.

According to Melone, the acceptance of duality enables Africans to become aware of something they lack and to formulate a wish for overcoming it. When they express this wish in literature, they generate a state of consciousness that possesses both them and their readers. Characterized by an intuitive insight into the unity of all things, this state of consciousness places people into contact with an absolute purity that transcends all earthly contradictions. Although the moment of insight cannot be sustained in a world of transitory appearances, it sanctions hope for those who must deny their blackness as defined by Europeans in order to reaffirm it in a form suggested by their desire. Under these circumstances, Melone believes that the African "will flee from the real to take refuge in the essential."[19] In this way, the words of authentic African writers acquire mystical qualities that allow them and their readers to overcome death through communal participation in a redemptive vision that remains inaccessible to European rationality.

Melone believes that such writers have given expression to the message of the black race. It is a message of hope for humanity, for it reveals modes of thought and perception that enable Africans to feel at home in the world while entering into dialogue with people from other cultures. Such a dialogue would be as beneficial for Europeans as for Africans, he argues, because these modes of thought and perception complement those of Europe. In fact, Melone believes that the example of black consciousness could contribute significantly to the spiritual well-being of everyone in a world menaced by overreliance on linear, analytical thought and materialistic assumptions about the nature of life. Like Senghor's "cultural cross-fertilization," Melone's definition of the Negritude message represents an attempt to overcome the legacy of colonialist oppression by promoting a new spirituality based on a reaffirmation of traditional Africa values.

Inspired by the Senghorian epistemology he described in *De La Négritude*, Melone drew upon French structuralism and psychoanalysis to develop a critical approach that he considered uniquely appropriate for the analysis of African literary works. The first premise of this approach is the assumption that African texts can be fully appreciated only when they are restored to the cultural context that permeates them and legitimizes the authority of their discourse. According to Melone, African critics are singularly well equipped to perform this task because they share points of cultural reference with the authors of such texts and because they have the capacity to grasp the meaning of an African text in the same intuitive, global fashion that was used to create it.

His model for this approach is the circle of listeners at the telling of an oral tale. Just as they participate in the creation and critical evaluation of the story, critics reconstruct and judge the writer's imaginary world. As critics take the text apart and put it back together again, they add supplementary information to bridge the spatio-temporal gap between author and audience—a gap that did not exist in the case of the oral story-teller. By projecting themselves into the text and allowing its rhythms to pulsate in them, African critics can, according to Melone, experience the inner reality of the text in the same way the traditional story-teller's audience grasped the inner reality of the tale being told.

Once African critics have obtained insight into a literary work, Melone believes their task is to help others experience it as fully as possible. Because there is always a gap between what authors wrote and what they intended to write, Melone is even convinced that genuine African critics can reconstruct the intended meaning of texts and restore their wholeness by sympathetically identifying with the imaginary worlds created in them. For example, he argues that all authors leave signatures in their work. These signatures are actually complex interweavings of personal motivation and the collective genius of the culture in which the author is embedded. If critics can identify this collective genius and render it accessible to others, they can authenticate the author's text in the eyes of its readers by enabling them to recognize themselves in it. When critics make it possible for readers to participate in re-creating the author's fictional world, they revitalize the written word by establishing, as

Melone suggests, an equivalent for the scene of the oral story-teller's performance.

Melone's *Mongo Beti, l'homme et le destin* was the first scholarly book to be written on a Cameroonian writer, and it provides a good example of how his Negritude critical approach functions when applied to actual literary texts. By projecting himself into the imagined worlds of Beti's fiction, Melone claims to have intuitively grasped their global significance. On the basis of his empathetic understanding, he proposes to fill the gaps in Beti's novels by reconstructing what the author intended to write. Intention in this case does not necessarily imply conscious purpose; in fact, Melone's thesis is that Beti's Negritude spoke through him, even though he himself did not realize it. To substantiate this idea, Melone argues that the signature in Beti's writing bears witness to a rediscovery of the "realm of childhood." Although Beti repressed a conscious awareness of this experience, it provided him with a clue to his own authentic nature, and he supposedly wrote his novels out of a subconscious desire to preserve the Negritude identity he vaguely sensed in himself.

According to Melone, the real power of Beti's fiction derives not from any overt political ideas in it but from the authenticity of the African world view that is embedded in it. This world view manifests itself in many different guises: the emotivity of Beti's characters, their intuitive understanding of situations, their mystical bond with nature, their sense of community, the rhythm of their speech, and the traditional wisdom of the common people. Beti himself never professed allegiance to this world view, but Melone contends that the Cameroonian novelist felt the lack of what he would have recognized if he had verbalized the insight offered him by his rediscovery of the realm of childhood.

To compensate for this lack, Beti allegedly envisioned a "perfect city" that incarnates the harmonious unity described by Tempels and Kagame as the goal of human life in Bantu belief systems. Melone asserts that all Beti's young heroes have the emotive sensitivity to repudiate the imperfect colonialist society in which they are imprisoned, but they fail to reach the perfect city because they merely wait for the intervention of a cosmic force to bring it into being. In other words, they do not accept the inevitable duality of life because they never successfully undergo an initiation that might have integrated them into a genuine African society. As a result, they become restless, frustrated individuals with dysfunctional personalities, and having lost the sense of being at home in the universe, they yearn for an unattainable perfection. Melone thus explains the ambiguous endings of all Beti's early novels on the basis of a "failed initiation" that prevents the young protagonists from embracing their own Negritude.

By extrapolating his interpretation of Beti's work into the real world, Melone concludes that the themes of failed initiation and unattainable perfection are actually expressions of Beti's alienation from an authentically African existence. According to him, Beti was never fully initiated because he never consciously adopted the authentic identity implicit in his rediscovery of the realm of childhood. Similarly, Melone argues that, as long as Beti's vision of the perfect city is not nuanced by an acceptance of duality, it remains an evasion of contemporary social problems.

Melone's interpretation of Beti's character has important ramifications for Cameroonian cultural politics because he is suggesting that all Africans have an essentially mystical identity. Although they might refuse to acknowledge it, it is an inescapable part of their nature and will find ways of expressing itself, just as Beti's Negritude supposedly manifested itself in spite of his conscious repudiation of it. Such an understanding of authenticity implies that national unity is simply an awakening to the latent brotherhood of people who share the same mystical view of the world. In light of this overarching goal, a socially critical approach that dwells upon the institutional and material causes of oppression can be dismissed as a preoccupation with the inessential, and this is precisely what Melone does with regard to the political content of Beti's novels. That this approach lends support to Ahidjo's nation-building rhetoric becomes apparent at the end of the book when Melone attacks Beti for refusing to admit that the abuses of the colonial period no longer exist in a Cameroon that, he claims, is moving toward a "perfection that asserts itself each day."[20]

This optimism with regard to the contemporary Cameroonian situation was an integral part of the government's ideology, especially after the former militant student leader and Negritude poet Sengat-Kuo became a principal adviser to the president in the mid-1960s. An admirer of Senghor and a protégé of Alioune Diop, Sengat-Kuo had been book review editor of *Présence Africaine* for five years during the 1950s, and he was largely responsible for introducing a Negritude slant to Ahidjo's speeches and official party pronouncements. In becoming a government functionary, Sengat-Kuo never completely abandoned his earlier revolutionary sentiments. He simply channeled them into a new faith in the nation-building process. For him, the world was still divided into oppressors and oppressed, but within the context of a politically independent Cameroon, he was convinced that the true liberation of the people could be realized only through constructive work. If the chief motivation for working toward the common goal of a prosperous, self-respecting nation is hope, Sengat-Kuo believed that the poet and the politician have a responsibility to inspire the people with hope and to galvanize them into action by helping them become aware of who they are and what they can become.

When he published a poetry volume, *Collier de cauris*, in 1970, Sengat-Kuo felt he was fulfilling the same responsibility that he had assumed in his public life. The title of his book, "A Necklace of Cowry Shells," suggests that he is stringing together the mundane words of everyday reality and transmuting them into objects of inestimable value. Each poem in the collection revolves around an image that embodies a sustaining ideal of black consciousness. The image can be a person, a place, or a thing, but it invariably reinforces a Negritude consciousness that assumes the unity of black experience, the need for cultural authenticity, and the dream of a future prefigured in the attitudes of heroic black personalities such as Senghor, Chaka, Martin Luther King, Myriam

Makeba, Louis Armstrong, and Mario de Andrade. Although individuals die, their ideals survive in the hearts of others. As Sengat-Kuo suggests in his poem about King, the image of the black American's raised fist outlives his assassination, for it has become a cowry shell in the necklace that symbolizes the rich heritage of black consciousness.

According to Sengat-Kuo, the colonial intrusion destroyed a preexisting sense of harmony in Africa, and the task of newly independent countries such as Cameroon was to restore that harmony. In his earlier open letter to Pouka, he had alluded to a proverb about a tree that could aspire toward the sun only by plunging its roots deeply into the ground. He revives this image in *Collier de cauris* to support his contention that the lost harmony of Africa can be recovered only if people reaffirm the values embedded in traditional customs. In the poem "Au Masque," for example, he celebrates his own experience of this insight when he recognizes the beauty of an African mask that Europeans had conditioned him to regard as ugly and primitive. Gazing at the mask, he found "myself in front of me."[21] In other words, his encounter with the traditional past revealed his own identity to him. Similarly, in the joyful dancing of the people he sees the model for an authentic African society, which he imagines as the "unrestrained dance of virile men."[22] In this dance, Sengat-Kuo prophesies, Africa's lost harmony will once again prevail.

In a Cameroonian setting, Sengat-Kuo's Negritude translated into a joyful sense of working with others to realize the promise of national independence. He believed that those who engaged themselves in this enterprise would become part of a community that transcended the sum of their individual identities. His eulogy to Ahidjo in *Collier de cauris* illustrates this conception of the nation-building ideal. He presents the Cameroonian president as a traditional hero who demonstrates the courage, ingenuity, grace, and majesty necessary to forge a new unity from the cultural diversity of the country. Yet throughout the poem, Sengat-Kuo employs the conditional tense, claiming that he would sing Ahidjo's bravery in subduing the tiger or praise his skill in taming the parrot if he were a griot. The ambivalence of this syntactical pattern suggests that the real Ahidjo might not possess these traits but that he symbolically represents a national ideal with which the people can identify. The image of Ahidjo is crucial to the nation-building process, Sengat-Kuo concludes, because it embodies the hope that motivates Cameroonians to work toward a utopian future.

The last major apostle of Negritude in Cameroon was the geologist and poet-musician Samuel-Martin Eno Belinga. Profoundly influenced by Senghor, Alioune Diop, and Cheikh Anta Diop, Eno Belinga sought to reconcile scientific pragmatism with mystical vision and the power of love in a world view that reflects both his respect for traditional African belief systems and his Catholic faith. This world view is an elaboration of Senghorian Negritude, and Eno Belinga believed it offered his countrymen their only hope of overcoming the cultural crisis from which all of Africa was suffering. After returning to Cameroon in the late 1960s after many years of study in France, he attacked

Senghor's critics for having reduced Negritude to a caricature. He insisted that Senghorian epistemology is not antirational but rather a necessary complement to European modes of thought and perception because emotivity, an intuitive grasp of essences, a holistic vision, and a receptivity to the rhythmic patterns of life can produce a richer, more fully dimensioned understanding of reality than can be obtained through an exclusive reliance on linear, analytical approaches to knowledge.

In his *De L'Authenticité négro-africaine*, Eno Belinga posits the existence of a black "logos" that embraces asymmetry because it tolerates differences without reducing them to polar oppositions. According to him, the world view implied in this "logos" is non-Aristotelian in the sense that it conceptualizes the world as a spectrum of graduated differences within a global unity rather than as a congeries of material entities that can be understood in isolation from one another. The organizing principle behind this world view is not linear logic but rhythm—rhythm in sound, movement, line, and color. Senghor argued that such qualities are intuitively experienced by Africans who project themselves into the objects of their perception, and Eno Belinga carried this argument a step further by proposing that modern scientists could profit from looking at the world in the same way.

As an example of how the black "logos" subsumes diversity into a larger unity through the use of rhythm, Eno Belinga cites the Bamun caduceus or two-headed snake. By comparing the organization of this traditional design with the movement of subatomic particles and the transmission of neural impulses, he demonstrates the congruence that exists between the way an African artistic symbol is constructed and the nonlinear behavior of phenomena that are just beginning to be understood by contemporary scientists. Eno Belinga's point is an important one, for if he could prove that Senghorian epistemology represents a scientifically valid approach to knowledge, he would be rebutting many of Senghor's critics who claimed that Negritude was incompatible with scientific and technological progress.

Eno Belinga's world view is a profoundly religious one that assumes the existence of a unifying Absolute beneath a superficial reality of illusory appearances. Three influences helped shape this assumption. As a child, he became familiar with the Bulu Bible that was read in his Protestant grandmother's house, and even then he was impressed with the way Christ's enigmatic parables were immediately comprehensible to those who had already accepted the truth of his message. Years later, he came to believe that poetry could function in the same way.[23] The second major influence on Eno Belinga was the Catholic mysticism he embraced as a young man, and the third was the Bulu belief system that he began to appreciate fully only during his stay in Europe.

A talented musician who plays the *mvet* and collects Bulu oral epics, he is intimately familiar with the possibilities of oral poetic performance—its playfulness, its educative value, and its role as a cohesive force in traditional society. According to Eno Belinga, the words of the *mvet* singer are "born of a single planetary breath" because the singer allows the people's sense of universal harmony to express itself through him.[24] His own verse employs *mvet*-like rhythms and sonorities to fulfill the same prophetic function because Eno Belinga views poetry as a vehicle for allowing the Absolute to speak through him and to provoke a heightened sense of awareness in his readers.

His individual poems can always be traced back to an encounter with another person, an object, or a set of circumstances. Each encounter is similar in the sense that it leads to the same truth—an intense experience of his own existence at a moment when he is harmoniously attuned to the mystery of the Absolute. In many cases, his encounters have been with women, and his poems about them bear witness to the possibility of momentarily escaping from the alienating, fragmented world of appearances. Each contact with another person serves as a catalyst that triggers an awareness of the mystery inside him. Once he opens himself to this mystery, he intuits a larger mystery that courses through him and lends unity to all that exists. It is as if the presence of the other person generated a field of light that permits the poet to realize that he is a privileged being in an inexpressibly beautiful world. Having penetrated beneath the arbitrariness of surface appearances, he composes poems in response to the creative urge that the feeling of divine harmony has evoked in him.

This process is a major center of focus in Eno Belinga's first collection of poems, *Masques nègres*. Like the lover and the traditional carver of masks, the poet at the center of this volume experiences luminous moments of unity with the Absolute, and these moments give birth to a godlike urge that can find satisfaction only in shaping fragmented, chaotic materials into forms capable of evoking analogous sentiments in others. The collection itself was inspired by an exhibit of African masks in Paris. The Bulu word for mask is *Eyema*, which derives from the verb *yem* (to know). Reflecting on this etymological relationship, the poet realized that, although the mask hides the face of its wearer, it reveals the wisdom of its maker. Embedded in the culture of the people, this wisdom expresses itself in a dialogue between the creative impulse of the inspired woodcarver and the telluric force of the wood he is carving. The result of his work is a symbolic object that celebrates life but can be fully understood only by those who have been initiated into the culture.

Each poem in this collection functions like a mask, embodying the knowledge of a concealed truth and inviting people to the celebration of life. "A song as silent as time, / And, in these faces the cosmic / Pulse of the hidden world."[25] In this poem, the mask and the poem are like the world created by God. Their rhythm is the cosmic pulse of time, and they testify to the underlying spiritual reality that found expression in the creative impulse of their makers. For anyone who knows how to read them, they communicate an experience of the ineffable Absolute.

The poet in *Masques nègres* has an unquenchable desire for this experience, but his own weakness and the imperfection of the material world repeatedly thrust him into despair. The experience for which he yearns is possible, but only because he already believes in a spiritual reality beneath the world of appearances. It is faith that sustains him in his moments of despair—"in darkness faith sings of hope."²⁶ His encounters, especially his encounters with women, open his heart to this experience by awakening his capacity to love, and love enables him to penetrate to the core of existence, whereas his rational faculties had merely permitted him to know the surfaces of things. By producing a state of consciousness that is in harmony with the Absolute, the act of love becomes an act of knowledge, and this knowledge is embodied in the poem he writes on the basis of his experience, although this knowledge will be accessible only to readers who already share Eno Belinga's faith in a mystical realm of truth.

Like the carver of masks, Eno Belinga's poet is guided in his creative efforts by an intuitive grasp of an underlying unity: "Wisdom is fair / And force wise: / Strong is beauty."²⁷ When these qualities emerge in a poem or in a mask, they imply a knowledge of the Absolute, but because the Absolute cannot be represented in concrete terms, this knowledge can be evoked only in symbolic form. Just as Eno Belinga felt possessed by a feeling of awe in the presence of the masks he saw in the Paris exhibit, the readers of his poems are expected to feel a sense of wonder in the face of an experience that is inexpressible in words. In the ever-changing world of appearances, love and the creative impulse are presented as having redemptive value in *Masques nègres* because they grant access to the wisdom, force, and beauty that are reconciled on a higher plane of truth.

Eno Belinga's support for the Ahidjo government was an extension of his poetic and philosophical principles into the sphere of politics. In his favorable account of recent Cameroonian history, *La Révolution pacifique du 20 mai 1972*, and in his second volume of poetry, *Ballades et chansons camerounaises*, he implies that a head of state can create a new nation in the same way a poet creates a poem. Just as the effect of his own poetry depends upon his readers' willingness to accept his assumptions about the nature of reality, he argues that Ahidjo's vision of national unity can be realized only if the people have faith in it, and because he himself has this faith, he exhorts them to share it with him.

In *Ballades et chansons*, he depicts the people and the countryside of Cameroon as a complex totality that tends toward the condition of music and beauty. By projecting himself into this totality, he claims to feel its "obligatory rhythms" pulsating in him. His poems about Cameroon resemble his earlier work in the sense that his encounter with the nation produces a state of consciousness that places him in harmony with a larger spiritual entity, in this case the unity of the country and its people. For him, this unity is an ultimately mysterious expression of the Absolute, and he is like the *mvet* singer who allows the spiritual reality of this unity to speak through him. It is this spiritual reality that generates his utopian vision of a society where love, freedom, and justice flourish. However, when Eno Belinga invites his readers to celebrate a knowledge that is supposedly latent in them, he is assuming they share his mystical Negritude view of reality. In actual practice, his concept of a Cameroonian spiritual identity lent support to the government's nation-building rhetoric at a time when the ideals it promoted stood in stark contrast to the realities of everyday life for most of the country's citizens.

By the time he published *La Prophétie de Joal*, Negritude had become seriously discredited in Cameroonian intellectual circles, and after Melone left the university, Eno Belinga became its principal spokesman. Having already linked the nation-building concept with an underlying cosmic unity, he expanded his vision in these poems to encompass all of Africa. The encounter that occasioned them involved a giant shell that he discovered while walking on the beach at Joal in Senegal. Joal is the birthplace of Senghor, and Eno Belinga adopted the name to designate the Africa he imagined during a vision he experienced while listening to the message of the shell. As in his earlier poetry, he presents himself as a seer and the object of his contemplations as an expression of the Absolute.

La Prophétie de Joal is organized around three major themes: the authentic heritage of Africa's traditional past, the momentary loss of that past during the colonial period, and the ideal city that Africans can construct in the future if they remain faithful to the values of their ancestors. Comparing African history with the Tower of Babel story, Eno Belinga suggests that traditional culture was moving toward the ideal city when the "master" became angered. During the centuries of his anger, Africans were sold into slavery, their land was occupied by strangers, and the wisdom embedded in their culture was forgotten. Under these circumstances, the poet-prophet keeps alive the vision of the ideal city and urges his fellow Africans to rededicate themselves to its construction:

> Let us erect the ark that pierces the clouds, for the ark
> Is the great abode in the land of the rising sun
> The great abode on which the kingdom of Joal is built.[28]

By relating traditional African culture to the Hebrew ark of the covenant, he is intimating that this culture houses a knowledge of the Absolute, and by exhorting his readers to help reconstruct the ark, he is suggesting that the ideal city of the future can be built on the traditional values of the past.

The poem culminates in a radiant image of the ideal city. Its four pillars —wisdom, force, beauty, and mystery—are already in place, but it will be completed only if Africans reaffirm their authentic identity and work intelligently toward the realization of its potential. To comprehend the grandeur of this goal, however, people need to have faith:

> The prophecy of Joal
> Is one, cannot be proven
> Like the song of the kora, music for
> The heart cannot be proven.[29]

As conceived by Eno Belinga, the authentic poetry of Africa aspires to the state of music. It does not present a rational argument. On the contrary, it is a symbolic object capable of triggering an emotional response during which readers experience a truth that is inaccessible to reason. Eno Belinga once wrote that it is urgent for his readers to rediscover a "taste for the eternal." His own world view is permeated with this taste for the eternal. It provides the rationale for his defense of an embattled Negritude concept and explains his allegiance to Ahidjo's nation-building rhetoric.

During the early 1970s Senghor vigorously reaffirmed his belief that cultural authenticity was a precondition for healthy economic and social development in Africa. When a conference was organized on this topic in 1971 at Dakar, the Negritude concept was staunchly defended by a number of speakers, including Mveng, Melone, and Eno Belinga. In Cameroon itself, Negritude reached the apogee of its influence and public visibility two years later when *Présence Africaine* collaborated with the Ahidjo government in sponsoring an international colloquium to commemorate the tenth anniversary of the University of Yaounde. Organized by Melone, the colloquium focused on the critic as a producer of African culture and clearly demonstrated the Ahidjo government's commitment to the Negritude concept.

In his opening remarks, the Cameroonian minister of information and culture announced that Negritude was the necessary starting point for the creation of an Africa in control of its own destiny. Although Alioune Diop was unable to attend the colloquium, he addressed an open letter to its participants. In the letter, he argued that Africans must become interpreters of their own culture rather than allowing others to interpret it for them. For this reason, he concluded that "the African critic holds the key to the future of Africa in his hands."[30] By linking the future of Africa with a Negritude appreciation for traditional values, both men lent support to the cultural nationalism that had become an integral part of the official ideology in Senegal and Cameroon. The rapprochement between the two countries was appropriately symbolized by Melone's dedication of a Festschrift to Ahidjo and to Senghor, who delivered the keynote address at the colloquium. In presenting the volume of essays on black writing to the two presidents, the chancellor of the university eulogized them for having established a sane equilibrium between traditional culture and modernization. In a political sense, the 1973 colloquium marked the apparent triumph of the Negritude position in Cameroon.

But this triumph was short-lived. The following year Melone left the university in a dispute over salary disparities between French expatriates and Cameroonians with equivalent titles and responsibilities. A spate of newspaper articles about cultural authenticity appeared in the mid-1970s as the country was preparing to send a delegation to the FESTAC celebrations in Nigeria; however, Melone's departure from the scene and Mveng's resignation as director of cultural affairs diminished the influence of Negritude on Cameroonian intellectual and political life. Sengat-Kuo and Eno Belinga continued to play important roles in the government, and cultural authenticity retained its central place in Ahidjo's cultural politics, but Negritude itself gradually faded into the background and came to be regarded by most educated Cameroonians as a historical phenomenon with little relevance to the problems of development in contemporary Africa.

Nevertheless, Negritude exercised a crucial influence over the national identity concept that was taking shape in Cameroon during the 1960s and early 1970s. Through a direct participation in formulating the government's cultural policies and by means of their own writing, Cameroonian adherents of Negritude reinforced the idea that the country was a latent spiritual community with a utopian potential. The underlying assumption was that this potential can be realized only if the people of the country accept a spiritually based conception of their African authenticity—an authenticity that can presumably be recuperated by pursuing a deeper understanding of the values embedded in traditional culture.

This commitment to authenticity rests on an essentially religious attitude toward life. It is hardly accidental that all Cameroonian proponents of Negritude had been profoundly influenced by Christianity. As early as the 1940s Tempels had pointed out the compatibility between African belief systems and a Christian view of the world; in fact, he regarded this compatibility as proof of his contention that Africans are philosophically predisposed to accept the Christian message. Especially after the Vatican Council in 1960, the churches themselves began to incorporate African forms of cultural expression into their services as a means of revitalizing the practice of Christianity on the continent. Mveng and Hebga were prominent spokesmen for this movement.

They and other Cameroonians presented Negritude as a mystical approach to reality, and this mysticism became part of the national identity concept espoused by the Ahidjo government. By promoting an ideology based on the assumption that a latent national community exists beneath the level of surface appearances, the government created a rationale for arguing that the unity and harmony of this community must be established before the material conditions of existence can be improved. Opponents of the Ahidjo regime countered that such an ideology was merely part of a hypocritical scheme to divert attention from the corruption and social inequity of the existing system. If the often heated debate between critics and defenders of Negritude had a profound impact on Cameroonian print culture during the 1960s and early 1970s, it was largely because this debate was also a conflict between opposing definitions of national identity.

CHAPTER
10

THE ANTI-NEGRITUDE
MOVEMENT

In the early 1960s socially engaged writers in Cameroon had already begun to attack Negritude as an irrational concept that diverted attention from the economic causes of poverty and oppression. They argued that national identity was not an essence to be discovered in the cultural practices of the past but a potential that could be realized only by working in the material world of the present to bring about a socially just society in the future. For them, the way to truth was not a mystical experience of the Absolute but a rational probing of concrete reality. In practice, the Ahidjo government did not abide by the Negritude principles it gradually incorporated into its official rhetoric. By espousing them in theory, however, it created a widely perceived gap between ideology and reality. As a result, criticisms of Negritude often functioned as veiled attacks on the existing situation in Cameroon.

The approach of the 1966 Festival of Black Arts in Dakar provoked several APEC writers into publishing statements against the Negritude identity concept that had inspired the historic event. The most articulate of them was the organization's executive secretary, René Philombe. Responding to Charles Ngandé's Negritude prescription for an authentic Cameroonian poetry, Philombe argued that any attempt to impose a single world view or source of inspiration upon all the country's writers would stifle creativity rather than foster it. According to him, a viable literary tradition can arise only when writers are free to choose the style, subject matter, and ideological content of their works. Confining writers to traditional ways of looking at the world and seeking to eliminate foreign influences would, he thought, merely narrow their horizons and oblige them to falsify their actual identities, which had been irrevocably changed through contact with a cosmopolitan, modern world.

Convinced that common people should be able to participate in a Cameroonian national literature, Philombe rejected the example of the early Negritude writers on the grounds that they had cultivated an esoteric idiom comprehensible only to a small elite readership. In his opinion, a poet could best contribute to the emergence of a national literature by speaking to the people in a vocabulary they can understand and by lending expression to their "profoundest aspirations and most sacred dreams."[1] When he employed the word *sacred* in this context, he was referring not to mystical intuition but to the people's yearning for freedom and dignity. A literature that translates this yearning into concrete form and awakens people to the need for a "cultural revolution" would correspond to his idea of a truly national literature. He concluded that Negritude is incapable of sustaining such a literature, for despite its professed concern for authenticity, it is the expression of a deeply conservative impulse that in practice tolerates the economic and cultural dominance of Africa by the former colonial powers.

The APEC novelist Rémy Medou Mvomo repeatedly attacked Negritude as "a dangerous dogma, a new form of alienation that lays a foundation for the neocolonialist penetration of Africa."[2] It is dangerous, he believed, because it locks Africans into a narrow range of fossilized ideas and ignores the economic and political factors that contribute to the ongoing oppression of Africans. For this reason, he sees Negritude as an impediment to the flowering of African cultures that would occur if they opened themselves to the eclecticism of modern international civilization. He baptized this approach "cultural pragmatism" and contended that, in contrast to Negritude, it would have attained its goal when Africans defined themselves no longer as black people but simply as people in the modern world.

Medou Mvomo asserted that traditional African societies were organized to perpetuate a specific way of life. When they fell victim to the spread of European colonialism, this way of life collapsed, and according to him, it is better to confront the anxiety caused by its collapse than to avoid it by fleeing into an idealized version of the past. For this reason, he suggested that Cameroonians should accept the existing situation and construct a new identity based on the real possibilities of the present. If Europeans had learned to control the environment for their own material well-being, he felt Africans should borrow what they needed from Europeans rather than seeking to rediscover it for themselves. Convinced that it is more important to plan for the future than to meditate on the past, he frequently cited postwar Japan to illustrate how a modern national society could be created by adopting European technology and retaining a distinctive cultural identity. Because he assumed that Africans cannot escape modernity, he concluded they should exploit the opportunities it offers and forge a practical culture without worrying about its authenticity.

Although the political views of Philombe and Medou Mvomo differed, both felt that Negritude was actually inauthentic in the sense that it failed to take the historical reality of contemporary Africa into consideration. Representatives of the UPC were even more critical of Negritude on these grounds. In *L'Economie de l'ouest africain*, for example, Osendé Afana denied there is an essence that distinguishes Africans from other people. For him, basic human needs and aspirations are everywhere the same, and if they are not being satisfied, people have the moral obligation to seek a rational understanding of the conditions that thwart their satisfaction.

In Cameroon, he argued, these conditions include the institutional and psychological mechanisms by means of which foreign interests collaborate with the local privileged class to exploit the majority of the people. According to him, the most urgent task facing the country was not a rehabilitation of traditional values but a consciousness-raising campaign that would enlighten people about the mechanisms of their own oppression and help them discover scientifically valid ways of satisfying their own needs. Viewed from this perspective, Negritude becomes an obscurantist myth that prevents people from comprehending the truth about their own situation.

Philombe, Medou Mvomo, and Osendé Afana rejected Negritude on the basis of its irrationalism, its hostility to technological progress, and its tolerance for social injustice. By the mid-1960s such criticisms had become relatively common in Cameroonian intellectual circles, and several writers undertook the task of adapting the Negritude concept to contemporary circumstances. The most prominent of these revisionists were Jean-Marie Abanda Ndengue, who coined the word *Negrism*, and Basile-Juléat Fouda, who introduced the term *Negrity* into the debate. Devout Catholic intellectuals who had spent considerable time in France, both Abanda Ndengue and Fouda wanted to preserve the spiritual aspects of Negritude while placing greater emphasis on scientific thinking and technological progress. They claimed to have transcended Negritude, although in reality their systems differed little from that of Senghor. However, by publicly promoting their ideas about cultural authenticity, they helped launch the Negritude debate in Cameroon.

In a series of lectures that were later published in the Catholic weekly *L'Effort Camerounais* and reprinted as *De La Négritude au négrisme*, Abanda Ndengue defined Negrism as the marriage of African values and modernism for the moral, intellectual, and spiritual liberation of black people. Rather than rejecting the Senghorian position, he assimilated it into his system, pointing out that Negritude's origins in European anthropology illustrate how a more humane attitude can result from the interpenetration of cultures. Abanda Ndengue argued that the recently independent countries of Africa needed to go one step further by opening themselves completely to European science, technology, and humanistic thought while at the same time taking stock of their own traditions to recover the spiritual values embedded in them. The Negrist approach thus synthesizes a new style of life by drawing upon the Negritude reverence for the past, the European cultural heritage introduced to Africa during the colonial period, pragmatic approaches to the solution of current problems, and the utopian dreams generated during the decolonization process.

The unifying factor in Abanda Ndengue's eclecticism is his respect for the sanctity of the human person. In the context of national independence, this attitude translates into a desire for traditional ethnic values to be applied on a much broader scale. For example, he suggested that the palaver of the ethnic group could be expanded into a national dialogue that would allow women as well as men to participate in the decision-making process. And if characteristically African traits—such as the capacity to live in harmony with the rhythms of life and the willingness to accept the unalterable givens of existence—could be integrated into a new national identity, he was convinced that technological progress might occur in an orderly fashion without occasioning the spiritual death that afflicted so much of European civilization. By adopting this newly synthesized national perspective, he implied, Cameroonians would become capable of creative engagement in an ongoing dialogue with people from other cultures.

Fouda's Negrity also involves the search for a revitalized African culture that would embrace both modern technology and the European ethos of purposeful work without renouncing traditional African spirituality. Although he dismissed Negritude as a "narcissistic senility complex," his own views remain firmly within the Senghorian tradition.[3] According to him, Negrity begins with the recognition that Africa is in a state of crisis, for the contemporary African is like a schizophrenic Janus condemned to gaze toward Europe and Africa at the same time. To overcome this anguished split, Fouda argued, Africans must realize that traditional belief systems evolve in response to specific historical circumstances. When these circumstances change, people's mentalities change with them, but if they desire to know themselves, they must maintain continuity with their own cultural heritage. By regarding African character as a flexible, organic structure capable of assimilating all the influences that impinge on it, Fouda believed Africans can adopt scientific modes of thought without relinquishing their past. In fact, he regarded this conception of character as a basis for transcending the fatalism of traditional African society while preserving its humanizing features.

According to Fouda, these features include both rationality and intuition in forms that reflect the history of Africans' attempts to understand the world in which they were obliged to live. Opaque and deterministic, this world confronts people with an unknowable immensity that contains the mystery of their own being. Yet people cannot simply resign themselves to the harsh arbitrariness of the world; they must exercise their freedom to create their own way of life. As Fouda declared, "man must make himself or disappear."[4] The result of this creative enterprise is culture, and culture varies greatly as it comes into being in different environments. By analyzing myths and folktales, Fouda demonstrated that traditional culture promoted rational attitudes of self-reliance in the affairs of daily life while at the same time fostering a respect for the unknowable.

Like Tempels and Kagame, Fouda defined existence in terms of a unitary force that gives rise to all the subsidiary forces in the universe. According to him, human reason is incapable of comprehending these forces, although their meaning can be intuitively grasped in symbols that express the collective wisdom of people whose cultures have evolved in a constant dialectic with the surrounding world. Preserved in oral literature, art, and religion, these symbols permit contemporary Africans to overcome the schizophrenic split in their historical situation by recognizing that the possession of things is less important than being in harmony with the underlying forces of nature and society. Negrity is thus a religious philosophy that draws upon traditional belief systems while remaining fully compatible with Fouda's Catholic mysticism as he proclaims the reconciliation of duality in a transcendent Absolute.

In his opinion, this philosophy provides the most appropriate psychological basis for economic and social development in Cameroon because it respects the interplay of forces that define the country's global identity. Fouda situated this identity in a field of choices and actions that occurred as the Cameroonian people forged their own cultures in a never-ending struggle with the surrounding world. The historical equilibrium that had existed before the arrival of Europeans was disrupted, but according to Fouda, the Cameroonian field of choices and actions continued to evolve according to the trajectory it had been following at the time, and he was convinced that the European influence could simply be incorporated into this trajectory. Within such a context, the nation is like "a vantage point inserted into a flexible, structured network of spiritual forces and meanings."[5] He therefore concluded that the basic objective of national development should be to place the country in harmony with the historical trajectory that defines its teleological goal. Negrity resembles Senghorian Negritude in this sense, for it too proposes to discover national identity in a pre-existing spiritual reality.

But Fouda also stressed the fact that the people of the country could not acquire this identity by passively waiting for it to manifest itself. They would have to synthesize it from the materials available to them, and they would have to work purposefully toward its realization. For example, Fouda claimed that Europeans had historically emphasized the Promethean urge to domesticate nature, whereas Africans had pursued the Apollonian impulse to utilize their rationality as an instrument for placing themselves in harmony with nature and society. During the colonial period, European technology entered the Cameroonian field of choice and action. It therefore became available for the solution of concrete problems in the present, and Fouda argued that using it to eliminate poverty would be compatible with the historical trajectory of a country where people have always had a highly developed sense of communal welfare. By placing African culture into a living, dialectical relationship with European culture, Fouda formulated a utopian vision that, like the ideas of other Cameroonian Negritude thinkers, resembled the unfulfilled promises of the Ahidjo government.

Also like the proponents of Negritude, Fouda envisaged a universal dialogue of cultures to which Africans could contribute their interiority and their intuitive understanding of the mysterious force at the center of all existence. Echoing Senghor's "civilization of the universal," he proposed a future colloquy of cultures and referred to it as a "civilization of the rose-window."[6] What he meant is that each culture would retain its own color and shape while fitting harmoniously into a larger unified pattern—like the individual pieces of glass in the rose window of a Gothic cathedral. As this example illustrates, Fouda often borrowed the ideas of Negritude and described them in slightly different terms. In reality, neither Negrism nor Negrity differed in any significant way from Negritude. Nevertheless, they were important because they represented a reformulation of the Senghorian position from a Cameroonian point of view and an attempt to salvage its spiritual definition of national identity at a time when Negritude was under assault as an impediment to progress.

During the late 1960s and early 1970s, Melone's impassioned support of Negritude and Fouda's strident defense of Negrity elicited responses from Cameroonian intellectuals who refused to accept the irrational premises on which philosophies of cultural authenticity were based. This opposition was particularly strong among philosophers at the university, and two of them— Marcien Towa and Ebenezer Njoh-Mouelle—eventually became the leading spokesmen of the anti-Negritude movement. Towa in particular attracted considerable notoriety for his public attacks on Senghor, whose version of Negritude he characterized as "the quasi-official ideology of neo-colonialism, the cement for the prison where neo-colonialism intends to imprison us."[7] According to Towa, Negritude and its offshoots Negrism and Negrity were politically reactionary religious systems that facilitated the exploitation of Africans by blinding them to the truth about their own situation. In light of Ahidjo's Negritude-influenced cultural politics, such contentions were often seen as veiled criticisms of the Cameroonian government.

Towa's primary objection to Senghorian Negritude involves its unphilosophical approach to truth. He pointed out that Senghor and his followers elevate assumptions about the existence of God, the essence of blackness, and the cogency of traditional belief systems to the level of absolute truths without subjecting them to rational analysis. Such a strategy is philosophically untenable, he argued, because the most basic human value is freedom, and freedom can be preserved only by a willingness to question all first principles. Strongly influenced by Hegel's emphasis on freedom and rationality, Towa criticized Negritude for relying on nonrational modes of cognition that remain inaccessible to those who do not already believe in its first principles. A philosophically defensible position should, he felt, be presented as a clearly formulated sequence of ideas that can be understood by any rational individual.

Towa also objected to Senghor's brand of Negritude on the ground that it is a racist escape into an imaginary world. It is racist, he contended, because it embraces the racial assumptions of early twentieth-century European anthropologists who believed that race determines culture. According to Towa, these assumptions are highly unscientific, and in the form promoted by Senghor, they condemn black people to perpetual inferiority by characterizing them as emotional, intuitive individuals who lack the rational faculties to master the intricacies of modern science and technology.

Furthermore, Towa felt that Senghor's Negritude is escapist because it draws inspiration from an idealized image of traditional society as recalled by the Senegalese president in his nostalgic memories of a happy childhood at

Joal. In Towa's eyes, this idealized image enabled Senghor to ignore the actual relations of dominance in the contemporary world and to avoid a recognition of the contradiction between his allegiance to Africa and his attachment to France. Even his concept of cultural cross-fertilization betrays a desire to flee the truth, for Towa suggested that Senghor imagines the redemptive qualities of blackness to compensate for Africa's lack of anything practical to offer in exchange for the political power, scientific knowledge, and literate culture of Europe. The real problem confronting contemporary Africa is, according to Towa, the need for people to gain rational control over their own destinies. Imaginary worlds like Senghor's realm of childhood prevent them from doing so by blinding them to the oppressiveness of existing conditions and by persuading them that they lack the capacity to change these conditions.

For Towa, the genuine liberation of Africa will occur only when people comprehend their present dependency in rational terms and devise pragmatic strategies for overcoming it. Because he was convinced that Senghor's emotivity and intuitive modes of knowledge are inadequate to this task, he exhorted Africans to embrace their own rationality, which is not a European attribute but a generically human potential. If Europeans developed science and philosophical speculation to a highly sophisticated degree, it behooves Africans to incorporate this sophistication into their own way of looking at the world. But rather than subordinating themselves to the economic and political ambitions of foreign interests, Africans should exploit this newfound sophistication to acquire the power that will enable them to work toward goals they have set for themselves or, as Towa declared, to regain the historical initiative they had lost. In his opinion, this approach to African identity is the opposite of religion, for it is no more than rational thought applied to concrete problems by Africans seeking to free themselves from oppression and ignorance.

Because Towa believed that a proper understanding of the present required a rational analysis of the past, he refused to accept the Negritude assumption that the true significance of traditional culture could be appreciated only by intuitive or mystical means. He thought people should investigate the practical consequences of traditional customs to determine their strengths and weaknesses. The reasons for Africa's vulnerability to European penetration must be explained, he felt, so that contemporary Africans can turn the secret of European hegemony to their own use: "only the destruction of traditional idols will enable us to adopt and assimilate the spirit of Europe, the secret of its power and of its victory over us."[8] If Europeans have dominated Africans culturally, politically, and economically in the past, it seemed to Towa that the only reasonable course of action is to acquire the intellectual and physical power to prevent them from doing so in the future. Asserting one's right to be black or seeking to restore the values of the past will do nothing to change existing relationships of dominance and oppression. Only power will permit Africans to overcome the tyranny of the present, and Towa was convinced that power could be acquired only through the use of reason.

Behind Towa's critique of Senghorian Negritude is a revolutionary ideology that drew inspiration from the works of another Negritude writer, Aimé Césaire. Whereas Senghor fled into an imaginary world in which the Zulu military leader Chaka could be transformed into a poet who announces a new world order based on the acceptance of black cultural values, Césaire recognized the need for oppressed peoples to acquire power and to liberate themselves through the agency of a rationally organized struggle in the material world. For Towa, Césaire's position offered Africans the possibility of regaining the historical initiative, which the Cameroonian philosopher regarded as a prerequisite for the flowering of any authentic culture. "What we need above all is freedom," he argued, "because with freedom, a true freedom, our originality will emerge of its own accord."[9] The exercise of this freedom implies that people have the power to make the decisions that affect their destiny, and because many Cameroonians felt they have been denied this power, Towa's advocacy of concrete revolutionary action proved particularly attractive to a generation of disaffected young people.

Although Towa never overtly criticized the Ahidjo government, his general statements were clearly applicable to its policies. For example, Towa argued that there is no preexisting unity of organization in Cameroonian society to serve as the basis for a viable national identity concept. He acknowledged that an identity crisis exists because people are aware of having lost their traditional sense of themselves, but rather than resurrecting the past, he asserted, people need to recognize what had been missing in traditional culture to make it susceptible to collapse. The first task of nation building would then be to remedy this lack so that people can rationally address the problems confronting them. Like Fanon, Towa concluded that national identity must constantly be reforged in the process of struggling with these problems.

Contrasting this approach with Senghor's cultural nationalism, Towa declared:

> National identity—an avatar of Negritude—is not a given; it is not an eternal, immutable essence. It will not magically appear by virtue of the incantations to which the black intelligentsia has abandoned itself for nearly half a century. It will be the unstable and always incomplete result of our theoretical and practical efforts to revolutionize our current situation of weakness, poverty, and other-directedness and to constitute ourselves into a living national entity. . . .[10]

According to this conception of national identity, Cameroonians were behaving irrationally when they defined themselves in terms of an idealized past, for only in the process of confronting their common problems and pursuing their common aspirations can they discover who they are. They would be acting rationally if they sought to determine the most effective solutions to these problems and then chose to implement them. By exercising their freedom in this way, Towa suggested, they would be regaining the historical initiative and affirming their real identity. For young people who felt stifled under Ahidjo's authoritarian regime with its Negritude-influenced cultural politics, such an approach offered the promise of liberation, and that is precisely why the government later imposed restrictions upon his right to address public audiences.

Although Njoh-Mouelle never acquired the notoriety that Towa enjoyed both inside and outside the country, his thoughtful critique of Negritude also functioned as a negative commentary on the existing situation in Cameroon. Like Towa, he reproached Negritude for being unphilosophical and irrelevant to the present concerns of Africans. He regarded both the Negritude movement and the traditional world views it sought to rehabilitate as products of a particular historical moment, not as expressions of a nonexistent black essence. In the face of colonialist attitudes toward Africans, he argued, it made sense for the early Negritude writers to proclaim the legitimacy of their cultural heritage and to depict the existential situation of black people in the contemporary world. However, a respect for the African past and a convincing rejoinder to white racism cannot provide an adequate basis for economic and social development in postcolonial Africa. The difficulty with Negritude arose, he concluded, when its proponents reduced the multifariousness of traditional culture to a single ahistorical world view and made it the touchstone of African authenticity.

According to Njoh-Mouelle, Africans had been imprisoned in a world of superstition and irrationality before the arrival of Europeans. In other words, they had been subject to the false determinism of their own ignorance. European colonialism imposed another false determinism on them. To liberate themselves from such false determinisms, Njoh-Mouelle contended, Africans need to adopt the rational, scientific approach to knowledge that Europeans had brought to Africa. As he said, "those who fail to master science and technology are exposing themselves to domination and enslavement in all their many forms."[11] What he meant is that a rational, scientific attitude would enable Africans to repudiate images of reality that allow them to be exploited by others. Such an attitude would also enable them to implement appropriate strategies for realizing goals they set for themselves.

From Njoh-Mouelle's perspective, Negritude is a false determinism because it seeks to impose on people an identity they do not feel. What was originally a slogan for awakening black people to their own alienation became a pseudophilosophy incapable of providing solutions to the practical problems that must be solved if Africans hope to become masters of their own fate. And what was originally a declaration of cultural independence became an acknowledgment of Africans' dependency on others for the accomplishment of their own development goals. The Bantu philosophy formalized by Tempels and Kagame is, Njoh-Mouelle contended, even less capable of sustaining development in Africa because it is the expression of a socio-economic organization that no longer exists. Besides, it often sanctioned beliefs that are no longer tenable in light of modern scientific knowledge. "A traditional African value that rests on a foundation of ignorance and superstition is not a value," he asserted. "Conserving it can only contribute to the stifling of Africans."[12] For Njoh-Mouelle, then, Negritude and its idealization of traditional belief systems are ultimately harmful because they reinforce stereotyped notions of African irrationality and divert attention from the real problems of developing countries.

In contrast to Towa's revolutionary socialism, Njoh-Mouelle's alternative to cultural nationalism is a meritocracy based on the "man of excellence." Influenced by Nietzsche and Bergson, Njoh-Mouelle assumed that, because there is no inherent meaning in the world, all people are responsible for forging their own identities and striving toward the realization of their own potential for excellence. Relating this project to African development, he began by distinguishing between "having" and "being." Most development programs are designed to give Africans possessions that others already have. In Njoh-Mouelle's opinion, this orientation distorts African priorities because, according to him, the primary goal of development ought to be an improvement in the quality of existence, not an increase in the quantity of possessions. As he himself declared, "man should be the end purpose of all development."[13] And when he used the term *man*, he was referring to the "being" of the individual.

"Being" in this sense implies a constant state of becoming or, rather, of overcoming obstacles. Njoh-Mouelle rejected all philosophical positions that hold out the promise of permanent happiness because he believed that the goal of human life—the complete realization of one's own potential—could never be reached. As a result, any willingness to be satisfied with a static happiness would be equivalent to the acceptance of mediocrity or the death of the spirit. If all development is self-development, as Njoh-Mouelle contended, then Africans should abandon stereotyped conceptions of themselves and assume responsibility for creating their own future in a process that ceases only with death. The reward for committing themselves to this process will be neither possessions nor a guarantee of permanent happiness. It will be the joy they experience in the exercise of their own creative faculties.

Njoh-Mouelle's man of excellence exemplifies this motivation when he undertakes any initiative in the world around him. His first step is to detach himself momentarily from the progression of historical events in order to comprehend their principles of organization. After repudiating all false determinisms and all clichés, he conceptualizes what he would like to accomplish. He then reinserts himself into the course of events so he can mold them in conformity with his idea of what they should be. The final step in this process requires work—an overcoming of the obstacles that nature and society oppose to the realization of his project. By countering such resistance, the man of excellence gains self-knowledge and experiences the pleasure of giving material form to an idea of his own conception. Because such actions threaten the status quo, the man of excellence runs the risk of antagonizing the most powerful people in society, but it is a risk he must assume if he hopes to realize himself.

The acceptance of this risk is the price of freedom, and freedom is the only state in which the man of excellence can thrive, for it allows him to make optimal use of his capacities in the ongoing process of raising himself above the false determinisms of nature and society. According to Njoh-Mouelle, freedom can never be given to anyone because it is a conquest that must be renewed each day. Even if not all people can attain the excellence he associated with creative activity in the realm of freedom, he was convinced that the recently independent countries of Africa would remain mired in mediocrity unless they could find ways of institutionalizing the conditions under which men of excellence can emancipate themselves and demonstrate to others that "having" should be placed in the service of "being."

The ideal society for Njoh-Mouelle is one in which excellence can flourish. According to him, all human beings have the rational and creative abilities to superimpose a state of law and culture on a state of nature, but for them to achieve excellence as a group, they must sublimate their instinctual selfishness and establish a social order that assures all individuals the freedom to realize themselves without infringing on the freedom of others. Such an order would encourage people to use their talents in creative, socially beneficial ways, and it would define personal relationships in terms of "being with" other people rather than "possessing" or dominating them. Njoh-Mouelle's utopian dream is not a society from which the elite have been eliminated but a society in which every citizen has become a member of the elite.

If this dream appears quixotic in contemporary Africa, Njoh-Mouelle refused to abandon it, insisting that people can realize it if they are willing to engage in a massive educational effort. The key to his concept of institutional reform is inculcating in everyone a commitment to the ideal of individual excellence. As he himself admitted, "the man of excellence cannot be excellent except insofar as others recognize him as such, that is to say, recognize themselves ideally in him."[14] What he meant is that the man of excellence should become the behavioral model for others to emulate. Implied is Njoh-Mouelle's conviction that the good society is one that has eliminated false determinisms and created an atmosphere in which people are free to develop their abilities in creative and humanly rewarding ways.

When Njoh-Mouelle's utopian vision is compared with existing conditions in Cameroon, it becomes evident that his critique of Negritude and his conception of human development are implicit commentaries on the pervasiveness of corruption, the obsession with stability, the lack of freedom, the stifling of talent, and the frenetic pursuit of wealth in his own country. Under such circumstances, Njoh-Mouelle concluded, neither a reaffirmation of cultural authenticity nor an authoritarian government can promote a viable national identity. According to him, the people of a country develop a sense of communality when they are free to pursue their individual proclivities for excellence. If their attempts at self-realization are continually frustrated, as in Cameroon, Njoh-Mouelle was convinced that national identity would remain a hollow concept with no real meaning for the people.

Because proponents of Negritude generally supported the cultural nationalism of the Ahidjo government and opponents tended to be obliquely critical of the existing system, discussions of the Negritude question attracted considerable public attention at a time when people had little or no opportunity to express their discontent openly. Senghor's visits were calculated to enhance the prestige of the Cameroonian president, but they also linked Ahidjo's cultural policies more closely with the Negritude concept.

As interest in the controversy grew, the École Normale hosted a series of Wednesday night lectures and discussions on the topic. CLE published a dozen books on Negritude and related issues. Most of them were written by Cameroonians. Philombe resurrected *Cameroun Littéraire*, and it became a forum for the discussion of questions raised by the debate. He himself reiterated his belief that African creative expression had to be rooted in the sufferings and aspirations of the people, not in any imagined racial essence. In his mind, those who quibbled over various forms of neo-Negritude were guilty of intellectual masturbation.[15] Towa dismissed them as ethnophilosophers. François Minyono-Nkodo devoted a university thesis to "Negritude and Narcissism." Rumors began to circulate that the government would close the philosophy department at the university and silence some of the most articulate spokesmen for the anti-Negritude position.

In this charged atmosphere, over a thousand people jammed into the auditorium at the Ecole Normale to attend a 1971 roundtable discussion among some of the principal adversaries in the Negritude debate—Melone, Abanda Ndengue, Fouda, Towa, and Njoh-Mouelle. Each explained his own position, and the audience participated animatedly in an ensuing discussion that lasted for several hours. Despite Melone's spirited defense of Negritude, there was a general feeling of disenchantment with Senghor's concept of a characteristically African world view, and some former proponents of Negritude publicly expressed their reservations about it.

For example, Jean-Baptiste Obama had once presented himself as "an ambassador of Negritude."[16] During the discussion that followed the roundtable, he cautioned people against imprisoning themselves in a movement that defined itself in opposition to something else, and although he reiterated his belief that a deeper knowledge of the African cultural heritage would enable people to reach a higher level of consciousness, he felt that, once they had attained this consciousness, they should be able to live their identity without having to reassert it *ad nauseam*. If there was a perceptible shift away from Negritude among popular audiences in Cameroon during the early 1970s, the issues at stake in a debate conducted largely by literary critics and philosophers continued to concern large numbers of people because they, like Obama, were personally affected by competing definitions of the national community to which they belonged.

After the 1971 roundtable, the criticism of Negritude redoubled in Cameroon. The well-known anti-Negritude philosopher from Benin, Stanislas Adotevi, visited Yaounde and reaped applause from his youthful audience when he proclaimed that Negritude was dead and deserved to be buried. The Cameroonian sociologist Jean Mfoulou delivered a "Requiem pour Dame Négritude." The literary critic Simon Mpondo offered a series of public lectures in which he attacked the Negritude tendency to regard all African literature as a vehicle for the expression of a single world view. Mpondo found Melone's prescription for an authentic African literary criticism to be psychologically implausible, and he condemned the coinage of terms such as *Negrism* and *Negrity* for blurring distinctions rather than clarifying them. By advocating reforms that would place African works at the center of the university's literature curriculum, he hoped to broaden the scope of literary study to include more than the European canon introduced by the French and the Negritude approach being promoted by Melone.

But no substantial reforms were made in the curriculum, partly because the Cameroonian authorities had become aware that literary and philosophical discourse could serve as a vehicle for the expression of political dissent. In response to the situation, the Ahidjo government encouraged the institutionalization of critical approaches that would focus more on cultural authenticity than on social justice. Government sponsorship for the 1973 conference on the African critic as the producer of civilization was part of this campaign, and sanctions imposed on Towa, Philombe, and other representatives of the anti-Negritude movement were designed to stifle opposing critical views. On an official level, Negritude seemed to have prevailed in Cameroon during the early 1970s, but many people regarded it with the same skepticism that colored their attitudes toward Ahidjo's nation-building rhetoric. After Melone left the university, the controversy subsided, and by the mid-1970s Negritude was no longer a burning issue for most Cameroonian writers and intellectuals.

A few years later, Hubert Mono Ndjana, a teacher and editor of the news magazine *Objectif*, published *L'Anégritude*, which might well serve as a postscript to the entire debate. Drawing heavily on the arguments of Towa and Njoh-Mouelle, Mono Ndjana denied the relevance of race to the discussion of African identity in the modern world. He described his project as the deconstruction of Negritude, Negrism, Negrity, and all other racially based authenticity movements on the ground that they ignore irreconcilable differences among traditional world views and seek to impose an oversimplified synthesis of them on all Africans. He also objected that the racial characteristics Senghor attributed to Europeans or Africans are actually qualities shared by people everywhere. In a sense, Mono Ndjana carried the original Negritude reaction against white racism to its logical conclusion by defining his own philosophy as the negation of Negritude.

According to Mono Ndjana, the real danger of Negritude lies in its monopoly over the media, the school curricula, and the publishing houses that determine the image of Africa held by millions of people on the continent. He felt that even the Negritude-inspired Africanization of Christian church services contributed to this monopoly by reinforcing a falsely romanticized conception of African cultural unity. According to him, this image of Africa even translates into the stereotyped scenes of village life that dominate Cameroonian theater with its countless portrayals of "bald-headed, asthmatic little old men crouching around a calabash of palm wine or a kettle of magical decoctions, munching on an eternal mouthful of kola nuts and spewing out a jumble of local proverbs that the author probably lifted from some specialized anthology. And that's supposed to be the quintessence of Negro-African culture."[17] By making the superstition, ignorance, and poverty of village life into inherent characteristics of the African personality, Mono Ndjana argued, writers in the Negritude tradition were avoiding the real issues that confronted the nation. He proposed to replace it with a new attitude, a "creationism" that would draw upon people's rational faculties and emphasize productive work as the only path to economic and social development.

By the mid-1970s the Negritude debate had run its course in Cameroon, but it continued to represent a crucial moment in the country's attempt to define itself as a nation. It opened a channel for the questioning of basic assumptions behind the Ahidjo government's cultural politics, and it identified the questions that would have to be answered if the country was to develop into a truly unified state. Both Negritude and anti-Negritude attitudes were utopian in the sense that they promulgated visions of what their spokesmen felt Cameroon could become. The government was a party to the debate because of its identification with the Negritude position, and the alternative utopian visions of anti-Negritude writers were among the few public criticisms of official government ideology during the 1960s and early 1970s. These debates profoundly influenced Cameroonian print culture, and because advocates as well as opponents of Negritude assumed that the people of the country were facing a common destiny, they reinforced the impression that a Cameroonian national identity was emerging in the network of shared references that such discussions helped establish.

CHAPTER

11

LITERATURE AND
THE PURSUIT OF THE SELF

With expanding educational opportunities and a rise in literacy, the number of writers in Cameroon multiplied rapidly during the 1960s, and as the unifying cause of anticolonialism receded into the background, literature increasingly became a vehicle for the expression of highly personalized views of the world. Feelings of solidarity with the newly independent country and an underlying fear of government reprisals prevented many Cameroonians from openly criticizing social inequities as the best writers of the colonial era had done. Besides, the conservative editorial policies of Présence Africaine and CLE, the two major publishers of francophone African literature at the time, militated against the emergence of a socially engaged literature in any of the former French colonies.

In a political environment where people were expected to show respect for an official rhetoric that many of them regarded as a hypocritical sham, writers often turned inward to find inspiration in their sense of themselves. Throughout the 1960s and early 1970s, Cameroonian poetry and fiction displayed a strong autobiographical strain. And as younger writers translated their own most deeply felt concerns into literary form, their preoccupation with individual identity became a dominant theme in the country's literate culture.

Several factors contributed to the rise of individualism in Cameroon. European-style schooling conditioned young people to regard themselves as individuals in competition with each other, and their familiarity with European assumptions about the autonomous self made them intensely aware of arbitrary limitations on their own dreams of self-realization. Modernization and the movement of rural populations toward the cities weakened traditional identity concepts and accentuated the tendency for people to pursue individual rather than communal goals. The very act of writing novels and poems reinforced the notion that individuals have unique sensibilities that deserve to be recorded for their own sake. However, in an authoritarian society wracked with political tensions, corruption, and vast disparities of wealth, the new individualism often produced the same anxiety and alienation that plagued contemporary European culture. Individualistic attitudes also clashed with basic assumptions of traditional society, and much Cameroonian literature of the early independence period betrays the ambivalence with which people viewed this conflict.

If the communal nature of traditional society seemed to offer an alternative to the anxiety and alienation of modern society, it also inhibited the freedom of young people to seek happiness on their own terms. However, modern Cameroonian society itself often proved a major obstacle to the self-realization that many young people had come to regard as the principal purpose of life. Since the new writers tended to be from the younger generation, the autobiographical materials they incorporated into their works generally reflected a yearning for freedom from social forces such as the traditional customs that frustrated their desires for self-realization in romantic love. Such pressures also originate in corrupt modern practices that block young people's attempts to exercise their talents in a meaningful, productive fashion. In either case, individuals were depicted as struggling against hostile circumstances to assert their right to an identity they felt inside themselves.

The definition of individual identity has been a major preoccupation of writers from all over the world since the beginning of the modern era. In fact, the spread of literacy encourages reflection on the nature of the self because writing is a solitary activity that makes people into intermediaries between their own consciousness and the universe of discourse available to them for the production of texts. Furthermore, each text preserves the unique sensibility of the person who composed it. Once people recognize that texts can function in this way, they begin to employ them as a means of recording their individuality. The novel and the poetry of the European Renaissance bear witness to this tendency, and when the same literary genres made their appearance in Africa, they served a similar purpose.

The concept of selfhood was not totally foreign to traditional society, but a new way of conceptualizing it became possible with the introduction of the written word and the assumption that every self merits attention for its own sake. In postcolonial Cameroon, as elsewhere in the contemporary world, fiction and poetry often focused on the personal experiences of people seeking to find an appropriate place for themselves in modern society. The result was a literature that foregrounded a consciousness of individual identity—its uniqueness and its potential for self-realization. The existential anguish that often characterizes this consciousness suggests that the problems confronting self-definition in the mass societies of Europe and America have also become dominant concerns in modern African countries such as Cameroon.

For the generation of Cameroonian writers who came into prominence after 1960, the quest for identity generally took the form of a meditation on the meaning of personal experience. François-Borgia Marie Evembe's *Sur La Terre en passant* provides a good example of this approach to the literary portrayal of Cameroonian reality. The novel's central character, Iyoni, recognizes how an overemphasis on the material dimension of human life has produced a society dominated by greed, pretention, and indifference to the suffering of others, but he persists in believing that people have a spiritual capacity that enables them to create a genuine community based on love and trust. Although Iyoni is eventually crushed by the corrupt society and betrayed by his own weakness, his struggle to uphold an ideal so impresses those who know him that, even after his death, he remains alive in their memories as an example of the human spirit's yearning to refashion an imperfect world. In fact, the narrative pretext for the story is an anonymous friend's desire to record Iyoni's life so that others might appreciate the unusual quality of the young man's character.

What distinguishes Iyoni from other people is his refusal to compromise with the prevailing standards of value in a decadent society. Having come to Yaounde in the expectation of receiving a responsible position from the government minister Nkilviagah, he fell victim to a mysterious illness that causes his body to eject clots of blood and horrible chunks of decaying organic matter. Because he has no money, he relies on friends for the basic necessities of life, and as he awaits the promised employment, he is repeatedly humiliated by people who refuse to acknowledge his need for help. Nevertheless, Iyoni has the imagination to conceive of a better, more humane world, and he has the force of character to work toward its realization. His models are Christ, the man of love, and Napoleon, the man of action. Christ offered people the vision of a community based on love and compassion, and Napoleon demonstrated the willpower necessary to create a just society in which careers would be open to all people of talent. Iyoni synthesizes their examples into an idealized image of what the new nation could become, and by seeking a government position, he hopes to help realize the promise of this image.

Thrust into a hostile, repulsive world, Iyoni senses the uniqueness of his individual consciousness and the value of the ideal with which it is imbued. Like the hero of Evembe's unpublished novel *Un Nègre épars*, he reasons that, "because there is nothing but ugliness and horror all around me, my mission as a *Heimatlos* is to pursue the perfection and authenticity that the established lie has put to flight."[1] Iyoni is a "man without a homeland" in the sense that the ideal community toward which he aspires has not yet come into being. The authenticity he seeks is not the Negritude essence of blackness. On the contrary, he realizes that, because there is no inherent meaning in the world, he must forge his own identity in the ongoing dialectic between his dreams and the material conditions of existence.

The difficulty arises when Iyoni proves too weak to overcome the obstacles that lie between him and the realization of his dream. Burdened by the suspicion that he is incapable of attaining the identity he has imagined for himself, he feels ashamed. His name literally means "shame" in the language of his native Kribi. Because he does not want to appear ridiculous in the eyes of others, he always tries to maintain a dignified pose, but his body often refuses to obey his commands, and he is overcome with shame at the impression he makes. He is ashamed of his poverty and dependency, and he is ashamed that he has accomplished nothing at an age when Napoleon had conquered half of Europe, but most of all, he is ashamed of being ashamed.

To avoid succumbing to this shame, Iyoni must continually struggle against two forces that threaten his idealism—self-doubt and the pervasive corruption of society. The illness that afflicts him plays an important symbolic role in the novel, for by depriving him of control over his bodily functions, it momentarily convinces him that he is like a factory whose production lines have broken down. However, to maintain his belief in the spiritual dimension of life, he must uphold the conviction that he is more than a mechanically functioning body that ingests food and expels a variety of disgusting wastes. He overcomes this reductionist image of himself by an excerise of will, but the self-doubt it engenders in him menaces his faith in his identity as a man capable of commitment to a transcendent ideal.

As a suffering human being, Iyoni offers a choice to everyone whom he encounters. Most choose to ignore him, and some even go out of their way to humiliate him, but each time he is rebuffed, his will to continue the struggle grows weaker. A scene near the end of the novel illustrates the relationship between his physical illness and the treatment he receives from others. Seeking to find solace from depression, he attends Mass at the Yaounde Cathedral, but when he faints, no one comes to his aid. After leaving the church, he stumbles and falls in the street, where a policeman accuses him of public drunkenness and kicks him in the small of the back. This beating and the indifference of the churchgoers contribute to the breakdown of Iyoni's body and spirit. As a result, he suffers a relapse. While he is recuperating, friends and colleagues ignore him, but as soon as his appointment to an important position in Nkilviagah's ministry is announced on the radio, they besiege him with solicitude. A short time later, he dies, the victim of a disease that has social as well as physiological causes.

The Cameroonian society in which Iyoni lives is largely unreceptive to his idealism. In the frenetic pursuit of wealth and status, most of the people he meets have repudiated the qualities that might enable them to participate in a productive, compassionate, morally responsible national community. They pretend to be other than they really are, and they speak in clichés. However, a few individuals respond to Iyoni's example, and some even help him. They give him the courage to pursue what he regards as his mission on this earth—helping others realize what life could be like if it were not distorted by hypocrisy, greed, and egotism. When he dies, his death signifies not only the body's failure to continue functioning on a mechanical level, but also a loss of faith in his ability to realize his image of himself. In a society where the masks and lies of others prevail over his ideals, shame and hopelessness conquer his will to live. But he does have an impact on those who remember how his idealism preserved a human quality that most people repress.

The life of Iyoni is an implicit commentary on many of the larger issues confronting Cameroonian society. His experiences reveal the corruption that is eroding the moral fabric of the newly independent country. They also illustrate the dubiousness of Negritude claims about the redemptive value of the black experience. As Iyoni's tragic fate demonstrates, modern Africans have no special dispensation from suffering and death. In fact, they are in the process of creating social systems that increase rather than diminish suffering in countries such as Cameroon. In light of such circumstances, Iyoni's life acquires an exemplary value. Despite the pain that overwhelms his consciousness, the corruption that demoralizes him, and the cruelty of others, he has the courage to believe that a better world is possible. The scatological details that have repelled some readers of *Sur La Terre en passant* must be seen within the context of Evembe's desperate hope that the humiliation and suffering they represent are not inevitable and that a change in people's mentalities can bring about the just, humane society that seemed to have been promised by independence.

Like Evembe, Rémy Medou Mvomo and Mbella Sonne Dipoko drew heavily upon autobiographical materials to express their intense preoccupation with self-definition. As Sonne Dipoko admits: "In autobiography we reap / Searching in the field of our past days."[2] Both he and Medou Mvomo recorded their personal quests for freedom and identity by projecting their own experiences and states of mind into the fictional characters in their novels. They rejected Negritude as incompatible with the modern world. Medou Mvomo's "cultural pragmatism," for example, addresses what has become the central question for many young Cameroonians: how can talented, energetic individuals realize their potential in a society that constantly blocks their initiatives? He himself believed that people need freedom to express themselves in creative ways, not prefabricated identities that the government or the guardians of African authenticity were seeking to impose on them.

Sonne Dipoko argued that the self-conscious quest for authenticity is a contradiction in terms because authenticity can be found only in the un-self-conscious experience of one's own being. He admitted that the Negritude response to white racism was a necessary step toward the liberation of black people, but he thought the movement ultimately foundered on its nostalgia for the past and its propensity for racial stereotypes that were as confining as those of the former colonizers. For him, the Negritude belief in a characteristically African mentality was also irreconcilable with modernization. But he felt that the most damning argument against Negritude was the failure of its advocates to remain committed to their own utopian visions once they assumed power in the newly independent countries of Africa.

His own dominant concern was with liberation—the liberation of individuals to experience the full intensity of life and the liberation of oppressed peoples to live in accordance with values they determine for themselves. When he became convinced that Negritude was a major obstacle to both sorts of liberation, he publicly broke with the editors of *Présence Africaine* and wrote a poem to explain his reasons for doing so:

> . . . the black colour of our skins
> And a common ancestry are not enough

To hold us together
For in Africa today
The class struggle is real indeed
And I have comrades beyond the colourline
And there are black oppressors who need interminable elegies to the past;
And there are black oppressed and exploited who need the future.
I stand by the latter against the former.[3]

His stance in this poem is unequivocal: social justice and human decency are goals that transcend racial solidarity, and the pious pretense of identifying with the past is often exploited by Africans to hold other Africans in bondage. In an earlier piece, Sonne Dipoko had written that "the art of writing in the hands of liberated men is a decisive weapon."[4] Throughout his own career, he repeatedly used this weapon to defend his own concept of freedom.

Both Medou Mvomo and Sonne Dipoko created fictional characters whose experiences and dreams resemble their own to the extent that their novels constitute thinly veiled self-portraits. At the center of these novels is a single dynamic individual who seeks freedom from arbitrary social constraints so he can realize the potential he senses inside himself. These fictional characters are talented men who desire to reconcile intense individual experience with a sense of community. However, their values place them in conflict with society, a situation that often engenders a profound sense of isolation. By projecting themselves into these characters, Medou Mvomo and Sonne Dipoko recorded the uniqueness of their own sensibilities and implicitly advocated a modern conception of selfhood.

Although both authors were profoundly influenced by their years of study in France, Medou Mvomo eventually returned to Cameroon, whereas Sonne Dipoko remained in Europe as a self-exiled Bohemian writer and artist. If Medou Mvomo's world view reflects the frustration of living in a society that offers few outlets for the exercise of his creative talents, that of Sonne Dipoko evolved in an ongoing struggle to reconcile his counter-culture passion for individual freedom with a yearning for the communal solidarity he had experienced as a child on the banks of the Mungo River. In Paris during the 1960s, he could freely pursue the intense pleasure he had always found in his relations with women; he could also follow his creative impulses in any direction they might lead him.

Yet the dominant attitudes in French society were hostile to his way of life. They were racist. They called for conformity to social conventions that condemned people to boring, senseless lives. And they condoned obscene disparities of wealth. In contrast to the sterility and hypocrisy of the French middle class, the warm sensuousness of the land and the people in the Mungo River region came to epitomize his idea of a truly human environment. When he returned to the area in the mid-1960s, he exclaimed, "this is home. It will always be home. This is my life."[5] But despite his attachment to the community where he spent his childhood, he could not remain there because he realized it was part of a stagnant, oppressive society that would deprive him of his freedom and stifle his creative impulses.

From Sonne Dipoko's vantage point as an expatriate, it was clear that the acquisitive individualism of Europe had spread to Africa and was already transforming countries such as Cameroon into hostile, dehumanizing societies. As early as 1962 he lamented that independence had not brought genuine liberation to Africa:

> We become like all mankind
> Decent without
> Indecent within
> Scaling the years on the backs of others.[6]

Rather than promoting the communal solidarity of traditional society, Sonne Dipoko argues, the new governments of Africa are merely paying lip service to it while sanctioning the viciousness of those who clawed their way to the top at the expense of others. The same mentality that prompted Europeans to mask their "indecent" motivations with "decent" appearances was, he believed, becoming characteristic of Africa as well.

To counter this tendency, he proposed to poetize the world:

> Let us all be poets
> Declaring certain places regional capitals of poetry
> And choosing a world capital of poetry
> Where we could meet to poetize the affairs of the world
> And relaunch those best dreams of mankind
> Which the politicians have betrayed.[7]

In Sonne Dipoko's utopian image, the poet is the truly liberated individual who experiences life with intensity and treats others with honesty and compassion. By keeping alive the dreams that politicians such as Ahidjo had betrayed, Sonne Dipoko's poet symbolizes a hope that the passionate intensity of individual experience can be reconciled with the African sense of community in a peaceful, just, and harmonious world. The protagonists in Sonne Dipoko's novels also yearn for this reconciliation, but because they have lost contact with a supporting community, their moments of intense pleasure are often followed by periods of melancholy, and the poeticized world remains an unrealized dream.

In African writing of the colonial period, the white woman was often portrayed as a forbidden fruit for black men, but as larger numbers of Africans studied and worked in France, relationships between black men and white women became more common, and it is symptomatic that both Sonne Dipoko and Medou Mvomo devoted their first novels to semiautobiographical accounts of love affairs with young French women. The liaisons depicted in Sonne Dipoko's *A Few Days and Nights* and Medou Mvomo's *Mon Amour en noir et blanc* clearly illustrate how young Africans had begun to adopt modern identity concepts that assume the individual's right to autonomy and hold out the promise of romantic love. At the same time, the black-white relationships in these two novels serve as foils to reveal the underlying racism of French society.

A Few Days and Nights is the first-person account of Doumbe's affair with Thérèse, a nineteen-year-old French student. The story relates how a growing intimacy bridges the gap between their racial and cultural differences, but although the shy, slightly overweight Thérèse blossoms into a self-confident woman under Doumbe's tutelage, she commits suicide when her parents forbid her to marry an African. However, the center of focus in the novel is not the affair but the "I" of the fictive narrator, who assumes his experiences are worth recording because they bear testimony to the unique identity he feels inside himself.

According to Doumbe, everyone has the capacity to experience life intensely, but the majority of French people repress this capacity to pursue wealth, power, and bourgeois respectability. Writing and women had served as the two principal sources of intensity for him. "I was going to write," he declared. "I had to live, and the pleasure which women gave, their life, was the very depth of existence. I liked women. I shall write and immortalize their names."[8] This intertwining of erotic and literary desire reveals how Doumbe conceives the purpose of life as a plunging beneath the surfaces of things to experience the core of existence. Such an experience is part of what Sonne Dipoko himself had in mind when he proclaimed the need to poeticize the world.

Doumbe's intensity principle conflicts with French middle-class norms of behavior, but he is convinced that his responsiveness to his own natural and creative impulses represents a higher order of morality. "I didn't subscribe to ordinary morals," he boasted, "and I didn't care. I lived."[9] By asserting his right to live according to his own values, he opens the possibility for a genuine self-realization inaccessible to the conventional bourgeois mentality that, for example, shrouds sexual pleasure in puritanical prohibitions while condoning the brutally obscene exploitation of third-world peoples. In contrast, the impulses that well up in him lend integrity to his world view by inspiring him with "a refusal to side with oppression or repression" and "hope, which is creation."[10]

Yet Doumbe's attitude is not without its own inconsistencies; for example, the naive young Thérèse assumes that their intimacy implies fidelity in sexual matters, while he cavalierly carries on affairs with her best friend, the Swedish au pair girl Bibi, and an African woman, Ndome. On the very afternoon he promises not to betray her, Doumbe makes love to Ndome and rationalizes away his guilt by assuring himself that art originates in such contradictions. Ultimately, his unwillingness to accept the reciprocity of moral obligation condemns him to loneliness. By the end of the novel, he himself recognizes the impasse toward which his relations with Thérèse, Bibi, and Ndome had been leading him. Thérèse is dead. Ndome will leave with someone else. And Bibi, who is carrying his child, has decided to return home. All that remains for him is the haunting memory of momentary happiness in the "prevailing despair." This happiness is far more valuable than the bourgeois decorum of Thérèse's parents, but unless Doumbe becomes part of a community that can sustain him between his moments of intense happiness, he will remain subject to a recurrent sense of loss.

The community for which he subconsciously yearns is symbolized by his idealized image of the Mungo River region where he lived as a child. However, as his relationship with his father illustrates, this community is based on the very reciprocity of moral obligation that he refuses to acknowledge in his affair with Thérèse. When his father requests him to return home and receive the wisdom of his ancestors, Doumbe respects the older man's wish because he feels the two of them are linked together by a spiritual bond that would be incomprehensible to most Europeans. Unlike Thérèse, he could never think of disowning his parents. And his father reciprocates Doumbe's trust in him, for although he preferred his son to marry a local woman, he accepted Doumbe's choice of Thérèse and immediately sent money so both of them could travel to Cameroon. The awareness of such mutual confidence merges in Doumbe's mind with memories of the Mungo River and coalesces into an idealized vision of social harmony that contrasts with the sterility of Parisian bourgeois society.

But like the author, the hero of *A Few Days and Nights* cannot resign himself to living in Africa because he knows that his quest for intensity would be stifled there. The paradox of Doumbe's existence is his desire for the personal freedom he enjoys in Europe and the sense of community he associated with Africa. In an ideal world, freedom and community would be complementary, but the real world is governed by relations of dominance and oppression that make it impossible for individuals to enjoy both qualities at the same time. Under these circumstances, Doumbe opts for freedom, although he, like the tortoise he mentions to Thérèse and Bibi, continues to carry his house (his African identity) with him. Without a community to sustain him, however, he repeatedly succumbs to loneliness in the never-ending struggle to keep his soul intact in a social environment that is unreceptive to his poeticizing impulses.

The basic issue is quite different for Ambroise, the autobiographical narrator in Medou Mvomo's *Mon Amour en noir et blanc*. Like Doumbe, Ambroise feels isolated and alone in bourgeois French society, and his relationship with the young white woman Genevieve serves as a pretext for drawing attention to the self-conscious "I" that is the true center of focus in the novel. In fact, Ambroise becomes seriously involved with her only in the second half of the story. Also like Doumbe, Ambroise recounts his experiences to preserve a record of his unique individual identity and to defend the nontraditional self-image he has forged for himself in a hostile European environment. However, the freedom he proclaims is far more conventional than that of Sonne Dipoko's hero.

The crucial moment in *Mon Amour en noir et blanc* occurs when Ambroise decides to disobey his father's command not to marry a white woman. The consequences of his decision are ambiguous, for Genevieve has not yet received her parents' permission, and even at the end of the novel, he has no assurance that the marriage will ever take place. Nevertheless, Ambroise's choice is significant because it asserts his right to be the person he has become during his years in France.

His father had originally sent him to Europe in the expectation that he would return and "become somebody" in Cameroonian society. The assumption is that Ambroise has a moral obligation to obey his father, who has already chosen an African wife for him; in fact, his anticipated marriage to her represents one of the ways he is supposed to reintegrate himself into the Bulu community from which he came. As his father writes upon learning of Ambroise's intention to marry Genevieve, "in our part of the world there are no individuals in the white man's sense of the word. There are members of a group who are closely linked together and interdependent."[11] According to his father, Ambroise is not free to make his own decisions because he remains subject to the will of the family that gave him life.

However, Ambroise's experience abroad has so altered his consciousness that he might never be able to reintegrate himself fully into African society. During his years in France, he was constantly aware of white people staring at him, and their stares made him acutely aware of his difference from them. To accommodate their stereotyped notions of Africans, he learned to play the role of the woolly-headed clown who laughs and dances upon command. But he also resisted pressures to internalize their reductionist conceptions of his humanity. In the process he suffered humiliation and loneliness. His response was to fashion a typically European idea of his own selfhood. His romantic love for Genevieve and his willingness to break with his father are expressions of this new identity concept. Whether or not he ever marries Genevieve, Ambroise's experiences in France have convinced him that he is an autonomous individual with the right to pursue his own vision of happiness.

In adopting such an image, Ambroise has recourse to the same clichés that Frenchmen often use in defining themselves. For example, he describes his love for Genevieve in the stock sentimental terms of popular French fiction. The first time he sees her, she smiles at him, and he immediately falls in love with her. In his fervor, he vows to become like a knight whose raised sword will enable him to overcome all obstacles and conquer the happiness he desires. Even in his dreams he envisions himself as a valiant knight battling the many-headed monster of French prejudice. If Sonne Dipoko's Doumbe demands his freedom to reject French social conventions, Medou Mvomo's Ambroise insists upon his freedom to assimilate them. Both characters assert their humanity in the face of French racism and defend their right to define themselves as unique individuals, but the identities they forge for themselves are based on different premises.

The contrasting temperaments of the two authors become even more apparent in their second novels, which are semiautobiographical accounts of individuals' attempts to cope with stagnating rural societies in Cameroon. Both the Bulu village in Medou Mvomo's *Afrika Ba'a* and the Mungo River region in Sonne Dipoko's *Because of Women* are clearly in decline. Abandoned houses and farms have fallen into decay and are gradually being reclaimed by the tropical forest. Populations have decreased precipitously as local populations have migrated to the cities in search of work. The social dynamism of the past has been replaced by lethargy and hopelessness. Under these circumstances, Medou Mvomo's hero succeeds in revitalizing the Bulu community by inspiring the people with a spirit of rationality and self-reliance, whereas the protagonist in Sonne Dipoko's novel becomes a symbolic embodiment of the Mungo River region's lost vitality and eventually falls victim to contradictions in his own view of the world.

The most popular of Medou Mvomo's novels, *Afrika Ba'a* has sold more copies than all the rest of his works combined, largely because the ministries of education in several African countries have included it on their school reading lists. The rationale for doing so was the belief that its depiction of a successful attempt to resurrect a moribund village would reinforce the self-help ethic being promoted as part of the development ideology in such countries. However, like the love affair between Ambroise and Genevieve in *Mon Amour en noir et blanc*, the regeneration of the village Afrika Ba'a (New Africa) occupies only the final portion of the novel.

The real center of focus is the consciousness of Kambara, a young man who leaves Afrika Ba'a to improve his fortunes in the city of Nécroville (Yaounde). But in fleeing from the despair of rural poverty, he encounters the even worse corruption of a large urban area; in fact, his experiences there trigger the insight that enables him to return to Afrika Ba'a and inspire his fellow villagers with a new confidence in their ability to determine their own fate. Thus, *Afrika Ba'a* is less the story of a village's rehabilitation than the account of an individual's struggle for psychological independence from the forces that threaten to imprison his generation in an endless cycle of meaningless, unproductive motions.

At the beginning of the novel, the only experience that makes Kambara feel alive in an otherwise bleak village setting is his relationship with Ada, a young woman whom he cannot marry because he has no money to pay the bride-price that her father demands. The happiness he feels in her presence catalyzes his resolve to escape from Afrika Ba'a, but his dream of finding a "true life" in the city proves illusory. Rather than freedom, Nécroville offers him a worse form of stagnation. After many fruitless efforts to find employment, however, Kambara responds to the absurdity of the system by rejecting its definition of people like him as nonpersons. He insists on regarding himself as an individual whose talents are being wasted, and he demands the freedom to exercise these talents.

The insight that allows him to attain his freedom is the recognition that he is responsible for realizing his own potential. After experiencing the frustration of urban life, he also realizes that the possibility for change is greater in the village than it is in the city. As he prepares for a civil-service examination, Kambara muses on the fate of rural areas such as Afrika Ba'a, and he becomes convinced that they can become idyllic places if people adopt a new attitude toward themselves. According to him, this attitude must include an openness to modern technology and a conviction that the people themselves control their own destiny. Such an attitude would, he concludes, liberate them from a self-defeating hopelessness and allow them to work together in pursuit of goals they had set for themselves. What Kambara envisions is a peaceful revolution that would transform rural villages into self-respecting, materially comfortable utopian communities.

Although he passes his examination and could accept a job in the city, Kambara decides to act upon his insight by returning to Afrika Ba'a and putting his ideas into practice. Because he succeeds in convincing the villagers to adopt his new attitude, a peaceful revolution does take place, and the village itself is completely rebuilt. There is even a sort of poetic justice in the fact that Ada runs away from her father and joins Kambara upon his return to Afrika Ba'a, working side by side with him and eventually bearing him a son. Their togetherness symbolizes their break with outmoded traditions and permits Kambara to preserve the happiness that first motivated him to seek a way out of the futility that had engulfed the village.

Ironically, he has discovered that his initial impulse to flee from it was based on the false assumption that life would be better somewhere else. Yet he perceives the truth about people's capacity to transform their misery into happiness because his stay in the city offered him a new perspective on the plight of the village. Having abandoned the illusions that continue to beguile many of his fellow countrymen, Kambara discovers an individual identity that gives purpose to his life and enables him to channel his talents into a productive communal enterprise. He makes a crucial contribution to the rehabilitation of Afrika Ba'a, but he can do so only after he has defined himself as an autonomous individual responsible for shaping his own fate.

In 1970 *Afrika Ba'a* was one of the finalists for the prestigious Ahmadou Ahidjo prize, and several years later a reviewer for the government-sponsored *Cameroon Tribune* declared that the book is primarily about "the green revolution, [which is] the leitmotif of our country's political economy."[12] Although the reviewer's interpretation is dubious, it helps explain the Ahidjo government's interest in the book. Like the authorities in other African countries where *Afrika Ba'a* was placed on school reading lists, government officials in Cameroon regarded it as an inspirational example of rural development. Beneath the surface of Medou Mvomo's novel, however, is a world view that challenges many of the Ahidjo government's development strategies.

In the beginning of *Afrika Ba'a*, it is clear that independence did not improve conditions in the village. On the contrary, it worsened them. The fall of commodity prices and the absence of employment opportunities combined with Christian forbearance and traditional superstition to produce a state of mind in which everything seemed to be determined by outside forces. Neither the government's national unity concept nor its Negritude-influenced cultural policies could liberate the villagers from this state of mind. According to Medou Mvomo, the only way to overcome their sense of powerlessness is to recognize, as Kambara does, that happiness and material well-being lie within reach of those who approach their problems in a rational, scientific way and work hard to achieve their own goals.

There is nothing miraculous about the rehabilitation of Afrika Ba'a. Every initiative that Kambara and his fellow villagers undertake is a rational step toward the realization of a well-defined objective. Because coffee and cocoa are no longer profitable, they replace their coffee and cocoa fields with a highly profitable collective farm. Huts that have deteriorated beyond repair are destroyed and replaced with permanent modern houses. Money is raised by selling fish and handicraft items in the local markets. Potential investors from the city are canvassed. Kambara makes certain that people eat properly, and he introduces adult education courses. Fruit trees are planted throughout the village. In short, the people have adopted a mindset that allows them to receive "the gift that nature offers to those who dare."[13] The crucial point is that everyone has a potential ("the gift that nature offers") and must assume responsibility for its fulfillment. By working together, people can create an environment in which individual self-realization is possible for everyone; however, when the utopian atmosphere in the new Afrika Ba'a is compared with the social climate in contemporary Cameroon, it becomes apparent that Medou Mvomo was indirectly criticizing a society that constantly blocks the initiatives of talented young men such as Kambara.

Sonne Dipoko depicts the situation of rural decline from an entirely different perspective in *Because of Women*. His hero, Ngoso, is an extraordinarily vital man who lives for his relationships with women and dreams of founding a family community on the site of his farm. Although the Mungo River valley where he lives is suffering from poor economic conditions and depopulation, Ngoso is never tempted to leave for the city because he feels a spiritual affinity with the river and with the land where his parents are buried. Even his passion for women is the expression of an impulse that vibrates in harmony with the world around him.

Like Doumbe, Ngoso embraces life and experiences an intensity that is inaccessible to those who let themselves be governed by artificial social conventions. Yet after a series of affairs with different women, he finds himself ill and alone. In the belief that he has lost both of the women who are carrying his children, he laments: "the sun will rise over Mungo River, . . . and I will be there alone like a widower, without a woman, without children. And the sun will set over me and my farm."[14] His words prove prophetic, for his depression erodes his will to live, and he dies a short time later, his dream of community unfulfilled. In a way, Ngoso resembles the region with which he identified so strongly. It too had once been vigorous and alive with dreams of future happiness, but it too was losing its vitality. At the end of the novel, Ngoso's brother weeps on the site of the deserted farm where Ngoso has just been buried, and his tears bespeak a profound sadness not only at the thought of a man's death but also at the spectacle of a dying world.

The action in *Because of Women* revolves around Ngoso's passionate affair with Ewudu; in fact, the story itself is framed by her engagement to another man before meeting Ngoso and her return to her fiancé after arriving too late to assure Ngoso that she still loves him. At the end, she too weeps in the realization that the intensity she experienced with Ngoso was merely an interlude in the mundane reality with which most people content themselves all their lives. Yet she herself had brought about Ngoso's depression by failing to meet him, as she had promised, because she was jealous that another woman, Njale, had moved back into Ngoso's house. Ironically, Njale had left him when he told her he was planning to bring Ewudu back to the farm with him. In their company and with all the other women he knows intimately, the focus is always on the intensity of the momentary pleasure he shares with them. Particularly with Ewudu, the rhythms of sexual intercourse seem to be in harmony with the larger forces of nature. However, intensity cannot be sustained permanently, and the conflicts that arise because of his multiple involvements with women actually prevent him from creating the small community he envisioned on the site of his farm.

Ngoso's problem is essentially the same as Doumbe's, for he wants to reconcile his desire for intensity with his dream of a warm and productive human community, but his pursuit of intensity precludes the reciprocal moral commitment necessary for the realization of his dream. In an ideal world where people respond honestly to their own impulses and refrain from participating in oppressive systems, such a reconciliation might be possible. In *A Few Days and Nights*, Doumbe mentions the "dreams of a better world" he had discussed with young people from all over the world, and Sonne Dipoko himself was inspired by the student revolts of May 1968 to write a series of essays in which he described his vision of a new socialism grounded in love and committed to the use of technology for the material well-being of all people. But like Doumbe, Ngoso is living in an imperfect world, and although his passion endows his life with a value that is absent from the lives of those who internalize the conventions of a corrupt social system, he remains a sad and lonely man because he is unable to create the community that might have sustained him between his moments of intense pleasure.

The protagonist in Medou Mvomo's last novel, *Le Journal de Faliou*, is also a lonely individual who is frustrated in his attempt to realize the potential he feels inside himself. As an itinerant musician and composer, Medou Mvomo himself traveled throughout Cameroon during the late 1960s, and the notes he took at that time were later transformed into the slightly fictionalized diary of Faliou. Like Ambroise and Kambara, Faliou pursues a dream of happiness in a society that is hostile to his aspirations. Having left Yaounde to seek his fortune as a musician in Douala, he experiences a few intermittent successes but ultimately falls into abject poverty and returns to Yaounde with less than he had possessed in the beginning. By recording his experiences in a diary, the narrating Faliou compensates for his failure by seeking to demonstrate that, despite appearances, he is a uniquely talented individual who desired the freedom to express himself but repeatedly found his way blocked by a social system that doesn't reward people according to their merits. Even in describing his most humiliating experiences, Faliou tries to project a favorable image of himself by emphasizing his insistence upon remaining free and his ability to withstand hardships that would have crushed others if they had been in his place.

In the act of composing his diary, however, Faliou reveals the self-imposed blindness that isolates him from others and contributes to his own failure. Whenever he suffers a momentary setback, he attributes it to the unjust social system or to individuals who plot against him, mock his destitution, rob him, betray him, besmirch his reputation, undermine his confidence, sabotage his success, deny his qualities, and generally seek to humiliate him. This tendency to blame others rather than looking into himself for the cause of his difficulties culminates in a self-pitying paranoia. "It seems to me that everyone is motivated by bad intentions toward me," he says at one point and later adds, "I am alone against the whole world."[15] He regards this mistrust of others as the price he must pay for attempting to realize his potential. In reality, it prevents him from establishing the warm human relationships for which he yearns. Faliou cannot experience the love of others because he is incapable of giving it to them in return.

Although the psychological profiles of Sonne Dipoko's semiautobiographical characters differ from those of Medou Mvomo's Faliou and Ambroise, they resemble each other in the sense that their individualism undercuts the sense of community that might have saved them from the solitude into which they are repeatedly thrust. Both Doumbe and Ngoso look upon women primarily as a means to their own pleasure, and although their ethics of intensity imply that women such as Thérèse and Ewudu share in this pleasure, neither man believes he has an obligation to fulfill other expectations that these women bring to the relationship.

For example, before Thérèse met Doumbe, she had been unhappy and insecure. Under his influence, she escaped the psychological prison into which her bourgeois parents had cast her, and she blossomed into a vibrantly alive young woman, but whereas she invested her entire being in their relationship, he regarded it as merely one episode in a lifelong series of adventures. He even proposed to marry her because he did not want to see her suffer, not because he wanted to live with her as husband and wife. When she committed suicide, she acted out of despair at the prospect of a future without him. In contrast, he quickly overcomes the momentary sadness he feels at the news of her death and looks forward to the next episode in his own life.

If Thérèse had lived, she would have discovered Doumbe's infidelities. Her escape from solitude and unhappiness was illusory in the sense that it was based on a false assumption about his commitment to her. In a situation where such a disequilibrium of moral commitment exists, Doumbe's moral stance is unfair because it allows him to take what he desires without fulfilling the expectations with which it is given. Ironically, his attitude is also self-defeating, for it undermines the reciprocity of obligation that is essential to the sense of community he also desires.

But modern society as portrayed in the works of Sonne Dipoko and Medou Mvomo is itself uncongenial to the idea of community. The Douala that Faliou had imagined as a freer, richer place than Yaounde is actually a filthy, stench-filled city where everything is for sale and everyone is trying to outwit everyone else. It is a city where excellence remains unrewarded and the incompetent are promoted because they know influential people. Even discounting Faliou's paranoid anxieties, Douala is a society that discourages the mutual trust on which decent human relationships are based. It also inhibits people from exercising their talents and realizing their potential.

In all the novels by Sonne Dipoko and Medou Mvomo, the major characters serve as foils to reveal the hypocrisy and corruption of the modern world. Although Sonne Dipoko places supreme value on the intensity of experience and Medou Mvomo on the rational capacity to forge one's own destiny, both focus on the typically modern problem of individual self-realization. In doing so, they reveal that Cameroonians like them are subject to the same internal conflicts and the same existential solitude that afflict non-Africans who define themselves in terms of a self that must constantly be reaffirmed in a hostile social environment. Implicitly, Sonne Dipoko and Medou Mvomo were criticizing that environment for placing obstacles in the way of their own self-realization.

The quest for individual self-definition was also a dominant theme in postcolonial Cameroonian poetry. Even Louis-Marie Pouka increasingly focused on personal subjects, although he also wrote patriotic eulogies to Ahidjo. The bridge that linked his public and private poetry was a belief in the spiritual dimension of life. Because he regarded himself as a prophet with privileged access to spiritual truth, he felt justified in depicting Ahidjo's nation-building ideal as a manifestation of this truth, while attacking the greed and corruption of contemporary Cameroon as an example of people's shortsighted attachment to the material world. At the same time, his belief in a spiritual world offered him solace in the face of his own mortality. In fact, in such collections as *Fusées* and *Ce Siècle est triste*, he almost yearns for death as a means of consummating his desire to be reunited with the spirit.

Yet just as Pouka had been condemned by Sengat-Kuo during the mid-1950s for his inauthenticity, he became the butt of repeated attacks in the 1960s by younger poets who reproached him for his sycophantic support of the Ahidjo government. His leading critic was the Bamileke poet Patrice Kayo, who eventually succeeded him as president of APEC. Rather than as a self-styled "magus of the Cameroonian people" or a "Cameroonian Parnassus," Kayo saw him as a man who had allowed himself to be mystified by the colonialist world view to the point that he no longer had any real convictions of his own. The documentary interest of this phenomenon so fascinated Kayo that he devoted his doctoral thesis to the man and his work. After accusing Pouka of being "so changeable that he's like a chameleon who takes its color from the plants among which he happens to find himself," he concludes that "his poetry is an opportunistic poetry that adapts itself to the circumstances."[16] The assumption behind Kayo's criticism is that poetry should be an honest expression of individual identity, and he contends that Pouka's poetry fails to express a coherent sense of identity.

Kayo's own poetry is the record of a painful search for emotional honesty. Having received most of his education in a Catholic seminary, he suffered a disillusioning experience that caused him to leave the church and become a militant spokesman for working-class solidarity, although he never abandoned his dedication to Christian ideals of love and spiritual community. He merely transformed them into a new vision that drew inspiration from Um Nyobé's radical nationalism and from the fraternal social relations that characterized traditional Bamileke society. The poetic voice that speaks through his poetry thus defines itself in terms of its commitment to a utopian ideal. If the contemporary world is hostile to this ideal, Kayo believes it is his duty to poeticize his experience of it so that others might recognize its relevance to them.

However, the task is not an easy one, and the poems that record Kayo's struggle to keep alive his hope in the ideal are filled with ambivalence and self-doubt. He knows that concrete revolutionary action is necessary to eliminate oppression, but he hesitates to engage in violence, and his verses are permeated with the anguished melancholy of one who fears disillusionment because his dreams have been shattered in the past. He yearns to be part of a larger community, but he constantly dwells in solitude. He preaches a doctrine of life and love, but he knows that all people are condemned to suffering and death in a world that is hostile to his ideals. All these conflicts reflect the fact that Kayo was only partially successful in reconciling his Christian view of the world with secular values after his loss of faith in the sustaining principles of the church.

Many of Kayo's poems express his desire to attain the spiritual harmony that Christianity had seemed to offer him. Often this harmony is contingent upon realizing his vision of perfection. Sometimes it entails the recovery of what has been lost—a person, a thing, a state of society. His quest for the object of his desire resembles the Christian's yearning to be united with a savior who is eternally elsewhere but always present to the spirit: "Dream or reality, I know not how to name you, / you for whom I search even when I have you, / you who are always absent and always present."[17] What he means is that the object of desire is always with him because it exists as an idea or an image in his own consciousness. As long as the idea or image persists, it functions like a star behind a cloud or a seed that falls on barren ground without losing its potential for growing into a plant. It is the principle of hope, and although the happiness of fulfilled desire is constantly deferred, the poet continues to live in anticipation of it. The pain and joy of this endless expectation become the real subject of his poems, for as he meditates in solitude on his hope and despair, he seeks to capture his evanescent feelings and transform them into poetry.

He is acutely aware that language is incapable of conveying the fullness of his emotion, and he fears that poetry might be futile in the face of tyranny, but he recalls that the word is "an act of faith, a note of hope sustained by the dawn that is gestating in the bosom of the night."[18] And then his own song bursts forth with its vision of a more just and humane world. In a sense, he is like the fireflies in another of his poems. Their light will never vanquish the darkness of the night, but it can inspire ideas that grow to fruition in the minds of those who see it, just as the ideas in poems can germinate in the minds of others and motivate them to liberate themselves from oppression. The ultimate justification for transmuting his personal struggle into poetry is a desire to preserve the light of hope; in fact, by engaging in the process of writing, he is defying the power of darkness.

Kayo's faith in the word derives partly from his familiarity with Bamileke oral culture. He himself has published collections of traditional proverbs and songs, and when he refers to the poetic word, he means the word that belongs to the people and speaks through him. In this sense, he is like Philombe because he regards the political vision in his poetry as an expression of the Cameroonian people's yearning for a better future. By giving concrete form to their inchoate feelings, he is offering them a light in the darkness, a seed from which revolutionary actions can grow. In contrast to Pouka, Kayo refused to support the Ahidjo government's nation-building rhetoric because he viewed it as a cynical pretext for maintaining a corrupt and oppressive regime in power. The integrity with which he adopted this stance expresses the coherence of the individual identity embedded in his poetry—an identity forged in the attempt to replace a Christian vision with values inspired by Bamileke traditions and by the UPC struggle for national independence.

As the writing of poetry became common in Cameroon, it increasingly served as a vehicle to express the uniqueness of the individual self. Behind much of this poetry was the assumption that a verse record of the poet's emotional life is intrinsically interesting, and many young Cameroonians became convinced that imagination can effortlessly transform strong feelings into poetry. One of them introduced his own first volume of poems by declaring that "poetry flows of its own accord, its practice becomes natural."[19] The lack of discipline that such an attitude implies frequently resulted in self-indulgent outpourings of personal sentiment. It also illustrated the heightened consciousness of individuality that was fostered by the spread of literate culture.

For example, the existential anguish that pervades the work of such poets as Etienne Noumé and Jeanne Ngo Mai bears witness to a sorrow that is experienced in solitude, not communally as it might have been in traditional society. Noumé is the pseudonym of Etienne Nkepndep, a young Bamileke teacher who wrote all his poetry by the age of nineteen before suffering several nervous breakdowns and disappearing without a trace in 1970. In the poems that his friend Kayo collected and published the following year, this Cameroonian Rimbaud focused almost exclusively on the anxieties of a sensitive individual who yearns for love and dignity but feels trapped in a world dominated by corruption, injustice, filth, and humiliation. As powerless as a bird whose nest is menaced by the winds of a storm, Noumé has no confidence in the redemptive power of poetry. All he can do is cry out at the senselessness of a world where dreams of perfection remain unfulfilled and all hope for the future is rendered vain by the inherent fragility of life.

The burden of daily existence gradually eroded Noumé's will to live, and a longing for death haunts the hallucinatory verses that emerged from his attempt to translate states of mind into literary form. Rejecting the stereotyped moral idealism that pervades much of Cameroonian poetry, he conveys the despair of gazing unflinchingly at the ugliness of contemporary society. Whereas the mother is usually presented as an example of selfless love, his poem on motherhood dwells on the way children survive by consuming her vital force and bequeathing her nothing but the prospect of future desolation. Imprisoned in a world view that offered him no solace but madness and death, Noumé wrote poetry that is a painful lament in the face of his own despair. This despair was partly a function of his own tormented psyche, but it also reflected the difficulties encountered by other sensitive individuals in a society hostile to their quest for freedom and a viable sense of identity.

Ngo Mai's *Poèmes sauvages et lamentations* also focuses on the suffering self and its despair at the loss of hope. The occasion for the major cycle of poems in this volume was the death of a young Bamun neighbor who was killed by a taxi she owned. The shock of the accident and her own guilt caused her to reflect on the assumptions that governed her life as an educated modern African. Conflating all her disappointments in life with the young man's death, she was overcome by the incomprehensibility of her own situation. Because she had experienced the joy of loving others, she longed for peace and harmony in a world where love might prevail, but death or departure seemed always to separate her from the object of her love.

As if perplexed by a God who endowed her with the power to love others and then deprived her of the opportunity to exercise this power, she laments the harshness of life and rages against the arbitrariness of divine will. In this frame of mind, she becomes intensely aware of her own death and fears that the world is crumbling around her. Writing poetry is her way of coping with solitude and with the pain of a loss that fills her with despair. The result is a series of poems that record a unique individual temperament as it struggles to find meaning in a world that appears to be without it.

Unlike Noumé, Ngo Mai ultimately overcomes her despair. She believes in the power of love and knows it can transport her into a realm of perfect harmony. Although her yearning for this harmony has repeatedly been frustrated, she recovers her capacity for love as she composes the cycle of poems dedicated to the dead young man. This thematization of love as a way of overcoming despair and death is a characteristically Christian approach to the definition of human potential; in fact, nearly all Cameroon's early poets were educated at mission schools, and their concepts of individual identity reflect what they learned there, whether or not they continued to be practicing Christians.

Poets as diverse as Paul-Charles Atangana with his classical French prosody, Ernest Alima with his eclectic modern style, and Charles Bebbe with his heavily cadenced free verse all project into their works an individual identity that is defined in terms of love and desire for union with a godlike perfection.

The Catholic church exercised a particularly strong influence over the expression of this identity concept in early postcolonial Cameroonian poetry. Not only had a majority of publishing poets attended Catholic schools, but a large number of them were priests and former seminarians. In Yaounde, the church operated the Saint Paul bookstore that brought out poetry collections by several young Catholics. In Douala, the Spiritain priest Henry de Julliot helped many aspiring Catholic poets publish their works. One result of this support was the emergence of an inspirational poetry that synthesized a new idealism from strong personal emotions, a religious faith in the power of love, and a patriotic attachment to the Cameroonian nation.

Samuel Nkamgnia and Toube Manga exemplify this strand of poetic creativity. Both had been influenced by de Julliot, whose Catholic humanism is echoed in their celebration of universal brotherhood, their acceptance of God's will, and their conviction that human love is the pathway to divine love. Nkamgnia employs common, everyday words to record his yearning for an impossible ideal, and Toube Manga depicts the world as if it were the scene for the drama of his soul's awakening to a profound spiritual truth. In both cases, the act of writing poetry is an exaltation of the individual self. Nkamgnia even scattered photographs of himself throughout the poetry volumes he published under the Saint Paul imprint. Similar to the Catholic Negritude intellectuals who projected their belief in a higher spiritual realm into their support for Ahidjo's cultural politics, Catholic poets such as Nkamgnia and Toube Manga proclaimed their faith in the government's nation-building ideal as part of their commitment to the divine order of the universe.

However, as the examples of Kayo and Bishop Ndongmo illustrate, Cameroonian Catholics were hardly unanimous in their support of the Ahidjo regime. Particularly in the Bamileke country, where French and Cameroonian troops had been extremely brutal in suppressing the UPC rebellion, many progressive priests and lay Catholics dedicated themselves to a utopian ideal that placed them in opposition to the government. Inspired by the wisdom of traditional Bamileke customs and appalled by the corruption and injustice that were eroding the people's dream of a genuinely independent Cameroon, the priests Jean-Louis Dongmo and Martin Nkamgang wrote intensely personal poems that define individual identity in terms of an allegiance to this utopian ideal.

Much of Dongmo's poetry focuses on the people or social practices of his own Bamileke village, but even when he is depicting traditional subject matter, his verses reverberate with a socially critical tone, as his image of the talking drum indicates:

> The talking drum sobs not
> shirks not

amuses not not not . . .
With tiny bites like drops of water on a rock
the talking drum gnaws
the chains of Africa bowed beneath the whips of all the nights.[20]

According to Dongmo, the chains that enslave Africa are not only the historical abuses of the colonial era but also the social injustice that obliges young
women to become prostitutes and the greed that transforms ambitious people
into swarms of voracious "grasshoppers." In this context, the talking drum
embodies the true spirit of Africa as it slowly erodes the mental constraints
that have kept people in bondage for centuries.

In "Libre, même si nu . . . ," Dongmo castigates poets who eulogize
those responsible for the country's misery:

> I hate those griots
> who bestow praises on command
> and make heroes of clever upstarts
> for a small consideration:
> I love liberty, . . .
> I love truth. . . .[21]

Two sorts of people are being criticized in these lines: the false poets who
compromise their integrity for material gain and the members of the privileged
class ("habiles parvenus") who inflate their public images with the aid of such
poets. Both criticisms are based on a standard of value that is located within
the poet who proclaims his love of truth and liberty. The center of Dongmo's
poetry is the individual "I" and its commitment to a vision of perfection that
contrasts sharply with the existing situation in Cameroon.

Like Dongmo, Nkamgang studied in France for many years before returning to Cameroon, where he too synthesized a utopian ideal from Christian
beliefs and traditional Bamileke values as they interacted in his sensitive soul.
A public enterprise that remains intensely individual, poetry was for him a
means of upholding this ideal and transmitting it to others. *O toi qui ne dors!*
is a spiritual autobiography in the sense that the poems collected in it trace
the evolution of his ideas during a fifteen-year period. *Chants et symbols d'unité*
contains three poems that show how people can achieve unity and progress
through collective effort and fraternal love, but only if the people's desire for
justice and equality is respected. As he repeatedly points out in his poems,
this was not the case in Cameroon during the 1960s and early 1970s.

As a Christian and a respected member of Bamileke society, Nkamgang
felt compelled to criticize a country that had turned its back on his most cherished values. In *O toi qui ne dors!*, he ascribes the existing malaise in Cameroon
to the greed of public officials who neglect the aspirations of the people and
condition them to treat each other like ruthless predators. As long as such
a social system prevails, he knows that his own vision will remain an unfulfilled
dream. He questions the divine purpose behind the misery he had witnessed

in the war-ravaged Bamileke region, but he invariably returns to God as the only hope for a humanity gone astray. Convinced that Christian charity and African traditions of communal solidarity offer the best foundation for a just society, he focused on his own sensitivity toward nature and his own compassion for the sufferings of others to reveal that the existing situation was neither normal nor natural.

During the late 1960s and early 1970s, the anglophone poetry of Sankie Maimo displayed a marked shift toward a similar sort of disillusionment with the broken promises of independence. In 1962, he wrote "Harken Boys to the Bugle Call," a fervently patriotic exhortation for people to abandon their frivolous pursuits and work toward national construction. With a typically British moralism, he assured his readers that the reward for their devotion to the national cause would be the satisfaction of a job well done. As the years passed, however, the inspirational tone of Maimo's poetry became tinged with irony and personal bitterness. Increasingly, his verses emphasized the political corruption, the crass materialism, and the scandalous waste of talent and resources in his country.

At the same time, the modern world view that permeated his preindependence poetry was gradually tempered with a more respectful attitude toward traditional values and the spiritual reality associated with them. He continued to believe in the importance of individual choice, but as he grew older, he began to view it in terms of a fundamental decision that all people must make in defining themselves. In many of his later poems, Maimo argued that evil is a function of people's blindness toward their own spiritual identity. Insofar as European modes of thought and behavior reinforce this blindness, he concluded that Africans should be prepared to abandon them—an opinion diametrically opposed to the ideas he had expressed in his earlier play *I Am Vindicated*.

The idea of individual choice and responsibility is central to the modern self-concept that the younger generation of Cameroonian writers implicitly defended in their works, and it became particularly prominent in their portrayals of romantic love. Influenced by the European cultural assumptions they had absorbed in the schools and by the French popular literature they had read for entertainment, young Cameroonians tended to believe they should be free to choose a marriage partner on the basis of strong emotional attachments. Many assumed that their own self-fulfillment was contingent upon their success in exercising this freedom.

Two novels written by Cameroonian women illustrate this linkage between individual identity concepts and the ideal of romantic love. Both Thérèse Kuoh-Moukouri's *Rencontres essentielles* and Yoko-Nana-Tabitha's *La Reine* are slightly fictionalized autobiographical accounts of women who suffered disappointment in their yearning for fulfillment through love. As Flo, the narrator in *Rencontres essentielles*, reflects back on her life, she still believes that men and women complete each other during "essential encounters" that permit them to achieve happiness. Although she desperately wants to regard herself as an independent individual who can bring an ennobling passion to such a relationship, she unwittingly reveals the character flaw that prevents her from attaining her goal.

Even as a schoolchild in Douala, Flo felt inferior to the Europeans who rented her father's villa, and France seemed to her like "a fantasyland that people entered through a golden doorway as in a paradise."[22] This lack of self-confidence and her tendency to idealize foreign culture reemerge clearly in her attitude toward Doris, an independent-minded white woman who has an affair with Flo's husband and bears him a child after Flo herself had suffered a miscarriage that prevented her from having any children. Doris had grown up in Douala, and although she was the same age as Flo, she was always ahead of her in school, and when they knew each other later in France, Doris seemed to be in control of her destiny, whereas Flo waited passively for her destiny to come to her. After the miscarriage, she became obsessed with her own inadequacy, and when Doris's child is born, Flo feels as if she has been reduced to "a minuscule point on the earth, a speck of dust in the universe."[23] There is a contradiction in Flo's view of the world, and it arises from her yearning for a romantic love that can be sustained only by what she does not possess—a self-confident willingness to pursue the object of her desire. All her essential encounters are accidental, and her sense of helplessness in the face of a hostile destiny suggests that she is incapable of becoming the autonomous individual she would have to be if she is to find fulfillment in love.

The narrator in Yoko-Nana-Tabitha's *La Reine* is a psychologically disturbed woman who also presents herself as an individual capable of great passion, despite the fact that her dream of romantic love has proved illusory. Claiming that she had been seduced and abandoned by Martin Nkamgang, who supposedly harassed her with magic spells, she became paranoid and felt completely isolated because "everyone hated me for no reason at all."[24] Like Flo in Kuoh-Moukouri's novel, she feels alienated and alone, but her mental state is in many ways a reflection of her own inability to achieve the clarity of vision that might have enabled her to become the individual she wanted to become.

What is significant about these two novels is the way they illustrate the belief that romantic love is the principal pathway to individual happiness. Despite their disappointments, the fictive narrators in *Rencontres essentielles* and *La Reine* tell their stories to leave a record of their own unique sensibilities. They also desire to justify themselves by showing how their present attitudes evolved as a result of unjustified sufferings in the past. However, if their individualistic self-images make it possible for them to define themselves in terms of the romantic love ideal, they also predispose them to solipsism and loneliness. As Flo concludes in attempting to generalize on the basis of her own experiences: "men and women pass in the fog, mute, indifferent, each lost in the dream of his or her own story."[25] The promise of happiness in a freely chosen, intensely emotional relationship has frequently motivated young Cameroonians to adopt such a self-image, but when the promise of happiness remains unfulfilled, they fall victim to the characteristic alienation of the modern world.

Another problem arises when this individualistic self-concept and the appeal of romantic love place young people in conflict with elders who assume they can still determine their children's marriages according to traditional custom. In fact, this conflict is the single most common theme in postcolonial Cameroonian fiction. It played an important role in novels by Medou Mvomo and Sonne Dipoko, and it is the center of focus in such semiautobiographical works as Patrice Ndedi Penda's *La Nasse* and Joseph-Jules Mokto's *Ramitou, mon étrangère*.[26] Both novels depict the difficulties encountered by younger people who insist upon their freedom to choose for themselves in matters of love and marriage.

In *La Nasse*, the two young people Dindè and Collette are in love with each other, and everyone in the village assumes they will be married, but when the high-ranking civil servant Ekandè offers an exorbitant dowry to Collette's family, her father accepts it. Although Dindè and Collette are outraged at the situation, they confront two obstacles to their happiness: the traditional custom of regarding marriage as an agreement between families or clans rather than as a bond between two individuals, and the power of an administrator who abuses his authority to obtain whatever he wants. Because the elders in Collette's family have a financial stake in the marriage, they will do anything to prevent Dindè from interfering with their plans, and Ekandè's control over the local police allows him to impose his will on the villagers, no matter how arbitrary it might be.

In the face of such obstacles, Dindè and Collette rely on the conviction that love and freedom of choice sanction their right to marry each other. What is really at issue in this case are two conflicting definitions of individual identity. Collette's family regard her as a member of the group that gave her life and supported her during her education. In return for their support, she is expected to obey their decisions. However, she and Dindè consider her father's acceptance of the inflated bride-price to be a crass attempt to sell her to the highest bidder. In their eyes, the cost of her education was the payment of a debt that all parents incur when they bring children into the world. For the two young people, Collette is an autonomous individual with the right to marry whom she pleases. For the elders of her family, she is a group member who has no choice in the matter.

Ekandè's arbitrary exercise of power raises a different issue. As citizens in a supposedly democratic society, Collette and Dindè should have the right to pursue any lawful interests they might have. But when Ekandè has Dindè's father arrested and beaten merely to intimidate him, his action reveals the hypocrisy of a system that preaches justice while allowing members of an emergent privileged class to oppress others with impunity.

Although the basic problem in *Ramitou, mon étrangère* is not the same, it too revolves around a conflict between the older and younger generations' concepts of individual identity. The novel's protagonist, Julot, is a Bamileke, and Ramitou, the woman with whom he falls in love, is a Bamun; their families object to their marriage on the ground that more appropriate partners could be found for them among members of their own ethnic groups. Despite this opposition, the two young people follow their romantic inclinations, marry, have a child, and move from Douala to a place near Bafoussam, where his business prospers. Three years later, Julot recounts his story to demonstrate how modern values such as romantic love and individual freedom can be reconciled with selected traditional beliefs to overcome the irrational prejudices that separate members of different ethnic groups from each other.

As in *La Nasse*, the young people's concept of individual identity differs from that of their elders. Throughout the early part of the novel, the narrating Julot draws attention to this difference by alternating episodes from his own life in Douala with scenes of his father's occupations in a small Bamileke village. Having received a European-style education, Julot has internalized a world view that allows him to orient himself in the modern world. Romantic love and individual freedom are important values for him, and he cannot imagine living for the rest of his life with a woman who is incapable of understanding his ideas.

In contrast, his father is convinced that Julot can be happy only if he returns to the village and marries the woman his family has chosen for him. The old man often prays that his son will remain on the "straight and narrow path" and considers him under an obligation to obey the wishes of a family that has sacrificed to send him to school. The difficulty with the father's position is that it renders him incapable of understanding the literate culture and the modern attitudes his son has absorbed as a result of his education. He himself had sent Julot to school so that at least one member of his family would be able to succeed in the contemporary world, but he irrationally expected the young man's conception of himself to remain unaffected by his schooling. What enables Julot and Ramitou to overcome the conflict that pits them against their parents is the underlying good will that imbues them with patience and allows them to incorporate elements of the traditional belief system into their own lives.

Such a reconciliation is not possible in *La Nasse*. After a "Romeo and Juliet" scenario in which Dindè and Collette each believe that the other has betrayed their love, she chooses to join Ekandè, who has been hospitalized after swallowing a potion that his first wife gave him in the hope of regaining his affections. In reality, Collette's decision is not a repudiation of Dindè. On the contrary, it is an acceptance of what cannot be changed. She recognizes that, if she persists in choosing for herself, members of her own clan might kill Dindè, and Ekandè will continue to harass his family. Placed before two equally unattractive alternatives by a corrupt social system, she chooses the one that is best for Dindè and his parents. In a situation where the individualistic conception of the self and the power of romantic love appear to have been crushed, they have actually been reaffirmed in a self-sacrificing gesture of great generosity.

But Dindè cannot recognize the magnanimity of Collette's decision. He knows only that she has turned her back on him. In anger and frustration, he rushes into a nearby river and tears apart a fish trap ("nasse"). His impulsive act is childish and immature, but it is also a turning point because it serves as a catharsis that enables him to read a symbolic meaning into what he has just done. Just as he demolished the fish trap, he would like to sweep away the corrupt system that allows the Ekandès of this world to frustrate the legitimate aspirations of younger people like himself.

Earlier Dindè had observed how a large crab could enter the fish trap and easily devour any fish that happened to be caught in it. The fate of the fish has nothing to do with fairness or justice. The structure of the fish trap gives the crab a momentary dominance over his prey. Analogously, the existing social system gave Ekandè an advantage over the young couple in love. As Dindè reflects on the situation, he realizes that his own disappointment is not an isolated case of injustice but the logical consequence of a corrupt social system. He therefore vows to change the system that deprives people of their freedom to seek self-realization in their own terms. By retaining his belief in a modern self-concept while gaining insight into the nature of power, Dindè becomes capable of working toward a world in which similar injustices will not be inflicted on others.

The image of such a world embodies the implicit utopian message of *La Nasse*, for the resolve of Ndedi Penda's hero at the end of the novel is based on a belief in the possibility of a society where all people would be free to realize their own potential without having to renounce the sense of community that prevents them from becoming solitary, isolated individuals. To the extent that social institutions in contemporary Cameroon resembled the fish-trap structure of Dindè's village, *La Nasse* is a socially critical work, for as Ndedi Penda himself said, "one cannot be a writer without engaging in politics."[27]

Mokto's *Ramitou, mon étrangère* also made a political statement, but rather than criticizing the injustice of the existing situation in Cameroon, it lent support to Ahidjo's ideology of national unity by suggesting a way of overcoming ethnic rivalries. The marriage of a Bamileke man and a Bamun woman symbolizes for Mokto the sort of reconciliation that could take place if all Cameroonians of good will regarded each other not as "foreigners" but as fellow human beings who have a common interest in working together. Despite differences in the two writers' political attitudes, however, they both defended the autonomous self and its right to the happiness of romantic love.

The pursuit of the individual self was a preoccupation that extended across the ideological spectrum during the early years of Cameroonian independence. Whether poets and novelists were critical of a social system in which individuals were denied the freedom to realize themselves or whether they promoted individual responsibility and interethnic tolerance as keys to the success of the nation-building process, they drew heavily on autobiographical materials to present the individual self as a touchstone of meaning and value in the contemporary world. In this way, Cameroonian literature reflected and reinforced the individualism commonly associated with the modern nation-state. At the same time, it manifested a decidedly utopian strain in response to the widespread desire for a society where this individualism could be reconciled with the sense of community characteristic of traditional society.

CHAPTER

12

GUILLAUME OYONO-MBIA
AND THE RISE OF
CAMEROONIAN THEATER

In literate cultures, drama differs from poetry or narrative fiction in the sense that its printed form is secondary to its performance before an audience. Although stage drama is a relatively recent phenomenon in Cameroon, many traditional practices were theatrical in nature. Unlike European plays, however, these practices assumed the participation of the audience, and when Cameroonians began to stage formal dramas, there continued to be considerable interaction between actors and spectators. This lack of distance between the audience and the action on the stage diminished the illusion that plays constitute a separate reality with their own laws of organization. Scenes regarded as tragic by European theatergoers who accept the conventions of dramatic representation often seem humorous to Cameroonian spectators who refuse to be deceived by the artifice. Responding to the nature of their audiences, Cameroonian playwrights have produced more comedies than any other kind of drama.

In countries such as Cameroon, the possibility of performance also heightens a writer's chances of reaching illiterate or marginally literate audiences. Plays in African languages could have a substantial impact on a broad spectrum of the population, but even dramas staged in French or English are often attended by people who seldom read books. Aware of this possibility, many writers turned to the theater in the hope of reaching more people. As René Philombe explained, "when I write a play, I'm . . . aiming for a much larger public than when I compose a novel or a short story."[1] Large audiences have been attracted to plays, not only in Yaounde and Douala but also in cities and towns throughout the country.

Yet the potential for a truly popular Cameroonian theater has never been fully realized, in part because the government adopted policies that restricted its development. By discouraging the use of African languages for high cultural purposes, the authorities blocked a possible source of critical commentary that it would have been hard for them to control, but they also prevented the emergence of local theater movements. During the 1960s and early 1970s, only a few plays were actually censored by the government, although a licensing system was implemented in the 1970s, and it impeded the evolution of a theater that had begun to flourish during the early years of independence. Actually, the government's attitude toward the performance of plays vacillated between tolerance and repressiveness, making it difficult for writers to know what would be acceptable on the stage.

If performance takes precedence over the written text in dramatic literature, there are still important differences between stage plays in a literate culture and theatrical representations in oral cultures. A stage drama is nearly always linked with a script, and it is generally presented for the entertainment of spectators who do not necessarily belong to the same ethnic community. Both of these characteristics reinforce the notion of individuality associated with modern national societies. The script is identified with the specific person who wrote it. It can also be read in isolation by other individuals, and it can be used as the basis for subsequent presentations by people who have no relationship to the author or to the group of actors who produced it for the first time. Although stage dramas often draw upon the cultural and historical background of a specific ethnic group, the heterogeneity of the intended audience prevents them from performing the social or religious functions that help preserve group cohesiveness in traditional settings. In this respect, they are undeniably modern, no matter how traditional their ideological message might be.

Cameroonians initially encountered this form of drama in the schools and seminaries, where the performance of European-style plays served a didactic or educational purpose. Seminary students at Akono and Mvolye staged several dramatic productions during the 1930s, and morality plays had occasionally been presented in mission churches even before this time. Throughout the 1930s, secondary-school classes in the French mandate territory occasionally performed scenes from French classical dramas. Some of those who participated in these productions realized that theater was a potentially popular form of literary entertainment, and many retained their interest in it after leaving school. In 1941, for example, Léopold and Abel Moumé Etia helped organize a Douala literary group that put on several plays during the war.

The first real outburst of creative dramatic activity occurred in the minor seminary at Akono during the 1940s. Like students at the William Ponty school in Senegal, the young seminarians were encouraged to familiarize themselves with traditional customs because it was assumed such knowledge would enable them to communicate more effectively with the people.[2] The bishop of Yaounde even challenged young seminarians such as Jean-Baptiste Obama and Adalbert Owona to write plays that might be staged for local audiences in their own languages. The result was two plays that enjoyed considerable success when they were staged in Ewondo and in French throughout the south-central and coastal regions of Cameroon. Loosely based on Molière's *Les Fourberies de Scapin* and adapted to an *mvet* style of performance, Obama's *Mbarga Osono* (Mbarga Pickpocket) tells the story of a young man who, taking seriously the

Biblical injunction to aid those in need, robs the wealthy and gives to the poor. In his *Fada Jean* (Father Jean), Owona created a Cameroonian version of the Bohemian martyr Saint John Neopomisine's refusal to reveal the secrets of the confessional to the king.

Both plays are based on the Christian premises of educated Africans who reevaluated traditional customs from a European perspective; however, Obama and Owona clearly recognized the disparity between colonialist practice and the Christian principle. They also became convinced that traditional culture contained many of the same values that Europeans had adduced to support their claims of cultural superiority. By structuring their plays around Christian values in a Cameroonian context, Obama and Owona did promote the ideals of the church, but they also called the unchristian practices of colonialist society into question, and this veiled social criticism, which later became a characteristic trait of postcolonial drama, was one of the major reasons for the popular success of *Mbarga Osono* and *Fada Jean*.

There were a few amateur acting groups in Yaounde and Douala during the 1950s, but a truly Cameroonian theater did not emerge until after independence, and when it did, it was intimately linked with small acting troupes that coalesced around dynamic individuals who directed plays written by themselves or their fellow countrymen.[3] Many of these groups were ephemeral and remained together for only a single production. Often they were supported by contributions from the actors themselves. All of them had to overcome the problem of inadequate rehearsal and performance space, the difficulty of publicizing their productions, and the public's unfamiliarity with the conventions of stage drama. Generally they performed in schools and cultural centers before relatively small audiences, although the French cultural center in Yaounde hosted an increasing number of francophone performances by local troupes after 1964. Despite obstacles, the enthusiasm for Cameroonian theater grew, and acting groups proliferated during the late 1960s and early 1970s.

Although improvisation is common in Cameroonian theater, these groups invariably worked from written scripts. At first their texts were produced only in rough mimeographed form for members of the acting company, but as interest in theater grew, authors of plays sold these mimeographed copies in bookstores and circulated them among friends. As a result, amateur acting groups and schools began to use them, frequently without the author's knowledge or consent. The most successful of these published plays was Guillaume Oyono-Mbia's *Trois Prétendants . . . un mari*, which was one of Edition CLE's first books when it began operation in 1963. Since then, it has remained the firm's best-selling literary work. Three years later, Adolph-Claude Mballa published several of the most popular locally produced dramas in a special issue of the *Bulletin du CFLC* (later reprinted as *Théâtre Camerounais*), and in 1968 CLE produced a series of cheap mimeographed plays that its editors proposed to sell by subscription to schools, theater groups, and individuals. Known as CLE-Théâtre, fifteen of these fascicles appeared during the next few years, including many of the dramas written for the local acting troupes.

The existence of the CLE-Théâtre series inspired young writers to submit scripts that had not yet been performed, and some of these were also published, promoting the idea that plays could also be read as literature. This idea was powerfully reinforced by the ORTF (French National Radio) when it instituted an annual competition for original radio dramas.[4] The winning entries were recorded and broadcast throughout francophone Africa; they were also published in attractive paperback editions and distributed by the French government's cultural exchange service. Cameroonians consistently submitted more manuscripts to this contest than did citizens of any other country, and their entries have frequently appeared under the ORTF imprint. In addition, Cameroonian playwrights have often subsidized the printing of their own works at local presses or with companies such as Pierre Jean Oswald in Paris. This flurry of publication fostered a growing tendency to regard drama not only as performance but also as an integral part of the country's literate culture.

During the early years of independence, there was little discussion of this nascent theater tradition in the public media. With the exception of a few articles by the playwright-director Jean-Pierre Dikongue Pipa, the country's daily newspaper, *La Presse du Cameroun*, ignored the production of Cameroonian plays, and they were never discussed on the national radio. Another dramatist, Abel Zomo Bem, wrote reviews and drama discussions for the Protestant weekly *La Semaine Camerounaise*, and Boé a Amang lectured on the educative value of theater at the French cultural center in Douala, but the most significant contribution to the development of an educated theatergoing public was the increasing availability of high-quality dramatic performances that accompanied the explosion of theatrical activity in Cameroon during the late 1960s and early 1970s.

The majority of plays written at this time were social comedies with a strong tendency to satirize the various forms of blindness that prevent individuals from recognizing the folly or inappropriateness of their attitudes toward the world. When set in the city, these social comedies tended to focus on the affectations of the newly wealthy, the corruption of the privileged class, or the foibles of villagers who did not know how to cope with the urban environment. When set in the village, these comedies usually depicted the local people's ignorance, superstition, greed, and abuse of traditional authority. Taken together, such plays represent a collective meditation upon a society that has not fulfilled the expectations generated by independence.

Because the blindness of characters who contributed to this corrupt reality was distorted to reveal its absurdity, the spectators of these plays could perceive what the characters themselves often failed to see, and this insight prepared them to recognize similar forms of blindness in the real world. Although the plays themselves almost never criticized the government, they often provoked laughter at forms of behavior that government policies had either fostered or failed to eliminate. Like the novels and poetry of the early independence period, these social comedies offered an obliquely critical view of Cameroonian society and sometimes held out the hope of utopian change. Apparent in the standards according to which the characters' blindness is judged, this hope generally found expression in happy endings that, at least temporarily, resolved the tension between the authors' desires for a better society and their awareness of imperfections in the existing one.

The problematic nature of individual identity in contemporary Cameroonian society is one of the dominant themes in these early social comedies. To the extent that individualism is associated with selfishness and the unbridled pursuit of wealth, it is often satirized as the root of corruption. But when the individualistic self-concept is linked with romantic love or with the right to self-realization, it tends to be portrayed in a positive light. In fact, the action of many Cameroonian social comedies revolves around individuals' struggles to achieve self-realization in situations where inflexible traditions, corruption, or the machinations of others threaten to prevent their doing so. Although there is a potential for tragedy in such situations, it is seldom realized on the Cameroonian stage, for most of these plays operate according to a principle of poetic justice that maneuvers the action toward a happy ending and reaffirms the belief that change is possible in the most corrupt system.

The best-known dramatist to emerge from the theatrical effervescence of the early independence period was Oyono-Mbia, whose *Trois Prétendants . . . un mari* is the most popular play ever to have been written by a Cameroonian. It is frequently staged in the schools and on public occasions, and its place in the national consciousness is suggested by the fact that it is the country's only literary work ever to have received the prestigious Ahmadou Ahidjo prize. Oyono-Mbia wrote the first version of *Trois Prétendants . . . un mari* while he was still a student in the Protestant secondary school at Libamba, and although he continued to revise it until the second edition was published by CLE almost ten years later, his initial venture into the theater was so successful that it set the tone for what was destined to become the dominant form of Cameroonian drama—the social comedy.

All of Oyono-Mbia's other plays are variations upon the social comedy format he adopted for *Trois Prétendants . . . un mari*, even though two of them, *Jusqu'à nouvel avis* and *Le Train spécial de Son Excellence*, were originally written in English and presented on the BBC. Having spent five years at the University of Keele in Great Britain, Oyono-Mbia is fluent in English, and he himself has translated his own works into both of Cameroon's official languages. When he directed the 1973 French premier of *Le Train spécial* at the Abbia movie theater in Yaounde, he also helped establish a precedent for using large auditoriums for the presentation of live drama.[5] Until that time, the largest theater used for this purpose was the one at the French cultural center, and it had less than one-sixth the seating capacity of a theater such as the Abbia. Written in the late 1960s, Oyono-Mbia's final play, *Notre Fille ne se mariera pas*, received first prize in the 1969 ORTF drama competition. With the exception of *Notre Fille*, all Oyono-Mbia's works were published by CLE and have enjoyed considerable popular success.

One reason for this success is Oyono-Mbia's extraordinary skill as a story-teller who recognizes how common, everyday occurrences can be transformed into dramatic episodes that stand for characteristic realities of contemporary African life. Cameroonians have no difficulty identifying with the types of characters, the speech patterns, and the actions in his plays. The comic structure and the theatrical conventions that characterize them owe a great deal to his reading of Molière, but the world view behind his depictions of contemporary Cameroonian reality differs greatly from that of the French classical dramatist.

As he demonstrated in his three-volume collection of short stories *Les Chroniques de Mvoutessi*, Oyono-Mbia has the capacity to elicit laughter while provoking people to reflect on the analogy between their own world and the imaginary one he has created for them. Although the humorous traits of the characters in these stories are exaggerated for dramatic effect, the characters themselves remain fully human, and readers laugh with them nearly as much as they laugh at them. This capacity to maintain the humanity of characters who are subjects of laughter carries over into Oyono-Mbia's plays and reflects elements of the traditional story-teller's world view. One early reviewer of *Trois Prétendants . . . un mari* remarked that the play's style was "nothing other than Bulu translated almost literally into French."[6] Projected into an essentially European theatrical form, this style and the world view associated with it help explain the extraordinary popularity of Oyono-Mbia's dramas.

One dimension of this world view also surfaces in the folktales of his native Bulu region. Many of these tales revolve around Kulu the tortoise, whose adventures illustrate characteristic aspects of traditional Bulu wisdom. For example, Kulu often triumphs over physically stronger creatures through the use of clever stratagems, but there is always an implicit acknowledgment that force —intellectual as well as physical force—will prevail in a harsh world where there is no poetic justice to right the wrongs inflicted on people. In such a world, Kulu can outwit stronger adversaries if they allow themselves to be blinded by pride, gullibility, or the obsessive pursuit of a goal they desire to reach. When they are outwitted, they become objects of laughter, reinforcing the idea that force is partly a function of intellectual discernment. Although these tales have comic overtones, they also express an awareness of life's tragic dimension. This same balanced view of the world reemerges in Oyono-Mbia's theater.

But Oyono-Mbia is not a traditionalist in the Negritude sense. The scene for many of his plays and stories is Mvoutessi, the village where he himself lived as a child. He realized that European colonization had introduced profound changes in villages such as Mvoutessi, and although people's values had changed in response to the altered situation, they often retained modes of behavior that were incompatible with their new values. Their failure to grasp the full significance of changes that had occurred in their society is a primary source of the comic effect in Oyono-Mbia's plays; in fact, the contradictions produced by this miscomprehension are often so great that society itself assumes a grotesquely comic appearance. The major change that had taken place in the world of Oyono-Mbia's characters was the introduction of a money economy, and all his plays revolve around the way characters define themselves in relation to the wealth and status made possible by money.

The principal preoccupation of these characters is the pursuit of wealth and the prestige associated with it. To reveal the folly of their approach to life, Oyono-Mbia exaggerates their attitudes in such a way that spectators cannot help but laugh at them. This laughter serves a dual function. Laughter at the foibles of the characters is the first step toward a socially critical appraisal of tendencies that exist in contemporary Cameroon, for when spectators reflect on the object of their laughter, they realize they have been laughing at attitudes often regarded as completely normal.

At the same time, laughter with the characters is a celebration of life that places their blindness and absurd pretentions into proper perspective. In a world governed by force, Oyono-Mbia believed that people should accept what they cannot change and rejoice with others in the awareness of being alive. For this reason, he construed the imaginary worlds of his plays as games in which the audience is invited to participate. In fact, three of his four plays culminate in celebrations that resolve the tensions that had surfaced during the previous action. Like his cousin Ferdinand Oyono, he perceives the world through the lens of an enlightened self-irony that enables him to regard laughter and joy as redeeming human possibilities in an implacably harsh world.

According to Oyono-Mbia, one of the greatest impediments to the realization of this possibility in contemporary Cameroon is a preoccupation with material wealth. In all his plays, this preoccupation is linked with villagers' attempts to benefit economically by exploiting the monetary value of a young woman from their family or ethnic group. For example, in *Trois Prétendants . . . un mari*, Atangana accepts a dowry payment from a local farmer who wants to marry his daughter Juliette, but when a high-ranking civil servant offers a substantially larger bride-price with the intention of taking her as his ninth wife, Atangana accepts it as well. Having attended school at Libamba where she developed strong convictions about freedom of choice in such matters, Juliette steals the two dowries and secretly gives them to Oko, the young classmate whom she desires to marry. At the end of the play, Oko disguises himself as a wealthy man and returns to the scene where the distraught villagers, who must reimburse the first two dowries, have been seeking to interest a Bamileke merchant in paying a bride-price large enough for this purpose. Oko then offers the money he received from Juliette as a dowry and agrees to marry her on the condition that she consent to the proposal.

The action of the play is humorous, but the underlying issue is serious. It involves competing definitions of individual identity and includes an attack on the acquisitiveness that is eroding the fabric of modern African society. Atangana and the other villagers view Juliette's marriage as a business transaction. They paid for her schooling, and they expect to reap a return on their investment by sharing in the bride-price and in the other presents that her future husband would presumably give them. In fact, nearly everyone in the village hopes to profit in some way from her marriage to the civil servant.

They assume that Juliette will obey her father's wishes because traditional social norms decree obedience and because she herself would enjoy prestige and wealth as the result of such a marriage.

However, the traditional practices on which they base their expectations evolved under socio-economic conditions that did not include monetary exchange or the possibility of individual self-realization. A contradiction arises when they accept the money economy but refuse to accept the other values that accompany it in the modern world. Their failure to recognize this contradiction produces humorous consequences. It also places their conception of Juliette's identity in conflict with her image of herself. When she proclaims her right to choose a marriage partner on the basis of romantic love, she is expressing her faith in the modern self-concept she acquired during her years of European-style schooling. And by devising a Kulu-like ruse to obtain the object of her desire, she demonstrates how the greed of the villagers blinds them to reality and allows them to be outwitted by someone who recognizes their vulnerability. The ending of *Trois Prétendants . . . un mari* thus serves as a vindication of Juliette's conception of herself.

Variations on the theme of the young woman as economic asset occur in all Oyono-Mbia's plays. *Jusqu'à nouvel avis* revolves around the villagers' expectations that their "daughter" Matalina, who has returned to the country after studying in France and marrying a doctor, will be the source of endless gifts and preferments for them. In *Le Train spécial*, a young university student returns to the village with her lover, whom the local stationmaster and a few older villagers mistakenly believe to be the "Excellency" whose presence in the region had been announced on the radio. Echoing the action in Gogol's *The Inspector General*, they seek to impress him so that he will bring "civilization and prosperity" to the village and secure a promotion for the stationmaster. And in *Notre Fille ne se mariera pas*, the villagers are intent upon preventing their university-educated daughter Charlotte from marrying because they have all staked claims to some portion of the salary she receives at the ministry where she works in Yaounde. One of the short stories in *Chroniques de Mvoutessi* even details the way in which a shrewd woman parlays the affairs of her mulatto daughter into a small fortune.

Yet just as Juliette's stratagem reveals the inadequacy of the villagers' attitude toward her in *Trois Prétendants . . . un mari*, the action in Oyono-Mbia's other plays discloses the harmful social consequences of the villagers' obsessive pursuit of their own economic self-interest. For example, in *Jusqu'à nouvel avis*, Matalina's father and the other villagers are anticipating her and her husband's first visit to the village since they returned to Cameroon three months previously. Her husband had initially desired to work in a backcountry hospital, but the government has offered him a prestigious position in the capital, and the villagers hope he will accept it because they expect to benefit from his wealth and status.

At the end of the play, the doctor's driver arrives with a letter explaining that he has just accepted the administrative position and will be obliged to postpone his visit "until further notice." The cases of beer, wine, and food that accompany the letter gladden the hearts of the villagers, who interpret them as an indication of what they can expect to receive in the future. In reality, Matalina's husband has sent the gifts as a surrogate for his own presence in the village, and the cold, formal tone of his letter suggests that he does not acknowledge the communal solidarity on which their claims to a share of his wealth are based. Furthermore, the doctor's acceptance of the administrative post means that he will not practice medicine in a part of the country where his expertise is most needed. In the long run, the villagers are harming themselves by their acquisitiveness because the global needs of society will never be fulfilled if everyone thinks as they do.

A similar mentality is evident in *Notre Fille ne se mariera pas*, for when the young woman becomes romantically involved with an agriculture specialist, her relatives object on the grounds that farming is not a sufficiently prestigious occupation. Yet like medicine, agricultural expertise is one of the greatest needs in rural Africa. In the background of all Oyono-Mbia's dramas is a profound social malaise, and the mentality of the villagers who pursue materialistic goals at the expense of their own long-term communal welfare is one of the primary causes of this malaise.

The satiric portrayals of individuals such as the money-grubbing sorcerer in *Trois Prétendants*, the pretentious stationmaster in *Le Train spécial*, and Charlotte's affectedly Europeanized friend Colette in *Notre Fille* illustrate the absurdity of this same mentality when it is viewed from the enlightened perspective of the dramatist and his audience. In fact, Oyono-Mbia is suggesting that the pervasiveness of this mentality in all its many guises helps explain why the promise of African independence has been deferred "until further notice."

The satiric depiction of this mentality is part of the entertainment that he views as the primary purpose of his drama. In his eyes, he has created artificial worlds that are not to be confused with reality, even though their impact on spectators depends upon a recognition of parallels between what happens on the stage and what happens in real life. To underscore this point, he frequently breaks the illusion of verisimilitude by having his characters allude to the roles they are playing. For example, when Juliette's cousin accompanies her fiancé, Oko, off stage after she has given them the two dowries in *Trois Prétendants*, he turns to the spectators in the audience and assures them that he will see them again in the fifth act. And when Colette in *Notre Fille* discovers that she is a character in a play, she complains that she wasn't given enough time to prepare her role. Such comments heighten the impression that Oyono-Mbia's dramas resemble games that are calculated to entertain the audience. They also draw attention to the role-playing that contributes to the social malaise in the background of all his plays.

The comic flaw of many Oyono-Mbia characters is the exaggerated seriousness with which they assume the roles they have invented for themselves. When they confuse these roles with their true identities, they cut themselves off from others and inadvertently reveal the absurdity of their pretentions. The villagers who seek to profit by exploiting the economic value of their young women illustrate how people can blind themselves to the human ties that should link them together. The earnestness with which they pursue their materialistic goals also prevents them from understanding how the world has changed around them.

Often Oyono-Mbia holds up these false identities to ridicule, as he does with the stationmaster who officiously orders the passengers to clean up the railroad station to impress "His Excellency" in *Le Train spécial*, or with Colette who, in *Notre Fille*, self-righteously insists that her son become cultured by learning to eat the Camembert cheese that she herself cannot tolerate. The stationmaster is deflated by a telephone call that reveals he has been trying to impress the "wrong Excellency," and Colette's affectations prevent her from engaging in honest relationships with other people. Nevertheless, most of Oyono-Mbia's plays culminate in celebrations, suggesting that the only real escape from false identities is to drop them in favor of a genuine engagement with life.

Laughter and celebration are leitmotifs in all Oyono-Mbia's plays, and at the end of *Trois Prétendants, Jusqu'à nouvel avis,* and *Notre Fille* they coalesce in a festive atmosphere that momentarily resolves the conflicts generated by the acquisitiveness of the characters and their earnestness in identifying with their own false masks. In *Trois Prétendants*, for example, the entire audience is invited to join in the dancing and singing that mark the announcement of Juliette's engagement to Oko. As the spectators mingle with the actors, the pretext for their participation is no longer important. By laughing, singing, and dancing with those who have dropped the masks they wore during the play, spectators are celebrating life in a way that contrasts with the acquisitiveness and the exaggerated attachment to social status they have seen on the stage as well as in real life. They are being encouraged to drop their own masks in the recognition that spontaneous outbursts of joy testify to the humanity they share with everyone around them.

Although the celebrations at the end of these dramas become an implicit standard according to which the characters' corrupt values can be judged, they do not constitute a solution to the social malaise that such values have engendered. Oyono-Mbia himself stated that "the endings of my plays should never be taken as an attempt to suggest solutions."[7] However, the catharsis they produce is premised on a profound insight into the nature of human life. Resulting from the same intellectual penetration that features so prominently in the Kulu tales, this insight allows people to comprehend the folly of obsessive preoccupations with wealth and status. At the same time, it shows them why they must accommodate themselves to the irrevocable changes that have occurred in African society as the result of modernization. Oyono-Mbia's form of social comedy is popular in Africa because it permits spectators to laugh at characters and situations similar to those they have encountered in their own lives. Spectators can also empathize with a comic vision that incorporates elements of a traditional world view without idealizing it as a means of diverting attention from the unpleasant realities of postcolonial society.

Like Oyono-Mbia's social comedies, the vast majority of the more than two hundred plays written by Cameroonians during the first dozen years of independence focus on situations that reveal how Africans can be blinded by an obsessive preoccupation with wealth, a pretentious attachment to status, or a naive belief in outmoded superstitions.[8] These social comedies of the early independence period can be roughly divided into two categories—those set in the city and those that take place in the village. Although interconnected in many ways, urban and rural societies confront different sets of problems in contemporary Cameroon, and these differences are clearly reflected in these two sorts of plays.

The social comedies with urban settings tend to depict the corrupt mentalities that result from the unbridled pursuit of wealth and status. They did not attack the Ahidjo government directly, but their portrayals of a society that contrasts sharply with the official nation-building ideal often represented an implicit criticism of the system that this government helped to create. At the same time, most of these urban social comedies could be interpreted as supportive of Ahidjo's nation-building ideal because the corruption they portrayed was presented as an impediment to the realization of this ideal. The central metaphor in these plays is blindness, for the characters in them often fail to recognize the values that might enable them to live in harmony with themselves and others. When this blindness causes them to betray such values, they are acquiescing in the "pitiless society" that Boé a Amang mentions in the preface to his *Course à l'argent*.

This "pitiless society" is the principal subject of Cameroonian urban social comedies, which generally seek to unmask the hypocrisy and greed that characterize it. This unmasking process implies a standard of value that is often utopian in nature. For example, Jacques-Mariel Nzouankeu's popular *L'Agent spécial* deals with corruption in the civil service, and in discussing the world view behind his approach to such phenomena, Nzouankeu declared: "I am firmly attached to the human person as the end purpose of any enterprise. I believe that man can perfect himself and the world."[9] Not all authors of urban social comedies would subscribe to Nzouankeu's humanistic optimism, but the utopian impulse is nearly always present in their works as a contrast to the corrupt society portrayed in them.

The issue that Nzouankeu raises in *L'Agent spécial* is a crucial one in Cameroon and in many other recently independent African countries. The special agent in the title is the government fiscal representative who collects, disburses, and safeguards public funds at the local level. When Nzouankeu's Ngantcha is appointed special agent in a provincial town, all his relatives descend upon him, assuming that the money in the government coffers is at their disposal. To fulfill his obligations toward them and to support a lifestyle commensurate with his new position, Ngantcha borrows heavily from the public treasury, but his malfeasance is discovered in a government audit, and he is sent to prison, although he is soon released on the condition that he repay the missing funds. Recognizing his previous folly, Ngantcha vows to live modestly and to perform the duties of his office with integrity.

This happy ending implies that people are capable of overcoming their blindness by learning from their past mistakes, but the action of the play also suggests the need for a reevaluation of the attitudes that impede progress toward a decent and equitable society in Cameroon. The embezzlement of government funds is endemic in many African countries, and Nzouankeu is inviting the spectators of *L'Agent spécial* to reflect on the complex ways in which this abuse of public trust originates in false assumptions about the individual's relationship to the national community. In traditional society, people who gain access to great wealth are expected to live in grand style and share their resources with members of their family. However, as Nzouankeu intimates, public funds belong to everyone, and social justice demands that they be administered responsibly. At the end of the play, Ngantcha accepts this principle, and his conversion expresses Nzouankeu's faith in people's capacity to recognize the common interest and to work toward it.

The major impediment to this sense of civic responsibility is the corrupting power of money among the newly wealthy classes of Africa, and it became one of the most prominent themes in Cameroonian urban social comedies of the early independence period. Amang's *Course à l'argent* presents a tableau of characters who lose touch with themselves because they equate happiness with economic self-interest. Samuel Nkamgnia's *La Femme prodigue* and Decatlas Philippe Ngassam's *La Première Paye* revolve around the extravagant expenditures of women whose pretentiousness causes them to argue publicly with their husbands. An excellent example of this materialistic mentality is contained in Abel Zomo Bem's *Le Patron noir*, a satiric farce in which the "black boss" Bingo mistreats his employees even more shamelessly than his European predecessor had done. Although he lives in luxury and indulges the whims of a secretary who doubles as his mistress, Bingo resists paying his creditors as long as possible, and he never gives his workers their pitifully low salaries on time. During the play, his employees revolt, forcing him to raise their salaries and to give them a check for what he owes them. His creditors also extract payment from him, and as the curtain falls, he is cursing in vain over the money he has been obliged to relinquish.

Beneath the humor of *Le Patron noir*, Zomo Bem is making a serious statement about the materialistic mentality that transforms Bingo into a lonely individual who values money more than people. This mentality is widespread, as one of the rebellious employees suggests when he asserts that "we must confront the situation created by the Bingo mentality on a national scale."[10] Within the context of Ahidjo's Cameroon, such a statement implies that the social malaise in the country results from the greed of a privileged class that continues to exploit the people after independence. According to one of Bingo's creditors, people desired independence so that everyone might live more happily than before, but what happened was that black bosses simply replaced white ones.

Frustration at the disappointed expectations of independence often found expression in Cameroonian urban social comedies such as *Le Patron noir*. For example, when one of the characters in Thomas Fotso Mangwa's *Le Triomphe de l'alcool* is struck by a policeman, he indignantly replies, "the time of the colonialists is over; the country's independent now, and we're citizens; and you can't strike a citizen like that."[11] Cameroonian audiences immediately recognized the irony of such protests, for they knew that the police were often more arbitrary after independence than they had been during the colonial era. As in *Le Patron noir*, the point is that the transfer of authority from white bosses to black bosses will make no difference to the majority of the people unless the corrupt mentality of the privileged class can be changed.

The hollowness of nation-building slogans is suggested in both plays. Despite paying lip service to the ideals of independence, Bingo profits unconscionably from his dealings with government ministries. And in *Le Triomphe de l'alcool*, the temperance crusader, whose pious words resemble the government's nation-building rhetoric, makes a fool of himself after taking a few drinks to steady his nerves in preparation for a major speech. Yet both Zomo Bem and Fotso Mangwa indicate that there is a possibility of overcoming the greed and hypocrisy that blind people to their own human needs.

The success of Bingo's employees in obtaining higher salaries suggests that the people of Cameroon could vanquish the Bingo complex if they acted with a similar solidarity. And two young people whose earlier dreams of romantic happiness had been frustrated by corrupt dowry practices in *Le Triomphe de l'alcool* discover that they can create their own happiness by simply ignoring the system. Plays such as *Le Patron noir* and *Le Triomphe de l'alcool* are socially critical in the sense that they invite audiences to compare the official optimism about national independence with the "pitiless society" that has been created by a corrupt privileged class.

One of the major inequities in this society involves the way incompetent individuals are rewarded while those of talent and good will are allowed to languish in poverty. Stanislas Awona's *Le Chomeur* addresses this problem, and its popularity suggests that his treatment of the subject struck a responsive chord in Cameroonian audiences. The major character in this urban social comedy is Eboutou, a sensitive and talented young man who remains unemployed at a time, shortly after independence, when two of his less well educated friends obtain lucrative civil-service positions that they see primarily as a means of acquiring wealth and status. Despite Eboutou's previous generosity toward them, the two friends disdain him for his lack of respectability. Yet when his maudlin letter to a government minister results in his appointment to an important position, he does not hesitate to extricate them from the difficulties into which their irresponsibility has precipitated them.

The action in *Le Chomeur* operates according to a poetic justice that allows

Eboutou, who treats people with respect regardless of their station in life, to obtain a position commensurate with his talents and his integrity. During a moment of discouragement at being unemployed, Eboutou once soliloquizes: "Am I without any value then? No. I feel capable of dedicating my whole life to a task that would be useful to my country."[12] This idealism was widespread among Cameroonian young people in the early independence period, and Eboutou's triumph at the end constitutes a form of wish fulfillment for them, but it hardly solves the underlying problem of the society's arbitrariness in distributing the work that needs to be done and the rewards for doing it. Eboutou's appointment and his intervention on behalf of his friends are possible only because he is enjoying the benefits of the same patronage system he had decried when he was unemployed. As in Rémy Medou Mvomo's *Les Enchaînés*, Awona's hero achieves wealth and happiness because he possesses moral qualities that should, in an ideal world, be recompensed by them. The assumption behind such happy endings is that the system itself is fair as long as it functions to reward ambitious, talented people such as Eboutou.

Although the predominance of social comedy on the Cameroonian stage owed a great deal to the success of Oyono-Mbia's plays, some practitioners of the genre distanced themselves from the farcical aspects of his works. For writers such as Hubert Mono Ndjana and Marie-Charlotte Mbarga, the humor of social comedy serves a morally edifying purpose that should not be obscured by mindless laughter. The underlying assumption in their social comedies is that people who fail to see themselves clearly often make fools of themselves and call disaster down upon their own heads. The dramatic conflict at the center of their plays is generally resolved by a form of poetic justice that predisposes members of the audience to accept the author's condemnation of attitudes that are prevalent in contemporary Cameroonian society. Insofar as these authors are exhorting people to liberate themselves from false appearances and to abandon the social masks that prevent them from dealing honestly with each other, their plays become part of an ongoing national discourse about freedom and identity.

The social comedies of Mono Ndjana clearly illustrate this tendency. Eschewing what he regards as the abstract or stereotyped thinking of Negritude, radical politics, traditionalism, and experimental theater, he insists that drama should entail the transformation of concrete reality into momentary illusions capable of entertaining people and provoking insights into the nature of real-world problems, particularly problems of self-definition. The values underlying his depiction of these problems are invariably the same—honesty toward one's self and others, independence of mind, and the capacity to transcend selfish motivations in acts of love. Each of his plays revolves around a series of incidents in which one or more of the major characters disregards these values.

In the first scene of *Vice-Versa*, for example, a Europeanized couple invites a traditional couple to dinner. Their roles are reversed in the final scene when each couple adopts the mannerisms that the other had initially cultivated. The point is that all four characters lack confidence in their own sense of identity.

The Europeanized husband in the first part of the play even confides in his traditional counterpart that "to be myself, I need to be somebody else, you for example."[13] Like the other characters, he attaches supreme importance to the mask he presents to the world rather than seeking to harmonize his outward appearance with what he actually feels himself to be. The solution to his problem lies neither in a European identity nor in a traditional one, but in a self-understanding that would enable him to be himself regardless of the clothes and habits he chooses to adopt. Without this understanding, he and the other characters are abdicating their freedom in the sense that their actions are determined not by their own honest impulses but by stereotyped models of behavior.

The same problem is approached from a different perspective in Mono Ndjana's *La Revenante*, where the major character learns that his attachment to an ambitious woman doctor is pointless in the sense that she is incapable of loving anyone but herself. He had initially been attracted to her because their relationship corroborated his image of himself as a modern man, but his experience with a woman dressed as a "revenante" (a person returned from the dead) teaches him to define himself in terms of love and honest self-awareness. As in his case, moral blindness engendered by the single-minded pursuit of a false self-image lies at the center of all Mono Ndjana's social comedies. Generally linked with a yearning for money or social status, this moral blindness transforms those afflicted with it into fools or victims, thereby illustrating the superiority of the human values they renounced when they accepted the commonplace aspirations of contemporary society.

This pattern of dramatic action is also apparent in many other social comedies of the 1970s. Joseph Kengni's *Un Amour adultère*, Rabiatou Njoya's *La Dernière Aimée*, Louis Kengne Fouamno's *Le Polygame*, Jacob Ndié's *La Place de la femme*, and Michel Magong's *Contrat* all depict the punishment suffered by characters whose preoccupation with their own self-interest blinds them to the truth about themselves and causes them to act in self-destructive ways. Marie-Charlotte Mbarga's *La Famille africaine*, *Le Charlatan*, *Une Fille dans la tourmente*, and *Les Aventures de Passa* follow a similar pattern as a means of provoking audiences into reflecting upon the connection between what they see on the stage and what they experience in society. She herself is convinced that "daily life is filled with theatrical scenes."[14] In her plays, some form of moral blindness usually precipitates a major character into a difficult situation that prompts the audience to reflect upon who is to blame. The implication is that, if they understand the nature of the character's blindness, they can avoid succumbing to it themselves.

For example, Mbarga's best-known play, *La Famille africaine*, deals with the ruinous demands that a young man's family make on him when he and his wife return home after having completed their studies in Europe. He is so blinded by his status as a "big man" that he accedes to every request. To sustain his false self-image, he embezzles government funds, issues bad checks, and sells civil-service examinations. Arrested and sentenced to prison, he is abandoned by his relatives, although his wife remains loyal, demonstrating how love can transcend the self-interest that had attracted the others to him.

The implicit question that hangs over the end of *La Famille africaine* is: who is responsible for the young man's debacle? Family members placed an enormous burden on him, but his own ego blinded him to the folly of attempting to sustain a role he could not play. The primary moral value in the play is his wife's honesty of emotion, which contrasts with his blindness and that of his greedy relatives. By reflecting on this contrast, spectators of the play are led to perceive that people can overcome moral blindness if they liberate themselves from dehumanizing identity concepts and act with emotional honesty. The underlying message in her work is therefore quite similar to that in Mono Ndjana's plays.

To unmask various forms of moral blindness, both Mono Ndjana and Mbarga have recourse to satire, which becomes the dominant vehicle for the communication of a social message in such plays as Georges Abelar's *Le Supporter*, Protais Asseng's *Trop c'est trop*, and Pabe Mongo's *Le Philosophe et le sorcier*.[15] In *Le Supporter*, the butt of the author's satire is a soccer fan whose passion for the national team is so excessive that he allows himself to be duped by a confidence man who persuades him that he will be named his country's representative to the international soccer federation. In *Trop c'est trop*, it is a husband who exhorts his wife to have a thirteenth child so he can be awarded a medal as a "National Papa." He changes his mind only after she has given him a potion to make his stomach swell and convinced him that he himself is pregnant. And in *Le Philosophe et le sorcier*, both the pompous philosophy professor and the charlatan who claims to have cured his wife of childlessness are exposed as self-centered individuals who pretend to be other than they really are. All three social comedies satirize the pride that causes such individuals to engage in self-destructive forms of behavior while attempting to defend false self-images.

Cameroonian social comedies that take place in village settings also deal with the way mentalities have been distorted by the repudiation of intellectual and emotional honesty. The moral blindness depicted in them frequently stems from an obsessive desire for money and status, although the conflict between traditional and modern values is more obvious in them than it is in urban social comedies. This blindness might result from an individual's ambition to "become somebody" in local society. Or it might originate in ignorance and superstition. In many rural social comedies, members of the older generation are blind to the changes that have inspired younger people with individualistic attitudes toward freedom and self-realization. The world view behind the dramatic action in these plays generally implies a utopian standard of value that finds expression in the poetic justice that discredits human blindness and in the satiric distortion that reduces blinded individuals to objects of laughter.

Both techniques are apparent in three of the most frequently produced plays of the period—Jean Mba Evina's *Politicos*, Patrice Ndedi Penda's *Le Fusil*, and

Joseph Kengni's *Un Père aux abois*. Like the works of Oyono-Mbia, they all culminate in a festive atmosphere, echoing the communal, participatory ethos of traditional village life, and marking the reestablishment of a just social situation that had been temporarily threatened by the corrupt mentalities of the modern world. *Politicos* lampoons a pretentious villager's ambition to "become somebody" by running for political office despite his lack of qualifications and his inability to identify with the common good. He even prides himself on not paying his taxes. However, after persuading the village elders to support his candidacy by plying them with palm wine, he is unsuccessful in his attempt to bribe a government official, who orders him sent to prison for nonpayment of taxes.

Although *Politicos* is critical of the electoral process in Cameroon, it was frequently staged under Ahidjo government sponsorship because its underlying message supports the nation-building process. In the play, the word *politics* serves as a many-layered metaphor for corruption in personal and public affairs. The candidate's father even regards politics as an illness, the primary symptoms of which are garrulousness, greed, and frequent trips to the city. Reminding his son that politics cannot cultivate the fields, the old man insists that people should attend to their vital needs first. Similarly, the government official admonishes the candidate for paying lip service to patriotic symbols while neglecting his civic duties.

Mba Evina's play focuses attention not on the shortcomings of the political system but on the foolish ambition that blinds villagers to the need for conscientious work and voluntary obedience to a just system of government. The author's moral perspective is implicit in the healthy common sense of the candidate's father and in the incorruptibility of the government official, both of whom serve as correctives to the blindness of an individual obsessed with politics as an avenue to personal aggrandizement. His imprisonment is a vindication of this moral perspective and a reaffirmation of political ideals like those espoused by the Cameroonian government.

Both *Le Fusil* and *Un Père aux abois* depict the tribulations of innocent villagers who experience difficulty with the corruption of modern society, although they ultimately receive what they desire because their honesty is rewarded by a form of poetic justice. In *Le Fusil*, the villager Ndo travels to Douala, where he seeks to collect payment for his cocoa harvest, cash a check at a bank, and obtain a gun permit from the police. The possession of a gun would be a matter of pride to him and to his entire village, but after paying bribes and losing the rest of his money to thieves, Ndo returns empty-handed to the village and encounters the scorn of those who had previously envied him; however, the unexpected gift of a gun from his niece in Yaounde rectifies the situation and allows him to "become somebody" in village society. Yet before the gift arrives, Ndo must confront his creditors, and to one of them he laments: "may the one who invented money be damned! Money sows discord, hardens hearts, ruins everything."[16] From the perspective of traditional village society, the introduction of a money economy did change everything, but one cannot simply wish away such change.

Ndo's own desire to be "somebody" is contingent upon his ability to acquire wealth. His blindness to his implication in the system he condemns is humorous, but when it is compounded by the corruption of the bribe-takers and thieves, it contributes to a larger social malaise that mirrors the situation in contemporary Cameroon. Waman, the major character in Kengni's drama, faces a similar dilemma when he attempts to obtain an authenticated birth certificate so that his son can continue his schooling. Although duped into paying a substantial bribe for a worthless scrap of paper, Waman eventually speaks with a higher authority and acquires the needed document. His commitment to the education of his children is rewarded by the principles of poetic justice that govern the play's dramatic action. In all three of these rural social comedies, blindness and corruption are unmasked from a point of view that assumes the need to reconcile modern rationality with a traditional sense of community.

This point of view and the moral didacticism associated with it are also apparent in the rural social comedies published in the CLE-Théâtre series. Works such as Jean-Laforest Afana's *La Coutume qui tue*, Simon Bibana's *La Case en péril*, and Rabiatou Njoya's *Toute la rente y passe* all demonstrate how traditional superstitions induce people into making tragic errors or entice them into being duped by others. The assumption behind the action in all these plays is that people must achieve a clarity of vision that permits them to overcome a blindness occasioned by outmoded beliefs.

A similar emphasis is apparent in plays such as Poincaré Tioguep's *Le Triomphe de l'amour*, Pabe Mongo's *Innocente Assimba*, and Timothée Ndzagaap's *La Fille du roi a menti*, where young people succeed in choosing their own marriage partners in the face of parental opposition that is rooted in a traditional concept of the individual's relationship to the family. Even though there is an atypically tragic ending in Léon-Marie Ayissi's *Les Innocents*, the play's hero recognizes the petty jealousies and self-destructive tendencies that masquerade beneath traditional customs, and he too defends the individual's right to the happiness of freely chosen romantic love. Under such circumstances, older people are generally depicted as blind to the changed conditions of life in the modern world, and the triumph of the younger generation vindicates the modern idea of selfhood.

By the mid-1970s, the conflict between young people and their parents over questions of love and marriage had become a stereotyped dramatic situation, and it began to lose its fascination for young playwrights. The question of self-realization remained pertinent, however, and Kengni poses it within a larger social context in his frequently staged *Dans Le Pétrin*, in which the brilliant young man Noutsa cannot continue his studies because no one is willing to pay his school fees. After his mother had conceived him, her father had insisted on prosecuting her lover, who remained in prison many years later. Convinced that, "whatever my origins might be, I have the right and the duty to educate myself like any other citizen of this country,"[17] Noutsa turns to his grandfather and to the courts for support, but both refuse to acknowledge their responsibility for his welfare, and he is left "dans le pétrin" (in a mess).

His dilemma mirrors that of many Cameroonian young people, for a viable identity in the contemporary world depends upon the possibility of realizing one's own potential, and many of them have been denied the opportunity to educate themselves in accord with their talents and ambitions. Kengni does not offer a solution to the problem, but by drawing attention to the moral blindness that lies behind it, he is unmasking the hypocrisy of claims that the society is a just and equitable one.

Both Lin Chindji's *Le Choix irrevocable* and Lucien Mailli's *C'était écrit dans le ciel* depict the ending of an age in which parents could define their children's identity and make important choices for them; the new era announced by the protagonists' success in challenging such traditional practices is one in which romantic love, freedom of choice, and Christianity are compatible with African authenticity. In these plays and many others like them, the younger generation's quest for freedom and individual identity becomes a melodrama with modern self-concepts being pitted against the traditionalist assumptions of village life. As in all the francophone social comedies of the early independence period, the principal thrust of such dramas is to unmask some form of blindness, whether it is brought about by traditional superstitions or by the obsessive pursuit of wealth and status. Oyono-Mbia was the most successful practitioner of this genre, but many others developed variations on the model he helped to popularize.

Throughout the 1960s and 1970s, the leading dramatist in anglophone Cameroon was Victor Musinga, who developed a unique sort of social comedy.[18] In many ways, his accomplishment is remarkable. Like Oyono-Mbia, Musinga had never seen a dramatic performance before he staged his own first play, but when he brought together a group of amateur actors to put on *Mr. No-Balance Tastes Bribery* at Victoria (Limbé) and Buea in 1966, the response was so enthusiastic that he wrote more plays and took them on tour throughout West Cameroon.[19] Since then, he has written, produced, directed, and acted in all the more than twenty-five plays that his Musinga Drama Group has brought to the stage.

The only anglophone acting company entered in the 1974 national drama competition to choose a Cameroonian representative for the FESTAC celebrations in Nigeria, Musinga's group won first prize, although it was deprived of the opportunity to travel abroad when the government decided to send a selection of francophone actors instead. Overcoming his disappointment, Musinga wrote a fictionalized account of the affair and staged it as *Mr. Director*, one of his most popular plays. For more than twenty years, Musinga has held together the only permanent acting troupe in anglophone Cameroon, and he has done so while supporting himself as a government clerk.

The popularity of his plays derives in large part from the fact that he conceives of them from within anglophone Cameroonian society and not as a detached observer who contemplates it from a position of social superiority. Attuned to the language spoken by the people in their homes and in the markets, he weaves their idiom into his texts. He does not hesitate to include outrageous puns, malapropisms, allusions to local events, farcical episodes, and long dialogues in pidgin. When he is on tour, he even visits public places to glean information that he later incorporates into his highly flexible script for the evening's performance. The people who attend his plays immediately recognize traits, attitudes, and impulses they have witnessed in the real world. What might seem like slapstick to a European observer can thus function as a critique of contemporary society for Musinga's audiences. Yet because improvisation and interaction with the audience are encouraged, the atmosphere at a performance by the Musinga Drama Group is more like a raucous, participatory social event than a European-style evening at the theater.

The social commentary in Musinga's plays is reinforced by the Christian-influenced moral didacticism that characterizes much of anglophone Cameroonian literature. Each play revolves around a problem that he believes should be brought to the attention of the public. Invariably this problem stems from some form of moral blindness, and as in many francophone Cameroonian social comedies, the true nature of this blindness is exposed by means of satire and a poetic justice that punishes people for their hypocrisy and pretentiousness. *The Trials of Ngowo* and *The Challenge of Yoé* deal with the dilemma of young women who desire to liberate themselves from outmoded marriage customs, *Madame Magrano* and *Night Marriages* with adultery, *Colofonco* with the dangers of cult practices, and *Accountant Wawah* with the corruption of a European-educated "been-to." In each case, the assumption is that the problems evoked could be resolved if people acted with good faith, love, and integrity. Underlying the exuberance of Musinga's plays is, therefore, an idealistic vision of what Cameroonian society could become if its citizens behaved in a morally upright fashion. This vision unites the comic and didactic elements of his work and lends them a moral seriousness that transcends their propensity toward farce.

The Tragedy of Mr. No-Balance provides a typical example of Musinga's approach to this kind of theater. Structured around the theme of petty bribery, it focuses on the one-dimensional comic figure of Z. K. No-Balance, an office manager who solicits illegal contributions from prospective employees and eventually receives a long jail sentence for attempting to bribe an undercover police officer who is investigating his corrupt practices. By presenting No-Balance as a caricature of the petty bribe-takers with whom Cameroonian audiences are intimately familiar in their day-to-day lives, Musinga unmasks the folly of a mindset that undermines a stable sense of individual identity, distorts relationships with others, and erodes the social fabric upon which any meaningful national development must be based.

After listening to an account of No-Balance's corruption, a police officer explicitly makes this connection when he refers to bribery as "one of the most nation-killing, prevailing vices of the twentieth century."[20] And when he is sentenced in court, No-Balance himself ruefully acknowledges, "I slept and dreamt that life was beauty, I awoke and found that life is duty."²¹ Such comments establish a set of norms that enable spectators to condemn the attitudes behind corruption while laughing at No-Balance's predicament and his hypocritical self-justifications for having fallen into it. Their judgment and their laughter are reconciled by the position of moral superiority they share with the author, for it provides them with the vantage point from which they can envision a country where people deal honestly with each other and resist the temptation of unearned wealth.

Although no other anglophone Cameroonian playwright has enjoyed Musinga's popularity, many of them have focused on the same themes of corruption and moral blindness that he depicted in plays such as *The Tragedy of Mr. No-Balance*. In general, they associate corruption with the materialistic individualism of modern society and advocate the adoption of moral values that would allow people to relate honestly to themselves and others. Sammy Kum Buo's *For Self, for Tribe, or for Country* and *The African Dilemma*, for example, are wish-fulfillment fantasies in which the author projects himself into the heroic role of foreign-educated young men who return to their country and receive important government posts as a reward for uncovering particularly egregious cases of corrupt behavior. The implicit message in such works is that a reform of mentalities must take place before Cameroonians can expect to develop a viable sense of collective identity.

Sometimes this message is linked with the reaffirmation of traditional values, as in Kemonde Wangmode's *Papa's Choice*, where the hero, a young plantation worker, rejects the modern conception of marriage and allows his father to choose a wife for him. In his eyes, the individualistic assumptions behind such ideas of marriage not only breed divorce and prostitution, they also transform Africans into "slaves" by subordinating them to foreign ways of defining themselves. Although dramatists such as Sankie Maimo and Bole Butake defended modern notions of selfhood in their early plays, their later works also reflect the conviction that traditional attitudes provide a viable alternative to the corrupt, fragmented world of Cameroonian independence.

In a complete reversal of the views he expressed in the preindependence *I Am Vindicated*, Maimo's *Sov-Mbang the Soothsayer* (the only anglophone Cameroonian work ever published by CLE) suggests that Africans can retain an adequate understanding of their own identity only by remaining rooted in the traditional awareness of a profound mystery at the core of all existence. The title character in the play is a genuine African spiritual leader, but his beliefs are dismissed as ignorant superstitions by the supercilious missionary Blunderblast, who seeks to have him banished from the village. Sov-Mbang comprehends the blindness of Blunderblast's cultural arrogance and contends that: "There are no values true for all times / And all places—without modification."²² By denying the universal validity of the white missionary's Christian message, Sov-Mbang eventually convinces the local *fon* (chief) that people can know their own spiritual identity only by preserving the wisdom of the ancestors. Even though the African wise man dies before the end of the play, he vanquishes Blunderblast in their struggle for the soul of the people. This ending confirms Maimo's movement away from his earlier faith in a modern world view and signals a growing disillusionment with the way it was being misused in the nation-building process.

Maimo's next play, *The Mask*, carries this development even further, for it exploits the mystical significance of the African mask to discredit the duplicitous roles that modern individuals play as they seek to take advantage of each other. The first part of the play is devoted to conversations between a final-year law student and two friends about the possibility of achieving happiness in this world. After the friends leave, the law student falls asleep and dreams that a masked figure enters his room and assures him that "happiness is the mystical experience of the Divine."[23] Arguing that such happiness is unattainable in the world of men, the masked figure seeks to persuade the student to lend his talents to the corrupt government. He refuses, but while he is asleep, two burglars tie him up and steal all his earthly possessions.

Despite the masked figure's guile and the student's loss, his dream contains an implicit reply to the question about the possibility of happiness. For Maimo, true happiness derives from contact with the mysterious core of human existence, but this contact has been broken by the assimilation of European values that predispose Africans to abandon all other considerations to the pursuit of material wealth. As a result, they lose contact with the mystery of life and mask their true feelings in the presence of others. By the end of the play, the student realizes that the traditional African mask symbolizes an awareness of the Divine and provides access to the happiness it offers people. Once this message has been understood, both earthly possessions and secular masks can be placed in proper perspective. In this sense, traditional beliefs become Maimo's touchstones of integrity and coherence in a corrupt modern world.

The rationale for this stance is made explicit in his most recent play, *Succession in Sarkov*, where the thoroughly Westernized *fai* (subchief) Kubena fails to unite his people behind him because he does not comprehend the need to maintain a sense of continuity with the past. Desiring to liberate himself from what he regards as barbaric and superstitious practices, he refuses to carry out the traditional sacrifices and repudiates the royal wives he inherited from his father. However, his sister warns him: "We are always slaves of a system / Into which we have been born and nurtured."[24] If it is true that people cannot escape from their own historical context, the implication is that they should accommodate themselves to it rather than seek to impose alien values upon it.

After the death of Kubena, who suffers a stroke as a result of the growing tension between himself and the people, his brother Saghen restores a sense of communal solidarity by conducting the sacrifices and accepting the royal wives. He recognizes what Kubena had ignored: continuity with the past is necessary if people desire to discover their true identity and to live in harmony with it, for continuity ensures the coherence of this identity from one generation to the next. A problem arises, however, when the person who succeeds to a position of leadership cannot maintain this continuity. Kubena's elder brother Siton should have become *fai* when Kubena was chosen for the position, but everyone knew that Siton was corrupt, and the elders feared that the community would be condemned to degeneracy if he was elected. Their dilemma reflects in microcosm the question of leadership succession on the national level, for if prospective rulers are corrupt, what principles should govern their selection? The example of Kubena proves that the solution does not lie in embracing "foreign gods." And Saghen's success in reuniting the community suggests that national identity in Africa is contingent upon rejecting corruption while maintaining continuity with traditional wisdom.

This same message is embedded in Butake's *Lake God*. After having published *Betrothed without Libation* and *The Rape of Michelle*, in which he defended modern concepts of individual identity, he was inspired by the 1985 Lake Nyos disaster to write a dramatized meditation on the psychological reality of a community being torn apart by religious and economic conflicts. Like Maimo's Kubena, the *fon* in Butake's play is a modern individual who sees no reason to maintain continuity with the traditional past. Under the influence of the European priest who raised him, the *fon* refuses to participate in ceremonies to propitiate the local gods and outlaws the traditional male and female associations. In a sort of neocolonialist alliance, both the *fon* and the priest have invested money in the cattle that were brought into the area by Fulani herdsmen. Outraged at the depredations these cattle have wrought on their crops, the women of the community band together to protest against the *fon*'s "enlightened" policies, and the older men resurrect their secret society in an attempt to "save the land" from the profanation that has been inflicted on it.

The primary spokesman for the disaffected villagers is the diviner Shey Bo-Nyo, whom the *fon* dismisses as a madman, although he himself is haunted by nightmares and plagued by the suspicion that he has betrayed the principles according to which the identity of his people has always been defined. One of the elders even explains to him, "you will never find peace, because you have denied your people peace."[25] However, the *fon* disregards all warnings and premonitions. The result is catastrophe. The anger of the gods finds expression in a mysterious poison cloud that arises from the nearby lake and engulfs the entire community. The only survivors are a man, a woman, a young boy, a young girl, and Shey Bo-Nyo. They are the remnant of a people brutally purged of its alienation from the land and from its own traditions, but when the diviner places a ruler's scepter into the young boy's hands, Butake is suggesting that the village can regain its true identity if this nucleus of survivors reaffirms the traditional values that the *fon* and the priest had denigrated. Like Maimo, then, Butake views continuity with the past as an antidote to the corruption that distorts human relationships in the contemporary world.

Within the Cameroonian context, drama has been viewed primarily as a form of entertainment. The popularity of social comedies by playwrights such as Oyono-Mbia and Musinga bears witness to the taste for humor among local audiences. At the same time, Cameroonian theater reflected the same preoccupations that characterized other forms of literate discourse in the country. It mirrored contradictions in postcolonial Cameroonian society and served as an arena for the expression of divergent views in a larger national dialogue over the meaning of freedom and identity in a society moving from colonial dependency to independence and from ethnically diverse oral cultures to the literate culture of a modern state.

CHAPTER
13

FRANCIS BEBEY
AND THE THEME OF
RECONCILIATION

Although Francis Bebey belongs to the same generation as Ferdinand Oyono and Mongo Beti, he did not begin to write seriously until the mid-1960s. The world view that emerges in his three major novels was shaped less by a resentment against colonialist oppression than by a desire for reconciliation in a world where the injustices of the past can be transcended if people accept what they cannot change and commit themselves to the creation of a society based on love and productive work. Inspired partly by the Christian humanism he absorbed as the son of a Protestant pastor and partly by his respect for traditional African wisdom, Bebey's dream of reconciliation expresses his belief in a spiritual reality that gives meaning to human life. When people lose contact with this spiritual reality, he contends, they become capable of the selfish, cruel, hypocritical behavior that prevents them from living peacefully with each other. Although couched in a tone of comic irony, his own writings subtly affirm a moral idealism that reflects his faith in the spiritual dimension of human life while implicitly condemning those who turn their backs on it.

In traditional African society, an awareness of this higher reality was embedded in cultural practices and artifacts that Europeans transformed into museum pieces with economic value. However, as Bebey attempts to show in his long poem *Concert pour un vieux masque*, their real value lies in their ability to convey the communal spirit, the vitality, and the sense of awe with which Africans had traditionally confronted the harshness and mystery of life. One of the best-known Cameroonian singers and composers, he had originally presented *Concert* as a song, but when its message was misinterpreted by one of his listeners, he expanded it into a narrative poem that recounts the story of a mask that an old Angolan chief had presented as a token of friendship to a white Brazilian. Many years after returning to his homeland, the Brazilian forgot the chief's proviso that the mask not be sold or given to anyone else, and he allowed it to be exhibited in the local museum; however, during its first night in a display case, it mysteriously broke in half.

The mask in the poem symbolizes the human values that had found expression in African cultural practices. The old chief's generosity made these values accessible to the Brazilian, but because he lived in a materialistic society where people did not comprehend the real significance of the mask, he eventually betrayed its gift of knowledge. His betrayal denies the original function of the object that incarnates traditional spiritual insights, but it does not invalidate the insights themselves. In fact, the words of Bebey's poem endow them with new meaning and communicate them to a much larger audience. "The power of the word is salutary," he proclaims:

> It enables the death of an old mask
> to be the beginning of a new life
> that nothing will ever annihilate
> For it is the true magic of the world.[1]

By intensifying traditional values such as respect for the mystery of life, the power of the word strips them of their incidental features and allows people to become bearers of the wisdom embodied in the mask. As the modern world encroaches upon traditional society, Bebey admits that cultural practices must change in response to changing circumstances and improved knowledge, but he insists that the insights themselves need to be retained. For him, writing is a means of keeping them alive.

All the major characters in his novels confront the opposition between modern and traditional values, and each of them ultimately synthesizes a hybrid world view that resembles Senghor's "cultural cross-fertilization." Having combined elements of European classical music and African rhythms in his own guitar performances, Bebey himself is an outspoken proponent of such a world view. Senghor even told him: "you have done what I expect of an African artist—rooted yourself in the black African tradition while welcoming all available influences from abroad. This is how we shall develop from folklore to great works that are truly African."[2] The traditional component of Bebey's world view is crucial to his synthesis of values, but it is not linked to outmoded forms of cultural practice, and it cannot be imposed on them from the outside, for it must be freely adopted by Africans in light of their present needs.

His attitude toward cultural synthesis is clearly illustrated in his third novel, *Le Roi Albert d'Effidi*, when the protagonist publicly criticizes a white priest for demanding that Africans praise God in their own languages and according to their own customs. Angered that Europeans, who had denigrated African traditions for decades, should determine what is authentically African in the contemporary world, he argues that customs change over time. In his eyes, authenticity resides in a willingness to be one's self, and in modern Africa, most people accept European as well as African values. Obliging them to resurrect cultural practices from the past would be a falsification of the identity they feel inside themselves. Like Senghor, Bebey regards Africa's dual heritage as an opportunity rather than a handicap. "We have had the good fortune to be living at the crossroads of two cultures," he explained. "We have thus come into the possession of two different cultural forces . . . that complement each other perfectly."[3] By drawing upon both forces, he concludes, Africans can forge a new identity that will be emotionally satisfying and intellectually defensible.

On one level, then, Bebey's concept of reconciliation involves the synthesis of traditional and modern values. This synthesis is reflected in the way he fuses elements of oral speech with written words to create a literary style that responds to the contemporary African sensibility. As a singer who has also worked in radio broadcasting, Bebey recognizes the power of the spoken word. He even conceptualizes his novels as stories that can be read aloud to African audiences.

Many people assume that written language represents an advance over oral communication, but as Mbenda, the narrating protagonist in Bebey's *Le Fils d'Agatha Moudio*, realizes, an exclusive reliance on writing predisposes people to ignore an important dimension of their own existence. As he says, the written word divorces people from life by deluding them into believing that the conventional signs for things are more important than the things themselves. "The spoken word signifies life," he asserts, "life that goes on and that one should respect at every moment because it is the only earthly thing that hardly passes away. People who know how to write lose this profound respect for life."[4] Although Bebey condones Mbenda's linkage of orality with an awareness of spiritual reality, he also knows that literacy is indispensable in the modern world; in fact, his goal in writing novels is to synthesize the written word and the spoken word into a new form of literary discourse. "My authenticity does not consist in repudiating the traditional proverb or Descartes," he declared, "it is composed of these two elements combined."[5] At the heart of his world view is thus an impulse to reconcile two cognitive styles that have frequently been regarded as antagonistic to each other.

This same impulse toward reconciliation is apparent in the balance Bebey strikes between individual demands for self-realization and African principles of communal solidarity, between scientific knowledge and traditional wisdom, between productive work and the joy of living. It also emerges in the forgiveness and tolerance that allow the characters in his novels to overcome their resentments against each other and to establish relationships based on love and trust. The mental attitude that enables them to achieve this reconciliation implies the belief in a higher ideal, and one person who exemplified this belief for Bebey was his older brother, Marcel Bebey-Eyidi, who raised him after the death of their father.

The first fully certified Cameroonian doctor in the territory, Marcel served in the French army during the Second World War and led the Cameroonian veterans' struggle for the government benefits they had earned. After holding an appointment in Aujoulat's Ministry of Colonial Affairs for several years, he returned to Cameroon in 1956 and became a leading proponent of free speech and representative democracy—a stance that culminated in his imprisonment several years after independence and indirectly contributed to his premature death as the result of health problems he incurred at that time. For Bebey, this remarkable man embodied the ideal around which a viable modern African society could be constructed.

Like his brother, Bebey was repelled by the hypocritical rhetoric of oppressive African regimes, and Marcel's death might have left him resentful and bitter. In the late 1950s, he himself had resigned from positions with the ORTF in France and with the Ghanaian national radio system because he objected to the role they were expected to play in disseminating cultural or political propaganda. However, his own yearning for reconciliation was in harmony with the Ahidjo government's call for national unity. And his belief in a higher ideal was compatible with the Negritude-inspired nation-building ideals that became a prominent part of its official ideology during the late 1960s and early 1970s. All three of his major novels were published by CLE, which generally declined manuscripts that might offend the government, and Bebey himself eventually became a member of the UNC, although he has resided outside the country since before independence and would not have faced the usual sanctions for failing to join the nation's single party. He has even played benefit concerts for the UNC.

Because the action in Bebey's novels takes place either before independence or in a non-Cameroonian setting, he never directly commented on the ambiguities of the contemporary situation in his own country. Yet each of these novels focuses on individuals who reconcile conflicting elements of traditional and modern culture to forge identities that allow them to cope with the modern world while retaining a sense of continuity with the past. The dilemma they confront resembles that of newly independent African countries such as Cameroon, and Bebey is implying that these countries can achieve a viable sense of identity in the same way that his principal characters do—through hard work, willingness to accept what cannot be changed, forgiveness of past offenses, and commitment to a morally idealistic vision of peace and harmony. According to him, both individuals and countries in Africa find themselves at a crossroads.[6] They must decide how to confront a changing world, and he believes they can best accomplish this goal by a process of reconciliation on all levels.

Among Cameroonian novelists published by CLE, Bebey has proved to be the most successful in cultivating a popular style that appeals to a broad cross-section of African readers. The simulated orality in his novels and their depictions of common people engaged in everyday activities provide reference points with which nonelite audiences can identify, and Bebey's fictive narrators reinforce this tendency by addressing their readers as if they were speaking directly to them. They digress from the main strand of action as an oral story-teller might do, and they frequently interject the proverbs and proverblike generalizations so characteristic of traditional African tales. Yet the novels themselves are far more sophisticated than they appear at first glance, for although Bebey projects elements of his own world view into his fictive narrators, he always maintains an ironic distance from them, allowing the reader to detect their blind spots and occasionally to laugh at their foibles.

The narrators in *La Poupée Ashanti* and *Le Roi Albert d'Effidi* are anonymous individuals who presumably observed many of the events they describe, whereas Mbenda in *Le Fils d'Agatha Moudio* tells his own story. Mbenda's situation is more fully developed than those of the narrators in the other two novels, but all three narrators function similarly in terms of their relationship to Bebey's actual readers, who eavesdrop on oral narrations that are not addressed to them. In each of the three novels, the major character evolves toward an acceptance of the reconciliation ideal that the narrator already shares with the author, although both this evolution and the narrator's description of it remain firmly embedded in Bebey's comic vision. By recognizing how this comic vision structures the imagined worlds in these novels, readers begin to grasp the hopeful message underlying a story that has been fashioned for their instruction and amusement.

Bebey's manipulation of the narrator's voice for this purpose is most obvious in *Le Fils d'Agatha Moudio*, for as Mbenda recounts the story of his marriage to two women whose firstborn children were fathered by other men, he is revealing how he acquired the humane perspective that governs his view of the world at the moment of narration. This perspective is the moral center of the novel, and the fact that it is held by a semiliterate Douala fisherman demonstrates that Bebey's vision of reconciliation lies within the reach of common people like Mbenda. His name means "The Law," and as a powerfully built young man who respects the values of traditional society, he is the law in the sense that he embodies the principles behind the coherence of the community. At the same time, the narrator's attitude becomes the law of Bebey's fictional universe insofar as his rudimentary synthesis of traditional and modern values, his acceptance of the children, and his reconciliation with their mothers reflect the same values that the author himself is advocating.

The narrating Mbenda's synthesis of values results from the insights he experienced as a result of reflecting on the events of his own life. This synthesis is symbolized by the harmony he enjoys with his two wives, for they correspond to conflicting definitions of himself. The young Fanny had been chosen for him in an agreement between his dying father and her father before she was born, and Mbenda's mother had trained her to be a perfect domestic companion for him; his marriage to her was arranged by negotiations among the elders, and it signaled his integration into a traditional world order. In contrast, the temperamental Agatha is a modern African woman who initiated him into the pleasures of sexual intimacy, and he chose to marry her in a gesture that proclaimed his freedom to pursue romantic happiness. His own indecisiveness caused both his wives to seek momentary solace with other men. As a result, they bore children whom he did not father. However, Mbenda realized that children should not be punished for the sins of their parents, and he vowed to raise them as if they were his own. By accepting what he cannot change and by forgiving those who have wronged him, he reconciles the impulse that inclines him toward a traditional definition of his place in society with the desire that pushes him toward a modern, individualistic conception of himself.

As a Christian and a man who respects traditional custom, the narrating Mbenda has found a solution to the conflict of cultures in the love and forgiveness that transcend both European and African views of the world. Although he accepts traditional superstitions as well as modern ideas, he presents both of them from an ironic perspective that subordinates them to his belief in a higher spiritual reality. He himself admits that "time and the proximity of people who 'know how to live' have given my reasoning a certain dose of 'civilization.'"[7] However, when he describes the benefits of modern life, he casts them in an ambiguous light that reveals the folly of the villagers' pride in them. For example, he points out that the road through the village has brought corruption as well as progress. He also observes that the new public tap provides a murkier water than the local springs and fosters a contentiousness that had not existed before it was built.

Similarly, he describes instances of sorcery as if he believes in its power, although he invariably undercuts his accounts of it by providing plausible alternative explanations for its effects. For example, he lends credence to the allegations that his uncle Gros Coeur had conjured a magical frog and laid a fateful curse upon the man who had spread the allegation. At the same time, he relates how Gros Coeur had angered the village elders by selling a parcel of communal land without consulting them, and he hints that the dead man had succumbed to natural causes. He also credits the old woman Mauvais Regard with supernatural powers to regulate births in the village, but the children born to his two wives (and those that are born to other women in the community during the absence of their husbands) suggest that she really has no power over the events she is supposedly capable of controlling. In effect, the mentality of the narrating Mbenda is a crucible where traditional and modern assumptions fuse into an enlightened perspective that allows him to present the story of his previous life as an example that corroborates his mature attitude toward life.

Seen in this light, the rhetorical thrust of Mbenda's narrative involves an attempt to persuade his audience to share his enlightened view of the world. Because one of his primary motivations for telling his story is to justify his present attitude toward life, he selects and omits details on the basis of their appropriateness to his purpose. For example, he realizes that the events he is recounting might be perceived as humiliating for a man of honor and as the subject of laughter for others. Desiring to downplay this aspect of his story, he acknowledges: "I reserve the right to remain silent on a number of points, all the more so since I foresee the amused smile with which you would be prepared to listen to my account."[8] Mbenda wants his listeners to take him seriously, for despite the humorous dimension of his experiences, he considers himself worthy of admiration as a man whose mature attitude toward life enabled him to overcome disappointments that would have defeated other men. The peace and harmony he enjoys at the moment of telling his story result from a spirit of reconciliation that makes him the primary standard of moral value in the novel.

Although the narrators in *La Poupée Ashanti* and *Le Roi Albert d'Effidi* are urbane observers who relate and comment on the stories of others, their roles are not altogether different from that of Mbenda. They digress, they interject their observations on the action, and they consciously shape their naratives as they seek to persuade their audiences to adopt the views they themselves hold. Like the narrating Mbenda, they are standards of value insofar as they embody Bebey's ideal of reconciliation and relate stories that illustrate the wisdom of adopting it.

The principal character in *La Poupée Ashanti* is the young and beautiful but illiterate Edna, who helps her grandmother tend a market stall in Accra. In many ways she resembles Mbenda. Just as his mother raised him to respect traditional values and planned his future by preparing for his marriage with Fanny, her grandmother taught her the lore of her ethnic group and groomed her for the life of a market woman. Yet both Mbenda and Edna feel constrained by the well-intentioned plans that others have conceived for them. Romantically attracted to people who have become part of the modern world, they desire the freedom to pursue their own visions of happiness. Their allegiance to a traditional concept of identity enters into conflict with a modern sense of individuality, and the ambivalence they experience is resolved only when they reconcile their traditional and modern inclinations in a new self-concept that allows them to envision the future with optimism. Essentially, they have evolved to the point where they adopt the world view that the fictive narrators of their respective stories already hold.

In *Le Fils d'Agatha Moudio*, Fanny and Agatha fulfill different needs for Mbenda: his need to remain in harmony with traditional society and his need to act as a mature individual with the right to make his own independent judgments. Difficulty arises when he cannot opt unequivocally for either alternative. Although he loves Agatha, he marries Fanny to satisfy his mother's wishes and to abide by the customs of the group to which he belongs, but he neglects his wife and continues to see Agatha. After Fanny gives birth to a child without ever having made love to him, he reconciles himself with her but insists upon marrying Agatha as a second wife; however, Agatha leaves in a huff when he does not come to her first after he returns from a fishing expedition, and her brief affair with a Frenchman results in the birth of a mulatto child. Once again Mbenda swallows his pride and forgives an errant wife. The adulterous origins of both children can be traced to his own indecisiveness, but by accepting these children as his own, he demonstrates a generosity of spirit that enables him to reconcile his conflicting impulses in a marriage that unites him with a traditional wife and a modern one.

Mbenda's relationship with his traditional wife, Fanny, reflects his desire to remain in harmony with the community and its customs, for he realizes that marriage in the traditional sense represents an alliance between two families or clans, an alliance that results from the negotiations of the elders rather than from the personal desires of the young people involved. When he solemnly declares, "I am the child of this village, and I will follow tradition all the way," he is committing himself not only to a marriage with Fanny but also to a particular definition of his place in society.[9] At the same time, his relationship with his first wife is a product of his mother's attempt to shape his life according to her image of what it should be. Maa Medi is proud of her son, but she is also proud of her role in making him into the man he has become. "Now you are big and strong and handsome and courageous," she tells him, "but I am the one who created you."[10] In marrying the woman she has chosen and trained for him, Mbenda makes his mother happy, as he desires to do, but he is also acquiescing in her conception of him.

The problem is that neither her conception of him nor the traditional definition of his place in society is adequate to encompass his impulse to act as a free individual, particularly after he has entered into his relationship with the independent-minded Agatha. But the potential for his rebellion against these overly restrictive conceptions of his identity were already present long before he met her. At the age of fifteen, he dropped out of school and became a fisherman because he felt intensely alive while exercising his powerful body in the company of loyal friends and surrounded by the rhythms of nature. The choice was his own, and he insists, "I became a fisherman because I myself chose to become one."[11] Although this insistence upon his freedom to be what he wants to be is potentially in conflict with tradition and with his mother's image of him, it becomes an issue only when he enters into a relationship with Agatha, of whom his mother and the villagers disapprove.

Having been virtually disowned by a father who had desired a son rather than a daughter, Agatha has become a "modern African woman" who believes she has the right to make her own decisions without consulting her father or the community that had sanctioned his attitude toward her. Notorious for her succession of white and black lovers, she contends that marriage should be based solely on the love that two individuals have for each other. As a liberated woman, she comes to his house and declares her love for him after observing how his imposing stature and resoluteness had cowed a group of white hunters into paying the tax that the village elders had been trying in vain to impose on them for hunting in the area. Partly as a consequence of his close ties with his mother, Mbenda has remained sexually inexperienced until this time, and Agatha's sensuous vitality literally bewitches him.

Despite Maa Medi's animosity toward a woman who would not, she was convinced, prepare her son's meals and work in his fields as a good wife should, Mbenda continues to see Agatha even after his marriage to Fanny, and for the first time in his life he conceals his thoughts and actions from his mother. The birth of Fanny's child catalyzes his resolve to act as a free person by making Agatha his second wife in defiance of his mother and the villagers. "I thought that I had obeyed enough in this way," he remarks, "and that it was time for me to make decisions myself."[12] When he says these words, Mbenda is defining himself in individualistic terms, and although Agatha eventually bears the mulatto child whom he could not have fathered, the simple wisdom that characterizes his attitude at the end of the novel embraces this modern self-concept as well as the traditional ideals represented by Fanny.

Although the conflict between traditional and modern concepts of identity is presented from a different perspective in *La Poupée Ashanti*, the basic issue is the same, and the principal character resolves it in a similar fashion. Like Mbenda, Edna feels two impulses inside her. The first, more traditional one is linked with her grandmother Mam, and the second is represented by her Aunt Princess, a "modern African woman" who insists upon maintaining her freedom to act as she pleases. After years of living under Mam's tutelage, Edna has acquired all the talents necessary to become a successful market woman like her grandmother, but when she becomes acquainted with the young civil servant Spio, she increasingly desires the freedom to enter into a modern relationship with him and to cultivate the skills she needs to cope with the contemporary world. Both Mam and Aunt Princess have an ideal image of what they would like Edna to become, but in the end she chooses a hybrid self-image that allows her to draw selectively upon what she has learned from both women while marrying the man she loves.

Like Maa Medi in *Le Fils d'Agatha Moudio*, Mam consciously seeks to transmit her view of the world to a younger person. As a clever businesswoman, she teaches Edna to calculate shrewdly on the basis of concrete facts and to deal pragmatically with the problems of survival. As a woman who respects traditional values, she initiates her granddaughter into the songs, tales, and proverbs she had learned during her own childhood. In Mam's eyes, Edna is a reincarnation of herself, and because she regards the market as a more reliable source of support than marriage to a man who could abandon her at any moment, she works hard to expand the small business that she expects Edna to inherit.

Yet Mam's conception of Edna's identity is inadequate for a young woman who desires to find a place for herself in contemporary society. It leaves no opportunity for her to pursue her dream of romantic love, and because Mam did not consider it important for her to read and write, Edna is incapable of dealing with some of her own basic needs in a complex, modern Ghana. Mam justifies her attitude by claiming that "everyone needs only to remain in his [or her] place, and life will go on very well this way."[13] However, if Edna internalizes Mam's attitude, many possibilities for self-realization in modern society will be blocked to her, and her relationship with Spio has awakened her desire to take advantage of them.

Aunt Princess represents an alternative to Mam's view of the world. She had raised Edna until the girl was eight years old, and during that time she had sought to shape her into a liberated African woman. She sent her to school and attempted to inculcate in her the idea that all people have the right to pursue their own self-interest. Aunt Princess maintains her freedom by marrying a wealthy polygamous man who allows her to do more or less as she pleases, but despite her material well-being, she lacks the sense of higher purpose that Mam derives from tradition and from her solidarity with the other market women. And when she was caring for the eight-year-old Edna, she was so preoccupied with her own affairs that one of her own lovers, the headmaster at Edna's school, took advantage of the situation and seduced the child. At this point Aunt Princess lost custody of the young girl because Mam was so shocked by the incident that she insisted upon taking Edna into her own household. If Mam's image of Edna is inadequate, Aunt Princess's conception of the liberated African woman is even less capable of providing her with a viable sense of identity.

Two of the qualities that Edna herself values most are the sense of community among the other market women and the love she feels for Spio. At first she believes they are incompatible with each other, but during the course of the novel she discovers the possibility of reconciling them in a new self-concept that combines traditional and modern values. Mam was a respected leader of the market women's association that had played a major role in Ghana's movement toward independence, and when one woman's sales license is withdrawn for arbitrary political reasons, Edna feels morally obliged to participate in the association's public demonstration against the government's unjust action. In fact, she assumes such a prominent part in the demonstration that she is wounded by shots that the police fire into the crowd. Spio had attempted to defuse the situation by speaking first with the inspector-general and then with a minister, and although he is sent to the northern part of the country as punishment for having questioned the inspector general's authority, he is eventually reinstated in his former position at Accra after a government commission determines his innocence.

By his words and actions, Spio shows Edna that commitment to the ideal of a new national society would enable her to remain a market woman while at the same time learning to read, to write, and to think in terms that transcend the shrewd calculations of Mam's approach to life. He encourages her to conceive of marriage as a freely chosen agreement between two individuals who complement each other as they work toward a goal they have set for themselves. In the light of such ideas, she becomes convinced she can have everything that is important to her, and this conviction motivates her to repudiate the identity that others had been trying to impose on her. As she says to Mam, "after all, I'm not going to marry my market stall . . . !"[14] Like Mbenda, she is asserting her right to be the individual she wants to be.

The marriage of Spio and Edna at the end of *La Poupée Ashanti* symbolizes a reconciliation of what had previously been regarded as disparate virtues. As the young people celebrate their engagement in the presence of Mam and Aunt Princess, they look forward to a future in which they will draw inspiration from Mam's industriousness, her sense of group solidarity, and her respect for tradition, but they will also be practicing Aunt Princess's independent-mindedness and the skills she regarded as necessary for success in modern society. Like Mbenda, Edna forgives those who have wronged her, for she realizes that she must accept that which cannot be changed. But what gives meaning and purpose to her new synthesis of values is her dedication to an ideal that places her in contact with the spiritual dimension of life. As she moves toward the same level of insight as that of the narrator, her story becomes an illustration of how Bebey's world view offers a solution to the problem of individual identity in contemporary Africa.

This same world view is the primary structuring principle in *Le Roi Albert d'Effidi*, which also culminates in a reconciliation of the conflict between traditional and modern values. The major focus of interest in Bebey's third novel is the rivalry between two men from the village of Effidi near Ngala.[15] King Albert is a successful fifty-year-old businessman who continues to respect many aspects of the traditional value system, whereas his rival is the stylish young civil servant Bikounou, who attended European-style schools and cultivated a modern, individualistic attitude toward life.

Both of them are attracted to the beautiful young Nani, the daughter of Toutouma, a trade unionist from the neighboring village of Nkool. And both of them become candidates in the election for the territory's first parliamentary assembly.[16] Although neither wins the election, Albert does achieve insight into the need for a new synthesis of traditional and modern values, and after many peripeties, his generosity of spirit enables him to gain the affections of Nani. His success with Nani reverses the usual pattern according to which young people must struggle against their elders to realize their dreams of romantic happiness, for in this case, the younger man, Bikounou, is eventually repudiated by the woman he desires. Nevertheless, the underlying theme of reconciliation remains the same as in Bebey's first two novels.

The conflict between Albert and Bikounou derives in part from their participation in the modern world, a participation symbolized by the road they take each day to reach the places where they work in Ngala. The first half of the novel is entitled "The Road," and the people of Effidi are proud that it passes through their village. But like the road in *Le Fils d'Agatha Moudio*, it is a mixed blessing for them. If it grants them access to the modern world of schooling, business, and the colonial administration, it also disrupts the equilibrium of traditional society by bringing the values of the modern world into the heart of the village. Because of their positions in the city, Albert and Bikounou are the two most prominent citizens of Effidi. Proud of the two men's success, the villagers expect to profit from Albert's wealth and from Bikounou's influence with the colonial government, but they resent the businessman's pretenses of poverty and his refusal to hire them to work in his store, just as they disapprove of the young civil servant's profligacy and his disrespect for traditional values.

The attitudes of both men reflect their partial assimilation of European values. Although Albert has remained attached to traditional ideas about marriage and the governance of communal affairs, he has adopted Western assumptions about work and the accumulation of material wealth. According to him, "everyone who works can rise very high while earning a good living."[17] In contrast, Bikounou's individualism is linked primarily with the pursuit of his own pleasure and prestige, for he devotes most of his leisure time to drinking and to seducing young women.

The antagonism that exists between the two men surfaces early in the novel when Albert returns from the city on his bicycle and distributes a few inexpensive gifts from his store among the villagers. At this moment Bikounou arrives on his motor scooter and mocks the villagers for paying court to a man who purchases their favor with trinkets. Albert counters by attacking Bikounou's drinking and his presumptuousness. Their verbal exchange is a minor incident in the life of the village, but it reveals the contrasting temperaments that determine their behavior as they compete against each other for Nani and for election to the territorial assembly.

As a fashionable, educated young man with money and the prospect of a lucrative civil-service career, Bikounou has a distinct advantage over Albert in their rivalry for Nani, especially since she is physically attracted to him and not to the older businessman. But her father, Toutouma, is sufficiently rooted in traditional custom to insist that marriage negotiations be conducted in the usual way by the elders from the suitor's village. The competition for Nani thus takes place on two fronts. Both men must overcome the resistance of Toutouma, who regards Albert as a capitalist exploiter and Bikounou as an arrogant, irreverent young man who has lost all sense of tradition. Albert and Bikounou must also persuade the elders of Effidi to speak with Toutouma on their behalf.

Initially there is some sentiment in Bikounou's favor, but after he offends the villagers and their traditions during a drunken escapade, the elders decide to support Albert's suit, and their efforts succeed in obtaining Toutouma's tentative approval for the marriage. Bikounou's failure at this point has not been imposed on him by others. On the contrary, it results from his own inability to empathize with the villagers and to reconcile his ideas of independence with their sense of communal solidarity. In response to this situation, Bikounou seduces Nani and appeals to the traditional custom according to which a woman is supposed to marry the man who deprives her of her virginity. His action is hypocritical because he himself does not believe in the traditional values on which this custom is based. He merely uses them to justify a self-indulgent pursuit of his own pleasure. In practical terms, his action is counterproductive because it angers the villagers and Toutouma, thereby hastening the marriage that he had been attempting to prevent.

But even after Albert's marriage to Nani, a feeling of tension remains, for it seems inappropriate that a young woman should be obliged to marry an older man when she herself is attracted to a man who is closer to her own age. The insight that resolves this tension occurs to Albert during the month he spends in jail after the young men of Effidi beat Bikounou nearly to death for his allegedly scandalous behavior during the electoral campaign. What Albert realizes is that times have changed and that "we can no longer force our daughters to marry men we have chosen for them."[18] Upon his release, he takes Nani back to her father and declares that he is releasing her from a marriage she never wanted.

However, his generosity evokes a sympathetic response in Nani, who voluntarily returns to his house, places a lamp on the table, and announces, "I am coming back to live here forever. I love this man because he understands everything about life."[19] At this moment, the flame in the lamp redoubles its intensity, and a new spark of life appears in Albert's eye as his face grows calm. The light of the lamp symbolizes the love, forgiveness, and wisdom that unite the couple. Resentments and previous misunderstandings are no longer important. They are simply the givens of a past that cannot be changed. This final scene in the novel also suggests the reconciliation of traditional and modern identity concepts, for if Nani originally married Albert according to customary negotiations during which her wishes were not consulted, she freely chooses to remain with him on the basis of her love for him.

The electoral campaign that takes place in the second half of *Le Roi Albert d'Effidi* demonstrates how the principle of reconciliation can also be applied to the society at large. Entitled "Toward a New World," this section of the novel depicts a change in political organization that will profoundly affect the traditional authority structure in villages like Effidi, where the voices of chiefs and elders will be subordinated to those of regional representatives in an assembly that legislates for the entire territory. The three principal candidates in the region that includes Effidi and Nkool are Bikounou, Albert, and Toutouma. Both Bikounou and Albert are motivated to seek public office by a desire for the prestige they imagine it would bring them, and this desire blinds them to inadequacies in their own understanding of the "new world" toward which their society is moving.

Bikounou hypocritically promises to respect the traditional wisdom of the elders while bringing progress and prosperity to the area. He boasts that he and other educated men like him are leading the territory toward national independence, and he cynically taunts Albert that he has continued to see Nani even after her marriage to the older man. As for Albert, he purchases a car he does not need because he wants to impress the local people with his wealth, and he allows himself to become so disturbed by Bikounou's insults that he begins to act foolishly. After one confrontation between the two men, a melee breaks out, and Albert's driver runs over a local hunter in his haste to escape the scene of the battle. At the man's funeral several days later, someone steals the wheels from Albert's car, and the general outrage at the effrontery of the theft is so great that the young men of Effidi inflict an exemplary punishment on the presumed culprit, Bikounou. With Bikounou in the hospital and Albert in jail as a result of his supposed implication in the beating of his rival, Toutouma wins election to the assembly.

In many ways, this outcome is appropriate. The two candidates who viewed the political process as a means to their own self-aggrandizement are defeated, and the trade unionist who had reflected seriously on the problems of social justice is elected. As a man who has recognized the need for modernization while continuing to respect the wisdom of African traditions, he is an ideal representative of people who are struggling to define a new collective identity during a period of transition. Yet Toutouma's election is a bitter pill for the people of Effidi because they had assumed that, just as the road passed through their village, the regional representative to the assembly would be from their community. As they hear the drums of Nkool boasting about Toutouma's victory, however, the chief of Effidi observes that his people must attend to voices from other places. His comment suggests that the secret of creating a better society lies in the same spirit of reconciliation that enables individuals like Albert and Nani to achieve happiness. The electoral subtheme in *Le Roi Albert d'Effidi* thus translates Bebey's vision of reconciliation into a political statement with unquestionable relevance for postcolonial Cameroon.

Although Bebey's fiction has often been regarded as apolitical, its consistent advocacy of a world view based on the necessity of reconciliation is in many ways a response to the conflict-ridden atmosphere in a country that had been deeply split by the suppression of the UPC and by Ahidjo's accession to power. If this situation were approached with the love and forgiveness that characterize the narrative perspective in Bebey's fiction, Cameroon itself might achieve the peace and harmony that Mbenda, Edna, and Albert enjoy at the end of their respective stories. The parallel between the microcosmic level of individual happiness and the macrocosmic level of social justice is particularly apparent in *Le Fils d'Agatha Moudio*, where reconciliation takes place on two levels.

On the first level, Mbenda forgives those who have wronged him and accepts the children of Fanny and Agatha as his own. On the second level, the entire village forgives Gros Coeur for having sold the parcel of communal land and kept the profits for himself. The subplot that stems from this transaction has potentially tragic ramifications because the man who had spread the story about Gros Coeur's magic frog died and is assumed to have been killed by a curse. To reveal Gros Coeur's alleged responsibility for the man's death, the villagers subject him to an ordeal that might have killed him. However, the colonial authorities intervene, and those who administered the ordeal are imprisoned for four years. During their absence, many of their wives bear children fathered by other men.

By this time, resentments have proliferated to the point where the village could never live in peace if all of them were acted upon. Besides, when vengeance is exacted for past injustices, it provokes the desire for countervengeance in an endless cycle of crime and retribution. According to Bebey, the only solution is to accept what cannot be changed, to forgive, and to work together for a better future. When Gros Coeur formally apologizes to the villagers, they forgive him and reintegrate him into village society, and when the prisoners return after four years, they participate in a ceremony that marks their willingness to live in peace with those who have wronged them. By adopting an attitude of reconciliation, the villagers even take pride in the imposing house that Gros Coeur has built with the profits of the land sale, just as Mbenda takes pride in the two children who play in the courtyard of his house. When placed into the context of postcolonial Cameroonian politics, such an attitude would enable people to live in harmony with each other while taking pride in the accomplishments of the Ahidjo government, even though these accomplishments were made possible by actions of dubious legitimacy.[20]

If the first principle of Bebey's political philosophy is reconciliation, the second is the need to engage in productive work. Each of his major characters —Mbenda, Edna, and Albert—has a positive attitude toward work, and they all experience joy in the exercise of their physical and mental capacities. Even the three shoeshine boys in his children's book *Trois Petits Cireurs* are described as possessing a virtue that is often lacking in Africa, the willingness to work hard. Bebey's own dedication to this ideal is cogently expressed in two lines of advice to an anonymous young African: "Live and work. / Then you'll be a man."[21] These lines appear in a poem that Bebey dedicated to his brother, Marcel Bebey-Eyidi, whom he admired as an exemplary man of thought and action. The implication is that countries, like individuals, will reach maturity only when they recognize that work is necessary to cope with a harsh, rapidly changing world.

Bebey's ideas about work, reconciliation, and the synthesis of values are all compatible with the country's nation-building rhetoric, and since he has refrained from any overt criticism of the Cameroonian government, it might be inferred that he was a supporter of the Ahidjo regime. In fact, he was repeatedly attacked by younger critics during the 1970s for failing to address the real problems of contemporary African society.[22] But such comments reflect a superficial understanding of the moral idealism behind Bebey's fiction. He was certainly aware of the injustices that had been perpetrated in Cameroon under Ahidjo. His own brother was a victim of them, and although *La Poupée Ashanti* is set in Ghana, it describes governmental corruption and totalitarian tendencies that also existed in Cameroon. The point of his writing is that these conditions are historical givens. According to him, people transcend such conditions not by committing additional crimes to eradicate them but by accepting them and by joining with others in working toward a world of peace and harmony.

In this respect, he resembles the anglophone Cameroonian songwriter Oigen Etah Elonge, whose best-known composition, "The Woodcock," presents a bird's nocturnal serenade as if it were an address by the president of the republic.[23] Neither Bebey nor Elonge was a proponent of political dictatorship. They yearned for a social harmony that corresponds to Ahidjo's nation-building ideal, and because they were convinced that this harmony could only be the expression of a profound spiritual reality, they placed more emphasis on a vision of human possibility than on an analysis of the reasons why this vision had not been realized.

Bebey's concept of reconciliation is regarded as naive by socially engaged critics, but it can also be seen as a noble ideal that reflects his faith in the power of love. As he himself writes:

We want to love
We *need* to love
Everything
Including the bitterness
that indelicately prolongs the past
To love tirelessly.[24]

As a singer and as a writer, Bebey strives to keep alive an appreciation of the spiritual reality that makes this love possible. Like René Philombe, Bebey consciously sought to forge a popular idiom in which common people could recognize the world in which they were living, but in contrast to Philombe, he based his appeal for future harmony on a religious belief in reconciliation rather than on a conviction of the need for collective struggle in the material world.

CHAPTER

14

CULTURAL POLITICS
IN AN AGE
OF TRANSITION

For most of the time since the early 1970s, Cameroon has enjoyed growing prosperity, particularly as the result of revenues from offshore oil and the construction of a major refinery near Limbé. The government's intermittent relaxation of constraints upon freedom of expression has also created the impression that Cameroonian society was becoming more open and tolerant of dissent. The crucial turning point during this period occurred when Ahidjo resigned from the presidency in 1982 and allowed his vice-president, Paul Biya, to succeed him. Despite an ensuing power struggle between the two men and an attempted coup in 1984, Biya managed to consolidate his control over the political process, and his liberalization policies were greeted with considerable popular enthusiasm.

However, the apparent stability of Cameroonian society was extremely fragile. By late 1986, the country was clearly plunging into the economic crisis that had already engulfed much of the African continent. Throughout this period, inequities in the distribution of wealth became increasingly obvious, and the scandals that erupted during the early years of Biya's tenure in office revealed that a few members of the privileged class had profited unconscionably from their access to the oil revenues that the Ahidjo government had shrouded in secrecy and refused to include in the official budget. Enormous sums of money were expended on factories that never functioned as planned, and corruption continued to plague the country. Cameroonians even coined a special term, *pajerocratie*, to designate the graft and embezzlement that had become common.

Furthermore, the Biya government's recourse to censorship and authoritarian methods of social control in the late 1980s alienated much of the support it had previously enjoyed, particularly in the anglophone western part of the country. In short, the malaise that had gripped Cameroonian society in the early independence period became even more pronounced in later years. At the same time, there was a growing consciousness of the fact that Cameroonians must confront their problems within a national context, and as the literate culture of the 1970s and 1980s demonstrates, this consciousness was accompanied by a yearning to identify with a moral ideal that could be linked with the destiny of the country.

On May 20, 1972, more than ninety-nine percent of Cameroonian voters approved Ahidjo's proposal that the federal republic be transformed into a unitary state. This "Peaceful Revolution of May 20" marked a decisive step in the centralization of power that had been taking place throughout the 1960s. According to the new constitution, West Cameroon lost its status as a semi-autonomous state within the federation and became two separate provinces in the new republic. Furthermore, the president's decrees were no longer subject to parliamentary review. By broadening the discretionary authority of Ahidjo and his close advisers, both changes reflected the assumption that national unity could be achieved though control from above. Even the nearly unanimous approval of the unitary state was hardly an expression of popular sentiment. On the contrary, it was simply the pro forma ratification of a policy that had been adopted by the government long before the vote was taken.

In economic terms, the declaration of the unitary state ushered in a period of sustained growth. With the cessation of UPC hostilities in the Bamileke territory and the discovery of offshore oil, Cameroon was increasingly regarded as an attractive investment opportunity for foreign capital. One consequence of this situation was a diversification of export-import relationships and a decreased dependency on France as a dominant trading partner.[1] As one of only two West African countries that remained self-sufficient in food production, Cameroon did not suffer the foreign-exchange crisis that afflicted many third-world nations at this time, and the seven to ten percent growth rate that prevailed throughout the 1970s enabled the government to improve the country's communication and transportation networks. Many Cameroonians benefited from this economic growth, and even Ahidjo's erstwhile political rival, the wealthy businessman Paul Soppo Priso, acknowledged that "it works. The Cameroonian experience is valid in comparison with what other countries have done under the same conditions."[2] Outside observers even began to rank Cameroon, along with the Ivory Coast, as one of Africa's rare success stories.

But beneath this apparent success, there were serious imbalances in the country's economic picture. In addition to the "planned liberalism" that had become the key term in Ahidjo's development ideology during the late 1960s, the new unitary state proclaimed its adherence to "auto-centered development" and the "Green Revolution." Both slogans disguised the stagnation that plagued many sectors of the economy. The term *auto-centered development* was intended to suggest that the country's resources would be exploited in an orderly fashion by the people and for their benefit, whereas *Green Revolution* implied that the government would support investment in new fertilizers and hybrid seeds to help farmers increase food production. Behind such terms was the idea that the people themselves needed to assume more responsibility for the attainment of national development goals.

However, increased levels of foreign investment intensified the existing division between Cameroon's privileged class and the vast majority of its citizens, who remained mired in poverty and powerless to participate in the decision-making process. Furthermore, the economic outlook was in many ways bleaker than the overall statistics suggested. Without the oil revenues, which constituted over sixty percent of the country's export earnings by the early 1980s, Cameroon would have recorded a severe balance-of-payments deficit. Industrial activity stagnated, and most government-sponsored agriculture projects never proved profitable. Because very little "Green Revolution" funding reached small farmers, their yields declined, and per capita food production decreased.[3]

Under these circumstances, the migration from the land to the cities accelerated rapidly. As late as 1970, only sixteen percent of the population lived in the major urban areas, but by the year 2000 the figure will have reached more than fifty percent, swelling the overcrowded slums in Yaounde, Douala, and other cities. Such trends are part of the modernization process that has generally accompanied the emergence of nation-states, but because employment opportunities in the urban areas failed to expand proportionately, the already high level of popular discontent rose appreciably. When Cameroonian oil revenues dwindle, as they have already begun to do, the artificiality of the country's prosperity becomes apparent. Behind a façade of political stability and economic growth, therefore, lurks a widespread conviction that the promise of independence remains unfulfilled for the majority of Cameroonians. And this conviction haunts much of the writing that has been published since the "Peaceful Revolution of May 20."

Yet the government and the party persisted in promoting the optimistic nation-building rhetoric that emphasized Ahidjo's heroic leadership in implementing the "great idea" he had articulated for the people. According to official versions of history, his vision and determination had transformed a divided and backward country into a unified and prosperous nation. To bolster this image, a spate of publications were issued during the mid-1970s in anticipation of the twentieth anniversary of his accession to power. *Hommage à El Hadj Ahmadou Ahidjo* included tributes by heads of state, journalists, and writers such as Pouka and Sengat-Kuo, who dedicated long poems to him. Jos-Blaise Alima's *Les Chemins de l'unité* and Eno Belinga's *La Révolution pacifique du 20 mai* presented Cameroonian unity as an accomplished fact and linked it with this idealized image of the president.

Alima concluded, for example, that "there was really no other path to follow except the one taken by Ahmadou Ahidjo toward the 'rendezvous with the universal.' It was the only one consistent with the wishes of a Cameroonian people who yearn for peace and progress."[4] Newspapers touted his unqualified success in forging a "fraternal, balanced, and prosperous society."[5] Lucien Mailli's color film *Ahmadou Ahidjo, batisseur infatigable de la nation camerounaise* was shown throughout the country, and the president was awarded an honorary doctorate during the 1978 national cultural week that commemorated his first twenty years in power. One anglophone commentator even described Ahidjo's "democratic authoritarianism" as an authentically African form of government that had carried out "one of the most successful processes of political integration so far experienced on the African continent."[6]

When a Belgian public-relations firm adopted the hardback comic-book format of the popular Astérix and Tintin series to present the glorified biographies of African heads of state, the Cameroonian government willingly provided a subsidy for its 1980 publication of *Il était une fois . . . Ahidjo*. Aimed at adults as well as children, the book presented a highly idealized image of the Cameroonian president in a form that even marginally literate individuals could understand.[7] In it, a venerable griot relates how an intelligent, patient, persevering young northerner overcame his humble origins and created a peaceful land where everyone loved and respected him as a national hero. Throughout Africa, the legend of the heroic leader has been cultivated in the attempt to promote feelings of national identity, but in Cameroon as elsewhere, it generally met with skepticism because such legends were clearly being used to sanction the consolidation of power in the hands of the few.

In fact, they clashed openly with most people's perceptions of reality. The same structural inequities that had bred discontent in the past continued to plague the country. The building boom triggered by the offshore oil discoveries and the construction of a lavish presidential palace on the outskirts of Yaounde merely underscored the growing disparity between the privileged class and the rest of the population. Cameroon's fifty thousand civil servants constituted only two percent of the working population in 1975, but they earned one-third of the country's national income, nearly as much as the more than two million farmers who represented ninety percent of the work force. Despite large public investments in the North, the wealth there remained concentrated in the hands of the minority Fulani, and people in other parts of the country grew increasingly bitter about the neglect of roads, hospitals, and schools in their areas. They also resented the preferential treatment accorded to northerners, who had to meet less rigorous requirements for entry into the university, the professional schools, and the civil service. But the most disturbing fact about the 1975–80 economic expansion in Cameroon was the rise in unemployment and poverty at a time when members of the privileged class were enjoying an unprecedented prosperity.[8]

Under these circumstances, the mythology surrounding Ahidjo and his nation-building rhetoric functioned primarily to obscure two of the most important facts about contemporary Cameroon—the increasing centralization of decision-making power at the presidency and the consolidation of a privileged class that had a vested interest in the existing situation. The members of this class pursued their own materialistic goals while ignoring the social inequities of a corrupt system that did not hesitate to impose ideological orthodoxy by the threat of imprisonment and torture. The paradox of their situation resides in the fact that they express support for a nation-building ideal based on a sense of common purpose while they live according to the same individualism that flourished during the emergence of nations in Europe and the Americas. By itself, this split consciousness does not necessarily weaken people's allegiance to the nation. It may even enhance their commitment to a system that works to their advantage. However, modern education and other forms of social conditioning awaken desires for individual self-realization and upward social mobility among the less privileged classes, and when they discover that their access to these goals is blocked, a potentially revolutionary situation develops.

During the years that followed the declaration of the unitary state, there were isolated examples of popular resistance to government policies—workers engaged in illegal strikes, people refused to purchase UNC party cards, students distributed antigovernment tracts, and several Kirdi villages rebelled against Fulani administrators in the North. In general, however, the discontent and cynicism that pervaded the country were expressed in only the most muted terms.[9] People had grown accustomed to corruption, nepotism, vast disparities of wealth, and the hyperbole of official party rhetoric. Even those who had not resigned themselves to this situation avoided making public statements because they feared police surveillance. The government's strict control over the news media and the secrecy of the decision-making process stimulated the spread of rumors in a society where most information was disseminated by word of mouth. In an atmosphere where the truth was often difficult to discern, many individuals made their separate peace with the regime in power, although there remained a strong undercurrent of resentment against what was generally perceived as a betrayal of the expectations aroused by independence.

This resentment found expression in the writings of Cameroonians who strove to maintain a counterversion of the truth in the face of Ahidjo's optimistic nation-building rhetoric. Although the Ouandié-Ndongmo trial had exercised a chilling effect on UPC militants living abroad, the radical nationalist party eventually regrouped its forces, and by the mid-1970s Woungly-Massaga and others were once again publishing antigovernment pamphlets. Works such as Abel Eyinga's *Introduction à la politique camerounaise*, Mongo Beti's *Main basse sur le Cameroun*, and Achille Mbembe's edition of Um Nyobé's writings in *Le Problème national kamerounais* recovered crucial elements of recent Cameroonian history that had been ignored in government-sanctioned accounts of the past.[10] Such publications became an implicit part of the ongoing debate over the identity of the Cameroonian nation, and they served as a standard against which the inflated claims of the Ahidjo government could be judged.

Shortly before Ahidjo left the presidency, his government began to rein in the lively intellectual life that had begun to emerge in response to a liberalization of cultural policies in the late 1970s. René Philombe was arrested and held without charge for several days. Marcien Towa was removed from his teaching post and prohibited from giving public lectures. Plays that had previously been produced in the country were banned, and all publications were placed under more rigorous censorship. The popular minister of education, Adamou Ndam Njoya, was dropped from the government. All these measures indicated that Ahidjo and his close advisers were intent upon reasserting their control over Cameroonian society, whether or not the newly elected Mitterand government in France continued to provide them with substantial economic and military support.

The case of Ndam Njoya is particularly striking because, just as Bernard Fonlon had evoked an idealistic strain in the people's consciousness during the 1960s, Ndam Njoya generated widespread enthusiasm for the "new morality" he advocated during his tenure as minister of education. Many people shared the attitude expressed by a prominent journalist who declared that "there is no morality in politics, there are only interests."[11] Nevertheless, a deeply rooted moral idealism made the majority of Cameroonians receptive to Ndam Njoya's plea for a society in which all people would have the opportunity to develop their individual potential while contributing to the nation's welfare.

If young people could be educated to respect the humanity they share with all other people, to familiarize themselves with traditional and modern culture, to adopt an attitude of intellectual curiosity, and to accept moral responsibility for the consequences of their actions, they would, Ndam Njoya argued, become capable of producing a national culture that they might pass on with pride to future generations.[12] He himself reduced class sizes in the schools, reformed abuses in the examination system, and revitalized a demoralized cadre of teachers, but in doing so, he incurred enmity by challenging the prerogatives of the privileged class. Although he was removed from his post after two years in office, the popular response to his "new morality" suggested the persistence of a widespread yearning for a more just and equitable society in Cameroon.

When Biya came to power and gradually distanced himself from Ahidjo, "moral renewal" became one of his key slogans, and there was considerable optimism that he would introduce the kind of reforms that Fonlon and Ndam Njoya had envisaged. After the unsuccessful coup attempt in 1984, Biya himself fostered this impression by changing the name of the country's single party from UNC to RDPC (Rassemblement Démocratique du Peuple Camerounais) and launching a campaign of national renewal. At first, Biya presented himself as a common man who understood the needs of the people and eschewed the inflated rhetoric of his predecessor. He championed civic responsibility and freedom of information, and his first presidential speech was delivered in English, an important symbolic gesture toward the disaffected anglophone population in the western part of the country. Even Biya's reputation as an efficient manager suggested that he would address the country's social and economic problems in a pragmatic, equitable fashion.

Among the more than half-dozen books that sought to establish a favorable image of the new president, Charly-Gabriel Mbock's *Cameroun: L'Intention démocratique* is one of the most convincing. According to Mbock, Biya's democratic socialism synthesizes a respect for the spiritual dimension of life with a recognition of the need to subject all experience to rational examination. It envisages a national community in which people earn their freedom by striving to actualize their potential as individuals. Mbock implies that Biya can inspire this new, more rigorous attitude toward life in the people, thereby enabling them to participate in the creation of the nation. "Cameroon will be the work of Cameroonians, or it will not be at all," Mbock argued, adding that "Cameroon still remains to be invented."[13] The implication is that the Ahidjo government had failed to define a viable national identity and that Biya would lead people toward the realization of a national vision based on democratic principles and the rational pursuit of truth.

Despite Biya's good intentions, however, structural inequities persisted in Cameroonian society, and authoritarian patterns of governance remained in place. Especially after the 1984 attempted coup, Biya became increasingly dependent upon the military, and he established closer ties with the French government. As the country's oil reserves are gradually depleted, constraints on government spending exacerbate the widespread discontent that resurfaced after an initial burst of enthusiasm for the new president, and revelations about the misappropriation of oil revenues reinforced the people's skepticism toward their country's government. Biya's 1985 appointment of former Ahidjo stalwarts to well-remunerated positions in parastatal corporations merely strengthened the impression that behind-the-scenes operations were still being conducted as they always had been. Besides, corruption and mismanagement contributed directly to the worsening economic situation. Smuggling, overbilling, payment for development projects that were never realized, and the skimming of percentages from government contracts cost the federal treasury billions of CFA francs, and with the fall of oil and raw material prices, Cameroon had become a debtor nation by the late 1980s.[14] Even before the coup, René Philombe and other writers had begun to decry the malaise that was once again settling over Cameroonian society.[15]

Confronted by problems over which it did not have complete control, the Biya government resorted to many of the same political techniques that had been employed under Ahidjo. Censorship was applied with new rigor. Socially critical writers were arbitrarily arrested. And in spite of Biya's earlier attempts to demythologize the presidency, a campaign to glorify his image gathered momentum. Mbock's book fostered this tendency when it described Biya's reappearance after the attempted coup in terms that suggest both the resurrection of Christ and the successful completion of an initiation rite. For Mbock, this experience transformed Biya from an individual into a chief worthy of governing his people. Hubert Mono Ndjana's *L'Idée sociale chez Paul Biya* presents a similar image of Cameroon's second president. Such idealizations served the same political function as they had during the Ahidjo years, for they sought to establish a symbolic identification between the country's leader and its destiny while drawing attention away from real social and economic problems.

One of the most influential spokesmen for this position under both Ahidjo and Biya was the party functionary and sometime minister of information and culture Joseph Charles Doumba, whose *Etre au carrefour, Monsieur le Maire: Lettre ouverte*, and *Vers le Mont Cameroun* focus on the civic responsibility of individuals in the nation-building process. According to him, the primary goal of politics in a developing country is the articulation of an ideal that can be implanted in the minds of the people through a process of open dialogue and self-criticism. He envisaged this process as a cultural one, for he defined culture broadly as "that which is essential in the life of a people, that which is positive and has survived from the past, that which gestates and is born to the present, that which seeks to transcend the existing situation and projects itself into the future."[16] All his books revolve around the kind of leadership needed to shape this culture in conformity with the national ideal that he symbolically associated with Mount Cameroon.

To inspire people with a commitment to this ideal, he argued, leaders should be capable of withdrawing into themselves, examining a broad spectrum of alternatives, and weighing the possible consequences of their actions. Then they must have the will to carry out their ideas and the skill to transform them into realities. In *Monsieur le Maire*, he exhorts the mayors of various thinly disguised Cameroonian cities to adopt this approach to the task of governance, which he compares to the design and cultivation of a garden. The objective in both cases is an aesthetically pleasing and functional well-orderedness, and the assumption is that it can be achieved through rational planning. With regard to literature and art, Doumba believes that such a policy, honestly and resolutely applied, can foster the emergence of works that reinforce the national ideology. His position in the government and in the party allowed him to act upon this conviction, thereby becoming a principal architect of the policy of channeling cultural activities into forms acceptable to the government.

A similar approach to cultural renewal is evident in the government economist Nicolas Atangana's *Problématique du développement en Afrique tropicale* and *Travail et développement*. Having been influenced by the Negritude philosophy of the *Présence Africaine* group during his student days in France, Atangana later became convinced that a viable national culture is largely a function of economic development, which depends on conceptual organization, habits of capital formation, and a conscientious attitude toward productive work. Although Atangana is more critical than Doumba of government policies, his underlying assumptions about civic responsibility and rational planning are quite similar. For example, he contended that the parasitism, corruption, and bureaucratic inefficiency in many African countries derive from an irrational attitude toward work, and he proposed to change the situation by enlightening people about the historical origins of this attitude.

According to him, the precolonial ethic of communal work was destroyed by the colonialist intrusion that deprived people of control over the products of their labor and eliminated any recognizable relationship between the amount or quality of work done and the reward received for having done it. Africans who understand this relationship will, he argued, be able to see that productive work confers dignity insofar as it enables people to realize their potential, to exercise mastery over nature, and to acquire the wealth they desire for themselves and their country. If the government engaged people in the decision-making process and made certain that rewards were distributed according to the amount and quality of work performed, it could then persuade them that conscientious work contributes to the satisfaction of their own needs. And if work can be institutionalized on the basis of social solidarity rather than individualistic competition, he concluded, the material conditions of life can be improved, thereby revitalizing a cultural identity that had been submerged beneath the legacies of colonialist oppression. Like Doumba, Atangana believed that cultural renewal demanded the solution of social problems that can best be addressed by rational planning and by the attempt to transform people's ways of thinking about their relationship to national development goals.

Under Biya, many of these ideas have been incorporated into a new official ideology that was initially shaped by François Sengat-Kuo, although it has gradually become the province of Georges Ngango, the architect of the "Renewal" and the renamed party's platform of "communitarian liberalism." The philosophy is clearly outlined in Biya's programmatic *Pour le liberalisme communautaire*, which acknowledges weaknesses in the Cameroonian system and proposes a liberal democratic vision of the country's future. The emphasis in Biya's book is on the creation of a socio-economic environment in which individuals can realize their own freely chosen goals while at the same time developing a heightened sense of allegiance to the Cameroonian nation.

Based on a modern concept of selfhood, his assumption is that allowing people to participate in the decision-making process will lead to the emergence of "a liberated Cameroonian, [who is] guided by reason, culturally free of alienation, and convinced that people are human only when they are acting creatively."[17] The mechanism for assuring this emancipation is, according to Biya, the principle that everyone should be rewarded according to merit. By recognizing the need to eliminate corruption, inequitable distributions of wealth, and arbitrary restrictions on freedom of expression, he holds out the promise of a democratic society in which individuals control their own destinies and deal honestly with each other.

If communitarian liberalism proposes an ethics of self-reliance and moral integrity on the individual level, it also envisages the integration of disparate individuals into a self-respecting national community. As Biya himself declares, "it is necessary to create in every Cameroonian the conditions of a national consciousness so profound that primary, instinctive attachments to tribal or regional values and interests can no longer disturb it."[18] For him, such an enterprise presupposes a spiritual dimension of life that makes human solidarity possible. A commitment to this spiritual dimension lies behind his rationale for reforming the government, the economy, and the country's foreign relations because he believes they should serve the spiritual well-being of the entire population rather than enslaving the majority for the benefit of a small privileged class. By identifying the universal truths embedded in traditional ethnic practices and by fostering interethnic contact, Biya hopes that Cameroonians will pass from multiple ethnic cultures to a single national culture without jeopardizing their rootedness in their own ethnic communities. On the ideological level, he is suggesting that Cameroon can become a unified nation by conceiving of itself as an expression of the people's will. In this sense, his liberal democratic vision differs markedly from his predecessor's more authoritarian public stance.

Presented as a statement of purpose for the RDPC, *Pour le liberalisme communautaire* stresses the need for a rational, pragmatic approach to the problems that stand in the way of the national unity he envisions. The educational system must be improved to enable all people to realize their potential as individual human beings and as participants in the national community. Communication and transportation networks must be expanded to embrace all parts of the country. Adequate housing and medical care must be provided for everyone. Institutions must be created to encourage saving, stimulate agricultural production, promote appropriate industrial development, and eliminate gross inequities in the distribution of wealth. Because he is convinced that people will support such projects only if they have a stake in their realization, he proposes to involve citizens in economic planning and to grant more decision-making power to rural communities and other local groups. Although he describes the country's single party as a transitional stage in the evolution toward a multiparty state, he regards it as a necessary step in defining an appropriate form of democracy for the specifically Cameroonian situation. The party thus remains a primary instrument of social and political mobilization in the nation-building process.

In his book, Biya vows to promulgate a "charter of freedoms" that will guarantee people, among other things, the right to subject the Cameroonian past and present to critical scrutiny. The corollary of this new openness is a democratic assumption that the truth will emerge in the free exchange of ideas, and this truth is regarded as essential to the successful governance of the country. During the mid-1980s, the publication of numerous books and articles on the "Cameroonian Renewal" lent credence to the government's liberalization policies, for writers such as Jacques Fame Ndongo, Alexandre Kum'a Ndumbe III, Hubert Mono Ndjana, Charly-Gabriel Mbock, Henri Bandolo, Jean-Pierre Fogui, Patrice Etoundi M'Balla, Biyiti bi Essam, and others did not hesitate to criticize the Ahidjo regime as they eulogized the initiatives of the country's new president. Even Victor J. Ngoh's secondary-school textbook *Cameroon, 1884-1985: A Hundred Years of History* acknowledges the Ahidjo government's mistakes in a way that would not have been possible before Biya came to power.

At the same time, Biya's new liberalism spawned a flood of books that examined contemporary Cameroonian history from a variety of perspectives. Published largely by L'Harmattan in Paris, these books expressed a strong impulse toward democratic reform as the basis for a new vision of national identity. Eugene Wonyu's *Cameroun: Plaidoyer pour le patriote-martyr Ruben Um Nyobé* seeks to reestablish the truth about the UPC's role in the country's struggle for independence. Emmanuel Kengne Pokam's *La Problématique de l'unité nationale au Cameroun* and Victor Kamga's *Duel camerounais: Démocratie ou barbarie* attack the Ahidjo government for the disparity between its idealistic rhetoric and its oppressive exercise of power, intimating that his policies had been particularly prejudicial in their effects on the entrepreneurial dynamism of the Bamileke.

Tjadè Eonè's *Radios, publics et pouvoirs au Cameroun* examines the role of the radio in Cameroonian public life and pleads for opening the government-controlled media to the free exchange of ideas that Biya himself was advocating. Referring to the suppression of opinion under Ahidjo as the "dark ages" and recognizing the dialogue that had begun to take place under Biya, Bassek ba Kobhio's *Cameroun, la fin du maquis? Presse, livre et "ouverture démocratique"* criticizes the privileged class for opposing the institutionalization of democratic reforms upon which he believes the country's future depends. As a plea for freedom of the press and universal access to books, Bassek's argument specifically links Cameroonian print culture to the evolution of a viable national identity concept.

Biya's democratic inclinations and his advocacy of rational problem-solving techniques reinforced this concept. They also brought about some changes in the contemporary Cameroonian political atmosphere. For example, when elections with secret ballots were held in 1986 and 1987, more than one-half of the party's officeholders at the local and national levels lost their positions. Dissidents have been arrested and imprisoned, but they do not disappear, as they did under Ahidjo, and they are generally released within several months. The sixth five-year plan—the first to be prepared completely under Biya—represents a departure from earlier ones in the sense that it foresees increased expenditures on social services for a broad spectrum of the population. Furthermore, the introduction of computers has reduced some forms of corruption by trimming absentee workers from the government payroll and by verifying the collection of import duties.[19]

Nevertheless, Biya's reform program has been seriously undermined by the worsening economic situation, the persistence of corrupt patterns of behavior, and the conviction among Biya's closest advisers that they have the right to shape the country according to their conception of its national destiny. Despite Biya's emphasis on interethnic solidarity, he has appointed overwhelming numbers of people from his own south-central region to high government positions, and latent feelings of ethnic and regional resentment have increasingly begun to surface. Many Bamileke believe they have been excluded from the exercise of political power, not only on the national level but also in cities such as Douala and Yaounde, where they now constitute a significant percentage of the population. In contrast, many Beti-speaking Cameroonians distrust what they regard as Bamileke aspirations for power.

Biya's Beti-dominated government has even fostered rumors that attribute the present crisis at least partly to massive Bamileke withdrawals of currency from the national economy. Hubert Mono Ndjana's March 1987 speech "De L'Ethnofascism dans la littérature politique camerounaise" confirmed this tendency by openly attacking an alleged Bamileke conspiracy to gain economic and social control over the country. A short time later, fifty priests from south-central Cameroon wrote a letter in which they accused the papal nunciate in

Yaounde of plotting to enhance the power of Bamileke in the church hierarchy. The Biya government's tacit approval of these declarations was signaled by the fact that journalists who criticized Mono Ndjana's speech were arrested and the priests' letter was allowed to circulate publicly.[20]

Against the background of this situation, the exile UPC activist Elenga Mbuyinga published his *Tribalisme et problème national en Afrique Noire: Le Cas du Cameroun*, a penetrating analysis of the "tribalist" motivations behind the nation-building rhetoric of leaders such as Ahidjo and Biya. Like the anglophone Cameroonian exile Ndiva Kofele Kale in *Tribesmen and Patriots: Political Culture in a Polyethnic African State*, Mbuyinga sees no contradiction between ethnic loyalty and allegiance to a modern nation; in fact, both writers contend that the primary obstacle to national unity is the existence of ethnically based bourgeoisies that compete with each other for dominance while collaborating to further their own interests at the expense of most people in the country. After discussing the tribalist and class interests inherent in the nation-building works of writers such as Mono Ndjana and Kengne Pokam (who defend opposing viewpoints on the Bamileke question), Mbuyinga proposes a new UPC approach to the national identity problem in Cameroon.

According to him, an appropriate first step would be to foster a heightened popular awareness of the class interests behind both ethnic conflict and the nation-building rhetoric. His assumption is that, if people recognize how they have been manipulated, they will become capable of working together and respecting each other's human rights without relinquishing a strong sense of ethnic identity. Although he regards ethnic groups as incipient nations and conceptualizes the long-run solution to Cameroonian political reorganization within a pan-African context, his practical suggestions indicate that he envisions the emergence of a Cameroonian state that would respond to the needs and desires of the people who live within its boundaries. To bring such a state into being, he argues, they themselves must repudiate the oppression to which the upper bourgeoisie from their own ethnic groups has subjected them. The historical precedent for this repudiation is, according to him, the UPC struggle for independence during the 1950s. If the vision of Um Nyobé could be revived, and if the country's socio-economic structure could be transformed through democratic participation, decentralization, and the elimination of private property, Mbuyinga concludes, the genuine will of the people could express itself in the creation of a truly free and independent Cameroon.

However, the utopian impetus toward freedom and democracy that characterizes recent books by Biya's apologists as well as his detractors has never been fully incorporated into the Cameroonian government's approach to cultural politics. During the last ten years of Ahidjo's presidency, cultural politics did play an increasingly prominent role in the official nation-building rhetoric, and the declaration of a unitary state offered him an opportunity to proclaim the need for a "cultural renewal" that would reaffirm a specifically Cameroonian identity. According to him, culture is the collective personality of a people, and because this personality is susceptible to influence, he felt that the party and the state have an obligation to shape it in conformity with their own nation-building goals—fostering a sense of transethnic unity, promoting modernization, and presenting a recognizable identity to the rest of the world.

He was calling for a transformation of mentalities in an educational and cultural process that would inspire all Cameroonians with an allegiance to the higher ideal of national unity. This higher ideal represents a synthesis of traditional and modern values. It also expresses his conviction that ethnic identities from all parts of the country can be maintained within a larger community of interests. Defined in these terms, Ahidjo's cultural politics were an instrument to consolidate a sense of collective identity and engage people in the party's struggle to create a unified, modern nation. In 1974, he charged two newly created councils—the Council on Higher Education and Research and the Council on Cultural Affairs—with the task of outlining ways in which these goals might be attained. The results of their meetings were formalized five years later in a Cameroonian cultural charter, and several government agencies were directed to implement the councils' recommendations. This attempt to create a national culture betrayed the influence of Senghorian Negritude. It also reflected the somewhat dubious assumption that an authoritarian government could impose its concept of cultural identity on an ethnically and socially diverse population.

On one level, Ahidjo's cultural renewal was intended to establish a network of cultural reference points that could be shared by all Cameroonians and become a part of their national identity concept. The Bureau of Cultural Affairs and the national research foundation were mandated to preserve a knowledge of traditional values by creating museums, libraries, and cultural centers throughout the country. In addition, the Ministry of Information and Culture subsidized documentary films about the country's various regions and ethnic groups. It also oversaw the production of the first national encyclopedia and helped organize cultural festivals to commemorate national holidays and anniversaries of important historical events.

Yet official government efforts to promote the idea of a national culture were only marginally successful. Financial resources were lacking to create museums, libraries, and cultural centers. Those that did exist in the larger cities were poorly equipped and had little impact on the population at large. The Chinese constructed an impressively furnished Cultural Palace in Yaounde, but when they donated it to the Cameroonian government in the early 1980s, its use was restricted for official functions, and it never became identified in the public mind with a national culture.

Similarly, the national encyclopedia was produced in a luxurious format with a gold medallion of Ahidjo embossed on the front cover of the first volume. Although some entries in it are informative, others are hastily written and poorly researched. The dominant tone throughout its four volumes is self-congratulatory and reflects the official rhetoric of the party. Nearly all seventy-five hundred copies of the encyclopedia were sold at a profit to Cameroonian civil servants, who were placed under some pressure to purchase it for more than ninety thousand CFA francs. The Cultural Palace and the national encyclopedia were monuments to the government, and like many of the government's initiatives, they did not register on the consciousness of most Cameroonians as an expression of their own culture.

On another level, Ahidjo's cultural renewal was part of his government's effort to gain control over all phases of public life. During the five years that the government was working out the country's cultural charter, Ahidjo emphasized in his speeches that there could be no legitimate cultural activity outside the framework of national development and its requirements for political stability. In essence, he was warning writers and other producers of culture that their intellectual efforts were part of a larger political program and would be judged on the basis of their contribution to that program. In practical terms, the work of the two councils and the cultural charter created more efficient mechanisms for channeling the efforts of individuals into projects the government considered appropriate to its conception of national identity.

One way in which this channeling took place was through the creation of a national theater company. In 1974, the national cultural council recommended its establishment as a means of preserving traditional culture and integrating it into a style that expresses an authentic Cameroonian character. As one aspect of what Ahidjo called the country's "cultural identity card," a national acting company was expected to sensitize the people to the traditions that unite them. At the same time, it was to showcase a composite image of these traditions for foreign audiences. The potential for such an undertaking was demonstrated by the success of the National Ensemble that had been formed in 1963 for a drama competition in Paris. Modeled in part on Keita Fodeba's Ballets Africains and the national dance troupes that had emerged in many African countries shortly after independence, the National Ensemble presented dances from various parts of the country and choreographed them into a self-contained spectacle. In the process, the significance of traditional materials changed. They lost their religious and communal functions, but they acquired the potential to symbolize cultural authenticity on a national scale. Unfortunately, the National Ensemble disbanded after its tour of France, and the government never again succeeded in bringing together such a dynamic group.

Despite the success of the National Ensemble, the dramatic group that represented Cameroon during the Festival of African Arts in 1966 proved disappointing, and the following year Minister of Education William Eteki summoned the well-known Cameroonian actor Ambroise Mbia from Paris to organize a "troupe d'essai" that was envisaged as the forerunner of a national theater. Mbia's training was entirely in the French tradition, and his directorship of the "troupe d'essai" established implicit standards for high-culture dramatic performances. Overall, the French influence on the concept of a Cameroonian national theater was pervasive. Alain Gheerbrandt, the former director of the French cultural service in Yaounde, helped organize the National Ensemble and served as an adviser for several other acting groups. Theater workshops sponsored by the French cultural service in 1965 and 1966 decisively influenced the acting styles of the country's leading performers. In fact, the "troupe d'essai" was partly an outgrowth of these workshops. Touring French theater companies also reinforced French models of stage production.

The 1967 "troupe d'essai" achieved a high level of proficiency in this style of performance, but it was short-lived because Mbia returned to France shortly after having directed it in the first major production of Oyono-Mbia's *Jusqu'à nouvel avis*. Two years later the absence of a national theater proved embarrassing when the Cameroonian entry in the drama competition at the Algiers festival was severely criticized. If the government's sporadic attempts to establish a national acting company before 1974 had failed, they nevertheless helped create a substantial cadre of highly professional actors.

The announcement of the FESTAC celebrations in Nigeria prompted the government to act upon the cultural council's recommendation by forming the nucleus of another national theater company in 1975. Known initially as the Théâtre de l'Essai and later as the Théâtre Ecole, it was directed first by the Frenchman Pierre Blondet and then by his countryman Philippe Dauchez. Many of the country's leading actors participated enthusiastically in the project. They did research in traditional cultures and explored various modern techniques in an attempt to develop an authentically Cameroonian acting style. By the fall of 1977 they were staging weekly performances at the Cameroonian Cultural Center and undertaking regular tours to other parts of the country. In the words of the director of cultural affairs, they were well on their way to fulfilling their mission, for their new style "should lead to a true affirmation of our cultural identity."[21]

Ironically, the transformation of the Théâtre Ecole into the National Theatre and the Cameroonization of its directorship resulted in the loss of the communal spirit that had characterized the group's earlier period. When Mbia returned to become artistic director in 1979, he abandoned the experimental approach of the Théâtre Ecole and reintroduced the high-culture acting style he had perfected during his nearly twenty years in Paris. Although Mbia was replaced by François Njoumoni in 1983, the company never regained the vitality of its early years. In fact, it produced fewer plays in ten years than its forerunner had in less than half that time, and its influence over drama production in the country has been minimal. In short, it never succeeded in playing the role envisaged for it as a symbol of the country's cultural unity.

An even more crucial aspect of the government's cultural politics during the Ahidjo and Biya years involves the Cameroonization of the educational system. After the "Peaceful Revolution of May 20," the Ahidjo government sought to bring school and university curricula into harmony with the official conception of national unity. The "baccalauréat" had been removed from the jurisdiction of the French Inspectorate of the Academy in 1968, and increasing numbers of students passed the Cameroonian examination each year, especially after the British-influenced school system in the western part of the country was modified to bring it into conformity with the French-based system in the

East. Students who wrote the "baccalauréat" examination in 1982 learned more about oral literature than did their predecessors during the 1960s, and most of the thirty-five literary works on their required reading list were African, although only four of them were by Cameroonian authors. The dominance of French literary works on earlier reading lists had been broken, and the shared cultural references of students who graduated in the 1980s were far less Eurocentric than those of preceding generations. The cultural renewal that accompanied the "Peaceful Revolution of May 20" thus resulted in an appreciable reduction of French influence over the country's school system.

The administration of the university and the national research institute also passed from French to Cameroonian hands in the early 1970s. By this time, more than two-thirds of the faculty at the university were Cameroonians, and French funding had declined to less than a third of the university's budget.[22] However, as the government assumed a greater portion of educational costs and replaced French teachers with Cameroonians, the tendency to regard schools, and particularly the university, as instruments of national development policy grew stronger. In his initial speech to the two councils, Ahidjo declared that university instructors were expected to serve the state as teachers of civic responsibility, and the Council on Higher Education and Research officially recommended that all instructors, researchers, and students should be "politically engaged in conformity with the political principles defined by the UNC."[23] In practical terms, such strictures meant that the university and the national research institute were being ordered to lay the intellectual groundwork for the nation-building goals already formulated by the country's political leaders. Such a task implied ideological orthodoxy, and the government did not hesitate to police these institutions to ensure that this orthodoxy was being respected.

The most intractable problem confronting the government at this time was the severe overcrowding that afflicted all levels of the educational system. Enrollments in Cameroonian secondary schools doubled between 1971 and 1976, and those in primary schools increased by fifty-three percent, although this explosive increase did not occur uniformly in all parts of the country: if ninety-four percent of school-age children were actually attending school in the Center-South by 1982, the figure was only thirty-one percent in the North at that time.[24] Public schools could not always cope with the influx of new students, and classrooms were strained beyond capacity. For example, class sizes at Lycée Leclerc in Yaounde often exceeded a hundred, and confessional schools continued to teach nearly a third of the student population as late as 1980. Because access to elite public schools was easier for children of the privileged class, a growing number of poorly equipped private schools emerged to satisfy the demands of parents who regarded education as the only avenue to social advancement for their children. Some Bamileke spent as much as three-fourths of their annual income on school expenses, which illustrates the power that this belief exercises over large segments of the country's population.

The university was also vastly overcrowded. Built to serve three thousand students in the 1960s, it was enrolling more than six times that number by the mid-1980s without having increased its physical facilities proportionately. Coupled with the corruption that plagued most sectors of the public sphere, the difficulty of teaching and learning under such circumstances intensified the skepticism of students and faculty toward the idealistic goals of the government's cultural politics.

Voices were raised in opposition to the education Cameroonian young people received under such circumstances. For example, arguing that "one cannot be modern by adopting the modernity of others," Léon Messi advocated the need to develop the whole person, not only the rational faculties. He suggested that traditional society offered instructive models for heightening people's ability to perceive the world and to make appropriate value judgments based on their observations.[25] In contrast, Charly-Gabriel Mbock's *Cameroun: L'Intention démocratique* criticizes the attitude that views schooling as a stage on the path to social privilege and not as an opportunity to acquire the knowledge and skills to perform the tasks that need to be accomplished in countries such as Cameroon.

As rural populations migrated to the cities and the economy proved incapable of absorbing ever larger numbers of former secondary-school and university students into the job market, a growing discontent surfaced among increasingly literate groups within the country's population. Recognizing the political dangers inherent in such a situation, the government supported educational programs that encouraged people to remain on the land, but such efforts often foundered on the resistance of parents who did not want their children relegated to second-class citizenship.

For example, the most ambitious project of this kind was the UNESCO-supported IPAR (Institut de Pédagogie Appliquée à Vocation Rurale), which emphasized practical experience, modern agricultural methods, and the acquisition of useful vocational skills. After eight years of research, the IPAR curriculum was ready to be introduced on an experimental basis in 1973, but the opposition of parents was so strong that its implementation was delayed for two years, and the program never attained the goals that had been set for it. In this instance, parents suspected that the new curriculum was designed to prevent their children from receiving the kind of education necessary to improve their status in society. As long as such attitudes persist, the government will encounter resistance to educational reforms that respond to social needs by narrowing the range of options for specific groups of people. Individualism has become so deeply ingrained in most parts of Cameroon that few people are willing to relinquish their access to upward social mobility, even if it is no more than an illusion.

One response to the blockage of opportunity in the educational system was a marked increase in the number of young people studying in other countries. West Cameroonians in particular turned toward Nigeria, where at least a thousand of them were enrolling annually at universities by the early 1980s.

At the same time, Cameroonian students also flocked to France, Germany, Canada, and the United States. Rather than strengthening popular commitment to the Ahidjo government's conception of national unity, the educational consequences of its cultural renewal policy merely provoked people into seeking ways of circumventing the institutions that had supposedly been created for their benefit.

The major unanswered question in the area of cultural politics involves the language issue. In the process of defining a national culture, the government recognized that the first language for the majority of Cameroonians is neither French nor English but an African language. Insofar as cultural identity is deeply intertwined with the use of language, an authentic culture for most Cameroonians would imply a culture in the language of the ethnic group to which they belong. However, in a country with a multitude of different languages, the government could not promote them all, and if it chose to favor the development of some at the expense of others, it would incur considerable opposition from those whose languages had been ignored.[26] Furthermore, the people around Ahidjo desired to exercise strict control over the dissemination of information, and the emergence of literate cultures in African languages would make such control difficult. In fact, the government has consistently discouraged African-language newspapers out of the fear that they might express dissenting opinions in terms that even uneducated people could understand.

This policy was reinforced by a change in French cultural policy during the early 1970s. Before this time, the French government had attempted to keep alive an attachment to the culture of France, but emphasis gradually shifted to the promotion of French-language cultural activity by Africans. Fewer French theater troupes visited the country, and the French cultural centers in Yaounde and Douala began to sponsor events such as film festivals devoted to the works of francophone African directors. Fewer books by French authors were distributed in the country, and more publications of French-language books by Africans were underwritten by the French government. The 1972 conference of education ministers from francophone African states met at Tananarive in Madagascar and seconded the new French policy by adopting an official resolution to incorporate African texts into the school curricula at all levels. By promoting the use of a European language for the expression of African cultural values, the new French policy and its endorsement by francophone African governments actually heightened the dominance of European languages in countries such as Cameroon.

The adoption of such a policy ensured that Cameroonian students would continue to read texts written in French. In fact, the proliferation of Cameroonian writing in French during the 1970s and 1980s reflected the younger generation's acceptance of the French language as an integral part of its own cultural heritage. The continuing presence of French teachers and technical advisers helped sustain the belief that their language was necessary for Cameroonian development, but by the mid-1970s the primary advocates for the continued use of French were educated Cameroonians for whom the European language had become an indispensable prop for their own sense of identity.

The status of English was slightly different. After the declaration of the unitary state, anglophone Cameroonians felt marginalized in the predominantly francophone state, and although they were initially heartened by Biya's gestures toward them, they have never been fully integrated into the country's political and cultural life. As a result, the English language has remained an important symbol of regional identity, and they defend it tenaciously against what they view as francophone infringements upon their prerogatives. In 1985 anglophone students and intellectuals grew more insistent in their demands for a greater recognition of their cultural heritage, and the lawyer Fowgum Gorka-Dinka was arrested for circulating a statement that branded the present government as unconstitutional because it failed to respect the articles of confederation on the basis of which the two parts of the country had originally been joined. At the same time, the anglophone opposition party in exile, the Cameroon Action Movement, became increasingly active. Yet the most significant development in anglophone literate culture during the 1970s and 1980s was the emergence of an English-language intellectual community in Yaounde. The absence of a major urban area in the former British Cameroons had always impeded the development of an anglophone literary tradition, but as substantial numbers of educated individuals from that part of the country came to study or work in the capital, they formed a nascent center of English-language cultural activity.

Although the government paid lip service to the importance of Cameroonian languages, it did little to foster their use as a vehicle of cultural expression. Instruction in the schools had to be given in French or English, and in 1977 the university ceased offering courses in Cameroonian languages. At about the same time, the government discontinued the publication of documents and bulletins in the country's major vehicular languages. Although nine of these languages were selected for regular use on the radio, there has been no serious attempt to incorporate them into the government's concept of a national culture.

This failure to promote the use of African languages has been criticized by Cameroonians who regard them as the sine qua non of an authentic national culture. For example, the linguist Pierre Ngijol Ngijol asserted that "development in our country can take place only through our languages, which alone are suitable for liberating the national genius and making it flourish."[27] Ngijol's point is that all people must have an opportunity to participate in the social, economic, and cultural development of the country if the sense of belonging to a national community is to take root among them. According to him, this participation remains impossible as long as most people are excluded from the process by the use of languages they do not fully understand. He and others have also contended that the obligatory use of European languages traps many Cameroonians in a split consciousness that prevents them from engaging spontaneously in the creation of a culture responsive to what they feel inside themselves. Only such a culture could, he concluded, serve as the basis for an authentic national identity.

Most Cameroonian writers adopt a pragmatic approach to the language question. They acknowledge that African languages contain a rich storehouse of philosophical wisdom, moral insight, and aesthetic potential. They also recognize that the preservation of these languages is crucial if Cameroonians hope to remain in contact with a traditional heritage that endows them with a coherent sense of who they are. But they also accept English and French as part of the Cameroonian national identity—the part that allows people to communicate across ethnic boundaries and grants them access to the rest of the world. Proponents of the anti-Negritude position, including Marcien Towa, Ebenezer Njoh-Mouelle, and Hubert Mono Ndjana, argued that the true basis for a national cultural identity is not linguistic but socio-economic. Once all Cameroonians become participants in the development of their country and receive a fair share of the benefits it has to distribute, a national personality will emerge, and according to them, such a personality can be expressed equally well in European and African languages. Others as diverse as the linguist Maurice Tadadjeu and the UPC writer Mbuyinga contend that the adoption of Cameroonian languages is a prerequisite to the emergence of a free and self-respecting country.

Despite the government's hesitancy to promote Cameroonian languages, important initiatives were undertaken during the 1970s and 1980s to preserve them and expand their use. Members of many ethnic groups were enthusiastic about efforts to develop a written form of their own languages, and UNESCO supported the use of African languages in the schools and in local newspapers. The real contribution to education and publishing in the national languages was made by privately funded institutions such as the Collège Libermann in Douala, the Protestant Bible-translating association SIL (Summer Institute of Linguistics/Société Internationale du Linguistique), and the Bamileke adult-education association Nufi.

A small group of teachers at the Collège Libermann created a linguistics section that pioneered the development of pedagogical methods for African-language instruction, introduced an African-language requirement for all students at the school, and conducted research on the Douala, Bassa, Bamileke, and Ewondo languages. The recent publication of the Douala epic *Les Merveilleux Exploits de Djeki la Njambe* bears witness to their role in keeping alive the country's oral literature heritage. In 1973 and 1974, the Collège Libermann attracted national attention to the language question by hosting well-attended conferences on the role of Cameroonian languages in national development.

By 1982, SIL volunteers had developed written forms for twenty-five Cameroonian languages and worked with native speakers of forty-three more to help them do the same for their own languages.[28] During the late 1970s and early 1980s, more than three thousand people completed the rigorous program leading to a Nufi certificate in the Bamileke dialect Fé Fé, and follow-up studies revealed that those who subsequently pursued their studies in French performed at a higher level than those who had never received instruction in their native language. Over fifty texts have been published by Nufi, which encourages former students to continue writing in Bamileke by publishing their essays and literary pieces in the monthly journal *Nsienken-Nkwé*.

In collaboration with the African-language group at the Collège Libermann, SIL, and linguists at the university, the government agency CERELTRA (Centre de Recherche sur les Langues et Traditions Orales) established a uniform alphabet for the transcription of Cameroonian languages, generated a lexicon of modern words in the major vehicular languages, and compiled the country's first authoritative linguistic atlas. One of CERELTRA's long-range goals is the comparative analysis of all Cameroonian languages to provide the basis for a coherent national-language policy. However, it is already apparent that no single African language could be elevated to the status of Cameroonian national language without an enormous expenditure of time and money. Until now, the government has been unwilling to lend its full support to such a project, and as long as people continue to view European languages as the primary avenue to upward social mobility, French and English will remain the principal vehicles of literate culture in Cameroon.

Within the context of Cameroonian cultural politics since the early 1970s, the media have generally been treated as instruments of national construction. The press, radio, and television are controlled by the government to the extent that they invariably support its political objectives and present the country's overall image in a favorable light. Radio is unquestionably the most important source of information in Cameroon. With over two million radio receivers in the country, government-sponsored broadcasting reaches all sectors of the population and influences far more people than does either television, which was introduced in 1985 and relies heavily on foreign programming, or print journalism.[29] Foreign radio stations can be heard in the country, but they seldom report on Cameroonian affairs, and the government enjoys a monopoly over the local news that is of greatest concern to the people.

One reason for the relative unimportance of print journalism in Cameroon has been the virtual disappearance of an independent press. The privately owned newspapers that flourished in the late 1950s were eliminated by the Ahidjo government during the 1960s, and although the popular Catholic and Protestant newspapers survived into the early 1970s, they too had ceased to appear by 1975. The French-owned *Presse du Cameroun*, which had never completely shed its original orientation toward an expatriate readership, declined steadily in quality, and shortly after the "Peaceful Revolution of May 20," the government took over its facilities, transferred them from Douala to Yaounde, and began to publish its own daily newspaper, the *Cameroon Tribune*. A weekly English version was added a short while later.

In contrast to its predecessor, the *Cameroon Tribune* focused on local news and included substantive accounts of Cameroonian cultural activities as well as reviews of books by Cameroonian authors. However, every issue of the paper was subject to prior censorship, and accounts of events usually reflected government policy. In 1976, at least two hundred fifty people were killed in a collision on the Transcameroonian railway, but the *Cameroon Tribune* reported only a minor accident with five or six fatalities. In 1979, government soldiers massacred more than two hundred Kirdi villagers who had rebelled against their Fulani mayor; no word of the incident ever appeared in the newspaper. When civil servants or government ministers are removed from office, explanations are seldom given. Yet people know something about such events, and they supplement what they know with rumors. Under such circumstances, the press contributed to an atmosphere in which half-truths often became accepted as truths and people became increasingly skeptical about the credibility of information filtered through official channels.

If the government succeeded in controlling the news media, it did so by stifling the independent press, but control of the media was merely part of a larger effort to mold the country's literate discourse into forms capable of consolidating a national consciousness. In dealing with writers, the Cameroonian government has vacillated between a relatively benign tolerance of constructive dialogue and a rigorous insistence on ideological orthodoxy. There has always been considerable ambivalence in the relationship between the government and the intellectual community in Cameroon. During the 1970s, the circle of Ahidjo's close advisers mistrusted highly educated individuals, although they were obviously needed to achieve the country's development goals. At the same time, intellectuals who worked for the government resented the fact that they could be arbitrarily removed from their positions when they fell into disfavor with their superiors.

The liberalization proclaimed by Biya seemed to promise an opening toward the intellectual community, but many of the Ahidjo government's restrictions on freedom of expression remained in place throughout the 1980s; independent newspapers that sprang up in response to an atmosphere of greater tolerance in the mid-1980s had been closed down by the end of the decade, and books by Mbembe, Kamga, Wonyu, Mbuyinga, and other socially engaged Cameroonian writers continued to be prohibited. A momentary relaxation of controls over the print media did help Biya consolidate his position by distancing himself from Ahidjo, whose authoritarian rule was discredited in many of the publications that appeared at this time. However, once his government established its hold on power, it adopted the same rationale as its predecessor for channeling public opinion into paths determined in advance by the state.

For example, the country's 1979 cultural charter stipulated that the work of Cameroonian writers should be authentic and committed. Because the government defined these terms according to its own nation-building ideology, any writing critical of the status quo could be labeled a "factor of alienation" and suppressed. The application of such policies was particularly resented at the university, where some faculty and students believed they should be calling established truths into question. Antigovernment tracts were distributed by students on several occasions during the 1970s, and conservative members of Ahidjo's entourage began to view the university as a seedbed of revolutionary activity. By the early 1980s, the philosopher Marcien Towa had been removed from his teaching post on this pretext, and an increasingly strict control was being exercised over the recruitment of new faculty and the authorization of campus cultural activities.

The government's ambivalence toward freedom of expression is clearly illustrated by the policies it has adopted to regulate theatrical productions. On the one hand, the government recognized the potential of theater as an exemplary expression of the national identity it was seeking to foster. On the other hand, many politicians remained suspicious of a literary medium capable of reaching large numbers of people with messages that contained an ideological content they could never completely control. Before the mid-1960s it had not been necessary to obtain official permission to stage a play, but to protect the rights of authors and to coordinate the scheduling of performances, the government subsidized the creation of FENAL (Fédération Nationale des Mouvements de Jeunesse des Arts et Lettres), a loosely organized federation of drama groups and cultural associations.

Under the direction of Jean-Marie Abanda Ndengue and Charles-Henri Bebbe, FENAL became responsible for maintaining a calendar of dramatic productions and cataloguing the plays of Cameroonian writers. The scheduling of plays is not the equivalent of censorship, but it does provide a mechanism by means of which censorship can be exercised, as it was in 1969 when Abel Zomo Bem's *La Mort de Martin-Paul Samba* was banned at the request of a German embassy official who feared that bad publicity might result from a reenactment of his country's role in the execution of the popular Bulu folk hero.

In the same year, Bebbe organized the first Festival of Dramatic Art in Yaounde. Nearly all the major theatrical troupes in the country participated in the event, which proved so successful that FENAL was able to stage an even larger drama festival the following year as part of the country's tenth-anniversary celebrations. But the role of FENAL changed as the government became more directly involved in controlling dramatic performances, and by 1972 the federation had become moribund. During the six years of its existence, it had fostered contacts among the country's acting troupes and inspired them with the idea that they were involved in a common enterprise. It had also lent currency to the idea that the intellectual and economic rights of authors should be respected. At the same time, it created a precedent for requiring authors and directors to obtain authorization for presenting their works in public. In the hands of government officials, this precendent became a means of stifling the socially critical theatrical activity that peaked in Cameroon during the late 1970s and early 1980s.

In late 1981, prior censorship was introduced in the sense that directors had to submit playscripts to the Ministry of Information and Culture before they could obtain authorization to stage any public performance. The bureaucratic difficulties entailed in this process were compounded by the creation of SOCADRA (Société Camerounaise pour les Droits d'Auteur) and by the rapidly escalating fees for the rental of theater space. Established to guarantee that authors received royalties for the use of their works, SOCADRA demanded a substantial advance deposit before according its permission for a performance to take place—a particularly galling situation for author-directors who realized that only a small portion of the deposit would ever be returned to them.

By the late 1980s, rental fees for the major movie theaters in Yaounde had risen to 400,000–600,000 CFA francs for a single performance. The seldom-used Cultural Palace boasts the most advanced theater equipment in the country, but its 1.5 million-franc rental ensures that it will be used only for government-sponsored performances. Even the French cultural center, which has once again become the most commonly used theater in the country, now charges 125,000 CFA francs for the use of facilities that were formerly free.[30] As the result of these financial and bureaucratic pressures, independent theater activity has declined precipitously.

The government also censored books and periodical publications during the 1970s and 1980s, but access to the country's print culture was limited even more drastically by social and economic factors. Despite a substantial increase in adult literacy, the only consistent market for books continued to be that for school texts.[31] Trade books remained too expensive for most people to purchase, and many former students lapsed into semiliteracy after leaving school. UNESCO acknowledged the gravity of this situation in 1970 when it organized the International Year of the Book to focus attention on the need to provide universal access to books, and it enthusiastically supported a 1975 Cameroonian initiative to establish CREPLA (Centre Régional du Promotion du Livre en Afrique) at Yaounde.

The primary function of the new organization was to promote the publication, dissemination, and reading of books appropriate for African audiences. During its first five years, CREPLA organized conferences for librarians, editors of children's books, and publishers; it also facilitated coproduction agreements among publishing houses, enabling them to draw upon their combined resources in undertaking more ambitious projects, and it sponsored an extensive reading campaign in Cameroon and other equatorial African countries. Yet the overall impact of CREPLA was minimal because the origins of the problem it confronted were socio-economic as well as educational.

Another government initiative proved far more successful. In the face of mounting costs for school textbooks, it created CEPMAE (Centre d'Edition et de Production de Manuels et Auxiliaires de l'Enseignement) in 1974.[32] By producing textbooks in the country, the government hoped to husband its foreign exchange and hasten the Cameroonization of the curriculum. It succeeded on both counts, for despite larger numbers of children attending school, the cost of imported textbooks declined during the following decade, and the new texts included specifically Cameroonian materials.

Large multinational publishing companies such as Hachette, Garnier, Heinemann, Longmans, and Macmillan continued to provide many of the textbooks used in the country, and foreign cultural services frequently made books from their countries available at little or no cost to Cameroonians. Largely excluded from the textbook-publishing market, Editions CLE suffered a series of financial setbacks and gradually lost its position as a dominant influence on Cameroonian print culture. The production of new books at CLE peaked during the 1971–73 period and then steadily declined. Partly as a result of the 1973 international monetary crisis, optimistic sales projections failed to materialize, and the Protestant-sponsored firm discovered that much of its capital was immobilized in an enormous stock of unsold books.

Rising costs and high import duties on ink, paper, and printing presses made it four times more expensive to produce a book in Cameroon during the early 1980s than it had been ten years earlier.[33] And as the retail prices of CLE books increased dramatically, slumping sales declined even further. The firm, which published an average of twenty-six new titles a year between 1971 and 1973, was reduced to bringing out less than one new book a year during the 1980s. In the decade before 1973, CLE published the vast majority of Cameroonian fiction, but the dozen Cameroonian novels it has published since then constitute less than a fourth of the country's novelistic output during this period.

An important factor in the decline of CLE was the founding of NEA (Nouvelles Editions Africaines) at Dakar and Abidjan in 1972. The initiative for the creation of a new francophone African publishing house originally came from Senghor, who helped bring together a consortium of Paris-based publishing firms (Armand Colin, Hachette, Fernand Nathan, Présence Africaine, and Seuil) with the governments of Senegal and Ivory Coast to provide financial backing for NEA at a time when CLE's situation was becoming precarious. From the beginning, NEA was self-supporting because it produced tourist guides and school texts, for which assured markets existed in the sponsoring countries, which later included Togo as well. In five years, NEA brought out more new books than CLE had done during its entire fourteen-year history, and authors who had been working with CLE began submitting their manuscripts to NEA.

Overwhelmed by the seven hundred to a thousand unsolicited manuscripts that arrived in its editorial offices each year, the shrinking staff at CLE abandoned its earlier policy of dealing personally with all submissions, and many authors waited for years to receive notification about whether their works had been accepted for publication. This situation was particularly frustrating for Cameroonian writers at a time when NEA was publishing more and more works by people from other parts of francophone Africa. Although CLE and NEA did develop a good working relationship for the copublication of several books, the availability of NEA's new titles adversely affected CLE's already declining sales, and by the late 1970s NEA had clearly supplanted CLE as the most important publishing house in francophone Africa.

To fill the vacuum left by the decline of CLE, several independent publishers emerged and began to print inexpensive editions of works by local authors. In Yaounde, René Philombe started a modest publishing enterprise under the

Semences Africaines imprint, and Joseph Ndzié launched Editions Le Flambeau. In Bafoussam, Timothée Ndzagaap's bookstore, Librairie Populaire, issued cheap editions of plays and poetry collections. Many of these small publishing houses required authors to pay publication subsidies, as did Parisian firms such as Pierre Jean Oswald and La Pensée Universelle. Another option for aspiring writers was to finance the printing of their own works on the presses operated by CEPMAE or by one of the country's Christian missions. Despite the costs of publishing under these circumstances, the volume of Cameroonian writing increased dramatically during the 1970s and 1980s.

The dearth of publishing opportunities in West Cameroon inhibited the growth of an anglophone literature in that part of the country, but English-speaking Cameroonians also began to subsidize the printing of their own works in Nigeria and in the United States. Works by several of them were brought out by major British publishing houses, and Buma Kor founded an anglophone publishing venture in Yaounde during the mid-1970s, although financial difficulties prevented him from expanding his list of offerings beyond a few titles. Anglophone Cameroonians have an intense interest in literary activity, as indicated by the hundreds of manuscripts they submitted to the Guiness Writers' Contest during the late 1970s, but the vast majority of their writing has remained unpublished.[34]

Like CLE, the principal Cameroonian cultural journals of the 1960s and early 1970s gradually lapsed into inactivity after the declaration of the unitary state, and they were replaced by a flurry of ephemeral publications that reflected a variety of individual viewpoints. Although Fonlon managed to keep *Abbia* alive until the early 1980s, it appeared with increasing irregularity and no longer served as an important forum for the exchange of ideas. *Ozila* was never revived, and with the exception of a single issue in 1982, *Cameroun Littéraire* was moribund. Literary magazines such as Antoine Chonang's *L'Acropole* and academic journals such as *Ngam*, *Recherches Ouvertes*, *The Mould*, and *New Horizons* were produced in inexpensive formats, but none of them could command a national readership, and the most widely distributed local sources of information about contemporary Cameroonian literature were the cultural columns in the *Cameroon Tribune* and *Objectif*, an independent monthly news magazine that appeared in the early 1980s. As in other areas of cultural activity, the government's attempt to channel literate discourse into forms compatible with its nation-building ideology resulted in a fragmentation of earlier efforts to express the ideal of national unity and a decline in the quality of periodical publishing.

On an international level, scholars and critics tended to regard Cameroonian writing primarily within the context of African or francophone African literature. In accordance with its shift in focus, the French cultural service subsidized the publication of two professionally produced journals, *Notre Librairie* and *Recherche, pédagogie et culture*, both of which emphasize work from francophone Africa. Because their distribution was assured by the French government, these journals reached a far larger audience than did those edited by

Africans themselves. Journals associated with the Negritude movement also presented African literature as part of a unified tradition, while supporting the cultural nationalism that had influenced conservative political leaders such as Ahidjo. However, the most important of these journals, *Présence Africaine*, gradually lost its position as the leading proponent of black consciousness, and younger African intellectuals began to consider it irrelevant to the contemporary situation on the continent. Senghor did support the founding of *Ethiopiques* in Dakar, and it too reflected the Negritude position, but neither it nor the more eclectic *L'Afrique Littéraire et Artistique* reached substantial audiences in Africa. At any rate, such journals were not readily accessible to most Cameroonian writers, whose dominant concerns revolved around situations that existed in their own country.

The awareness of a specifically Cameroonian literature existed on two levels by the 1980s. On one hand, the government touted it as an expression of the national consciousness it claimed to have fostered; on the other, writers and intellectuals began to regard their country's literate culture as a body of writings to which they themselves were contributing. These two levels of understanding were not always compatible. The Ahidjo government's concept of literate culture presupposed that national consciousness can be planned by the country's political leadership and allowed to express itself in the writings of those who have assimilated this consciousness. In contrast, most writers merely recognized that their work reflected a particular set of socio-cultural realities and contained allusions to a network of shared reference points.

In response to Ahidjo's policy of cultural renewal, the university sponsored a major colloquium on Cameroonian literature and literary criticism in 1977. The announced goals of the colloquium were to establish a systematic inventory of oral and written Cameroonian literature, to define the most appropriate techniques for understanding and appreciating Cameroonian texts, and to make concrete proposals for the future development of a national literature. Many of the papers delivered on that occasion sought to identify the specificity of Cameroonian literature. Several touched upon the relationship between national literature and national identity. And the final recommendations of the colloquium participants included proposals for disseminating the country's literate culture to a wider popular audience. In her opening and closing remarks, the vice-minister of education, Dorothy Njeuma, declared that the government considered literature to be an integral part of the nation-building process. For this reason, it expected genuine Cameroonian writing to be firmly rooted in the realities of national life and committed to the positive values of national construction.

The national literature concept was discussed and defined in a flurry of articles that appeared in the *Cameroon Tribune* during the years that followed. According to the author of one such article, a national literature "must serve as a catalyst of the national consciousness which it expresses and from which it emanates."[35] Only a writer with a true Cameroonian soul could produce such literature, which would, he asserted, be dedicated to the ideal of national unity and the virtues associated with it. This was presumably the soul that the government was seeking to inculcate in Cameroonians by channeling their cultural activities in conformity with the official ideology, as it did in 1982, for example, by offering a substantial prize for the best literary text on the subject of "unity as a factor of national construction."

In a lecture to UNC party members, Polycarpe Oyié Ndzié discussed the application of this channeling approach to theater, which he described as a means of instructing people in civic responsibility while providing them with a communally oriented source of entertainment. According to him, properly conceived plays foster development and a sense of national unity by stimulating people to reflect critically on the problems confronting society, by exhorting them to participate in the solution of these problems, and by demonstrating the unity that underlies ethnic diversity. Although he decried the stereotyped portrayals of simple-minded villagers in the popular comedies of the period, he believed that retrograde attitudes can be corrected if they are turned to ridicule on the stage. At the same time, he was convinced that drama can help define an authentic Cameroonian identity by keeping alive elements from the traditional past. He concluded that "theater can participate actively in the necessary mobilization of the nation's positive energies to erect a free, strong, and prosperous Cameroon."[36] And in his eyes, it does so by transforming spectators into "militants" of development.

The effects of the government's cultural channeling were apparent during the 1981 general assembly of APEC. After years of inactivity, the national writers' association had sponsored a two-week festival of film showings, lectures, seminars, drama productions, concerts, poetry readings, and book exhibits in 1980 to celebrate its twentieth anniversary. Although Philombe, Fonlon, and others spoke eloquently at this time in support of granting writers the freedom to create a national culture that would truly reflect Cameroonian realities, the minister of information and culture, Guillaume Bwélé, made the government's position clear when he declared that "culture must have a civic, didactic, constructive content that is capable of contributing effectively to the consolidation of national unity."[37] Under the leadership of Philombe and a handful of writers who shared his populist views, APEC had obviously not fulfilled the cultural role prescribed for it by the government.

With the support of Bwélé, a group of university-educated writers and civil servants gained control of the organization the following year. Led by the dramatist and professor of German Alexandre Kum'a Ndumbe III, the new executive council of APEC vowed to promote a more vigorous intellectual and literary life in the country. A single issue of *Cameroun Littéraire* was published under the editorship of Ebenezer Njoh-Mouelle, but the organization lapsed into quiescence again. Nevertheless, the leadership change at APEC was a turning point. It demonstrated how the Ministry of Information and Culture could assume control over the national writers' association, and it transformed the group's dominant orientation from an independent-minded populism to a socially sophisticated, middle-class modernism.

Events such as the 1977 colloquium and the 1980 APEC festival reinforced public awareness that Cameroonians had produced a substantial body
of literary works in response to the socio-political realities of their country.
Attempts to define the common characteristics of these works on the basis
of a uniquely Cameroonian soul were bound to prove aleatory, but the fact
that such attempts were being made testified to a growing consensus that the
country had given birth to a national literature. Throughout the 1970s and
1980s, books and articles about Cameroonian literature proliferated; national
anthologies and reference guides were published, and theses at the university
increasingly focused on the work of Cameroonian writers.[38]

Among the many publications that appeared at this time, Philombe's *Le
Livre camerounais et ses auteurs* was particularly significant because it contained
reliable information on more than two hundred Cameroonian writers and illustrated how Cameroonians themselves had begun to employ the national literature concept. Recognizing the ever-present drama of writers who are entrapped
in a tension between tradition and modernity as well as between African and
European languages, Philombe presented the history of his country's literature
as a people's struggle to emancipate itself from ignorance and oppression. According to him, writers have a central role to play in this process, for they
have the capacity to inspire others with a respect for truth and for the ideals
on which a better society can be built.

But he insisted that writers can perform this role only if the government
accords them the freedom to express the truth as they perceive it. He concluded
that "there is no utopia more dangerous than believing that the Cameroonian
fatherland can be constructed without [writers] and in opposition to them.
For national unity to become a living reality, they are the ones who must give
it a spiritual dimension."[39] Philombe's own book demonstrates how the yearning for an unfettered freedom of expression can culminate in the consciousness
of a national literary tradition that the government could never impose on
people by demanding an orthodox adherence to its nation-building ethos.

At the time that Philombe was writing his *Livre camerounais et ses auteurs*,
a group of younger critics was already applying modern linguistic and sociological analyses to Cameroonian literature. Charly-Gabriel Mbock, Jacques Fame
Ndongo, Gervais Mendo Ze, Mathieu-François Minyono-Nkodo, and others
challenged many commonly held assumptions about the nature of literature
in their attempts to discover the underlying structures behind Cameroonian
literary texts. As an editor of the *Cameroon Tribune*, Fame Ndongo was the
most widely read of these younger critics, for he discussed a large number
of Cameroonian novels in the columns he wrote for the country's daily newspaper.

In 1975, Mbock coined the term *soporific literature* to describe what he
viewed as the failure of postcolonial Cameroonian writers to deal adequately
with the complexities and conflicts of contemporary society. Two years later,
Fame Ndongo adopted the term for his presentation at the 1977 colloquium
and for a series of articles he wrote in the *Cameroon Tribune*. Drawing upon

Goldmannian structuralism, he sought to demonstrate how the novels of Oyono and Beti were governed by literary structures that corresponded with the mental structures of Cameroonians subjected to colonialist oppression, whereas the works of Bebey and other novelists published by CLE lacked an analogous correspondence with the mental structures of contemporary Cameroonians.

Fame Ndongo extends this line of argument and gives it a political coloration in his *Le Prince et le scribe*. After demonstrating how the most dynamic postcolonial African novelists are preoccupied with the depiction of sterility on three levels (individual, social, and political), he suggests that their opposition to enlightened government leaders such as Biya reflects an obsession with unrealizably idealistic goals. Nevertheless, he believes these leaders should heed the constructive criticisms of their country's best writers, and he advises them to profit from the corrective feedback that is offered to them. At the same time, he exhorts opposition writers to return to their homelands because "the exalting task of national construction requires the participation of everyone."[40] With regard to Cameroon, Fame Ndongo's thesis implies that all writers should seek to incorporate into their discourse a realistic acceptance of the mental structures that Biya has articulated in coping with the limitations that impede his efforts to create a modern, democratic state. By characterizing the literary works of their fellow countrymen in such a global fashion, critics such as Mbock and Fame Ndongo reinforced the notion that these works belong together in a common tradition and form part of what can be regarded as a national literature.

The 1970s also witnessed the emergence of a heightened self-consciousness among anglophone Cameroonians with regard to literary productivity from their part of the country. The moral idealism that pervades the essays of Fonlon and the later works of Sankie Maimo is also apparent in the writings of other anglophone Cameroonians. To a large extent, it derives from the dominant role played by Christian missions in educating the first several generations of intellectuals from the area. In the face of French and francophone Cameroonian attempts to marginalize English-language culture in the country, these intellectuals compensated for their lack of political power by identifying their European language with a sense of moral superiority over the corruption they associated with the country's French-dominated central government.

Although the 1977 colloquium focused primarily on francophone Cameroonian literature, it offered anglophone writers such as Buma Kor and Maimo an opportunity to draw the attention of a national audience to the problems confronting literary creativity in their part of the country. Both insisted that western Cameroon had the potential to produce a dynamic English-language literature if the government would support the aspirations of the anglophone minority rather than attempting to suppress them. As Buma Kor explained, "what we want are the simple ingredients which will help us find our own voice, an authentic voice."[41] These ingredients presumably included support for publishing and other English-language cultural activities in the western provinces. During the years following the colloquium, anglophone Cameroonians themselves hotly debated the causes of what Sam-Kubam decried as "the paucity of literary creativity in anglophone Cameroon." Behind this debate lay the need of West Cameroonians to reaffirm a sense of self-worth that had been implicitly called into question by the volume and reputation of writings by their francophone compatriots.

Sam-Kubam launched the debate with a provocative 1978 essay in *Abbia* when he suggested that the literary talents of anglophone Cameroonians needed to be cultivated by more imaginative teaching methods, writers' clubs, radio programs, the creation of literary prizes, and the expansion of publication possibilities. In the next issue of *Abbia*, Fonlon blamed the British educational system's emphasis on vocational training and the popularity of British-style drinking clubs for the failure of anglophone Cameroonians to produce a flourishing literature. Maimo then riposted in a *Cameroon Tribune* article that a pedantic preoccupation with European literature and the absence of English-language publishing houses were primarily responsible for having stifled anglophone literary creativity.[42]

Despite their disagreements over the causes behind the situation, all three men assumed that anglophone Cameroon had produced little of lasting literary value. Partly in response to this assumption, several young critics at the university argued that "a great literature is flourishing in English-speaking Cameroon."[43] The only reason it has remained unknown, they contended, was the dearth of publishing opportunities. To prove their point, one of the most prominent of them, Bole Butake, published an anthology of anglophone Cameroonian poetry and collaborated with Nalova Lyonga to write a brief history of anglophone Cameroonian writing.

During the 1980s, Yaounde became the country's major center of anglophone literary activity: university-related journals such as *The Mould*, *New Horizons*, and *Ngam* published creative works and critical essays in English, several English-language theater groups were formed, Buma Kor's publishing house was founded, and a number of English-language bookstores opened. This heightened literary activity reflected the anglophone Cameroonians' resolve to prevent their British-influenced identity from being submerged beneath the centralizing tendencies of a government that had been shaped by French political and cultural models.

Both anglophone and francophone writers articulated their own sense of identity at least partly in opposition to the cultural renewal that originated in the "Peaceful Revolution of May 20." The Ahidjo government's channeling of literate culture into forms compatible with the government's official ideology implied that a sense of national identity could be defined by those in power and projected into the consciousness of the people. However, Cameroonian writers tended to regard national identity as an ongoing process in which people describe the truth as they perceive it and openly discuss their differences to reach common ground on as many issues as possible. Although Biya's democratic rhetoric seemed to constitute an acceptance of this principle, his government continued to practice repressive measures against dissenting points of view. Under such circumstances, Cameroonian writers often subjected their work to a self-censorship that rendered it incapable of expressing a critical vision of society.

Yet as Philombe, Towa, Kayo, Fonlon, Kum'a Ndumbe III, Fame Ndongo, Maimo, and many others repeatedly pointed out, such a vision is necessary if writers are to perform their task of critiquing the existing society and giving concrete form to the ideals by means of which it can be transcended. According to them, honest dialogue can take place only when writers are free to express their perceptions of the truth, and such a dialogue is a prerequisite for the sense of community on which any lasting national unity must be based. "These are suspicious times," proclaimed Maimo at the 1977 colloquium. "Only very few people can afford to raise their head and say what they think is right, without fear of being crushed. The other group that is likely to be heard [are] the sycophants, and what they write now will not outlive the present generation."[44] Kum'a Ndumbe III was equally emphatic in his 1981 lecture on the writer's responsibilities to the people. He insisted that freedom of expression is not a luxury in countries such as Cameroon but a necessity, for only by attending to the insights of its writers and thinkers can a government bring about the just and equitable society that it professes as an ideal. Fame Ndongo reaffirmed the same message in his *Le Prince et le scribe*.

Cameroonian society settled into a period of apparent stability after the declaration of the unitary state in 1972, and as writers sought alternative publishing possibilities in the wake of CLE's decline, a wide range of perspectives on individual and collective identity surfaced in their works. At the same time, historical studies of ethnic groups laid the groundwork for the kind of national history that Wonyu envisaged in a series of lectures he delivered at Yaounde and Douala during the mid-1970s. He argued that, by drawing upon oral traditions and recognizing that different groups evolved in different ways, people could overcome the Eurocentric bias that had been perpetuated by an overreliance on written documentation—a necessary first step toward an accurate understanding of Cameroonian history.[45]

Popular biographies of Rudolph Douala Manga Bell, Martin-Paul Samba, and Sultan Njoya appeared in NEA's Grandes Figures Africaines series, reinforcing their status as Cameroonian culture heroes and solidifying the network of shared references that constitute a national consciousness. Thus, although the world views expressed in Cameroonian writing became increasingly heterogeneous in the 1970s and 1980s, the dissemination of historical and cultural information multiplied the number of reference points that are commonly recognized by writers and their audiences within the country.

Perhaps the most important of these reference points is the idea of the Cameroonian nation itself. Despite the cynicism and demoralization bred by an obvious disparity between the government's official rhetoric and its actual practice, there abides a persistent desire to identify with something like Ahidjo's "great idea"—a yearning to realize the promise of national independence. People continue to admire the idealistic vision of men such as Fonlon and Ndam Njoya. They respect the moral courage of Philombe. And like Jean-Baptiste Obama, many of them feel compelled to ask, "what are we going to leave our children in terms of a uniquely Cameroonian culture after a hundred years of existence?"[46] Most writers share this concern for the future of Cameroon, and their almost unanimous refusal to accept the implicit values of a corrupt, materialistic society helped sustain the hope that justice, decency, and a true national unity might someday prevail in Cameroon. An authoritarian government's attempts to channel their writing in predictable directions and use it as an instrument of national construction created a tension that is evident in much of their work, but their representations of Cameroonian reality also record a remarkable quest for freedom and identity, and this quest is a principal component of the Cameroonian national consciousness.

CHAPTER
15

WRITING AND
POPULAR CULTURE

The Protestant-sponsored publishing house CLE never succeeded in creating a truly popular literature. Even when its editors attempted to reach larger audiences, as they did in launching the Pour Tous series of inexpensive, short books in simplified French, their initiatives usually met with failure because their offerings did not respond to the tastes of people who knew how to read but did not usually buy books. Many of these people had some disposable income, for they often attended movies or consumed European pulp fiction like the popular photo-novels from France. They would undoubtedly have bought Cameroonian books as well, if these books had offered them the same sort of entertainment. In fact, when the French librarian Fannie Lalande Isnard experimented with innovative selling techniques in Douala, she discovered that Cameroonians would purchase books at affordable prices if they encountered them in accessible locations. She also discovered that CLE books were inappropriate for this market because they cost three to four times more than what most people were willing to pay.[1]

Although foreign films and pulp fiction purveyed attitudes that were sharply criticized by government officials, religious leaders, and intellectuals, they appealed to large numbers of Cameroonians for the same reason that soccer matches attracted enormous crowds. All three forms of entertainment provide a vicarious escape from the monotony of everyday life. They also enable people momentarily to forget the country's pressing social and economic problems. One critic of the government even referred to the officially sanctioned soccer mania as the present-day "opium of the people."[2]

With regard to films, the government exercised little control over them and allowed three large French firms to dominate the market. These firms provided European and American films to large, big-city theaters and cheaper Indian, Chinese, and Egyptian films to the smaller ones. Both sorts of films tended to glorify violence, romantic love, sentimental pathos, and wealth. Stereotypical characters and melodramatic plots were characteristic of them. The same is true of the European photo-novels, detective thrillers, and romances that were sold second- and third-hand by street vendors in the larger cities. As in Europe and America, the formulaic clichés in these forms of popular culture gradually entered the consciousness of many Cameroonians and shaped their expectations of the real world as well as their tastes in literature.

Echoes of these clichés exist in some of the novels published by CLE, but by the mid-1970s enterprising authors had already begun to explore other publishing possibilities for works that would respond in a more immediate way to the interests of literate Cameroonians who viewed novels primarily as an escapist form of entertainment. Disregarding CLE's implicit standards of moral propriety and literary merit, these authors translated the stereotyped patterns of European popular culture into African settings and, in the process, reinforced many of the assumptions associated with individualism and romantic love. The emergence of a Cameroonian popular culture signaled an increasing interest in the opinions of common people, some of whom were already beginning to inject their own ideas into the country's literate culture. For example, the homespun philosopher Chrétien Timamo was a simple blind man who published his reflections on the human condition at his own expense. Similarly, the self-taught poll-taker Justin Bengono Ewondo subsidized the printing of four volumes based on the results of public-opinion surveys he conducted among Africans living in France.[3] Behind the publication of such books lies the quite modern assumption that the opinions of all people are valuable and worth recording.

In Cameroon, familiarity with popular culture stereotypes was widespread, and by the mid-1970s, a number of writers were drawing upon these stereotypes in novels that they often published at their own expense. The dominant characteristic of these novels was an overlay of moral didacticism. Even when they focused on violence, corruption, or sexuality, they invariably established a context of values according to which some moral could be drawn from their depictions of undesirable behavior. There are several explanations for the pervasiveness of this moral sentiment: it was present in European popular fiction and in the Nigerian market literature that had penetrated West Cameroon; it reflected the Christian assumptions that many Cameroonians had imbibed from the mission schools; and it echoed moral principles like those emphasized in traditional oral literature. In any case, readers of these novels expected to extract a moral from them, and authors gave them every opportunity to do so, although the principal attraction of such fiction was its promise of a vicarious escape from reality.

A good example of this tendency is Omo Ya Eku's *La Prison sous le slip d'Ebela*. The title itself has pornographic connotations, although the paradise that men seek "beneath Ebela's underpants" is characterized from the beginning as a "prison." Ebela is a beautiful prostitute who beguiles the narrator's friend Zambo into giving her expensive presents to prove that he is a "big man" worthy of enjoying her favors. However, the moral center of the novel is the narrator himself. He demonstrates restraint by resisting Ebela's charms and the illusion that physical pleasure or material possessions can guarantee happiness. Both Zambo and Ebela are prisoners of this illusion, and their fates illustrate the folly of their blindness. Zambo is ultimately jailed for having embezzled government funds to purchase the presents he gave her, and Ebela is beaten to death by another lover who was humiliated by his inability to satisfy her sexual demands. From the narrator's perspective, this poetic justice illustrates the folly of an obsessive preoccupation with wealth and sexual desire, for such obsessions produce a state of mind that is symbolically implied by the title— "The Prison beneath Ebela's Underpants."

The appeal of Omo Ya Eku's melodramatic novel for Cameroonian readers is at least partly contingent on their recognition that characters like Zambo and Ebela exist in real life. In fact, the common reader's propensity to identify with the major characters of popular fiction suggests that these characters reflect the literate public's assumptions about individual identity more accurately than do the heroes of many novels in the high culture tradition. What is striking about Cameroonian fiction of this kind is that it focuses almost exclusively on the individual consciousness and its attempts to cope with modern life.

For example, Martin Enobo-Kosso's *Monologue d'une veuve angoissée* recounts the story of a woman who recognizes the self-destructiveness of her own attitudes and reshapes them in such a way that she can live peacefully with her second husband. Like Ebela, Ngon-Minlan had been a prostitute. Although attached to the material comfort this profession allowed her to enjoy, she was troubled by the instability of her situation and by the solitude to which her customers abandoned her. To escape such a life, she married one of them, but because she never felt confident that he loved her, she constantly placed unreasonable demands upon him. On a subconscious level, her actions were appeals for him to demonstrate his love for her, but he failed to interpret them in this way and fled from the tensions of their marriage into drunkenness and affairs with other women, thereby contributing to his own premature death. The novel itself consists of a short letter written by her first husband shortly before he died and a much longer one in which Ngon-Minlan explains, four years later, how she gained insight into her own blindness and atoned for the perversity of her attitude toward him.

Focusing on the individual consciousness of Ngon-Minlan as it reveals itself in her letter, Enobo-Kosso demonstrates the necessity of love and trust in a modern marriage. He also presents a psychologically plausible account of how the absence of these emotions can destroy a marriage and condemn two people to unhappiness. The real problem for Ngon-Minlan is the self-image she brought into her first marriage. As she relates in the letter, her father withdrew her from school at an early age and then disowned her after she was raped by four men who pretended to be friends of his. Because she was unable to prepare herself for a legitimate career, her only recourse was prostitution. Having grown vain and mistrustful as the result of her commercial dealings with men, she maintained the same attitudes after she married her first husband, for she wanted to harden herself against the possibility of being abandoned by him. Not until several years after his death does she realize her mistake and adopt a new self-image based on love and trust, a self-image that allows her to find happiness with a second husband. The breakdown in communication between husband and wife is a common problem in contemporary Cameroonian society, and Enobo-Kosso's solution to it reflects his belief in a modern concept of individual consciousness and romantic love.

This concept is characteristic of Cameroonian popular fiction and appears in both anglophone and francophone examples of the genre. In Abossolo Zoobo's *Contrat de mariage*, it is even linked with the French colonial administration, for the first-person narrator in this novel relates how a French official had refused to perform the obligatory civil ceremony between himself and the woman his family had chosen for him. The reason for this refusal was the objection, raised by another woman, that he was bound to her by an implicit "marriage contract" in the sense that they truly loved each other. *Contrat de mariage* is the story of this love, and the fact that it is sanctioned by the French legal system in defiance of traditional custom reveals the author's modern understanding of the human personality.

In anglophone Cameroon, one of the most common variations on the individualism theme involves the scoundrels featured in the pamphlet novels that are occasionally sold in local bookstores or markets. The protagonists in these novels tend to be unsympathetic characters who are presented as examples of immoral behavior, and although the cleverness of their ruses provides a major center of focus, they themselves are invariably unmasked and punished for their misdeeds. In John Menget's *Adventures of Tita* and Peter Akum Fomundam's *The Agony of an Early Marriage*, for example, the roguish protagonists succeed in duping other people, but they enjoy the fruits of their dishonesty for only a short time because they inhabit fictional worlds that operate according to the rules of poetic justice. However, the real tragedy of their lives derives from the hypocrisy of their relationships with other people. If Menget and Fomundam condemn the materialistic individualism of contemporary society through the depiction of such characters, they are also implying that the antidote to it is a heightened sense of individual responsibility.

This sense of responsibility is a crucial ingredient of the nation-building process, and several anglophone Cameroonians have published pamphlets in which they employ fictionalized accounts of individual experience to promote morally responsible behavior in this context. In *The Other Cameroonian*, for example, John S. Dinga presents imaginary scenarios in which one or more people exhibit the symptoms of a disease such as sickle-cell anemia, malaria, hookworm, filaria, or amoebic dysentery. He then relates these symptoms to their biological causes and demonstrates in passing why traditional methods of treating such diseases have little chance of success. Under such circumstances, he argues, the only morally responsible stance is to address the problem of endemic diseases in a modern scientific fashion, not only for the sake of afflicted individuals but also because widespread illness saps the nation's productive potential and condemns it to perpetual dependency. He therefore concludes that every individual in the country should be concerned with "the other Cameroonian"—the person who is chronically but unnecessarily ill.

The emphasis on individual responsibility in a society permeated with ignorance and corruption is also apparent in such pamphlet novels as F. C. Ngam's *Tricks of a Smuggler* and B. A. Ranndze's *The Adventures of a Mosquito*. Both present variations on the popular rogue theme. In *Tricks of a Smuggler*, a reformed smuggler describes the ruses he employed to avoid paying import duties and concludes that every Cameroonian has the moral obligation to cooperate with customs agents in eliminating smuggling because the government depends upon import duties for eighty-seven percent of the revenues it needs to build schools, hospitals, and roads. In *The Adventures of a Mosquito*, the insect-hero listens to conversations in which people divulge their participation in various corrupt practices; it then bites them as a punishment for their immoral behavior. In both books, the major point is that Cameroonians must, as individuals, assume responsibility for the consequences of their actions, for this is, as Ngam's reformed smuggler insists, the only way to "build our cherished peace on a solid foundation."[4]

At the same time that individual responsibility is frequently linked with national destiny in Cameroonian popular fiction, a dominant subtheme of this literature is unmerited suffering. Characters such as Ebela in *La Prison sous le slip d'Ebela* and Ngon-Minlan in *Monologue d'une veuve angoissée* became prostitutes and developed self-destructive attitudes because they were victimized by a society that allowed them to be mistreated by others. Edmond Mvogo Nkoussou's *Le Gibier de Kondengi* focuses on a young student who inadvertently becomes the "prey" of such a society. After his girlfriend is killed in a hit-and-run accident, her father, an important government official, accuses him of having murdered her. The lawyer who defends him is more concerned with demonstrating his own eloquence than in establishing the facts of the case. As a result, the young man is sentenced to three years in prison, where he suffers repeated beatings at the hands of other prisoners. The injustice of his fate illustrates the perversity of a society that destroys its young people rather than nurturing them into responsible citizens who interact openly and honestly with each other.

Similarly, Jean-Clément Aoué-Tchany's *Du Folklore en enfer* recounts how another young student, Sam Jona, is humiliated, exploited, and ignored by many people after he suffers painful burns over most of his body in the explosion of a gas stove. Even his fiancée abandons him to pursue the material advantages she can extract from a lesbian relationship with the wife of a Dutch missionary. But when a kindly Swiss doctor sends Jona to a Lausanne hospital, he recovers completely and marries a young Swiss woman, who persuades him that his life is intrinsically valuable and can serve as an inspiration to others. With ironic appropriateness, Jona returns to Cameroon after the overthrow of a corrupt government and becomes a living symbol of the new president's pledge that every person in the country will be treated with compassion and respect, whereas his original fiancée becomes blind and deaf after swallowing poison in frustration at having wasted her life by accompanying the Dutch missionary's family to Europe.

Nearly all these stories were based on real-life experiences in Cameroon, but they were elaborated according to the melodramatic conventions and popular culture stereotypes that common people had come to expect in literary works and films. None of the protagonists in these novels are particularly noteworthy for their accomplishments. They are all ordinary individuals like those whom Cameroonians encounter in their daily lives. Yet when such characters become the heroes of novels, they affirm the principle that, no matter how insignificant a life might appear to be, it is important because some lesson can be learned from it. In addition, readers of these novels feel reassured about their own sense of themselves as they reflect from a superior vantage point on the suffering or blindness of fictional characters who resemble them in some ways. Within the context of the nation-building experiment, this popular culture focus upon the value of common people's lives translates, as writers such as Dinga and Ngam explicitly stated, into the assumption that the efforts of individuals are crucial in determining the fate of the country to which they belong.

This message is at the center of Pierre Epato Nzodam's *Sur les pistes d'aventure*, the story of a young man's participation in a youth camp sponsored by the government to revitalize a Cameroonian village and endow it with the modern infrastructure it needs if its inhabitants are to enjoy the higher standard of living promised by independence. Reminiscent of Medou Mvomo's *Afrika Ba'a* in terms of its emphasis on a self-help ethic, Nzodam's narrative is accompanied by comic-strip-like illustrations that reinforce the moral lessons to be drawn from the protagonist's experiences at the camp. Although ignorance among the villagers and corruption in the society at large represent obstacles to the realization of the volunteer project, the principal challenge is to convince individuals that they must accept responsibility for shaping their own future.

Like many other examples of Cameroonian popular fiction, *Sur les pistes d'aventure* depicts an ordinary person in terms of modern individuality concepts. It then uses his life to illustrate moral truths that must be respected if people desire to cope successfully with the contemporary world. The writing of such a book reflects the influence of the nation-building enterprise in the sense that the assumptions behind it are part of the modernization process, and the fact that these assumptions are linked with popular culture stereotypes indicates the extent to which they have spread through the Cameroonian population.

The most successful author of Cameroonian popular fiction was Naha Désiré, a young tailor who attended school in Cotonu (Dahomey) before wandering across Nigeria and settling in Yaounde, where he brought out two short novels in the late 1970s and early 1980s. As a tradesman in daily contact with the unemployed and marginally employed Cameroonians who frequent the local market, he developed an idea of what they were interested in reading. When he published *Sur le Chemin du suicide* and *Le Destin a frappé trop fort* at his own expense, he calculated his production costs so that his modest volumes would be affordable for most people. Written in a simplified, cliché-ridden style, both books focus on a suffering victim who wallows in self-pity and fantasizes about unattainable desires while living in a world dominated by the concrete objects of everyday life.

Thousands of copies of these two novels were sold in a relatively short time, and they proved far more popular than most of the Cameroonian novels published by CLE. This popularity was largely due to Naha's focus on nonheroic protagonists whose misfortunes evoked a sense of pathos with which common readers could identify. An advertising flier that he distributed to promote his first book illustrates the approach he adopted in seeking to attract their interest: "After having lost all his relatives in an automobile accident at Cotonu, after having been defrauded and poisoned, Naha Désiré, commonly known as the Child of Misfortune, was able to tell the story of his sad and miserable life in a novel of 100 pages. In Yaounde, the young writer is now anticipating a slow and painful death that lurks in wait for him because cancer never spares anyone. If you have ever suffered in your life or if you would like to know about the suffering of others, read *Sur le Chemin du suicide*."[5] Naha's appeal to popular culture stereotypes of sentimentality and melodrama is obvious, but equally obvious is the fact that such appeals were successful because they responded to the sensibility of the audiences CLE had been unable to reach with its books.

Sur le Chemin du suicide and *Le Destin a frappé trop fort* revolve around a series of misfortunes that befall the central characters despite their good intentions. Naha in *Sur le Chemin* and Albert Goussi in *Le Destin* experience variations on Naha Désiré's own journey from Cotonu to Yaounde, and both are cheated by fate and by other people before discovering that they are suffering from incurable cancers. Yet Goussi and the fictional Naha are attracted to idealistic visions of societies in which peace and harmony reign. During his childhood in Dahomey, Naha is persuaded by several Jehovah's Witnesses to abandon his schooling and work toward the Kingdom of God, for he can supposedly help bring about a world where "death will be no more, [where] there will be no more suffering, no more war, no more hatred, no more crime. Sickness and hunger will be things of the past."[6] Similarly, Goussi frees himself from a mental illness that has kept him confined in a Yaounde asylum for seven years when he dreams that he is participating in the overthrow of the apartheid government in South Africa and contributing to the unification of an Africa where "there will be bread for anyone and everyone."[7] Yet neither the fictional Naha nor Goussi succeeds in realizing his idealistic vision because both are overwhelmed by circumstances beyond their control.

In fact, the dominant sentiment of both characters is injured innocence. Jehovah's Witnesses prove less idealistic than their rhetoric when they poison the fictional Naha and defraud him of the reweaving business he had established in Cotonu. The poison affects his liver in such a way that he develops a disagreeable odor, and everyone begins to shun him. Cheated on numerous occasions as he works his way across Nigeria and reestablishes his reweaving business in Yaounde, the poor Naha learns that he has cancer and that his sisters have been killed in an automobile accident. At this point he resolves to commit suicide, and the novel ends with the note he writes to his mother.

Although Goussi is more successful with women (he makes love to four secondary-school students at the same time, to an extremely wealthy light-skinned Igbo woman, and to a white South African woman who is a leader in the struggle against apartheid), he too succumbs to the rigors of an unjust fate. The four secondary-school students are burned to death in a gruesome train wreck, and his later mental illness results from the guilt he feels for having escaped the accident that took their lives. Within days of leaving the asylum, he learns of his cancer, and he dies shortly after seeing the son that the Igbo woman has borne him. The narrative pattern in both novels is the same, for both central characters are self-pitying victims of undeserved suffering. They dreamed of contributing to a utopian future, but fate and the duplicity of others betrayed them.

The success of Naha's novels reveals something about the taste of literate but socially and economically marginalized Cameroonians who are not generally interested in the sort of fiction published by CLE. By referring to concrete, verifiable details such as the exact amounts of taxi fares, the prices of everyday objects, the addresses of houses, and the specific numbers of bank accounts, Naha encourages such readers to imagine that his works are true accounts of individuals like themselves. In this way, they could read a book such as *Sur le Chemin* or *Le Destin* as if it were conveying a moral lesson relevant to their own lives. When actual readers of these books were interviewed, they cited a number of different lessons they had found in them: one should never be discouraged by misfortune, for there is always someone whose situation is worse than one's own; one should always be alert because others are lurking in wait for the unwary; helping those who suffer will give one courage to endure one's own suffering.[8] Such responses indicate that these readers were consciously looking for a moral purpose to justify their interest in such novels.

However, the extraordinary popularity of Naha's fiction also suggests that his readers recognized a part of themselves in his portrayals of Goussi and the fictional Naha. Like these characters, many young men in Yaounde and Douala fantasized about bringing peace and harmony to the world, about making love to rich and beautiful women, about living in luxury. Yet also like these characters, they usually failed to realize their dreams and needed the assurance that they themselves were not to blame for their misery. *Sur le Chemin* and *Le Destin* gave them that assurance. In doing so, such novels captured the feelings of powerlessness and unmerited suffering that characterize large numbers of marginalized young people in countries such as Cameroon.

Other writers attempted to exploit the popular culture formulas that Naha had used, but none proved as successful as he had been, although Kumé Talé's *Journal d'une suicidée* and Samuel Nkamgnia's *Si Mon Mari se rend compte* did vary the pattern by introducing female protagonists. The heroine of *Journal* is a seventeen-year-old schoolgirl who commits suicide after being abandoned by a young man who had deployed all the sentimental clichés of European movies, photo-novels, and popular music to seduce her, whereas the central character in *Si Mon Mari* is a naive young wife who feels she cannot tell her husband about her encounters with a gangster, an unsolved murder, and the police in Paris, where she has come to live with him. The former mistakes platitudes for the pure and absolute love that she desires; the latter experiences the reverse of the usual European excursion to exotic Africa when she travels from her familiar Cameroonian homeland to the mysterious civilization of Europe. One question dominates the reflections of both women: why is this happening to me? The same question lies at the center of Naha's novels, but no answer is ever given because, from the point of view of the average person, there is no answer. The question itself remains a symbol of the powerlessness that afflicts a large segment of the Cameroonian population.

One way to escape this sense of powerlessness is through fantasy, and several Cameroonian writers have adapted heroic popular culture stereotypes like the James Bond character to create a vehicle for the expression of such fantasies. For example, Jean-Pierre Dikolo published four detective novels in which "Scorpion the African" serves an African secret-service agency run by "The Old Man" in Addis Ababa. Thanks to his physical prowess and his absolute command of modern technology, the fearless Scorpion extricates himself from one difficult situation after another to defeat an assortment of enemies: white colonialists in southern Africa, representatives of the Ku Klux Klan in America, gunrunners attempting to foment coups in independent African countries.

Scorpion is not a specifically Cameroonian hero, but "The Baron" in Evina Abossolo's *Cameroun/Gabon: Le D.A.S.S. monte à l'attaque* is, and he displays many of the same characteristics as Dikolo's hero. Serving under "The Uncle" in the Cameroonian secret service and following the well-known pattern of the popular Bond films, The Baron transforms an apparent triumph of evil at the beginning of the novel into a victory for the forces of good at the end. In this case, the enemy is the Soviet Union, which is establishing a clandestine communications network along the west coast of Africa to destabilize Europe-friendly nations such as Cameroon and Gabon. The Baron's intelligence, lightning-quick reflexes, technical expertise, and daring allow him to penetrate this network and destroy it in a violent series of episodes during which he demonstrates an easy familiarity with luxury and proves irresistibly attractive to women.

Obviously modeled on the James Bond stereotype, both Scorpion and The Baron are projections of an African desire to escape the sense of powerlessness that repeatedly surfaced in the popular fiction of writers such as Naha. Yet despite their reassertion of African manhood in the face of racism and against the background of colonialist oppression, the heroes of Dikolo and

Abossolo reinforce an essentially conservative ideology within the contemporary African context. Their efforts on behalf of existing African governments imply that virtue lies in defending the status quo, and no mention is ever made of the corruption that pervades these governments. Furthermore, Scorpion and The Baron are idealized embodiments of the materialistic, macho values that had sanctioned the European colonialist adventure in the first place. *Cameroun/Gabon* and the Scorpion novels were published in Paris, and unlike the more modest popular fiction published in Cameroon, they promoted acquisitive individualism, but it too is merely another aspect of the modern identity concepts that were rapidly emerging among the common people of the country.

Besides the novel, varieties of Cameroonian theater with popular culture overtones began to emerge during the late 1970s and early 1980s, and they often attracted enormous followings. Actor-directors such as Daniel Ndo, Dieudonné Afana, and Deiv Moktoï regularly performed before more than a thousand spectators at the major movie theaters in Yaounde and Douala. They toured other parts of the country with their shows, and they made popular recordings. Moktoï even published his plays *L'Homme bien de là-bas* and *La Femme bien de là-bas* in an illustrated comic-book format. The performances of Ndo and Afana were more like extended monologues than actual plays. Having invented the colorful characters "Uncle Otsama" and "Jean Miché Kankan," they merely presented them in a variety of humorous situations. However, the popular performances of Ndo, Afana, and Moktoï shared two important characteristics: they borrowed from other forms of entertainment to create a variety-show atmosphere, and they deformed standard French to make it more expressive of Cameroonian realities.

Ndo pioneered this sort of theater in the early 1970s. After winning first prize at the 1970 Cameroonian drama festival for his interpretation of Mbarga in Oyono-Mbia's *Notre Fille ne se mariera pas*, Ndo adapted a similar character for the dramatic sketches that were part of the variety-show performances he staged with his Théâtre Expérimental and its successor, the Atelier d'Art et d'Animation. By 1975 this group was staging large-scale spectacles that included jazz, dancing, mime, folktales, riddles, poems by Birago Diop and Charles Ngandé, jokes, and character sketches. According to Ndo, this mixture of genres was the most appropriate form of African drama because "we need a complete and total theater that can embrace African life in its globality."[9] Although the search for a total theater took on many forms in Cameroon during the late 1970s, Ndo was one of the first proponents of the concept.

During the time he spent in Italy on an acting fellowship, he polished his Mbarga-like character into a stereotyped old villager whom he baptized "Uncle Otsama" when he played him on the radio after his return to Cameroon in 1978. The character soon became well known, and when Ndo produced his first full-length dramatization of the white-bearded, bareheaded old villager, *Les Aventures de l'Oncle Otsama en ville*, more than fifteen hundred people attended the premiere in Yaounde. During the next three years, Ndo developed thirteen additional Uncle Otsama sketches, always interweaving the dramatic action with musical performances, singing, dancing, mime, and humorous skits.

The textual content of these sketches is less important than Ndo's ability to sustain the credibility of a comic character who continually misunderstands the significance of what is happening in the world around him. The effect of Ndo's performances depends partly on his mastery of Uncle Otsama's rustic accent and speech patterns, which echo local Ewondo usage. By exaggerating the forms of speech actually used in the Yaounde area, Ndo developed a comic idiom that responded to the sensibility of his fellow countrymen. Although his performances often rely on slapstick techniques and one-line gags, the Uncle Otsama sketches would soon have lost their appeal if they had not touched upon problems that concern substantial numbers of Cameroonians.

Even Ndo's outrageous word plays often carry a deeper significance. In *L'Oncle Otsama à la banque*, for example, the "sous-directeur" (deputy director) becomes the "directeur plein des sous" (director full of money). Within the context of widespread corruption, such puns contain a veiled commentary on the venality of dishonest individuals in high places. The same is true of the action. In *La Convocation*, Uncle Otsama trembles when he receives a summons to police headquarters, and he rehearses all the possible reasons why the police might be interested in seeing him. In reality, they merely want to return his lost wallet, but it is ironic that the police commissioner should be overcome with a similar anxiety at the end of the play when he is summoned without explanation to the capital. The action and Uncle Otsama's hilariously embellished account of it produce uproarious laughter among Cameroonian audiences, but the point on which the humor turns is a serious one in contemporary Cameroonian society—the fear of being arbitrarily arrested and having no recourse against an irrational bureaucracy.

Similarly, *Les Aventures de l'Oncle Otsama en ville* revolves around the old man's willingness to let his daughter pay an enormous bill for the round of drinks he orders at a Yaounde bar while visiting her in the capital. The action and his account of it upon his return to the village are humorous, but the expenses incurred by city-dwellers to satisfy the demands of their rural relatives represent a problem that preoccupies many Cameroonians, and Ndo's comic treatment of the issue is a form of social criticism that reached large numbers of people who do not habitually attend dramatic performances.

The same is true of Afana's Jean Miché Kankan, who was originally created for Albert Mbia's popular radio program "Radio Trottoir." When Afana adopted Ndo's variety-show format and presented *Les Mésaventures de Jean Miché Kankan* at one of the large movie theaters in Yaounde, he scored an impressive popular success that was repeated during a series of presentations in other parts of the country. Like Otsama, Kankan is a stereotyped character—a rich but miserly merchant whose fractured French and exaggerated Bamileke intonations proved hilarious to Cameroonian audiences, partly because he was a caricatural distortion of what was generally regarded as a typical Bamileke mentality. Also like Otsama, Kankan often alluded to serious social problems. For example, his complaints about his difficulties with government bureaucracy or about what his son is (and is not) learning at the local school reflect concerns shared by many Cameroonians.

But Moktoï was the one who transformed the variety-show format and popular culture stereotypes into an overtly critical form of theater. His Uhuru Drama began as a collective of former university students who desired to unmask "the new contradictions of African society" and to provoke audiences into repudiating the institutions that stand in the way of "a global and balanced development" on the continent.[10] Their first production was *Remember Soweto*, a mélange of blues music, dancing, poetry, and dramatic sketches of racial oppression. However, the group did not attract a significant popular following until it staged Moktoï's *L'Homme bien de là-bas* in 1979. During the next two years, the play drew capacity crowds to the large movie theaters in Yaounde and Douala as well as to performances in other Cameroonian cities.

On the surface, *L'Homme bien de là-bas* is a farce. But beneath the humorous names, the one-line gags, the stereotyped characters, and the melodramatic action of the play, there is a penetrating critique of the vulgar materialism that characterizes Cameroon's privileged class and prevents the country from evolving into a just and equitable national community. *L'Homme bien* consists of five tableaux in which Newrichard Proudlove reveals his corrupt mentality in a variety of settings—the government office where he profits shamelessly from his position as director, the university where he sells his lecture notes at exorbitant prices and seduces a succession of female students, and the villa where he flaunts his illicitly acquired wealth while haggling over the pitifully small wages he pays his servants. The corruption that pervades these settings and the willingness to accept it are the real sources of contradictions between the nation-building ethos and actual conditions in countries such as Cameroon. Moktoï's caricatural depiction of them makes it impossible for audiences to ignore such contradictions in their own society.

The name Newrichard Proudlove suggests both the enormous fortunes recently amassed by members of the privileged class and the arrogance with which they display their wealth while treating their poverty-stricken countrymen with disdain. Proudlove's thick American accent evokes connotations of vulgar materialism and parodies the affectedness of the French spoken by many newly wealthy Cameroonians. The structural inequity of the situation that Proudlove exploits to acquire his six automobiles and ten villas is underscored by his willingness to give high-class prostitutes a hundred thousand CFA francs for a few hours of their time while threatening not to pay his maid her four-thousand-franc monthly salary on account of her need to care for a sick child. As a Professor of Social Affairism at the "Académie Supérieure Royale" in a country where the Royal Radio and the *Great National Daily* report the activities of government agencies such as the Ministry in Charge of Improving the Situation of the People, Proudlove lectures on authentic black capitalism and on ways to describe dishonest activities so they cannot be called thievery.

The real crime exposed by Moktoï in his satirical *L'Homme bien* is society's acquiescence in the corrupt values of people like Proudlove. When Proudlove imagines that he has overheard a critical remark about his behavior, he turns to the audience and declares piously, "Ah gets along. Gettin' along ain't stealin'. Ah'm no crook!"[11] Behind his protestation of innocence is the implicit claim that he is merely taking care of himself and that anyone in his position would do the same. This assumption is of course widespread in Cameroonian society, but by placing it in the mouth of an exaggeratedly comic figure, Moktoï challenges audiences to laugh at it, for if they reflect on the cause of their laughter, they will be obliged to recognize that such assumptions also obtain in the real world.

At the end of the play, Proudlove is arrested, and justice seems to have been served, but upon closer examination, it becomes evident that Moktoï's character has come to grief not because of what he did but because he did it so brazenly. As the police inspector who charges him with the embezzlement of public funds reminds him, "you need to embellish the façade, Mr. Newrich."[12] In essence, he is condoning Proudlove's attitude and implying that most people share it, but he is also recognizing that, if the profiteering of the privileged class is to continue, those who benefit from it must respect a certain decorum in camouflaging their thefts. The implication is that the corrupt employees in his office will continue to be corrupt and that the new director will operate according to the same standards as he did. The justice that apparently prevails is thus undercut, suggesting that the story of Proudlove is actually an indictment of the society that has bred him and so many others like him.

In addition to the music and poetry recitations that are introduced into performances of *L'Homme bien*, an off-stage announcer comments on the action and invites audiences to ponder the significance of what they are witnessing. A prologist assures them that theater is but the imitation of life. At one point, the announcer even reads Philombe's "Dénonciation civique," a poem that lampoons those who demand a thousand and one meals while their fellow countrymen are starving to death. By constantly breaking the illusion of verisimilitude in this way, Moktoï prevents spectators from dismissing the play as frivolous entertainment. The farcical aspects of *L'Homme bien* are not gratuitous. They actually rip the veil of respectability from attitudes that people often regard as normal in their own society.

The performances of Ndo, Afana, and Moktoï were not universally appreciated by Cameroonians. Intellectuals lamented what they regarded as a penchant for mindless laughter in comedies without any redeeming social value. One commentator referred to their drama as "the exploitation of tribal prejudices and, at the same time, of behavior triggered by an inadaptation to rapid modernization. The most vulgar farces, misperceptions, images, and puns in the work of all three rely upon a rustic pidgin that evokes laughter among city people who are convinced they are above all that."[13] Yet Ndo, Afana, and Moktoï did develop a comic style that enlisted an enthusiastic response from many Cameroonians. Unlike the more conservative popular fiction of the period, their dramas contained elements of social criticism, and by late 1981, when the Ahidjo government began to scrutinize theatrical productions more closely, Moktoï in particular experienced difficulty in obtaining official permission to stage works such as *L'Homme bien*.

The emergence of a Cameroonian popular culture during the late 1970s and early 1980s illustrated how writers draw upon the stereotyped expectations of common people to create literary works capable of interesting them. As in many European societies, this popular culture reached a larger segment of the population than did the high culture supported by the country's intellectual establishment. If the identity concepts implicit in Cameroonian popular fiction and drama are highly conventional, they are also modern in the sense that they place primary emphasis on individual consciousness. Although popular literatures in most parts of the world exhibit the same characteristics, their presence in countries such as Cameroon is significant because it indicates that people who do not belong to the intellectual elite have begun to adopt modern notions of self-definition. Such notions are often commonplaces, but they enter into the collective consciousness of the people and influence the way they think about themselves. In this way, they become reference points that contribute to a sense of shared identity in nations such as Cameroon.

CHAPTER
16

THE REEMERGENCE
OF MONGO BETI

When *Main basse sur le Cameroun* appeared in 1972, it was the first book that Mongo Beti had published in fourteen years. Having settled into a teaching career at a secondary school in Rouen, he had not returned to Cameroon since before independence, although he remained passionately interested in what was happening there. The Ouandié-Ndongmo trial and accounts of it that appeared in the French press convinced him that the false images of postcolonial Africa were as harmful to Africans as the false images of colonial Africa had ever been. A writer with a profound social conscience, he once again felt compelled to expose the falsity of these images by offering a counterversion of contemporary African history as an alternative to the nation-building rhetoric of oppressive governments and the newspaper reporting that reinforced it.

For him, the Ouandié-Ndongmo affair demonstrated the failure of the decolonization process in Cameroon by revealing the social and economic injustice of the system that had emerged under Ahidjo. However, the case was presented in an entirely different light by French journalists, who ignored blatant human rights violations and supported the Cameroonian government's description of the issues at stake. *Main basse* was Beti's attempt to provide an accurate account of the events surrounding the affair, but the French government was so intent upon suppressing his "counterhistory" that it seized all copies of the book and unsuccessfully sought to deport its author.[1]

This incident merely confirmed one of Beti's major contentions in *Main basse*: beneath the idealistic nation-building rhetoric of the Ahidjo government was a cynical alliance between the Cameroonian privileged class and French interests that benefited from the existing relationship between the two countries. According to Beti, the true nature of this situation was obscured by the myth that Africans were inherently dependent upon European benevolence. He charged that both parties to the alliance desired to prevent this myth from being challenged because they knew that the public's acceptance of it helped assure the stability of a system that functioned to their advantage. *Main basse* represented such a challenge, and the French government's response to it revealed the importance it attached to preserving the myth intact.

After the appearance of *Main basse*, Beti published five novels, a documentary account of his difficulties with the Biya government, and countless articles. For more than a decade, he has kept alive *Peuples Noirs/Peuples Africains*, one of the few independent progressive journals with a focus on Africa. Throughout this flurry of publication, Beti was motivated by many of the same considerations that had prompted him to write *Mission terminée*, *Le Pauvre Christ de Bomba*, and his other preindependence novels. By juxtaposing the true historical situation with the self-serving myth that had been fabricated to disguise the beneficiaries of the collaboration between vested interests in France and Cameroon, Beti hoped to prod his readers into a critical consciousness that would enable them to liberate themselves from the new forms of oppression being imposed on them. As in his earlier work, he argued that Africans themselves must forge the image according to which they shall be known in the world, for only then will they be able to control their own destiny.

By repudiating the false images of Africa promulgated by a new alliance of oppressors, Beti contended, Africans could expose the fraud perpetrated on them by the illusory promises of political independence. Convinced that this alliance retains its power by cultivating a resigned acceptance among the people, he concluded that revolutionary social and political change is possible only if a heightened sense of awareness can be communicated to the general public in countries such as Cameroon. From this perspective, the act of writing becomes a gesture that sweeps away false images and lays the groundwork for a rational understanding of contemporary Africa in its socio-historical context. On the basis of this understanding, Africans can participate actively in the struggle for freedom and identity that, according to Beti, each people must undertake for itself.

The people in this case are the people who live within the boundaries of a single country. In contrast to Beti's earlier fiction, his writing after 1972 focuses on questions specifically related to national identity in Cameroon, although the situation there is sufficiently typical that his descriptions of corruption and oppression have considerable relevance to other African countries as well. Nevertheless, his allusions to people, places, and events in Cameroonian history make it evident that the novels, essays, and documentary exposés he wrote in the 1970s and 1980s are part of a larger attempt to reestablish the true story of Cameroonian independence and to offer it as a counterimage for the false one that had gained currency because the country's privileged class and its French allies controlled access to the mass media. His five novels from this period—*Perpétue et l'habitude du malheur*, *Remember Ruben*, *La Ruine presque cocasse d'un polichinelle*, *Les Deux Mères de Guillaume Ismaël Dzewatama*, and *La Revanche de Guillaume Ismaël Dzewatama*—are thus designed to provoke a rethinking of what national identity might mean in a free and independent Cameroon.

Shortly after the publication of *Le Roi miraculé* in 1958, Beti visited Cameroon for the last time. By then he had already identified the principal characteristics of the soon-to-be-independent country: the growing split between an unproductive privileged class and the impoverished majority, the demoralization of young people with no legitimate outlets for their energies and talents, the stagnation of rural areas where older men clung to the vestiges of traditional power, and the appalling degradation of life in the big-city slums. Realizing that this state of affairs benefited the privileged class in Cameroon as well as the French, he accused them of engineering an internal autonomy that was "an (apparently) elegant solution for maintaining things just as they have always been."[2] Two years later, he declared that corruption and tyranny had transformed the independence of his country into "a masquerade of grinning puppets."[3]

In contrast to the artificial, dependent society that was emerging in Cameroon, he remained committed to Um Nyobé's vision of a free Cameroonian nation that would emerge naturally as an expression of the people's will. Although he knew that Um Nyobé's death had left a leadership vacuum at the head of the country's nationalist movement, he was convinced that the UPC leader would always remain the true soul of the Cameroonian nation—the embodiment of an ideal toward which the people must continue to strive if they hope to realize their national destiny. Beti's attitude toward the Ahidjo regime was unequivocal, but he remained largely silent about it until the Ouandié-Ndongmo trial motivated him to protest the false images of Africa that sanctioned such miscarriages of justice and made them seem inevitable.

By the early 1970s, the convergence of Senghorian Negritude and the nation-building ideology had culminated in a cultural nationalism that linked Cameroon's supposedly authentic destiny with an idealized Ahidjo and condoned the heightened influence of French cultural and economic interests. Those who publicly criticized this conception of national identity were subjected to reprisals by a government that regarded them as unreasonable opponents of legitimate development goals. Within the conceptual framework of this nation-building rhetoric, French assistance to Cameroon was presented as a gesture of disinterested benevolence toward people who are unable to help themselves. Most Europeans and many Africans accepted this picture of reality because no alternative sources of information were available to them. Beti, however, believed such images were part of a public-relations campaign that predisposed people to accept the continuing exploitation of Africa. He was also convinced that it reinforced the dependency complex that prevented Africans from assuming responsibility for their own destiny.

Beti himself knew how critics such as Thomas Melone had distorted his own earlier novels in an attempt to reconcile them with the Negritude conception of cultural authenticity, and he resented the resultant misinterpretation of his efforts to expose the socio-economic causes of colonialist oppression and its psychological consequences for Africans. Similarly, he felt that

Negritude-influenced cultural nationalism in countries such as Cameroon obscured the true nature of postcolonial society. To discredit such concepts, he refined a theory of neocolonialism that draws upon the "political economy" approach to third-world societies and reflects his analysis of actual historical circumstances in contemporary Africa. This theory lies at the heart of everything he has written since 1972.

For Beti, neocolonialism is the oppressive system that links petty dictators and the privileged classes in third-world countries with large international firms and foreign cultural interests in mutually profitable schemes that disenfranchise most people in these countries and reduce them to abject poverty. To illustrate the nature of these schemes, he pointed out that French private investment in Cameroon has often generated exorbitant profits that are repatriated to France and remain unavailable for reinvestment in the country itself. Some Cameroonians benefit from this arrangement by virtue of their positions in government or the private sector, but their money tends to be spent in unproductive ways such as the purchase of imported luxuries. Furthermore, he continued, French economic assistance is invariably expended for French goods and services; the money itself remains in French hands. The result of this situation is a net outflow of the capital needed to create the foundation for a viable modern economy in Cameroon.

Under these circumstances, Beti thought that the real traitors to the national cause are the members of the privileged class that opposes economic independence and social equity because their personal wealth and status depend upon maintaining the status quo. Producing nothing of value and lacking the entrepreneurial spirit of the European middle class, the members of this class are, in Beti's eyes, no more than parasites who consume the national patrimony. He also accused them of hypocrisy, for they rationalize the impoverishment of rural populations, the lack of adequate medical care, the overcrowded schools, and the totalitarian state as unavoidable consequences of African underdevelopment, whereas such conditions actually result from the neocolonialist system that accords them their privileges.

According to Beti, the neocolonialist alliance can enlist the compliance of Cameroonians and the tacit support of French public opinion, for people accept the false image of Africa promoted by the Ahidjo government, the French cultural service, supporters of the Negritude movement, European technical advisers, Africa experts, and the French journalists who profoundly influence the public image of Cameroon because there is no free press in the country itself. By unmasking the self-serving rhetoric that obscures the nature of neocolonialist exploitation, Beti proposed to destroy the credibility of this false image. He himself argued that every African intellectual has an obligation to "defend the culture of his people and to control its image in the media" because those who fail to do so "submit to the image that the master's culture has been pleased to impose on us and, in the end, internalize it."[4] What he means by culture is not an outmoded set of superstitions but rather the actual life conditions and aspirations of the people. Rational thought, modern technology, and freedom of expression are, he insists, as much a part of this culture as traditional values, and a critical consciousness that rejects false constructions of reality is necessary for the emergence of any truly national culture in contemporary Africa.

All his recent writings seek to provoke readers into adopting this critical consciousness, but they differ from his earlier works in the sense that they offer an explicit revolutionary solution to dilemmas left unresolved for the protagonists of *Ville cruelle*, *Mission terminée*, *Le Pauvre Christ de Bomba*, and *Le Roi miraculé*. His assumption is that, by persuading African and European readers to disavow false images of Africa, he can weaken the neocolonialist system because it needs both the support of European public opinion and the passive acceptance of people in countries such as Cameroon. The most important of these audiences is of course the most difficult for him to reach. It consists of the disenfranchised Africans whom he desires to convince that they are not powerless in the face of neocolonialist oppression. If the common people of Cameroon could be persuaded to accept Um Nyobé's vision of national destiny and if they worked rationally toward its realization, Beti was certain they could liberate themselves and develop an authentic national culture.

According to him, the key to the success of this enterprise is the people's willingness to take the initiative for shaping their own image of themselves rather than allowing it to be imposed on them by others. His attitude toward the use of the French language provides a good example of what he means by initiative in this context. Beti had no objection to retaining French as a primary vehicle of expression for Africans, but he insisted that they must be free to adapt it to their own purposes rather than merely serving as receptacles for the cultural assumptions embedded in it when it is used in France. For French to become a dynamic medium of communication in Cameroon, for example, the government would have to cease relying upon French expatriates to teach the language to schoolchildren, upon the ORTF to provide programming for the national radio, and upon French literature to serve as a model of stylistic excellence.

Beti himself declared that "the totally free creation of French-language works by Africans is the ideal means of imposing their imagination, their genius, their sensibility, and the natural tendencies of their pronunciation on a language that would otherwise remain a foreign dialect, a mere instrument to keep them in their place, a new pretext for their secular servitude."[5] Within a Cameroonian context, his advocacy of a French-language literature capable of reflecting the true concerns of the people implies an acceptance of French as an integral part of the national culture. For him, the crucial issue is not the choice of language but the freedom with which language is used to express people's understanding of the world in which they are living. By recording his conception of the truth about Cameroon, he forged the French language into a weapon in his struggle against the neocolonialist system and its stereotyped images of Africa. And by examining the country's history since independence from the perspective of critical consciousness, he established a major reference point in the country's awareness of its own identity.

The process of writing *Main basse* represented a turning point in Beti's career as a writer because it encouraged him to formulate the neocolonialism concept that undergirds everything he has written since 1972. Its publication also announced his determination to challenge the "monopoly of the word" that the neocolonialist alliance enjoyed in Cameroon and elsewhere in francophone Africa. In this polemical exposé, the Ouandié-Ndongmo affair symbolically embodies the "long night of neocolonialism" that Cameroon endured under Ahidjo. If the government's reason for prosecuting the guerilla leader Ouandié was clear, its rationale for trying the bishop of Nkongsamba was initially puzzling to Beti. However, by pursuing his investigation into Ndongmo's background, he discovered a set of facts that enabled him to comprehend the success of the neocolonialist system.

During the 1960s, Ndongmo had become convinced that Africans could assume responsibility for their own economic well-being by working together and by relying on their own resources rather than waiting for the foreign capital and expertise often considered necessary for third-world development. For this reason, he committed his influence and financial backing to help create a series of cooperative ventures—a bookstore, a hotel, a farm, a meat market. His most ambitious undertaking was the sponsorship of Mungo Plastique, a factory that employed over fifty people in Douala and, after only a few months of operation, earned a profit by manufacturing cheap plastic objects for local consumption. Ndongmo's approach was innovative insofar as it promoted economic initiatives among groups that prospered without foreign investment or the active support of the government.

But as Beti pointed out in *Main basse*, this successful attempt to convince people that they can shape their own fate was a crime in the eyes of the Ahidjo government because it posed a threat to "the psychological and socio-economic foundations of an unjust, hypocritical order of things."[6] According to him, the government and its French advisers perceived this threat and fabricated the case against Ndongmo as a pretext for dismantling enterprises such as Mungo Plastique. It also enabled them to eliminate from the public scene a man who encouraged people to repudiate the assumptions behind a system that enslaved them as effectively as French colonialism had ever done.

If Beti's explanation of the rationale for Ndongmo's trial is accurate, the role of the French press in propagating the Cameroonian government's version of the affair becomes clear. Attached to the notion of French cultural superiority and convinced that a continued French presence in Africa was necessary for the development of the continent, respected journalists such as Pierre Biarnès and Philippe Decraene viewed moderate governments in Cameroon, Senegal, and Ivory Coast in a positive light and considered local opposition to them pernicious. For this reason, Beti concluded, they branded both Ndongmo and Ouandié as criminals who had sought to disrupt the legitimate political order in Cameroon. However, Beti refused to regard the established order as legitimate. When French journalists assume that it is, they are, according to him, reinforcing a false image of Africa and anesthetizing public opinion with regard to a criminally unjust system.

To place the Ouandié-Ndongmo affair into historical perspective and to show how it represents the neocolonialist situation in microcosm, Beti devoted a large part of *Main basse* to an account of the political evolution that had taken place in Cameroon during the previous twenty-five years. He interrogated this evolution in the same way that he had examined the prosecution of Ndongmo. First, he established what had actually happened. He then described what French journalists had written about it. In analyzing the divergence between his account of events and newspaper reports of them, he discovered the same neocolonialist situation that he had encountered while examining the case against Ndongmo.

Beti viewed recent Cameroonian history as the struggle between progressive forces striving to emancipate the people from oppression and colonialist (or neocolonialist) forces intent upon maintaining the existing relations of dominance. For him, the progressive forces represent a true nationalist movement, and their first leader, the martyred Um Nyobé, was a true national hero. When Um Nyobé was killed and Ahidjo ascended to the presidency of the newly independent country, the neocolonialist alliance prevailed and, according to Beti, instituted a more oppressive system than the one that had preceded it.

In his eyes, Ahidjo was a cowardly buffoon whose public image had been created for him by his French advisers, and the real benefactors of independence were the large French firms that conducted business in the country and the privileged class of Cameroonians who arrogated a disproportionate share of the country's wealth to themselves. Subjected to a police-state atmosphere that enforced a semblance of allegiance to the Ahidjo regime, most Cameroonians resigned themselves to a situation they felt powerless to change, but Beti remained convinced that they could regain control over their own fate if they recognized the truth about neocolonialist exploitation and renewed their faith in the progressive nationalist ideal symbolized by Um Nyobé.

However, human rights violations went unreported in highly regarded newspapers such as *Le Monde*. The UPC was characterized as a band of terrorists bent upon disrupting the development process. Ahidjo was presented as a stabilizing influence and credited with having brought prosperity to the country. For more than ten years, these newspapers and the Cameroonian government exercised a virtual monopoly over the flow of information that determined how the country would be viewed by foreigners and, to a certain extent, by its own citizens.

The French government's attempt to suppress *Main basse* reaffirmed Beti's conviction that he had an important mission to perform, for he knew he could make people aware that the commonly accepted image of his country did not correspond to reality. He also felt he could keep alive Um Nyobé's revolutionary vision despite the efforts of French journalists, foreign-aid experts, and the

Ahidjo government to extirpate it from the national consciousness. These two goals motivate all five of the novels that he has written since the "Peaceful Revolution of May 20."

After the seizure of *Main basse*, Beti reformulated his accusations against the neocolonialist system and presented them under the guise of fiction because he knew the French government would not want to appear ridiculous by censuring works of imaginative literature. One of the first novels he published at this time was *Perpétue et l'habitude du malheur*. It relates how the major character, Essola, pieced together the truth about the death of his younger sister Perpétue, just as Beti had unriddled the truth about the neocolonialist usurpation of power in Cameroon. He himself admitted that "in *Perpétue*, I'm redoing *Main basse sur le Cameroun* in a sense."[7] Both books are structured around a movement toward the critical consciousness and revolutionary commitment that Beti considered necessary if the Cameroonian people hoped to create the just and humane national community that Um Nyobé had envisioned.

Perpétue focuses upon Essola's gradual awakening to the truth about the neocolonialist situation, which is symbolically encapsulated in the story of his dead sister, and upon his development of a new strategy to cope with it. Having spent six years in a political prison, Essola purchases his freedom by publicly renouncing his allegiance to the PPP revolutionary movement and accepting a teaching post in the underdeveloped eastern part of the country. Shortly before his release, he learns of Perpétue's death, and six months after taking up his teaching duties, he returns to his village and begins to reconstruct the story of her life on the basis of interviews and the school notebooks in which she had recorded her thoughts. What he discovers is a complex web of causality that culminated in the tragic waste of an extraordinary young woman's talents.

Perpétue's unhappy fate and the misery that is routinely inflicted on the majority of Cameroonians are, as Essola learns, two faces of the same problem. Like the people of her country, Perpétue possessed the energy, the intelligence, and the desire to create a better life for herself and others, but her idealistic quest for fulfillment was constantly blocked by a corrupt system and by the individuals who have internalized the values of that system. Her name echoes that of an early African martyr, and her childhood friend Crescentia regarded her as an "angel." In any case, Perpétue was a person of decent human impulses, a touchstone of virtue that unmasks the perversity of the system in which she was entrapped.

Although she dreamed of becoming a doctor, her mother, Maria, withdrew her from school and forced her to marry the ignoble Edouard in order to collect the bride-price that she in turn gave to her son Martin. Edouard mistreated her and obliged her to become the mistress of a highly placed civil servant so that he himself could obtain a government position. Rebelling against the degradation into which her husband had thrust her, Perpétue borrowed a sewing machine and created a successful dressmaking business. She also took another lover, the soccer star Zeyang, and became pregnant with her third child, but when Edouard imprisoned her in his new villa and continued to beat her, she lost her will to live and died in her sleep one night. Despite her energy and idealism, Perpétue was defeated by a system that refused to recognize her full humanity.

Such a system can function only when individuals like Maria, Edouard, and Martin act in ways that perpetuate it. They all pursued their own self-interest by reducing her to the status of an object that could be manipulated for their own purposes. Their attitude toward life poisoned the existence of everyone else who, like Perpétue, cannot escape its dominance; it also condemns them to a state of mind that prevents them from ever experiencing the joy of decent human relationships. For example, Edouard was a weak and stupid man who acquired the illusion of power by imposing his will on Perpétue, but his fortunes improved only when he became a police informer, pushed his wife into the affair with the civil servant, and organized the first cell of the government party in the Zombotown section of Oyolo (Yaounde). People feared him because the entire police apparatus of the neocolonialist state stood behind him, and as a climate of terror settled over Zombotown, Edouard became a "miniature Baba Toura [Ahidjo]." Just as the country's petty dictator exploited the people and blocked their aspirations for a just and decent society, Edouard used Perpétue and prevented her from realizing her potential.

The collective action of the people could change this corrupt system, but they have become so accustomed to what Beti calls "the habit of unhappiness" that they have resigned themselves to it as if it were inevitable. Perpétue's response to this situation proves that it is not inevitable at all. Her dream of becoming a doctor, her dressmaking business, her affair with Zeyang, and her revulsion at the filth and degradation she encounters in Zombotown all testify to the fact that she is not an object but a human being with the capacity to feel and the desire to shape her own destiny. The name Zombotown suggests that its inhabitants are the walking dead, and her momentary resistance to their habit of unhappiness proves that the impulse toward life endures even under the most oppressive conditions. For this life to flourish, the habit of unhappiness must be broken. People must understand that their misery is not inevitable, and the first step toward this understanding is the critical consciousness that Essola demonstrates in reconstructing Perpétue's story and the meaning behind it.

The second step is commitment to the overthrow of the neocolonialist system and its replacement by a just and humane social order. This commitment enables Essola and all the other heroes of Beti's recent fiction to transcend the ambivalence that plagued the protagonists of his earlier novels. In *Perpétue*, the ideal of revolutionary commitment is symbolized by the legendary Ruben and the recently assassinated guerilla leader Bifanda (Osendé Afana), whose examples inspire Zeyang to recognize the relationship between Perpétue's death and the neocolonialist system that brought it about. Although he is publicly executed after committing himself to the overthrow of Baba Toura, Zeyang represents an idea that will remain etched in the minds of others and remind them that resistance to oppression is necessary if people expect to maintain their human dignity. For Essola, the symbol of this resistance is the memory of Perpétue. By the end of the novel, he vows he will no longer accept the endless cycle of miseries that the people have come to regard as normal, and insofar as his image of Perpétue embodies his insight into the nature of the neocolonialist system, she will remain alive as the motivating force behind his resolve to eradicate the habit of unhappiness by communicating this truth to others.

His actions at the end of the novel must be understood within the context of this resolve. Having concluded that the true revolutionary imperative was the education of the people, he encourages his profligate brother Martin to drink himself into a stupor, ties him to a tree, and leaves him to be eaten alive by brown ants. Although such a punishment seems unnecessarily cruel, its significance is primarily symbolic. Martin represents the unproductive, parasitical class that must be destroyed if a just society is ever to be established in the country. Ironically, his own weakness for alcohol places him in a situation where he will be eaten, just as he had feasted upon the profit extracted from Perpétue's enslavement to a husband who was unworthy of her. Furthermore, Maria's obsessive attachment to Martin had caused her to treat her other children in a criminal fashion, and when he is no longer alive, she will be obliged to recognize the emptiness of her own life. Her punishment for the role she played in denaturing Perpétue's life is also ironically appropriate because she must live with the same solitude she had imposed on her daughter by treating her as a saleable commodity.

In a well-ordered society, Essola would have been held accountable for the death of Martin, but in a neocolonialist society such as Cameroon, the attitudes of the authorities are shrouded in ambiguity. For example, when Essola reports his crime to the police chief, Norbert, and openly acknowledges his disaffection with the existing system, Norbert minimizes the seriousness of the affair and promises to submit a report that will exonerate Essola completely. On the surface, Norbert is acting in a self-interested fashion because he senses that Essola could become an important man in the party and might someday be in a position to return the favor; however, Norbert might also be surreptitiously signaling his support for resistance from within the system. By asking Norbert to transmit a message to his dead sister's best friend, whom he invites to meet him in the town where he is teaching, Essola reveals his intention to structure his life around the memory of his sister. In practical terms, he will devote himself to educating people about the truth he has learned in piecing together the story of Perpétue.

On an allegorical level, *Perpétue* recapitulates the story that Beti told in *Main basse*. The truth that Essola unearths is essentially the same as what Beti had discovered as he pieced together the background of the Ouandié-Ndongmo affair. Just as Maria married Perpétue to Edouard for a substantial dowry that was squandered by Martin, France married Cameroon to Ahidjo, and the windfall that accrued to a privileged class of Cameroonians was wasted on luxury consumer items. In both cases, the transaction reduced the bride to an object that could be bought and sold, exposing her to the arbitrary injustices of a tyrannical husband. The parallel between Perpétue's death and the widespread misery in her country is actually pointed out by one of her Zombotown neighbors, who observed: "confronted by an Africa that is pregnant and calling for help, our so-called governments . . . turn the other way."[8] In other words, Edouard treated his wife the same way Ahidjo treated Cameroon, and the mechanisms that brought about Perpétue's tragic death are the same as those that had reduced Cameroon to a corrupt, oppressive state.

The first step in preventing a recurrence of the fate suffered by Perpétue (and by extension Cameroon) is to analyze its causes. The second is to devise a strategy capable of eliminating those causes. Both Essola and Beti concluded that the major obstacle to revolutionary change is the lethargy of people who believe they have no control over their own destiny. Acting upon this insight, the two men undertake to enlighten people about the nature of the system that oppresses them. And if the idealized image of Perpétue endowed Essola with a hope that the people will recognize their power to change this system, the idealized image of Ruben Um Nyobé inspired Beti with the same hope.

The epic cycle that includes *Remember Ruben* and *La Ruine presque cocasse d'un polichinelle* reflects Beti's resolve to perpetuate the memory of Um Nyobé. It also exemplifies the new revolutionary strategy that he felt was necessary in light of the neocolonialist situation in contemporary Africa. Although the two novels focus primarily on the story of Mor-Zamba, a mild-tempered giant of a man whose name means "man of god,"[9] their real subject matter is the liberation of the forest town of Ekoumdoum from the oppressive rule that had been imposed on it by colonial domination and the ensuing neocolonialist alliance between an illegitimate chief and a European missionary. The key to this liberation lies less in heroic military opposition to the regime in power at Ekoumdoum than in the ideal that Mor-Zamba and his two companions, the wily former delinquent Jo the Juggler and the schoolboy Evariste, communicate to the people of the town by their very presence in the area. This message is essentially Um Nyobé's vision of a free and independent society, and it gives people confidence in their capacity to forge a new identity grounded in critical consciousness and commitment to a democratic, socialistic form of government.

If the story of Perpétue allegorically encapsulates the history of neocolonialist domination in Cameroon, Beti's epic account of Ekoumdoum's liberation evokes the revolutionary transformation that could take place on the national level if people repudiated the false images that enslave them. Such a challenge to the sustaining myths of neocolonialism would presumably exacerbate the inherent contradictions of the corrupt system to the point where the system itself would self-destruct, as it did in Ekoumdoum. As an object lesson in the creation of a genuine national community, *Remember Ruben* and *La Ruine* provide a counterhistory of the decolonization process as an alternative to the blandly optimistic views promoted by the official nation-building rhetoric. At the same time, they offer a blueprint for liberation from neocolonialist oppression in Cameroon and other parts of Africa. By translating the spirit behind Um Nyobé's vision of national identity into a modern epic, Beti challenged false images of Africa and gave concrete form to an ideal capable of motivating his fellow countrymen to participate in the shaping of their own destiny.

In the two novels of this epic cycle, the story of how Mor-Zamba evolved from a wandering orphan to the chief of a liberated Ekoumdoum is told to the people of the town by an older man who, like a griot, has gleaned his material from personal observation, oral tradition, and the testimony of participants in the events he is describing. The revolution that overthrew the neocolonialist alliance between the illegitimate chief Mor-Bita and the white priest Van den Rietter had taken place one year after the declaration of national independence in 1960, and the narrator recounts his story three or four years later.

By this time, Mor-Zamba has been recognized as the legitimate chief of Ekoumdoum, and he has already helped implement a new form of social organization that combines communal values from the precolonial past with modern technology. A scientific approach to health care has been adopted, and an efficient system of economic exchange enables everyone to obtain consumer goods at reasonable prices. The rational, cooperative organization of work and the return of social justice permit the people of Ekoumdoum to become self-sufficient while regaining the sense of self-worth they had lost during the colonial period. In contrast to the moral decadence that characterized the town when Mor-Zamba first arrived there in the late 1930s, an atmosphere of hope and fraternity prevails.

Within this context, the narrator's epic cycle sanctions the proud new identity of the people and reinforces the critical consciousness that played a crucial role in their liberation. But as the narrator himself admits in his final comment, the struggle for true independence is just beginning, and critical consciousness will remain necessary to sustain the revolutionary impulse and expand its influence into the larger society that continues to be dominated by the petty dictator Baba Toura and his French advisers. By allowing readers of *Remember Ruben* and *La Ruine* to eavesdrop on the simulated telling of an oral epic that defines the collective identity of its listeners, Beti has created a model for the understanding of national identity in Cameroon and elsewhere in Africa.

The values associated with this national identity concept are chiefly embodied in Mor-Zamba, and *Remember Ruben* is devoted to the informal education that prepares him for the role he eventually plays in the liberation of Ekoumdoum. From the beginning, Mor-Zamba incarnates the positive values of traditional society. His grandfather had been the last duly elected chief of Ekoumdoum before the French replaced him with Mor-Bita, an ex-soldier from a different area. All the legitimate chief's children were banished from the town, but Mor-Zamba's mother attempted to return, although she died on the way, and her young son wandered into Ekoumdoum without knowing who he really was. Like the legendary common ancestor Akomo, Mor-Zamba appears mysteriously on the outskirts of the city and develops into a man with prodigious strength, a beautiful face, a thundering voice, a noble tread, and a generous heart.[10] The suggestion is of course that Mor-Zamba represents the true identity of Ekoumdoum and can help the town regain its lost dignity.

However, the people of Ekoumdoum have been so demoralized by colonialist oppression and the corrupt rule of Mor-Bita that they develop an irrational hostility toward Mor-Zamba. The other young men harass him, and one of them even tries to drown him in a nearby river. Despite his good-natured willingness to help others, most of the older people also resent his presence, and no one protests when the chief delivers him into the hands of the French for service in a forced-labor camp. Their repudiation of him reflects the extent to which French colonialism had eroded the communal solidarity that at one time would have prevented them from treating him in this way. The elders of the town had come to accept the colonial situation as a means of preserving their own prerogatives, and in the face of French military support for Mor-Bita's arbitrary regime, the people became resigned to their own powerlessness and withdrew from the modern world in superstitious fear. In other words, they succumbed to the "habit of unhappiness," and their apathy contributed to the emergence of a society in which the man who epitomizes their own traditional virtues is reviled.

Yet a remnant of human decency persists in the town. A generous old man adopts Mor-Zamba and later seeks to incorporate him into the community by giving him land on which to build a house. Also, disdaining the rebuffs of the other young men in the town, Mor-Zamba's agemate Abena works with him to build his house. The solidarity that unites them in this endeavor is a model of the honest, fraternal relationships that would be characteristic of a truly free society. Abena is the one person who has a clear vision of this free society. His name means "the one who refuses."[11] Recognizing that Mor-Bita is the principal source of a degeneracy that is destroying the moral fiber of the community, he passionately desires to overthrow the corrupt system. He possesses the critical consciousness necessary for effective revolutionary action, but he lacks the means of carrying out his intentions.

Abena knows he must acquire power if he wants to participate in shaping the destiny of his people rather than allowing others to determine it for them. The gun becomes for him a symbol of this power, and after Mor-Zamba is taken to the forced-labor camp, he voluntarily leaves Ekoumdoum and joins the French army to procure the gun he needs. Twenty years later, Abena returns to the country and becomes a renowned guerilla leader in the struggle against neocolonialism. Although he appears only briefly one more time in the entire epic cycle, he is constantly present as an ideal of revolutionary commitment. He inspires Mor-Zamba and, through him, the progressive forces of Ekoumdoum to undertake the revolution that liberates the town from the oppressive rule of Mor-Bita.

But twenty years elapse before Mor-Zamba returns to Ekoumdoum, and during this time the moral atmosphere in the town continues to degenerate.

At about the time of Mor-Zamba's abduction to the forced-labor camp, Father Van den Rietter founded a mission in Ekoumdoum. In his parishioners he inculcates an attitude of resignation toward the corrupt social order that has been imposed on them by the colonial administration. He eventually becomes the dominant force that keeps Mor-Bita on his throne. However, because the narrator is telling his story from the perspective of the successful revolution, he barely mentions the events that take place in Ekoumdoum during Mor-Zamba's absence. They are not crucial to the social upheaval that will later transform the town into a free, independent community. Truly central to the narrator's purpose are the experiences that teach Mor-Zamba what he needs to know in order to cope with a modern world in which traditional values are not, in themselves, sufficient to prevent the demoralization of African society.

At the forced-labor camp in Oyolo (Yaounde), Mor-Zamba acquires the rudiments of modern medical knowledge by caring for his sick and injured comrades. After his release, he remembers Abena and vows to preserve his own life in anticipation of his friend's return. Almost instinctively he identifies with the revolutionary vision that Abena had articulated years ago in Ekoumdoum. Guided by his new mission in life, Mor-Zamba travels to Fort-Négre (Douala) and begins to live in Kola-Kola (New Bell), the center of anticolonialist agitation in the country. During the twelve years he spends there, his employment with a corrupt African businessman teaches him the workings of a modern economy and familiarizes him with the operation of machines. Even more important, he gains an intensely personal insight into the nature of colonialist oppression and gradually develops an enlightened commitment to the goals of the national liberation movement.

Mor-Zamba's commitment to the revolutionary cause is naive at first, but he takes a step toward critical consciousness by repudiating the false images propagated by the colonialist system. The intellectual dimension of his commitment is solidified as a result of his conversations with Jo the Juggler, who discusses the structure of colonial society with him at great length. On the basis of what Jo tells him about the political machinations of the school director Sandrinelli and other Frenchmen who manipulate the future chief of state Baba Toura and write his speeches for him, Mor-Zamba gains a new insight into the fraud being perpetrated on his countrymen by the emerging neocolonialist alliance between French interests and the local privileged class.[12] By the end of *Remember Ruben*, Mor-Zamba is intensely aware of the fact that Africans must be free to conceptualize their own identity in order to regain their sense of self-worth.

In the closing pages of the novel, Mor-Zamba attains the goal he set for himself in Oyolo, for he is briefly reunited with Abena, who has returned from twenty years of foreign military service with the guns and expertise he left Ekoumdoum to acquire. After the death of Ruben, he has become the leader of the national liberation movement, and when he enters the room where Mor-Zamba and Jo are waiting for him, he calmly tells them to "turn up the light." In metaphorical terms, the light that can shine more brightly is the truth he is bringing them.

After revealing to Mor-Zamba that he is the eldest surviving descendant of Ekoumdoum's last legitimate chief, Abena charges his childhood friend with a new mission—the liberation of Ekoumdoum from the tyranny of Mor-Bita and the establishment of a just and equitable social order in its place. He gives Mor-Zamba guns and a medicine chest, intimating that, although he might have to use force, he must also know how to heal, for the power to cure is ultimately more important than the power to destroy. His final words are "Remember Ruben," the revolutionary password that expresses his hope that Mor-Zamba will act with the courage, patience, and vision symbolized by the heroic example of Um Nyobé. The ending of *Remember Ruben* resembles the ending of *Perpétue* insofar as it implies the hero's resolve to remain faithful to the memory of an admirable individual who was martyred by the existing system.

In *La Ruine*, the focus shifts from the education of Mor-Zamba to his role as the bearer of this ideal. The action in the second volume of Beti's epic cycle begins on the day when independence is declared and Baba Toura is installed as the country's first president. This is the day on which Mor-Zamba and his two companions, Jo and Evariste, set out on the "long march" that ultimately takes them to Ekoumdoum. Although Baba Toura and the neocolonialist alliance claim to control the new state, guerilla attacks disrupt the independence celebrations (as they did in Cameroon itself), and the three Rubenists' conversations with a truck driver and an old villager demonstrate that not everyone has been duped by the falsely optimistic nation-building rhetoric of the new regime. The truck driver transports them for the first sixty kilometers of their journey, and the old man later accords them a generous hospitality, suggesting that there is considerable support for their revolutionary project among the people.

Yet the small band of Rubenists faces countless difficulties, not the least of which is the conflict that arises as the result of their differing temperaments. Mor-Zamba is a sensitive, idealistic humanist with an absolute sense of integrity. Tempered by the ordeals described in *Remember Ruben*, he has learned patience and perseverance. In contrast, Jo is a cynic who assumes that mask wearing and clever ruses are necessary for coping with a corrupt world. He invariably desires to act quickly and decisively to obtain an advantage that he can exploit with a certain ruthlessness, but his often cruel stratagems are deeply disturbing to Mor-Zamba, who is convinced that all people can be dealt with honestly and compassionately. Tensions between them threaten the cohesiveness of their group on several occasions and persist even after the revolution in Ekoumdoum, but the two men remain linked by a sense of common purpose, and it enables them to contribute their complementary talents to the success of their enterprise.

The three Rubenists must learn the basic principles of revolutionary strategy by trial and error. The most important of these principles is that a successful revolution must be based on the enlightened participation of the people. Initially, Jo does not act according to this principle because he has faith in the stereotyped notion that a revolutionary avant-garde can play a heroic role by manipulating people as if they were pawns on a chessboard. According to Beti, however, the principal objective of the revolutionary avant-garde should be to raise the consciousness of the people so that they can comprehend the nature of their own oppression and act rationally to overcome it.

In the case of Ekoumdoum, the infirm chief Mor-Bita, his vicious son Zoabekwe, and the white priest Van den Rietter constitute a typical neocolonialist alliance that maintains itself in power through the threat of violence. Their rule is posited on the assumption that Africans lack the technical expertise to modernize their society and should resign themselves to suffering in this world. Under such circumstances, the elders of the town abdicated their responsibility for the welfare of the community, and the young men became mired in endless rounds of purposeless activity. Therefore when Jo and Evariste enter the town for the first time, their initial task should be to enlighten people about the inequity of this archetypically neocolonialist system and the falsity of the myths that sustain it.

However, Jo fails to recognize the necessity of raising the people's consciousness, and his elaborate plan to enlist the support of the young men in overthrowing the Mor-Bita/Van den Rietter alliance miscarries disastrously. Rather than identifying the truly progressive forces in the town, Jo assumes that the young men who openly criticize their oppressors are his natural allies, and he attempts to manipulate them into playing roles he has imagined for them. He even conceals his revolutionary sympathies beneath a mystifying charade of his supposedly occult powers, but despite the blood oath he imposes on the young men, one of them betrays his plan to Van den Rietter, who arrests the two Rubenists, tortures them, and imprisons them in the dungeons that his fellow priest, Brother Nicholas, had built beneath Mor-Bita's palace. They escape with their lives only when the chief's youngest and most rebellious wife, Ngwane-Eligui, secretly descends to their prison and leads them to safety. The point is that genuine revolution requires the conscious participation of the people, and Jo's disregard for this principle dooms his initial assault upon the neocolonialist alliance in Ekoumdoum.

In a larger historical context, his failure does have several salutary effects that advance the cause of the revolution. When Evariste is bitten by a snake, Mor-Zamba, who had been hiding in the nearby forest during his two companions' visit to Ekoumdoum, is obliged to lead the group to the city of Tambona, where he has the opportunity to perfect his knowledge of modern medicine by working with a Protestant missionary doctor. This knowledge ultimately becomes a powerful symbol for the alternative social order that the Rubenists offer the people of Ekoumdoum. Furthermore, by arousing the suspicions of Mor-Bita, Van den Rietter, and Zoabekwe, Jo's aborted rebellion incites them to commit a series of irrational actions that reveal the inherent contradictions of the neocolonialist system. And by planting the seed of resistance to unjust authority in the minds of the people, the presence of Jo and Evariste catalyzes a new hope among the truly progressive forces that will eventually assure the success of the revolution in Ekoumdoum.

The paranoid responses of Van den Rietter and Zoabekwe illustrate the vulnerability of the neocolonialist alliance. After the mysterious escape of the two Rubenists, the rulers of Ekoumdoum create a small army and establish a network of spies and informers. Forced labor is introduced to build a mud wall around the chief's palace because Zoabekwe's ability to control the women in his father's harem has become, in his eyes, a symbolic measure of his power over the people of Ekoumdoum. Van den Rietter even counsels the chief's son to confine all his subjects in an invisible prison of fear, for, as he explains, "a man who trembles is a caged and paralyzed man."[13] The supposedly Christian missionary himself grows increasingly sadistic in his attempt to ferret out every secret and to control every aspect of life in Ekoumdoum.

For a while, his police-state tactics seem to work. The young men whom Jo had regarded as his natural allies rally to the neocolonialist cause and are converted into storm troopers who zealously serve the regime in power. An attitude of resigned acceptance descends upon the rest of the town. But in the long run, the totalitarian objective of absolute control is impossible to sustain. Haunted by fear, Van den Rietter and Zoabekwe can trust no one, and although they seek to appear invincible, they expect to be attacked at any moment from any quarter. Under the pressure of this anxiety, their irrational behavior heightens the contradictions in their system of social control and provokes opposition among those who had, until then, tolerated it.

Like Drumont in *Le Pauvre Christ de Bomba,* Van den Rietter desires to control the image Africans have of themselves because he obtains psychological gratification from the conviction that he is playing a heroic role in shaping the destiny of an inherently inferior race. But he can continue to believe in himself only as long as Africans agree to play the subordinate roles he assigns them in his conception of reality. When he forcibly organizes the young men of the village into work gangs that clear fields, build new docking facilities on the river, and construct a soccer stadium, he exhorts them: "Let yourselves be molded by your superiors, like a vase between the hands of a potter who shapes the clay as he pleases, without encountering any resistance, because the least intractableness in the clay would ruin his work. I am the potter, and you, you're the clay. It is God who ordained it so."[14] As his choice of metaphor indicates, Van den Rietter's real motivation is not a desire to help Africans but a hope of subordinating them to his image of what they should be.

The image is a demeaning one for Africans because it presupposes that they are incapable of conceptualizing their own future. The underlying issue revolves around the question of who controls the image of Africa. Should this image be conceived by Europeans and imposed on docile Africans, or should it be forged by free Africans and reconciled with goals they have set for themselves? For Beti, the answer is clear. The emergence of self-respecting societies in Africa is contingent upon the repudiation of false images, like those promoted by Van den Rietter, and upon the recognition that Africans are the only ones who have the right to define their collective identity.

In addition to the impact of Jo's failed scheme on the leaders of the neocolonialist alliance in Ekoumdoum, it exercises an important influence over the potentially progressive forces of the town. The knowledge that two strangers escaped from the old chief's dungeons after entering Ekoumdoum to foment a rebellion against the existing order plants the seed of an idea that grows .. the minds of the people and flourishes in ways the Rubenists themselves had never anticipated. As a result of the handbills dist ι. uted by Jo and Evariste, the promise of Abena's return inspires many individuals with a hope that gives them courage to resist an oppression to which they had become accustomed. The vast majority of these individuals are women. In fact, one of the major flaws in Jo's original plan was his failure to realize that women constitute an enormous potential for revolutionary change in Africa.

According to Beti, women are the most oppressed class of people in contemporary Africa, but they also possess a rudimentary form of critical consciousness. Because they do most of the productive work, they have an implicit understanding of what constitutes effective action. And because they raise the children, they are profoundly concerned about the future society in which these children will live. By crystallizing the hope of the women in Ekoumdoum, the Rubenists' presence activated an existing potential, rather than providing heroic leadership that directed the course of social change.

The revolutionary commitment of these women is triggered by the outbreak of a flu epidemic that mainly afflicts the town's male infants. When Van den Rietter and Zoabekwe refuse the women's pleas for help in obtaining modern medicines with which to treat their dying children, they recognize how the existing system prevents them from satisfying their most basic needs. Spurred by the determination of Ngwane-Eligui and encouraged by the hope injected into the community by the earlier audacity of Jo and Evariste, the mothers of Ekoumdoum occupy the palace and insist that a delegation be sent to Tambona for the purchase of antibiotics. Zoabekwe accedes to their demand and allows a group of adolescent girls to leave town under the supervision of a particularly malicious palace guard, but while in Tambona, the girls encounter the three Rubenists and, with Jo's help, participate in the murder of the guard who had brutalized them. The series of events that culminate in the guard's death represent a turning point in the history of Ekoumdoum. The solidarity of the town's mothers had forced the corrupt regime to do something it did not want to do, and the Rubenists' collaboration with the girls unites them for the first time with a genuinely progressive group of people from the town.

The second stage of the revolution occurs when Mor-Zamba and his companions accompany the girls back to Ekoumdoum, where his medical expertise allows him to save the lives of children and, as a result, to consolidate the women's opposition to the regime that had refused to help them. Their massive show of defiance is by itself sufficient to topple the neocolonialist alliance because its leaders are powerless when the population challenges their pretense of invincibility. At this point, the people of Ekoumdoum must still repudiate the false images they have internalized during many years of colonial and neocolonial oppression. The public renunciation of these images constitutes the third stage in the revolutionary process. It begins when the disgruntled Van den Rietter parades in front of the assembled women and nonchalantly shoots five hawks to reassert his superiority as a white man who has mastered technology. In response, Jo strolls forward with a gun and calmly shoots a sixth hawk. His flamboyant gesture purges the town of its inferiority complex and effectively annihilates Van den Rietter's image of Africa. The crowd's jubilation reflects the birth of a new hope, for by performing a feat that the white man implicitly claimed to be beyond the reach of Africans, Jo has demonstrated that there is no justification for the black man's subordination to the white man.

The myths that sustained Mor-Bita's illegitimate reign and Van den Rietter's role as technical adviser are permanently discredited in two subsequent incidents. First, the women from the chief's harem organize a series of public confessions during which it becomes apparent that the old chief was sterile and had fathered none of the children who lived on the palace grounds. He actually leaves no heirs to the throne when he dies shortly after the successful uprising. Second, Jo delivers an antisermon from Van den Rietter's pulpit, rebutting the priest's doctrine of white superiority and presenting the history of European colonialism as a series of morally indefensible actions. In both instances, false images are swept away, and the people of Ekoumdoum become free to articulate a new sense of collective identity.

If no town can be truly free until it exists within a free country, a model for the liberation of the entire country is implicit in the story of Ekoumdoum. In fact, Ekoumdoum is the country in miniature, and Mor-Bita's corrupt regime parallels the system that emerged under Ahidjo. The outcome of the revolution is different in Ekoumdoum than it was in Cameroon, but the contrast suggests that Cameroonians could also do what the people of Ekoumdoum did. The implication is that, by promoting a sense of critical consciousness, progressive forces in Cameroon could persuade people to repudiate the neocolonialist system and the false images that sanction its oppression of them. Once they recognized the true nature of this system, they would work toward the overthrow of their oppressors, who are far weaker than they seem because they cannot escape the inherent contradictions of their own system. According to Beti, the authentic identity of Cameroon resides in the yearning of its people for a just and humane society, and since Um Nyobé initially articulated the vision of such a society, Beti concludes that Cameroonians must acknowledge their legitimate national hero just as the people of Ekoumdoum needed to acknowledge Mor-Zamba as their legitimate chief before they could forge a collective identity in conformity with their own needs and aspirations.

Beti realized that the success of genuinely nationalist movements in countries such as Cameroon requires more than a heightened level of consciousness and commitment within these countries. It is also contingent upon public opinion in the industrialized countries that collaborate with petty African dictators to perpetuate the neocolonialist situation from which they both benefit. As Beti discovered in writing *Main basse*, the French press had portrayed this collaboration as a benevolent and necessary part of the nation-building process. After the seizure of *Main basse*, he became more convinced than ever that one of the most effective ways of promoting social change in Africa was to inform Europeans about oppressive conditions in countries such as Cameroon, thereby disabusing them of the false images upon which their tacit approval of their own governments' policies toward Africa was premised.

He himself became active in this campaign, although when he tried to alert the French section of Amnesty International about human rights violations in francophone Africa, he encountered considerable resistance, in part because the president of this organization was employed by a government agency that was charged with presenting French aid to developing countries in a favorable light. On one occasion, Beti lectured on the subject in Lyon, where he met a young Frenchwoman who was seeking to influence French public opinion as a means of aiding her Cameroonian husband and others who had been unjustly imprisoned by the Ahidjo government. This woman later served him as a model for Marie-Pierre, the central character in *Les Deux Mères de Guillaume Ismaël Dzewatama* and *La Revanche de Guillaume Ismaël Dzewatama*.

Like the Mor-Zamba cycle, these two novels are parts of a single unified story that focuses on the major character's gradual recognition of the truth about the neocolonialist situation in a country that resembles Cameroon. It too culminates in an action that demonstrates the power of enlightened political commitment to a revolutionary ideal. As the wife of an African lawyer who had participated in antigovernment activities during his long stay in France, Marie-Pierre knew his country only from a distance before she traveled there to live with him when he accepted a position as deputy public prosecutor in the capital. At first, contemporary African society seems confusing to her. She does not realize that Guillaume, the young boy who came to live with them, is actually her husband's son with a woman he had married in his village many years previously. She herself does not know whether her husband has betrayed the progressive principles he had advocated while in France or if he is merely concealing them so he can work for change within the system. The ambiguity of the situation produces a growing estrangement between her and her husband, but it also propels her into a closer relationship with Guillaume, who had been somewhat of an orphan during his father's prolonged absence from the country.

Although initially naive, Marie-Pierre possesses two qualities that enable her to perceive the truth about neocolonialist society. She is incapable of the hypocrisy that might allow her to enjoy her own privileged status in such a society, and she has a passionate commitment to justice. Although Marie-Pierre is disgusted by the way many of the radical students she had known in France were participating in the corruption and conspicuous consumption they had once denounced, she senses that members of the country's privileged class remain somehow unfulfilled. Everyone is competing against everyone else for status and material possessions. No one can trust anyone else. Driven by selfish impulses and haunted by the fear that the government can at any moment precipitate them into disgrace, they are not working toward the utopian society they had once envisioned for the future of their country. After years of living under such conditions, most of them have come to regard the existing situation as normal. In light of the misery she observes among the common people and the police-state atmosphere that affects everyone, Marie-Pierre considers this lack of critical consciousness to be a crime, but until she comprehends the full extent of her own country's complicity in the neocolonialist situation, she will not recognize what she can do to change it.

In the final pages of *Deux Mères*, Marie-Pierre discovers several important facts that dispel some of the ambiguity that had troubled her relationship with her husband. When she meets Guillaume's mother in the house that her husband had purchased for members of his family in the overcrowded Niagara section of the city, she realizes the pain and humiliation that have been inflicted on the African woman. At this point, Marie-Pierre accepts full responsibility for helping Guillaume find ways of realizing his potential. Shortly afterward, she learns that an attempted coup against the country's petty dictator was betrayed to the authorities and that her husband is about to be arrested for his role in it. Although she regrets his lack of frankness with her, she is reassured by the knowledge that he had, despite appearances, remained faithful to his progressive principles.

When he orders her to return to France, she refuses, admonishing him, "don't decide for me, please!"[15] Her reply announces her intention to act as a free individual who accepts responsibility for the consequences of her own choices. She refuses to be patronized any longer, as she had been by him when he failed to confide in her about his clandestine opposition to the regime. This fierce independence of mind sustains her after his imprisonment and motivates her campaign to liberate him in *La Revanche*. At the beginning of this novel, Marie-Pierre's contact with the European wives of imprisoned Africans and with the rural women of her husband's village shows her how the injustice inflicted on her husband is merely one aspect of a much larger phenomenon—the neocolonialist exploitation of Africa. When she visits her husband's village, she develops a strong bond of affection with the women who welcomed her so warmly into their midst, and she dreams of how she might help them improve the quality of their lives, but she knows such dreams will remain unrealizable as long as the country's petty dictator maintains his hold on power. Just as she insisted on making her own decisions when her husband ordered her to leave the country, she realizes that Africans will be able to lead satisfying lives only when they become free to define their own identity and participate fully in the political process.

She knows they have been deprived of this freedom by a government that seeks absolute control over the population. She also knows that the French benefit from their relationship with this dictatorial government. What she does not yet fully comprehend is the influence of French technical advisers in shaping the image of reality that is inculcated in Africans by the threat of force and the dissemination of false information. In the Cameroon-like country where she is living, the most powerful representative of this French presence is Hergé Xourbes, who advises the president on internal security matters.[16] To intimidate Marie-Pierre into abandoning her increasingly revolutionary ideas, Xourbes and his cohorts lure her to the local police headquarters on the false pretext that she will be allowed to see her husband. Once she is in their power, they interrogate her and abuse her physically. But rather than being cowed by their vulgarity, Marie-Pierre determines to combat it by returning to France and speaking out against the myth of French benevolence in the African nation-building process. As she now understands, the French public's acceptance of such myths allows Xourbes and others like him to perform criminal actions while helping African dictators impose the worst kind of oppression on their own people.

Ironically, the best way of procuring her husband's release from prison is to campaign in France against the media monopoly that Beti had described in *Main basse*. Because the oppressive practices adopted by African dictators with the support of French advisers are much easier to implement when the French public remains ignorant of them, the neocolonialist alliance is vulnerable to any voice that can inform a large number of people in France about what is actually taking place in francophone Africa. The voice of a white woman who has personally experienced the injustices of a corrupt African regime has the capacity to reach such an audience. In fact, Marie-Pierre's publicity campaign in France creates sufficient anxiety among Baba Saoulé's advisers that they eventually agree to release her husband and all other political prisoners when another kind of pressure is exerted on them.

This pressure is provided by Guillaume, who in the meantime has become one of the best soccer players in the country. By refusing to play on the national team unless the prisoners are released, he places the government in a difficult situation, because success in international matches is viewed as a way of distracting the people's attention from their misery. If Guillaume and others like him do not play and the team loses, it is likely that riots will break out in the big-city slums, and in light of Marie-Pierre's revelations to the French public, the government can ill afford additional bad publicity in the country from which it receives the support it needs to remain in power.

Guillaume's ploy actually constitutes his revenge against the neocolonialist system that had made his own existence so "precarious and bumpy" during his earlier years. His Cameroonian name is a neologism that means "why are you insulting me?"[17] It suggests the humiliation to which he is subjected when government representatives harass his family in retaliation for his father's political activities in France and, later, when the children of the city ostracize him in the belief that his father had betrayed the nationalist cause by becoming a public prosecutor. In neither case is he to blame, and under such circumstances he feels powerless to influence his own fate. He himself is convinced that "his life would be marked by unforeseeable and threatening rebounds, like the path of an extraordinarily capricious soccer ball."[18] Like so many Africans in the modern world, he fears he is being bandied about by forces beyond his control.

Yet even as a child, he yearns to exercise some control over the world in which he is living. In response to the ostracism of the other children when he comes to live with Marie-Pierre and her husband in the capital, he frequently withdraws into a small niche near his father's garage and daydreams about driving a truck. This habit explains the "future truck driver" epithet in the subtitle of *Deux Mères* and expresses his fantasy of being in control. In the real world, however, he can gain control over his own destiny only if he achieves insight into the nature of the neocolonialist system and frees himself from its influence over his image of himself.

His heightened consciousness in such matters results from his relationship with Marie-Pierre, for when he accompanies her to France, he not only hones his remarkable athletic talents; he also recognizes that the real struggle in the world is between the forces of progress and the forces of oppression. After returning to Africa, he proves capable of directing the flow of a soccer game at will. No longer does he think of himself as an erratically bounding ball, for as his "revenge" on the neocolonialist regime demonstrates, he has become a free human being who is capable of taking the historical initiative.

As in *Perpétue* and the Mor-Zamba cycle, the ending of the Guillaume Ismaël sequence implies the dawning of a new era. The story of that era is not told. It remains in the narrative future, but the principles for the creation of a truly independent African nation have been formulated by individuals who acquired a critical consciousness that enables them to understand the functioning of the neocolonialist system and to promote social change by undermining the false images of Africa that sustain it. In writing *Main basse*, Beti developed a neocolonialism concept that provides a convincing explanation for the persistence of oppressive, brutal regimes in many parts of Africa. This concept also helps explain widespread popular disappointment with the consequences of national independence.

His model for this concept was obviously Cameroon. The five novels he wrote to illustrate it mirror Cameroonian reality and contain allegorical allusions to recent Cameroonian history. Their implicit blueprint for revolutionary social change applies specifically to Cameroon. In the context of an ongoing dialogue about Cameroonian national identity in the country's print culture, Beti's writing since 1972 represents a major statement, for it shows how the Cameroonian people's quest for freedom and identity has been in direct opposition to the national unity rhetoric of the Ahidjo and Biya regimes.

As he himself suggested in his recent *Lettre aux Camerounais*, the national identity of Cameroon resides in the suppressed aspirations of the people for a just and humane society like the one envisioned by Ruben Um Nyobé. For this identity to find expression in the political organization of the state, he concluded, the people must finally become masters of their own destiny. The neocolonialist system has until now prevented them from doing so, but his novels and his polemical writings emphasize this system's vulnerability to the truth and to the solidarity of those who aspire toward a better society of the future. Both qualities respond to profoundly human sentiments, and as Beti once wrote, "it is always wrong to despair of the human race."[19] He himself has never despaired of humanity, and the hope that humanity will prevail in Cameroon and elsewhere in Africa is the unifying thread that runs through all his works.

CHAPTER
17

THE RADICAL CRITIQUE
OF POSTCOLONIAL SOCIETY

Beti's image of Cameroon as an oppressive neocolonialist society stood in direct opposition to Ahidjo's optimistic nation-building rhetoric. During the 1960s, variations on this image had been widespread among opponents to the government, but not until the 1970s did it play a major role in the country's print culture, where it served as a foil to the national identity concept promulgated by the government. Four groups of writers were primarily responsible for this proliferation of radical perspectives on postcolonial Cameroonian society: established authors disillusioned with the directions independence had taken, philosophers and theologians seeking to reconceptualize the decolonization process, exiles living in Europe, and militant younger people.

What they have in common is a passionate repudiation of the neocolonialist society that had emerged in Cameroon under Ahidjo. They regard the act of writing as a means of raising the general level of consciousness about the inequity of the system, and they emphasize the need for Africans to take the initiative for changing it. In particular, they argue that the people must participate in making the choices that shape their national destiny, for a destiny imposed on them from above by a totalitarian government will inevitably imprison them in feelings of alienation and powerlessness.

United in their opposition to Ahidjo's Negritude-influenced cultural nationalism, these radical critics defined national identity in terms of process, not as a set of static concepts that could be distilled from tradition or decreed by the government. Recognizing that process always occurs in a specific socio-historical context, they tended to emphasize how the existing system had come into being and how it could be changed. The utopian vision embedded in their works bears eloquent testimony to the quest for freedom and identity in Cameroonian literate culture.

Among the established writers who became increasingly militant in the works they published during the 1970s were René Philombe, Patrice Kayo, Benjamin Matip, and Patrice Ndedi Penda, all of whom attacked the Ahidjo government's rhetoric and condemned its role in sanctioning the emergence of a corrupt society. Like Epanya Yondo, who left Cameroon in disgust over the results of independence, these writers regarded Um Nyobé, not Ahidjo, as the symbolic embodiment of national identity, and they urged people to resist the tyranny that was being imposed on them. In one way or another, they all echoed Epanya Yondo's exhortation to

> Fight! Love! Hope
> And fight again
> To offer man
> The fruit of his FREEDOM.[1]

Their vision of a truly just society in Cameroon gave expression to the widespread discontent in the country, and many of them suffered harassment as a result of their outspokenness.

Throughout the 1960s, Philombe had written socially critical poetry, but little of it circulated publicly at that time, and his prose works published by CLE were muted in their criticism of the existing situation. By the mid-1970s, however, he had become convinced that "the indolent calm of good but timorous souls" produces an invidious self-censorship that contributes to the persistence of corruption. Acting upon this conviction, he published five collections of poetry and a satiric political drama under his own Semences Africaines imprint. He also wrote a novel, *L'Ancien Maquisard*, that CLE refused to publish unless he excised politically sensitive portions of the text. Although NEA initially accepted it in an unabridged form, the editors at Dakar decided not to bring it out when they discovered that the Ahidjo government would not allow it to be distributed in Cameroon. What distinguishes these works from Philombe's earlier published writing is their overt invitation for readers to engage themselves in a collective, revolutionary effort to transform society into a just and equitable national community.

The clearest expression of Philombe's militancy occurs in his poetry, where it reflects a profoundly humanistic response to the harsh reality of contemporary Cameroon. In an age when greed, cynicism, and government-sanctioned brutality prevail, he insists on ripping the façade of respectability from the behavior of those who had betrayed the promise of national independence. In his poetry, decolonization marks the passage from one form of slavery to another: "The whites having left / the blacks are dancing / but the blacks are dancing on the backs of blacks."[2] This refrain from one of Philombe's best-known poems draws attention to the dominant image in the verse that he published during the 1970s and 1980s—the image of neocolonialist society as a jungle where individuals devour each other like wild beasts rather than cooperating with each other for the common good.

Such a society contains the eaters, whom he portrays as panthers or hyenas, and the eaten, who are depicted as sheep. A primary objective of this poetry is to make people understand the criminal nature of the panther-man's mentality. In "Dénonciation civique," he exhorts readers:

Open your eyes, look at him:
He can eat but one tiny meal
Yet he wants to bolt the meals
Of a thousand and one mouths
At once![3]

By reducing the complex neocolonialist situation to a simple parable, Philombe is attempting to raise the consciousness of his readers so they can comprehend the true nature of the society in which they are living. The implication is that, if they recognize injustice, they will act to eliminate it. At the end of this poem, for example, he calls upon readers to arrest the panther-man and punish him as the most dangerous of terrorists.

Confronted with the jungle mentality of neocolonialist Africa, Philombe believes that the writer has an obligation to become the voice of the people. "He must have the courage to put himself in the place of this muzzled, gagged, beaten people and become their interpreter. . . . His mission is to overturn taboos, to invite the people to vomit the indigestible, and to provoke responsible reflection about the problems of the moment."[4] For him, poetry is a weapon in the struggle against oppression. By prompting Africans to recognize the truth about their own situation and by giving concrete form to their aspirations, he hopes to incite them to revolutionary acts that would enable them to define their collective identity in the process of liberating themselves.

The applicability of this objective to Cameroon is apparent in Philombe's controversial political drama *Africapolis*. The events in the play echo the Ouandié-Ndongmo trial, and the fall of a dictator who bears some resemblance to Ahidjo reinforces the idea that the dream of a better society can be realized if the people join together to support it. The revolutionary hero of *Africapolis* is Boki, who was dismissed from his position as director of the national bank because he refused to grant preferential treatment to members of the privileged class while facilitating loans to farmers, small businessmen, and unemployed workers. At this point, Boki realizes that the entire society must be restructured so that no individual will ever again be relegated to the garbage heap.

Along with the popular poet Kwassi Tamtam and nearly a hundred other people, Boki is arrested and placed on trial for allegedly participating in a UPC-like revolutionary movement. The police brutality and the tendentious questioning to which they are subjected illustrate the totalitarian atmosphere that has been institutionalized by King Ekamtid. Under his totalitarian rule, the privileged class prospers, and anyone who objects to official corruption is dispatched to a "center for civic reeducation." The single party and its doctrine of national construction are touted as the only avenues to development, while health care and schooling are neglected. History has been rewritten to sanction Ekamtid's claim to be the father of his people. Newspapers are suppressed. Arbitrary house searches are routinely conducted. The parallel with the situation in Cameroon is obvious, and it is not surprising that government officials repeatedly denied authorization for *Africapolis* to be staged in Yaounde.

Philombe's publication of the play was a defiance of the government, for its ending is a deliberate provocation of the established order. At the moment when Boki and Kwassi Tamtam are about to be convicted on the false charge of treason, Ekamtid's government falls to a band of armed revolutionaries, and the play culminates in an outburst of popular enthusiasm for the dawning of a new era. The release of the prisoners heralds the country's liberation because it finally creates an opportunity for the people to define their own identity. The revolutionary message proclaimed by Boki and Tamtam does reach them, and with their support, the corrupt government is toppled. Within the Cameroonian context, Philombe's moral is clear: people can bring a genuine national community into being if they repudiate neocolonialist myths and take their destiny into their own hands.

This same revolutionary optimism characterizes *L'Ancien Maquisard*, the novel that francophone Africa's two major publishing houses declined to publish on the basis of its political content. Modeled in part on Philombe's own experiences, *L'Ancien Maquisard* recounts the story of Bedi-Ngula between the time he is released from prison for having participated in the UPC guerilla movement until his rearrest after becoming chief of his village and organizing the local farmers into a successful cooperative movement. He himself tells the story from his prison cell as he awaits an uncertain fate, but he does not despair, because his experiences in the village have convinced him that revolution is possible. Despite his imprisonment, Bedi-Ngula is a man, not a slave. He recognizes the truth about neocolonialist exploitation, and his intense awareness of his own humanity defeats all attempts to break his spirit.

Bedi-Ngula's narrative consists of two parts: his alienating experiences in Yaounde shortly after having been released from prison, and his involvement in the life of his village when he returns there to cultivate his family's long-neglected cocoa fields. The first part presents a panorama of neocolonialist society in independent Africa—the arrogance and indifference of the privileged class, the brutality of the police, the lethargy and despair of the urban poor. His former friends have either accommodated themselves to the dominant morality of acquisitive individualism or abandoned themselves to alcoholism and idleness. Independence has clearly not brought his country the just society that he and his UPC companions had envisaged.

The second part of *L'Ancien Maquisard* revolves around Bedi-Ngula's rediscovery of communal solidarity among the people of the village and demonstrates how an enlightened individual can foster a sense of critical consciousness among them. The villagers greet his arrival with joy and dancing, and when he starts to clear his fields, all the young men of the village help him. After three years, the village elders elect him chief, and for eight months his revolutionary optimism mobilizes a good-natured frenzy of constructive activity. Work brigades clear weeds from the village, cultivate fields, and replace dilapidated shacks with solid, new buildings. At this point, the government intervenes, ordering the villagers to select a new chief and sending Bedi-Ngula back to prison. As a radical critique of neocolonialism, Philombe's novel focuses attention on the demoralization of contemporary African society and the possibility of reviving the idealism that had motivated the national independence movement during the colonial era. In fact, Philombe implies that it must be revived if countries such as Cameroon are ever to become truly independent.

In Cameroon itself, the man identified with this vision of independence is Ruben Um Nyobé, and like Philombe, Patrice Kayo regards himself as a spiritual heir of the martyred UPC leader. Kayo's commitment to the revolutionary transformation of neocolonialist society has become increasingly apparent in the works he has published since the early 1970s. Particularly in his short-story collection *Tout le long des saisons*, he attacks the corrupt system that permits some people to wallow in luxury while others are deprived of the most basic necessities. For example, the old villager who writes to his son in the title story of this volume displays a naive awareness of the structural injustice behind this situation. Describing the exactions imposed upon the villagers to support lavish receptions for visiting dignitaries and the unpaid work they must do in the fields of a tyrannical chief, he declares that independence "didn't change our situation, only our masters." He later explains, "the perpetual bane of our existence [is] to toil so the bosses and the authorities can get fat. . . . For the rich, everything is permitted. The poor have only duties."[5] The old man's insight into the perversity of a system points toward the conclusion that Kayo himself draws: the people must topple the corrupt regime and liberate themselves from a neocolonialist mentality that disenfranchises them.

This same conclusion is apparent in the final pages of Benjamin Matip's *Laisse-nous bâtir une Afrique debout*. Dedicated to Um Nyobé, this dialogue novel is a rewriting of Matip's successful 1961 play *Le Jugement suprême*, revised to serve as a critique of postcolonial African society. This society is obviously not the one that Um Nyobé had envisioned, and as several characters in the novel observe, conditions are in many ways worse after independence than they were before. The action in *Laisse-nous bâtir une Afrique debout* takes place in the village of Nko-Njok, about one hundred miles from the capital Nedayou (Yaounde) in the "Democratic, Social, Popular, and African Republic of Banibil-Lon," and it revolves around the return of Dr. Bisseck, an enlightened young man who had left the village many years earlier to study medicine in Europe. The principal conflict in the novel springs from the difference between Bisseck's concept of national independence and that of the local party functionaries.

An oppressive system has been imposed on the villagers by the threat of force, and although their understanding of the situation is clouded by outmoded superstitions, Matip insists that a continuity with their past must be maintained by incorporating traditional values into a modern view of the world. In his book, the spokesman for this position is the wise village elder Mandeng. According to him, African society is like a house that should be rebuilt on its existing foundation rather than being burned to the ground and abandoned. But Mandeng's vision remains unrealizable as long as the local party functionaries are free to impose their will on the villagers. Representatives of the country's privileged class, they enjoy a luxurious standard of living and regard the exercise of power as an opportunity to enrich themselves. In fact, Nko-Njok is the country in microcosm, and for Matip the same principle applies on the local and national levels: if those in power are corrupt, the system they impose on others will be corrupt.

When Bisseck returns after many years of study, Mandeng and the other villagers greet him with enthusiasm, for they have vested their hopes in him as a man who, having acquired the white man's knowledge, can help them rebuild Nko-Njok into a place where they can once again hold up their heads with pride. In actuality, Bisseck is a potential leader. He respects tradition and the laws of the ancestors. He accepts the validity of some herbal medicines, although he approaches the solution of practical problems in a rational, scientific manner, and he has no qualms about working among the people. However, he confronts two major problems. The villagers begin to doubt his powers when three old men die from what are thought to be supernatural causes, and the party functionaries plot to arrest him because they fear that his independent-mindedness will inspire the villagers to rebel against their arbitrary rule. In both cases, others come to Bisseck's defense, and their solidarity enables him to form the nucleus of a revolutionary band that will oppose the functionaries and the troops they summon from Nedayou at the end of the novel.

Just before Mandeng dies, he urges the villagers to have faith in Bisseck's approach to reality, and they have the opportunity to follow his advice when the commandant of the gendarme brigade shoots the political functionaries and arms a small group headed by Bisseck. The ending of *Laisse-nous bâtir une Afrique debout* brings together a cross-section of progressive forces from the village. Together, they constitute a revolutionary movement that will seek to implement the vision of Mpodol (Um Nyobé), whom Bisseck cites as his model. The members of this group are representatives of the people in whose name Bisseck demands, "let us . . . build a new Africa, an Africa with its head held high."[6] By drawing the parallel between Nko-Njok and Cameroon, Matip is exhorting his fellow countrymen to rebel in a similar fashion against the neocolonialist alliance that is oppressing them.

Although the revolutionary message is not as clearly stated in Ndedi Penda's play *Le Caméléon*, it becomes the dominant concern in his unpublished novel *Samakopé*. But even *Le Caméléon* was sufficiently critical of the electoral process in Cameroon that the authorities banned it after its initial performance in 1981. The major character in the play is a retired civil servant who aspires to a seat in the legislature as a reward for his loyalty to the state. He assumes he can conduct business as usual by flattering and bribing the party functionary who draws up the official slate of candidates. He even orders his daughter to spend the night with the man. However, she refuses, and when her father is confronted with the possibility that her fiancé, a young veterinarian, might receive the nomination, he objects, "the whites passed on the power to us, not them [the younger people]. It's our power."[7] This proprietary attitude toward power is characteristic of the privileged class in Cameroon, and as in his earlier novel *La Nasse*, Ndedi Penda depicts it as a principal cause of social injustice.

The ending of *Le Caméléon* is ambiguous, for if the young veterinarian receives the nomination, he appoints his future father-in-law as a technical adviser, and the local prefect hints that the younger man was chosen so he could be coopted into the system. The method of selecting candidates for a single-party election remains as arbitrary as it was when the veterinarian observed, "there aren't elections anymore, there are investitures."[8] Despite his success in becoming the party's official candidate, he will have to operate within the corrupt system. Ndedi Penda recognized the pervasiveness of this corruption in Cameroon, and he felt strongly that it should be portrayed on the stage because it is "a gangrene that is in the process of progressively devouring everything."[9] Only by subjecting it to open and honest scrutiny, he argued, could a new and healthier society emerge.

That such scrutiny would culminate in a commitment to the revolutionary overthrow of the neocolonialist system becomes clear in *Samakopé*, which is an expansion of Ndedi Panda's 1973 short story "Le Fils du propriétaire." The focus of the novel is on the evolution of a young man's consciousness. After having initially adopted the stereotyped patterns of selfish, dishonest behavior in a corrupt society, the young man, Mboma, develops strong friendships with his uncle and a friend, both of whom have repeatedly suffered the injustice characteristic of neocolonialist society. Mboma's crucial insight occurs near the end of the novel when he hires a snake charmer to help him extort money from the arrogant playboy, who, however, dies after being bitten by his companion's deadly snake. At this point, Mboma flees into the nearby forest. Within the context of Ndedi Penda's views on corruption, the playboy represents the privileged class. The term *Samakopé* signifies a vine that climbs local fruit trees and sucks on their sap until they die. By extension, it is analogous to the privileged class that leeches the country's lifeblood to assure its own luxurious lifestyle.

What is needed, Ndedi Penda implies, is a huge fire capable of sweeping away this parasitical class in the same way that farmers' fires consume the "Samakopé" that strangles their trees. And this is precisely what happens when Mboma is joined by his friend, his uncle, and the snake charmer, for like the small group of revolutionaries at the end of Matip's *Laisse-nous bâtir une Afrique debout*, they have committed themselves to take up arms against the neocolonialist system in the hope of replacing it with a more just and equitable society. They are convinced that their movement will grow, for as Mboma's friend declares, "every injustice committed in contempt of human dignity, every affront imposed on people, every act of vandalism is a fire kindled in some corner of the bush. And this fire is going to grow until it becomes a conflagration that will be fed with the blood of those who are digging the nation's grave."[10] The gravediggers of the nation are those who squander its resources in a show of conspicuous consumption. By implying that they will be destroyed by a popular uprising, Ndedi Penda is suggesting that the same thing can happen in Cameroon.

As established Cameroonian writers became increasingly radical in their depictions of postcolonial society, a new source of radical thinking emerged among Cameroonian philosophers and theologians who, having rejected Negritude and cultural nationalism, focused on the concrete historical circumstances necessary for development. Their goals were not always the same. Influenced by the growing popularity of liberation theology, several Cameroonian theologians attempted to redefine their faith in terms of the need to free people from the repressive political environment into which independence had precipitated them. In contrast, most academic philosophers insisted that rational thinking was the only viable approach to the solution of pressing social and economic problems in third-world countries. But these theologians and philosophers were united in their condemnation of neocolonialism, and they all grounded their opposition to it in their definitions of freedom and identity.

The most influential philosophical statement of the 1970s was Marcien Towa's *L'Idée d'une philosophie négro-africaine*. He had originally intended to present the argument developed in this book as a lecture at the 1977 FESTAC celebrations in Nigeria, but Cameroonian officials had grown increasingly suspicious of his ideas, and they prevented him from attending the event. Later, he delivered an expanded version of this lecture to a philosophy department colloquium at the university, and CLE published it in this form along with comments by Engelbert Mveng, Ebenezer Njoh-Mouelle, and others who participated in the discussion. The thrust of Towa's argument did have radical implications within the Cameroonian context, and two years after the book's publication, he was removed from his teaching post and prohibited from speaking in public.

Developing an implicit corollary of Towa's earlier anti-Negritude stance, the central thesis of *L'Idée d'une philosophie negro-africaine* involves a defense of freedom—in particular, the freedom to engage in the practice of philosophy, which is, according to Towa, the process of thinking through the conditions of human life. Because the essential tool of philosophy is rational thought and because he assumes that rational thought is the same for all people everywhere, he concludes that there can be no uniquely African philosophy. Characteristically African traditions exist, he admits, but like traditions in other parts of the world, they are creations of the human spirit. Insofar as philosophy engages people in the critical examination of who they are and what they are capable of becoming, it presupposes a willingness to subject all assumptions to rational scrutiny. In this sense, it is a liberating activity, for by reaffirming people's capacity to think for themselves, to conceive their own goals, and to move effectively toward the realization of these goals, it enables them to become fully human in the exercise of their rational faculties.

Conflict is inevitable between Towa's philosophical project and any social, religious, or political system that demands an unquestioning adherence to the assumptions that sanction its existence. As Towa himself declares, "philosophy is the courage to think the absolute."[11] Whenever a state or a religion refuses to allow its fundamental postulates to be examined in the light of reason, it is creating a set of absolute values. Towa believes that all people who accept these values without reflecting critically on them have renounced their freedom because they are acknowledging a higher authority than their own capacity to think. But for him, the individual's capacity to think must be the highest authority. "I place nothing above the human spirit," he said, implying that even the most hallowed religious and political principles should be subjected to rational analysis.[12] Any institution that demands absolute obedience to these principles seeks to prevent such analysis, inhibiting genuine philosophical thought and enslaving the minds of those who conform to its doctrines.

Within the Cameroonian context, Towa's defense of the rational individual's right to question the fundamental assumptions of the official nation-building rhetoric served as the basis for a radical critique of the existing system. Declaring that no authority is infallible, Towa concludes that blind obedience to any authority is a form of folly. In contemporary Africa, he identifies two types of authority that often lead to folly. The first is the authority of tradition and the cultural authenticity movements, such as Negritude, that elevate traditional concepts to the level of absolute truths. The second is the neocolonialist system that spawns petty dictators and corrupt privileged classes, while relegating the majority of people to poverty and imposing on them a set of absolute truths that supposedly justify the existing situation. According to Towa, both forms of authority obscure the real nature of problems confronting countries such as Cameroon. Convinced that such problems can be solved only by addressing them in a truly philosophical manner, he suggests that the critical examination of prevailing authority systems should be one of the African philosopher's primary missions.

In response to those who object that he is merely applying European modes of thought to African problems, he argues in *L'Idée* that there are African precedents for the sort of rational analysis he is advocating. For example, he points out that West African trickster tales featuring the hare, the tortoise, and the spider emphasize the use of rational intelligence as the best way of coping with concrete problems of survival in a harsh, conflict-ridden world that is inherently neither just nor benevolent. In these tales, the characters who renounce their own capacity for thought and naively trust in the authority of others render themselves vulnerable to being manipulated by the trickster figures. When powerful creatures fail to employ their own rational faculties, they lose the advantage that their superior physical strength had bestowed on them. Extrapolating the implicit lesson of these tales into the modern world, Towa concludes that they provide a model for approaching the truth through a critical interpretation of concrete historical circumstances.

Towa's approach to philosophy has practical implications for action in the world, for as he says, "when one has an idea of what is, it is necessary to think of what should be."[13] If what exists does not conform with what should exist, he believes the philosopher has a moral obligation to utilize the tools at his disposal to change the world. Like Fanon, he is convinced that national cultures arise out of this desire for change on the part of rational individuals struggling to free themselves from oppression. By regarding identity as a constantly evolving process rather than as a stable constellation of attributes and cultural practices, he provides a convincing justification for revolutionary opposition to the neocolonialist regimes of contemporary Africa. To the extent that a government does not reflect the dialogue of rational individuals who enjoy access to the best available knowledge and have committed themselves to the social good, it deserves to be overthrown and replaced by a government that does. Although Towa never publicly applied this thesis to Cameroon, the thrust of his argument is clear, and the authorities understood that his concept of national identity diverged sharply from the official one.

The same is true of the new Christian theologies outlined by writers such as Jean-Marc Ela and Fabien Eboussi Boulaga, although for slightly different reasons. Unlike their Negritude predecessors Mveng and Hebga, whose principal goal was to forge a culturally appropriate vehicle for the transmission of Christian values in Africa, Ela and Eboussi Boulaga undertook a radical rereading of the Gospels to justify the transformation of neocolonialist society into a just and humane community. By drawing attention to the historical situatedness of Biblical narratives, they stripped away the European cultural overlay that had been imposed on missionary Christianity. Once they had distilled what they regarded as the essential message of Christ, they examined the sociohistorical situation in Africa to find the best way of reinserting this message into it.

While working among the farmers of south-central Cameroon and later in the impoverished Kirdi village of Tokombere in the North, Ela wrote four books in which he developed his version of liberation theology.[14] In reflecting on the essential message of Christianity, he concluded that two fundamental tenets must be respected in formulating a Christian world view that would be appropriate for African circumstances. First, if Christ was declaring his solidarity with a suffering humanity when he shouldered the cross, any Christian who desired to emulate Christ's example in Africa must adopt the same attitude toward the disinherited multitudes of the continent. Second, if God manifests himself only through interventions in the course of history, as He did during the Jewish exodus or the passion of Christ, then hope is justified for those who place themselves in harmony with His will by working toward the realization of His kingdom within the existing socio-historical context.

Couched in these terms, Ela's Christianity necessarily enters into conflict with the neocolonialist government of his own country. According to him, the starting point for any viable theology in Africa must be the concrete problems of existence for the people who live there, and the best way to address these problems is to help these people acquire a critical understanding of their historical situation so they can devise effective strategies for satisfying their needs within the limitations it imposes on them. When he examined countries such as Cameroon from this perspective, he recognized that the collaboration between foreign interests and the local privileged class invariably leads to the pauperization of rural populations.

Emphasis on cash crop agriculture produces a high level of indebtedness among farmers, and profits from export sales are seldom reinvested at the place where the crops are grown. The inequity of this situation is exacerbated by official corruption, police-state brutality, bureaucratic incompetence, the conspicuous consumption of the privileged class, the hypocrisy of the nation-building rhetoric, and a vulgar mass culture that diverts the people's attention from the true causes of their misery. Under these circumstances, Ela concludes that a truly Christian attitude is by definition a condemnation of the neocolonialist system.

Deprived of spiritual and physical well-being by the corrupt institutions of the existing social order, millions of Africans have become marginalized and can express themselves only in a cry of anguish that Ela wants the rest of the world to hear, as the title of his second book, *Le Cri de l'homme africain*, suggests. He wants the church in particular to hear this cry, for it must fulfill its historic mission as the conscience of society if it is to prevent countries such as Cameroon from becoming "cemeteries of [human] intelligence."[15] In his eyes, the church can best perform this function by awakening people to the causes of their oppression, not by blinding them to it, as the Negritude theologians had done. Because Ela believes that Genesis invites people to acquire mastery over nature and history, he argues that the church should also foster their engagement in the creation of self-reliant communities where they are free to define their own identities. Like Philombe, Beti, Kayo, and other socially engaged Cameroonian writers, he insists that a genuine community is an expression of the people's will and cannot result from their conformity to concepts imposed on them by the government.

Ela realizes that the church can never liberate Africans. It can only give them the tools to liberate themselves. "Our task is clear," he declares, for we must "enable man to be reborn to a life of freedom and communion."[16] By awakening people to the full potential of their own humanity and by inspiring them with hope, the church could, he maintains, offer them what they most need in order to achieve this utopian dream—a sense of power over their own destiny. Essentially, he is advocating a liberation of the African imagination so that it can function without coercion in its own intellectual space, rejecting both Western consumerism and outmoded traditional superstitions. Such an imagination would, he feels, be capable of grasping the revolutionary content of Christ's message and translating it into twentieth-century African terms.

Like Ela, Eboussi Boulaga starts with the premise that social and religious phenomena can be properly understood only within the socio-historical context that made them possible. Influenced by Kierkegaard and Sartre, his existentialist approach to the problem of identity assumes that all views of the world are frameworks of knowledge that place necessary but arbitrary limits on people's freedom of expression and action. According to him, individuals should become consciously aware of the way they frame knowledge, for they can then compare their own historical situatedness with that of other people and determine whether the philosophical propositions advanced by such people have any validity for them. In agreement with the French philosopher Michel Foucault, Eboussi contends that those who proclaim the universal validity of their own philosophical position and deny its contingency upon their own framework of knowledge are taking the first step toward transforming philosophical discourse into the tool of a dominant ideology. For this reason, he concludes that African religion and philosophy can preserve a respect for human freedom only if they are elaborated in full recognition of the particular historical conditions that allowed them to come into existence in the first place.

Such a stance is anathema to political and religious leaders who demand unquestioning allegiance to propositions they present as absolute truths. In defiance of traditional church doctrine, for example, Eboussi declares in *Christianisme sans fétiche* that Jesus did not reveal a preexisting truth, but rather created a new truth within the limitations of a specific socio-historical context by converting a group of individuals into a community of love and hope. By voluntarily taking upon himself the suffering of others and by freely accepting the loss of his temporal identity in the ordeal of the cross, Jesus established a model of human behavior that Eboussi feels can be emulated under different historical circumstances—a model that presupposes a society of free individuals who are ends in themselves and who joyfully celebrate the triumph of hope over despair.

However, the vital significance of this model became submerged, he argues, when it was institutionalized in a context of European social norms that were later exported to Africa by the missions. By renouncing Western Christianity's accidental attributes, including acquisitive individualism and materialistic positivism, he proposes to recapture this vital significance and redefine it in terms appropriate for the historical situation of contemporary Africa. Like Ela, Eboussi employs a line of argument based on the historical situatedness of all philosophical positions to justify a utopian vision that serves as an implicit critique of neocolonialist systems such as the one that evolved in Cameroon after independence.

This same line of argument lies at the heart of his reflections on the Negritude debate in *La Crise du Muntu*. By demonstrating that proponents as well as critics of Negritude lacked self-consciousness with regard to the socio-historical determinants of their own discourse, Eboussi lays the groundwork for an African philosophy capable of addressing the problem of identity. As he points out, advocates of the Negritude position blurred distinctions among different ethnic groups to create a generalized African culture that allowed them to take refuge in an imaginary past as a means of avoiding the knowledge that they were being exploited by others. Their refusal to recognize the internal weaknesses that contributed to the collapse of these ethnic cultures prevented them from incorporating African traditions into a progressive, modern view of the world, and many of them promoted what Eboussi regarded as the misconception that philosophy can be found in cultural practices or language rather than being forged in a confrontation with the concrete problems of a specific historical situation.

Yet he is convinced that the academic philosophers who attack Negritude are also prisoners of a historical situatedness that they fail to acknowledge. By relying almost entirely on scientific, rational modes of thought and by relegating traditional wisdom to the realm of the nonphilosophical, they implicitly accept European claims about the universal validity of Western philosophical thought, although it too is, for Eboussi, no more than the expression of a particular socio-historical situation. He argues that the very nature of academic philosophy in Africa is contingent upon its legitimation in the cultures of the former colonizing powers. Those who uncritically adopt its methodologies are relinquishing an important part of themselves and losing contact with the vital concerns of most Africans, in whose name they claim to be speaking.

Eboussi seeks to overcome the deficiencies of both sides in the Negritude debate by incorporating Muntu (or African authenticity) into a modern consciousness that situates itself objectively in the socio-historical process and strives to achieve a more humane future by addressing concrete problems in the present. According to him, Negritude thinkers had an important insight when they realized that black people were different from but equivalent to white people. They defined this difference in terms of culture and sought to articulate it in a universally comprehensible form, but they did not, Eboussi insists, liberate their insight from the alien idiom in which they described it, and they failed to reinsert it into the concrete historical process that is taking place in modern African societies.

Actual traditional practices are, he admits, anachronisms, but because all philosophical and religious thought occurs within a necessarily arbitrary framework of knowledge, an awareness of African traditions provides an indispensable set of mental landmarks for the orientation of any intellectual undertaking aimed at the liberation of Africans. For example, rather than being judged solely by foreign criteria, one could draw upon African traditions to determine the relevance of the questions being posed in contemporary Africa, to expand the horizons within which answers to these questions will be sought, and to formulate the standards according to which such answers will be accepted or rejected.

When freed from the dream of a nonexistent past and projected into the future, he argues, the idealization of tradition can become part of a utopian vision that critiques the debased present and provides a motive for seeking to transform it. People could identify with such a vision because it would maintain a sense of continuity with their own historical particularity while enabling them to generate new traditions that are consistent with it. In Eboussi's view, tradition is not a static condition but a dynamic process that can assimilate modern scientific techniques and make them accessible for the satisfaction of basic human needs. The intellectual project that he outlines in *La Crise du Muntu* and *Christianisme sans fétiche* is similar to that of Ela in the sense that he too proposes a Christian world view designed to foster development by helping people recognize who they really are and what they need to do in order to free themselves from neocolonialist oppression.

Such questions also preoccupied Cameroonian writers living in exile, and because they were not subject to the same restraints as people inside the country, many of them denounced the situation in their homeland more explicitly than they could have done if they had been living there. For example, Abel Eyinga specifically applied the neocolonialist analysis to Cameroon in his *Mandat d'arrêt pour cause d'élection*. The point of departure for his documentary exposé was the warrant issued for his arrest on the grounds that his attempt to run against Ahidjo in the 1970 presidential elections constituted a threat to public order.

In recounting the incident, Eyinga explains his rationale for opposing the government. By citing numerous examples of economic exploitation, oppression, torture, corruption, and misinformation, he seeks to demonstrate that Ahidjo and his supporters betrayed the people and deserve to be overthrown. And by outlining a participatory, socialistic form of government as an alternative to tyranny, he offers people a vision capable of motivating them to work toward this objective. According to him, Ahidjo was an intellectual mediocrity, a French puppet who had contributed nothing to the heroic struggle for national liberation. Preferring loyalty to merit and uttering only words written for him by others, Eyinga's Ahidjo is a petty-minded, greedy individual whose example corrupted the entire nation. His collaboration with the French and with the privileged class in his own country resulted, Eyinga claimed, in a form of government that controlled and marginalized the people rather than serving as a vehicle for the expression of their aspirations.

Although the self-exiled poet and publisher Paul Dakeyo is less concerned with the political analysis of neocolonialist oppression, his five volumes of poetry reflect a radical stance similar to that of Eyinga. If Dakeyo's experience of exile convinced him of the need for solidarity among oppressed peoples everywhere, his own poetic sensibility was shaped by memories of the atrocities and arbitrary injustices he had witnessed while growing up in the war-ravaged Bamileke territory during the 1960s. It also reveals a profound yearning for a genuinely independent Cameroon that is no longer subject to the exactions of a petty dictator and the neocolonialist alliance that stands behind him. Dakeyo himself sees poetry as an expression of this yearning, and when he set out to publish a major anthology of Cameroonian poetry, he proposed to include only poems that would "raise people's consciousness about contemporary reality, not the folklore reality of Negritude poems."[17] This goal was a primary motivating factor in everything he himself has written.

In *Les Barbelés du matin*, *Le Cri pluriel*, *Chant d'accusation*, *Soweto soleils fusillés*, and *J'appartiens au grand jour*, Dakeyo consistently fuses his experience of selfhood with a utopian vision that contrasts sharply with the brutality, the hypocrisy, and the injustice of contemporary society in Cameroon and elsewhere in Africa. The poems in these volumes are all part of his ongoing attempt to make sense of a world where he feels obliged to live in exile from the land where his sense of identity took shape. For him, exile is a painful state of transition between the past with its unsettling memories and the future with its promise of a new world order in which he could return to the land of his birth.

The past in Dakeyo's poetry is filled with scenes of horror that symbolize the neocolonialist oppression he opposes. He recalls burned-out villages being assaulted by hordes of vultures, people being whipped and herded into concentration camps, blood flowing in the schools and marketplaces. He himself admits that "a thousand dead people walk through my memories."[18] Gathering impressions as he wandered from city to city during a "famished childhood," a "childhood filled with tears" in a "barbed-wire space," he developed a nightmare image of neocolonial Africa. "My land is an immense prison where vultures hover overhead," he declares.[19] Yet when he escaped from this "prison," he sensed that he lost something precious—the warmth of relationships with other people and the grandeur of a landscape that he had experienced as a part of himself. This remnant of love and beauty convinces him that the country itself has the potential to become a utopian community if those who hold it in bondage can be dislodged and replaced by leaders who respect the people's desire for peace and harmony.

As an exile, however, he finds himself in a society where his outrage at oppressive conditions in his homeland is met with silence and indifference. "I'm but a stranger in this glacial country," he laments, "plodding through forbidden space in search of my faithful land."[20] Repeatedly he voices his desire to abandon an exile that condemns him to a dark night of silence and solitude in an alien setting, but as long as his world remains subject to neocolonialist exploitation, there is really nowhere for him to go. Under these circumstances, the writing of poetry becomes an act of liberation that celebrates the individual's capacity to love, the people's right to determine their own destiny, and the poet's transformation of the oppressor's language into an instrument of defiance. As a result, his poems challenge the existing system and unmask the hypocrisy behind the nation-building rhetoric that sanctions it.

The key to emancipation is the light of human awareness that makes possible a vision of purity. In *Soleils fusillés*, for example, each of the "suns" in the title represents the bright individual consciousness of a schoolchild killed in the Soweto massacre by a criminally unjust government. By analogy, these "suns" stand for all those who have suffered under similar regimes, including the victims of the Cameroonian government's brutality in suppressing the UPC rebellion in his native Bamileke territory. Within this context, Um Nyobé is presented as a light that was extinguished by the forces of oppression. But despite the deaths of such people, Dakeyo maintains that the light they represented can be rekindled in the word of the poet. Similar to the light of the sun, this poetic word testifies to the fact that, although tyrants might murder individuals, the human spirit and the vision of purity that emanates from it cannot be killed. As the expression of what endures, Dakeyo's poetry illuminates the "prison-dark night" of government-sanctioned crimes against humanity and awakens people to the possibility of reinventing society on the basis of love.

The anger that reverberates through his poems springs from a conviction that neocolonialist interests prevent such societies from coming into being. Behind this anger is the frustration he feels at being deprived of the utopian possibilities heralded by national independence in countries throughout Africa. These possibilities are variously symbolized in his poetry by the flower, the rainbow, and the sun. Because he realizes that a vision of purity cannot by itself loosen the hold of petty dictators and their supporters on the instruments of social control, he hopes to inspire anger among his readers by revealing the disparity between the society in which they live and the utopian society in which they could be living. If his own anger were to spread and unite the oppressed of the world in a common cause, they could, he believes, overthrow their oppressors and implement a new international order based on universal justice. His poetry is not only a "song of accusation" but also a beacon of hope, announcing the "volcanic eruption" that will purge the world of injustice and create the possibility for a more humane future. With regard to Cameroon, this radical stance translates into the assumption that the neocolonialist system must be swept away before a genuine national unity can be attained.

In Dakeyo's poetry, this unity is often symbolized by the act of love, for just as revolutionary activity is envisioned as a movement toward the social harmony in which the exiled poet might once again feel at home, lovemaking culminates in a euphoric sense of oneness that banishes the alienation he feels on a personal level. By offering a contrast to the brutality of the neocolonized world, the tenderness of an intimate personal relationship reassures the poet that love, not coercion, must be the basis for a new social order. Especially in *J'appartiens au grand jour*, images of the sun, the flower, the rainbow, the volcanic eruption, and the sowing of seed suggest a progression that leads to the reconciliation of opposites in a new peacefulness that is social as well as personal. In this sense, the poet's experience of love in a woman's embrace serves as a metaphor for the liberation of oppressed people everywhere. The political and the personal become one.

On another level, lovemaking recapitulates for Dakeyo the self-liberating act of poetic creation, which also strives toward a purity that transcends the ugliness and injustice of the contemporary world. As he says in *Soweto soleils fusillés*, poetry is "the unbound word, the essential gesture, the plural dance."[21] To be freed from the control of the oppressors, the language of poetry must, he feels, be reinvented, its syntax broken, and its habitual meanings shattered, so that it can penetrate the silent darkness, awakening people from their torpor and motivating them to act. In this sense, the poetic word is the essential gesture that names the reality of the existing situation and gives concrete form to the hope for a better future. It conveys the light of truth and love that liberates the genuine aspirations of the people and allows them to speak through him in a "plural dance."

The title of his collection *Le Cri pluriel* suggests that their cries of sorrow and anger reverberate in his poetic voice. When he declares that every child who dies of hunger, every brutal act that imposes suffering on people, and every executed freedom fighter should become "the verse of a poem, a word that saves, a verbal icon that reproduces itself," he is explaining his own poetic practice.[22] By transforming the everyday reality of neocolonialist society into poetry, Dakeyo seeks to convince people that their servitude is avoidable and to inspire them with a faith in the dawning of a new day. He is offering them the possibility of awareness and love, but they must embrace this possibility and act accordingly if they hope to liberate themselves from oppression. Dakeyo's poetry is an exhortation for them to do so. At the same time, it is the record of one Cameroonian's quest for freedom and identity on three levels of experience—personal, political, and poetological.

His depiction of this quest reflects his exile from a homeland to which he felt he could not return until it had been liberated from its neocolonialist masters. Yet it remained his homeland, and his vision of what it could become was a powerful refutation of the Ahidjo government's official rhetoric about national identity. The same is true for the work of two other exile Cameroonian poets, Nigoue na Bato and Bekate Meyong. Influenced by the black power ideologies of the early 1970s, Nigoue na Bato's *Métamorphose* and *Poésie primaire* attack the technocratic materialism that transforms people into robots. It also prophesies a revolt against the privileged classes that collaborate with Euro-American economic interests to exploit the African continent for their own benefit.

Like Dakeyo, Nigoue na Bato believes there is a historical continuity between his struggle and that of the UPC martyrs who died in the hope of creating a truly free and independent Cameroon. He too views his own exile as a metaphor for the alienation that had been imposed on his neocolonized homeland. As his fantasies of African liberation merge with images of his day-to-day life in Paris, his pursuit of personal freedom becomes an analogue for the revolutionary process. What he proudly calls his "bastard poetry" is an attempt to shock readers into an awareness of their own oppression and their need to liberate themselves from it.

Meyong's *Mânes sauvages* also seeks to shock readers into repudiating the mechanical sterility of the Western world and the myth that Africans must remain perpetually under the tutelage of others. As he looks around himself in Paris, he remarks that people have lost the ability to rejoice in life as they run to catch up with time and honor their only god, money.

> The white man's smile is frozen in place
> or prefabricated
> or calculated
> or false
> Sometimes useful.[23]

The joyless single-mindedness suggested by this smile enabled Europeans to colonize Africa. It also helped them exploit it efficiently both before and after independence.

Meyong specifically decries the dehumanization that accompanied independence in Cameroon—the political assassinations, the atmosphere of mistrust, the vast disparities of wealth. Like Dakeyo and Meyong, he challenges the nation-building ethos of the Ahidjo regime and reminds people of their own humanity, which he believes should constitute the starting point for any definition of national identity. Also like them, he is convinced that the neocolonialist system will collapse under the weight of its own contradictions as soon as Africans oppose it in a rational but determined way. Implicit in the works of all these exile poets is the assumption that the true identity of the Cameroonian people will emerge in their struggle to liberate themselves from an unjust political order, not in their passive acceptance of the existing situation.

Even before the Ouandié-Ndongmo trial, the exile writer Daniel Ewandé's *Vive le Président! La Fête africaine* offered a satiric indictment of African dictators and the neocolonialist mentality that keeps them in power. Based largely on the situation in Cameroon, Ewandé's polemical novel provokes readers into reflecting critically on the nature of neocolonialist exploitation and on the rhetoric used to support it. Like Beti, Ewandé believed that the truth about Africa had been obscured by scholars, journalists, and "ethnophilosophers" who claimed that Africans think differently from Europeans. In reality, he argued, all people have similar desires—freedom, dignity, material well-being, peace, and emotionally satisfying relationships with others. According to Ewandé, totalitarian governments in countries such as Cameroon fail to fulfill such aspirations. Rather than liberate people, they subject them to new forms of domination. His book focuses attention on the corrupt mentality that acquiesces in these forms of domination, and when it was banned in Cameroon, the government was tacitly acknowledging that Ewandé's fiction echoed the existing situation there.

Vive le Président! is presented as a series of reflections by Dakou-Bolé, a forty-eight-year-old party loyalist who enjoys the confidence of President Kabouganga in an independent African country. Kabouganga is a typical neocolonialist despot, and Dakou-Bolé sycophantically approves of everything the president does until he himself assumes the country's highest office after a coup. The real center of focus in the novel is Dakou-Bolé's mentality, for it is a major pillar of support for neocolonialism in Africa. This mentality is symbolically embodied in the expression "vive le président," which is repeated at the end of each chapter. Since every chapter deals with some abuse of presidential authority, the interjection reflects Dakou-Bolé's willingness to praise anything the president does simply because he is president. The "African celebration" in the book's subtitle is an ironic allusion to all those who profit from the system Dakou-Bolé is describing. *Vive le Président!* thus has a dual focus—the nature of neocolonialism and the attitudes that permit people like Dakou-Bolé to prosper under it.

During his service as a minor functionary in the colonial administration, Dakou-Bolé had learned that those who support the regime in power enjoy the amenities of life. The coming of independence represented a chance for him to assure his future by transferring his loyalty to the petty dictator who ascended to power at that time. "Politics is like war," he observes in retrospect. "The important thing is to be on the right side. You win when you're still alive after the firing is over."[24] By placing an absolute value on survival, he acknowledges his willingness to defend any policy his superiors happen to proclaim. In fact, he is ostensibly writing his "pamphlet" to counter the slanders of those who oppose Kabouganga's government and refuse to admit that "everything is for the best in the best of all possible Africas."[25] Dakou-Bolé has the mentality of an obedient but cynical servant, and Ewandé's point is that such a mentality enables petty dictatorships to flourish in neocolonized countries such as Cameroon.

Often Dakou-Bolé's praise of Kabouganga's reign is ironically undercut by the content of his statements. For example, he boasts that even torture is democratically administered in his country, and he claims casuistically that a minister's worth is proved by the fact that he earns more in one month than a laborer can earn in fifteen years. One of the most visible consequences of independence was the emergence of a privileged class, and Dakou-Bolé lauds its ostentatious display of wealth. Even though he admits that his wealthy countrymen are "capitalists without capital," he vaunts their trips to Europe and their imported luxuries as evidence that Africans can enjoy the "American way of life" and occupy the same positions that white men had once occupied. By predisposing readers to adopt a critical perspective toward the objects of Dakou-Bolé's eulogies, Ewandé is encouraging them to recognize the absurdity of similar behavior in real life.

Because he believes that African intellectuals have abdicated their responsibility toward the people, some of the most acerbic satire in *Vive le Président!* is reserved for them, especially those who, like Senghor, helped create the neocolonialist system and invented the rhetoric that obscures its inequities beneath a web of specious rationalizations. Dakou-Bolé refers to francophone Africa's most prominent intellectual as an exemplary "good president," a standard by means of which all other intellectuals might be judged. Inverting the narrator's opinion according to the satiric conventions of the book, readers realize that Ewandé's conception of the intellectual's role is just the opposite of Senghor's implicit definition of it. According to the Cameroonian satirist, intellectuals have a moral obligation to analyze the nature of the neocolonialist alliance and enlighten people about its impact on them, not to sanction its dominance in contemporary Africa.

To illustrate the sort of analysis he has in mind, Ewandé occasionally drops the satirically distorted narrative voice of Dakou-Bolé and openly challenges readers to examine the neocolonized world. At one point, he even poses a series of mathematical problems to demonstrate how aid to developing countries can actually impoverish them. Instead of competing for colonies, he argues, the developed countries cooperate to exploit the rest of the world. For example, they control the international markets that hold down the prices of raw materials while allowing the prices of finished products to rise. Under such circumstances, he concludes, genuine economic development is impossible, and foreign aid merely enables the donor countries to appear generous while perpetuating the psychology of dependency in third-world countries.

Dakou-Bolé of course praises this sort of aid and the "good presidents" who scurry around the world in search of it. However, in light of the foreign aid that is squandered on armies, prestigious buildings, and projects that enrich the privileged class, it is clear that most Africans benefit very little from arrangements that leave them hopelessly mired in poverty. The neocolonialist mentality represented by Dakou-Bolé accepts this situation and profits from it. From Ewandé's perspective, this mentality constitutes a betrayal of the people. His satiric portrayal of it is sufficiently general that it could be applied to many African countries, but specific parallels with the Cameroonian situation suggest that his radical critique of postcolonial society was also intended as an attack against the Ahidjo regime.

The radical image of a neocolonialist Cameroon served as the model for one of the most talented young novelists to emerge during the post-1972 period. A political exile living in France, Yodi Karone published two socially engaged works of fiction, *Le Bal des caïmans* and *Nègre de paille*, during the early 1980s. Both deal with the consequences of political repression in a fictional country that resembles Cameroon. *Le Bal des caïmans* is a fictionalized reenactment of the Ouandié-Ndongmo affair and an attempt to place the issues it raised into a perspective from which the government's bad faith would be apparent. The "dance of the crocodiles" in the title refers to the macabre celebration that the government and the privileged class hold during a series of events that culminate in the execution of a guerilla leader and the imprisonment of a priest.

Narrated by a griot who alternately presents the story through the eyes of the guerilla leader Adrien and those of the priest Jean, *Le Bal des caïmans* is intimately linked with the idea of national destiny in the sense that the major characters' preoccupations express an entire people's quest for freedom and identity in the oppressive environment of a neocolonialist state. The first part of the novel is devoted to their respective arrests, interrogations, and tortures. The second revolves around the show trial at which the charges against them are presented in public. Neither Adrien nor Jean is by nature violent, yet both are subjected to physical and psychological torture by a regime that accuses them of terrorist activities.

In response to this situation, both the rebel leader and the priest reexamine their basic assumptions and, in the process, shed light on questions that frequently trouble men of good will in repressive societies: why uphold a revolutionary ideal in the face of overwhelming government force and the apparent indifference of the people? Why live according to religious principles when society is dominated by ruthless individuals who oppress the majority of the population at will? Both questions are answered during the course of the griot's narrative, but in an ironic reversal of roles, it becomes apparent that the accusers of Adrien and Jean are actually the accused within the larger framework of Karone's fictional universe.

The griot's tale begins with the gruesome scene of a public execution in the municipal stadium of a large unnamed city. A holiday atmosphere reigns among the people who gather to sanction the punishment of a "subversive rebel leader," but there is a tinge of nervousness in their laughter. Although the government seems to have succeeded in imposing its version of the truth on the people, its execution of the rebel leader reveals its vulnerability when the event is placed in its historical context. Beneath the government's official rhetoric about a benevolent leader, a unifying national party, a doctrine of "planned liberalism," and a cultural policy based on "authenticity," there is an oppressive system that manipulates people without the slightest regard for truth and justice. For example, the presiding magistrate at the trial admits he has little interest in the prisoners' defense because the official version of their guilt has already been determined. Because Adrien and Jean are depicted as principled individuals with a commitment to the welfare of the people, the story of their brutalization actually exposes the moral bankruptcy of the system that condemns them.

As a former student who became politically conscious during the years he spent in Europe, Adrien joined the revolutionary nationalist party because he wanted to be "free in a more just society."[26] He knew he could attain such a goal only by siding with the people against a corrupt government that imprisoned them in a net of poverty and fear. Throughout his long career as a guerilla leader, he always sought to convince people by words rather than coercing them by the threat of violence, and when the police arrested him for a curfew violation, he had been visiting his wife and their three-year-old son. In other words, Adrien's opposition to the government was sustained by his vision of a better society and the conviction that he was fighting for a just cause.

When government officials discover that they are holding a major leader of the revolutionary underground, they decide to make an example of him, but despite torture and the lies of false witnesses, he maintains his dignity by proclaiming his version of the truth. "I am a man who is fighting for true independence," he retorts in the face of outrageous lies about his character, "for freedom, for justice, for a new world."[27] Although Adrien realizes that he never overcame the inertia of the people, he doesn't regret having committed himself to the revolutionary movement because he still believes the people can grasp the nature of their oppression and take the initiative for eliminating it. This belief supports him even in front of the firing squad, and it enables him to become the symbol of an idea that the government cannot kill.

In contrast, Jean loses faith in the Christian religion during his ordeal. Having been recruited into the church by white missionaries, he initially sought to place himself in harmony with the will of God by trying to alleviate the misery of the people, but when he resisted the unjust policies of the state and the hypocrisy of his superiors, he was ordered to avoid politically sensitive issues. Resigning himself to the impossibility of reforming an imperfect world, he withdrew to a hermit's existence in the forest. He claimed to be apolitical and even referred to "our beloved and venerated President."[28] On the night of his arrest for a curfew violation, Jean was in the city to replenish his supplies and to pray in the church, but because he had picked up one of Adrien's revolutionary tracts to wrap around his tobacco, the police assumed he was a subversive and subjected him to a series of vicious beatings.

Although he knows he is innocent, Jean cannot withstand the pressure of his situation. He is a profoundly decent man who empathizes with the suffering of his fellow prisoners, but the blatant injustice of the situation remains incomprehensible to him. He attempts to view it as a punishment for some forgotten sin or as a trial to test his faith, but prayer fails to sustain his integrity when the chief interrogator places a basket of snakes in front of him. Terrified, Jean confesses to his participation in a (nonexistent) plot to assassinate the president and implicates innocent people whom he does not even know. He implores God's forgiveness, but he knows he has irrevocably compromised the ideal he had worshipped for so many years. When he prays for enlightenment, it doesn't come. When he reflects upon his life as a hermit, the memory fails to inspire him with courage. On the contrary, it reminds him of the shame, guilt, and sense of impurity that continually assailed him. He is no longer certain of his religious vocation. Although his compromise with the truth allows him to escape with a five-year prison sentence, he is a defeated man. Never again will he be able to pray without laughing at what became of his faith when it was put to the test.

The contrast between his reaction and that of Adrien illustrates Karone's conviction that Adrien's revolutionary commitment provides a more reliable basis for the articulation of a stable identity concept than does Jean's faith in God. In fact, religious belief in *Le Bal des caïmans* represents a form of false consciousness that predisposes people to accept the neocolonialist situation as a given of their existence.

At the end of the trial, the government has apparently triumphed. Supposed revelations about the activities of men such as Adrien and Jean reinforce the idea that a devious enemy is menacing the public order. The corollary is that the state must continue to rule with an iron fist. The exemplary punishments meted out to the two men also send a warning to anyone else who might be tempted to challenge the regime in power. Finally, by taking decisive action against reputed subversives, the government hopes to convince foreigners that the country is a safe place in which to invest capital. However, the government's victory is a pyrrhic one, for Adrien and Jean represent the decent impulses that even the most corrupt regime cannot completely suppress. When viewed from their perspective, the events surrounding the trial reveal the perversity of a society ruled by greedy, power-hungry individuals who camouflage their rapaciousness behind a cloak of political legitimacy.

The vulnerability of the neocolonialist system derives from the impossibility of imposing a lie on all people at all times. An incident that takes place at the independence-day celebrations shortly after Adrien's death illustrates the point. As everyone is cheering the president's optimistic nation-building platitudes, someone shouts "Viva la Revolucion," and the crowd replies "Viva!" This spontaneous repudiation of the official rhetoric indicates that the spirit behind Adrien's resistance to corruption and injustice did not die with him. It constantly resurfaces among others who also yearn for truth and compassion in an environment dominated by falsehood and cruelty. Karone's point is that human values persistently undermine the corrupt system by calling its hypocritical rationalizations into question. His fictional rewriting of the Ouandié-Ndongmo affair thus culminates in a reaffirmation of the revolutionary ideal.

In *Nègre de paille*, Karone adopts an entirely different approach to the quest for freedom and identity in neocolonialist society. One of the principal obstacles to the creation of self-respecting national communities in the independent countries of Africa is the complex of guilt and impotence that has been imposed on many Africans by a long history of oppression. By focusing on the hallucinatory dream of the recently released political prisoner Yoyo Dibanga as he rides the train toward his home on the outskirts of Douala, Karone allegorically evokes the solitude and alienation that accompany this complex. He also suggests that it can be overcome only if the African accepts the past with all its injustice and humiliation, repudiates illusions about the superiority of Europe, and acts decisively in defense of his own dignity.

Yoyo's dream is the purgation of a psychological complex that haunted him long before he was imprisoned eighteen years previously for having accidentally run over a ten-year-old girl with his taxi. Already at that time he had felt humiliated by his inability to have children with his wife, Carlota. On the day of his scheduled return to Douala, Carlota awaits him at the railroad station, and her memories of the past enable readers to comprehend the subjective reality behind Yoyo's surrealistic dream. But she waits in vain. Her husband doesn't get off the train, and she never sees him again. The incident even acquires a certain notoriety because a local griot transforms Yoyo's mysterious disappearance into the subject of a popular ballad. But whatever the outside world may have thought, Yoyo had become engaged in an imaginary journey into himself, where he discovered the source of his guilt and feelings of inadequacy.

The crucial event in Yoyo's past was the accident in which the young girl, Emily, was killed, for it was associated in his mind with the daughter he never had and with Carlota's infidelity in her attempt to have a child. Imprisoned in his memory of the accident, he knows he has not regained his freedom at the moment of his release from the Paille Noire prison camp. And although he hears the president's optimistic radio broadcast announcing plans for a new "Freedom Boulevard," his experience of arbitrary injustice has convinced him that he must seek his freedom far from his own country. During the colonial period, he had been conditioned to regard Paris as the center of civilization, a place where people could be truly free. For this reason, he heads north on his imaginary journey.

His path leads through the realm of death, which represents both an ultimate reality he must accept as part of life and an allegorical tableau of the living dead who inhabit neocolonialist Africa. In the seemingly endless labyrinth through which he wanders before emerging in a Paris Metro station, he encounters the figure of Politics, who has no useful advice to offer him about his quest. And Paris itself proves incapable of giving him his freedom, for it is the opposite of what he had expected it to be. Rather than a center of civilization, it is a place where people ignore the suffering of others and titillate their jaded sensibilities with pornography, gluttony, and voyeurism. This insensitivity to the horror of modern life is symbolized by the nonchalance with which a beggar kicks a severed hand onto the subway tracks and by the indifference with which bystanders watch the rats carry it away. Yet this insensitivity was at the heart of the colonialist enterprise that initially imposed the complex of guilt and inadequacy on Africans. If Yoyo is ever to gain his freedom, he must see Europe for what it is and renounce his illusions about its superiority.

He must also accept the past and acquire a sense of self-worth. But he can do so only by repudiating the false images that have been imposed on him. At first, he thinks he can liberate himself from his guilt by finding the dead Emily or a surrogate that would allow him to pretend that the accident had never happened. Thus, when a young white girl approaches him on the Metro platform and announces that her name is Emily, he exults to himself, "here is my freedom."[29] But the girl is a capricious hippie who acts with gratuitous cruelty and takes him to a commune, a false paradise of drugs and promiscuity. After he declines her invitation to make love, she cavorts with a band of naked young people and taunts him with his impotency, as Carlota had done years before.

But when she calls him a "dirty nigger," he becomes furious and kills her. Although his act results in his own death, it frees him from a burden he had carried with him all his life. On a symbolic level, the white Emily in his dream represents all the false images he had carried around inside himself—the idea that he could eradicate all memory of the accident by finding the girl who had been killed, the idea that he was powerless in the face of his wife's taunts, the idea that Europe could somehow give him his freedom. The only way he can attain freedom is by acting on the basis of a self-image he has forged for himself, and this is what he does in killing the symbolic embodiment of his own illusions. Nègre de paille is thus the allegorical representation of a psychological process capable of liberating Africans from the complexes that colonialist and neocolonialist oppression have inflicted on them.

The radical vision of utopian possibilities and a profound resentment at the inequitable distribution of wealth also reverberated through the socially engaged poetry of a younger generation that began to publish during the mid-1970s. Many of these poets came from the Bamileke area. Like Kayo and Dakeyo, they often had vivid memories of the brutality with which the UPC rebellion had been suppressed, but whether or not they were Bamileke, they openly expressed their disaffection with the Ahidjo regime and its nation-building rhetoric, and they castigated the obscene indulgences of the privileged class in the face of widespread poverty in the country. These young poets linked their own quests for personal freedom with the struggle for national liberation, and they tended to advocate militant opposition to the existing system. Nearly all of them suffered some form of government harassment.

Behind their militancy, there was invariably a yearning for peace, love, and social harmony. Even moderate Bamileke poets such as Timothée Ndzagaap and Paul Tchakouté, who were profoundly influenced by Christian idealism and traditional values, felt constrained to repudiate the excesses of the Ahidjo government. Although much of Ndzagaap's poetry is a melancholy, self-pitying reflection on the meaning of his own experiences, he also eulogizes Martin Luther King, implying that the black American's demands for freedom and dignity must be raised in Africa as well. Reflecting on contemporary Cameroon, he asks rhetorically, "where is freedom then?"[30] This question underlies all radical Cameroonian poetry of the period.

It is the central question for Tchakouté, a doctor who spent many years in Europe before returning to Cameroon in the mid-1970s, when his poetry began to appear under Ndzagaap's Librairie Populaire imprint. Convinced that all people have the same capacity to experience joy and suffering, he envisions the poet as one who articulates the people's own truths for them. "Each man's cry is but the echo of the eternal sigh," he once wrote.[31] Because he believes that everyone shares a common humanity, he believes people can live together peacefully in a society based on compassion and communal solidarity. He also realizes that an unjust and irrational world order imposes vast amounts of unnecessary suffering on people.

In the poems he wrote in Paris, he often attributes this dehumanizing situation to a widespread preoccupation with wealth and power. As a temporary exile from his homeland, he defines himself in terms of his capacity to experience beauty, justice, love, and everything else that seems to be lacking in European society. In such poems as the long *Journal d'un matin*, the real standard of value is the poet's sensibility. His own experience of a morning in Paris might be unique, but when transformed into poetry, it generates insights that readers can apply to their own lives, and such insights are, he believes, the seeds of revolutionary social change. The poet's sensibility thus symbolizes an awareness that is accessible to all people. At the end of *Journal d'un matin*, he grabs his gun and descends into the street to participate in a revolution. Within the context of his own return to Cameroon and the publication of his poetry there, his ideological message is clear: the utopian vision of a genuine national independence implies the need for people to join together and purge Cameroonian society of the hypocrisy and greed concealed beneath the idealistic slogans of those who profit from the existing system.

In the even more militant verse of Enoh Meyomesse, Epale-Ndika, Nkame Ntane, Augustin Millam, and Jean-Pierre Ghonda-Nounga, the poet's self identifies with the oppressed and upholds the conviction that change can occur if people unite in defense of a common cause. Often these young poets sought to shock readers into an awareness of the intolerable conditions that Cameroonian independence had brought in its wake. One reviewer of Epale-Ndika's *La Mort en silence* remarked that the young man's poems were like spittle in the face of his readers.[32] However, the violent imagery in Epale-Ndika's poems is not gratuitous. It is calculated to evoke an emotional response—compassion for a starving child, revulsion at the ugliness of poverty, disgust at the general indifference to suffering. In his eyes, this emotional response is what distinguishes people from animals. It is also a forestage of critical consciousness and a stimulus to revolutionary action. Such poetry demythologizes the nation-building rhetoric as a first step toward the creation of a truly independent and self-respecting Cameroon.

Millam also emphasizes the hypocrisy of the official ideology. In "Grand-père se souvient," for example, he allows an old man to compare his memories of the colonial period with his perceptions of the present. His conclusion is that independence is worse than what preceded it, for the "black shadow" merely followed the "white shadow," bringing a new form of slavery along with it. In his "Cauchemar et réalité," the nightmare quality of the present becomes apparent during a police raid on his house:

> I was sleeping soundly at home that night,
> When "they" approached like wolves, shadows in
> The darkness, silent, avoiding the least sound. At the
> Crowing of the cock, they suddenly burst in and,
> Without even letting me dress, without explanation,
> Menacingly ordered me out. And binding my wrists in handcuffs of injustice,
> The executioners of this century led me to torture.[33]

In a mad society where officially sanctioned violence is regarded as normal, the poet's sensitivity becomes a touchstone of sanity. Although he perceives postcolonial society as a "sea of false freedom," it reassures him that the human spirit can eventually prevail over the "executioners of this century."

Deeply marked by his childhood experiences in the Bamileke area during the 1960s, Ghonda-Nounga also depicts neocolonialist society as a scene of horrors. Images of massacred children, fires, rotting corpses, napalm bombs dropped from French airplanes, and the display of severed heads bear witness to government brutality. For him, this brutality expresses a historical evolution that originated in man's desire to subjugate other men. In *Chants pour Ruben*, he offers a disarmingly straightforward account of how such a system came into being:

> In the beginning was the word
> and the word was human.
> . . . .
> Then man created the tool
> he saw it was good and smiled.

. . . .
. . . soon a master arose among men.
seized the tool
and enslaved the slave
who had never been enslaved before.
The master saw that all this was good
and smiled
and is still smiling today.[34]

Ghonda-Nounga's basic idea is simple: people create the societies in which they live, and if some classes gain dominance over others, they do so by usurping a power that should belong to everyone.

When an awareness of this fact is obscured by the false myths of neocolonialist society, the potentially revolutionary impulses of the people are often dissipated in trivial pastimes such as soccer mania and cheap films. Under such circumstances, Ghonda-Nounga believes the poet has a responsibility to enlighten people about their own oppression and motivate them to liberate themselves from it. Like Beti, Philombe, Kayo, and other opposition writers, he proposes to accomplish this goal by preserving the utopian ideal articulated by Um Nyobé and other martyred UPC leaders.

In one poem, he depicts Um Nyobé holding up the body of a dead child in sorrow while donning the skin of a panther in anger. Surrounded by ugliness and misery, the legendary UPC leader symbolizes the people's pain as well as their determination to resist further oppression. In the face of a similar situation twenty years later, Ghonda-Nounga urges his readers to take up arms against the neocolonialist alliance because "in violence alone is FREEDOM invented here."[35] According to him, revolutionary violence is the only practical way to cope with the existing situation. It is also the only justifiable response to the violence that has been perpetrated against Africans for centuries. Adamantly opposed to the Ahidjo government's cultural nationalism, he concludes that the Cameroonian people will define their collective identity only by fighting to liberate themselves from neocolonialist oppression. Like nearly all the radical Cameroonian poets of the 1970s and early 1980s, Ghonda-Nounga links his personal quest for freedom with that of the Cameroonian people while presenting the sensitive self of the poet as a repository of humane values and a guardian of the revolutionary utopian dream.

Radical critiques of postcolonial Cameroonian society were embedded in a variety of world views, but despite differences, the authors of these critiques were linked together by a common opposition to the neocolonialist society that had come into being during the Ahidjo years. Implicit in their writing was a utopian dream that contrasted with the corrupt reality of contemporary Cameroon and offered an alternative to the government's nation-building rhetoric. This utopian dream reflected the individual values and tastes that were projected into it, but it also proposed an image of communal well-being with which large numbers of Cameroonians could identify. Although government officials often tried to suppress the radical perspective when it was specifically applied to the Cameroonian situation, they proved incapable of discrediting the neocolonialist analysis and its utopian possibilities. Because the radical counterversion of Cameroonian reality reflected and reinforced a widespread disaffection with the regime in power, it engaged the official version of the truth in an implicit dialogue that decisively influenced the country's universe of discourse. In fact, the tension between these two approaches to the definition of national identity was one of its most prominent features.

CHAPTER
18

INDIVIDUAL IDENTITY AND MORAL IDEALISM
The Theme of Reconciliation in Recent Cameroonian Fiction

As the euphoria of independence and the brutal suppression of the UPC rebellion in the Bamileke territory faded into the past, Cameroonian novelists increasingly focused on the problem of self-definition. They tended to view individual identity in a modern way as a process that takes place during an ongoing series of interactions between the self and society. To depict this process, they drew heavily upon autobiographical materials; in fact, their claim to the reader's attention often hinged on the assumption that they were providing an emotionally honest expression of their own feelings and convictions. In recording the responses of an individual consciousness to its social milieu, they reinforced the notion that the unique identity of individuals is worth preserving because every life is valuable in its own right. At the same time, they remained profoundly aware that contemporary Cameroonians confront a characteristic set of dilemmas in seeking to define themselves within a system that offers them few viable alternatives and subjects them to many unresolved conflicts.

For example, the conflict between tradition and modernity lies at the heart of the identity question as it has been portrayed in recent Cameroonian fiction. Yet there is no general consensus about how to resolve it, and writers have approached it from a variety of perspectives. A striking development in the literature of this period has been the reexamination of this conflict in light of the role of women in contemporary African society. The emergence of women writers has contributed to this new focus, but even the writings of men exhibit a heightened awareness of women's aspirations for self-realization.

The moral idealism that characterized Cameroonian writing during the 1960s persisted in much of the literature that appeared after the "Peaceful Revolution of May 20." Although the establishment of Editions CLE in Yaounde provided considerable impetus for this tendency, it did not decline appreciably with the eclipse of the Protestant-sponsored publishing house because it reflected a widespread yearning for peace and harmony among Cameroonian writers. Often they found support for this yearning in beliefs that had been influenced by traditional precedents or by Christianity, and their works tend to define individual identity in terms of its relationship to a moral ideal. Sometimes the characters in contemporary Cameroonian fiction evolve toward a heightened awareness of this ideal. Sometimes the ideal serves as a standard of value by means of which they are judged. In cases where society is portrayed as blocking access to the ideal, the ideal functions as a foil that reveals the corruption of this society. In one form or another, moral idealism is intimately related to the definition of the self in contemporary Cameroonian fiction.

One of the most powerful accounts of this process is contained in Bernard Nanga's prize-winning novel *La Trahison de Marianne*, a semiautobiographical meditation upon an African student's disillusionment with the France he had idolized since his schooldays in colonial Cameroon. Modeled on Nanga's own experience, the story in *La Trahison de Marianne* is told by a mature narrator fifteen years after the events he is describing. In the intervening years, he has philosophically accepted the ambiguity of a world where corruption and injustice cannot be eliminated by good intentions. He has also married the beautiful but unorthodox Frenchwoman Dany, whom he had long admired from a distance. "We are living between two worlds," he explains, "two worlds that complement each other without repudiating our identity. Perhaps that's the only way to be free. . . ."[1] By refusing to define themselves in terms of the stereotyped assumptions of their respective cultures, they have created an identity for themselves, and this act of self-creation is an expression of their freedom. From this perspective, the narrator's story recounts the evolution that enabled him to adopt the enlightened world view on the basis of which this freedom is possible.

Before attaining the insight that lies behind this view of the world, he must shed the illusions and misconceptions that have prevented him from realizing the truth about himself and his world. As a schoolboy in Africa, he developed an exaggeratedly idealistic image of France, which for him embodied the heroic spirit of a civilization that had subdued the barbarian hordes. Fusing the female profile on French coins with the map of his idealized France, he also regarded it as the epitome of beauty. At first he called this woman "Liberty" because the word was inscribed on the reverse side of a French coin that he religiously carried in his pocket. When he discovered that Marianne was another name for the French Republic, he adopted that name and vowed to remain eternally faithful to her.

His fascination with Marianne transformed him into a surrogate European who read French books, played games with French heroes, ate French food, wore French clothes, hung European paintings in his room, and played European composers on the piano. In his village, he became known as the "white man" who disliked the sound of drums. He himself admits, "I had a French soul."[2] In other words, he vested his entire identity in the belief that

France represented an ideal he must pursue if he hoped to achieve happiness. He had become what the colonial educational system intended for him to become—a completely acculturated African.

Yet once he arrives in a provincial French city to study economics, he discovers that reality does not conform to his idealized image of it. Rather than the paradise he had been conditioned to expect, he encounters the isolation and alienation that so many African students have experienced in Europe. He is painfully aware of the curious, hostile stares that follow him wherever he goes. He compares himself to an insect on the verge of being devoured by an animal, and he wishes he could become invisible to avoid meeting the French people he had idolized from a distance. As he reflects on the gap between the real France and his ideal, he begins to understand the reason for his despair.

In French society, everyone is preoccupied with acquiring things. The statues of heroes who symbolize the country's idealistic values have become fouled with bird droppings, and the people themselves forget these values in their trivial day-to-day activities. In the eyes of the narrator, the sterile, mechanical world that the French created with their wealth devours them and reflects the death of their gods. Because the people he idolized are spiritually dead, his own Europeanized self-concept is no longer tenable. Marianne has betrayed him, and his loss of faith in what she represented obliges him to redefine himself in more realistic terms.

Like Nanga himself, the narrator in *La Trahison* was profoundly influenced by his reading of André Gide, whose antibourgeois skepticism convinced him that all social values are merely conventions. Although momentarily attracted to the material comfort enjoyed by a Cameroonian friend who has accommodated himself to the French way of life, he ultimately refuses to exchange his former ideal for a banal imitation of it. But he is reawakened to something real in himself by his chance encounter with a group of half-starving African workers who had been lured to Europe by false promises of work. Despite their misery, these Africans share what little they have. They laugh together, sing together, and dance together. Suddenly he becomes aware of what he forsook in becoming a surrogate European. "I recognized my native Africa. An Africa without history, but also without ruse and prevarication, humiliated through the centuries, plundered, but always proud and alive, confident in man and without malice."[3] These Africans are not spiritually dead. In fact, they are closer to the narrator's original idea of purity than the French with whom he had identified.

The part of himself that he rediscovers in the company of the destitute workers provides him with a counterbalance to the stereotyped images of Africa he sees reflected in the eyes of Frenchmen who pass him on the street. Having felt imprisoned in an endless labyrinth of mirrors that continually reminded him that he could never become the European he had wanted to become, his insight allows him to relinquish his naive illusions about France and to devote himself to the task of self-definition. As he himself says, "it was a matter of finding my lost unity again, of being myself."[4] This unity is not the Negritude conception of black culture, which he also regards as a conventional notion, but the unity of himself as a human being with the capacity to relate with other human beings in emotionally honest ways.

The force that enables him to consolidate this unity is the love that unites him with Dany. Like him, she rejects the conventions of bourgeois society and yearns for relationships that transcend surface appearances. When he first saw her in the lower-class restaurant where he usually took his meals, she was reading a book, and he immediately associated her with his own literature-influenced image of Marianne. At first, he admires her from a distance, but gradually all the psychic energy he had once invested in Marianne is transferred to her. Although they become friends, she ceases coming to the restaurant, and he loses sight of her for a long period of time. But when they meet again, he recognizes that they are truly kindred spirits who share a belief in the possibility of an ideal love.

Their elective affinity is confirmed when he spends a summer on her family's farm to recuperate from injuries received during a student demonstration at which he had been an innocent bystander. On the farm, he regains a feeling of harmony with the natural world, and their love ripens in the absence of oppressive social conventions. In a sense, Dany's presence allows him to become fully himself, for in satisfying his need to love and to be loved, he is realizing his potential as a human being. The "betrayal of Marianne" in the novel's title thus has a dual significance. It refers to the French people's betrayal of their own ideals, but it also has a positive connotation insofar as it alludes to his broken vow of fidelity to the idealized Marianne. He had to betray Marianne in order to find Dany, and his relationship with her represents the final stage in the evolution of his mature personality. By recognizing the need to love and to be loved in a world where greed, loneliness, and hypocrisy militate against the honest expression of emotion, he succeeds in articulating a modern self-image that permits him to reconcile his desire for freedom with his yearning for a moral ideal.

The process of individual self-definition depicted in Nanga's *La Trahison de Marianne* is a dominant concern in the Cameroonian writing that proliferated during the 1970s and 1980s. Although relatively few autobiographies were published at this time, novelists drew heavily on personal experience, and their fictions were often thinly veiled accounts of their own lives. The primary value in such works was nearly always the emotional honesty with which individuals revealed the truth about themselves, and emphasis tended to be placed on the process by means of which they became who they are. The works that appeared at this time did reflect many of the same tendencies that had characterized the literature of the 1960s, particularly the linkage between the evolving self and the quest for freedom within the context of a morally idealistic view of the world. Autobiographies such as Pabe Mongo's *Un Enfant comme les autres*, Jean Mba Lenou's *L'Enfant Bamileke*, and Victor Fotso's *Tout pour la gloire de mon pays* clearly illustrate this relationship, for they all relate how morally upright individuals overcame obstacles to become successful in their own terms. In each case, they implicitly exhort readers to follow their example of Christian self-reliance.

The novels published by CLE at this time were not overtly supportive of the government, and they occasionally engaged in a moderate form of social criticism, but their general thrust was morally uplifting in a way that remained compatible with the official ideology. In none of these CLE novels, for example, is Cameroonian society portrayed as a neocolonialist system that defrauds the people of an equitable share in the nation's wealth. On the contrary, the concerns that dominated the CLE novels of the 1960s remain prominent in the firm's later publications. In particular, emphasis is placed on individual quests for the freedom to pursue self-realization and romantic love in a society where traditional superstition or materialistic acquisitiveness places arbitrary limits on them.

Sentiment and melodrama predominate in many of these works, and the strong influence of Christian moral values is evident, for example, in the way their authors rely on poetic justice to reward those who are emotionally honest while punishing those who are not. Underlying this use of poetic justice is the assumption that the world functions to bring about a benevolent order if people place themselves in harmony with the principles behind it. The implication is that emotional honesty, self-reliance, and commitment to an ideal can lead to reconciliation and social progress in a peaceful evolutionary fashion. Nearly all the CLE novels of this period reflect an ideological position that implicitly supports the government's national unity concept and contrasts sharply with radical critiques of contemporary Cameroonian society.

Works such as Charly-Gabriel Mbock's *Quand saigne le palmier*, Daniel Etounga Manguélé's *La Colline du fromager*, and Pabe Mongo's *Bogam Woup* typify this approach to the depiction of Cameroonian reality. All three writers blend traditional values with a psychologically plausible account of character development, and in each case the narrative culminates in the promise of a new social order to replace the disequilibrium engendered by some form of emotional dishonesty. For example, *Quand saigne le palmier* revolves around the relationship between the unjust chief Bitchoka and the upright farmer Lién during the colonial era. Before Bitchoka had become chief, he had tried to commit suicide because he could not face the shame of admitting his sexual impotence in light of his impending marriage. Lién saved him and introduced him to a healer who cured his impotency but not his infertility. Some time later, Lién agreed to make love to Bitchoka's wife so that the chief's lineage might continue into the next generation. To consummate the agreement, the two men entered into a blood oath beneath the sacred palm tree of Lién's family. Whoever betrayed the oath was to be punished (bled) by the spirit of the tree.

The drama in the novel arises from the conflict between the anxiety-ridden, hypocritical chief and the noble, emotionally honest Lién. As the son born to Bitchoka's wife grows older, his resemblance to Lién becomes unmistakable, and the chief finds it increasingly difficult to endure the humiliating rumors that circulate about him. Although his position endows him with power and authority, he fears that his weakness makes him unworthy to occupy it, but rather than admitting his vulnerability, he denies it, even to himself, and dons the mask of a self-confident despot. This pose leads him to act in ways that ultimately prove self-destructive. For example, believing he can escape his shame by eliminating the man who had saved his life and honor, he sends Lién to a forced-labor camp, where he dies. However, the chief cannot escape the anxieties that plague him, and when he steps on a thorn beneath Lién's palm tree, he develops blood poisoning and dies.

In contrast to Bitchoka, Lién displays an absolute integrity that stems from a determination to act in accordance with the values of his ancestors, whose spirits are embodied in the tree. Regardless of the injustices inflicted on him, he remains faithful to his oath and never reveals the attempted suicide or the chief's sexual incapacity because he feels bound to act as his ancestors would have wanted him to act. For him, the chief is a symbol of tribal unity, and he has a moral obligation to support that unity. In light of the chief's harassment, he explains his refusal to protest by declaring, "I serve the village, not a man."[5] But when Bitchoka orders him to wrestle a man who represents the throne, Lién is placed in an impossible dilemma: either he fights according to his abilities and risks humiliating the chief, or he betrays his own values and allows the chief's representative to defeat him. He decides to fight, and although he wins, he incurs the bitter resentment of the chief, who avenges himself by sending Lién to the forced-labor camp. Yet even then Lién does not seek to escape his fate. His nobility lies in an unflinching honesty toward himself and his environment.

Bitchoka's dishonesty appears to triumph over this nobility, but through a stroke of poetic justice, Lién's values ultimately prevail. In the final scene of the novel, as Bitchoka writhes in agony with the infection in his leg, the young prince that Lién had fathered thrusts his spear into the last of the royal cocks, a decrepit old bird symbolically identified with the chief. At that moment, Bitchoka dies. Within the context of the story, his death is plausible on several levels. In modern medical terms, he died of blood poisoning. In psychological terms, his insecurity caused him to confront a humiliating reality by seeking to maintain an illusion of power, but he was not actually in control, and his pride blinded him to the self-destructive consequences of his actions. And in terms of traditional belief, Bitchoka was justly punished by the gods for having broken a blood oath. With ironic appropriateness, Lién's son will become the next chief, and Lién's heroic example will inspire future generations. The moral order that was disturbed by the dishonest Bitchoka's elevation to the chieftaincy has been restored.

Quand saigne le palmier is not only about emotional honesty on the personal level, for the relationship between Bitchoka and Lién also constitutes Mbock's commentary on the nature of any polity. As one of Lién's friends explains, there are two sorts of people in the village: those who climb and those who form the ladder on which the others climb. Because the chief is traditionally among those who climb, he should make certain that the ladder is strong enough to support him. By ruling in an arbitrary and unjust manner, he weakens the ladder and places himself in jeopardy. The prerequisite for just government is the kind of honesty that Bitchoka experienced on only one occasion, the moment when he told Lién the truth about himself and swore a blood oath with him. All the rest of his life he is pretending to be someone he is not. This mask wearing is as detrimental to the social fabric as it is to the individuals who engage in it. When projected onto the society at large, Mbock's moral stance implies the need to reform government so that people can relate honestly with one another, and in his later *Cameroun: L'Intention démocratique* he claims that Biya created a political climate in which such relationships can flourish.

The spiritual basis for Mbock's ideal of emotional honesty becomes apparent in his second novel, *La Croix du coeur*. The central idea in this work is suggested by the Gandhi quotation he cites as an epigraph: "He who has reached the very heart of his own religion has reached the heart of all religions."[6] The novel itself depicts a series of conflicts that arise in the village of Song Mboua as a result of Christian missionary activities, but beneath these conflicts it is clear that those who believe in traditional African religions and those who adopt the new religion are pursuing the same truth. Difficulties occur not because one religion is wrong and the other is right, but because people fail to live according to the spiritual insights they could have obtained from either of them.

The most faithful Christian in the village is an old woman who yearns for the purity promised by the church, and her son becomes the new catechist at the end of the novel. Recognizing the arbitrariness of European assumptions about religion, he intends to build on the wisdom inscribed in traditional cult practices, for he regards his essential task not as the preservation of doctrinal orthodoxy but as a search for the divine and an attempt to live in harmony with it. *La Croix du coeur* thus culminates in the reaffirmation of a spiritual truth that can be reached by different paths. The point is that individuals who become aware of it will act in the emotionally honest ways that Mbock regards as crucial for their own well-being and that of the society in which they live.

But the Christians who established the church in Song Mboua did so in a spirit of confrontation with traditional beliefs, not in a spirit of reconciliation. They insisted that the villagers destroy their totems, and they built their church on a sacred hill to mark the triumph of the new religion over the old one. The nephew of the white missionary's assistant is named catechist and placed in charge of the local congregation. Despite his naiveté and his susceptibility to the temptations of the flesh, he recognizes the compatibility of Christian and traditional African beliefs, and he knows that people's material needs cannot be neglected in the search for spiritual perfection. However, the truly wise man in the village is the guardian of traditional cult practices, for he understands the nature of spiritual truth and lives according to it. When the catechist and the schoolteacher lust after the nurse from the local infirmary, he devises a solution to the social problem created by their illicit rivalry. In the end, the pious old woman's son marries the nurse, suggesting that the young couple will minister to the physical and spiritual needs of the village, but the crucial point is that their efforts will be based on a respect for the spiritual dimension of human life, a respect sanctioned by both Christianity and traditional African religion.

The emotional honesty of the hero in Manguélé's *La Colline du fromager* is linked less with spiritual truth than with the ideal of a country where people would be free to contribute their talents and energies to the construction of a better society. At the moment of telling his story, the European-educated engineer Ntam has decided to return to his village, where he plans to develop cooperative agricultural and small-scale manufacturing projects. When he originally returned to Cameroon, he wasted six months in the futile attempt to obtain a civil-service position, and although he detests the mind-deadening consumerism of Europe, he almost goes back because the corruption and social injustice of postcolonial Africa seem even worse to him.

Having just visited his village, however, he realizes that he doesn't need a high-paying government job to accomplish what he had hoped to accomplish. The communal values of the village have not yet been distorted by the materialism that is eroding the moral fiber of urban society, and the people there desperately need the skills he has to offer. If he succeeds in mobilizing the will of his fellow villagers, he can help them reconcile modern scientific techniques with traditional social values to form the basis for a happy and prosperous microsociety. His attitude at this point represents a model for others to follow, and the evolution through which he passes to attain it reveals how individual identity can be defined in terms of commitment to a social ideal.

As a schoolboy in Dola (Douala) during the final years of the colonial period, Ntam and his companions had been inspired by the heroic idealism of the national independence movement. All of them identified with the destiny of their country and vowed to work toward the creation of a free and just society after independence. Ntam himself was imbued with a desire to absorb the white man's knowledge so he could help his fellow countrymen regain their lost sense of dignity. But when independence is declared, many young men like him abandon their idealism and cynically accommodate themselves to the prevailing mores in a corrupt society. Others succumb to despair and take refuge in alcoholism. During this time, Ntam is studying in Europe, where he becomes acutely aware of his African identity, for even after establishing himself professionally and marrying a French wife, he knows he will never feel at home unless he returns to his native country.

He possesses the expertise that his country needs, but when he returns, he discovers that his credentials are less important than his political opinions and his willingness to bribe public officials. He also learns that he is no freer to discuss opposition politics than he had been as a schoolboy during the colonial era. The utopian dreams he shared with his schoolmates at that time had obviously failed to materialize. But Ntam's decision to stay in Cameroon is a profession of faith in the possibility of achieving that dream on a smaller scale. It is also a repudiation of ideology, for his example suggests that individual integrity and commitment are more important than abstract theory for the development of countries such as Cameroon.

Pabe Mongo's *Bogam Woup* also focuses on the transformation of mentalities that is necessary for development to occur in the country's rural areas, although the major obstacle he sees to such development is not the corruption and greed that reigns in the cities. It is the lethargy and superstition of the villagers themselves. Before writing the novel, Mongo had attended the Université des Mutants on the island of Gorée in Senegal—an adult education program that emphasizes self-reliance and a pragmatic approach to the solution of concrete problems. The influence of this experience on him is suggested by the novel's subtitle, *Allégorie de la mutation*. It is also apparent in the attitudes expressed by the fictive narrator, an educated semi-outsider who resembles Mongo in many ways.[7] His story is related in a tongue-in-cheek fashion, but he is clearly seeking to enlist his readers' support for the attitudinal change he would like to see occur in all such villages.

The events described in the first part of *Bogam Woup* set the stage for the dramatic confrontation that occurs in the second part. The village of Mbamais (the name means "metropolis" and suggests the villagers' inflated sense of their own importance) had settled into a lethargy symbolized by a giant baobab tree with its scarred trunk and stumps of branches. According to local legend, the god Mekouk Mpouomb had planted the tree before he created the rest of the universe. The villagers' belief that it embodied the essence of their spiritual existence enhanced the power of the chief, the sorcerer, and the catechist, who constituted an informal alliance that supported the existing social order and promoted the passivity it engendered. The catechist stood beneath the baobab to call his parishioners to services, and all important assemblies were held there. Someone had even attached a "metal parrot" (radio) to its trunk. The tree was truly "the heart of Mbamais."

The mindset symbolized by the half-dead tree was called into question by modernization, but until the arrival of the former soldier Bogam Woup, the ruling triumvirate and the apathy of the villagers had successfully warded off all attempts to introduce modern ideas. When the government sent a teacher, a male nurse, and an agricultural extension agent to instruct the villagers, there was an initial spurt of enthusiasm for their ideas, but the tempo of village life soon settled into its usual monotony, and the three representatives of modernity resigned themselves to their failure. Bogam, however, is different. A giant of a man who was decorated for valor during the government's suppression of a guerilla movement, he has returned to his father's village to carve out a peaceful existence for himself. He is not particularly intelligent and has no well-defined political opinions, but he regards traditional superstitions with skepticism, and he uses modern techniques to build an impressive house and lay out flourishing gardens. Most of the villagers scorn his accomplishments as being "against nature and, above all, against custom." Nevertheless, like the idealized father in Mongo's novella *Tel père quel fils*, Bogam disregards the opinions of others because he believes in the work ethic.

The chief, the sorcerer, and the catechist might have allowed him to pursue his idiosyncratic way in such matters, but when he dismisses their taboos or intervenes in legal affairs involving the authority of polygamous husbands, he is threatening their source of power, and they decide to teach him a lesson by casting a spell on him. Actually, the sorcerer shoots a small pellet with a poisonous insect into Bogam's neck, and the former soldier falls seriously ill. For a moment, the forces of lethargy and superstition seem to prevail, and people expect Bogam to become more submissive. Instead, he becomes a local hero when he throws two gendarmes out of his adoptive wife's bar after they attempt to harass the villagers gathered there. As the first part of the novel ends, Bogam and the ruling triumvirate of Mbamais remain on equal footing with regard to the appeal of the positions they represent.

The second part of *Bogam Woup* relates the former soldier's victory over his adversaries. Because Bogam can speak French and is respected by the people in the area, the government appoints him administrative chief and charges him with translating official directives into a language the villagers can understand. However, he lacks any real understanding of development policy, and when he tells the people how they can liberate themselves by renouncing sorcery and superstition, they merely gaze at him in uncomprehending amazement.

Since his limping rhetoric fails to have the desired effect, he devises a stratagem that does succeed in transforming mentalities by appealing to existing belief structures. He engages two men who dress like marabouts, enter the village surreptitiously, and direct the people in quasi-traditional ceremonies that culminate in the felling of the baobab tree, the deaths of seven old people linked with sorcery, and the ritual purgation of the entire village. When Mbamais is declared free of sorcery, the people feel as if a burden has been lifted from them. They celebrate and adopt new attitudes toward themselves. What Bogam was unable to do with words, he has achieved through trickery. Pragmatically, he uses the villagers' belief in superstition and their identification with the tree to wean them from their outmoded attitudes.

As a result of Bogam's ruse, Mbamais experiences a rebirth. However, liberation from superstition is only the first step toward development. As the narrator implies, the real motivation for change will be the villagers' own self-interest. Freed from the customs of the past, the people of Mbamais become tolerant of individual differences. They no longer insist that everything remain as it always had been, and they no longer object when some villagers acquire possessions that others are unable to enjoy. One of the villagers buys a bicycle. Another purchases a radio. Still another uses his savings to put a corrugated metal roof on his house. What promises to transform the village is the materialistic individualism that so many Cameroonian writers have decried as the primary source of corruption in contemporary Africa. In contrast to them, Pabe Mongo regards the rational pursuit of self-interest as the key to development, rather than as a cancer that is eroding the country's moral fiber. By linking Bogam with this mentality, Mongo demonstrates that individual self-definition can sustain the nation-building effort, even when the person involved is not fully conscious of the role he is playing.

The theme of reconciliation was a dominant motif in novels published by CLE during the 1970s and 1980s—reconciliation between Christianity and African religions, between tradition and modernity, between the older generation and the younger one. It was a central structuring principle in works by Mbock, Manguélé, Mongo, and Francis Bebey. It also lies at the heart of Etienne Yanou's *L'Homme-dieu de Bisso* and Samuel Mvolo's *Les Fiancés du grand fleuve*, both of which illustrate how Christianity and traditional beliefs can be synthesized into a modern African identity based on emotional honesty and a respect for individuality. Like many other CLE novels, *L'Homme-dieu* and *Les Fiancés* reflect the impact of missionary Christianity upon the concept of self-definition among literate Cameroonians, particularly with regard to the emphasis they place on love and hope as the agents of reconciliation.

In the first part of both novels, an African construction of the world nearly prevails over Christian assumptions, but the balance is redressed in the second part as the limitations of a traditional world view become apparent. Both end in a Christian marriage that symbolizes the reconciliation of positions that had previously been regarded as incompatible. For example, *Les Fiancés* is the story of a fantastic journey that passes through jungle swamps and evolves into a love idyll. Although the adventure itself took place in the early 1940s, it is being told after independence by Sondo, the man who experienced it and subsequently became a legend in the community for his integrity as well as for the love that unites him with his wife, Tonia. Despite the injustices of the colonial era, he and Tonia had developed a viable sense of identity by repudiating superstition and by relating to others in a spirit of emotional honesty. Their successful integration of African and Christian beliefs into a modern self-concept is presented by Mvolo as a model to be emulated by younger people in the postcolonial period.

The process that culminates in Sondo's mature personality occurs in two movements. The first is like an initiation rite that tests his courage and manliness. Having entered the swamp area of the upper Nyong River to collect latex for the French war effort, he becomes lost and traverses a series of islands, where he confronts a nightmare reenactment of the various stages in human life. To prove his worthiness, he must demonstrate self-reliance and an ability to overcome the horror of, for example, falling into a mudhole where a boa is eating an antelope. It is as if he has to gaze upon the land of the dead without losing his sense of reality. Buoyed by his Christian faith and his boy scout training, Sondo does not despair. His strength of character prevails over all the ordeals to which he is subjected.

The reward for his perseverance is a reunion with the young Tonia, whom he had known before she disappeared and presumably drowned at the age of five. Actually, her uncle had taken her from the village to protect her from the chief's wives, who were jealous because Tonia's mother had become the chief's favorite. The uncle himself had been unjustly treated by the villagers, so he withdrew with his niece to an island paradise in the middle of the swamp. When Sondo reaches their asylum, the uncle is dying, but he did not live in vain, for he has formed the young woman's character by inculcating her with Christian virtues; in fact, she is like a tree that grew from the seed he planted. After his death, the two young people return to the village and are reintegrated into the society there. Having undergone a spiritual journey during which they learned enough about themselves and the world to live virtuously and peacefully, the two of them exemplify the possibility of self-realization. By the end of his narrative, Sondo has reconciled traditional African wisdom with the values of his Protestant upbringing. He is, in other words, a modern individual with a Christian sense of moral responsibility.

If *Les Fiancés* is a naive fantasy, *L'Homme-dieu* is the realistic account of a confrontation between traditional religious practices and Christianity in a village that, Yanou implies, needs both in the attempt to realize its potential for spiritual and material development. At the beginning of the novel, local cult values seem to have triumphed over the faith of the Catholic congregation in the village of Bisso, for the well-intentioned Father Voulana, who grew up there, finds himself in an empty church at a time when the usually popular Christmas Eve services should be taking place. In preparation for a ceremony during which the village elders will name a new man-god, they have announced that a man-panther is roaming the area, and Voulana's parishioners have elected to stay home.

In reality, the ceremony is part of the elders' plan to counteract population declines and social disorders that they attribute to the felling of the community's sacred tree by the European owner of a local lumber company and to the Christian practices that incline people to neglect their duties to the ancestors. The traditional rites prove to have a salutary effect on the village, and Voulana himself participates in a ritual purification after he inadvertently pollutes himself by touching a taboo corpse. As word of the man-god's powers spread, people stream toward Bisso in hopes of obtaining miraculous cures or magical powers, and the village prospers, but when desires for money and power replace communal well-being as the primary motivation behind the man-god's presence, the meaning of traditional religious practices is distorted.

Furthermore, the reign of the man-god constitutes a masquerade that is difficult to sustain. In fact, the man-god is actually the young villager Men'Si, and unlike a real god, he experiences the need for human companionship. Tired of being manipulated by the elders, he abandons his throne, takes refuge with Voulana, and eventually marries the young Christian woman who cared for him when he fell ill. What appeared to be a defeat for Voulana at the beginning of the novel is transformed into his triumph, for he converts the symbolic representative of traditional cult practices into a member of his congregation. However, within the context of the entire story, Yanou demonstrates how traditional ideas such as communal solidarity and purification can be reconciled with the modernizing, universalistic thrust of Christianity. The renewal of Bisso required a return to traditional roots, but as the ending implies, this return can best be achieved under the aegis of a Christianity that proclaims the power of love and the human dimension of individual identity.

The traditional ceremonies in Bisso are initially successful because they respond to deep-lying psychological needs. Any community that hopes to recover a lost vitality must find some way of renewing its faith in its collective symbols, and such a renewal can take place only if the disabling emotions of guilt and mistrust are purged from the consciousness of the group. The dedication of a new sacred tree and the naming of a man-god effectively reestablish belief in symbols that had lost their power as people increasingly adopted European values and migrated to the cities. By eating together and by mourning all those who have recently died, the villagers ritually acknowledge their common past and reaffirm their solidarity with each other. Public confessions eliminate the tensions and anxieties that had prevented them from acting freely upon generous impulses. Even the white lumber company owner, his wife, and his son gain insight into themselves and reconcile their differences as a result of their contact with the new spirit of Bisso. And Voulana's purification enables him to integrate himself into the community in a new way because he has finally undergone the equivalent of a traditional initiation.

Yet traditional practices are not by themselves sufficient to sustain the development of the village. Because they can be exploited for personal profit, they prove vulnerable to corruption, and because they are based in part on outmoded superstitions, they often prevent people from approaching the problem of development in a pragmatic fashion. Furthermore, the story of Men'Si demonstrates the validity of the Christian principle that, although human beings can participate in a communion with the divine, they can never supplant God. Like Mbock's *Croix du coeur*, Yanou's *L'Homme-dieu* reaffirms the possibility of synthesizing a new African identity from traditional religious beliefs and Christianity. Because the reconciliation depicted in their novels parallels the thrust of Ahidjo's national unity concept, CLE's bias in favor of such works certainly conformed to the spirit of the government's cultural politics.

As larger numbers of women pursued higher levels of education in Cameroon, they became increasingly aware of the inequities they suffered. Within the context of modernization, they too were beginning to conceive of themselves as autonomous individuals with the right to forge their own identities. The government minister Delphine Zanga Tsogo gave voice to these aspirations in her two novels, *Vies des femmes* and *L'Oiseau en cage*. For Zanga Tsogo, feminism implies both a more intense awareness of female individuality and a heightened solidarity among women. Each of her novels focuses on the life of a woman who achieves insight into this imperative by reflecting upon her own experiences and by comparing them with the experiences of other women whom she encounters. The simulated autobiographies of these women are important for two reasons: they record the unique sensibilities of individual people, and they reveal characteristic features of women's lives in contemporary

Africa. Zanga Tsogo's implicit thesis is that men as well as women need to realize that dominant attitudes and prevailing social institutions must be changed if Africans are ever to enjoy the fullness of their own humanity.

She develops this thesis by showing how such attitudes and institutions distort the lives of women. For example, in *L'Oiseau en cage*, the central character, Ekobo, is a brilliant pupil who dreams of creating an existence for herself, but her father, who desires a high bride-price to recompense him for the "investment" he made in her education, has no qualms about marrying her at a young age to a man she does not know. The situation of her mother and her grandmother had been even worse, for they grew up in an era when women did not attend school and had no protection against arbitrary treatment by men. The attitude behind this situation is clearly expressed by Ekobo's uncle when he objects to her schooling because "woman is made for working in the fields, having children, and feeding a family."[8] As long as women remain subject to social institutions premised on assumptions of their instrumentality, they will continue to be frustrated in their attempts to realize their potential.

The story of Dang in *Vies des femmes* illustrates the same point from a different perspective. She too had wanted to pursue her education, but after a young man seduces her and flees when she becomes pregnant, she finds herself at the mercy of a succession of lovers who use her for their own purposes and then discard her. Scarred by her previous experiences and burdened with several children, she cannot even accept the genuine love that is offered to her by a young man from the village where she has obtained a position as social welfare worker. In the context of contemporary Cameroonian society, women such as Dang are placed before an impossible alternative: either they accept relationships on the humiliating terms sanctioned by a corrupt system, or they maintain their independence by renouncing the promise of romantic happiness. As in *L'Oiseau en cage*, Zanga Tsogo uses the story of Dang and other women in *Vies des femmes* to expose the true nature of a male-dominated society and its effects on women.

One of the most invidious of these effects is the way it conditions women to accept their own subservience. As Ekobo realizes when her husband begins to live with another woman and gives her barely enough money to feed the children, she had always been conditioned to obey. Her parents, her education, traditional customs, the legal system, and even the church assume that women ought to be subordinate to men. As her mother tells her when she protests her father's intention to marry her to a man she does not know, "it's not a question of loving. You have to obey. You don't belong to yourself, and you don't have any say in the matter. Your father is the master, and your duty is to obey. For us, things have always been this way."[9] Such resignation in the face of arbitrary male dominance was also inculcated into Dang in *Vies des femmes*, and it is, according to Zanga Tsogo, the real prison that prevents women from becoming what they are capable of becoming.

To break out of this prison, she believes, women must first become aware of their own situation and then assume responsibility for changing it. Dang and Ekobo are exemplary characters in the sense that they achieve this insight and act upon it. Even at an early age, both instinctively resented the system that denied them any opportunity to realize the potential they felt inside themselves, but at that time they were too unsure of themselves not to comply with its demands upon them. Later, however, their resolve is strengthened when they obtain jobs and meet other women. By giving them a sense of purpose in life, the jobs reassure them of their own self-worth. Their encounters with other women show them that the injustices inflicted on them are part of a much larger system that can be changed only if women themselves insist on changing it.

As these two women look back upon their own lives, they comprehend what has happened to them, and they proclaim their right to make their own decisions in the future. Ekobo explains succinctly that she and women like her "only ask to be recognized as human persons, to belong to ourselves before belonging to others."[10] Both novels culminate in an atmosphere of hope. Neither Dang nor Ekobo has yet succeeded in reconciling the romantic love for which they yearn with the independence they have forged for themselves, but their heightened consciousness makes such a reconciliation possible for the first time.

An essentially modern preoccupation with the evolution of the individual self is characteristic of most novels published by CLE during the 1970s and 1980s. In some of them, such as Lydie Dooh Bunya's *La Brise du jour* and Patrice Etoundi M'Balla's *Lettre ouverte à Soeur Marie-Pierre*, this preoccupation becomes the major center of focus. Both novels are simulated autobiographies in which a narrator recounts previous experiences to gain perspective upon them. In each case, the narrator has suffered disappointment or disillusionment, but an emotionally honest account of what he or she felt at the time reflects the underlying assumption that a written record of the unique individual personality is worth preserving.[11]

Although Dominique Akoa's *Survivances du clocher* was not published by CLE, it provides an excellent example of the motivation behind much of the simulated autobiographical fiction that was. The "survivances" (survivals, relics) in the book's title refer to the narrator's childhood memories of his parents' village and to the valuable lessons he gleaned from his visits there. By reconstructing these memories, he preserves a personal history that remains important to him because it contributed to his present identity. And by relating this history to others, he projects himself as a man who has carefully winnowed the traditions of his people, separating the wisdom they contain from the ignorance in which they are often embedded. The important point is that these "survivances" exist in the mind of a particular individual who perpetuates his own self-image by recording them.

This same motivation colors the narrating Zinnia's account of her idealized love for her cousin Pat in Dooh Bunya's *La Brise du jour*. The memory of her disillusionment with him is still painful, but although he proved unworthy of the love she offered him, she knows that her own life was decisively shaped by her relationship with him, and she tells her story partly to understand how she has become the person she is. At the same time, she believes there is something valuable in her capacity to love and to transform reality into an idyllic dream. Convinced that her naive but emotionally honest sentiments were betrayed, she also tells her story to justify her image of herself as a sensitive, morally pure soul who was deceived by appearances and her own yearning for love.

Zinnia's childhood predisposed her toward her romantic idealization of Pat. Her own parents had divorced when she was a small child, and after the death of her grandfather, she felt the need for an intense personal relationship that would enable her to escape the solitude and despair she felt inside herself. As a good student and a voracious reader of European literature, she had internalized Western assumptions about romantic love and individual freedom. Modeling her feelings for Pat on what she had read in books, she believed she had the right to choose her own husband, even if such a step would oblige her to defy a Douala taboo against marriage between cousins. Besides, Pat knew how to play upon her romantic sensibility. He called her "Aurora" and participated in a regular exchange of letters, even though they lived in the same neighborhood. A devout Protestant, she fully intended to preserve her chastity until marriage; however, the distance she maintained between herself and Pat was also a precondition of her love for him. If she approached him too intimately, she would realize that he did not correspond to her idealized image of him, and she desperately wanted to believe in this image because it validated her romantic conception of herself.

However, this self-imposed blindness prevents her from recognizing Pat's incapacity to play the role she has envisaged for him. His repeated infidelities and his insensitivity toward her feelings lead to the breakup of their relationship on several occasions, but having defined herself in terms of a grand passion, she cannot renounce her idealized image of him without losing a part of herself. Whenever he renews his pledge of undying love, she represses her doubts and accepts his words at face value. This pattern of rupture and return is repeated several times, but Zinnia herself never wavers in her fidelity to the romantic conception she has created for herself.

After a series of further betrayals, she finally accepts the fact that Pat is unworthy of the emotions she has invested in him. The incident that enables her to free herself from her obsession with him occurs shortly before his marriage to another woman. When he nonchalantly tries to seduce her, she realizes that he looks upon her just as he would have looked at a prostitute. This insight enables her to realize that their love had existed largely in her own mind. "It was a beautiful idyll," she concludes.[12] By the end of the novel, she knows that Pat is unworthy of her love, but she refuses to repudiate the idea of romantic happiness, which she regards as a liberating possibility for African women. *Brise du jour* thus recounts the maturation experience of a young woman who perceives the naiveté of her previous behavior but reaffirms the romantic and religious values upon which this behavior was based.

Like Dooh Bunya's novel, Etoundi M'Balla's *Lettre ouverte à Soeur Marie-Pierre* is the story of a narrator whose identity has evolved in response to a tension between his romantic image of himself and a world that denies the validity of this image. The narrating Joseph in *Lettre ouverte* resembles Zinnia in the sense that he too focuses on his failure to establish an emotionally honest relationship with a person whom he had transformed into an idealized love object. He tells his story in the form of an open letter to the woman, Pauline, after she has renounced the world and entered a convent under the name Sister Marie-Pierre. As in *Brise du jour*, the primary structuring principle in Etoundi M'Balla's novel is the coherence of the process that culminates in the identity of the mature narrator. Joseph reflects on the meaning of his experiences partly because he desires to preserve a record of his own life and partly because he feels compelled to justify himself in the light of events that others might consider shameful.

The self-justificatory dimension of Joseph's narration is undercut, however, by his inadvertent revelations of character flaws that prevent him from achieving the happiness he had envisioned for himself. For example, in seeking to project a favorable image of himself, he idealizes the love that had supposedly united them. "You and me," he writes, "we are pure beings, without falsity and cleansed of all sin, because together we savored a true love, as violent as the storms of November and as tender as the forgiveness of a friend."[13] In light of the story he tells, it is apparent that he and Pauline were hardly "pure beings," and the sentimental clichés he employs to characterize their "true love" merely obscure the fact that the two of them never succeeded in communicating their feelings to each other. In fact, Joseph's attempt to cloak their aborted relationship in idealized terms provides a further illustration of the blindness he has inflicted on himself by adopting a romantic self-image that beguiles him into misconstruing his own reality.

Aware that readers of his "open letter" might blame him for his behavior toward Pauline, Joseph attempts to exculpate himself by suggesting that right and wrong are relative values. "Crime in itself does not exist," he claims. "Crime is created solely by our own conscience or, more often, by the conscience of the society in which we are living."[14] As an abstract principle, Joseph's point is valid; however, within the context of his own quest for an ideal love, he would have to act consistently with the moral purity it implies if he expects to enjoy the reward it promises. Because he betrays this purity in his dealings with Pauline, he destroys the possibility of attaining romantic happiness with her, and the ethical relativism with which he rationalizes away his moral responsibility is a hypocritical pretense to avoid looking into himself for the cause of his failure.

Like Zinnia, Joseph developed an obsessive passion for a person whom he transformed into a romantic ideal. He saw Pauline for the first time when she was an adolescent schoolgirl and he was a student at a nearby seminary, but his image of her was influenced less by her actual identity than by his readings of European literature and his yearning for the absolute purity to which his religious education had introduced him. He fell in love with this image of unattainable perfection, not with her. He devoted entire nights to the contemplation of this image. He wrote poems about her, and on the few occasions when their paths crossed, he sought to impress her with his generosity and his piety, although he never told her of his love, and he felt pangs of guilt when his awakening sexuality plagued him with visions of her nakedness.

The psychological gratification he receives from his idealization of Pauline is the assurance that, if she is as pure as he imagines her, his love for her justifies him in regarding himself as noble. He needs to believe in her purity in order to believe in his image of himself. That is why he resists the temptation to see her in sexual terms. His dilemma is a characteristic one for the romantic lover: he yearns for union with the object of his desire, but he dares not approach it too closely for fear that intimate contact will disillusion him about the perfection he worships from a distance.

This syndrome governs their entire relationship, for Joseph can sustain his adoration of her only as long as she is not physically present. For example, he writes to her during the two years he is studying in France and even proposes to her through the mail, but when he returns to Cameroon, he refuses to consummate their relationship because he wants to regard her as a "pure being." His indecisiveness prevents him from communicating honestly with her. To compensate for his anxiety about his own inability to live according to his image of himself, he treats her in a cruel, spiteful way, and when his behavior drives her into an affair with a Greek merchant, he beats her mercilessly to avoid recognizing his own responsibility for what he interprets as her betrayal of his romantic ideal. At this point, she tells him that she has never loved him. Her words destroy the self-image of a man who yearns to believe himself capable of inspiring a perfect love. They also deprive him of the illusion that he is in control. In the wake of this incident, she enters the convent, and he adopts a pose of studied indifference in his relationships with other women because he does not want to suffer the same humiliation again.

The ending of Etoundi M'Balla's novel is ironically appropriate in the sense that Pauline's retreat to the convent allows Joseph to reestablish an unbridgeable gap between himself and her. Under these circumstances, he can once again believe in her as a symbol of absolute purity. Because she herself is no longer present to contradict his idealization, he can define himself as a noble individual who upholds its sanctity, and that is precisely what he does when he writes his open letter to her. Rather than question his own role in her renunciation of the world, he prefers to look upon her as a victim of the "intransigent cruelty of our decadent society."[15] What he fails to realize, even at the moment of telling his story, is that the principal source of decadence lies within himself and his inability to cope with real people in an emotionally honest fashion. By devoting herself to the religious vocation he had abandoned, Pauline actually comes closer than he does to living the moral purity toward which he aspires in vain.

As CLE published fewer and fewer titles, Cameroonian writers who treated the themes and subject matters favored by the Protestant-sponsored publishing house began to find other outlets for their work. Francis Bebey, Pabe Mongo, Delphine Zanga Tsogo, and others who had published their first works under the CLE imprint brought out new books with NEA. Writers such as Sévérin Cécil Abéga and Joseph Nkou began their careers with the Dakar-based firm, and others managed to find publishers for their work in Europe. Therefore, despite the decline of CLE, the preoccupations characteristic of CLE novels remained prominent in works by writers such as Nkou and David Ndache Tagne, whose *La Reine captive* was brought out by a Parisian publishing firm. Etoundi M'Balla's second novel, *Une Vie à l'envers*, is particularly interesting in this respect because it links the moral idealism of *Lettre ouverte* with the Biya administration's ideology of renewal. Printed on the government presses at SOPECAM, *Une Vie à l'envers* was extensively promoted by the *Cameroon Tribune* and other public media. Etoundi M'Balla himself was officially proclaimed the country's "best writer of 1987."[16]

The Cameroonian government's enthusiasm for *Un Vie à l'envers* is not difficult to explain. Beneath its utopian vision of a peaceful, harmonious society, Etoundi M'Balla's novel is actually a civic instruction manual that preaches docile obedience to the regime in power. Having returned to his village during the school vacation, the eighteen-year-old Balita is kidnapped by the spirits of the ancestors, transported to their world, and subjected to a trial. Although he persists in regarding himself as a prisoner who has been unjustifiably abducted from his home, the spirits treat him kindly and answer his questions with patience. Their real goal is to acquaint him with the truth about their world in the hope that he will carry this truth back with him to the world of the living, as he does at the end of the novel. The first stage in this instruction process is the trial. The second is a walking tour that he takes through the land of the spirits in the company of a guide. The primary focus of the narrative is on the exchanges that occur between Balita and the spirits, especially his guide, whose teachings often assume the form of a Platonic dialogue.

The novel's underlying message is communicated to readers in two ways: through the pronouncements of the spirits and by means of the perspective that Balita's "upside-down life" in their world provides upon the distorted values of human society—values that he had previously accepted without reflecting on their true meaning. For example, the spirits attach no importance to individual identity. They do not even have names, and because they do not fear death, suffering, or the passage of time, they recognize the folly of individuals who define themselves in terms of wealth or power. Committed to truth and communal solidarity, the spirits eschew polite formulas and the sophistical arguments that living people use to manipulate others, although they do engage in a sincere friendship marked by discreet smiles and frank laughter. Their straightforward logic is irrefutable, and in the sense that they are never obliged to do anything against their will, the spirits are free, but because their will is a function of their absolute commitment to the common good, they always act to preserve the well-being of the entire spirit world. In essence, they enjoy the freedom of choosing to obey what they cannot change and to do what is in their own best interest.

In this setting, Balita is less a prisoner than he had been in the world of the living, where people are hopelessly entrapped in their fears and petty aspirations. Yet despite his insight into the vanity of earthly things, he clings to the individual identity he would have to transcend if he were to live according to the wisdom of the spirits. "He didn't want to die," affirms the narrator, "even to enjoy freedom and truth without restraint."[17] According to Etoundi M'Balla, Balita's refusal to relinquish the satisfactions associated with individual identity will prolong his subjection to the illusions of the material world, but the point of the novel is that people can discover better ways of coping with these illusions. As a child, Balita had learned one of the songs that the spirits sing for him. This song announces a vision of peace and universal justice that provides people with clues about the sort of society they should be striving to create. Unfortunately, their attachment to the illusory satisfactions of individual identity prevents them from realizing the ideal they can glimpse in such ways. In fact, Balita's situation symbolizes the paradox of mankind's ability to envision a perfection that people feel compelled to pursue, even when they suspect it can never be attained.

Under these circumstances, a practical question remains: how should an individual like Balita behave toward the government of his own country? The response that Etoundi M'Balla provides is not entirely consistent with his idealistic view of the world, but it did prove congenial to the Cameroonian authorities because it lent support to their contention that citizens are morally obliged to obey the rules of a political system that has been created to serve their interests. The novel's implicit justification of this attitude exists on three levels: the wisdom of the spirits is presented as analogous to the Biya government's ideology of national renewal, the statements of the spirits explicitly sanction the practices of this government, and individuals are portrayed as being so powerless that any attempt to oppose the existing government would be futile.

If Balita's abduction parallels political arrests that have occurred in Cameroon, the kindness with which he is treated and the solicitude with which he is instructed about the "true" nature of reality suggest that the Biya government is similarly motivated with regard to the political prisoners it has taken into custody. Balita's guide even informs him that "people . . . don't really agree to live in peace and unity unless placed under a certain constraint, under the rule of a persuasive authority.[18] Properly understood, this authority will be exercised to promote freedom, justice, and dignity for all, but because human beings remain subject to worldly fears and desires, the spirits explain that tyranny will always seem to be present in the world of the living.

Nevertheless, they do propose two justifications for tyranny in human society. They regard it as an instrument employed by fate to assure that "everything happens in conformity with the superior and indefeasible laws that govern the order of the world."[19] Even the arbitrary imprisonment of Balita's uncle during the colonial period can be viewed as part of a larger evolution toward national independence. In addition, the spirits claim that tyranny is not as widespread as the critics of existing governments pretend, for it is often no more than the imposition of the constraints needed to assure the survival of a peaceful, unified society.

As Etoundi M'Balla makes clear, the role of the individual in such a society is to obey. The spirits repeatedly emphasize the powerlessness of individuals acting alone. They also insist that the efforts of artists and intellectuals must be channeled in the service of a "higher idea" that has been formulated for them by the government in power. Just as the spirits kidnapped Balita to make him aware of a "higher idea" about his own place in the world, Etoundi M'Balla suggests that the Biya government is intent upon inculcating in the citizens of Cameroon the "higher idea" of national unity. In both cases, the thought of rebellion against the established order is depicted as foolish and vain. "The only form of engagement you should choose," advises Balita's guide, "is to remain silent and to let things happen as they will."[20] Etoundi M'Balla thus defines political freedom in the same religious terms that he used in describing the spirits' acceptance of what is in their own best interest and cannot, in any case, be changed. *Une Vie à l'envers* is a clear example of how writers in the CLE tradition could focus on individual consciousness (the entire novel revolves around Balita's subjective responses to the ideas he encounters) while espousing the collective goals of the government in power.

In Joseph Nkou's *Edima* and *Le Détenteur*, the theme of reconciliation is specifically linked with the nation-building concept, but these morally uplifting novels also defend ideas associated with modern notions of selfhood—individual freedom, romantic love, emotional honesty, self-reliance, and the repudiation of superstition. An Adventist teacher, Nkou obviously shares the world view that characterizes most of the books published by CLE. For example, *Edima* revolves around a woman's attempt to choose her own destiny rather than have it imposed on her by others. Although there is considerable affection among the members of the title heroine's family, conflict arises when her father announces his intention to marry her to the wealthy vice-mayor of Mbalmayo. Everyone assumes she will obey her father's wishes, especially since most of the villagers believe their own prestige is implicated in the match. However, Edima has attended school, and she is convinced that marriage should be based on a pure, disinterested love that allows two people to assume responsibility for creating their own shared future. She also believes that people should be free to choose their marriage partners.

The conflict between these divergent views of her role is enacted in public when she is asked to take a bank note symbolizing the proffered dowry payment and either indicate her assent by giving it to her father or return it to the wealthy suitor. In front of the entire village, Edima opts for freedom and incurs the wrath of her family. Later, after fleeing from this intolerable situation, she returns, and the scene is repeated with the father of the man she loves. On this occasion, she hands the money to her father. The parallel scenes and the story in which they are embedded function like a parable for the modern world, illustrating that freedom of choice can be reconciled with traditional custom. In light of the fact that other young women from the village have committed suicide or become prostitutes as a result of being obliged to follow the wishes of their families in such matters, Edima's insistence upon being the person she feels herself to be is presented as the only viable alternative.

The world is changing, Nkou implies, and people need to change their customs in order to survive in it. Edima's pursuit of self-realization is better suited to assure her integration into a modern society than is the traditional concept of marriage. Yet she refuses to renounce her family and their traditions. She does participate in the second dowry ceremony according to custom. Her gesture reveals that tradition and modernity, love of family and individual freedom, are compatible when considered in a reasonable manner. The fact that she is Beti and the man she chooses to marry is Bamileke reinforces the theme of reconciliation and projects it onto the level of national unity. But Edima's most important insight is into the nature of happiness in the modern world of free individuals: "true happiness is not given as a gift," she says. "It is conquered. It is earned."[21] The moral behind Edima's success is the need to inculcate in people the conviction that they are responsible for creating their own happiness. This sort of self-reliance is of course a major tenet of the nation-building ideology.

Le Détenteur deals with another aspect of this same ideology—the need to eliminate harmful traditional practices without abandoning the valuable lessons that had been learned by previous generations. To perform this winnowing, Nkou believes, Africans must acquire a clarity of vision that never ceases to question its own assumptions. The character who possesses this clarity of vision in the novel is the schoolteacher Mambé, for when the villagers persecute an old man whom they accuse of killing young people by occult means, he realizes that their fears are causing them to treat an innocent man unjustly. Such fears also paralyze the village and prevent people from improving the quality of their lives by solving concrete problems in a rational manner.

Confronted by a legal system that prohibits the tortures they inflict on the old man, the village elders insist that they have the right to act according to their own customs. The motivation behind their resistance to modern legal thinking is comprehensible. They are convinced that their dignity requires them to maintain their traditions in the face of the humiliations they had suffered during the colonial period. However, Mambé realizes that no honor accrues to people who persist in following traditions that are harmful to them. According to him, they must select traditions capable of helping them forge a better life, and he perceives such possibilities in, for example, the healing practices of a medicine man whom he visits during the course of his story.

As in *Edima*, the ending of *Le Détenteur* affirms the possibility of reconciliation, for although Mambé's point of view prevails over the superstitions of the villagers, it is a point of view based on the assumption that a modern African identity can embrace both the scientific method and traditional cultural values. Individual identity is a central preoccupation in Nkou's novels, and his concept of it embraces Edima's idea of freedom as well as the intellectual penetration of Mambé; however, Nkou invariably defines this concept within the context of a larger enterprise—the construction of a national community in which the individual can feel at home. At least on a theoretical level, the Cameroonian government itself was promoting a similar message.

Ndache Tagne's *La Reine captive* is another moral parable that supports the nation-building ideology by demonstrating how individuals can positively influence history even under the most adverse circumstances if they work to achieve their own goals rather than blaming others for their misery. The well-known proverb "The goat grazes where it has been tethered" is cited several times in the book. Often misinterpreted as a justification for accepting bribes in contemporary society, this proverb is actually an admonition for people to make the best use of the resources at their disposal, even though these resources might be limited.

The heroine, Mangwa, adopts this attitude after being forced to become the fiftieth wife of the powerful chief of Bakamtsché (Bangangté) near Tishon (Bafoussam). At first, she is extremely bitter. As an excellent student and the daughter of a local catechist, she had imagined her future life as a free and independent individual, not as a captive slave who must toil in the fields and obey every arbitrary whim of her husband. "Poor me," she laments. "They've ruined my life."[22] Yet despite her misery, which is compounded by childlessness, Mangwa works within the limitations that have been imposed on her. She adopts the young son of a recently deceased co-wife. She creates a network of open-air schools, where she teaches French to adults and inspires them with the modern ideas she acquired when she was a student. Ultimately, her resistance to the injustice of the male-dominated social order in Bakamtsché obliges her to take refuge in Tishon, but her influence makes it possible for the village to become a modern, prosperous place, for her adopted son ultimately becomes chief, and his implementation of the ideas she inculcated in him is facilitated by the receptiveness of her former students.

The key to Mangwa's influence is her spirit of resistance. She does not accept the traditional definition of her role in society because she is not satisfied with the explanation that things have always been done in a particular way. If a tradition is unjust or ignorant, she sees no reason not to change it. Yet the chief and the majority of the villagers refuse to tolerate change, which they regard as a threat to their identity and, in many cases, to their privileges.

The rupture between Mangwa and the ruling hierarchy in Bakamtsché occurs when she is ordered to pay the exorbitant fees for her adopted son Foba's initiation into the secret society. She had projected herself into his academic success and dreamed of making him what she herself had wanted to become. Because she alone had been informed of the chief's decision to name Foba as his successor, she knows that initiation is the first step toward preventing him from realizing the destiny she had envisioned for him. Furthermore, the contribution demanded of her is so large that she could never pay it without going deeply into debt. For a long time, she had resented a social system that

places a disproportionate share of the work on women and accords a disproportionate share of the rewards to men. She therefore refuses to pay and flees
from the village just before the chief's men burn down her house to punish
her for defying the system.

During her life as a "captive queen" in Bakamtsché, Mangwa had always
recognized that development would never occur unless there was a transformation of mentalities. She envisages a time when people from the village will
learn modern farming techniques and adapt them to local circumstances, when
men will share the work with women and help create a just society where
no one is exploited for the profit of others. For this reason, she pushes Foba
into the study of agricultural engineering. But when she leaves the village,
her dream seems far from realization. The chief is more powerful than ever.
He even succeeds in thwarting the government representatives and European
engineers who begin to clear the nearby forest for the construction of a modern
hotel complex; however, his triumph is illusory, for he himself dies shortly
after a French engineer shoots his totemic lion, and his death marks the end
of a rigid adherence to traditional values.

One of the primary causes of social unrest in the Bamileke area during
the time of the UPC rebellion was the frustration of the younger generation
at being subjected to the authoritarian control of the elders. The opening scene
of *La Reine captive* illustrates the arbitrariness and injustice that often characterized this control. Not only is Mangwa arrested and forced to join the chief's
harem because she inadvertently violated a taboo space, but a prosperous, enterprising young farmer is exiled from the village and his property seized because
he has ostensibly practiced sorcery. The real reason for his banishment is his
wealth, which has excited the jealousy of the elders. In both cases, dynamic
young people suddenly find themselves thrust into misery. But by "grazing
where she was tethered," Mangwa prepared the way for peaceful change because her ideas shaped the mentality of Foba, who later transforms Bakamtsché
into the modern village she had envisioned. The relationship between his project and the nation-building ideology would have been clear even if he had
not specifically mentioned it.

However, although Mangwa's influence on Bakamtsché was positive, she
herself falls victim to the second great danger of postcolonial society—the triv-
ialization of life among the privileged class. In Tishon, she meets a successful
young doctor who declares his love for her. She obtains a job as a hospital
administrator, and when she marries the doctor, she lives in an expensive villa,
drives a car, and even becomes pregnant with the child she had wanted for
so many years. Yet this idyllic existence seems pointless to her. To her husband,
she admits, "I no longer know who I am."[23] In her despair, she aborts the
child and commits suicide. Ironically, her miserable life as a captive queen had
been more fulfilling than her comfortable existence as a member of the privileged class. Her resistance to the injustice of her imprisonment in the chief's
harem had given her a sense of purpose. What she lacked in her materially
comfortable life was something that many of the people of Bakamtsché still

had—the sense of belonging to a community that retained its links with the past. Foba acquires this sense during the initiation he undergoes before becoming chief, and by reconciling it with his stepmother's legacy of modern ideas, he forges a viable identity for himself and his village.

A modern sense of selfhood and the theme of reconciliation also feature prominently in the anglophone writing that gradually emerged after the declaration of the unitary state in 1972. Because school reading lists define the only assured market for books in West Cameroon, much of the literature from this part of the country has been consciously written for young readers. One consequence of this tendency has been a pronounced emphasis on the colonial past and a relative neglect of contemporary problems. The motivation behind this emphasis is twofold. West Cameroonian writers desire to preserve a record of their specific history as a way of defining their unique identity in the present. At the same time, they view the colonial period as a time of transition when African and European values came into conflict with each other, and because nearly all of them advocate a synthesis of these values, a focus on the colonial past helps them delineate the issues at stake in the present. A second consequence of their orientation toward younger readers has been the morally uplifting tone of their writings. In West Cameroonian fiction, for example, characters are often presented as exemplars of the moral idealism, the emotional honesty, and the spirit of self-reliance that the authors desire to inculcate in the minds of their readers.

The assumption that the unique individual life is worth recording for its own sake is apparent in naive fictionalized autobiographies such as Jedida Asheri's *The Promise* and René Simo's *The Little Gringo*, both of which defend the modern self-concept adopted by the narrators during the course of the events they are describing.[24] The same pattern characterizes Nsanda Eba's *The Good Foot*, which is even more explicit in presenting the emergent self of the main character as an example of what others might accomplish if they worked hard and persevered in the face of difficulties. Set during the late 1930s and early 1940s in the coastal plantations of western Cameroon, the novel is a success story that follows the young Mbamu from his childhood in the village to his graduation from the school he attended on a scholarship from the company for which his father worked after having moved his family to a plantation work camp. He had decided to seek work there after stubbing his right foot (a sign of good luck according to local belief), and in the sense that Mbamu's success results from his access to advanced schooling, the prophecy of the "good foot" did come true.

In Eba's novel, colonialism is presented as both an advantage and a disadvantage for Africans. On the one hand, the racist assumptions of the white overseers are demeaning, and the intolerable conditions in the work camps breed dishonesty, despair, and misery. On the other, the British attitudes and values that Mbamu assimilates at school represent an opportunity for him and others like him to overcome the ignorance that prevents the people in his village from enjoying the benefits of a self-aware life in the modern world.

Two assumptions make it possible for Mbamu to profit from this opportunity. The first is Eba's conviction that the world operates in a morally intelligible fashion, rewarding those who do good and punishing those who do evil. This view of the world is clearly illustrated by the reinstatement of Eba's father, who had been dismissed from his job after being falsely accused of stealing company property. When the truth emerges, his accusers are exposed as the true culprits and appropriately punished. The second assumption is that commitment to education is a virtue that will be rewarded in such a world. By weaving these assumptions into the fictional universe of *The Good Foot*, Eba encourages his readers to believe that their duty is to realize their potential just as Mbamu did, for they too will presumably be rewarded for their efforts.

Self-reliance and moral idealism are also major themes in the work of such anglophone Cameroonian novelists as Kenjo Jumbam and Joseph Ngongwikuo. Both of them set their novels in the past as part of an attempt to articulate a world view that respects the cultural identity of their own ethnic group while acknowledging the limitations of traditional behavior patterns. They believe that Africans can liberate themselves from outmoded customs by distinguishing between what is life-enhancing in traditional culture and what impedes progress toward an enlightened, equitable society. Like Eba, they view the European intrusion as a mixed blessing that brought both injustice and opportunity in its wake. Accepting the fact that the past cannot be changed, they use fictional narrative to make people, particularly younger people, aware of the need to synthesize a modern sense of identity from the European and African elements in their historical heritage.

The best-known post-1972 novel by an anglophone Cameroonian is Jumbam's *The White Man of God*, which depicts this challenge in terms of a young boy's struggle to comprehend the complex reality of a world that is interpreted in one way by European missionaries and in another by the adherents of traditional cult practices in his native Banso village. From the author's perspective, these practices are often compatible with Christianity, but young Tansa lacks the discernment that would enable him to reconcile them in his own mind. Nevertheless, as he naively grapples with alternative approaches to reality, the readers of his story recognize how a viable African world view might be elaborated on the basis of Christian love, openness to technological progress, and traditional values that give people a sense of their place in the universe.

Jumbam's books for children, *Lukong and the Leopard* and *The White Man of Cattle*, also invite readers to exercise their own independent judgment in drawing conclusions about the relevance of traditional and modern values to life in contemporary Africa. For example, *The White Man of Cattle* revolves around a British veterinarian's attempt to establish an experimental farm and to improve sanitary conditions in the Banso area; however, the villagers distrust his inoculations of their cattle and develop an irrational hatred of him. When a woman dies after having been accidentally bumped by his horse, the hostile reaction of the local population obliges him to leave the village. What remains behind is the abandoned experimental farm, a decaying monument to the villagers' lost opportunity for a better life. Similarly, *Lukong and the Leopard* reveals how the *fon*'s (chief's) prerogative to marry any woman he desires can produce injustices that threaten even the innocent children of those who defy him. In both instances, Jumbam assumes that readers will perceive the self-destructive limitations of the traditional world view.

This same intellectual penetration enables readers to discern the strengths and weaknesses of the various perspectives that Tansa encounters in *The White Man of God*. Tansa has been raised in the Catholic faith by a strong-willed, pious mother, but he accepts its doctrines in a vaguely superstitious way, although he is sufficiently attracted to the local religion that he participates in a traditional sacrifice. His mother is incensed at this lapse in Christian devotion, but his wise old grandmother is more tolerant, for she has two major objections to Christianity. She cannot understand why Africans should request someone else's ancestors to intercede for them, and she cannot believe that a true god would be so cruel as to condemn any of his children to everlasting punishment. Her skepticism influences Tansa and causes him to question some of the Christian ideas he had previously accepted. Despite her reservations, however, the grandmother allows herself to be baptized shortly before her death because she is attracted to the doctrine of love—the aspect of Christianity that, in the end, exercises the greatest appeal for Tansa as well.

The problem is that European missionaries did not always act in the spirit of love. As Tansa was growing up, there were two priests in the village. Father Cosmas was a true "white man of God" in the sense that he attempted to understand the people he had come to serve. He learned their language. He danced with them. He played with their children. And he introduced useful skills such as bricklaying, carpentry, and the rudiments of modern medicine to the community. In contrast, Big Father excoriates them for their pagan practices, imposes conformity to European ideas of decorum, and exploits their labor in building his new church. Supremely confident in the rightness of his own world view, Big Father fails to recognize the human values embedded in the traditional practices he attacks so fervently that he forgets the essence of the Christian message.

From Tansa's perspective, Cosmas represents the true spirit of Christianity, but his observations also lead him to appreciate valuable aspects of traditional belief. For example, when Cosmas falls gravely ill, Big Father refuses to allow the local healers to treat his fellow priest and sends him to a hospital, where he dies. Tansa remarks that the healers have often cured people with similar symptoms. The implication is that they might well have succeeded where the European doctors failed. Similarly, when Tansa's sister transgressed against a taboo, she underwent a purification rite attended by everyone in the village. Her sin was forgiven, and she was welcomed back into the community. For Tansa, the attitude behind this ceremony seemed far more reasonable than the idea of eternal punishment that his grandmother found so objectionable.

The latent conflict between Big Father and the village surfaces when the villagers mourn the death of Cosmas in a traditional ceremony with *juju* dancers. Infuriated at the pagan rites, the priest attacks the most powerful juju only to discover his trusted catechist beneath its mask. His self-assurance shaken, Big Father eventually leaves the village, but more important than his sense of defeat is his failure to realize that the collective identity of the villagers is based on their attachment to the land and symbolized by the *juju*. From an enlightened perspective, neither the *juju* nor what it represents is incompatible with the doctrine of love. In fact, they are closer to the essence of Christianity than is Big Father's ethnocentric condemnation of them. Tansa does not consciously integrate this insight into his own self-image, but his awareness of the situation makes it possible for readers to recognize the desirability of combining positive elements from Christianity and traditional belief systems into a modern African identity.

Like Jumbam, Ngongwikuo was imbued with the ideal of reconciliation. Everything he has written implicitly supports his belief that traditional and modern values can be synthesized into a world view that responds to the needs and aspirations of contemporary Africans. His children's stories as well as his novel *Taboo Love* focus on characters who assert their right to act as modern individuals with the freedom to pursue self-realization and romantic love. Although an awareness of individuality was intensified by the European intrusion into Africa, Ngongwikuo insists that impulses toward such an awareness existed in precolonial society and occasionally challenged the assumptions of rigidly hierarchical systems such as the one in his native Kom region.

In fact, *Taboo Love* is in many ways about the rise of the modern individuality concept in Mukomangoc society. Initially, two young people defy the system because they regard their love as more important than the laws of the tribe. They feel what others have also felt, but people are accustomed to repressing their sentiments on the assumption that the tribal laws are immutably inscribed in nature. Anyone who infringes on these laws is branded a criminal and subjected to severe punishment. But as Ngongwikuo makes clear, the laws of precolonial Mukomangoc support a tyrannical hierarchy that deprives many people of the right to a decent life.

The *foyn* (chief) is an absolute ruler who can conscript any young man into his service as a *chindo* (warrior, messenger, domestic servant) and any young woman as a *wintoc* (wife). His enormous retinue is entirely supported by the people, who construct houses for him, cultivate his fields, and supply him with game. In addition, the *foyn* receives substantial tributes from men who desire to build their own houses or wear honorific articles of clothing. To enforce obedience to this system, people who disobey its laws are poisoned and pushed over a five hundred-foot precipice. For most people in Mukomangoc, life is characterized by a lack of individual freedom.

The heroine of Ngongwikuo's novel is Iyafi, a young woman who would have married her childhood companion Jam if she had not been forced to become a *wintoc*. Before she enters the *foyn*'s bedroom for the first time, she visits her parents and takes refuge from a storm in Jam's house, where they consummate their love in defiance of the tribal laws. Both of them realize they will be put to death as soon as their secret is discovered, but they do not regret their action. As Iyafi explains to the *foyn*'s first wife, "I offered myself to love and die rather than to live without experiencing love."[25] Such a sentiment is anathema in Mukomangoc society because it places individual freedom above traditional order and therefore challenges the assumptions on which the *foyn*'s power is based.

The real issue in *Taboo Love* is the identity of people under the *foyn*'s jurisdiction. If the laws that define them as vassals of the *foyn* are inviolable, Iyafi and Jam are criminals who deserve to be punished for breaking these laws. But if people are autonomous individuals with the right to pursue the goals they set for themselves, the two young people are martyrs to an unjust system. After their trial, Jam is executed in an atrocious torture scene, and the pregnant Iyafi commits suicide rather than face death after the birth of Jam's child. However, their example sets a precedent. They did not act from the motivations that presumably governed all behavior in Mukomangoc—the desire for status and the fear of punishment. Their assertion of freedom remained alive as an idea in the minds of others who could no longer believe in the immutability of the tribal laws.

During the years that follow the young couple's death, the people of Mukomangoc increasingly disregard the laws and the *foyn*'s authority over them. The German colonial authorities and later the British restrict his powers over his subjects. A mission church and school disseminate modern ideas about individual freedom and identity. When the *foyn* and the elders conspire to regain their lost privileges by burning down the mission, they are prevented from doing so by the people themselves, for having examined the traditional social order from the perspective of their new identities, they realize that it does not serve their interests. The idea symbolized by Iyafi and Jam's resistance has spread through the entire populace, and by the time the village becomes part of an independent Cameroon, the people have already adopted the concept of individuality usually associated with citizenship in modern nations.

The literary productivity of West Cameroon lagged behind that of the East, but by the early 1980s, many of the same themes that dominated the portrayal of individual identity in francophone Cameroonian fiction also began to emerge in English-language works from the former British trust territory. Although anglophone Cameroonian fiction tended to be strongly marked by didactic purpose, it resembled work from the eastern part of the country in its emphasis on the individual self and its relation to a moral ideal that could often be related to the nation-building project. The values of emotional honesty, individual freedom, self-reliance, and romantic love are frequently linked with portrayals of the self in literature from both parts of the country, and the theme of reconciliation is a recurrent leitmotif in anglophone as well as francophone Cameroonian writing of the post-1972 period.

CHAPTER

19

THE CORRUPT SOCIETY AND THE SENSITIVE SELF
Literary Anatomies of Contemporary Cameroon

Among Cameroonian writers and intellectuals of the post-1972 period, there was widespread agreement that the promise of national independence had been compromised by the materialistic individualism that found exaggerated expression in the conspicuous consumption of the privileged class. Supporters of the nation-building concept regarded the greed, corruption, and favoritism fostered by this attitude as obstacles to the realization of their goals, whereas radical social critics interpreted them as reflections of values inherent in the neocolonialist system. From both perspectives, however, it was clear that the promise of independence remained unfulfilled.

Although the disparity between the government's official rhetoric and the reality of everyday life was apparent to nearly everyone, the existing socioeconomic system had become so firmly entrenched that people gradually resigned themselves to it. Under such circumstances, the sensitive self often served as a touchstone of value for the novelists and poets who came into prominence after 1972. They tended to regard the self as a repository of humanizing knowledge that illuminates the truth behind deceptive appearances and sustains the emotional honesty necessary to preserve decent human relationships in society.

One of the most trenchant commentaries on the corruption of contemporary Cameroonian society is Bernard Nanga's satiric novel *Les Chauves-souris*. The title is an allusion to the bats that dart through the gathering dusk each evening in Eborzel (the name means "bribery" or "corruption" in Bulu and designates Yaounde). In symbolic terms, these bats are the government functionaries who emerge at night and zigzag through the city in search of pleasure, status, and wealth. The fact that they enjoy their privileged lifestyle at the expense of the people is suggested by an explicit parallel between unemployed workers clustering around city streetlights and the swarming insects that the bats devour.

The bat metaphor draws attention to the rapaciousness with which members of the civil-service establishment pursue wealth and status in independent African countries. Success in such systems often depends less on merit than on the Machiavellian maneuvering by means of which careers are made and broken. The prevailing assumption is that anything can be purchased if one has enough money to pay for it. According to Nanga, this materialistic individualism is eroding the basis for trust and human decency in contemporary Cameroonian society, and he wrote *Les Chauves-souris* at least in part to reveal how it deforms the minds of people and denatures their relationships with each other.

If such a critique had been couched in general terms, the Ahidjo government would undoubtedly have tolerated the novel, but because Nanga caricatured identifiable individuals and touched upon issues that the authorities regarded as sensitive, the book was banned, and all copies of it were seized.[1] In actual fact, many Cameroonian institutions are satirized in *Les Chauves-souris*, where the single-party government proclaims its commitment to the creation of an earthly paradise under the benevolent leadership of the "Father of the Nation." The party itself is known by the acronym PDPUR (pure homosexual), a veiled allusion to Ahidjo's rumored penchant for sodomy.

As was the case in Yaounde at the time, the presidential palace in Eborzel is the former colonial governor's residence, and it symbolizes the graft and corruption that reign in the country. Adherents of the nation-building rhetoric exhort the people to work selflessly for the common good, while the privileged class flaunts its unearned wealth. A ruthless police apparatus suppresses all dissent. There are no medical supplies in the hospitals because the funds appropriated for them have been embezzled by government officials. Soldiers are called out to break a strike by the underpaid workers of a French entrepreneur who pays enormous bribes to the authorities and has no qualms about spending a million CFA francs during an evening of debauchery in Sansanboyville (Douala). In contrast, the penury of the disinherited is evoked by the madmen who wander the streets of Eborzel just as they do in Yaounde.

The major point of focus in *Les Chauves-souris* is the mentality of Robert Bilanga, a representative example of the African functionary who subordinates everything to his lust for money and status. In Bulu, the word *bilanga* signifies a maliciously inclined practical joker. It is also a play on the name of Eno Belinga, who served Nanga as a model for some of the character's principal features.[2] But Bilanga is far more than the caricature of a single individual. His approach to life is typical of the "bats" in countries throughout Africa. By offering an insight into the hypocrisy of such characters, Nanga demonstrates how the idealistic promise of independence had been betrayed by those who claimed to be defending it.

Bilanga is ambitious in the sense that he wants to be a "big man" in a society that respects only wealth and power. For this reason, the villa he owns in the Bordelchic (Stylish Brothel) section of Eborzel and the luxuriously appointed house he has constructed for himself in his village of Vémélé are essential to him. They are important in the same way his Mercedes, his influential government position, and his countless mistresses are important. Such symbols of wealth and power reaffirm his conception of himself as a man who can have whatever he wants.

In human terms, the cost of this reassurance is high, for Bilanga achieves it by becoming a hypocrite who relates to others solely on the basis of his desire to exploit them. Despite appearances, he is an empty, solitary man. He is loyal to the government because loyalty to the government is a prerequisite for social advancement, but he never reflects seriously on the real problems that the government of an independent country should be addressing. And he never experiences love or trust because he regards others—his mistresses, his son, his colleagues, his wife, his fellow villagers at Vémélé—as objects to be manipulated rather than as human beings with whom he can communicate in an emotionally honest fashion.

The result of adopting such an attitude is pain for others and anxiety for himself. The anxiety arises from his fear that there is nothing real behind the mask he presents to the world. It also reflects a suspicion that nothing he can acquire will ever really satisfy him. Occasionally Bilanga glimpses the truth about himself. As he watches his mistress of the moment dancing with another man whom he desires her to influence on his behalf, he drinks heavily and muses on the futility of his life. "It seemed to him he had gone through life like the wind that caressed and touched everything without settling on anything. And the moment he had wanted to hold on to something, he embraced nothing but emptiness. A many-faceted emptiness that was merely the reflection of the emptiness inside himself."[3] Yet Bilanga cannot bear to draw the obvious conclusion from such insights because it would threaten the image he has created for himself. Instead of questioning the premises on which his attitude toward life is based, he flees from any situation that calls this self-image into question.

However, he cannot always escape the consequences of his cynical behavior toward other people. Even if he represses an awareness of his responsibility for the suffering he causes them, they continue to exercise some control over what he needs in order to believe in himself. For example, when he is nominated for a seat in the national legislature, he believes he can buy the support of the villagers in Vémélé with gifts of money and food. But they have a long-standing grudge against his family because Bilanga's father had persuaded them to entrust their best lands to him so that he could construct a large cocoa plantation. Contrary to their expectations, the profits from the plantation were never shared with them, and Bilanga exacerbated the situation by building an ostentatious house in the village and refusing to help them in any way. They had responded by placing him under a form of social quarantine during which none of the villagers speak with him.

Although the government radio has promoted an idealized image of Bilanga during the electoral campaign, the villagers recognize his true nature. One of them had visited Eborzel and learned how he had betrayed his wife, his mistress, his son, and others whom he had used for his own selfish purposes. Thus, when Bilanga begins to harangue the people of Vémélé with the usual nation-building clichés, they confront him with his own dishonesty, and in the ensuing melee, a powerfully built villager throws him across the assembled crowd. He is seriously injured and loses his chance to be elected to the legislature. The villagers burn the truckloads of food with which he had intended to purchase their votes, and they disdain to pick up the money that fluttered from his pockets as he flew through the air like a bat. Life in Vémélé will continue much as it had before the election, and Bilanga will salvage his tarnished self-image by flying off to Europe after spending several months in the hospital, but the village has lived up to its name by ejecting him like a glob of spittle or snot.[4]

Les Chauves-souris does not end on an optimistic note. On the contrary, its harsh satiric portrait suggests that the corrupt mentalities of the bats will remain dominant and that poor villagers will remain poor. However, the satire in the novel is effective because there is an underlying belief in the possibility of emotionally honest relationships. The contrast between Bilanga's cynical self-centeredness and the generosity of his victims implies that a just society could come into being if people treated each other with love and trust. The villagers of Vémélé know that national independence has aggravated their misery rather than alleviated it, and they accurately place the blame for this situation on individuals such as Bilanga, "the false brother, the heartless man" who unconscionably pillages the country's wealth in the pursuit of selfish desires that can never yield true sastisfaction.

Others also recognize that this mentality is a primary cause of the malaise that afflicts the country. After Bilanga seduces and abandons his son's girlfriend, she commits suicide, and the son tries to follow her example in despair at his father's duplicity. At the hospital where his son is being treated, Bilanga offers the doctor a bribe, which is summarily refused because the doctor views corruption as a cancer that is eroding the people's ability to recognize the truth about themselves. And this ability is, he implies, a prerequisite for progress toward the better society promised by independence.

During the final scene of the novel, Bilanga's mistress visits his wife to return the key to a villa he had built for her. In unspoken accord, the two women glance at a retouched photograph of Bilanga and intimate their recognition of the fact that, beneath the image he presents to the world, he is a pitifully empty person. Yet, as *Les Chauves-souris* demonstrates, empty individuals threaten the cohesiveness of Cameroonian society. Whether or not they prevail will depend on the resistance of people, like Bilanga's wife and mistress, who possess the insight and emotional honesty to establish relationships on a basis different from the one he was offering them.

The moral condemnation of the privileged class in *Les Chauves-souris* also features prominently in works that offer a panorama of contemporary society.

Invariably, these works attack the mentality that precipitates people into the single-minded pursuit of wealth and power behind hypocritical masks of respectability. After not having published a major prose work for many years, François-Borgia Marie Evembe published a collection of short stories, *Les Morts . . . de demain*, in which he applied the psychological realism of *Sur la terre en passant* to a broad spectrum of everyday situations in postcolonial Cameroon. The motivation behind this collection is twofold.

On the one hand, Evembe desired to awaken readers to the horror of a reality that was gradually being accepted as normal. Each story in the collection focuses on lonely, alienated individuals who live in a nightmare world where no one can trust anyone else. Victims and victimizers alike are entrapped in this world because of a widespread addiction to "sociatine," which Evembe defines as "a substance secreted by modern society and consisting of the rape of conscience, the rape of minors, the theft of public property, honors coveted, power coveted, wealth amassed. . . . It is the pollution of human authenticity."[5] "Sociatine" is Evembe's symbol for the materialistic individualism that drives people to sacrifice their most decent impulses in the vain hope of achieving satisfaction in the frenetic pursuit of wealth, status, and power. By depicting the effects of this addiction on recognizable types of people, he is hoping that his readers will perceive its effects on their own society and repudiate its hold over them.

On the other hand, each sketch in *Les Morts . . . de demain* is an image in the author's mind. He presents that image as one might cite a proverb that encapsulates an entire world view in a single brief phrase. If this compression of significance is capable of triggering insight, it also expresses the character of the person who utters it. The working title of Evembe's collection was "Les Morts de ma conscience de demain," suggesting that each vignette bears witness to the fact that he, a unique individual, lived and created a poetic statement that endures. Just as the cry of a young peasant in "Monoko et son cri" reverberates like a siren through a nearby culvert and arouses the latent anxieties of all who hear it, Evembe is crying out against the dehumanized society spawned by an addiction to "sociatine," and he is hoping that his voice will evoke a response in the hearts of others. There are images of ugliness embedded in his cry, but it is not a cry of despair. It is one man's assertion of his individual identity, of his capacity to remain human in a society that rewards conformity to the values of a spiritually dead privileged class.

Similarly, Marie-Thérèse Assiga-Ahanda's *Sociétés africaines et "High Society"* is a semiautobiographical sketch that employs the description of a European-educated young couple's experiences in Pala (Yaounde) to unmask the hypocrisy and greed of the country's social elite. Both husband and wife are appalled by the pressures exerted on them to spend extravagantly as a means of demonstrating the status of their family. They are dismayed by the disingenuousness of those who snub them when they first arrive but court their friendship after the husband secures an important government position. Yet the worst feature in this society of "arrivistes" is the mentality according to which everyone believes it necessary, as one of the characters explains, "to wage a merciless war against his counterparts for fear of losing his job to them or simply for the pleasure of preventing them from enjoying the same possessions that he has."⁶ As in *Les Chauves-souris* and *Les Morts . . . de demain*, the dominant social attitude in *Sociétés africaines* is a profound cynicism that reflects a breakdown in public morality and a general unwillingness to engage in the emotionally honest relationships that give meaning and purpose to human life.

In such an environment, the young couple's love for each other and their vision of a better society function as positive poles of values that reveal the inadequacy of the corrupt attitudes they encounter, just as some of the secondary characters in *Les Chauves-souris* and the authorial voice in *Les Morts . . . de demain* provide implicit standards by means of which the bats and the addicts of "sociatine" can be judged. All three books are motivated by a desire to raise people's consciousness about the need for change if the promise of independence is ever to be realized. But unlike the radical critiques of contemporary society, they place less emphasis on the need for institutional change in a neocolonialist context than on the need for people to behave more generously and honestly in their dealings with one another. At the heart of their portrayals of Cameroonian society is a plea for people to respect the individual personality and its potential to serve as the basis for a genuine sense of community.

As these works indicate, the corrupt society affects individuals in two important ways. On the one hand, it distorts their mentalities in such a way that they become selfish, empty people. On the other, it makes them vulnerable to being victimized by others who have internalized its materialistic, individualistic system of values. During the post-1972 period, novelists increasingly focused on each of these phenomena in an attempt to illuminate the psychological crisis to which the individual self is subject under such circumstances. For example, Honore-Godefroy Ahanda Essomba's *Le Fruit défendu* and James Ndeng Monewosso's *Pris entre deux forces* depict the corrosive influence of contemporary society on the moral character of individuals who harm themselves and others because they have internalized its values. Works such as Séverin Cécil Abéga's *La Latrine*, Calixthe Beyala's *C'est le soleil qui m'a brûlée*, and Albert Mukong's autobiographical *Prisoner without a Crime* emphasize the fate of those who are entrapped in this society and condemned to suffer as a consequence of its callous disregard for their humanity.

Le Fruit défendu and *Pris entre deux forces* place the individual's dilemma in the context of an unresolved conflict between traditional and modern modes of self-definition. Blinded by their attachment to selfish, materialist goals, the central characters in both novels fail to recognize that their exploitation of other people is, by extension, an implicit denial of the principle according to which they themselves might expect honest treatment from the world. In their anxiety about the possibility that others might treat them as they have treated others, both Ahanda Essomba's Alima and Ndeng's Kamé become alienated, solitary individuals. *Le Fruit défendu* ends with an insight that enables Alima to purge himself of his corrupt mentality, whereas *Pris entre deux forces* culminates in Kamé's puzzlement. In fact, the final words of Ndeng's novel are "what is to be done?" However, in the background of both works is the implicit message that Africans should synthesize a new sense of identity from traditional and modern values without succumbing to the blind spots of either.

The origins of both characters' difficulties lie in their relationships with their fathers and with their fathers' villages. In *Le Fruit défendu*, the evolution of Alima's corrupt mentality is equally plausible when viewed in modern psychological terms or as a function of his disregard for the values of traditional society. Having amassed considerable wealth through questionable business dealings, his father lives in the city and distances himself from his village, although he takes Alima there shortly after his birth to receive the blessing of their relatives. Because the father had been overjoyed at the birth of his only male heir, he is extremely solicitous of the boy's welfare and, in conformity with his usual skepticism about traditional usage, refuses to allow the villagers to administer the customary herbal potion. They in turn express their premonition that an evil fate is hanging over the child. As Alima grows older, he has little contact with the village, and his father's indulgence enables him to develop into a brilliant, handsome young man who always obtains whatever he wants—clothes, women, academic success. He has, in other words, become an arrogant, selfish, modern individual.

Although Kamé's father still lives in the village, he too has prospered through dishonest business dealings, and he too is more concerned with his own prestige than with what might be best for his son. When Kamé receives a scholarship to study in France, his father opposes the idea because he and the village elders believe the young man already has the qualifications to obtain a job from which they all can benefit. In defiance of their wishes, Kamé goes to France, for he is convinced that a foreign education will assure him success in his own recently independent country. After two years abroad, he returns to the village on vacation, and his father imposes a local wife on him, despite the fact that he conceives of himself as a modern individual who should have the right to choose his own wife. He accedes to their wishes, but he also marries a French woman and brings her back with him when he returns to a highly paid government position a few years later. By this time Kamé has become thoroughly Europeanized, and he turns his back on his African family and their fellow villagers.

The "two forces" that pull Kamé in opposite directions are the expectations of the villagers and his own desire for material success in the corrupt society that has emerged in his country since independence. Neither force is unequivocally positive. The villagers fail to comprehend the conditions of life in contemporary society, and they hope to exploit Kamé's career for their own personal gain. At the same time, Kamé's preoccupations with wealth and status alienate him from other people and motivate him to deal dishonestly with them. Both forces lead toward unsatisfying definitions of the self in the modern world.

In *Le Fruit défendu*, the emotional dishonesty of Alima's egocentric self-concept becomes apparent in his obsessive passion for his sixth cousin Mengue Rose, whom he is forbidden to marry by local incest taboos. She grew up in the village, and the taboo was an integral part of her world view. Furthermore, her Catholic education inculcated in her the desire to preserve her virginity until after she was married. In contrast, Alima believes, like Julien Sorel in his favorite novel, *The Red and the Black*, that nothing lies beyond the grasp of his ambition. For him, incest taboos are outmoded superstitions, and romantic love should be the only criterion for determining whether two people are suitable for each other. Yet marriage is not his primary concern. He wants to make love to her, and her resistance merely inflames his passion.

Unable to control himself and believing he has the right to take anything he desires, Alima rapes Mengue Rose in a secluded spot. She is devastated, but she is also convinced that she has participated in a crime so heinous that she dare not tell anyone else about it. She feels polluted and desires above all to conceal her shame. Alima's self-centeredness becomes apparent in his response to the situation. He had never truly loved her. He merely wanted to possess her as a means of reaffirming his image of himself. For him, she is merely the forbidden fruit to be plucked for his own delectation, and he is willing to flaunt ancestral taboos as well as the most basic tenets of Christian charity to pluck it. His lack of concern for her is evident in his threat to kill her if she ever reveals what has taken place.

The crisis in Kamé's life is less dramatic, but it derives from the same self-centeredness. After his return to Cameroon, he distances himself as much as possible from his village. He changes the spelling of his name from Kamé to the Europeanized C'Kammey, and he adopts a thoroughly French style of living. Yet his success proves illusory, for it is based on a set of false appearances that he has erected to avoid admitting the weakness of his own character. For example, when his African wife comes to the city, Kamé subjects her to a series of humiliations, but his French wife discovers the truth and leaves him. He loses his government position for having been involved in the sale of civil-service examination questions. Unable to find another white wife and learning of his eldest son's death in France, Kamé tries to commit suicide. From the pinnacle of success, he has fallen to the depths of despair.

For the people of his village, the only way for him to recover his equilibrium is to undergo a purification ceremony, but because he no longer believes in the efficacy of such rituals, he cannot subject himself to it. Lacking the force of character to shape his own destiny through individual effort, he also cannot overcome his identity crisis by realizing himself in modern terms. When the trappings of his success are taken from him, he is revealed as an empty, solitary figure with no real identity of his own. For Ndeng, Kamé's situation at the end of *Pris entre deux forces* illustrates the existential dilemma of Africans who have internalized the corrupt value system of the privileged class.

In *Le Fruit défendu*, Alima eventually realizes the sterility of a life based on these values, but only after he and Mengue Rose have been obliged to suffer atrociously. She marries another man, who beats her when she refuses to reveal the name of the person who deprived her of her virginity, but although she wins a legal suit against her husband, she remains adamant in her refusal to identify the man who raped her. However, when her parents convince her to reveal her attacker's name in front of the assembled villagers as a prerequisite for undergoing a purification rite, Alima drives furiously away from the scene and, in a form of poetic justice, loses his leg in a high-speed accident. Whether viewed as a punishment of the gods or as the consequence of a troubled psyche that compelled him to behave in a self-destructive manner, the artificial limb he is later obliged to wear becomes the symbol of his corrupt mentality.

But Alima achieves insight in a way that Kamé never did. As he lies in a hospital bed, Alima relives the rape, the trial, the village assembly, and the accident in a series of nightmares. Encouraged by his father's retelling of a traditional tale about a foolish young man's insistence upon entering a forbidden part of the forest, he recognizes the truth about himself and agrees to participate in the purification rite. In traditional terms, he humbles himself before the gods and reintegrates himself into the community. In modern psychological terms, he gains a new sense of equilibrium by accepting responsibility for the crime he committed. The reconciliation that occurs at the end of *Le Fruit défendu* is one of the most common themes in contemporary Cameroonian literature, and in this case, it serves as a foil by means of which the perversity of Alima's earlier corrupt mentality can be judged.

When writers such as Abéga, Mukong, and Beyala focus on the innocent victims of a society in which this mentality predominates, they draw attention to the implicit contrast between the sensitive self of an individual and the indifference or cruelty with which that individual is treated. The nightmare world evoked by these writers is the psychological equivalent of imprisonment in a society where individuals are regarded as expendable. By depicting the fates of such individuals, these writers shock readers into an awareness of the fact that such societies should not exist and can, in fact, be changed if people learn to interact honestly and compassionately with each other.

The cruelty of urban society in modern Africa is the principal theme in Abéga's *La Latrine*. Neither the five-year-old boy who falls into a latrine behind his father's house nor the older brother who tries to obtain help is identified by name, and their anonymity underscores the typicality of their plight. The salient fact in the story is that no one except the older brother cares enough about a suffering human being to expend the effort necessary to save him. In the final scene, after the older brother has stolen some rope from his father's shop and descended into the latrine to haul up his younger brother, all that he finds is a corpse. By the time other people arrive, he is sitting beside the black hole, cradling his dead brother in his arms and weeping. "Around their besmeared bodies," reports the narrator, "flies were singing songs of victory."[7] The victory of the flies is the defeat of the human. Everyone whom the older brother alerted to the situation had been too preoccupied with some petty concern to aid the young victim, and their indifference is an expression of the corrupt mentality that pervades modern society.

The dead boy's father is the principal villain in the story because he remains calmly in his shop while his son is suffering at the bottom of the latrine; he even regards the boy's predicament as an appropriate punishment for his disobedience. However, all the people who ignore the older brother's pleas for help must bear some responsibility for the younger child's death. Neighbors refuse to lend the rope from their well to assist in the rescue. Taximen won't take the boy to the fire station, and when he finally arrives there, the firemen pay no attention to him. After they reach the boy's house, the local administrative chief insists upon inviting them to a bar. Then they must intervene in a fight between the shopkeeper and his wife. The general lack of concern for the young boy's suffering is an index of the extent to which the sense of community has disintegrated under the pressures of the modern urban environment.

In this environment, the major positive value is the older boy's capacity to empathize with his brother. He had been ashamed when his father whipped his brother the previous day for playing near the latrine, and he was beginning to rebel against the shopkeeper's tyranny. In fact, he had discovered his brother's dilemma after he stole his father's whip and was about to throw it into the latrine. Later, he also steals the rope he needs to descend into the stinking black hole, but first he must appropriate his father's keys, and they trigger in him an insight that goes to the heart of the social malaise in contemporary Africa. In his own naive way, he realizes that, when people need locks and keys to protect their wealth, they are no longer capable of enjoying it. As in the short stories collected in his *Les Bimanes*, Abéga's novella focuses on people who are more concerned with wealth and status than with human values. These are the people who create an atmosphere in which the death of a young child can occur simply because no one cares enough to help him. As a parable for modern times, *La Latrine* shocks readers into an awareness of the unnecessary suffering that such an atmosphere engenders.

Mukong's autobiographical *Prisoner without a Crime* deals with the same corrupt society that Abéga, Nanga, Assiga-Ahanda, and Evembe were portraying. The crucial turning point in Mukong's life occurred in 1970 when he was arrested and transported to Yaounde. There he was placed in the same prison cell as the UPC leader Ernest Ouandié. He was never charged with a crime or brought to trial, but he spent more than six years in political detention camps, including Tcholliré, where Bishop Ndongmo served four years of his prison term. When Mukong was released, he had nothing. His wife had left him, his friends feared to be seen in his company, and he had no means of supporting himself. Yet two preoccupations sustained him. While in prison, he had begun to write about his own experiences in thinly veiled fictional form, and he had become a devout member of a Catholic group committed to universal reconciliation. Years later his writing efforts culminated in *Prisoner without a Crime*, and his religious faith provided him with a perspective from which to judge the society that had inflicted so much suffering on him.

Mukong's book has a dual focus. It recounts the inner evolution of a sensitive individual who discovers what he believes to be the truth about himself, and it exposes the corruption of contemporary Cameroonian society. It is not a radical critique of that society, for its underlying values are religious rather than political, but it does offer a rare glimpse of life inside the Cameroonian gulag, and this life is presented as a reflection of conditions in the country as a whole. For Mukong, the most important experience during his confinement was the recognition of his own spiritual identity. Rather than cowing him, his incarceration actually liberated him from a dependency on earthly vanities. When life was stripped to its barest essentials, he endured, and this endurance taught him that man's relation to the divine transcends all the corrupt forces that seek to subdue it. The self at the center of *Prisoner without a Crime* is thus presented as a touchstone of moral good in an evil society.

While interned at the Mantoum political detention camp near Fumban, Mukong realized that the prison was really a microcosm of this evil society. The prisoners who spied on each other to curry favor with competing administrators thought they could gain some advantage over the others, but like oppressed people everywhere, they were actually contributing to their own oppression by internalizing the corrupt mentality of their oppressors. According to Mukong, the only way they can liberate themselves is by repudiating this demeaning mentality and refusing to compromise with it.

Viewed from the perspective of the corrupt society, Mukong might appear to be mad for rejecting Ahidjo's offer of freedom and a lucrative UNC party position in return for a declaration of loyalty to the government; however, if the society itself is mad, Mukong's insistence upon integrity in the face of a dehumanizing lie becomes a mark of sanity. It is one human being's assertion of his freedom to maintain the truth as he perceives it. And the truth that he perceives is a government that murdered thousands of its citizens in torture chambers and imprisoned tens of thousands on political grounds. He himself had heard the victims of this system screaming in anguish, and he describes the instruments of torture in great detail. In the face of such inhumanity, he continues to believe that human beings can live together in love and mutual respect. When a society prevents them from doing so, it is, in his eyes, a criminal institution. In contrast with his own moral idealism and independence of mind, the repressiveness of Cameroonian society stands condemned.

Beyala's *C'est le soleil qui m'a brûlée* is an entirely different sort of book—the surrealistic account of a young woman's lesbian yearnings in a big-city slum. Nevertheless, the young woman, Ateba, is as much a prisoner of society as Mukong was. Abandoned at the age of nine by her prostitute mother, Ateba lives with her aunt and a long succession of her aunt's lovers. She herself feels stifled by the atmosphere of the slum. As a child she had dreamed of escaping to a life of opulence, and as a young woman she expresses her intellectual pretentions in letters to other women and to God, but her dreams remain unfulfilled, and her letters are deposited in the litter-strewn stream that flows through the neighborhood. In a promiscuous environment, she has retained her virginity, but she is haunted by the fear that no one really cares for her, and she yearns for sensual fulfillment. In response to such feelings, she takes refuge in a rich interior world where the exploitative hypocrisy of men and the ugliness of her immediate surroundings are absent.

Narrated by a disembodied spirit that watches over Ateba and becomes united with her in a final hallucinatory scene, *C'est le soleil qui m'a brûlée* presents the female self as the custodian of joy and love in a decadent society. In Ateba's eyes, redemption lies in the solidarity of women, and her entire life is a frustrated attempt to achieve union with them. Ever since her mother left her, Ateba has regretted that she never told her "I love you." She dreams of being with her mother again, of entering her and purging the pollution that countless men had deposited there. She also dreams of embracing her prostitute friend Irene and freeing her from the men who defile her body. Yet in the society where she lives, Ateba can find no way of satisfying her longing for purity. Repeatedly she undresses herself and caresses her own naked body, but her sensual reveries are invariably interrupted by the unwanted intrusions of an ugly, male-dominated reality.

Ateba encapsulates her view of the world in a legend she recounts to the unreceptive crowd of mourners assembled at the wake of her friend Irene, who has died after undergoing an abortion. According to this legend, women were originally stars in the sky, and they existed long before the arrival of men on earth. When men were created, they lived in misery, and women, taking pity on them, descended to the earth and comforted them. However, men proved treacherous, imprisoning women and preventing them from returning to the sky. In their sorrow, women wept for seven days and seven nights. Their tears formed the oceans. Ateba's point is that the consciousness of women originated in a state of harmony and must be liberated from its present bondage to fulfill its joyful destiny. She herself has dedicated her life to the quest for this liberation. When she says, "I have married the stars,"[8] she is affirming her commitment to womanhood.

Two obstacles stand between her and the realization of her dream—the dominance of men and the pervasive despair that expresses itself in the ugliness she sees all around her. In *C'est le soleil qui m'a brûlée*, men are portrayed as having produced this ugliness by their selfish pursuit of their own gratification. Men have distorted the lives of her mother, her aunt, Irene, and all the other women she has known. All the men she encounters seek to dominate her and force themselves on her. And their corrupt mentalities have produced the ugliness in which she feels entrapped. The slum where she lives was at one time the scene of a civil war, the ravages of which remain visible in the overcrowded, stench-filled streets. The people living there came to the city in the hope of finding a better life than the one they knew in the villages, but they found something worse. Everyone mistrusts everyone else, and just as the government paves a few streets and paints a few buildings to impress foreigners, the people of the slum mask the depth of their own despair behind façades of insouciance. They are, as Ateba observes, "ambulatory prisoners tied to their own filth."[9] She cannot believe that such a society is natural, and her lesbian fantasies represent her way of escaping from it.

The final scene of the novel depicts her attempt to translate her revolt into a concrete action that symbolizes her revenge upon men and the cruel, ugly society they have brought into being. She goes to the discotheque where her dead friend Irene had plied her trade and sells herself to a man for five thousand CFA francs, but when he attempts to force her into performing oral sex, she rebels and kills him. He is an accidental victim but a symbolic one, for in her mind he represents the male principle that has imprisoned her and all other women in a corrupt, revolting world.

As she walks away from the man's apartment into the rising sun, the spirit narrator dons her wedding dress and announces, "I am your soul."[10] By her violent act, Ateba achieves the union for which she has been yearning all her life, for after embracing the corpse as if it were Irene, she regains the sense of being at one with the stars and the seas that symbolize womanhood. The progressive consummation of a similar union provides the narrative framework for Beyala's second novel, *Tu t'appelleras Tanga*. The two protagonists in this novel are the French Jewish secondary-school teacher Anna-Claude and the seventeen-year-old black woman Tanga. Both had yearned for an ecstatic fulfillment of their female potential, but they were frustrated in their dreams by the corruption of a male-dominated world and by the anxiety of solitude. Only when they find themselves together on the floor of a stench-filled prison cell in the African country of Iningué do they succeed in sharing a love that enables them to transcend the despair of being trapped in such a world.

Even as a child, Anna-Claude had been painfully aware that her Jewishness made her an outcast in French society. Having studied philosophy and dabbled in the occult, she invented an imaginary African lover, Ousmane, and spent years looking for him. She had come to Iningué as a teacher in the hope that she would find him there, but she discovered that reality did not correspond to her dream. She was eventually arrested as a "subversive" when she wandered through the city carrying signs that demanded information about students who had disappeared, presumably into political detention.

In contrast, Tanga is a young black woman who experienced the nightmare of life in the slums of an African city. Seduced by her father and sold into prostitution by her mother, she continues to yearn for a love that takes on concrete form after an ecstatic encounter with Hassan, a man whom she refuses to regard as a customer, but Hassan is already married, and when she meets him again, he proves incapable of sustaining her image of him. To participate in the joy of a selfless love, she begins to care for a crippled young boy. However, he dies in her arms at a revival meeting, where the success of the white preacher's solicitation inspires her determination to acquire as much money as she can. A short while later, she is arrested for her involvement with a gang of forgers.

As the novel opens in the wretched prison cell, Tanga announces her impending death to the white woman whom she does not know. Anna-Claude treats the black woman's wounds, holds her hand, and entreats her to recount the story of her life. After Anna-Claude is beaten by one of the guards, the two women embrace on the floor, and Tanga's story flows almost wordlessly into the French woman until she herself can say, "I am Tanga." The merging of the two women's identities in the face of death, despair, and decay symbolizes the possibility of achieving the ideal love they had formerly associated with their illusory images of Ousmane and Hassan. Although Tanga herself has disappeared from the prison cell by the end of the novel, the meaning of her life survives in Anna-Claude's consciousness, suggesting that the love of women can transcend the ugliness of the prison world into which they have been thrust by the cruelty and indifference of men.

The meaning of Tanga's life is crucial to Beyala because it reflects the living death to which African children are born. It also helps explain the breakdown of the African family as a sanctuary for the love that people need in order to lead decent, emotionally fulfilling lives. As a child, Tanga had been instructed by her father to keep her eyes on the ground, but she wanted to raise them to the stars, for she aspired to something better than the filth that surrounded her in the city. Yet she was constantly being drawn into its depravity. When she was only six years old, her father made love to one of his mistresses in front of her; his insatiable lust drove him to humiliate his wife by bringing other women and eventually even his own daughter into their bed. Tanga's mother in turn took a man with an ugly wound as her lover and became obsessed with money that she hoped would help her ward off the fear of death. For this reason, the older woman pushed her daughters into prostitution. They were charged with obtaining the money that would save her. But money could not protect her from death, and Tanga suffered the profound solitude of a woman who had embraced hundreds of men without ever being able to offer them the love that she wanted to give. Her African childhood was desolate and empty, yet its texture was no different from that of countless others.

What distinguishes Tanga is her commitment to a dream of perfect love, to the inner spark that reflects the brilliance of the stars. She initially projects this dream into visions of a happy marriage with Hassan, but he cannot play the role she has assigned to him. Later, she enters into a relationship with a cripple who presides over a community of young thieves, but as she recalls the thousands of children growing up in a world without love, she knows she can never fulfill her lover's desire for a son. Vacillating between a desire to die and a wish to share her love with these deprived children, she visits a cemetery in the rain and symbolically plugs her vagina with mud, signaling her resolve to remain childless and her refusal to continue serving as the instrument of men's selfish impulses. She does find momentary happiness in her relationship with the young crippled boy, whom she allows to suckle her breast in a gesture that suggests the selfless giving she associates with her ideal. But the boy dies, and she momentarily abandons herself to the pursuit of money.

Only in the prison cell with Anna-Claude is her dream fulfilled in the ecstasy of complete union with another person.

The fact that her story does not die with her but survives in Anna-Claude's consciousness suggests both the power of women's love for each other and the possibility that others will also take cognizance of the horrors routinely inflicted upon children in Africa's urban slums. Tanga herself empathized with all those who had been alienated from life, and her adoption of the crippled boy reflects her intention to share her dream of love with them. "The world is broken," she laments. "It needs to be glued back together."[11] Her generosity is a small step toward repairing this world. It is also a part of her attempt to transcend her destiny by making it correspond to her vision of what it should be. Her allegiance to this vision in the face of dehumanizing pressures bears eloquent testimony to the enduring spirit of womanhood. Although Beyala's lesbian approach to the reality of contemporary Cameroon is unusual within the context of the country's literate culture, it is not altogether different from the methods adopted by Mukong and Abéga, for it too juxtaposes the sensitive self with the corrupt society to expose the malaise that afflicts countries such as Cameroon.

The tension between the sensitive self and the corrupt society also characterizes much of the Cameroonian poetry that has been published since 1972. This poetry serves as a vehicle for recording the uniqueness of the individual poet's sensibility while at the same time offering the poet's emotional honesty as a touchstone of value in a society where the moral fabric has been rent by hypocrisy, greed, and a criminal disparity of wealth. Along with Paul Dakeyo, one of the two major Cameroonian poets to emerge during this period was Fernando D'Almeida.

For him, the act of self-definition was rendered particularly intense by feelings of exile in a country that differed from the one where he spent his early childhood. Of mixed Brazilian, Togolese, and Cameroonian parentage, D'Almeida lived in Dahomey until the age of sixteen, when he migrated to Douala after the death of his father. Working for *La Presse du Cameroun* and educating himself through voluminous reading, he began to compose poems that express the anguish of a sensitive individual questing for a knowledge capable of healing the wound of separation from the place where he was born. Lacking the ties that most Africans have with a specific ethnic community, he became preoccupied with the question of individual identity and placed it at the center of his four volumes of poetry.

D'Almeida's verse traces the spiritual evolution of a young man who gradually acquires the assurance of belonging to his adoptive country, although even his latest work continues to be haunted by feelings of loss and doubt. Influenced by St. John Perse's images of exile, solitude, and the melancholy comfort of the sea, many of D'Almeida's early poems reflect his attempt to reorient himself in a situation where he lives in the hope of regaining what he has lost. His first collection, *Au Seuil de l'exil*, expresses his conviction that he can obtain the knowledge he covets by looking into himself and discovering a clue to the meaning of life. He claims his verses were dictated to him "by a crystalline voice, that strange voice that speaks to you silently from within."[12] On a personal level, he is acutely aware of his non-African name and his confused genealogy. "I don't know my true identity,"[13] he laments, recalling images from the country he left and addressing an unnamed "tu" from whom his exile has separated him.

This "tu" is occasionally associated with a princess or a fiancée who shares his feelings of solitude, but he is also speaking to a part of himself and to other Africans who suffer from the sense of being adrift in a world where traditional landmarks no longer guarantee a stable sense of identity. The malaise he is describing thus constitutes a metaphor for the spiritual reality of contemporary African youth. But the ambiguity of identity, the painfulness of exile, and the yearning to recover something that has been lost are not entirely negative because they motivate him to overcome self-pity. They also oblige him to recognize that hope lies in his capacity to love and his willingness to reforge his own conception of himself.

The vehicle for this reconceptualization is the act of writing poetry, for when transmuted by love and imagination, the experience of exile offers him concrete images with which to express the aspirations of all Africans who are faced with a world over which they have little control. Fettered by corrupt governments and exploited by their own countrymen, many of them live in fear, like the poet who explains that "night is approaching, and I'm afraid of the shadows that trumpet [like elephants]."[14] Yet by raising his own voice and unshackling language from the rhetoric of oppression, he proposes to overcome this fear and become a spokesman for the people. His uniquely personal sense of loss is translated into an expression of hope for all of modern Africa. In the process of awakening readers to this hope, D'Almeida creates a new identity for himself as the bearer of a message that insight into his own situation has enabled him to decipher.

In his second volume of poetry, *Traduit du je pluriel*, the dialectical relationship between the poet and the people emerges clearly, for if they speak through him, his reformulation of their thoughts makes them more fully conscious of what they are saying. On a personal level, he rejects the inheritance of slavery and colonialist oppression to reclaim his dignity as a human being. By extension, his gesture becomes the model for a redefinition of society, and the poetic word is his means of communicating this insight to others:

> The word was bequeathed me
> to rip aside the mask of lies
> The word was given me
> to engage in the rutting of my people.[15]

The recognition of his role as one who can raise the people's consciousness and participate in their vital impulses endowed D'Almeida with the sense of purpose he needed to overcome the crisis occasioned by his exile.

Yet the confidence he draws from his conception of himself as a poet of the people is not a permanent acquisition. It must be continually reforged in an ongoing struggle against doubt and despair. For him, the poetic impulse is linked with love, life, and the dream of a better future. Each time he sets out to write, he reaffirms these impulses as a part of his own identity. When he acknowledges his intention to recover his origins, he is not acquiescing in the Negritude project but seeking to "rediscover the scattered debris of my Self."[16] By repeatedly plunging into his own solitude in his "fervent quest for identity," he finds that his misery links him irrevocably with all the oppressed people of Africa, for their common suffering is a function of the humanity he shares with them, not of the accidental blackness that colors their skin.

In his eyes, concrete experience has given him access to that which all people have in common. "I am born in the particular," he says, "to finally attain the universal."[17] Like Eno Belinga, whom he admires, D'Almeida perceives the truth as a light inside himself, a light that enables him to write poems capable of triggering a similar insight in the minds of his readers, but unlike Eno Belinga's Negritude, his light culminates in a declaration of solidarity with all those who suffer hunger and injustice.

D'Almeida's yearning to transcend the state of exile and his hope of participating in the creation of a new Africa are two facets of the same endeavor. As he makes clear in *L'Espace de la parole*, the knowledge that sustains him in this endeavor is a self-knowledge that derives from direct encounters between the individual self and the real world. "To engage myself in life," he asserts, "I burned my schoolbooks."[18] In this instance, the schoolbooks represent commonly accepted modes of perception, and his repudiation of them constitutes a profession of faith in his ability to know the truth through the independent use of his own faculties. The truth or light that D'Almeida discovered was the liberating possibility that people could shape their lives according to their own powers of love and imagination rather than allow themselves to be shaped by the dehumanizing forces of a corrupt society.

To make this light accessible to others, he created highly personal poems that are like rituals in the sense that they predispose readers to adopt a reverential attitude toward themselves and others. According to him, such an attitude is a precondition for both social justice and a viable sense of individual identity. It is also the motivating impulse behind the "poetry of totality" he seeks to create—a poetry that reconciles the exiled "I" with the absent "you" and unites the self of the poet with the collective identity of a suffering African humanity. If the act of poetic creation is a liberating self-realization, he feels that the people can express the same creative impulse by conceptualizing new social forms based on love and imagination. Such individual and collective acts of creation constitute refusals to condone the pervasive lack of respect for the human in contemporary African society. But as D'Almeida realizes, they are acts that must be continually repeated because truth and freedom can never be possessed like objects; they must be reacquired each day in an ongoing interaction between the self and society.

The world view that D'Almeida articulated in his first three volumes of poetry becomes specifically focused on Cameroon in *En Attendant le verdict*. Written in response to his arrest and harassment by the Cameroonian police, the poems in this collection reflect a newfound conviction that he is part of a national community struggling to define itself within the context of an oppressive social system. Realizing that his nostalgic memories of an irretrievable past must be placed behind him if he is ever to overcome the anxiety of exile, he understands that his view of the world makes sense only if he identifies with the people in the country where he has chosen to live. In spite of his temporary imprisonment, he feels that he has finally become a Cameroonian. "I am at home," he writes for the first time, "I am truly at home."[19] The underlying thrust of D'Almeida's poetry remains the same as it always has been, but by fully accepting his rootedness in a specific time and place, he acquires a new politically engaged perspective on the relationship between self-knowledge and social change.

As a mature poet with a heightened confidence in his own identity, D'Almeida achieves a sense of wholeness in *En Attendant le verdict*. The "I" and "you" of his earlier poems become "we," and vague ideas about the need for change become the seeds of a conflagration that he hopes will "rouse the consciousness of my people to rebellion" and sweep away the hypocrisy of a pseudoindependence that imprisons them in fear and poverty. He still believes in an ineffable truth that can be grasped only through introspection, but it is a truth accessible to everyone, and he conceives of his poetry as a means of awakening them to it. This truth gives meaning to all that exists, and even though a consciousness of it must be constantly reacquired, he remains convinced that it must be respected in any just society.

His experiences with the Cameroonian police obliged him to apply such beliefs in a concrete situation, and as he reports in *En Attendant le verdict*, the result was an overcoming of the identity crisis into which his exile had propelled him many years previously. D'Almeida's four books of poetry trace the evolution of an individual sensibility from alienation to commitment, and because the writing of poetry played such an important role in this process, his self-awareness is largely a function of his engagement in the creation of his own works. The assumption that individuals can articulate their own identity in this fashion illustrates one of the most important relationships between the act of writing and the implicit acceptance of modern individuality concepts in contemporary Cameroon.

In contrast to Dakeyo and D'Almeida, a substantial number of Cameroonian poets from the post-1972 period continued to identify the self with a complex of ideas commonly linked to Senghorian Negritude and the nation-building concept. The yearning for reconciliation was one of the most common themes in this poetry, and it often reflected the influence of a Christian moral idealism. For example, Valère Epée's *Transatlantic Blues* reaffirms the unity of the black experience by paralleling the laments of the black American son and the African father. Through a history of slavery and the nominal freedom of

"Jazzonia" (Harlem), the American Sonny Boy keeps alive echoes of his African patrimony in the music he creates and in his dreams of a place where he would be free of suffering and oppression. On the other side of the Atlantic, the African Epesse yearns for the return of his lost son and senses a redemptive vitality in the rediscovery of an African authenticity that had been suppressed by the colonialist presence.

To him, the ocean replies that he must listen to the blues rhythms in the pulsing of the waves. This message is essentially a reassurance that Africans and black Americans still belong to a spiritual community based on a knowledge of the natural rhythms that have been absorbed into African music and recuperated by the black music of the New World. Without realizing it, Sonny Boy and Epesse incorporate these rhythms into their own recollections of past suffering and their dreams of freedom. The form of *Transatlantic Blues* thus becomes part of its content, reinforcing the Negritude sensibility that inspired it.

The idealistic thrust of Epée's long poem can also be found in the works of the many Bamileke poets who began publishing during the 1970s and 1980s. In fact, one of the striking literary phenomena of this period was the remarkable rise of published poetry by writers from the Bamileke region. In contrast to more radical poets such as Patrice Kayo, Paul Tchakouté, and Jean-Pierre Ghonda-Nounga, a large number of young Bamileke responded to the troubled period of the UPC insurrection not by proclaiming the need for further revolution but by giving voice to their yearning for peace in a chaotic world. Throughout the works of such poets as Christophe Nguedam, Antoine de Padoue Chonang, Claude Joseph M'Bafou-Zetebeg, Vincent Boujeka Fodieng, Pierre Epato Nzodam, Michel Simeu, and Martine Djoupé, this yearning is linked with an introspective focus on the sensitive self and a strong tendency toward sentimental moralizing.

Influenced by Patrice Kayo, Nguedam provides a good example of this inspirational response to a contemporary world that often seems oppressive. Acutely aware that he is part of a vast, nameless humanity, he describes himself as a "poet in a tattered world where good and evil are confused."[20] Because values have become ambivalent in this world, he admits he has become lost in the frenetic search for his true identity. "Heavens!" he exclaims in one poem, "I've become lost at midday in the dense forest of my being."[21] By focusing on the mundane events of day-to-day life, he shows how his poetic consciousness distinguished patterns that Christianity and traditional Bamileke values helped him shape into a wisdom capable of shielding him against despair. A gentle rain, a red crab, the face of a passerby, or the death of his son can thus occasion poems that convey his insights into the vanity of earthly things, the inevitability of death, and the deceptiveness of appearances. His propensity for repetition and aphorism echoes the sources of his wisdom, but the center of his poetry always remains the sensitive "I" that links concrete experience with the principle it illustrates.

In fact, the poetic self is Nguedam's primary standard of value in a corrupt world where some people pride themselves on their wealth and privilege while others are suffering in poverty. One of his poems depicts a beggar railing against a joyful crowd's indifference to the suffering all around them. The people in the crowd dismiss him as a madman, but his example suggests that, because all people are subject to suffering and death, they should recognize their common destiny and treat each other with compassion. According to him, exploitative social systems result from the suppression of this awareness, which he believes the poet has an obligation to keep alive. He himself sows his own poems in the wind, he says, so they might sprout and bear fruit in the hearts of others. From this perspective, his own sensitive self becomes a reservoir of values inspired by his reconciliation of Christianity, traditional belief, and the nation-building ethic.

The poetry of Chonang, M'Bafou-Zetebeg, Boujeka Fodieng, Simeu, Epato Nzodam, and Djoupé resembles that of Nguedam in the sense that they too ascribe the corruption of Africa to moral shortcomings that can be corrected if people listen to the voice of a self that has reconciled traditional wisdom with Christian idealism. All of them discovered this enlightened perspective by looking into themselves. It becomes their justification for hope, and their poetry reflects their desire to share this hope with others. M'Bafou-Zetebeg, for example, imagines himself revealing his innermost being to his readers as if he were opening eggshells before them and allowing them to see the marvelous rainbows contained in them. Chonang's symbols for this hope—the midnight rainbow, the flaming star, the height of a mountain peak—all reflect his belief in the need for vision. In the poetry of all these Bamileke writers, the sensibility of the poet becomes a primary locus of value because it is inspired by such a vision.

In most cases, these poets identify their own yearning for peace and harmony with the idea of political reconciliation inherent in Ahidjo's conception of national unity. Boujeka Fodieng even eulogizes the Cameroonian president as a "One-Man Nation" and exhorts his fellow countrymen to heed the call of "our great national party."[22] In general, these poets are imbued with a universal humanism that inspires them with the conviction that utopia is possible if people can learn to see everyday reality in the light of their own capacity for love and understanding. Chonang justifies this belief by pointing out that all human beings are capable of experiencing wonder and awe. The cultivation of these feelings is, he argues, the key to developing a spirit of generosity.

According to all these Bamileke poets, such a spirit is the basic prerequisite for the birth of a genuinely Cameroonian nation. It is also necessary for the emergence of a free Africa. When Epato Nzodam pleads, "Africa that belongs to others, become ours once again,"[23] he is acknowledging that these goals have not yet been attained. The first step in moving toward them is self-knowledge, and these poets offer accounts of their own experiences as examples of how they as individuals acceded to such knowledge. Some of them regard nation building as the reflection of a divine impulse toward goodness and harmony, and all of them define the individual in relation to a utopian future that gives them the courage to face an imperfect present.

Among the non-Bamileke poets who adopted this inspirational approach to self-definition are Etienne Nkeunbang, Théophile Bikoula Abessolo, Bitha Balla, Jean-Marcel Meka d'Obam, Jacques Mahi Matiké, and Titus Nguiagain. In "Cameroun, pays bien aimé," Meka d'Obam even provides an example of how a mutually supportive linkage between the sensitive self and the nation can lead to self-parodying sentimentality: "You are everything for me, everything for the children who love you / You are a gilded pearl for those who know your history."[24] Yet even in these patriotic clichés, the underlying sensibility is assumed to constitute a standard of value that reflects the individual's freedom to proclaim the truth as he or she perceives it. If this freedom culminates in an expression of patriotic fervor, a sense of national identity has clearly taken root in the consciousness of literate Cameroonians such as Meka d'Obam.

The tendency to fuse humanistic sentiments with an idealistic attachment to traditional values can also be found in the work of such francophone Cameroonian poets as Vincent Tsoungi-Ngono, Marcel Mvondo II, Léon-Charles Tijoufack, Hermann Mingole, James Oto, and Georges Tchianga. Jean-Paul Nyunaï's *10 Poèmes traduits du ME AN* even offer a philosophical account of how the poetic "I" comes into being in the interplay between the word, the thing, and a deeper reality that people share with one another. His understanding of the poetic word and its capacity to evoke subjective responses in readers represents a synthesis of traditional Bassa values and Christianity—a synthesis that provides a plausible account of how the individual psyche functions in its never-ending quest for freedom and identity.

The anglophone Cameroonian poetry that began to appear in print during the 1970s and 1980s was often moralistic with overtones of nostalgia for a more peaceful era. Although seldom explicitly acknowledged, anglophone poets often regarded the corruption they depicted in their works as a result of the French influence on their francophone compatriots. The satiric thrust in poems by writers such as Babila Mutia, Peter Abety, Adamu Musa, Bole Butake, Gregory Achu Ashi, and James Malia draws attention to the greed of politicians, the hypocrisy of priests, and the pretentious lifestyles of francophone Cameroonians. The Christian moralism in poetry by Buma Kor and Mesack Takere also reflects an underlying desire to inject justice and decency into a social order menaced by corruption and unnecessary suffering.

In some cases, moral outrage resulted in the reaffirmation of a traditional sense of identity. For example, Ayuk Tabe-Ebob rejects European-inspired models of behavior and proclaims, "I am the proud offspring of a savage race."[25] In other cases, poets such as Kitts Mbeboh denied that poetry had anything to do with social commentary. Strongly influenced by European modernist techniques, his own poems do express a unique individual sensibility, but because the idiom he employs is foreign to most literate people in his part of the country, his poetry remains largely unpublished. Much more common is a morally didactic, inspirational verse that can be taught in the schools. In fact, collections such as Fokwang John Koyela's *The Busy Spider and Other Poems* and Jacob Ndifor's *Old Men Are Libraries* were specifically conceived as supplementary reading texts. The poems in them convey a moral and seek to inculcate a respect for traditional values. Often they emphasize self-reliance and Christian moral sentiments. What links them with some of the francophone Cameroonian poets of the period is the personal, confessional tone they adopt to record the evolution of unique individual sensibilities at the crossroads of traditional and modern culture.

Buma Kor's *Searchlight Poems* and Takere's *Kingfisher Poetry* provide characteristic examples of the moralizing, character-building strain in anglophone Cameroonian poetry. *Searchlight Poems* is a three-part spiritual autobiography that traces the poet's attempt to reorient himself as he moves from the village to the city. In the first part, he becomes aware of the corruption and ugliness that pervade modern society. The underlying question is whether one needs to be corrupt to survive in such an environment. The second cluster of poems answers this question by indicating that God has shown him the path to virtue and helped him overcome temptation. The third section, entitled "Breakthrough," registers the poet's resolve to become the torchbearer (or searchlight) of God's truth in a society where falsehood and injustice hold sway. Fusing the traditional wisdom of his people with Christianity, he defines individual identity in terms of its commitment to a moral ideal.

The same is true of Takere, who specifically relates this ideal to the nation-building effort. Convinced that moral commitment is essential in this process, he promises to contribute his part:

> I pledge to you my country,
> A faith strong in loyalty
> To uphold truth and unity
> In honour and responsibility.[26]

The opposite of this patriotic, morally upright attitude is depicted in Takere's poem about Peter X, whose drinking, slander, and dishonest dealings blind him to the truth about himself and prevent him from living in harmony with the other members of his community. In a concluding comment, the poet warns his readers against becoming like Peter X and implies that God will reward them if they eschew the temptations of lust and greed.

The underlying assumption in such poems is that divine justice will assure the triumph of the virtuous. On the national level, this assumption translates into the idea that, if individuals behave as the poet has vowed to do, the sum of their actions will produce "a nation great and virtuous." The naive sentimentality of Takere's verses resembles the stereotyped patriotism of Meka d'Obam's poetry, both of which ground individual identity in the communal concept of a Cameroonian nation.

Kewai Nyamgha's *Spectres on Scale* differs from the majority of published anglophone Cameroonian poetry in the sense that his work focuses on scatological imagery to "break the boil" of social injustice and to "let the pus" drain from it. For example, he compares members of the privileged class with the voracious locusts that are feared in the grasslands region of his native Banso because they deprive the people of the crops on which their survival depends. Yet the people themselves are partly to blame for the political corruption that robs them of their sustenance: "We have voted locusts into power / Locust-shit has made umbrellas / For crop-leaves in Africa."[27] By drawing attention to the parallel between a natural plague, which people recognize as a danger, and an equally devastating plague they have brought upon themselves, Nyamgha jolts readers into an awareness of the moral turpitude that is often regarded as normal in Cameroonian society. Fashioned in the mind of the poet, the locust metaphor is the expression of a poetic sensibility that once again serves as a standard of value according to which the corrupt society is judged.

Whether Cameroonian writers view corruption as a result of the nation-building process or as an impediment to it, they are almost always sustained by the belief in an ideal. Even the most bitter condemnations of a cruel society can be communicated only by establishing a set of countervalues that serve as a contrast to the existing situation. However, Cameroon has also produced a few dark poets—poets who cannot fully believe in a sustaining ideal when a corrupt, indifferent world continually thrusts them back into solitude and misery. In works such as Claude Nana Sunji's *Bonheur du misère*, Joseph Sop's *Pleurs d'une jeunesse en deuil*, Christophe Ndessenfong Fotso's *Désenchantement*, and Mommadou Modibbo Aliou's *Sur les Chemins de la Sa'iira*, despair constantly threatens to vanquish the poet's will to live.

The focus in all these works is the sensitive self of the poet and its response to a corrupt environment. The nightmare quality of this environment weighs on their consciousness. In *Sur les Chemins de la Sa'iira*, one of the rare volumes of francophone poetry by a northern Cameroonian, Aliou compares the inhabitants of this environment to the lost souls in the seventh hell of the Islamic cosmogony, and he is among them. Nana Sunji is rendered apprehensive and unsure of his own inclinations by the pressures it exerts on him: "The softest chirp of an insect makes me uneasy / I am obsessed by a thousand vain desires."[28] And Ndessenfong feels himself to be a "miserable exile" who is perpetually among the hunted in a "universe of poor wretches without hope." Yet in spite of their despair, each of these poets is intent upon finding a voice to express the unique identity he feels inside himself.

For all of them, Cameroonian independence had engendered a society where the frenzied pursuit of money and status had transformed people into solitary individuals who treat each other as enemies to be outwitted rather than as human beings to be loved and trusted. They are the condemned souls, the living dead, in Aliou's Sa'iira. Both Ndessenfong and Nana Sunji depict the hypocritical earnestness with which people pursue their selfish goals and conclude that contemporary society is a comedy in which the actors are duped by their own roles. Their images of this corrupt society resemble those of Nanga, Abéga, Evembe, Assiga-Ahanda, and others, but in contrast to them, poets such as Ndessenfong see no escape from the despair that this society imposes on them. Overwhelmed with the superfluity of their own existence, they see death as a respite from suffering, and although Nana Sunji and Sop eventually find a justification for living, even their final poems are steeped in self-pity.

The most talented of Cameroon's dark poets from the post-1972 period was Antoine Assoumou, whose work was discovered in several school notebooks after his death at the age of seventeen. Grouped together, his poems constitute the fragmentary spiritual autobiography of a young man who sought in vain to make sense of a chaotic world for which the stereotyped value systems of contemporary Cameroon seemed woefully inadequate. In his quest for a viable self-image to replace the bourgeois identity that his parents and the schools had attempted to inculcate in him, Assoumou yearned to know more about Bulu customs, and he read voraciously. In the novels of Dostoevsky, he discovered a "vast interiority" that suggested analogues for his own intimations of mortality.

But Assoumou lacked Dostoevsky's faith in the spiritual dimension of life, and he speculated that death might offer him the only possibility of discovering who he really was: "Adieu, I'm leaving to doff my mask / Beneath the metallic shadow of the lake . . . / To recognize myself at last in its silvery mirror."[29] The real problem for the young Assoumou was the unriddling of his own identity because he was convinced that "the power to proudly say *I* has been lost."[30] Like the Bamileke poet Etienne Noumé, Assoumou was a solitary, tormented individual who could not overcome his despair at being imprisoned in a hypocritical society that placed ultimate value on superficial, materialistic goals.

His fate might almost serve as a symbol of the tragic conflict between the sensitive self and the cruel society in contemporary Cameroon. Obviously the majority of Cameroonian writers did not succumb to despair, but they were aware that the reality of independence did not correspond to the idealistic hopes that had been vested in it. In contrast to the radical critics who ascribed the failure of independence to the structure of neocolonialist society, large numbers of them blamed it on a breakdown of morality. The premature death of Assoumou is merely one example of the way in which sensitive individuals are victimized by the conditions that result from this breakdown. Paradoxically, however, the sensitivity of these victims is also the value upon which writers as diverse as Nanga, D'Almeida, Evembe, and Abéga place their hope for the future. The self can be distorted by the pressures of a corrupt society, but it can also keep alive the humane values on the basis of which a better society might be built. That Cameroonian writers focused on both cases illustrates the extent to which modern concepts of individuality have come to be taken for granted in Cameroonian society.

CHAPTER
20

NEW VOICES IN
CAMEROONIAN THEATER

Cameroonian theater experienced an explosive growth during the post-1972 period. The vast majority of the more than two thousand playscripts estimated to have been written by Cameroonians came into being at this time, and although most of them were social comedies, there was considerable experimentation as dramatists explored new forms and techniques in their search for a theater responsive to contemporary African sensibilities.[1] Like the poets, novelists, and other writers of the period, Cameroonian playwrights tended to confront the disappointed expectations of independence with a utopian vision of what their society might become if the existing situation could be changed.

The values according to which they thought such change should occur were not always the same, but they were invariably defined in relation to an ongoing quest for freedom and identity. Within the African context, drama is distinguished from other forms of literary expression by its potential for reaching large numbers of people who do not habitually read books. In Cameroon, a heightened popular interest in theater reflected this potential and helped catalyze a rethinking of its role in society. In the late 1970s and early 1980s, the emergence of an experimental, socially critical drama and the success of popular comic performances by Daniel Ndo, Jean Miché Kankan, Deiv Moktoï, and others triggered a public debate over the purpose of Cameroonian theater in the *Cameroon Tribune*, *Objectif*, and other local publications. Animated roundtable discussions took place at the university, and discussions of the topic were broadcast on the national radio.

As in the period before 1972, play production in Cameroon continued to revolve largely around independent acting groups organized by writer-directors who staged their own works or by dynamic directors such as Charles Nyatté, who often produced dramas by Cameroonian writers. Most of this activity was centered in Yaounde, where more than thirty troupes were active in late 1981, although by this time there were also a dozen troupes in Douala, where Jean-Pierre Dikongue Pipa, Boé a Amang, and Edouard Henri Zoé maintained a high level of artistic achievement.[2] Other groups sprang up in Garoua, Bafoussam, Nkongsamba, Bertoua, Dschang, Sangmelima, and Buea. Several Yaounde troupes toured the country with some regularity, and school classes became increasingly involved in the production of plays. Works such as Oyono-Mbia's *Trois Prétendants . . . un mari*, Mba Evina's *Politicos*, Wole Soyinka's *Lion and the Jewel*, Guy Menga's *Marmite de Kola Mbala*, and Baba Moustapha's *Maître des Djinns* became known to a substantial public in Cameroon. By the late 1980s, familiarity with the idea of theatrical production had become far more widespread than it was during the 1960s.

The development of a theater arts program at the University of Yaounde in the 1980s provided an additional source of innovation and theatrical talent while helping to create an audience for experimental drama. The francophone component of this program was under the direction of the Frenchwoman Jacqueline Leloup, who arrived at the university in the mid-1970s as a "coopérant" and founded the Club d'Art Dramatique, which gained a reputation for the professionalism of its productions. After joining the theater arts program, her group became known as the Théâtre Universitaire and created a dynamic acting style that artfully combined the traditional and the modern. In *Gueido* (an adaptation of the Oedipus theme to a Cameroonian setting) and *Meyong Meyeme au royaume des morts* (a modern variation on a Beti folktale), characters are presented as emanations of an oral story-teller who bridges the gap between the real world of the audience and the imagined world on the stage. Music, dance, song, masks, color symbolism, and interaction with the spectators transform the texts of these plays into vivid experiences that have impressed local as well as international audiences. By elaborating a Cameroonian style of acting, Leloup's group did what the National Theater had been mandated to do but never quite accomplished.[3]

The government-sponsored production of Gervais Mendo Ze's *Boule de chagrin* at Yaounde's cultural palace in 1985 did, however, demonstrate the professionalism with which the National Theater could adopt similar techniques. Like Mendo Ze's *La Forêt illuminée*, *Boule de chagrin* consists of sequences rather than acts. These sequences alternate between a village scene, where the story-teller, Ndondoo, recounts the experiences of a young person who had left the village, and a succession of scenes that depict his or her misadventures in the settings where they actually took place. The plots of both dramas involve familiar themes: a European-educated young man's difficulty in overcoming a corrupt environment after his return to Cameroon, and a young woman's rebellion against her father's attempt to marry her to an aging chief. The morals drawn from these stories are predictable and clearly support the ideology of national unity. But if there is nothing unusual about the plot and intellectual content of these plays, Ndondoo's playful exchanges with the villagers are interwoven so naturally with the performance of events from his story that *La Forêt illuminée* and *Boule de chagrin* might well be regarded as reinforcing the initiatives undertaken by the Théâtre Universitaire.

The anglophone component of the theater arts program at the university was under the leadership of Hansel Ndumbe Eyoh, whose Baromi Players became the University Theater in the early 1980s. Although lacking the resources of the francophone section, this group became particularly active in producing works by anglophone Cameroonian dramatists such as Bole Butake. In addition, Eyoh pioneered the "theater for development" concept in Cameroon by working with villagers in the western part of the country to conceptualize and perform dramas that address the problems they confront in their daily lives.[4] However, with Leloup's departure from the country in 1987 and Eyoh's appointment as director of culture at the Ministry of Information and Culture, their initiatives were in danger of remaining without lasting consequences.

By the mid-1980s, university academics had become deeply involved in the study of theater. Their interest led to the founding of a major journal, *African Theatre Review*, and the organization of a 1987 colloquium on Cameroonian theater. The presentations at this colloquium were later published as *Théâtre camerounais/Cameroonian Theatre*, and many of them focused on the relationship between traditional culture and theatrical practice. Several contributors provided detailed descriptions of ethnic rituals, which they regarded as authentically Cameroonian forms of theater. Others called for the incorporation of traditional story-telling techniques, ritual conventions, or participatory settings in the production of modern Cameroonian plays. At least one claimed that Cameroonian drama will acquire a distinctive identity only when playwrights succeed in synthesizing the traditional and the modern. The significance of this discussion lies less in the solutions it proposes than in the fact that scholars and critics are theorizing about the nature of Cameroonian theater on the assumption that a substantial corpus exists. Their competing opinions help structure the universe of discourse in which the awareness of a national literary tradition is already being taken for granted.

The most innovative development of the post-1972 period was the emergence of a mixed-genre, "total" theater that was conceptualized as an authentically African way of entertaining audiences while prompting them to reflect seriously about themselves and their society. One of the most outspoken proponents of this view was Joseph Tagne, whose "théâtre englobant" (total theater) was based on the assumption that music, dance, mime, traditional performative techniques, and multiple slide projections could be integrated into a "total effect" that would raise important political issues and stimulate spectators to become participants in a drama that embraced them and the actors in a single communal space. During the late 1970s and early 1980s, he created such controversial plays as *La Rage de ce peuple*, *Je l'accuse*, and *L'Auto-déchirement* by drawing on a wide variety of existing texts. His own troupe performed them with mixed success in Yaounde and other Cameroonian cities. But Tagne's "théâtre englobant" was merely the most radical example of a search for alternatives to social comedy and European stage conventions.

Alexandre Kum'a Ndumbe III and Werewere Liking were particularly successful in synthesizing new forms of dramatic performance from traditional precedent and modern staging techniques, although many of their innovations were anticipated in plays from an earlier period. Music, dance, and the participatory impulse are characteristic elements of daily life in the country, and play-wrights such as Oyono-Mbia, Nzouankeu, and Dikongue Pipa had integrated them into their works during the 1960s. Actors such as Ekéké Moukoury, Abia Moukoko, Marcel Mvondo II, and members of Joseph Sop's "Art-Pro" group produced montage presentations along experimental lines in the 1970s. In fact, the tendency to defy European stage conventions and break down the separa-tion between actors and audience was evident in many plays that were per-formed at this time.

Improvisation, dance, mime, and musical interludes often made them longer in performance than a reading of them would suggest. In fact, the texts of Cameroonian plays provide but a vague idea of what they will be like when they are produced on stage, and unpublished dramas can prove more successful in front of live audiences than plays that have been accepted for publication on the basis of their literary qualities. When critics such as Eyoh and Ferdinand Tewafo began to call for a new theater in the 1970s, they were in a sense suggesting that such tendencies be carried to their logical conclusions.

Two of the most important ingredients of the new theater that emerged in Cameroon at this time were the attempt to adapt traditional materials or techniques for the modern stage and the cultivation of a historical consciousness that placed the country's existing situation into perspective. Precedent existed for both tendencies. Writers of 1960s social comedies often incorporated tradi-tional elements such as proverbs, songs, and dances into their productions. The festive atmosphere at the end of Oyono-Mbia's plays, the musical interludes in Mba Evina's *Politicos*, the Bulu passages in Zomo Bem's *Le Patron noir*, and the funeral drumming at the beginning of Afana's *La Coutume qui tue* all illus-trate an urge to remold what had initially been a European genre into an African form of literary expression. Martin Tchou-Tchou's plays about Bamileke village life and David Eyombwan's Douala-language productions exemplify this same tendency.

At the same time, there was a Negritude-inspired attempt to create an authen-tic African drama. Plays such as Jean-Baptiste Obama's *Assimilados*, Antoine Epassy's *Les Asticots*, Tsino's *Nyia Bariba*, and James Oto's *Ngonrogo-le-fou* all sought to evoke traditional modes of perception as they focused on a search for harmony, peace, wisdom, and communal solidarity. Although these earlier dramas never achieved the popular success enjoyed by Oyono-Mbia and other authors of social comedies, they represented a first step toward the integration of traditional culture into a modern Cameroonian theater.[5]

The Negritude influence over these writers is apparent in Tsino's conception of the African writer's purpose, for he insists that "the modern poet actually needs to perform creative acts with the materials that tradition places at his disposal, to create modern works worthy of being contributed to the Culture of the Universal."[6] The materials that he, Obama, Epassy, and Oto found at their disposal were oral tales and *mvet* performances. Like such traditional nar-ratives, their plays function like parables that make philosophical statements about the nature of human existence and the search for wisdom and harmony.

The extensive use of dance, song, and stylized recitation elevates them into total spectacles that seek to engage the participation of African audiences in ways that would not be possible in a standard, European-style drama.

Obama was the most prolific of the early Cameroonian playwrights who emphasized the need for a culturally authentic theater, and his plays exemplify Tsino's definition of the modern poet. *Assimilados*, *Emvandoumba*, *Le Mariage héroïque*, and *Le Harem du monogame* are all constructed around a traditional tale, song, or custom and embellished with music and dancing. This form lent an aura of festiveness to his plays. It also framed a moral message that Obama felt was particularly relevant in the contemporary world. The didactic quality of his plays reflects the fact that he used them as part of his program at FEU, where they were presented by young adult students in a general education program. The assumption behind this use of theater was that actors and spectators can learn to comprehend contemporary problems by participating in the enactment of similar problems on the stage. The moral vision behind this enterprise reflects traditional cultural values as well as the humane ideals that Obama absorbed during his years at the seminary and through his contact with the Negritude movement when he was living in France. Invariably his plays hold out the possibility of reconciliation in peace and brotherhood.

His most well known drama is *Assimilados*. Borrowing the story line from a Yoruba tale about the birth of a mulatto child and setting the action in Angola, Obama employed an *mvet* style of performance to create a French-language stage drama that suggests how racial mistrust can be overcome if people recognize the humanity they share with each other. The action in the play is simple. The wife of a poverty-stricken griot works for a Portuguese administrator who fathers her mulatto child. When the griot sings a song of white oppression and black misery, he concludes by accusing the administrator of failing to support his own child. Becoming aware of the situation for the first time, the administrator acknowledges the child and offers the griot an "assimilado" identity card so that he and his family can become "as rich as the white man."[7]

The action in the play is like that of a parable. The colonialist situation engendered an unjust disparity of wealth that was perpetuated by Europeans who enslaved Africans and profited from their work. Throughout the play, a recurrent refrain questions the justice of a world in which the black brother was born poor and under the curse of God, whereas the white brother was born rich and blessed by the Lord. The griot, who sings for the labor gangs created by the Europeans, lives the reality of this injustice, and the administrator plays the role of exploiter, albeit unwittingly. When he gives the "assimilado" identity card to the griot, he is recognizing the humanity he shares with him—a humanity symbolized by the mulatto child. By accepting the identity card, the griot is acquiescing in Obama's belief that reconciliation rather than revolution is the best solution to the historical injustice of colonialism.

The implication is that both races can live together in peace, harmony, and material well-being if they forgive past injustices and treat each other as fellow human beings. There are similar moral observations at the center of Obama's other plays. In *Emvandoumba*, for example, the materialistic attitudes of modern society become apparent when a group of students canvass the city for contributions to aid the sick and the poor. Their singing, dancing, and miming are based on a village custom, but unlike the villagers, the city-dwellers in the play are too preoccupied with their own affairs to contribute to the welfare of others, and one of the group is fatally wounded when a night watchman fires a warning shot at them. The play culminates in a question: why must a young man die if his actions are motivated by love? In the implied answer to this question lies Obama's commentary on the dehumanization of contemporary Cameroonian society. Yet the full impact of plays such as *Emvandoumba* and *Assimilados* depends upon the entire spectacle of music, dance, and mime that Obama weaves into them, for he was one of the first Cameroonians to realize the potential for creating a total theater that would combine traditional customs and ritual practices with modern stage techniques to produce plays responsive to a modern African sensibility.

Epassy's *Les Asticos*, Tsino's *Nyia Bariba*, and Oto's *Ngronrogo-le-fou* employ similar techniques. They too function like moral parables that seek to enlighten spectators about the attitudes they should adopt in seeking to cope with a harsh world. The maggots ("asticots") in Epassy's play serve as a metaphor for the two primary causes of human misery under such circumstances: the decay of the flesh that leads inevitably toward death and the corruption of a society in which people feed upon the suffering of others to sustain themselves. The wandering madman who reappears periodically in the play and the example of a family afflicted by a series of misfortunes suggest that acquisitive individualism is self-defeating in a world where people can find solace only in a sense of community.

A similar moral viewpoint characterizes the other two plays. The title of Tsino's drama means "the mother of Bariba" in Ewondo, and it refers to a woman whose love of her children is so great that she braves the terror of being swallowed alive by the dreaded spirit of the forest to save them. And in *Ngonrogo*, the supposedly mad title hero has the independence of mind to realize that freedom, not obedience to authority, is what makes people human. By exercising this freedom to aid his fellow creatures in distress, he creates the bonds of love that render the harshness of existence tolerable. By striving to create a culturally authentic theater, playwrights such as Oto, Tsino, Epassy, and Obama reaffirmed the traditional values of intellectual penetration and communal solidarity in the face of dehumanizing pressures in the modern world.[8] Such values were adduced to support Ahidjo's cultural nationalism, but they could also be used as a standard according to which contemporary Cameroonian society might be judged, and this is precisely the use for which they were adopted by experimental dramatists in the 1970s and 1980s.

Historical drama emerged somewhat later than the cultural authenticity movement of the 1960s, but it tended to serve a similar ideological function in the nation-building process. For example, plays by Adamou Ndam Njoya, Paul Tchakouté, and René Bell focused on ethnic heroes such as Martin-Paul

Samba, Rudolph Douala Manga Bell, and Sultan Njoya, endowing them with virtues that transcend their ethnic affiliation and reinforce their status as shared cultural references for Cameroonians from different ethnic backgrounds. In addition to fostering pride in a common past, such historical depictions suggest traditional precedents for the type of behavior that is needed in the present; they also create the possibility of commenting on the values of present-day Cameroon by implicitly comparing them with the values that motivated heroic individuals in the past.

The most successful of these dramas was Ndam Njoya's *Dairou IV*, which has been staged somewhere in the country every year since its first performance in 1973. Exploiting a fictionalized account of the transition from arbitrary tyranny to benevolent leadership in Bamun history, Njoya created a play that illustrates the "new morality" he believes is capable of transforming Cameroon into a unified national community. The title character in *Dairou IV* is a sultan who, having lost sight of the fact that successful political organization requires a harmonious relationship with the cosmic order, devotes all his kingdom's resources to a war of conquest against neighboring tribes. Rather than concerning himself with the welfare of his people, he views them as objects to be manipulated for the gratification of his own desires; however, they spontaneously acknowledge the young Nad as their leader because they sense that his commitment to love and reconciliation is more attuned to the cosmic order in which they are living. Unable to bear the thought of living without power, the Sultan commits suicide, and Nad becomes the new ruler without incurring the guilt of having shed his predecessor's blood. At the end of the play, the off-stage voice of the Divine reinforces the idea that love is more powerful than the will to dominance and that people can eliminate the evils that beset them.

On one level, *Dairou IV* is an idealistic meditation upon the role of morality in government. Njoya himself admitted that his goal in writing the play was to "offer a reflection of that divine perfection toward which we aspire without ever attaining it."[9] Even if this perfection is unattainable, he argues, the image of it inspires people to work toward a society based on love rather than the struggle for dominance. By showing how Dairou's failure to unite his people was caused by his failure to recognize the true nature of the world, Njoya implies that the Sultan's vocabulary, which is the vocabulary of contemporary Cameroonian society, cannot promote national construction because it is rooted in materialistic individualism and the ethics of conflict.

Because Njoya finds more appropriate values in the traditional past, he suggests that the revival of history in works such as *Dairou IV* can help create a new vocabulary adequate to his vision of a national society based on communal solidarity and harmony with the cosmic order. From this perspective, Nad offers a model of political leadership. He incarnates the heroic virtues of the people and symbolizes their common purpose. At the same time, his moral idealism serves as an implicit commentary on the abuse of power in contemporary Cameroon, for it implies that integrity and social justice are prerequisites for a viable sense of collective identity. In this way, Njoya's historical drama engages in the ongoing dialogue that was taking place in Cameroonian print culture about the country's national destiny.

Paul Tchakouté also wrote historical dramas that present Cameroonian ethnic leaders as embodiments of the ideals upon which a genuine national unity might be built. He too implicitly contrasts their pursuit of reconciliation and social justice with the corruption that pervades the existing system, but by focusing on Martin-Paul Samba and Sultan Njoya's opposition to colonial rule, he is implying that a true nationalist position demands a similar opposition to neocolonialist oppression. In his *Samba*, for example, the Douala King Akwa embraces Samba upon his return from Germany and declares that all Cameroonians are bound together by their history of subjection to the same tyranny. This expression of transethnic solidarity culminates in the assertion that they share a common destiny and must fight for a common cause. Wronged by the colonial government and convinced that it is better to die in defense of one's freedom than to live in slavery, Samba becomes a martyred symbol of the nationalist cause.

His defiance of unjust authority resembles the revolutionary stance of UPC leaders such as Um Nyobé and Ouandié more than the nation-building rhetoric of Ahidjo, although Tchakouté's ultimate goal of peace and reconciliation is strikingly similar to that of Ndam Njoya. As his earlier play inspired by Sultan Njoya demonstrates, Tchakouté believes in the possibility of a just society that reflects the cosmic principle of universal love. Published under the pseudonym Franz Kayor, *Les Dieux trancheront* portrays the Sultan's judicious handling of two threats to the integrity of his kingdom: a son's treasonous behavior and a German military invasion. After both threats have been rebuffed, he instructs the court historian to record the events, embellishing them, where necessary, to create an ideal image of his people's collective identity. Realizing that the ruler is merely the trunk of a tree that cannot survive without strong roots (the people), he proposes to exploit this idealized history as a means of inspiring virtuous civic behavior, just as Tchakouté manipulates the stories of Samba and Sultan Njoya to reinforce his conception of Cameroonian national identity.

Similarly, René Bell's *Le Seigneur de la terre* focuses on Rudolph Douala Manga Bell's refusal to acquiesce in the local German administration's decision to remove the Douala from lands guaranteed them by the 1884 German-Douala treaty. The play also reaffirms the status of this incident as a shared reference point in the Cameroonian national consciousness. Although the author changes the names of the major characters to suggest the general nature of injustice under colonial rule, his story of Nguila is a compressed but accurate account of Douala Manga Bell's confrontation with the German authorities. Like Ndam Njoya's Nad and Tchakouté's Sultan, Nguila aspires to establish a harmonious social order that combines justice, continuity with the past, and openness toward modern technology. Prevented from realizing his utopian dream by the Germans' decision to execute him as a traitor for opposing their plans, he refuses to flee, despite his awareness of their intentions, because he accepts his destiny as the leader of an unjustly treated people. René Bell's play preserves the memory of this heroic gesture and etches it in the minds of Cameroonian spectators.

Ndam Njoya, Tchakouté, and René Bell drew upon the ethnic past as a means of illustrating traits they believe should become part of an ideal national character. At the same time, they helped consolidate a network of shared references with which people from different ethnic backgrounds could identify. Jean-Pierre Dikongue Pipa's *La Mort héroïque du Lamido de Banyo* and Pierre Messomo's *Que cela change* deal with historical materials in a similar fashion, but even works set in foreign countries often allude obliquely to the question of Cameroonian national identity. For example, Tchakouté's *Les Femmes en cage*, Abel Zomo Bem's *Fini le temps des boys*, and Joseph Ngoué's *La Croix du sud* take place in Rhodesia and South Africa, but they illustrate world views that Cameroonian audiences could easily recognize as relevant to their own society. Tchakouté's play reinforces the idea that society can evolve toward a state of peace and harmony if people align themselves with the cosmic order through love and heightened consciousness, whereas Zomo Bem's and Ngoué's dramas suggest that people can achieve freedom and a viable sense of identity only by banding together and combating the forces of injustice and oppression.

None of these historically oriented plays encountered difficulties with the Cameroonian government because they did not contain direct attacks on the institutional structure of the existing political system. And when a group of young playwrights did attack this system in plays they wrote during the late 1970s and early 1980s, a momentary relaxation of government controls enabled them to stage some of the most socially critical drama that has ever appeared on Cameroonian stages. Moral blindness had always been a dominant theme in the country's theater, and as early as Nzouankeu's 1964 *L'Agent spécial*, dramatists had drawn attention to the problem of public corruption, but until the mid-1970s, they almost always portrayed it as a function of individual weakness. The assumption was that existing social norms constitute a standard of value according to which guilty people can be brought to judgment.

However, plays such as Philombe's *Africapolis*, Messomo's *Que cela change*, Dikongue Pipa's *Le Crépuscule des vautours*, Isaac Monthé's *Ce n'est pas un péché d'aimer l'abbé*, and Ferdinand Kongou's *La Corruption* began to call this assumption into question. They depicted society itself as corrupt and held out little hope that the situation could be improved by punishing individuals without changing the system that had produced them. By the late 1970s, young students and former students were forming troupes to stage original plays that expanded this approach to include overt attacks on the Cameroonian system and the rhetoric that had been created to justify it.

Deiv Moktoï's popular boulevard theater originated in this politically charged atmosphere, although his Uhuru Drama group later developed a comic style that set its productions apart from the more "serious," often experimental work of author-directors such as Bassek ba Kobhio, Raymond Ekossono, Bidoung

Mkpatt, Jean-Pierre Ghonda-Nounga, and Joseph Tagne. Most of these "young Turks" had been influenced by the socially critical views of Marcien Towa. They sometimes worked together, and they felt they were engaged in a common enterprise—raising people's consciousness about the structural inequity of neo-colonialist society and exhorting them to liberate themselves by joining the struggle to change it.

Belonging to a generation that had grown up with a consciousness of film techniques and a profound skepticism toward Ahidjo's nation-building rhetoric, these young playwrights regarded experimental staging techniques and political engagement as mutually reinforcing aspects of the same enterprise. For example, Tagne defends his participatory, mixed-genre "théâtre englobant" as an antidote to the sick consciousness of neocolonialist society. According to him, it can shock people into recognizing the perversity of this sick consciousness and committing themselves to the democratic socialism he associates with writers such as Towa and Philombe.[10] Such attitudes inevitably brought these young writers into conflict with the government, but they were prepared to take this chance, for as Bassek ba Kobhio said, "people have to take risks if they want to remain honest with themselves."[11] By early 1982, the government had begun to refuse them authorization to perform their plays, but for a few brief years they had transformed Cameroonian theater into a dynamic medium for the airing of controversial social and political issues.

Mkpatt's *Monsieur le Préfet* and his trilogy (*Les Charognards, Les Parasites,* and *Les Malicieuses*) provide excellent examples of the young Turks' attempt to shock audiences into a heightened awareness of the corrupt mentalities that dominate contemporary society. In all his plays, major characters act out of self-interest and betray anyone from whom they expect to extract a profit. The dehumanizing consequences of this rapacity are suggested by the titles of the plays in his trilogy, for they define such characters as vultures, parasites, and malicious individuals. All three plays deal with episodes that take place in the household of a wealthy businessman, Elias, and their real subject is the acquisitive individualism that motivates people to mask their true intentions while preying on each other. As this mindset becomes widespread, it fosters an atmosphere in which everyone is profoundly alone because no one can trust anyone else.

The irony of this situation is particularly obvious in a scene from *Les Parasites,* where Elias has become convinced that everyone is stealing from him. At this point, his wife places her head on his shoulder and assures him that she will always be at his side even if everyone else is cheating him. What she fails to mention is that she herself is embezzling money from him. As a shrewd businessman, he has always lived according to an ethic that denies the necessity of acting honorably; as a result, he cannot expect others to act honorably toward him. Without trust, however, he is condemned to an empty, solitary existence—a fact that becomes evident in *Les Malicieuses* when his mistress reduces him to a helpless invalid and juggles his finances to enrich herself. Convinced that the value of people can be measured by the number of cars and villas they own, she exploits Elias exactly as he had exploited others, but in a sick society, no one can expect to be treated in any other way. Mkpatt's trilogy lays bare the psychological reality of living in such a society.

Men like Elias invent rationalizations to justify their attachment to a way of life that is so detrimental to their psychological well-being. In *Les Charognards*, for example, he defends his usurious loans and duplicitous business dealings by arguing, "I am a useful man, . . . I serve my brothers, . . . the nation, . . . the people. . . . I am among those who have sacrificed themselves to improve the lot of others."[12] Such posturing echoes the self-righteousness with which members of the privileged class in Cameroon justify their own positions. Even when their dishonest schemes are exposed, as those of Elias's mistress are at the end of *Les Malicieuses*, people will continue to deal dishonestly with each other because they believe they can realize themselves only by amassing as much wealth as possible.

The point of Mkpatt's portrayal of this situation is to discredit the assumption that such attitudes are natural. The appearance of a brilliant young student in *Les Charognards* suggests the possibility of defining the purpose of society in a different manner. This student reveals the falsity of Elias's hypocritical self-justifications and imagines a society in which people work together for the common welfare rather than competing for disproportionate shares of the country's wealth. The young man's intervention suggests that corrupt mentalities will prevail as long as the institutions that breed them remain in place. The implication is that fundamental social change is necessary if countries such as Cameroon are to escape from the malaise into which the attitudes of individuals like Elias have precipitated them.

The perverse functioning of the present social system and the need for revolutionary change become even more apparent in plays by Ghonda-Nounga and Ekossono. Each of their works invites spectators to form their own judgments about the society it portrays. Employing music, dance, mime, choral responses, and Brechtian distanciation techniques, Ghonda-Nounga's *L'Ivrogne aux cieux* prods members of the audience to reflect on their own complicity in the corrupt system. The action is simple. A man who died in a drunken quarrel with one of his mistress's other lovers appears before a panel of three recently deceased individuals, all of whom recount their own lives before listening to his story. The common element in the four autobiographies is a social organization that blocks their good intentions and denies them access to a decent life. At the end of the play, the three judges refuse to condemn the man. They merely line up next to him, acknowledging their own guilt and intimating that the members of the audience should be standing next to them because everyone is responsible for acquiescing in a system that robs people of a chance to realize their human potential.

Before he died, the man had killed his rival, but his real crime is not murder. It is a failure to recognize that both he and his opponent were victims of a system that allows the privileged class to exploit the rest of the people in the country. Because all human beings have the light of reason, the judges conclude that everyone has a moral obligation to think. If they think clearly, one of them adds, they will perceive the truth and protest against the unjust structures that imprison them. By succumbing to drunkenness and jealousy, the man had abdicated his duty to think and act rationally. Applied to contemporary Cameroon, this line of argument lends support to Ghonda-Nounga's conviction that the people will overthrow the existing system once they understand how it affects their lives.

This same conviction informs Ekossono's *Ainsi s'achève la vie d'un homme* and *Le Soleil rouge*, both of which are harsh indictments of prevailing institutions in Cameroon. In his introduction to *Ainsi s'achève*, he himself describes the play as a demand for freedom of expression in the face of an emergent class structure that condones social injustice and emotional dishonesty. Based on events that took place in his own family, *Ainsi s'achève* is the story of Mballa, a man who repudiates his first wife and ceases to support their children because he is infatuated with a second wife whose influential connections have made possible his promotion to a prestigious civil-service position. However, to pay for his second wife's extravagances, he embezzles government funds, although she is hardly grateful, for the first time he refuses one of her demands, she abandons him.

When Mballa is arrested for his crime, his spirit has been broken, and he dies in misery. His fate illustrates the self-destructiveness of a mentality that beguiled him into preferring a prestigious government post and the surface glamor of his second wife over the human emotions and moral obligations that should have bound him to his first wife and their children. However, this mentality is widespread and, as Ekossono implies, contributes to the malaise from which his country is suffering.

Like the student in Mkpatt's *Les Charognards*, the houseboy in *Ainsi s'achève* serves as a foil to unmask the hypocrisy behind this corrupt mentality. In reality, Lukas is a student conducting research into middle-class behavior, and his trenchant comments expose the cynicism with which his master spouts nation-building clichés about equality and social justice while pursuing unearned rewards for himself. After quitting his job in disgust, Lukas explains how a genuine African revolution must be based upon a collective effort to eliminate ignorance and poverty, not upon self-aggrandizing individual accumulations of wealth and status. But the state does not tolerate such opinions. Lukas is arrested as a "dangerous element" who is spreading "intoxicating ideas" through the city. The real tragedy in the play is not Mballa's wretched death but the systematic suppression of the truth about what he represents.

The relationship between this suppression of the truth and the waste of intellectual talent in countries such as Cameroon is the dominant theme in *Le Soleil rouge*, which relates how a brilliant economics professor is tried on spurious charges and executed by representatives of the corrupt system, despite an irrefutable defense by his equally brilliant lawyer. The professor's crime was a public lecture in which he outlined socialist development options for his country. His idealism and analytical rigor were applauded by students disillusioned with the government's nation-building rhetoric, but the local police commissioner felt humiliated by the laughter that greeted his attempt to refute the lecture, and he instigated the false accusations that led to the professor's death. His trial is a mockery of justice. He is tortured. His lawyer is denied access to the files containing the charges. The press is not permitted to enter the courtroom. Before the case has even been heard, the presiding judge characterizes the professor as "the incarnation of evil" and "one of the greatest criminals our peaceful nation has ever known."[13] After the verdict is announced, the lawyer is so disturbed by this miscarriage of justice that he goes mad and never pleads another case.

Both the professor and the lawyer had enjoyed successful careers in Europe before returning to Africa. They could have continued living there in comfort, but they wanted to contribute their talents to the construction of their homeland. In contrast to the government, however, they believed that national development requires a never-ending search for truth, not an unquestioning acceptance of political dogma. As the lawyer explains, "truth does not proclaim itself: it must be sought, worked out, pieced together."[14] Because a corrupt system denies people the opportunity to pursue the truth in this way, genuine national development remains impossible unless the institutional structure of society is changed. The government's attempt to prevent such change merely produces injustice and wastes the potential contributions of talented, well-intentioned men like the professor and the lawyer.

Yet their efforts are not in vain, for the ideas they injected into the national discourse survive in the minds of others—those who heard Essindi's lectures or read his book *Le Soleil rouge*, a second lawyer who recounts the story of the case to his apprentice, the spectators of the play. Because the play's action parallels events that took place in Cameroon, Ekossono is suggesting that, on the stage as in real life, the quintessentially human search for truth will frustrate any regime's insistence upon political orthodoxy. According to him, honest men might be eliminated, but the yearning for truth endures, and future generations will draw inspiration from the example of those who suffered for its sake.

The assumption that ideas can survive the apparent defeat of their proponents and become the seeds of future revolutionary change is the center of focus in Bassek ba Kobhio's *Demain peut-être* and *La Première Récolte*. The former deals with an old villager's journey to the city in an attempt to bring back his son, who, unbeknownst to the father, is awaiting execution because he killed his employer in a gesture of rebellion against the corrupt system. The latter focuses on a young teacher who ignores the prescribed curriculum at a village school and offers his students an opportunity to acquire practical skills and to gain an understanding of the neocolonized world in which they are obliged to live. However, he loses his job when his unorthodox teaching methods antagonize the principal and other prominent villagers whose privileged positions are contingent upon an unquestioning popular acceptance of the status quo.

In both plays, the bearer of revolutionary insight is apparently defeated by the system, although his ideas live on in the minds of others. Inspired by his son's example, the father in *Demain peut-être* returns to his village, where he topples the corrupt chief and encourages the people to transform local institutions into instruments for satisfying their own needs. His son's pregnant fiancée accompanies him to the village, and in conjunction with the heightened consciousness he has engendered there, the birth of his grandson presages the dawn of a new age, perhaps tomorrow, as the title of the plays suggests. In *La Première Récolte*, the schoolchildren and their parents have learned to think rationally about the merchants who defraud them, the catechist who obscures the causes of their oppression, and the chief who arbitrarily makes decisions concerning their welfare. As the teacher leaves the village, his former pupils offer him the fruits of "the first harvest" from the gardens he had taught them to cultivate. Quite literally, the seeds of ideas he had sown are beginning to sprout. The major point in both plays is that people can liberate themselves if they understand the material conditions of their existence and if they assume responsibility for changing them. This lesson endures, despite the schoolteacher's dismissal and the execution of the villager's son.

Taken together, the dramatic works of the young Turks represent a powerful indictment of social inequity in the waning years of the Ahidjo regime. Mkpatt, Ekossono, Ghonda-Nounga, Bassek ba Kobhio, Tagne, and the early Moktoï all attacked the mask-wearing, acquisitive society that had emerged in Cameroon to frustrate the utopian hopes that had been generated by independence. According to them, the privileged class had erected a system that functions to its benefit, and the members of this class had a vested interest in convincing the rest of the population that such a system provides the best foundation for the construction of a unified nation. The young Turks felt that such attitudes must be challenged, and the theater offered them an opportunity to argue publicly that the defiance of political orthodoxy is not futile. As the executed man's fiancée asserts in *Demain peut-être*, "to have an ideal is already to realize it in part."[15] The plays of these writers are themselves gestures of defiance that embody ideals of a better society. When applied to the Cameroonian situation, such ideals suggest alternative ways of defining national identity, and they motivate people to liberate themselves by taking their destiny into their own hands.

The critique of acquisitive individualism and the moral blindness it entails reappeared during the mid-1980s in plays such as David Ndache Tagne's *M. Handlock ou le boulanger politique*, but the dynamism of the earlier movement had effectively been stifled by a tightening of government controls over public performances in 1981. Many of the young Turks embraced the "total theater" idea during the years of their greatest activity, but the two innovative and prolific advocates of this concept—Alexandre Kum'a Ndumbe III and Werewere Liking—produced most of their plays outside the country. All of Kum'a Ndumbe's plays were written and staged in Europe, whereas Liking has lived in the Ivory Coast for more than ten years. Nevertheless, their substantial body of published plays constitutes a major contribution to Cameroonian literate discourse about the ongoing quest for freedom and identity. Both playwrights engage spectators in a participatory, mixed-genre theater that is calculated to raise their consciousness about the mask-wearing, acquisitive, individualistic society in which they are living. The ultimate goal of such performances is to prod people toward a self-liberating redefinition of themselves in terms compatible with their cultural heritage.

Kum'a Ndumbe spent many years as a student and as a teacher in Europe, where he became familiar with the distanciation techniques of Bertolt Brecht and the carnivalesque atmosphere of Jerome Savary's Grand Magic Circus. However, he claimed that the principal impetus for his concept of theater came from traditional African society. "The essential influence for me," he declared, "is the African celebration, the village entertainment in which everyone participates and during which there are not really two camps but a community that creates and improvises. There the 'true' actors serve more as instigators; they invite the others and set in motion a scene that is different each time it is performed because improvisation and the contribution of the 'spectators' (participants) vary every night."[16] Drawing upon this model, he transforms the entire theater into a stage where actors and spectators collaborate to interpret the significance of the performance. In a sense, they become like a collective consciousness moving toward insight.

To facilitate this process, Kum'a Ndumbe continually breaks the illusion of verisimilitude, reminding spectators that his drama is not an entertainment to be purchased for a few moments of vicarious escape from everyday reality, but rather a sequence of imaginary events that have been designed to provoke serious reflection on the world outside the theater. Actors slip out of their roles to discuss the meaning of their lines or to pose questions to members of the audience. Music, dance, and mime are integral parts of his plays, and spectators are invited to join the festivities in which the dramatic action generally culminates. In *Lisa, la putain de . . .* , one of the actors even passes through the audience at the beginning of the performance, handing out hats, false noses, and fake beards to give the impression that everyone present will be playing a role.

The goal of all Kum'a Ndumbe's plays is the same—a heightened awareness of the causes behind the failure of African independence and a reaffirmation of the need for Africans to liberate themselves from the various forms of oppression to which they have been subjected. His assumption is that people desire to live decent, fulfilling lives and that, if they can be shown the obstacles to the fulfillment of this desire, they themselves will remove these obstacles. As one of the actors in *Kafra-Biatanga* declares, "the play doesn't have a meaning unless it brings about understanding."[17] Among the primary obstacles to understanding are the colonialist and neocolonialist clichés that the exploiters of Africa inculcate in the minds of the people.

Because the internalization of these clichés leads to the docile acceptance of one's own subjugation, Kum'a Ndumbe provokes a reexamination of them by showing how they serve the interests of the exploiters. If his plays achieve their goal, the nascent community of actors and spectators will arrive at a shared understanding of the present historical situation as it relates to their own lives. The festive atmosphere that unites them at the end becomes an expression of their new collective vision. It in turn presupposes a commitment to changing the oppressive institutional structures that reflect the outmoded clichés and protect the privileges of the exploiters.

Like Sonne Dipoko, Kum'a Ndumbe participated enthusiastically in the 1968 student demonstrations in France, for he saw them as a rebellion against the same cultural and political system that had become entrenched in postcolonial Africa. One of his earlier plays, *Cannibalisme*, schematizes the evolution of this system from the racist clichés of the colonialist era through Negritude to the hypocritical nation-building rhetoric of the postcolonial period. In the opening scenes, which are reminiscent of Jean Genet's *Les Noirs*, a group of whites confronts a group of blacks, and each momentarily acts as a judge of the other. The whites accuse the blacks of having been ignorant barbarians before the arrival of Europeans, and when the blacks obey a white judge's command to dance, he regards the charge as having been substantiated, gives them European clothes, and pronounces them civilized.

The blacks then accuse the whites of murder, pillage, corruption of African mentalities, and the rewriting of history to conceal the heinousness of their own crimes. When the whites reply that they were merely obeying the law of survival of the fittest, a black judge dismisses their defense and sentences them to death. The irony of the situation is that the true "cannibals" in the history of colonialism were the very whites who justified their presence in Africa on the basis of stereotyped images that branded the local inhabitants as savages. In a clever ploy to avoid execution, however, the whites propose to compromise by praising Negritude.

At this point, one of the blacks advises his fellow Africans to accept their Negritude:

> Dance Negritude
> And let yourselves be exploited . . .
> Sing Negritude
> And bow your heads
> Dance
> Negritude
> forget
> your rights.[18]

Although this mock exhortation presents Negritude as a means of reconciling one's self to servitude, the black judge accepts it and enters into an agreement that allows the white judge to retain his position as well. In historical terms, the two judges reenact the bargain that enables Europeans and the privileged classes of Africa to collaborate in the continued exploitation of the continent.

Just as the actors had slipped out of character to discuss the meaning of earlier episodes, they all drop their roles at the end of the play and say "no" to the preceding scenario, which symbolizes the beginning of the neocolonialist alliance in francophone Africa. The real villains in *Cannibalisme* are the exploiters, white as well as black. They are those who subordinate justice and human decency to the pursuit of their own self-interest. What enables them to succeed in this endeavor is their ability to beguile people with abstractions such as Negritude or "survival of the fittest"—abstractions that camouflage the oppressiveness of the system they have created to preserve their unearned power and wealth. By the end of the play, actors and spectators have presumably grasped the hypocrisy of these abstractions and repudiated them.

Focusing on the duplicity with which Western powers encourage mineral-rich provinces such as Biafra and Katanga to secede from African countries so that large multinational companies can exploit them more effectively, *Kafra-Biatanga* exposes the way foreign businessmen, politicians, journalists, scholars, and clergymen manipulate false images of Africa to sanction the pillage of the continent while deceiving Africans into believing that they are benefiting from the situation. At one point in the play, oil and mining company agents don black masks and act out the tragedy that is about to take place in secessionist Kafra. The point is that all Africans—Kafrans as well as Biatangans—are merely pawns in an international struggle for the material wealth that lies buried in their soil. By recognizing the falsity of the terms in which this struggle is usually described in the West, the play's actors and spectators become capable of saying no to further exploitation while celebrating the sense of community they have achieved in reaching consensus on this question.

A similar insight is specifically applied to countries such as Cameroon in *Le Soleil de l'Aurore*. As in much of Kum'a Ndumbe's drama, the underlying question in the play is: how could the struggle for independence have led to an even worse form of slavery? *Cannibalisme* and *Kafra-Biatanga* offer partial responses to this question. *Le Soleil de l'Aurore* examines another facet of it —the growth of petty dictatorships and their disastrous effect on the quality of life in Africa. The action in the play revolves around an authoritarian president who must decide the fate of his brother, the captured leader of an opposition guerilla movement. Ultimately, his brother's stance leaves him no choice, for the guerilla leader refuses to relinquish his belief that no one can be free in a country where anyone is enslaved. He dies before a firing squad after a blatantly fixed show trial.

A thumbnail history of his country is provided in a series of flashbacks. After seeking to suppress a popular movement for national liberation, the colonial administration installed a puppet government to protect their economic interests in the country. Over the years, the president of this government grew increasingly autocratic. A privileged class emerged to share in the wealth formerly reserved for Europeans, while the standard of living for most people declined. Police surveillance intensified, and informers were everywhere. The government preached the nation-building rhetoric and extolled the country's economic development, although it was actually kept in power by the financial and military backing of the former colonial power. Parallels with the Cameroonian situation and the Ouandié trial are obvious. By presenting such incidents as part of an ongoing conflict between the people and their oppressors, Kum'a Ndumbe is inviting spectators to recognize the falsity of the clichés that dictatorial governments use to keep themselves in power.

From his perspective, the primary cause for the failure of African independence is the materialistic individualism that impels people to exploit others for their own profit rather than working together for the common good. The inadequacy of this mindset is the real subject of *Lisa, la putain de*. . . . During a celebration hosted by the generous-hearted brothel owner Lisa for the thieves and prostitutes of a city such as Douala, the guests discuss the mass arrests that had taken place in their neighborhood after an influential politician was robbed there. The assumptions behind the government's action are called into question by one of the petty thieves who asks:

> Why do they arrest us
> Instead of giving us bread
> Why do they beat us
> instead of telling us how
> to earn our bread in this city.[19]

His rhetorical question obliges spectators to reflect on the motivation of "them," the privileged individuals who persecute the poor and the weak.

As the Robin Hood–like Dragon Sauvage remarks, everyone in the existing society is a thief, and those who steal on a large scale under the pretext of doing business are the biggest thieves of all. But they and their allies in government have created a society that cloaks their crimes in respectability while punishing the poor, who must steal and prostitute themselves to survive. In contrast with Lisa and Dragon Sauvage, the hypocritical "they" in the petty thief's rhetorical question are imprisoned behind their own masks, and the carnivalesque atmosphere at Lisa's party evokes the intensity of experience and the sense of community they prevent themselves and others from enjoying.

These values are central to the utopian vision at the heart of Kum'a Ndumbe's world view. Lisa and Dragon Sauvage have created a small countersociety that preserves such values and erects them into a set of norms according to which corrupt postcolonial African societies can be judged. The acceptance of these values is part of the heightened consciousness that unites actors and spectators at the end of each play. For example, Lisa's final words are an exhortation for people to demand freedom so they can realize their potential for life. In simplified terms, she is telling them to resist the pressures of a crassly individualistic society and become self-respecting Africans who perceive the truth clearly, live in solidarity with others, and respect a traditional wisdom that has been adapted to the conditions of modern life.

The heroes who embody this utopian vision do not always survive in Kum'a Ndumbe's plays. The president's brother in *Le Soleil de l'Aurore* is executed, and Cabral in *Amilcar Cabral, ou la tempête en Guinée-Bissao* is assassinated. However, they do not die in vain because their ideas remain alive to inspire others with a spirit of resistance in the face of injustice and oppression. Their example provides an alternative to the existing system and the false myths that sustain it. Kum'a Ndumbe's plays are posited on the same principle, for the ideas they generate in the minds of participant-spectators persist long after the end of the performance.

Although Werewere Liking's ritual drama does not have an overtly political message, it resembles Kum'a Ndumbe's work in the sense that its mixed-genre format was inspired by traditional precedent and serves to move spectator-participants toward a heightened awareness about themselves and the world around them. Liking comes from the Bassa area, and after working together with two French scholars on a book about the theatrical potential of local rituals, she began a long collaboration with one of them, Marie-José Houran-tier, in the writing and producing of modern plays that are intended to fulfill the same healing, community-reinforcing function that rituals performed in traditional society. In contrast with Kum'a Ndumbe's goal of revolutionary social change, her plays culminate in the rediscovery of a lost harmony with the cosmic order. Both writers attribute the malaise of contemporary African society to Western-influenced acquisitive individualism, but where his vision is political, hers is religious.

Liking's conception of ritual drama took shape during her intensely personal relationship with Hourantier. Their co-authored *A la rencontre de . . .* tells the story of this relationship, presenting it as the vital encounter between two races that had been separated by a long history of mistrust and stereotyped thinking. In their contemplation of traditional ritual, they discover that their approaches to reality are complementary. The representative of Europe contrib-utes an understanding of psychotherapeutic processes and an analytical rigor that enable them to translate the wisdom of ethnically specific practices into universally comprehensible terms. But her knowledge is abstract and theoretical. The representative of Africa brings to their relationship a sense for lived experi-ence that permits them to achieve the enlightenment they are seeking.

What they discover is that the purpose of human life is a movement toward love and a consciousness of harmony with the cosmic order. The representative of Europe eventually undergoes an initiation rite, and the two of them experi-ence a love that transcends the self by reintegrating them into what they call "Universal Consciousness." As Liking declares, "we were but one and the same body."[20] They saw themselves as the symbol of a new race, and their collective insight into the recovery of a lost harmony gave them a sense of mission in creating the ritual drama they produced until 1985, when their relationship came to an end.[21]

During their study of Bassa ritual, Liking and Hourantier became convinced that the cosmic force is present in every individual. However, they also observed that people in the contemporary world habitually suppress an awareness of this force as they betray each other and seek to conceal their crimes from public view. In light of the malaise produced by these tendencies, the two of them recognized the wisdom of purification rituals that allow people to expiate their crimes and realign themselves with the force that gives order to the universe. In Bassa, this force is called Um, and when it descends upon purified individuals, they will act unselfishly, for Um is the principle of love and community. Such individuals will also become capable of a heightend creativity because their gestures and words will be infused with the power of this force. Convinced that purification rituals offer a model that can be adapted to the contemporary stage, Liking and Hourantier developed an innovative dramatic form that they called ritual theater.

Hourantier once referred to Bassa purification ritual as a "danced psychotherapy" during which the "patient" is liberated from anxiety and the community purged of its underlying tensions through the expulsion of negative forces that had previously remained hidden from view. The use of color symbolism, drumming, singing, and mime establishes an emotional atmosphere that facilitates the "patient's" reintegration into the community and restores the community itself to harmony with the cosmic force. The ritual process is not a rational one, and when Liking transforms it into drama, she retains its spiritual dimension by presenting a series of emotionally charged images that bring actors and spectators together into a harmonious community at the end of the play.

Within the contemporary African context, Hourantier and Liking believe that ritual theater offers the possibility of overcoming social and psychological neuroses that express themselves in the form of parasitical privileged classes, petty dictators, outmoded traditional hierarchies, and the lethargy of the common people. If Africa is to recuperate its true identity, they argue, the tensions underlying these symptoms need to be brought to the surface and exorcised. Many of these tensions were introduced to African society under the influence of Western ideas, and in her poetry volume *On ne raisonne pas le venin*, Liking characterizes them as a poison. The antidote she prescribes is an acceptance of the cosmic force, for if people allow it to work through them, they can regain their lost sense of harmony with others and with the world around them. Those who disregard this force in seeking to realize their own desires will, she contends, be condemned to alienation and the fragmentation of their personalities. This view of the African situation has universal ramifications because, as Liking and Hourantier point out, a similar procedure could be applied to the neuroses that exist in other parts of the world.

In addition to purification rituals, Hourantier and Liking studied initiation rites, which they also viewed as a pathway to self-knowledge and harmony with the cosmic force. To adapt such rituals for the theater, however, the two women felt the need to purge them of the ideological biases that had often become associated with them. For example, their introduction to the initiatory tale *Liboy li nkundung* describes how Bassa secret societies declined when they became dominated by ambitious, materialistic individuals during the colonial era. As a result, younger people turned away from traditions that could have offered them the self-confident sense of identity they needed to act in a creative, morally responsible fashion while placing European influences in proper perspective.

Similarly, Liking's book about Amadou Hampaté Ba's *Kaydara* interprets it as an initiatory tale with an overlay of gerontocratic assumptions that obscure its central meaning.[22] As in *Liboy li nkundung*, this central meaning is relevant to contemporary African youth in a way they do not always recognize. What is essential for Liking in both tales is the insight that all individuals must descend into the depths of their own being and confront the monsters (the fears, the complexes, the ignorance) that lurk there. Only by doing so can they align themselves with the cosmic force and integrate themselves into a genuine human community.

The focus on this essential message is evident in Liking and Hourantier's collaboration on *Orphée Dafric/Orphée d'Afrique*. The first part of this volume is a novella by Liking, who models her narrative on the stages of a Bassa initiation ritual. The second part contains Hourantier's transformation of this novella into a ritual drama. Liking's novella takes place on the wedding night of an African, Orpheus, and his bride, Nyango. In a dream, he imagines that she has been swept away by the nearby White River. Motivated by love, he goes in search of her and, after overcoming many trials, discovers a fundamental truth. "Alone, I can do nothing," he realizes. "I need to be imbued with a force that keeps me within myself, that prevents me from fleeing this troubled body which fills me with so much anxiety."[23] When his physical body trembles with fear, he needs to believe in a power greater than his own will; otherwise he would despair.

Earlier, Orpheus's father had told him he would find God within himself by remaining silent and listening, by replacing self-will and materialistic desire with an acceptance of the cosmic force and a willingness to let it work through him. By the time he awakens from his dream, he realizes the pertinence of his father's counsel and the implication it has for his own role in the community. He has acquired the self-confident sense of identity that renders him worthy of his bride and equips him to lead his people out of their poverty and their falsely materialistic state of mind. Having discovered that the force behind everything that exists is also present in himself, Orpheus has successfully undergone an initiation experience and retrieved a traditional wisdom that was in danger of being lost. In one form or another, this experience is at the center of all the ritual dramas that Liking herself has written.

In plays such as *La Queue du diable*, *Du Sommeil d'injuste*, and *La Puissance de Um*, Liking assumes that a reenactment of repressed fears and hostilities will enable actors and spectators to coalesce into a community that emotionally repudiates the false values behind such feelings. For example, the mimed flashbacks in *La Queue du diable* reveal the truth about a man's incest with his daughters and the hatred that inspires his wife with a desire to kill them. The death of her son impresses upon her the horror of the situation she has helped create. A chorus of wailing women comments on the fate of women in their society, and actors planted in the audience cite proverbs in judgment of the events being enacted in front of them.

In *Du Sommeil d'injuste*, an ailing chief is portrayed by two actors—one playing the actual individual lying on his sickbed, the other portraying the persona he presents to the public. Throughout the play, the public persona refuses to recognize that he is terminally ill and continues to believe that he can control the world through an exercise of will. Although his "nation-building" policies have brought the people to the verge of starvation, he insists that everyone pretend to be happy. In the end, the figure on the bed arises, gazes into the mirror, and collapses dead on the floor. By participating in the process by means of which the truth emerges in spite of people's attempts to repress it, the spectators of both plays presumably open themselves to the cosmic force that can endow their own lives with purpose, meaning, and joy. In this state of mind, they become capable of recognizing and repudiating the false consciousness that has been foisted upon them by petty dictators like the terminally ill chief.

A similar movement toward heightened awareness characterizes *La Puissance de Um*, in which a woman initially refuses to mourn her dead husband because he never created anything with his own hands during a life governed by out-moded customs and the obsessive pursuit of wealth and pleasure. As she begins to reflect, however, she and the rest of the community realize they are all respon-sible for the man's death. Living at the crossroads of modern and traditional cultures, they now understand that his assimilation of corrupt norms was merely a symptom of what was happening to the entire village, for it too is menaced with fragmentation and purposelessness. By acquiescing in his false construc-tions of reality, the other villagers helped obscure the truth that could have liberated them from this malaise.

With the aid of the *hilun* (griot), the villagers confess the errors of the past and begin to perceive solutions to problems that had previously seemed insolu-ble. What had been repressed has come to the surface, and they have recovered the creative use of language. When the woman finally expresses love for her dead husband, the corpse arises and exhorts the power of Um (love, peace, force, and power) to descend upon the village. Liking's use of color symbolism, dance, music, and mime emotionally predisposes the audience to participate in the spiritual reconciliation that unites the village at the end of the play.

According to Liking, contemporary African society must undergo a similar catharsis if it is to regain its lost vitality and sense of purpose. Both her ritual drama *Une Nouvelle Terre* and her rituallike poetic novel *Elle sera de jaspe et de corail* suggest this possibility by focusing upon the regeneration of entire communities through the healing process that is applied to individual situations in many of her other works. For example, the villagers in *Une Nouvelle Terre* no longer have a firm sense of their own identity because they have lost contact with their traditional gods. In order to reconstruct their community at a differ-ent site, they must reestablish a deep emotional rapport with the force behind all that exists. But such rapport is possible only if they recognize past errors and relinquish the false values that presently govern their lives.

The purification ritual that brings about this rapport is facilitated by three intermediaries—the Ndinga (artist), a wise man, and a child. The errors and false values of the community are evoked during the Ndinga's chaotic dance and by the introduction of characters who represent different types of individuals, each of whom blames the others for the decline of the village. However, the appearances of the wise man and the child catalyze the Ndinga's ability to recognize the primordial force that links them all to the ancestors and to the surrounding world. When the child speaks through an initiatory mask to announce that he is the sum of the past and the present, his symbolic gesture breaks through the villagers' false consciousness. Renouncing the petty animosities that had previously alienated them from one another, they dance together as an expression of their harmony with the cosmic force.

At the end of *Une Nouvelle Terre*, all the participants arrange themselves into a star-shaped pattern that symbolizes this harmony. As Hourantier explained in her 1983 thesis on the subject, the star is a primary structural element in ritual drama as she and Liking have practiced it. According to her, the five points of the star represent the body, the emotions, the intellect, the will, and consciousness. When the villagers form this pattern, they are performing what Liking calls the "alchemy of the place"—the formal recognition of their reintegration into a genuine community that draws its creative energies from the cosmic force residing in all of them. In many ways, the village in *Une Nouvelle Terre* is a microcosm of the state, and the ritual process by means of which it purged itself of false values could also be applied to the corrupt national societies in Africa.

This possibility becomes explicit in *Elle sera de jaspe et de corail*, an extended narrative during which the enlightened reflections of a female diarist are interspersed with descriptions and conversations overheard in the country of Lunaï. Scattered through the novel, the nine pages of her diary represent stages in a ritual initiation that culminates in heightened awareness and the vision of a utopian future. The "elle" in the novel's title refers to the new race that the diarist hopes to bring into being by proclaiming her rediscovery of the "word-force" or "total language" that can expose the falsity of Lunaï's current value system and motivate its citizens to place themselves in harmony with the cosmic force. But before she achieves this goal, she, like the major characters in *Liboy li nkundung* and *Orphée Dafric*, must descend to the bottom of an abyss and regain contact with her own true self.

In this case, the abyss is the reality of present-day Lunaï. The gods had once granted the people of Lunaï access to wisdom in the form of symbolic masks, but after the colonialist intrusion and the widespread acceptance of its materialistic ethic, they turned their backs on this wisdom. The possession of things has become more important to them than the knowledge of who and what they are. They reduce everything to the status of an object that can be bought and sold. They have lost the creative power of the word, and their willingness to lie and betray their fellow citizens has completely destroyed any sense of community that might have bound them together. They are drifting without hope or purpose. In short, they have become like animals, and the diarist mockingly refers to them as tse-tse.

Among the people of the city are Grozi and Babou, whose conversations constitute a substantial part of the novel. They sense the need for an initiation experience, but Grozi's stereotyped European thinking and Babou's abstract African authenticity prevent them from realizing that they must participate in their own salvation rather than waiting for it to come to them. The voice of "Nuit-Noire" (Black-Night) haunts the abyss of Lunaï, but the diarist needs to bring it to the surface of her consciousness before she can align herself with Um, the cosmic force that will enable the new race of "jasper and coral" to come into being.

She discovers the key to the birth of this new race in her own womanhood. In mythological terms, she explains that woman first came into contact with the cosmic power of love and consciousness, but because she was afraid, she called man, who usurped the power, distorting its meaning and keeping it from her. Yet because woman experienced this power first, she retains the ability to enlighten man about its true meaning and to guide him out of the corrupt mental state into which his desire for dominance precipitated him. As the diarist realizes by the end of her meditations, the woman's message implies a new world view based on unselfish love, freedom from false constructions of reality, and the creative urge that wells up in people who allow the cosmic force to work through them. In the sense that *Elle sera de jaspe et de corail* relies on a series of images to induce a heightened sense of awareness among a community of readers, it is the narrative equivalent of Liking's ritual theater.

Like Kum'a Ndumbe and the young Turks, she aspired toward a form of total theater that could liberate spectators from the false consciousness of post-colonial society. Her orientation was predominantly spiritual while theirs was political, but such distinctions are somewhat artificial since all their works have both spiritual and political dimensions. As responses to the disappointed expectations of national independence in Africa, the new voices that surface in Cameroonian plays of the 1970s and 1980s redefine individual and collective identity in terms of utopian possibilities. Drawing upon history and ethnic cultural practices, they synthesized traditional and modern elements into a form of dramatic expression that revitalized the Cameroonian quest for freedom and identity. In the process, they helped shape the universe of discourse in which a sense of national consciousness was taking shape.

CONCLUSION
NATIONAL LITERATURE AND NATIONAL IDENTITY IN CAMEROON

Since the Second World War, an extensive print culture has developed in Cameroon. Embedded in the texts that constitute this culture are the diverse world views that literate Cameroonians have adopted in response to the social, cultural, political, and economic realities of their country. These world views reflect the aspirations of Cameroonian writers to articulate a viable sense of identity for themselves and for the community to which they belong. In many cases, this community is an explicitly national one, and although print culture is not the only source of discourse about questions of freedom and identity at the national level, it is undoubtedly the most important. Radio, film, and television do reach beyond the literate population and disseminate ideas that become commonplaces in the country. Yet even these media remain dependent upon the culture of the written word for scripts, institutional organization, and source materials.

The participation of the general public in Cameroonian print culture is limited by several factors. Literacy rates remain low in some areas of the country, and the majority of the people do not have sufficient income to purchase books. Furthermore, as the popularity of African-language radio broadcasts makes clear, Cameroonians continue to identify strongly with their own languages, whereas most of the country's writers publish their works in French or English. Unlike European countries, where the defense of national languages played a major role in the emergence of national identities, Cameroon witnessed the flourishing of a literate culture in the languages of the former colonizing powers. The use of English by writers from western Cameroon even heightened a sense of disunity insofar as it became a symbol for their determination to maintain a regional identity that set them apart from the country's francophone majority.

Nevertheless, the European-language print culture of Cameroon has decisively shaped a universe of discourse that enables its citizens to recognize their participation in a shared destiny. Within this print culture, individual texts have broached fundamental issues of national concern and proposed various ways of resolving them. These texts have also helped establish a network of reference points that large numbers of Cameroonians have internalized.

The implicit reading audience in Cameroon has expanded enormously since independence, and much of what appears in published texts eventually finds its way, in a slightly modified form, into the discourse of illiterate populations as well. For example, the *Cameroon Outlook* never enjoyed a large circulation in western Cameroon, but when its irreverent "Ako Aya" column reported in pidgin English on local scandals, the stories soon passed by word of mouth to many people who had not read the newspaper. Similarly, Cameroonians are often familiar with issues raised in school texts or books by local authors, even though they themselves may never have read them.

The shared reference points that characterize the collective consciousness of the implicit reading audience in Cameroon are of several kinds. Some are historical or social markers: the German colonial period, forced labor, independence, reunification, the UPC, planned liberalism, Ahidjo's national unity slogans, the Ouandié-Ndongmo trial, Biya's call for moral rigor and renewal, the feared secret service, and even political detention camps (ironically called "centers for civic reeducation") evoke specific connotations that most members of this implicit reading audience could identify. Other shared reference points include ethnically specific allusions that have become familiar to people throughout the country. The heroic resistance of Rudolph Douala Manga Bell and Martin-Paul Samba to the arbitrary measures of the German colonial authorities, the intellectual accomplishments of Sultan Njoya, the stolen and recovered statue of Afo-a-Kom, the stories of Kulu the Tortoise, the designs on Abbia stones, and the casting of spells such as the *kong* fall into this category.

Cameroonian writers have reinforced an awareness of such reference points by defining the kinds of situations in which Cameroonians see their own preoccupations reflected. For example, the most widely read texts of the preindependence period depict the injustice of the colonialist system and express a need to be liberated from it. The dilemma of self-definition is a dominant concern for the authors of these texts because neither traditional nor modern values alone offered them adequate models of identity. While such concerns were not limited to Cameroon, the novels of Mongo Beti, Ferdinand Oyono, and Benjamin Matip did place them in Cameroonian settings and project them into a shared universe of discourse that provided subsequent generations of readers with commonly accepted images of the colonial past.

Problems depicted by postcolonial Cameroonian writers performed a similar function. Among other concerns, these writers focused on moral blindness occasioned by outmoded traditions or the frenetic pursuit of wealth, on the obstacles to self-realization in a corrupt environment, on the tensions created by conflicting views of the world, and on the utopian possibilities of national development. Guillaume Oyono-Mbia, René Philombe, Francis Bebey, Bernard Fonlon, Marcien Towa, Bernard Nanga, and others defined the nature of these problems in ways that eventually became familiar to a broad cross-section of the Cameroonian population. The literary representation of such contemporary events as the Ouandié-Ndongmo trial in works by Beti, Philombe, Yodi Karone, Raymond Ekossono, and others also helped establish shared reference points in a Cameroonian universe of discourse.

Networks of intertextual relationships have also become increasingly apparent in Cameroonian literate culture, especially since the expansion of educational opportunities and local publishing during the 1960s and 1970s. Beti has undoubtedly exercised the greatest influence over subsequent generations of Cameroonian writers. Bebey, Philombe, Karone, Lydie Dooh Bunya, Patrice Etoundi M'Balla, Samuel Mvolo, Patrice Ndedi Penda, Rémy Médou Mvomo, Bernard Nanga, Vincent Boujeka Fodieng, and many others have testified to the impact of his work on them. For example, Ndedi Penda admitted that his reading of *Mission terminée* initially awakened in him the desire to write. As a schoolboy he had until then read works only by Europeans, and the fact that a fellow Cameroonian had written a novel was an illumination to him. "It liberated me to know that I was somehow authorized to write," he said.[1] Philombe even modeled the narrative structure of his *Sorcier blanc à Zangali* on Beti's *Pauvre Christ de Bomba* in such a way that the reader's full understanding of the text depends upon a recognition that the major character in Philombe's novel is capable of insights that transcend the Eurocentric mentality of Beti's Father Drumont.

Yet Beti is not the only Cameroonian writer whose influence over his fellow countrymen can be detected in their works. For example, the epigraph in Charly-Gabriel Mbock's *Quand saigne le palmier* is taken from Matip's *Afrique, nous t'ignorons*, and its reference to the giant baobab's function as an implacable arbiter suggests the dominant role of the tree in Mbock's novel. In *Bogam Woup*, Pabe Mongo also focuses on a giant baobab that is at the center of village affairs, but only to demythify it. Similarly, Philombe and Towa have inspired an entire generation of younger writers, just as François Sengat-Kuo's criticism of Louis-Marie Pouka's inauthenticity influenced later Cameroonian poets, and the success of Oyono-Mbia's plays spawned a veritable flood of Cameroonian social comedies.

In addition to verifiable intertextual relationships among Cameroonian literary works, such works contain common ideas, preoccupations, themes, and image complexes because the materials in them are drawn from the same environments, experiences, and historical situations. Such parallels have been reinforced by the emergence of formal and informal networks of communication among Cameroonian writers. The national writers' association was founded shortly after independence, and because most of the country's writers have had some contact with it, they have developed personal relationships that enable them to become familiar with each other's work. Collaborative efforts, including the production of plays, the editing of journals, and the organization of public events such as the Negritude roundtable at the Ecole Normale, strengthened these networks, as did the existence of local publishing houses. Public awareness of a national print culture has been heightened by the increasing, although still limited, use of Cameroonian books on school reading lists and the reviews of books and plays in local publications. Against this background, writers have begun to regard themselves as being engaged in a common enterprise, as Philombe suggests when he characterizes Cameroonian literature as a people's ongoing struggle to emancipate itself from ignorance and oppression.

A major impetus for Cameroonian writing during the colonial period was the desire to challenge European misrepresentations of Africa by portraying African realities from an African point of view. This anticolonialist project presupposed the right of Africans to define themselves in their own terms rather than accept the demeaning stereotypes of their colonialist masters. After independence, anticolonialist sentiment remained popular, but censorship and the threat of government sanctions prevented postcolonial writers from criticizing contemporary Cameroon in the same way that writers such as Beti, Oyono, Matip, Sengat-Kuo, and Epanya Yondo had criticized colonialist society. For this reason, those who began to publish in the 1960s generally treated subjects that were compatible with Ahidjo's nation-building ideology.

This conservative tendency in the depiction of contemporary social reality was reinforced by the 1963 founding of Editions CLE in Yaounde. Because the Protestant-sponsored publishing house's editorial policy favored morally uplifting texts that dealt with characteristically African situations, it tended to publish works that promoted reconciliation and the nation-building ideal. The recurrent themes in these works included the quest for individual identity, the critique of moral blindness, the universalization of ethnically specific materials, the recuperation of history from an African point of view, the definition of authenticity, and the search for appropriate ways of achieving development goals. Among the most successful of CLE's publications were the novels of Francis Bebey, whose moral idealism and synthesis of traditional and modern values were in harmony with the overall thrust of the government's nation-building ideology. Like the social comedies that proliferated on Cameroonian stages during the 1960s and early 1970s, such works seldom called the institutional structure of the existing system into question, although UPC polemicists in exile did continue to attack the Ahidjo government.

Modern literature throughout the world has focused on the experience of the individual self, and writing by Cameroonians is no exception. As in other parts of Africa, the problem of self-definition in Cameroon was exacerbated by the conflicting appeals of traditional and modern values. Some early Cameroonian writers, including Louis-Marie Pouka and Joseph Owono, adopted an assimilationist view of the African personality, and even such militant anticolonialist writers as Beti, Matip, and Sengat-Kuo espoused Western concepts of selfhood and human rights in calling for national liberation. One of the best depictions of this conflict is contained in Oyono's novels, where the vulnerabilities and false premises of the assimilationist dream are laid bare in the lives of the protagonists.

The Negritude movement represented an attempt to resolve the problem of identity by reaffirming the unity and redemptive value of the black experience, but when it was transformed into a development ideology by Senghor and others, it encountered increasing opposition from those who argued that it relegated Africans to perpetual dependency. In postcolonial Cameroon, the proponents of Negritude claimed that people could preserve their authentic identity only by reintegrating traditional values into a contemporary way of life; however, Negritude eventually became identified with the Ahidjo government's brand of cultural nationalism, and many Cameroonian intellectuals attacked Negritude as a means of commenting obliquely on the negative aspects of a political system they dared not criticize openly. In any case, the ongoing dialogue over authenticity and national development helped clarify the alternatives available to individual Cameroonians as they sought to define a viable sense of their own identity.

This concern with individual self-definition was the center of focus in most of the Cameroonian novels published by CLE during the 1960s and early 1970s, but it also characterized the works of Cameroonian poets and novelists living in exile, where they constantly confronted the need to define themselves in a foreign environment. However, a preoccupation with individual identity in a broad spectrum of Cameroonian writings is merely symptomatic of a larger social trend. Mass education, urbanization, and other aspects of the modernization process continually reinforce the idea of the autonomous self, which in any case exercises a strong appeal over the younger generation of Cameroonians. The fact that the evolution of the individual self lies at the center of so much recent Cameroonian literature hardly distinguishes it from other modern literatures, but it does illustrate the impact of individualism on the way Cameroonians conceive of themselves—a way characteristic of national discourses in most parts of the world.

Because individual identity concepts are always nested in an image of one's place in the group to which one belongs, the individual quest for identity in works by Cameroonian writers implies a parallel attempt to define a sense of collective identity. The initial utopian image of an independent Cameroon was formulated by the UPC during the colonial era. It assumed that the new nation would be a socialist, democratic expression of the people's will. However, when the Ahidjo government consolidated its power after independence, it acted in the belief that a new national identity could be forged by a ruling elite and imposed on the people from above. At the same time, it promoted an alternative utopian vision based on unity, development, cultural nationalism, and discipline. In reality, the society that emerged under Ahidjo contrasted sharply with this utopian vision, and popular disillusionment with the promise of independence became a dominant theme in the writings of postcolonial Cameroonian writers.

They in turn elaborated utopian visions that served as norms according to which the abuses of the existing system could be judged. Philombe provides a good example of this tendency, for although he identifies with the nation-building ideal in some ways, he condemns the acquisitive individualism that motivates members of the privileged class to covet unearned luxuries while their fellow countrymen remain imprisoned in hopeless poverty. According to him, the Cameroonian system is mired in corruption, hypocrisy, dependency on foreign capital, and subjection to alien cultural models. As a populist writer, he proposes to enlighten people about this situation, for he assumes that, if they become aware of the causes behind their oppression, they will eliminate them and work toward the creation of a genuine national community.

Mongo Beti, Yodi Karone, Marcien Towa, the radical young dramatists of the late 1970s and early 1980s, Paul Dakeyo, and other socially engaged writers share the general thrust of Philombe's utopian vision. Even those who envision a different ideal tend to acquiesce in the criticisms he levels against the existing system. The important point is not the disagreement among them but the fact that large numbers of Cameroonian writers have engaged themselves in an ongoing dialogue over the shape of their country's future. In this way, they helped establish the network of shared reference points by means of which Cameroonians can discuss the common destiny they are obliged to confront as the result of their historical and geographical situation. In other words, the print culture of Cameroon has been largely responsible for creating the universe of discourse that enables people to conceptualize a national identity.

Within the Cameroonian context, national identity usually implies a series of nested identity concepts that include ethnic affiliation and a commitment to pan-African ideals. For example, the protagonist in Beti's *Mission terminée* exists in a cultural environment modeled on that of the author's own Bané people, but as this character struggles to articulate a viable identity in a harsh, rapidly changing world where neither traditional nor modern values provide him with adequate guidance, he experiences difficulties similar to those encountered by young men throughout Africa. One might say that the novel reflects ethnic group identity on the level of narrative content and a concern for African problems in terms of its ideological message. Consciousness of a Cameroonian identity is definitely muted. By the 1970s, however, the national context had become a primary point of reference in Beti's fiction. Even when a specific ethnic setting is evoked, as in *La Ruine presque cocasse d'un polichinelle*, it often functions as a microcosm of the Cameroonian nation. There is a similar focus on national identity in a broad spectrum of works by other writers—historical plays, patriotic poetry, polemical essays, dramatic and novelistic critiques of the existing system, exile literature, and popular fiction. It is even present in the implicit communities that the "totalizing theater" of writers such as Alexandre Kum'a Ndumbe III and Werewere Liking brings together for their performances.

Just as much of what constitutes a sense of national identity is defined after the fact, the concept of a national literature is always constructed in retrospect on the basis of texts that have already been written. In both cases, the concepts involved acquire idiosyncratic shapes as they evolve in the dialectic between individual consciousness and the prevailing universe of discourse in a particular society. As in the Americas, national identity and national literature concepts initially surfaced in Cameroon among literate elites who desired the same rights and privileges that were accorded to the citizens of the colonizing country. After independence, the print culture that consolidated this implicit reading community remained linked with the use of French and (to a lesser degree) English. This linkage excluded a large segment of the population from participation in the national discourse and assured the perpetuation of a privileged class, whose members owed their status in part to their mastery of European languages. Nevertheless, the European-language writing of Cameroonians preserves a mosaic of world views that often undercut the assumptions of this privileged class, just as the assumptions of the colonizers were undercut in the anticolonialist works of an earlier period.

Like national literatures everywhere, Cameroonian literature is a concept that has been constructed by critics, historians, literary scholars, journalists, radio broadcasters, members of the national writers' association, publishers, journal editors, schoolteachers, government officials, university students, and others who have contributed to an ongoing dialogue over the meaning and significance of Cameroonian writing. Numerous literary histories and anthologies have appeared. The majority of dissertations on literary subjects at the national university are devoted to Cameroonian topics. And although the schools have never placed primary emphasis on Cameroonian works, these works have increasingly appeared on school reading lists. As this process of dissemination and critical evaluation gains momentum, a canon of Cameroonian authors and characteristic traits of Cameroonian literature are being "discovered" in the same way they have been discovered in national literatures from other parts of the world.

Because Cameroonian literate culture has come into existence only during the past fifty years, the term *national literature* should be applied with caution, but this literature has clearly evolved in much the same way as national literatures elsewhere. With the expansion and diversification of written culture in Africa, the national literature concept has certain advantages. It draws attention to the ways in which written literature is influenced by social institutions and networks of intellectual exchange that are different in different parts of the continent. It also helps to situate individual works within the universe of discourse that prevails in the national environment where they were conceived.

Yet the term *national literature* is like any other schema that is used to describe a complex, ambiguous reality. It can reveal only a portion of that reality. In the case of Cameroon, it does not do justice to the ethnically based oral literature that still shapes the dominant universe of discourse for millions of people. It also minimizes the pan-African sentiment that continues to inspire many Cameroonians. Nevertheless, a detailed examination of Cameroonian literate culture has revealed the usefulness of the national literature concept in seeking to comprehend the complex interrelationships between national identity, written discourse, and the aspirations of the people. Similar relationships exist in other countries, and although the national literature concept may not prove as fruitful elsewhere in Africa as it has in Cameroon, we will be able to comprehend the specific nature of such relationships only if we subject the print cultures of other African countries to similar detailed examinations.

NOTES

1. NATIONAL IDENTITY AND NATIONAL LITERATURES IN AFRICA

1. Historically speaking, the word *nationalism* is itself a recent coinage. Although occurrences of it can be found in late nineteenth-century England and France, it did not enter the Italian or German vocabulary until the twentieth century, at which time its connotations were influenced by the emergence of a highly conservative nationalist movement in France. See Raoul Girardet, "Autour de l'idéologie nationaliste: Perspectives de recherche," *Revue Française de Science Politique* 14 (1964): 423–45.

2. The African National Unity Project at Northwestern University gathered considerable empirical evidence to support this claim. See John N. Paden, ed., *Values, Identities, and National Integration: Empirical Research in Africa* (Evanston: Northwestern University Press, 1980). The strength of national identity concepts obviously varies from one country to another. In Uganda, Zaire, and Chad, for example, internal conflict and/or corruption has produced situations in which popular acceptance of a national identity is probably weaker now than it was shortly after independence. For other reasons, there has never been a particularly strong sense of allegiance to the nation-state in a country such as Burkina Faso. Furthermore, problems of sheer physical survival are so pressing in some areas of Africa that national identity is a consideration of minor concern for the majority of the population.

3. Benedict Anderson develops this thesis at some length in his book *Imagined Communities: Reflections on the Origin and Spread of Nationalism* (London: Verso, 1983).

4. The consequences of this situation are authoritatively described in Crawford Young, *The Politics of Cultural Pluralism* (Madison: University of Wisconsin Press, 1976), and Jean François Bayart, *L'Etat en Afrique* (Paris: Fayard, 1989).

5. In two important essays, "Sur la culture nationale" and "Fondements réciproques de la culture nationale et des luttes de libération," Frantz Fanon defines national culture as the aggregate of all intellectual efforts to describe, justify, and celebrate the actions by means of which a people has constituted itself and maintained a coherent sense of its own identity. According to him, this culture is a dynamic and constantly evolving expression of a people's struggle to free itself from oppression while working out in practice the self-confident sense of identity that enables it to assimilate influences from other peoples while contributing to their cultural evolutions in return. Fanon's recognition of the role played by national cultures and his analysis of their relationship to colonized peoples' aspirations for freedom and identity are extremely insightful, although he perhaps underestimates the importance of the complex interplay between conservative and revolutionary ideologies in the shaping of a national consciousness, particularly in the postcolonial era. See Fanon, *Les Damnées de la terre* (1961; rpt. Paris: Maspero, 1968), pp. 141–75.

6. For many people, *collective memory* suggests Jungian connotations of inherent knowledge. However, in *La Mémoire collective* (Paris: Presses Universitaires de France, 1950), Maurice Halbwachs defines it as shared patterns of acquired knowledge, and it is in this sense that I am using the term.

7. In *Nations and Nationalism* (Oxford: Basil Blackwell, 1983), Ernest Gellner develops the idea that the nation as a form of socio-political organization emerged to meet the demands of industrialization and then elaborated the myths that justify its existence in its own eyes. According to him, there are many cultural communities, but only some of them have evolved into nations in response to the contingencies of pursuing modernization. The concept of reading audiences and their role in creating a sense of national identity has been insightfully discussed in Anderson's *Imagined Communities*.

8. For a fuller discussion of the cognitive mapping concept, see Richard Bjornson, "Cognitive Mapping and the Understanding of Literature," *Sub-Stance* 30 (1981): 51–62. In *The Tree of Knowledge: The Biological Roots of Human Understanding* (Boston and London: Shambhala, 1987), Huberto Maturana and Francisco Varela speak of the "world" that every individual brings forth in part through interactions with other members of his or her cultural group. Although they prefer *structural coupling* over *mental representation* as the appropriate term to define the way people organize and store information, their account of knowledge acquisition supports the general line of argument being advanced here.

9. In *Culture and Inference: A Trobriand Case Study* (Cambridge: Harvard University Press, 1980), Edwin Hutchins discusses the relationship between inference procedures and schemas in a litigation that took place in a Trobriand village. Hutchins's model helps explain how cultural codes enable people to generate a large number of propositions on the basis of fragmentary evidence.

10. For an account of the way African philosophies of authenticity evolved from European anthropological and missionary discourse, see V. Y. Mudimbe, *The Invention of Africa* (Bloomington: Indiana University Press, 1988). In "Out of Africa: Topologies of Nativism" (*The Yale Journal of Criticism* 2, 1 [1988]: 153–78), Anthony Appiah relates this situation to the question of identity in contemporary Africa.

11. A good account of this development is contained in John M. Meyer, "Myths of Socialization and Personality," in Thomas Heller, Morton Sosna, and David Wellberry, eds., *Reconstructing Individualism: Autonomy, Individuality, and the Self in Western Thought* (Stanford: Stanford University Press, 1986), pp. 208–21.

12. An excellent account of the privileged class and its formation in postcolonial Africa is contained in Bayart's *L'Etat en Afrique*.

13. An interesting psychoanalytical account of the way writers and artists project their own identities into their works is contained in Anton Ehrenzweig, *The Hidden Order of Art: A Study in the Psychology of Artistic Imagination* (1967; rpt. Berkeley: University of California Press, 1976).

14. For an extensive account of this phenomenon, see Albert S. Gérard, *African-Language Literature: An Introduction to the Literary History of Sub-Saharan Africa* (Washington, D.C.: Three Continents Press, 1981).

15. In Africa, the existence of transnational publishing ventures and the inclusion of works from all over the continent on school reading lists keep alive a sense of pan-African identity that in some ways competes with the national identity concept.

16. In *Les Lieux de mémoire: I. La République* (Paris: Gallimard, 1984) and *Les Lieux de mémoire: II. La Nation* (Paris: Gallimard, 1986), Pierre Nora refers to these reference points as "lieux de mémoire," which can include historical events, flags, laws, monuments, encyclopedias, geographical locations, and other allusions that acquire a commonly recognized symbolic significance.

17. Somalia represents a partial exception to this statement, and in *African-Language Literature*, Gérard discusses several literatures that could form the basis for such a development.

18. Ngugi wa Thiong'o, "The Language of African Literature," in *Decolonizing the Mind: The Politics of Language in African Literature* (London: James Currey, 1986), p. 27.

19. In "Nécessité d'une langue nationale" (*Abbia* 7 [1964]: 83–99), the Cameroonian scholar Pierre Ngijol asserts that "une nation est nécessairement une langue" (92) and claims that it would be relatively easy to force ("amener par la contrainte") the entire population of a nation to learn a single African language.

20. Bernard Dadié, "De la Problématique d'écrire dans une langue qui n'est pas votre langue maternelle pour rendre votre identité," in *Congrès mondiale des littératures*

de langue française: Actes (Padua: Centro Stampa di Palazzo Maldura dell'Università di Padova, 1984), p. 627. [". . . l'emploi de la langue française n'est pas un obstacle à me réaliser pleinement."]

21. This suggestion has been made by Pierre Alexandre in his "De l'oralité à l'écriture: Sur un example camerounais," *Études Françaises* 12 (1976): 70–78. It has also been perceptively discussed by Albert Gérard in his "Reflexions sur le destin de la francophonie littéraire en Afrique noire," *Congrès Mondiale . . . Actes*, 3–14.

22. The term *affective style* was introduced by Robert P. Armstrong in his *The Affecting Presence: An Essay in Humanistic Anthropology* (Urbana: University of Illinois Press, 1971). By adopting it, he focuses attention on the techniques and conventions that artists or writers from a cultural community habitually employ when seeking to evoke the psychological equivalent of experiencing an event, rather than merely communicating information about it.

23. There has been considerable debate over this issue in recent years. Conferences on the subject were held in Limoges and Dakar in the early 1980s. Special issues of *Research in African Literatures* 18, 3 (1987) and *Notre Librairie* 83, 84, and 85 (1986) have been devoted to the subject. The latter has also brought out special issues on Senegalese, Congolese, Zairean, Malian, Benin, and other national literatures in Africa. Anthologies and histories of national literatures have proliferated in recent years. Among the treatments of individual national literatures are Roger Chemain and Arlette Chemain-Degrange's *Panorama Critique de la littérature contemporaine congolaise* (Paris: Présence Africaine, 1979); Adrien Huannou's *La Littérature béninoise de langue française* (Paris: Karthala, 1984); Dorothy Blair's *Senegalese Literature: A Critical History* (Boston: Twayne, 1984); Mukala Kadima-Nzuji's *La Littérature zaïroise de langue française* (Paris: Karthala, 1984); and Richard Priebe's *Ghanaian Literature* (New York: Greenwood, 1988). One of the most outspoken opponents of the "national literature" concept is Guy Ossito Midiohouan, who regards it as misleading insofar as it draws unmerited attention to works of minor significance and sanctions the pseudoindependence of African countries that remain subject to the cultural, political, and economic domination of Europe. See his "Anthologies et littératures nationales en Afrique noire d'expression française," *Peuples Noirs/Peuples Africains* 37 (1984): 55–64, and his "The Nation-Specific Approach to African Literature," in Kenneth Harrow, Jonathan Ngaté, and Clarisse Zimra, eds., *Crisscrossing Boundaries* (Washington: Three Continents, forthcoming), Annual Papers of the African Literature Association. In his *L'Idéologie dans la littérature négro-africaine d'expression française* (Paris: L'Harmattan, 1986), he attacks the balkanization of African literature on the grounds that, when the national literature concept is applied to Africa, it imposes a false construction of reality and a Eurocentric mode of criticism on the continent's literary production. In *La Question des littératures nationales* (Abidjan: CEDA, 1989), Huannou responds at length to Midiohouhan's arguments and provides a convenient summary of opinions about the national literature question. For him, *national literature* is a descriptive term with no ideological connotations; it merely designates the total corpus of oral and written literary works produced in any language by authors from a given nation. If all African states are nations, as he claims, then the literatures of these states are national literatures, and there are as many national literatures in Africa as there are states. After criticizing the overgeneralizations characteristic of pan-African approaches, he concludes that the future of literary studies lies in the examination of works within their national contexts. The opposing positions of Midiohouhan and Huannou are defined in categorical terms, although the issue itself can be treated in a far more flexible manner. It might simply be the case that the national literature concept is more applicable in some African countries than in others.

2. THE AMBIGUOUS BLESSING

1. The word *acculturation* has also been used to describe this process. Those recognized as "assimilés" in French colonial Africa or as "assimilados" in Portuguese Africa were formally accorded rights and privileges denied to the majority of the population in these areas.

2. Considerable credit for the spread of literacy in this area should be given to Alfred Saker, who compiled a Douala-English dictionary, wrote a grammar and a textbook of the language, and translated the Bible as well as a hymnal into Douala during more than twenty-five years of missionary activity. See Alfred Saker, *Pioneer of the Cameroons* (London: Carey Press, 1929).

3. See Iwiyé Kala Lobé's *Douala Manga Bell: Héros de la résistance douala* (Paris: ABC and Dakar, Abidjan: NEA, 1977). Richard Joseph links the Douala protest movements with the later independence movement in *Radical Nationalism in Cameroun: Social Origins of the U. P. C. Rebellion* (Oxford: Clarendon Press, 1977), p. 37. For additional information about Douala history, I am indebted to interviews with Léopold Moumé-Etia (Jan. 25, 1982) and Jacques Kuoh-Moukouri (Jan. 28, 1982). Martin Lobe Bebe Bell composed his profoundly patriotic song "Tet'Ekombo" (Father of the People) in honor of Douala Manga Bell in 1929, and it is still sung on August 8 each year in commemoration of his death.

4. For a brief account of Njoya's life and the alphabet he created, see Adamou Ndam Njoya, *Njoya: Réformateur du royaume bamoum* (Paris: ABC and Dakar, Abidjan: NEA, 1977). An authoritative study of the *shümon* script can be found in A. Schmidt's *Die Bamun-Schrift* (Wiesbaden: O. Harrasowitz, 1963). In addition to his creation of a Bamun alphabet, Njoya built one of the most impressive palaces in West Africa, supervised the first topographical survey of the region and the preparation of its first map, reorganized his military and civilian administrations along more efficient lines, invented a grain mill and a printing press, revolutionized the local fabrication of textiles, reformed Bamun agriculture, and patronized a burgeoning colony of artists and craftsmen.

5. Ferdinand Oyono, François Sengat-Kuo, René Philombe, and many lesser-known writers were all children of secretary-interpreters. Their own later accomplishments may well have something to do with the fact that their fathers were among the few Cameroonians who kept books, magazines, and other printed materials in their homes. Jacques Kuoh-Moukouri's *Doigts noires* (Montreal: A La Page, 1963) contains a description of the role played by secretary-interpreters in the French colonial system. For further details about their activities, I have drawn upon interviews with Kuoh-Moukouri (Jan. 29, 1982), Léopold Moumé Etia (Jan. 25, 1982), and Louis-Marie Pouka (June 29, 1977), as well as upon conversations with René Philombe.

6. Patrice Kayo, *Panorama de la littérature camerounaise* (Yaounde: Librairie Panafricaine, 1979), p. 9.

7. The most complete account of Pouka's life is contained in Patrice Kayo, "Louis-Marie Pouka, l'homme et l'oeuvre," unpublished thesis (Yaounde, 1973). For additional biographical details, I am indebted to interviews with Pouka on June 29 and July 7, 1977.

8. Louis-Marie Pouka M'Bague, "Souvenir d'enfance," *Eveil des Camerouniens* (Dec. 10, 1934): 2.

9. Pierre-François Lacroix, ed., *Poésie peule de l'Adamawa* (Paris: Julliard, 1965), I, 28. Ajami is a non-Arabic language that has been transliterated into Arabic script. Lacroix claims that there were still 1,759 Koranic schools and 170 Koranic secondary schools in the northern part of the French mandate as late as 1956. However, the majority of the population in northern Cameroon is neither Fulani nor Muslim, for indigenous ethnic groups were subjected to domination by Fulani Muslims from the

West only at the beginning of the nineteenth century. They have been lumped together under the somewhat pejorative Fulani term *Kirdi*, but in reality they exhibit a broad spectrum of ethnic practices, responses to Fulani hegemony, and receptiveness to Western-style schooling. For an account of the Fulani adaptation to the colonial situation, see Victor Azarya, *Dominance and Change in North Cameroon: The Fulbe Aristocracy* (Beverly Hills: Sage Publications, 1976), Sage Research Papers in the Social Sciences 90–030.

10. The "corvée" (forced or statutory labor) was introduced in the colonies long after it was abandoned in France, where it was a common practice before the Revolution.

11. Victor T. LeVine, *The Cameroons: From Mandate to Independence* (Berkeley: University of California Press, 1964), p. 8.

12. David E. Gardinier, "The French Impact on Education in Africa," in Wesley Johnson, ed., *Double Impact: France and Africa in the Age of Imperialism* (Westport, Conn.: Greenwood, 1985), pp. 333–44.

13. *Nnanga kôn* is discussed in Pierre Alexandre and Jacques Binet, *Le Groupe dit Pahouine (Fang-Boulou-Beti)* (Paris: P.U.F., 1958), p. 126; Kayo, *Panorama*, p. 58; and Albert Gérard, *African-Language Literatures: An Introduction to the Literary History of Sub-Saharan Africa* (Washington, D.C.: Three Continents Press, 1981), p. 285.

14. The *mvet* is a stringed instrument with a resonating gourd. It is used by oral story-tellers as an accompaniment to their songs and narratives. The oral epic in this region is also known as an *mvet*.

15. René Philombe, *Le Livre camerounais et ses auteurs* (Yaounde: private, 1977), p. 85.

16. For a discussion of the school situation in the former British Cameroons, see D. and G. Courade, *L'Ecole du Cameroun anglophone* (Yaounde: Centre Géographique National, 1977).

17. Interview with Jeanne Ngo Mai (Feb. 18, 1982).

18. In addition to Isaac Moumé Etia, who printed his works privately and sold them from his home, the Protestant pastor Martin Itondo published a number of works during the 1930s—a history, a biography of Mandesi Bell, a collection of proverbs, and several religious works. Dualla Misipo, a young medical student living in Germany, also published an autobiography, *Der Junge aus Douala* (1930), in which he seeks to make African culture and his own encounter with European society comprehensible to a German reading audience. In any case, the rate of literacy was extremely high among the Douala.

19. Joseph, *Radical Nationalism*, p. 55.

20. Claude Welch, *Dream of Unity: Pan-Africanism and Political Unification in West Africa* (Ithaca: Cornell University Press, 1966), p. 157.

21. Willard R. Johnson, *The Cameroon Federation: Political Integration in a Fragmentary Society* (Princeton: Princeton University Press, 1970), pp. 117–18. Johnson's information is based on an interview with Betayéné.

22. Interview with Paul Soppo Priso (Apr. 9, 1982). See also Joseph, *Radical Nationalism*, pp. 71–73.

23. *Conférence Africaine Française: Brazzaville (30 janvier 1944–8 février 1944)* (Paris: Ministère des Colonies, 1945), p. 28.

24. *Conférence Africaine Française*, p. 22. ["dans la grande France, il n'y a ni peuples à affranchir ni discriminations raciales à abolir. Il y a des populations qui se sentent Français . . . [et] qui n'entendent connaître autre indépendance que l'indépendance de la France."]

25. Interview with Léopold Moumé Etia (Jan. 25, 1982). See also Joseph, *Radical Nationalism*, pp. 64–67.

26. Paul M. Kale, *Political Evolution in the Cameroons* (Buea: Government Printer, 1967), p. 50.

27. Neville Rubin, *Cameroun: An African Federation* (New York: Praeger, 1971), pp. 79–80.

28. Tambi Eyongetah and Robert Brain, *A History of the Cameroon* (London: Longman, 1974), p. 128.

29. Jacques Chastenet, "Eurafrique, chance suprême d'Europe," *La Presse du Cameroun* 1488 (Apr. 22, 1955): 4. ["notre méthode est, tout considéré, la meilleure."] The newspaper's refusal to print Um Nyobé's letter is described in Um Nyobé, "Je n'ai jamais préconisé la manoeuvre de diversion," *Lumière* (Apr. 30, 1956): 7. For an account of the Cameroonian press at this time, see Ignace-Bertrand Moundolock, *La Presse écrite et la liberté au Cameroun du mandat à la tutelle* (Yaounde: private, 1975).

30. J. Repiquet, "Préface," in R. P. A. Albert, *Bandjoun* (Ottawa: L'Arbre, 1943), Series France Forever, pp. 14–15. [". . . contraires aux principes de la civilisation. . . . il s'agit de la grande pitié des Noirs et du devoir éminent de les élever au-dessus de leur condition morale et matérielle."]

31. Jean-Marie Carret, *Kel'lam, fils d'Afrique* (Paris: Alsatia, 1958), pp. 254 and 98. ["Je vous apporte la liberté."]

32. The letter is in the possession of René Douala Bell, who discusses it in his unpublished manuscript "La Maison Bell."

33. In "Alexandre, un prince d'autrefois" (*La Presse du Cameroun* 2934 [Oct. 10, 1966]: 4), de Julliot wrote, "le prince aurait pu . . . dominer de haut la littérature camerounaise."

34. David Gardinier, *United Nations Challenge to French Policy* (London: Oxford University Press, 1963), p. 32, supplemented by figures in *L'Effort Camerounais* 16 (Mar. 25–31, 1969): 2. In *Verstärkung von Unterentwicklung durch Bildung? Schulische und ausserschulische Bildung im Kontext gesamtgesellschaftlicher Entwicklung in Kamerun* (Bonn: Neue Gesellschaft, 1978), Schriftenreihe des Forschungs-Instituts der Friedrich Ebert Stiftung, Band 134, Renate Nestvogel gives slightly different figures for secondary-school enrollments, which according to her increased from 855 to 9,290 between 1949 and 1957 (p. 116).

35. Lucien Anya Noa, "Le Cercle d'Etudes du Grand Séminaire d'Otélé," *Abbia* 3 (1963): 154–56.

36. Louis-Marie Pouka M'Bague, "Première Poukiade" (1959), rpt. in *Poèmes* (Yaounde: Lumen, 1971), p. 52. ["Je reconnais bien que vous êtes mon maître."]

37. D. and G. Courade, *L'Ecole du Cameroun anglophone*, p. 12.

3. ANTICOLONIALISM AND REVOLUTION

1. The writings of Um Nyobé have become more accessible since the publication of J. A. Mbembe's selected edition of his works in Ruben Um Nyobé, *Le Problème national kamerunais* (Paris: L'Harmattan, 1984). See also Ndong Lolog Wonyu II, *Cameroun: Plaidoyer pour le patriote martyr Ruben Um Nyobé* (Paris: L'Harmattan, 1988).

2. In *France and the Africans, 1944–1960: A Political History* (London: Faber and Faber, 1969), Edward Mortimer provides information on UPC membership figures (p. 214). For a discussion of local organizing activities, see Richard Joseph, "Ruben Um Nyobé and the 'Kamerun' Rebellion," *African Affairs* 73, 293 (1974): 428–48.

3. Willard Johnson, *The Cameroon Federation: Political Integration in a Fragmentary Society* (Princeton: Princeton University Press, 1970), p. 156, and Joseph, "Ruben Um Nyobé," p. 442.

4. At least 149 such publications were registered with the colonial authorities at this time, and there were undoubtedly more that were not registered. See Ignace-Bertrand Moundolock, *La Presse écrite et la liberté au Cameroun du mandat à la tutelle* (Yaoundé: private, 1975).

5. For a discussion of church attitudes toward the nationalist movement, see Emma-

nuel Kengne Pokam, *Les Eglises chrétiennes face à la montéé du nationalisme camerounais* (Paris: L'Harmattan, 1987), esp. pp. 27–103.

6. For a good account of this influential newspaper, see Jean-Paul Bayemi, *"L'Effort Camerounais," ou la tentation d'une presse libre* (Paris: L'Harmattan, 1989).

7. Victor T. LeVine, *The Cameroons: From Mandate to Independence* (Berkeley: University of California Press, 1964), p. 84.

8. "Congrès extraordinaire de la Fédération des Etudiants d'Afrique Noire en France," *Présence Africaine*, n.s. 17–18 (1959): 250–55.

9. Interview with Vroumsia Tchinaye (Mar. 24, 1982).

10. Originally published in the Feb. 20, 1954, issue of the *Bulletin*, Sengat-Kuo's letter has been reprinted in René Philombe, *Le Livre camerounais et ses auteurs* (Yaounde: private, 1977), pp. 212–14.

11. François Sengat-Kuo, "Lettre à un camerounais," cited in Philombe, *Le Livre camerounais*, p. 214. [". . . l'arbre ne peut croître qu'en enfonçant ses racines, et le plus profondément possible, dans la terre nourricière."]

12. Sengat-Kuo, "Ils sont venus," *Fleurs de latérite/Heures rouges* (Yaounde: CLE, 1971), p. 11. ["ils sont venus / civilisation / bibles sous le bras / fusils en main"]

13. Sengat-Kuo, "Fidélité," *Fleurs/Heures*, p. 16. ["on a 'blanchi' ma cervelle / mais mon âme est restée noire indomptée / elle pulse au rhythme chaud du tam-tam / elle pulse au rhythme vivant des choses"]

14. Interview with François Sengat-Kuo (Mar. 26, 1982).

15. Elolongue Epanya Yondo, "Souviens-toi," *Kamerun! Kamerun!* (Paris: Présence Africaine, 1960), p. 93. ["Il n'avait que quinze ans / Quinze ans d'âge, d'espoir et de courage / Il a été tué. . . ."] The poems in this volume were originally written in the Douala language and then translated into French; both versions were published on facing pages.

16. Jean Ikelle-Matiba, *Cette Afrique-là* (Paris: Présence Africaine, 1963), p. 51. ["Depuis la colonisation, l'opinion internationale a été trop mystifiée, car seul le colonisateur disposait des moyens d'information. Pour ériger son mode de vie en système universel immuable, il a crée une littérature, un style et même une éthique et c'est à travers ces clichés que nous sommes jugés."] The text of *Cette Afrique-là* was completed in 1955 and revised several times during the late 1950s, although it was not published until 1963.

17. Matip, *Afrique, nous t'ignorons*, p. 75. ["Ma politique, c'est moi."]

18. Matip, *Afrique, nous t'ignorons*, p. 61. ["Il est des âmes qui doivent être maintenues dans l'ignorance. . . . Il n'y a pas de guerre."]

19. Ikelle-Matiba, *Cette Afrique-là*, p. 83. [". . . les plus beaux moments de notre vie."]

20. Ikelle-Matiba, *Cette Afrique-là*, p. 113. ["Je me sentais de plus en plus camerounais. J'étais complètement détribalisé."]

21. Their numbers were substantial. In *Dream of Unity: Pan-Africanism and Political Unification in West Africa* (Ithaca: Cornell University Press, 1966), Claude Welch estimates that twenty percent of the people living in the Victoria subdivision in 1951 had been born in eastern Cameroon. Throughout the 1950s, Douala and Bamileke cultural associations in the French trust territory were very supportive of reunification.

4. DREAM AND DISILLUSIONMENT IN THE NOVELS OF FERDINAND OYONO

1. The difference between Oyono's orientation and that of Beti can be gauged by the way they responded to the conservative coalition that came to power shortly before independence in Cameroon. Oyono accepted the Ahidjo regime as compatible with his conception of national independence and served it faithfully as a diplomat in various

European, American, and African cities before returning to Yaounde and becoming a minister after Paul Biya acceded to the presidency in 1982. Beti rejected the Ahidjo government as a neocolonialist betrayal of the genuine nationalism that had come to expression in Um Nyobé's UPC, and he remained in France, eventually becoming an outspoken critic of Ahidjo and Biya.

2. In *"Une Vie de boy": Oyono* (Paris: Hatier, 1977), Jacques Chevrier contends that Oyono's favorite readings were the works of realist writers such as Balzac, Zola, Maupassant, and Erskine Caldwell. The Cameroonian novelist's view of life as a series of harsh realities may have been influenced by them, but as François Minyono-Nkodo points out in "Le Monde romanesque de Ferdinand Oyono ou pour une esthétique de décadence" (*Colloque sur littérature et esthétique négro-africaine* [Dakar, Abidjan: NEA, 1979], pp. 173–81), a similar world view can also be found in Bulu oral tales such as those about Kulu the Tortoise, who generally succeeds in an implacable world of power relationships by resorting to clever but often cruel ruses.

3. Ferdinand Oyono, *Une Vie de boy* (Paris: Julliard, 1956), p. 88. ["La rivière ne remonte pas à sa source."]

4. Oyono in an interview reported by Jean Marcenac in "Jacques-Stephen Alexis, Mongo Beti, René Depestre, Ferdinand Oyono: Les Littératures noires et la France," *Les Lettres Françaises* 643 (Dec. 1–7, 1956): 6. [". . . le Cameroun a été un pays sur lequel on avait tiré un certain rideau de fantasmagorie. L'écrivain camerounais doit donc, avant tout, essayer de lever ce rideau. . . ."]

5. Victor Turner, *The Ritual Process* (1969; rpt. Ithaca, N.Y.: Cornell University Press, 1979), esp. pp. 111–16 and 176–77.

6. In "Le Tragique dans les romans de Ferdinand Oyono" (*Présence Francophone* 7 [1973]: 24–30), Douglas Alexander points out that the actual climax in Oyono's novels is not an event that takes place but the major character's insight into the meaning of what has taken place; he suggests that Toundi and Meka are like Oedipus in the sense that they recognize the significance of their previous actions only when it is too late to alter the situation that has arisen as a consequence of them.

7. Oyono, *Une Vie de boy*, p. 32. [". . . le chien du roi est le roi des chiens."]

8. In "Ferdinand Oyono: *Le Vieux Nègre et la médaille*" (*Der Unabhängigkeitskampf im afrikanischen Gegenwartsroman französischer Sprache* [Bonn: Bouvier, 1979], pp. 122–55), Werner Glinga suggests that the term *vieux nègre* was a stereotyped French colonial expression for the harmless "good nigger" who was too old to be exploited further. Both Samuel Ade Ojo ("Ferdinand Oyono, chroniquer de la réalité coloniale au Cameroun," *Présence Francophone* 20 [1980]: 32–56) and Kofi Awoonor ("James Ngugi, Ferdinand Oyono, and the Anticolonial Novel," in *The Breast of the Earth* [Garden City, N.Y.: Anchor, 1976], pp. 281–305) point out the irony of awarding Meka a medal on a day that symbolizes liberty, equality, and fraternity for Frenchmen but also serves as a pretext for glorifying the enslavement of colonized people throughout the French empire.

9. The priest's casting of the sugar cubes among the children also recalls Christ's parable of the seeds, but rather than offering the people ideas that can sprout into truths in their own minds, he is sowing discord among them and leading them into the assimilationist trap.

10. In "Jungian Archetypes and the Main Characters in Oyono's *Une Vie de boy*" (*African Literature Today* 7 [1975]: 117–22), Charles Nnolim argues that Toundi's experiences are archetypal examples of universal human concerns as portrayed under the influence of Judeo-Christian mythology. Such an approach might be equally appropriate for an analysis of the humorous cataclysm scene in *Le Vieux Nègre*.

11. The police chief Gosier d'Oiseau is the only character who appears in both novels.

12. Oyono, *Le Vieux Nègre et la médaille* (Paris: Julliard, 1956), p. 163. [". . . chemin qui mène aux fantômes."]

13. Oyono, *Le Vieux Nègre*, p. 170. [". . . ce qui est arrivé à l'homme mûr appelé Meka nous est arrivé à tous par lui."]

14. The name Barnabas is an allusion to the criminal whom the Jews chose to free instead of Christ when they were given the choice by Pontius Pilate. By selecting such a name, Oyono is suggesting that the central character in *Chemin d'Europe* is a dishonest man who succeeds in a corrupt society where more righteous individuals fail, and that he does so because he enjoys the support of unperceptive people.

15. A. J., "Rencontre à Bruxelles: M. Ferdinand Oyono," *Le Soir* 309 (Dec. 30, 1965): 9. [". . . lui permet de devenir un homme comme les autres."]

16. Oyono, *Chemin d'Europe* (Paris: Julliard, 1960), p. 103. ["Pauvre, sans relations, sans amis, moqué dans mes espérances, je n'en fus pas découragé. Je dois confesser que j'étais . . . un monstre d'optisme dans un pays où l'appétit du gain, du pouvoir, le culte de l'intérêt, avaient déshumanisé l'homme."]

17. The group is called "Renaissance Spirituelle" in the novel. In *The Literature and Thought of Modern Africa* (1964; trans. and 2nd ed. Washington, D.C.: Three Continents Press, 1979), Claude Wautier claims that Oyono was satirizing "Moral Rearmament," a well-financed revivalist group that was active in West Africa during the 1950s.

18. There are numerous allusions to Stendhal's *Le Rouge et le noir* in the text. It is plausible for Barnabas to have read such novels, for they would have been on the reading list at the seminary.

19. Oyono, *Chemin d'Europe*, pp. 80, 81. ["cette sensation effrayante du vide"; "un sentiment d'impureté qui me donnait le dégout de moi-même."]

20. The name Cimetierre is a commentary on the nature of European ethnology that treated elements of African culture as if they were dead objects to be arranged in a museum (cemetery).

5. MONGO BETI

1. A. B. [Alexandre Biyidi, who is better known under his pseudonym Mongo Beti], "Afrique noire, littérature rose," *Présence Africaine* 1–2 (1955): 137. ["La réalité actuelle de l'Afrique noire, sa seule réalité profonde, c'est avant tout la colonisation et ses méfaits."]

2. Eza Boto [Mongo Beti], *Ville cruelle* (1954; rpt. Paris: Présence Africaine, 1971), p. 151. ["Mais non, c'est faux! Ça ne s'est pas passé ainsi; on vous a mal informé; on vous a menti. Ça n'est pas vrai. Ecoutez donc, moi je connais bien l'histoire."]

3. Bernard Mouralis describes Mongo Beti's perspective as a sociological one and suggests that it was influenced by the work of Georges Balandier, who began publishing his sociological studies of Africa in the early 1950s. According to Mouralis, the adoption of this perspective was crucial in Beti's development as a realistic novelist because it enabled him to view modern African society as an evolving, syncretistic process. See Mouralis, *Comprendre l'oeuvre de Mongo Beti* (Issy-les-Moulineaux: Les Classiques Africains, 1981), pp. 16–18, and his "Mongo Beti et la modernité," in Eileen Julien, Mildred Mortimer, and Curtis Schade, eds., *African Literature in Its Social and Political Dimensions* (Washington, D.C.: Three Continents Press, 1986), Annual Selected Papers of the African Literature Association 9/1983, pp. 85–90.

4. Essomba Mendouga is based on Frédéric Foé-Ndi, the actual chief of Beti's own Bané people. In "Tumultueux Cameroun" (*Preuves* 103 [Sept. 1959]: 28–29), Beti described Foé-Ndi in the following terms: "Sa misère morale se concrétisa, voilà peu de temps, à l'occasion d'une maladie grave, par un retour soudain à la religion catholique, après quoi il dispersa aux quatre vents un harem riche de plus de soixante unités."

5. Some French readers of course recognized the subversive content of Beti's early novels. For example, French supporters of the colonial empire attacked his *Le Pauvre*

Christ de Bomba as a defamatory portrayal of missionary Christianity and the colonial administration in Cameroon. The Catholic church placed it on the Index, and the colonial authorities succeeded in having it banned from all French African territories.

6. In *"Le Pauvre Christ de Bomba* expliqué" (*Peuples Noirs/Peuples Africains* 19 [1981]: esp. pp. 117–19), Beti explains that his reading of Twain, Harriet Beecher Stowe, and Richard Wright helped him recognize how literature could subvert the generally accepted stereotypes of a dominant culture that held black people in bondage. The difference between his conception of intended audience and that of Oyono emerges clearly in the interview reported by Jean Marcenac in "Jacques-Stephen Alexis, Mongo Beti, René Depestre, Ferdinand Oyono: Les Littératures noires et la France," *Les Lettres Françaises* 643 (Dec. 1–7, 1956): 1 and 6.

7. Beti, *Le Roi miraculé* (Paris: Buchet-Chastel, 1958), p. 156. ["Pourquoi les gens acceptent-ils toujours de se laisser piétiner ainsi?"]

8. Boto [Beti], *Ville cruelle*, p. 18. ["des haches . . . les équarissaient, les arrondissaient, les réduisaient aux proportions de l'usine et de la civilisation. Un petit train . . . les emmenait blanchies, numérotées, sagement couchées dans de longues voitures. . . ."] Charly-Gabriel Mbock discusses the significance of this metaphor in his *Comprendre "Ville cruelle"* (Issy-les-Moulineaux: Saint Paul, 1981), p. 15. Tanga is modeled on Mbalmayo, where Beti spent part of his youth. According to Jacques Fame Ndongo in *L'Esthétique romanesque de Mongo Beti* (Paris: A.B.C. and Présence Africaine, 1985), the name Tanga was derived from the Beti word *ntángán*, which means "white" and suggests that the cruel city is largely owned by white men.

9. Boto [Beti], *Ville cruelle*, p. 21. ["un certain penchant pour le calcul mesquin, pour la nervosité, l'alcoolisme et tout ce qui excite le mépris de la vie humaine. . . ."]

10. Beti, *Le Pauvre Christ de Bomba* (1956; rpt. Paris: Présence Africaine, 1971), p. 201. [". . . je me suis élevé dans mon esprit au niveau de Napoléon traçant sur une carte ce fameux plan qui devait lui valoir la victoire d'Austerlitz."]

11. Beti, *Le Pauvre Christ*, p. 64. [". . . j'avais interdit d'avoir recours aux services des sorciers."]

12. Beti, *Le Pauvre Christ*, p. 189. ["Je suis inutile ici; personne n'a besoin de moi."]

13. The sixa was an institution where young women were obliged to spend several months before they could receive the sacrament of marriage in the Catholic mission churches of south-central Cameroon. These women received instruction in religious doctrine and in domestic skills such as hygiene, sewing, and cooking, but they also worked without pay in the vegetable gardens and kitchens of the missions. The word *sixa* is an Ewondo deformation of the English *sisters*, for the institution itself was created by German priests and placed under the jurisdiction of nuns at a time when pidgin English had already become a lingua franca in the area. When French priests adopted the practice, they generally confided the governance of the "sixa" to a local catechist or a married Christian. The system was susceptible to abuse, and it was often deeply resented by the people.

14. Beti, *Le Pauvre Christ*, p. 222. ["le Diable est en toi. . . . tu as gâté le sixa."]

15. Beti, *Le Pauvre Christ*, p. 265. ["Vous me faites honte. Vous déshonorez ma maison. Je ne veux plus vous revoir."]

16. Beti's reading of Richard Wright helped him recognize how religion obscures the truth about the oppression of black people. In *"Le Pauvre Christ de Bomba* expliqué," he describes the Christianization of Africa as "notre déportation morale" and contends he wrote the novel to show how Christianity helped reduce Africans to slavery. On another occasion he declared unequivocally, "je considère le mysticisme et toute religion comme une aliénation." See Anthony Biakolo, "Entretien avec Mongo Beti," *Peuples Noirs/Peuples Africains* 10 (1979): 106.

17. Arlette Chemain discusses Banda's attitude toward his mother in *"Ville cruelle*: Situation oedipienne, mère castatrice," *Présence Francophone* 13 (1976): 21–48. Che-

main's observations are perceptive, although her application of Freudian concepts to African situations is questionable.

18. Boto [Beti], *Ville cruelle*, p. 219. [". . . la petite soeur dont il avait rêvé toute sa vie."]

19. Beti, *Le Pauvre Christ*, p. 194. ["On dirait qu'un étranger a pénétré en moi, qu'il s'y installe lentement, qu'il se substitue peu à peu à moi-même."]

20. Beti, *Le Pauvre Christ*, p. 246. ["Je ne devrais pas me laisser aller à de pareilles idées: j'e risque d'y perdre ma foi!"]

21. Medza directs questions and comments to this audience on a number of occasions. In "African Discourse and the Autobiographical Novel: Mongo Beti's *Mission terminée*" (*French Review* 55 [1982]: 835–45), Arthur Flannigan argues that this narrative situation reflects a synthesis of the autobiographical "I," commonly found in the European novel, and the traditional oral story-teller who speaks to a plural "you." According to him, the "I" and the "you" evolve toward a communal "we" during the course of the novel, enabling the narrator's experiences and observations to be incorporated into a communal system of values. Although Beti consciously eschewed oral story-telling techniques in his early fiction, Flannigan's basic description of the narrative situation in *Mission terminée* is quite perceptive. It should be pointed out that the tongue-in-cheek content summaries at the beginning of each chapter are addressed to a singular reader and supplied by the author, who models them on the précis that often appeared in seventeenth- and eighteenth-century French novels.

22. According to Melone (*Mongo Beti*, pp. 49–50), the name "Medza" is derived from the Beti verb *a dza* (to criticize); in fact, Medza's critical attitude is one of the traits that prevent him from participating fully in the gay insouciance he admires among the people of Kala.

23. Beti, *Mission terminée* (Paris: Buchet-Chastel, 1957), pp. 250–51. [". . . le drame dont souffre notre peuple, c'est celui d'un homme laissé à lui-même dans un monde qui ne lui appartient pas, un monde qu'il n'a pas fait, un monde où il ne comprend rien. C'est le drame d'un homme sans direction intellectuelle, d'un homme marchant à l'aveuglette, la nuit, dans un quelconque New York hostile. Qui lui apprendra à ne traverser la Cinquième Avenue qu'aux passages cloutés? Qui lui apprendra à déchiffrer le 'Piétons, attendez'? Qui lui apprendra à lire une carte de métro, à prendre les correspondances?"] The mention of the subway map is an allusion to the ending of Camara Laye's *L'Enfant noir*, where the protagonist has a subway map in his pocket as he flies toward Paris. In light of Beti's earlier attack on Laye's novel, *Mission terminée* can be seen as a rewriting of *L'Enfant noir* to include the effects of the colonialist presence that Beti accused Laye of omitting from his novel.

24. In "The *Bildungsroman* in Africa: The Case of *Mission terminée*" (*French Review* 59 [1986]: 418–27), David Mickelsen suggests that Beti's novel is an *Entbildungsroman* because Medza fails to articulate a positive philosophy of life and makes essentially negative decisions in repudiating all groups that attempt to assimilate him. Inasmuch as Beti is concerned with discrediting false images of Africa, Mickelsen's thesis could be expanded to include Medza's unlearning of the assumptions behind his formal education.

25. Beti, *Mission terminée*, p. 94. [". . . si je continuais dans la voie où je m'étais engagé malgré moi, je ne serais jamais moi-même."]

6. INDEPENDENCE AND THE MYTH OF NATIONAL UNITY

1. Hans F. Illy, *Politik und Wirtschaft in Kamerun: Bedingungen, Ziele und Strategien der staatlichen Entwicklungspolitik* (Munich: Weltforum, 1976), p. 352. See also Willard Johnson, *The Cameroon Federation: Political Integration in a Fragmentary Society* (Princeton: Princeton University Press, 1970), p. 323. An excellent account of privileged class

formation in Africa is contained in Jean-François Bayart, *L'Etat en Afrique* (Paris: Fayard, 1989).

2. Jean-François Bayart, *L'Etat au Cameroun* (Paris: Presses de la Fondation Nationale des Sciences Politiques, 1979), p. 229.

3. Samuel Kamé, "L'U.C. doit-elle être un parti de masse ou un parti d'élites?" *Premier Stage de formation des responsables de l'Union Camerounaise* (Yaounde: Imprimerie Nationale, 1961), p. 108.

4. Cited in David Gardinier, *Cameroon: United Nations Challenge to French Policy* (London: Oxford University Press, 1963), p. 123. See also Johnson, *The Cameroon Federation*, p. 251.

5. *Le Cameroun chante son unité: Cameroon Sings Her Unity* (Yaounde: Ministry of Information and Tourism, 1966), pp. 9–10.

6. This statement was made in the party newspaper *L'Unité* (no. 180). It is cited in Abel Eyinga, *Mandat d'arrêt pour cause d'elections: De la démocratie au Cameroun* (Paris: L'Harmattan, 1978), p. 29. [". . . en raison de leur fidelité au parti, c'est-à-dire au regime, de leur capacité à être des pions efficaces et loyaux sur l'échiquer du parti."]

7. In *Analyse du sous-développement en Afrique Noire: L'Exemple de l'économie du Cameroun* (Paris: Presses Universitaires de France, 1968), Philippe Hugon estimates that a moderately well paid civil servant earned almost 130,000 CFA francs per month in 1965, whereas a typical farmer in the relatively prosperous Yaounde area received slightly more than 3,500 per month (p. 231). Cotton growers in the North averaged about 1,300 a month, and Kirdi farmers less than 200. Since 1965, this disparity in incomes has increased.

8. Interview with François Sengat-Kuo (Mar. 11, 1982).

9. Béat Christophe Baeschlin-Raspail, *Ahmadou Ahidjo, pionnier de l'Afrique moderne* (Monaco: Paul Bory, 1968), p. 119. ["Nous devons nous incliner devant lui."]

10. Hugon, *Analyse du sous-développement en Afrique Noire*, pp. 107 and 121. See also Neville Rubin, *Cameroun: An African Federation* (New York: Praeger, 1971), pp. 172–73, and Abel Eyinga, *Introduction à la politique camerounaise* (Paris: Anthropos, 1978), p. 317. Since the early 1970s, the situation has become somewhat more favorable to Cameroon. The government now participates in the enterprise, and Alucam produces aluminum articles for domestic consumption.

11. *L'Unité* 200 (Jan. 15–22, 1971): 1. ["La vérité finit toujours par triompher."]

12. Ndeh Ntumazah, *Statement at the Conference of African Freedom Fighters* (June 4, 1962), p. 6.

13. The heavily Islamicized northern portion of the British Cameroons had never been fully integrated into the German or British colonial systems, and its people did not participate in the political activities that preceded the plebiscite in the southern part of the trust territory. Because they voted to become part of Nigeria and because they played virtually no role in the evolution of Cameroonian literate culture, they have not been included in this study.

14. Rubin, *Cameroun: An African Federation*, pp. 113–14, and Johnson, *The Cameroon Federation*, p. 290, n. 3.

15. For a detailed account of how reunification affected the CDC, see Sanford Bederman and Mark Delancey, "The Cameroon Development Corporation," in Ndiva Kofele Kale, *An African Experiment in Nation-Building: The Bilingual Cameroon Republic since Reunification* (Boulder: Westview, 1980), pp. 251–78. Several years after reunification, the CDC became a state-owned corporation, diversified its activities, and eventually became one of the more successful economic enterprises in the country.

16. Jacques Benjamin, *Les Camerounais occidentaux: La Minorité dans un état bicommunautaire* (Montreal: Presses de l'Université de Montréal, 1972), p. 12.

17. West Cameroon Press Release 909 (July 18, 1960).

18. Illy, *Politik und Wirtschaft*, p. 356.

7. CULTURAL POLITICS AND THE NEW NATION

1. *La Presse du Cameroun* 6924 (July 12, 1973): 10. ["... liées entre elles par la langue française qui porte, au-delà de sa signifiance pratique, les vertus d'une certaine conception de l'homme et présente l'avantage d'une subtilité où le rationnel intransigeant peut servir toutes les transactions de la sensibilité."]

2. Robert Cornevin, *Le Théâtre en Afrique Noire et à Madagascar* (Paris: Le Livre Africain, 1970), p. 164.

3. André-Marie Atangana-Zang, *Les Relations socio-culturelles franco-camerounaises* (Yaounde: private, 1975), p. 74. See also Jacques Benjamin, *Les Camerounais occidentaux: La Minorité dans un état bicommunautaire* (Montreal: Presses de l'Université de Montréal, 1972), p. 133.

4. "Coopérants" are French men and women who do public-service work in foreign countries, often as an alternative to military service. The number of "coopérants" in Cameroon varies from year to year. In 1969, there were 1,450 of them. See Benjamin, *Les Camerounais occidentaux*, p. 134.

5. Emmanuel Kegne Pokam, "La Religion face au pouvoir politique au Cameroun," unpublished thesis (Yaounde: 1980), II, 611–12.

6. Ndiva Kofele-Kale, "Introduction," in Kofele-Kale, ed., *An African Experiment in Nation-Building: The Bilingual Cameroon Republic since Reunification* (Boulder, Colo.: Westview, 1980), p. xliii.

7. D. and G. Courade, *L'Ecole du Cameroun anglophone* (Yaounde: Centre Géographique Nationale, 1977), p. 17. See also Neville Rubin, *Cameroun: An African Federation* (New York: Praeger, 1971), p. 167.

8. Claude Wauthier, *The Literature and Thought of Modern Africa* (1964; trans. and rev. Washington, D.C.: Three Continents Press, 1979), p. 298.

9. By 1974 this library with its 52,000 bound volumes and 618 periodicals had become the largest in the country.

10. During this time, there were always more than a thousand Cameroonian students attending French universities. According to Jean-Pierre N'diaye, nearly one-fourth of all francophone African students in France during the 1965–66 academic year were from Cameroon. See his *Elites africaines et culture occidentale: Assimilation ou résistance* (Paris: Présence Africaine, 1969), p. 29.

11. Benjamin, *Les Camerounais occidentaux*, p. 121.

12. Jean Zoa's statement appears in the newsletter *Nova et Vetera* 17 (Sept. 1963): 14. ["... à être lui-même, sans être esclave des formes parasitaires de son passé et sans être esclave de formes périphériques que les autres peuvent lui avoir apportées."]

13. The acronym CLE stands for Centre Littéraire Evangélique and suggests that books are the key ("clef") to knowledge. CLE's role in promoting a Cameroonian literary tradition will be discussed more fully in the following chapter.

14. The visit of this heterogeneous group to Paris was recorded in a film, *Tam-tam à Paris* (1963), by Thérèse Sita Bella.

15. Mveng's declaration was reported in *La Presse du Cameroun* 6118 (Oct. 13, 1970): 2. ["... créer une âme camerounaise, une âme nourrie culturellement d'un même idéal, des mêmes aspirations, consciente des valeurs traditionelles."]

16. Gabriel Mballa, "Conférence sur la presse," in *Premier Stage de formation des responsables de l'Union Camerounaise* (Yaounde: Imprimerie Nationale, 1961), p. 112.

17. For a partial list of government prohibitions of Cameroonian newspapers, see Abel Eyinga, *Introduction à la politique camerounaise* (Paris: Anthropos, 1978), p. 198. In his *Le Livre camerounais et ses auteurs* (1977; rpt. Yaounde: Semences Africaines, 1984), René Philombe estimates that the number of little magazines published in Cameroon fell from twenty-nine in 1958 to three in 1962 (p. 130).

18. Bernard Malang, "Chronique littéraire," *La Semaine camerounaise* 4 (Oct. 1,

1961): 4. ["Quand l'économie d'un pays tombe en ruines; quand la misère physique ou morale s'installe dans le peuple, et avec elles, le long cortège du mal; quand la richesse nationale s'éparpille dans le faste insolent et gratuit ou fuit à l'étranger ou dans les caisses noires, aucun épanouissement culturel n'est possible. On s'enfonce dans l'abrutissement. Malgré les voitures étincelantes et les grands discours."]

19. André-Marie Mbida, Marcel Bebey-Eyidi, Charles Okala, and Theodore Mayi Matip, "Open Letter to the Central Committee of the U.C.," in David Gardinier, ed., "Documents of Camerounian History" (mimeographed collection, n.d.), p. 27. ["A quoi servirait l'indépendance nationale si c'est pour créer un néo-totalitarisme en vue de remplacer le colonialisme de l'extérieur par un colonialisme de l'intérieur?"]

20. Mbida, Bebey-Eyidi, Okala, and Mayi Matip, "Manifeste du Front National Unifié" (June 23, 1962), in Gardinier, ed., "Documents," p. 36. ["La vie ne vaut la peine d'être vécue que si on la vit en homme libre. Dans le cas contraire il serait préférable de mourir plutôt debout que de vivre à genoux."]

21. Engelbert Mveng, "Perspectives nouvelles sur l'histoire africaine," *La Presse du Cameroun* 6766 (Dec. 26, 1972): 6. [". . . qui il était, qui il est et qui il veut devenir."]

22. David Kom, *Le Cameroun: Essai d'analyse économique et politique* (Paris: Editions Sociales, 1971), p. 74. The books by Ewandé and Beti will be discussed more fully in later chapters.

8. IN SEARCH OF A POPULAR IDIOM

1. Philombe's real name is Philippe-Louis Ombedé. He chose the Christian name René to suggest rebirth in the dual sense that all people are reborn when they decide to live a public life and that he himself had been reborn after a long period of suffering and mental depression. Philombe is simply a contraction of his original name.

2. René Philombe, "L'Hymne des révolutionnaires" (1958), reprinted in Philombe, *Le Livre camerounais et ses auteurs* (1977; rpt. Yaounde: Semences Africaines, 1984), p. 115. ["Nous sommes les élus d'une aube salutaire. / Le peuple, dans nos coeurs, tamtame ses chansons."]

3. Lilyan Kesteloot, "Pour une littérature nationale," in *Anthologie 1962 de l'A.P.E.C.* (Yaounde: APEC, 1962), pp. 5–7.

4. Louis-Marie Pouka M'Bague, *L'Entrevue d'outre-tombe ou message de Ruben Um Nyobé* (Yaounde: private, 1960), p. 11. [". . . le grand Leader du Nord guide bien le pays."]

5. Pouka, *Hommage à Son Excellence Ahmadou Ahidjo* (Yaounde: private, 1961).

6. *Le Manifeste des Apécistes* (Yaounde: APEC, 1964), p. 5. ["La meilleure révolution qu'un homme puisse faire pour son peuple est une révolution culturelle."]

7. René Philombe, Editorial, *Cameroun Littéraire* 1 (Jan. 1971): 1. [". . . où toutes les mentalités semblent obéir aux lois d'un matérialisme vulgaire."]

8. See Philombe, "Le Cameroun en quête de sa personnalité culturelle," *Cameroun Littéraire* 4 (Apr. 1971): 1–2 and his "Halte à notre étoffement culturel," *Cameroun Littéraire* 6 (June 1971): 1–3.

9. Buma Kor, "Encouraging Literature from the Schools," *Cameroun Littéraire* 6 (June 1971): 28.

10. Présence Africaine published a third of all francophone African literary works that appeared between 1958 and 1965. See Robert Cornevin, *Littératures d'Afrique noire de langue française* (Paris: PUF, 1976), p. 25.

11. *La Semaine Camerounaise* 14 (Mar. 1, 1962): 3.

12. P. Feuter, "C.L.E.," *La Semaine Camerounaise* 54 (Nov. 15, 1963): 7. [". . . devient de plus en plus un organe efficace des Eglises. . . . Il n'y a pas de doute que le Cameroun joue un rôle de pionnier dans le travail accompli pour la littérature chrétienne en Afrique d'expression française."]

13. Interviews with Jean Dihang (Nov. 8, 1976, and Dec. 13, 1976).

14. *La Semaine Camerounaise* 119 (Nov. 15, 1966): 4 and 6. One of the two most popular titles ever published by CLE was *Comment élever les poules*, which was still selling between 200 and 500 copies per month as late as 1982.

15. S. Van der Werf, "Edition et diffusion du livre en Afrique," *Culture Française* 19 (1970): 24. Van der Werf was the director of CLE's distribution network for many years.

16. The two market novels are J. E. A. Ngoh's *Flowers in the River of Temptations* and the francophone Rémy Medou Mvomo's *Nancy in Blooming Youth*. A good example of the flourishing manuscript literature in West Cameroon is Vincent Nchami's "The Fon's Anointed," a novel about the successful rebellion of young people against the unjust authority of a local chief who wants to anoint one of them his forty-sixth wife. The young people affirm their right to choose their own spouses and their own careers, but they cannot remain in their village after having defied its laws. The generational conflict depicted in "The Fon's Anointed" is one of the most common themes in this manuscript literature. The popularity of literary activity in the area became evident in the 1970s, when hundreds of manuscripts were submitted to the Guinness Writers' Contest.

17. Penda, *La Corbeille d'ignames* (Yaounde: CLE, 1971), p. 61. [". . . un des plus brillants, des plus prospères et des plus florissants de l'Afrique Centrale."] Penda's little book appeared in the "Pour Tous" series that emphasized the use of basic French and was addressed to a popular audience.

18. Lazare Sanduo, *Une Dure Vie scolaire* (Yaounde: CLE, 1972), p. 47. ["Si les hommes sont méchants, Dieu est bon et n'oublie aucun malheureux."]

19. Ndembiyembé-Bakoumé, "Simon Rifoé: Goliath sur les rings," *Cameroon Tribune* 850 (Apr. 20, 1977): 5. [". . . on n'est pas loin assurément de notre réalité quotidienne confuse, ambiguë, trouble."] For an account of Rifoé's life, see *Cameroun Tribune* 2009 (Feb. 22–23, 1981): 10. Gérard Markoff described the process by means of which Rifoé's *Tour* came into being during an interview on April 13, 1977.

20. Philombe, *Le Livre camerounais*, p. 17. ["La seule vraie histoire d'un peuple est celle que raconte ce peuple lui-même."]

21. Philombe, Interview in *Cameroon Tribune* 1934 (Nov. 22, 1980): 9. ["C'est au coeur de la vie quotidienne des hommes que nous situons notre principale source d'inspiration. Un homme de lettres trahit sa mission historique s'il ne puise pas ses sèves créatrices dans les réalités humaines de notre époque."]

22. Philombe, "Petit poème de minuit," *Petites Gouttes de chant pour créer l'homme* (Yaounde: Semences Africaines, 1977), p. 48. [". . . un chant d'homme / pour créer l'homme / au fond de l'homme."]

23. As executive secretary of APEC and editor of *Cameroun Littéraire*, Philombe was well acquainted with Cameroonian written literature. Like Beti, he had attended the Catholic mission school at Efok north of Yaounde and was familiar with the Eton people's legendary resistance to Christianization. During the early 1960s, Philombe undertook a study of Beti's works and published the article "Que voulait dire Mongo Beti?" (*Cameroun Littéraire* 2 [Nov. 1962]: 9) under the pseudonym Philémon Obout. The structural parallels between *Le Pauvre Christ* and *Un Sorcier blanc* are numerous, and Philombe's novel contains echoes of Beti's *Le Roi miraculé* as well, but the rhetorical thrust of *Un Sorcier blanc* is entirely different from that of Beti's novel.

24. Philombe, *Un Sorcier blanc à Zangali* (Yaounde: CLE, 1969), p. 128. ["Les morts sont les morts."]

25. Philombe, *Sorcier blanc*, p. 173. ["Il m'est apparu urgent et plus important de leur sauver la vie. Pendant que je leur prodigue des soins, je me borne à leur demander de se recommender à Zamba, l'Incréé. Je tâche de les mettre en confiance avec moi; et je leur parle de la religion naturelle qui fait de tous les hommes des frères condamnés

à vivre ensemble sur la terre. Je leur prouve, chaque jour, par mes actes, que les 'sorciers blancs' veulent le bonheur des hommes noirs."]

26. Philombe, *Choc anti-choc* (Yaounde: Semences Africaines, 1978), pp. 12–13. ["Mon nom à moi est *Homme!*"] See also his "L'Homme qui te ressemble," in *Petites Gouttes de chant pour créer l'homme*, pp. 41–42. Although these poems were not published until the late 1970s, most of them were written much earlier.

9. CAMEROONIAN REFLECTIONS ON NEGRITUDE AND AUTHENTICITY

1. For discussions of this development, see Abiola Irele, "Contemporary Thought in French-Speaking Africa," in Isaac Mowoe and Richard Bjornson, eds., *Africa and the West: The Legacies of Empire* (Westport, Conn.: Greenwood, 1986), pp. 122–58, and Valentin Y. Mudimbe, "On the Question of an African Philosophy: The Case of French-Speaking Africa," in Mowoe and Bjornson, *Africa and the West*, pp. 89–120. See also Mudimbe, *The Invention of Africa: Gnosis, Philosophy, and the Order of Knowledge* (Bloomington: Indiana University Press, 1988), esp. pp. 35–43, 83–97, and 135–86, and Robert W. July, *An African Voice: The Role of the Humanities in African Independence* (Durham: Duke University Press, 1987), pp. 20–44 and 201–26.

2. *Presse du Cameroun* 5913 (Feb. 2, 1970): 4. ["Un nègre qui ne croit pas à la négritude, c'est vraiment un suicide. Qu'on le mette au tombeau."]

3. Interview with William Eteki Mbumua, Mar. 31, 1982. ["L'homme camerounais, dans son désir d'épanouissement, doit d'abord appréhender ses propres valeurs culturelles, et la négritude est tout simplement l'identification culturelle."] Eteki's cultural philosophy is explained at length in *Un Certain Humanisme* (Yaounde: CLE, 1970) and in *Démocratiser la culture* (Yaounde: CLE, 1973).

4. Bernard Fonlon, "A Case for Early Bilingualism," *Abbia* 4 (1963): 89.

5. Bernard Fonlon, *La Poésie et le reveil de l'homme noir* (1960; Kinshasa: Presses Universitaires du Zaïre, 1978), p. 20. ["La vie de chaque nègre qui se heurte à l'hostilité négrophobe résume entièrement l'histoire de cette race qui se tord d'angoisse à travers les siècles."]

6. Fonlon, "Ten Years After—A Foreword," *Abbia* 27–28 (1974): 8.

7. Fonlon, "Idea of Cultural Integration," *Abbia* 19 (1968): 9.

8. Fonlon, *As I See It* (Buea: Catholic Press, 1971), p. 42.

9. Fonlon, "Le Devoir d'aujourd'hui," *Abbia* 29–30 (1975): 21. [". . . le fondement de la liberté, c'est la vérité."]

10. Fonlon, "Idea of Culture," *Abbia* 11 (1965): 27.

11. Fonlon, *Education through Literature* (Yaounde: private, 1977), p. 19.

12. Fonlon, *Education through Literature*, p. 35.

13. Lilyan Lagneau-Kesteloot, "Problèmes du critique littéraire en Afrique," *Abbia* 8 (1965): 21. [". . . des racines authentiques de leur personnalité."]

14. Engelbert Mveng, *Si Quelqu'un . . .* (Tours: Mame, 1962), facing plate VI. ["Tout nous racontait Ton visage: / Le vagissement du bébé dans son berceau de bambou, / Le péan nocturne des Initiés vanqueurs de la Mort, / Et le chant des nourrices, et le clameur des guerriers, / Et le voix des pleureuses autour des cases, autour des berceau, autour des tombeaux. . . ."]

15. Mveng, *Lève-toi, amie, viens* (Dakar: Clairafrique, 1966), facing plate XII. ["Le péché opprime plus que ne fit jamais négrier aux plantations des Iles."]

16. Charles Ngandé, "Indépendance," in Lilyan Kesteloot, ed., *Neuf Poètes camerounais* (Yaounde: CLE, 1965), p. 33. ["Où retrouver la tombe de l'Ancêtre . . . dans quelle source repimenter notre sang."]

17. Ngandé, "Indépendance," in *Neuf Poètes*, p. 35. ["Et le soir, nous danserons autour du même feu / Parce qu'ensemble, sur la tombe de l'Aieul, / Nous aurons fait germer une grande Cité."]

18. Thomas Melone, *De La Négritude dans la littérature négro-africaine* (Paris: Présence Africaine, 1962), p. 29. ["Pour Chaka l'Occident représente la source des principes qui ont inspiré sa protestation mais aussi l'obstacle qu'il faut supprimer pour accéder au bonheur."]

19. Melone, *De La Négritude*, p. 131. ["Il fuira . . . le réel pour se réfugier dans l'essentiel."]

20. Melone, *Mongo Beti, l'homme et le destin* (Paris: Présence Africaine, 1971), p. 237. [". . . perfection qui s'affirme chaque jour."]

21. François Sengat-Kuo, "Au Masque," *Collier de cauris* (Paris: Présence Africaine, 1970), p. 19. ["moi-même en face de moi"]

22. Sengat-Kuo, "Reviendra Chaka," *Collier de cauris*, p. 33. ["la danse libre des hommes virils"]

23. Interviews with Samuel-Martin Eno Belinga, Feb. 21 and Feb. 28, 1982. Many details in the following discussion are based on material collected during these two interviews.

24. Eno Belinga, "Prologue," *Ballades et chansons africains* (Yaounde: private, 1981), p. 132. [". . . nés d'un seul souffle planétaire."]

25. Eno Belinga, "Eyema," *Masques nègres* (Yaounde: CLE, 1972), p. 18. ["Un chant discret comme le temps, / Et, dans ces visages le pouls / Cosmique du monde secret."]

26. Eno Belinga, "Les Trois Epouses," *Masques nègres*, p. 33. ["La foi chante l'espérance dans les ténèbres."]

27. Eno Belinga, "Art royal," *Masques nègres*, p. 19. ["Belle la sagesse / Et sage la force: / Forte la beauté."]

28. Eno Belinga, "Huitième Chant," *"La Prophétie de Joal" suivi de "Equinoxes"* (Yaounde: CLE, 1975), p. 42. ["Faisons l'arche qui perce les nues, car l'arche / Est la grande demeure dans le soleil levant / La grande demeure qui est fondement du royaume de Joal."]

29. Eno Belinga, "Septième Chant," *La Prophétie*, p. 35. ["La prophétie de Joal / Est une, ne se démontre point / Comme chant de kora musique pour / Le coeur ne se démontre point."]

30. Alioune Diop, "Message de Alioune Diop," in *Le Critique africain et son peuple comme producteur de civilisation* (Paris: Présence Africaine, 1977), p. 528. ["Le critique africain tient entre ses mains la clef de l'avenir de l'Afrique."]

10. THE ANTI-NEGRITUDE MOVEMENT

1. René Philombe, "Préface," *La Voix des poètes camerounais/Voice of Cameroonian Poets* (Yaounde: APEC, 1965), p. 6. [". . . les rêves les plus sacrées et les aspirations les plus profondes."] Philombe's attack on Ngandé's position can be found in his "Réponse à Charles Ngandé: L'Avenir de la poésie camerounaise," *Abbia* 5 (1964): 170. He also wrote several anti-Negritude articles in the early issues of *Cameroun Littéraire*.

2. Rémy Medou Mvomo, "Pragmatisme culturel," unpublished manuscript, p. 28. [". . . un dogme dangereux, une nouvelle forme d'aliénation qui sert d'assise culturelle à la pénétration néocolonialiste en Afrique."] Medou Mvomo also wrote a series of anti-Negritude articles in the early issues of *Cameroun Littéraire*.

3. Basile-Juléat Fouda, *De La Négrité: Critique négro-africaine de la raison historique* (Yaounde: private, 1970–71), p. 6. [". . . complèxe de sénilité narcissique."] Fouda apparently borrowed the term *négrité* from Albert Memmi, who employed it in *L'Homme dominé* (Paris: Payot, 1950), p. 4.

4. Fouda, "Mythes camerounais et reflexion philosophique," in Fouda and Sindjoun-Pokam, eds., *La Philosophie camerounaise à l'ère du soupçon: Cas Towa* (Yaounde: Le Flambeau, 1980), p. 67. ["L'homme doit se faire ou disparaître."]

5. Fouda, "Philosophie et devenir national au Cameroun," in Fouda and Sindjoun-Pokam, *La Philosophie camerounaise*, p. 104. ["La nation apparaît ainsi comme un centre de perspective enserré dans un réseau mobile et structuré de forces spirituelles et de significations."]

6. Fouda, "Culture négro-africaine et civilisation occidentale," unpublished manuscript (1973), p. 8. ["civilisation de la rosace"]

7. Marcien Towa, *Essai sur le problématique philosophique dans l'Afrique actuelle* (Yaounde: CLE, 1971), p. 47. [". . . l'idéologie quasiment officiel du néo-colonialisme, le ciment de la prison où le néo-colonialisme entend nous enfermer."]

8. Towa, *Essai*, p. 52. ["C'est la destruction des idoles traditionelles qui seule permettra d'accueillir et d'assimiler l'esprit de l'Europe, secret de sa puissance et de sa victoire sur nous."]

9. Towa, cited in "Grand Débat public à l'Ecole Normale Supérieure," *Cameroun Littéraire* 5 (May 1971): 27. ["Ce que nous devons surtout c'est la liberté, car avec la liberté, une vraie liberté, notre originalité viendra d'elle-même."]

10. Towa, "Identité nationale, mythe ou réalité? (1)," *Annales de la Faculté des Lettres et Sciences Humaines de Yaoundé* 4, 7 (1976): 46. ["L'identité nationale—un avatar de la négritude—n'est pas donnée, elle n'est pas une essence éternelle et incorruptible. Elle ne surgira pas magiquement par la vertu des incantations auxquelles l'intelligentsia noire se livre depuis près d'un demi-siècle. Elle sera le résultat instable et toujours dépassable de nos efforts non seulement théoriques mais également pratiques pour révolutionner notre situation actuelle de faiblesse, de pauvreté et d'extraversion, et nous constituer en entité nationale vivante. . . ."]

11. Ebenezer Njoh-Mouelle, *Jalons II* (Yaounde: CLE, 1975), p. 74. [". . . ceux qui ne maîtrise pas la science et la technologie s'exposent à la domination et à l'asservissement sous toutes leurs formes."]

12. Njoh-Mouelle, *De La Médiocrité à l'excellence* (Yaounde: CLE, 1970), p. 51. ["Une valeur africaine traditionnelle qui repose sur un fond d'ignorance et de superstition n'est pas une valeur. Sa conservation ne peut que contribuer à l'étouffement de l'humanité de l'homme africain."]

13. Njoh-Mouelle, *Développer la richesse humaine* (Yaounde: CLE, 1980), p. 5. ["L'homme doit être la finalité de tout développement."]

14. Njoh-Mouelle, *De La Médiocrité*, p. 140. ["L'homme excellent ne peut être tel que dans le mesure où les autres hommes le reconnaissent tel, c'est-à-dire, se reconnaissent idéalement en lui."]

15. Interview with Philombe, *La Presse du Cameroun* 6924 (July 12, 1973): 8.

16. Interview with Jean-Baptiste Obama, *Cameroun Littéraire* 2 (Nov. 1964): 2. ["un ambassadeur de la négritude"]

17. Hubert Mono Ndjana, *L'Anégritude* (Yaounde: private, n.d.), pp. 112–13. [". . . petits vieillards asthmatiques à la tête chenue, accroupis autour d'une calebasse de vin de palme ou d'une marmite de décoctions magiques, mâchonnant une éternelle bouchée de kola et débitant en vrac les proverbes du terroir, que l'auteur aura puisé dans quelqu'anthologie spécialisée. Et cela s'appelle la quintessence de la cult... négro-africaine."]

11. LITERATURE AND THE PURSUIT OF THE SELF

1. François-Borgia Marie Evembe, "Un Nègre épars," unpublished manuscript, p. 53. [". . . parce qu'il n'y a que laideur et horreur autour de moi, ma mission d'heimatlos est de pourchasser la perfection et l'authenticité qui fuient sous le mensonge établi."]

2. Mbella Sonne Dipoko, "Night," *Présence Africaine* 77 (1971): 154.

3. Sonne Dipoko, "A Parting of the Ways," *Black & White in Love* (1972; rpt.

London: Heinemann, 1976), p. 67. Sonne Dipoko expressed his ideas about Negritude in "Cultural Diplomacy in African Writing," *Africa Today* 15, 4 (1968): 8–11. The same essay appears in Per Wastberg, ed., *The Writer in Modern Africa* (New York: Africana, 1968), pp. 59–70.

4. Sonne Dipoko, Review of Kwame Nkrumah's *I Speak of Freedom*, *Présence Africaine* 40 (1962): 180. ["L'art d'écrire aux mains des hommes libérés est une arme décisif."]

5. Sonne Dipoko, "The First Return," *Présence Africaine* 64 (1967): 176.

6. Sonne Dipoko, "Our Destiny," *Black & White in Love*, p. 29.

7. Sonne Dipoko, "The Tenderness Manifesto," *Black & White in Love*, p. 52.

8. Sonne Dipoko, *A Few Days and Nights* (1966; rpt. London: Heinemann, 1970), p. 65.

9. Sonne Dipoko, *A Few Days and Nights*, p. 5.

10. Sonne Dipoko, *A Few Days and Nights*, pp. 125–26.

11. Rémy Medou Mvomo, *Mon Amour en noir et blanc* (Yaounde: CLE, 1971), p. 106. ["il n'existe . . . pas chez nous d'individus ainsi que l'entendent les blancs. Il y a des membres du groupe qui sont étroitement liés entre eux et interdépendants."] Although *Mon Amour* was published after Medou Mvomo's *Afrika Ba'a*, it was the first of his novels to have been written.

12. Gabriel Deeh Segallo, Review of *Afrika Ba'a*, *Cameroon Tribune* 704 (Oct. 24–25, 1976): 2. [". . . la révolution verte, le leitmotif de la politique économique de notre pays."]

13. Medou Mvomo, *Afrika Ba'a* (Yaounde: CLE, 1969), p. 138. [". . . le don que la nature fait à ceux qui osent."]

14. Sonne Dipoko, *Because of Women* (London: Heinemann, 1970), p. 95.

15. Medou Mvomo, *Le Journal de Faliou* (Yaounde: CLE, 1972), pp. 107 and 137. ["Il me semble que tout le monde est animé de mauvaises intentions à mon égard." ". . . je suis seul contre tous."]

16. Patrice Kayo, "Louis-Marie Pouka, l'homme et l'oeuvre," unpublished thesis (University of Yaounde, 1973), p. 91. [". . . est si changeant qu'il ressemble à un caméléon qui prend la couleur des herbes parmi lesquelles il se trouve. Sa poésie est une poésie opportuniste qui s'accorde avec les circonstances."] Pouka was so infuriated by the contents of Kayo's thesis that he addressed a letter of complaint to Ahidjo.

17. Patrice Kayo, "Vertige," *Déchirements* (Yaounde: private, n.d.), p. 23. ["Rêve ou réalité, je ne te sais nommer, / toi que je cherche même quand je te possède, / ô toi toujours absente et toujours présente."]

18. Kayo, "Chanter encore," in Kayo, ed., *Anthologie de la poésie de langue française* (Yaounde: Le Flambeau, n.d.), p. 66. [". . . un acte de foi, une note d'espérance / qu'entretient l'aurore dans le sein de la nuit."]

19. Samuel Nkamgnia, "Introduction," *Jeunesse et patrie* (Yaounde: Saint Paul, 1969), p. 5. ["La poésie coule d'elle-même, sa pratique devient naturelle. . . ."]

20. Jean-Louis Dongmo, "Le Tambour parlant," *Présence Africaine* 60 (1966): 120. ["Le tambour parlant ne sanglotte pas / ne s'évade pas / ne divertit pas pas pas . . . / A petits coups de dent de la goutte d'eau sur le roc / le tambour parlant ronge / les chaines de l'Afrique ployée sous les chicottes de toutes les nuits."]

21. Dongmo, "Libre, même si nu . . . ," in Kayo, *Anthologie*, p. 60. ["Je n'aime pas ces griots / qui distribuent de louanges sur commande / et sacrent héros d'habiles parvenus / pour quelques billets de banque: / J'aime la liberté, . . . / J'aime la vérité. . . ."]

22. Thérèse Kuoh-Moukouri, *Rencontres essentielles* (Paris: Imprimerie Edgar, 1969), pp. 11–12. [". . . lieu féerique où l'on entre comme dans un paradis par une porte dorée."]

23. T. Kuoh-Moukouri, *Rencontres essentielles*, p. 100. ["... un minuscule point sur la terre, une poussière dans l'univers."]

24. Yoko-Nana-Tabitha, *La Reine* (Paris: La Pensée Universelle, 1972), p. 77. ["Tout le monde me détestait sans raison."]

25. T. Kuoh-Moukouri, *Rencontres essentielles*, p. 121. ["Des hommes et des femmes passent dans la brume, muets, indifférents, chacun perdu dans le rêve de son histoire."]

26. In an interview with M. B. Cissey ("Patrice Ndedi Penda, écrivain camerounais," *L'Afrique Littéraire et Artistique* 25 [1972]: 10–14), Ndedi Penda declared, "*La Nasse* est un sujet que j'ai vécu personellement," and later added, "j'en ai été absolument marqué" (11–12). Mokto made the same acknowledgment in an interview with the *Presse du Cameroun* (6374 [Aug. 25, 1971]: 3). The autobiographical nature of *Ramitou, mon étrangère* is underlined by the fact that the protagonist's nickname, Julot, is the same as the author's.

27. Interview with Ndedi Penda, *Presse du Cameroun* 6925 (Aug. 30, 1973): 6. ["... on ne peut pas être écrivain sans faire de la politique."]

12. GUILLAUME OYONO-MBIA AND THE RISE OF CAMEROONIAN THEATER

1. René Philombe in Wolfgang Zimmer, "'Chanter pour ceux qui n'ont pas le droit de chanter': Entretien avec René Philombe sur son oeuvre dramatique," *Peuples Noirs/ Peuples Africains* 51 (1986): 61. ["Quand j'écris une pièce de théâtre, je vise . . . un public beaucoup plus large que lorsque je compose un roman ou une nouvelle."]

2. For a discussion of the theatrical activity that emerged as a result of this policy at the William Ponty school, see Bakary Traore, *Le Théâtre négro-africain et ses fonctions socials* (Paris: Présence Africaine, 1958), pp. 25–53. Details about the dramas produced at Akono were provided by Jean-Baptiste Obama in an interview on April 3, 1982. See also the interview with him in *Cameroun Littéraire* 2 (Feb. 1971): 25–29.

3. Among the most successful of these troupes were Charles Nyatté's highly professional Tréteaux d'Ebène, Adolph-Claude Mballa's Negro-Star, Louis-Camille Nono's Cercle Camerounais d'Art Dramatique, Jacques-Mariel Nzouankeu's Conservatoire Populaire de Musique et d'Art Dramatique, Lucien Mamba's Théâtre Saisonnier, Jean-Pierre Dikongue Pipa's Avante-Garde Africain, and Marcel Mvondo II's Compagnons de la Comédie. As early as 1955, Stanislas Awona had formed his Association des Jeunes Artistes Camerounais, which later became linked with the Catholic adult improvement society Nova et Vetera; the group's performances of Awona's *Le Chomeur* made it one of the country's most popular dramas in the early 1960s. Mvondo II's group was associated with APEC, and it often performed plays by René Philombe. In addition to Dikongue Pipa's productions of his *L'Inévitable Compromis*, *La Vérité de ce pays*, and *La Légende du sorcier* and Nzouankeu's of his *L'Agent spécial*, other dramatists who successfully staged their own works included Boé a Amang, whose Théâtre Populaire Camerounais repeatedly put on his *Course à l'argent*, Joseph Kengni, whose Théâtre de l'Espoir presented many performances of his *Père aux abois*, Thomas Fotso Mangwa, whose Institut Populaire d'Art Dramatique made his *Le Triomphe de l'alcool* into a well-known drama, and Marie-Charlotte Mbarga, whose Etoiles de la Capitale staged her *La Famille africaine* on numerous occasions. Jean-Pierre Mendogo's Théâtre Populaire, Louis-Balthasar Amadangoleda's Les Amis de la Scène, and Claude Manfreidini's Les Amis du Théâtre were also active at this time. The history of dramatic performance in Cameroon has been studied in dissertations by Ndumbe Eyoh and Martin Kenkeu. Additional details are provided in Adolph-Claude Mballa's drama anthology, *Théâtre Camerounais* (Yaounde: CFLC, 1971), and in Bole Butake and Gilbert Doho, eds., *Théâtre camerounais/Cameroon Theatre* (Yaounde: BET, 1988).

4. For a discussion of the role played by the French National Radio in this area,

see Alain Ricard, "The O.R.T.F. and African Literature," *Research in African Literatures* 4 (1973): 189–91.

5. Three years earlier Jean-Pierre Dikongue Pipa directed a performance of his *L'Iné-vitable Compromis* at the Abbia as part of the country's tenth-anniversary celebrations, but the use of large movie theaters for drama productions remained relatively rare until the late 1970s.

6. J. M. Koulou, Review of *Trois Prétendants . . . un mari, La Semaine Camerounaise* 64 (Apr. 15, 1964): 4. [". . . rien d'autre que du bulu traduit presque littéralement en français."]

7. Guillaume Oyono-Mbia in Lee Nichols, ed., *Conversations with African Writers* (Washington, D.C.: Voice of America, 1981), p. 238.

8. For a listing of Cameroonian dramas, see Wolfgang Zimmer, *Répertoire du théâtre camerounais* (Paris: L'Harmattan, 1986).

9. Jacques-Mariel Nzouankeu in Thérèse Sajoux, "Dialogue avec Jacques-Mariel Nzouankeu," *France: Euroafrique* 235 (1972): 31–32. ["Je suis fermement attaché à la personne humaine en tant que fin de toute entreprise. Je crois que l'homme peut se perfectionner et perfectionner le monde."]

10. Abel Zomo Bem, "Le Patron noir," unpublished manuscript, p. 17. ["Il nous faut faire face à la situation créée par le Bingo national."]

11. Thomas Fotso Mangwa, *Le Triomphe de l'alcool* (Bafoussam: Institut d'Art Drama-tique, n.d.), p. 29. ["Nous ne sommes plus au temps des colons; le pays est déja indépen-dant et nous sommes des citoyens; et on ne bat pas un citoyen comme ça."]

12. Stanislas Awona, *Le Chomeur* (Yaounde: CEPMA, 1968), p. 31. ["Suis-je donc sans valeur? Non. Je me sens capable de consacrer ma vie entière à une tâche utile à mon pays."]

13. Hubert Mono Ndjana, *Vice-Versa,* in *Théâtre complet* (Yaounde: private, 1979), p. 17. ["Pour être moi, il faut que je sois un autre, vous par exemple."]

14. Interview with Marie-Charlotte Mbarga, April 2, 1982. ["La vie quotidienne est faite de scènes théâtrales."]

15. The same tendencies are evident in Asseng's *L'Homme-femme,* René Philombe's *Les Epoux célibataires* and *L'Amour en pagaille,* Jean Oloa-Bala's *Les Nouveaux Patriarchs,* Essindi Mindji's *Salifou* and *Curriculum vitae,* Pabe Mongo's *La Guerre des calebasses,* and many other Cameroonian social comedies.

16. Patrice Ndedi Penda, *Le Fusil* (Paris: ORTF, 1973), p. 102. ["Maudit soit celui qui a inventé l'argent! L'argent sème les discordes, durcit les coeurs, pourrit tout."]

17. Joseph Kengni, *Dans le pétrin* (Yaounde: private, n.d.), p. 15. [". . . quelles qu soient mes origines, j'ai le droit et le devoir de m'instruire comme tout fils du pays."]

18. There was not nearly as much drama produced in the Western Cameroons as there was in the eastern part of the territory. According to Hansel Ndumbe Eyoh ("The Development of Drama in Cameroon: 1959–1979," unpublished thesis [Leeds: 1979], pp. 41–42), the first original drama in Western Cameroon was *White Flows the Latex, Ho!,* a musical farce in English, pidgin, and Douala by the Kumba school principal Charles Low and two of his students. Similar initiatives may have been undertaken at St. Joseph's-Sasse, but there is no record of them.

19. Musinga has published his first and best-known play under several different titles. It is most readily available as *The Tragedy of Mr. No-Balance.* The best account of Musin-ga's approach to drama can be found in Stephen Arnold, "A Comparative View of the Career and Aesthetic of Victor Musinga, Cameroun's Most Popular Playwright," in Bernadette Cailler, Russell Hamilton, and Mildred Hill-Lubin, eds., *Toward Defining the African Aesthetic* (Washington, D.C.: Three Continents Press, 1982), Annual Papers of the African Literature Association, vol. 6, pp. 53–71. See also Michael Etherton, "The Dilemma of the Popular Playwright: The Work of Kabwe Kasoma and V. E. Musinga," *African Literature Today* 8 (1976): 26–41.

20. Victor Musinga, *The Tragedy of Mr. No-Balance* (1976; rpt. Buea: Catholic Printing Press, 1980), p. 23.

21. Musinga, *The Tragedy of Mr. No-Balance*, p. 42.

22. Sankie Maimo, *Sov-Mbang the Soothsayer* (Yaounde: CLE, 1968), p. 24.

23. Sankie Maimo, *The Mask* (Yaounde: Cowrie, 1980), p. 61.

24. Maimo, *Succession in Sarkov* (Yaounde: SOPECAM, 1982), p. 19.

25. Bole Butake, *Lake God* (Yaounde: BET, 1986), p. 65.

13. FRANCIS BEBEY AND THE THEME OF RECONCILIATION

1. Francis Bebey, *Concert pour un vieux masque* (Paris: L'Harmattan, 1980), p. 65. ["La puissance du verbe est salutaire. . . . / Grâce à elle la mort d'un vieux masque / est le commencement d'une vie / que plus rien n'abolira / Car elle est la vraie magie du monde."]

2. René Balbaud, "Francis Bebey," *Africa Report* 15, 8 (1970): 22.

3. Armin Kerker, "'Je suis le produit de la culture africaine et de la culture européenne': Un Interview avec le compositeur, poète et chanteur africain, Francis Bebey," *Afrika* 20, 9 (1979): 23. ["Nous avons eu la chance de nous mouvoir à la croisée de deux cultures. Nous sommes ainsi parvenu à posséder deux forces culturelles différentes qui . . . se complètent de manière parfaite."]

4. Francis Bebey, *Le Fils d'Agatha Moudio* (Yaounde: CLE, 1967), p. 25. ["La parole signifie la vie, la vie qui continue, et que l'homme doit respecter à tout moment, parce qu'elle est la seule chose d'ici-bas qui ne passe guère. Les hommes qui savent écrire perdent ce profond respect de la vie."]

5. Guy Riboreau, "Francis Bebey: A la croisée des chemins," *AGECOP-Liaison* 46 (1979): 40. ["Mon authenticité ne consiste pas à rejeter le vieux proverbe ou à rejeter Descartes, elle n'est faite que de ces deux éléments réunis."]

6. Wilbert Curtis Schade develops this idea at some length in his unpublished dissertation "Africa at the Crossroads: The Fiction of Francis Bebey" (Indiana, 1986).

7. Bebey, *Le Fils d'Agatha Moudio*, p. 184. [". . . le temps et la proximité des gens 'sachant vivre' ont donné à mon raisonnement une certaine dose de 'civilisation.'"]

8. Bebey, *Le Fils d'Agatha Moudio*, p. 172. [". . . je me réserve d'autant plus le droit de me taire sur bien des points, que je sais deviner le sourire amusé avec lequel vous vous disposeriez à écouter mon récit."]

9. Bebey, *Le Fils d'Agatha Moudio*, p. 62. ["Je suis l'enfant de ce village-ci, et je suivrai la tradition jusqu'au bout."]

10. Bebey, *Le Fils d'Agatha Moudio*, p. 58. ["Tu es aujourd'hui grand et fort et beau et courageux, mais c'est moi qui t'ai fait."]

11. Bebey, *Le Fils d'Agatha Moudio*, p. 30. [". . . je suis devenu pêcheur parce que j'ai moi-même choisi de le devenir."]

12. Bebey, *Le Fils d'Agatha Moudio*, p. 154. [". . . je considérais que j'avais assez obéi ainsi, et qu'il était temps pour moi de prendre des décisions, moi-même."]

13. Bebey, *La Poupée Ashanti* (Yaounde: CLE, 1973), p. 29. ["Chacun n'a qu'à rester à sa place, et la vie se portera très bien ainsi."]

14. Bebey, *La Poupée Ashanti*, p. 143. ["Après tout, je ne vais pas épouser mon étalage au marché . . . !"]

15. The action in *Le Roi Albert d'Effidi* occurs in south-central Cameroon, and if Ngala is the equivalent of Ongala, the original Ewondo name for Yaounde, then Effidi is an Ewondo village on the outskirts of the Cameroonian capital. However, Bebey employs Douala as well as Ewondo names for people and places in the text, suggesting that Effidi is a representative village and that the events of the narrative could have taken place in many other parts of the country as well.

16. In Cameroon, the first elections to the territorial assembly were held shortly after the promulgation of the *Loi cadre* in 1956.

17. Bebey, *Le Roi Albert d'Effidi* (Yaounde: CLE, 1976), p. 76. ["... chaque homme qui travaille peut monter très haut, en gagnant bien sa vie."]

18. Bebey, *Le Roi Albert d'Effidi*, p. 180. ["Il ne faut plus forcer nos filles à épouser des hommes que nous avons choisis pour elles."]

19. Bebey, *Le Roi Albert d'Effidi*, p. 181. ["Je reviens habiter ici pour toujours. J'aime cet homme parce qu'il sait comprendre toutes les choses de la vie."]

20. Bebey himself drew attention to the possibility of reading his novels in this way when he referred to the resentment that many Cameroonians felt about being ruled by the northerner Ahidjo. See Norman Stokle, "Entretien avec Francis Bebey," *Présence Francophone* 16 (1978): 175–90.

21. Bebey, "Un jour, tu apprendras," in *Nouvelle Somme de la poésie du monde noir*, *Présence Africaine* 57 (1966): 13. ["Vis et travaille. / Alors, tu seras un homme."]

22. In "Le Roman soporifique" (*Cameroon Tribune* 831 [Mar. 27–28, 1977]: 2), Jacques Fame Ndongo accused Bebey of fleeing from the social problems he depicted in the most superficial terms, and in "Qu'est-ce qu'un écrivain?" (*Cameroun Tribune* 870 [May 15–16, 1977]: 2), Betsen a Nwatsok criticized him for the falsity and banality of his portrayals of African life. Groups of young people have even jeered him at concerts he has given in Cameroon.

23. For an account of Elonge's work, see Stephen Arnold, "The Ch-Oral Literature of Sir O. E. Elonge, Anglophone Cameroonian," in Norman Simms, ed., *Oral and Traditional Literatures* (Hamilton, N.Z.: Outrigger, 1982).

24. Bebey, *Concert pour un vieux masque*, p. 39. ["Nous voulons aimer / Nous *devons* aimer / Tout / Y compris l'amertume / qui prolonge indélicatement le passé / Aimer inlassablement."]

14. CULTURAL POLITICS IN AN AGE OF TRANSITION

1. Between 1973 and 1982, France's share of Cameroonian investment capital fell from 73% to 23.6%. After having monopolized foreign trade with Cameroon during much of the 1960s, it provided only 44.7% of the country's imports and bought only 21.8% of its exports in 1980. See Mark W. DeLancey, "Cameroon's Foreign Relations," in Michael G. Schatzberg and I. William Zartman, eds., *The Political Economy of Cameroon* (New York: Praeger, 1986), pp. 189–217.

2. Interview with Paul Soppo Priso (Apr. 9, 1982). ["Ça marche. L'expérience camerounaise est valable par rapport à ce que d'autres pays ont fait dans les mêmes conditions."]

3. In "The Practices of a Liberal Political Economy: Import and Export Substitution in Cameroon (1975–1981)" (in Schatzberg and Zartman, eds. *The Political Economy of Cameroon*, pp. 11–32), Jean-Claude Willame describes the artificial nature of the industrialization process in Cameroon and the general failure of agribusiness initiatives supported by joint venture capital, loans from the world bank, and government funding. One exception to this overall trend is the CDC, which was transformed into a successful parastatal enterprise and remained (after the government) the largest single employer in the country. See Mark DeLancey, "The Cameroon Development Corporation (1947–1977): Cameroonization and Growth," in Ndiva Kofele Kale, ed., *An African Experiment in Nation-Building: The Bilingual Cameroon Republic since Reunification* (Boulder, Colo.: Westview, 1980), esp. pp. 274–75. For a discussion of the agricultural situation in Cameroon, see Virginia DeLancey, "Agricultural Productivity in Cameroon," in Schatzberg and Zartman, eds., *The Political Economy of Cameroon*, pp. 133–60.

4. Jos-Blaise Alima, *Les Chemins de l'unité* (Paris: ABC, 1977), p. 176. ["Il n'y avait vraiment pas d'autre voie à suivre que celle empruntée par Ahmadou Ahidjo vers le 'rendez-vous de l'universel.' C'était la seule conforme aux voeux d'un peuple camerounais qui aspire à la paix et au progrès."]

5. Jacques Fame Ndongo, "Semaine culturelle nationale," *Cameroon Tribune*

1173 (May 19, 1978): 3. [". . . une société fraternelle, équilibrée et prospère."]

6. John W. Forje, *The One and Indivisible Cameroon: Political Integration and Socio-economic Development in a Fragmented Society* (Lund: University of Lund, 1981), Lund Political Studies 35, p. 151.

7. For a discussion of this publishing venture and its role in supporting leadership cults in francophone Africa, see Victor T. LeVine, "African Leaders as Comic Book Heroes," *Africa Report* 29 (Mar.-Apr. 1984): 64–66.

8. Willame, "The Practices of a Liberal Political Economy," p. 131.

9. In *Afriques indociles: Christianisme, pouvoir et Etat en société postcoloniale* (Paris: Karthala, 1988), Achille Mbembe demonstrates how people in newly independent countries such as Cameroon have developed silent and sophisticated means of resisting the hypocritical propaganda and the arbitrary exercise of power to which they have been subjected.

10. Non-Cameroonians also contributed to this rewriting of Cameroonian history. In this regard, particular attention should be drawn to Jean-François Bayart's *L'Etat au Cameroun* and Richard Joseph's *Radical Nationalism in Cameroun*.

11. Conversation with Jacques Fame Ndongo (Feb. 3, 1982). ["Il n'y a pas de morale dans la politique, il n'y a que des intérêts."]

12. Interview with Adamou Ndam Njoya (Feb. 17, 1982).

13. Charly-Gabriel Mbock, *Cameroun: L'Intention démocratique* (Yaounde: Institut des Sciences Humaines, 1985), pp. 119 and 123. ["Le Cameroun sera l'oeuvre des Camerounais ou ne sera pas." ". . . le Cameroun reste à inventer."]

14. For an account of the country's economic situation in the 1980s, see Jean Ngandjeu, *Le Cameroun et la crise* (Paris: L'Harmattan, 1988).

15. René Philombe, "Lettre ouverte à Paul Biya," *Peuples Noirs/Peuples Africains* 39 (1984): 1–15.

16. Joseph Charles Doumba, *Etre au carrefour* (Yaounde: CLE, 1977), p. 96. [". . . la culture est l'essentiel de la vie d'un peuple, ce qui, de positif, a survécu du passé; ce qui, en pleine gestation, surgit du présent; ce qui, en quête de dépassement, se projette dans l'avenir."]

17. Paul Biya, *Pour le liberalisme communautaire* (Lausanne and Paris: Pierre-Marcel Favre and ABC, 1987), p. 102. [". . . un homme camerounais libre, guidé par la raison, culturellement désaliéné et convaincu que l'homme n'est véritablement homme que s'il est créatif."]

18. Biya, *Pour le liberalisme communautaire*, p. 33. ["Il faut alors créer en chaque Camerounais les conditions d'une conscience nationale si profonde que l'attachement primaire et instinctif aux valeurs et intérêts tribaux et régionalistes ne puisse plus la perturber."]

19. An account of Biya's initiatives in these areas can be found in Mark W. DeLancey, *Cameroon: Dependence and Independence* (Boulder, Colo.: Westview, 1989), pp. 76–77.

20. For a description of these events, see Elenga Mbuyinga, *Tribalisme et problème national en Afrique Noire: Le Cas du Cameroun* (Paris: L'Harmattan, 1989), pp. 36–37.

21. Interview with J. M. Essomba, *Cameroon Tribune* 1606 (Oct. 20, 1979): 3. [". . . devrait donc conduire à une véritable affirmation de notre identité culturelle."]

22. André-Marie Atangana-Zang, *Les Relations socio-culturelles franco-camerounaises* (Yaounde: private, 1975), p. 81, and Jean Bahoken, *Cultural Policy in the United Republic of Cameroon* (Paris: UNESCO, 1976), p. 54.

23. *Fondements du renouveau culturel au Cameroun* (Yaounde: Saint Paul, 1974), p. 21. [". . . politiquement engagés conformément aux principes politiques définis par le parti de l'Union Nationale Camerounaise."]

24. Emmanuel Kengne Pokam, "La Religion face au pouvoir politique au Cameroun," unpublished thesis (Yaounde, 1980), pp. 611–12, and J. P. Biyiti bi Essam, *Cameroun: Complots et bruits de bottes* (Paris: L'Harmattan, 1984), p. 88.

25. Léon Messi, "Développons l'homme et tout l'homme," *Cameroon Tribune* 997 (Oct. 16–17, 1977): 4. ["On n'est pas moderne de la modernité des autres."]

26. The definition of language is a vexed question in this context and depends to a large extent on the way one distinguishes between languages and dialects. Estimates on the number of Cameroonian languages range from 60 to 250; the linguist Maurice Tadadjeu is an authority on the subject, and he places the figure at between 150 and 170.

27. Pierre Ngijol Ngijol, *Etudes sur l'enseignement des langues et cultures nationales* (Yaounde: Centre National d'Education, 1978), p. 3. ["Le développement dans notre pays ne peut s'opérer qu'à travers nos langues, seules propres à libérer et à épanouir le génie national."]

28. Interview with Clinton Robinson, Director of SIL (Mar. 2, 1982).

29. According to a survey reported in Tjadè Eonè's *Radios, publics et pouvoirs au Cameroun* (Paris: L'Harmattan, 1986), 87.2% of a sample population in Douala listened regularly to the radio, whereas only 14.1% regularly read the country's daily newspaper, the *Cameroon Tribune* (pp. 37–38). For a discussion of the government's attitude toward the media's role in cultural politics, see Bassek ba Kobhio, *Cameroun, la fin du maquis? Presse, livre et "ouverture démocratique"* (Paris: L'Harmattan, 1986), pp. 65–70.

30. Eyoh, "Cameroon Theatre," in Butake and Doho, *Théâtre camerounais/Cameroonian Theatre*, pp. 123–39.

31. According to Bassek ba Kobhio in *Cameroun, la fin du maquis?*, 74% of all books sold in Cameroon are school texts, and 14% are comics or photo-novels (p. 50).

32. In 1972, the Cameroonian government spent 55.8 million CFA francs to import school texts; spurred in part by large enrollment increases, that figure jumped to 117.8 million CFA francs the following year. See *Cameroon Tribune* 70 (Sept. 20, 1974): 2.

33. Interview with Jean Dihang, Director of Editions CLE, *Cameroon Tribune* 2308 (Jan. 23, 1982): 2.

34. Stephen Arnold has discussed this work in his "Preface to a History of Cameroonian Literature in English," *Research in African Literatures* 14 (1983): 489–515. Arnold is also preparing to publish the results of his preliminary survey of works submitted to the Guiness Contest.

35. Georges Tchianga, "Pour une littérature camerounaise," *Cameroon Tribune* 1319 (Nov. 9, 1978): 5. [". . . doit servir de catalyseur à la conscience nationale, dont elle est l'émanation et l'expression."]

36. Polycarpe Oyié Ndzié, "Cameroun et renouveau théâtral," unpublished m.s. (1982), p. 2. See also his "Problématique du théâtre négro-africain," *Cameroon Tribune* 1559 (Aug. 26–27, 1979): 2 and 1571 (Sept. 9–10, 1979): 2. ["Le théâtre peut participer réellement à la mobilisation nécessaire de toutes les énergies positives de la Nation pour l'érection d'un Cameroun fort, libre et prospère."]

37. Cited in *Cameroon Tribune* 1932 (Nov. 20, 1980): 1. ["La culture doit avoir un contenu civique, didactique, constructif, susceptible de contribuer efficacement à la cimentation de l'unité nationale."]

38. In addition to Roger Lagrave, Henry de Julliot, and Basil-Juléat Fouda's *Littérature camerounaise*, which was reprinted in 1971, historical and critical accounts of Cameroonian literature can be found in Adolph-Claude Mballa's *Le Théâtre camerounais des origines à nos jours* (Yaounde: Centre Fédéral et Linguistique, 1971), Jarmila Ortova's *Etude sur le roman camerounais* (Prague: Oriental Institute, 1971), Jacques Rial's *Littérature Camerounaise de langue française* (Lausanne: Payot, 1972), Patrice Kayo's *Panorama de la littérature camerounaise* (Yaounde: Librairie Populaire, 1979), Romain Konka's *Histoire de la littérature camerounaise* (Paris: private, 1983), René Philombe's *Le Livre camerounais et ses auteurs* (Yaounde: Semences Africaines, 1984), Josette Ackad's *Le Roman camerounais et la critique* (Paris: Silex, 1985), David Ndache Tagne's *Roman et réalités*

camerounaises (Paris: L'Harmattan, 1986), and Claire Dehon's *Le Roman camerounais d'expression française* (Birmingham, Ala.: Summa, 1989). Bibliographies, anthologies, and a partial list of university theses on Cameroonian literature are contained in Richard Bjornson, "A Bibliography of Cameroonian Literature," *Research in African Literatures* 17, 1 (1986): 89–90.

39. René Philombe, *Le Livre camerounais et ses auteurs* (Yaounde: Semences Africaines, 1984), p. 297. ["Aussi n'y a t'il utopie plus dangereuse que celle de concevoir la construction camerounaise sans eux et contre eux. Pour que l'unité nationale devienne réalité vivante, c'est à eux qu'il appartient de lui donner une dimension spirituelle."]

40. Jacques Fame Ndongo, *Le Prince et le scribe* (Paris: Berger-Levrault, 1988), p. 320. ["L'oeuvre exaltante de construction nationale exige la participation de tous."]

41. Buma Kor, "The Rough Edges," paper delivered at the First Colloquium on Cameroon Literature and Literary Criticism (Apr. 22, 1977).

42. For a detailed account of this debate, see Karen and Curtis Keim, "Literary Creativity in Anglophone Cameroon," *Research in African Literatures* 13 (1982): 73–77.

43. Bole Butake, "Introduction," *Thunder on the Mountain: An Anthology of Modern Cameroon Poetry* (Yaounde: private, 1981), p. iv. See also Butake and Nalova Lyonga, *Cameroon Literature in English: An Appraisal* (Yaounde: private, 1980). In addition to those who write in standard English, a few West Cameroonians have composed works in pidgin. For an account of this literature, see Abioseh M. Porter, "Smohl no bi sik: A Preliminary Survey of Pidgin Literature in Cameroon," *Pacific Quarterly (Moana)* 6, 3–4 (1981): 62–69.

44. Sankie Maimo, "Problems Facing Cameroon Literary Creativity," paper delivered at the First Colloquium on Cameroon Literature and Literary Criticism (Apr. 22, 1977), p. 6.

45. *La Presse du Cameroun* 7090 (Feb. 4, 1974): 3 and 7. Eldridge Mohammadou had already demonstrated the possibilities of this approach in his work on northern Cameroon. Mention should also be made of regional and ethnic historical studies by René Bell, Martin Njeuma, Martin Nkamgang, Albert Dongmo, Rabiatou Njoya, and Adamou Ndam Njoya. Achille Mbembe's work on the Bassa and Philippe Laburthe-Tolra's study of the Beti are particularly noteworthy in this regard. Tambi Eyongeteh and Robert Brain's *A History of the Cameroon* (London: Longman, 1974) redressed the imbalance of earlier francophone accounts by placing the political and cultural evolution of the anglophone West into the context of national history, but the overarching synthesis suggested by Wonyu remains to be done.

46. Interview with Jean-Baptiste Obama (Apr. 3, 1982). ["Qu'est-ce que nous allons laisser à nos enfants comme originalité culturelle camerounaise après cent ans d'existence?"]

15. WRITING AND POPULAR CULTURE

1. Fannie Lalande Isnard, "Vendre des livres en Afrique: Une Expérience," *The African Book Publishing Record* 6, 3–4 (1980): 205–207.

2. Interview with Léopold Moumé Etia (Jan. 26, 1982).

3. Chrétien Timamo, *Reflexions sur la condition humaine et sur quelques problèmes actuels de l'Afrique* (Yaounde: Le Flambeau, 1981). All four of Bengono Ewondo's surveys were published under the Quoi de Neuf imprint in Paris; they are *Les Jeunes Femmes* (1972), *L'Accueil des étrangers* (1976), *De l'amitié* (1979), and *La Solitude et l'union* (1980).

4. F. C. Ngam, *The Tricks of a Smuggler* (Victoria: private, 1980), p. 25.

5. Advertising flier "*Sur le Chemin du suicide*." ["Après avoir perdu tous ses parents dans un accident de circulation à Cotonu, après avoir été détourné, empoisonné, Naha

Désiré dit l'Enfant Maudit, a pu raconter sa vie triste et misérable dans un roman de 100 pages. Le jeune écrivain attend actuellement à Yaoundé une mort lente et impitoyable qui le guette car le cancer ne pardonne jamais. Si vous avez souffert dans votre vie ou si vous aimez connaître la souffrance des autres, lisez *Sur le Chemin du suicide.*"]

6. Naha Désiré, *Sur le Chemin du suicide* (Yaounde: Edition du Démi-Lettré, 1979), p. 21. ["... la mort ne sera plus, il n'y aura plus de souffrance, plus de guerre, plus de haine, ni de crime. Les maladies et les disettes seront choses du passé."]

7. Naha, *Le Destin a frappé trop fort* (Yaounde: Les Editions Populaires de Yaounde, 1980), p. 26. ["... il y aura du pain pour tout un chacun."]

8. These interviews were conducted by Karen Keim and reported in her "Popular Fiction Publishing in Cameroon," *The African Book Publishing Record* 9 (1983): 7–11.

9. Interview with Daniel Ndo, *Cameroon Tribune* 67 (Sept. 17, 1974): 4. ["Il faut un spectacle complet et total qui puisse embrasser la globalité de la vie africaine."]

10. Interview with Deiv K. Moktoï, *Cameroon Tribune* 1271 (Sept. 14, 1978): 2. ["... les nouvelles contradictions des sociétés africaines ... un développement global et équilibré des peuples africains."]

11. Deiv K. Moktoï (David Kemzeu), *L'Homme bien de là-bas* (Yaounde: Uhuru Drama Productions, 1980), p. 37. ["Je débrouille. Débrouiller n'est pas voler. Je ne souis pas un voleur!"]

12. Moktoï, *L'Homme bien*, p. 49. ["Il faut embellir la façade, Mr. Newrich."]

13. Antoine Ahanda, "1981: Bilan de l'année culturelle," *Cameroon Tribune* 2275 (Jan. 14, 1982): 2. ["... l'exploitation à la fois de préjugés tribaux et de comportements nés de l'inadaptation au modernisme rapide. Chez les trois, les farces les plus basses, les quiproquos, les images et les calembours utilisent un langage petit nègre qui fait rire des citadins convaincus d'être au-dessus de tout cela."]

16. THE REEMERGENCE OF MONGO BETI

1. In 1976 a new edition of the book became available in France, but it remained prohibited in Cameroon throughout Ahidjo's presidency.

2. Mongo Beti, "Lettre de Yaoundé: Cameroun 1958," *Preuves* 94 (1958): 58. ["... une solution élégante (apparement) pour maintenir les choses telles quelles."]

3. Beti, "L'Unité Africaine," *Revue Camerounaise* 14–15 (1960): 2. ["... une mascarade de marionettes grimaçantes."]

4. Beti, "Les Médias, voilà le vrai pouvoir!" *Peuples Noirs/Peuples Africains* 34 (1983): 3. ["... défendre la culture de son peuple et contrôler son image dans les médias ... se plier à la représentation que la culture du maître voulait bien donner de nous et, finalement, à l'intérioriser."]

5. Beti, "Les Langues africaines et le néo-colonialisme en Afrique francophone," *Peuples Noirs/Peuples Africains* 29 (1982): 116. ["La création totalement libre par les Africains d'oeuvres en français est le moyen idéal pour plier à leur fantaisie, à leur génie, à leur mentalité, aux tendances naturelles de leur prononciation une langue qui, autrement, demeurerait un idiome étranger, un simple instrument de mise en condition, un prétexte nouveau de leur séculaire esclavage."]

6. Beti, *Main basse sur le Cameroon: Autopsie d'une décolonisation* (1972; rpt. Paris: Maspero, 1977) p. 162. ["... les fondements psychologiques et socio-économiques d'un ordre de choses hypocrite et injuste."]

7. ORTF interview with Mongo Beti (Oct. 10, 1974). Cited in Arlette Chemain, "*Ville cruelle*: Situation oedipidienne, mère castatrice," *Présence Francophone* 13 (1976): 22. ["Dans *Perpétue*, je refais un peu *Main basse sur le Cameroun*."]

8. Beti, *Perpétue et l'habitude du malheur* (Paris: Buchet-Chastel, 1974), p. 79. ["Devant une Afrique enceinte et qui réclame les soins, nos prétendus gouvernements ... tournent le dos."]

9. Jacques Fame Ndongo, *L'Esthétique romanesque de Mongo Beti* (Paris: ABC and Présence Africaine, 1985), p. 316.

10. Akomo is the hero of many *mvet* cycles in south-central Cameroon. In *Le Roi miraculé*, he was the common ancestor from whom Essomba yearned to be descended, and in *Perpétue*, Essola was momentarily regarded as a reincarnation of Akomo by the people of his village. Martin Besterman discusses Mor-Zamba's relation to Akomo in "Structure du récit et mécanique de l'action révolutionnaire dans *Remember Ruben*," *Présence Francophone* 23 (1981): 61–77.

11. Fame Ndongo, *L'Esthétique romanesque*, p. 297.

12. Nearly all the French plotters in the scheme to impose a neocolonial system on the imagined country in Beti's novel have real-world counterparts. Langelot is a parody of Aujoulat, and Sandrinelli suggests the colonial administrator Pinelli as well as Gandolfi, who was a close collaborator of Ahidjo during his rise to power during the late 1950s. Both the administrator of the colonies, Godefroy, and the territorial governor, Jean Ramadier, were reputed to have written many of Ahidjo's early speeches. Characters such as Brède are mentioned in *Remember Ruben* under their real names. The point is that Beti clearly intends his description of the larger political scene to be read as an allegory of recent Cameroonian history.

13. Beti, *La Ruine presque cocasse d'un polichinelle* (Paris: Editions des Peuples Noirs, 1979), p. 184. ["Un homme qui tremble est un homme clôturé, paralysé."]

14. Beti, *La Ruine*, p. 237. ["Laissez-vous modeler par vos supérieurs comme un vase entre les mains du potier, qui pétrit la glaise à sa guise, sans rencontrer de résistance, car la moindre indocilité de la glaise gâcherait son ouvrage. Je suis le potier, et vous, vous êtes la glaise. C'est Dieu qui l'a voulu ainsi."]

15. Beti, *Les Deux Mères de Guillaume Ismaël Dzewatama, futur camionneur* (Paris: Buchet-Chastel, 1982), p. 195. ["Ne décide pas pour moi, je t'en prie."]

16. Hergé Xourbes is an obvious allusion to Hervé Bourges, who served as director of the International School of Journalism in Yaounde from 1970 to 1977. His arrival in Cameroon coincided with the Ouandié-Ndongmo trial, and Beti speculates that he orchestrated the Ahidjo government's badly needed public-relations efforts at that time.

17. Fame Ndongo, *L'Esthétique romanesque*, n. 4, p. 19.

18. Beti, *Deux Mères*, p. 53. [". . . sa vie devait être marquée de rebonds imprévisibles et menaçants, comme le trajectoire d'un ballon de football monstrueusement capricieux."]

19. Beti, "La Dormeuse et les flibustiers," *Peuples Noirs/Peuples Africains* 17 (1980): 100. [". . . on a toujours tort de désespérer du genre humain."]

17. THE RADICAL CRITIQUE OF POSTCOLONIAL SOCIETY

1. Elolongue Epanya Yondo, "Chants villageois," *Présence Africaine* 70 (1969): 119. ["Lutter! Aimer! Espérer / Et lutter encore / Pour tendre à l'homme / Le fruit de sa LIBERTE."]

2. René Philombe, "Les Blancs partis, les nègres dansent," *Les Blancs partis, les nègres dansent* (Yaounde: Semences Africaines, 1974), p. 12. ["Les blancs partis / les nègres dansent / mes les nègres dansent sur les nègres."]

3. Philombe, "Dénonciation civique," *Petites Gouttes de chant pour créer l'homme* (Yaounde: Semences Africaines, 1977), p. 22. ["Ouvrez les yeux, regardez-le: / Il ne peut prendre qu'un seul petit repas / Mais il veut engloutir les repas / De mille et une bouches / A la fois!"]

4. Philombe in Wolfgang Zimmer, "Chanter pour ceux qui n'ont pas le droit de chanter," in Reinhard Sander and Wolfgang Breitinger, eds., *Interviews avec les écrivains africains francophones* (Bayreuth: University of Bayreuth, 1986), Bayreuth African Stud-

ies Series 8, p. 94. ["Il faut qu'il ait le courage de se substituer à ce peuple baillonné, muselé, matraqué pour être son interprète. . . . Il a pour mission de bousculer les tabous, d'inviter le peuple à vomir l'indigeste, de susciter une reflexion responsable sur les problèmes du moment."]

5. Patrice Kayo, "Tout le long des saisons," *Tout le long des saisons* (Paris: Silex, 1983), pp. 34, 37–38. ["Elle n'a pas changé notre condition, mais nos maîtres." ". . . le perpétuel calvaire de notre existence, à savoir trimer pour que s'engraissent les patrons, les autorités. . . . Pour le riche, tout est permis. Le pauvre n'a que des devoirs."]

6. Benjamin Matip, *Laisse-nous bâtir une Afrique debout* (Paris: Africascope, 1979), p. 146. ["Laisse-nous . . . bâtir une Afrique nouvelle, une Afrique debout."]

7. Patrice Ndedi Penda, *Le Caméléon* (Yaounde: CLE, 1981), p. 40. ["C'est à nous que les Blancs ont passé le pouvoir, pas à eux. C'est notre pouvoir."]

8. Ndedi Penda, *Le Caméléon*, p. 35. ["Il n'y a plus d'élections, il y a des investitures."]

9. Interview with Patrice Ndedi Penda, January 27, 1982. [". . . une gangrène qui est en train de tout dévorer progressivement."]

10. Patrice Ndedi Penda, "Samakopé," unpublished m.s., p. 74. ["Chaque injustice commise au mépris de la dignité humaine, chaque souillure imposée à l'homme, chaque acte du vandalisme, est un brasier allumé dans un coin de la brousse. Et ce feu va grandir jusqu'à devenir un incendie qui sera nourri du sang des fossoyeurs de la nation."]

11. Marcien Towa, *L'Idée d'une philosophie négro-africaine* (Yaounde: CLE, 1979), p. 7. [". . . la philosophie est le courage de penser l'absolu."]

12. Interview with Marcien Towa, February 8, 1982. ["Je ne place rien au-dessus de l'esprit humain."]

13. Towa, *L'Idée*, p. 113. ["Lorsqu'on a une idée de ce qui est, il faut penser à ce qui doit être."]

14. Jean-Marc Ela, *La Plume et la pioche* (Yaounde: CLE, 1971); Ela, *Le Cri de l'homme africain* (Paris: L'Harmattan, 1980); Ela, *L'Afrique des villages* (Paris: Karthala, 1982); and Ela, *La Ville en Afrique Noire* (Paris: Karthala, 1983).

15. Ela, *Le Cri de l'homme africain* (Paris: L'Harmattan, 1980), p. 84. [". . . cimitières de l'intelligence."]

16. Ela, *Le Cri de l'homme africain*, p. 120. ["Notre tâche est claire: permettre à l'homme de renaître à une vie de liberté et de communion."]

17. Interview with Paul Dakeyo, *Presse du Cameroun* 6935 (July 25, 1973): 4. [". . . porter l'homme à la prise de conscience de la réalité actuelle, non pas la réalité folklorique des poèmes de la négritude."]

18. Dakeyo, *Soleils fusillés* (Paris: Droit et Liberté, 1977), p. 47. ["Mille morts marchent / Dans mes souvenirs."]

19. Dakeyo, *Le Cri pluriel* (Paris: Saint-Germaine-des-Prés, 1976), p. 37. ["Ma terre / Est une immense prison / Où planent les vautours."]

20. Dakeyo, "Si tu regardais," *Chant d'accusation* (Paris: Saint-Germaine-des-Prés, 1977), p. 35. ["Je ne suis qu'un étranger / Dans ce pays glacial / . . . / Foulant lourdement l'espace illicite / A la recherche de ma terre fidèle."]

21. Dakeyo, *Soweto soleils fusillés*, p. 22. ["La parole deliée / Le geste essentiel / La danse pluriel."]

22. Dakeyo, "Poésie et sociétés africaines," in Eugene van Itterbeck, *Europe/Afrique* (Louvain: Association Européenne pour la Promotion de la Poésie, 1984), p. 65. [". . . le vers d'un poème, une parole qui délivre, un verbe qui se reproduit."]

23. Bekate Meyong, "Au Pays des blancs," *Mânes sauvages* (Paris: Pierre Jean Oswald, 1975), p. 36. ["Le sourire du blanc est figé / ou préfabriqué / ou calculé / ou faux / Parfois utilitaire."]

24. Daniel Ewandé, *Vive le Président! La Fête africaine* (Paris: Albin Michel, 1968),

p. 109. ["La politique est comme la guerre. Il s'agit d'être du bon côté. On est victorieux lorsqu'on est vivant après la canonnade."]

25. Ewandé, *Vive le Président!*, p. 113. [". . . tout est pour le mieux dans la meilleure des Afriques possibles."]

26. Yodi Karone, *Le Bal des caïmans* (Paris: Karthala, 1980), p. 50. [". . . libre dans une société plus juste."]

27. Karone, *Le Bal des caïmans*, p. 116. ["Je suis un homme qui lutte pour l'indépendance réelle, pour la liberté, pour la justice, pour un monde neuf."]

28. Karone, *Le Bal des caïmans*, p. 43. [". . . notre bien-aimé et vénéré Président."]

29. Karone, *Nègre de paille* (Paris: Silex, 1982), p. 57. ["Là voici ma liberté."]

30. Timothée Ndzagaap, "Révélation," *Amoureuses Flammes* (Bafoussam: Librairie Populaire, 1977), p. 21. ["Où est donc la liberté?"]

31. Paul Tchakouté, "Manovers (cris absurdes)," *Corps jumeaux* (Bafoussam: Librairie Populaire, 1978), p. 24. ["Le cri de chaque homme / N'est que l'écho / De l'éternel soupir."]

32. J. M. Abanda, *"La Mort en silence," Cameroon Tribune* 2230 (Nov. 18, 1981): 2.

33. Augustin Millam, "Cauchemar et réalité," in Patrice Kayo, ed., *Anthologie de la poésie camerounaise de langue française* (Yaounde: Le Flambeau, n.d.), p. 72. ["J'étais profondément endormi cette nuit-là chez moi, / Alors, à pas de loup, 'ils' se sont approchés, ombres dans / l'obscurité, silencieux, évitant le moindre bruit. A l'heure / où le coq chante ils pénétrèrent brusquement, et me donnèrent / sans même me laisser m'habiller, sans une explication, / l'ordre menaçant de sortir; et poignets liés aux menottes d'injustice, / les bourreaux de ce siècle me conduisirent à la torture."]

34. Jean-Pierre Ghonda-Nounga, "Chant deuxième," *Chants pour Ruben . . . chants pour les martyrs* (Yaounde: private, 1980), p. 36. ["Au commencement était le verbe / et le verbe était l'humain. / Puis l'homme créa l'outil / il vit que cela était bon et sourit. / . . . un maître surgit bientôt d'entre les hommes / s'empara de l'outil / et asservit l'esclave / qui ne l'avait jamais été encore. / Le maître vit que tout cela était bon / et sourit / et sourit aujourd'hui encore."]

35. Ghonda-Nounga, "Appel à la race des déshérités," "Nausées Tropicals", unpublished m.s., p. 42. [". . . car dans la violence seule / s'invente ici / la LIBERTÉ."]

18. INDIVIDUAL IDENTITY AND MORAL IDEALISM

1. Bernard Nanga, *La Trahison de Marianne* (Dakar, Abidjan, Lomé: NEA, 1984), p. 243. ["Nous vivons entre deux mondes, deux mondes qui se complètent sans renier notre identité. C'est peut-être la seule façon d'être libre. . . ."]

2. Nanga, *La Trahison*, p. 30. ["J'avais l'âme française."]

3. Nanga, *La Trahison*, p. 151. ["Je reconnaissais mon Afrique natale. Une Afrique sans histoire, mais sans ruse ni mensonge, humiliée tout au long des siècles, saignée, mais toujours vivante et fière, confiante dans l'homme et sans rancune."]

4. Nanga, *La Trahison*, p. 160. ["Il s'agissait de retrouver mon unité perdue, d'être moi-même."]

5. Charly-Gabriel Mbock, *Quand saigne le palmier* (Yaounde: CLE, 1978), p. 85. ["Je sers le village, non pas un homme."]

6. Mbock, *La Croix du coeur* (Yaounde: CLE, 1982), p. 6. ["Celui qui est parvenu au coeur même de sa propre religion est parvenu au coeur de toutes les religions."]

7. Pabe Mongo is a pseudonym for Pascal Bekolo Bekolo, who grew up near the eastern Cameroonian city of Doumé. He freely admits that all the characters in the novel, including Bogam Woup, were inspired by actual people in his village. Interview with Bekolo Bekolo, February 14, 1982.

8. Delphine Zanga Tsogo, *L'Oiseau en cage* (Abidjan, Dakar, Lomé: NEA and Paris: EDICEF, 1983), p. 14. ["La femme est faite pour travailler dans les champs, avoir des enfants et nourrir la famille."]

9. Zanga Tsogo, *L'Oiseau en cage*, p. 66. ["Il n'est pas question d'aimer. Tu dois obéir. Tu ne t'appartiens pas et tu ne dois rien valoir. C'est ton père qui est le maître et ton devoir est d'obéir. Les choses sont ainsi, pour nous, depuis toujours."]

10. Zanga Tsogo, *L'Oiseau en cage*, p. 9. [". . . nous ne demandons qu'à être reconnues comme des personnes humaines, qu'à nous appartenir avant d'appartenir aux autres."]

11. *La Brise du jour* and *Lettre ouverte à Soeur Marie-Pierre* closely parallel the author's own lives. Etoundi M'Balla even unwittingly uses his own first name rather than that of his fictional hero on several occasions. In any case, the point being made here about the fictive narrator's relationship to his or her past also applies to the two authors' elaboration of the autobiographical materials in their respective texts.

12. Lydie Dooh Bunya, *La Brise du jour* (Yaounde: CLE, 1977), p. 347. ["Ce fut une belle idylle."]

13. Patrice Etoundi M'Balla, *Lettre ouverte à Soeur Marie-Pierre* (Yaounde: CLE, 1978), p. 17. ["Toi et moi, . . . nous sommes des êtres purs, sans tricherie et lavés de tout péché, parce que nous avons savouré ensemble un amour vrai, violent comme les rages de novembre et tendre comme le pardon d'un ami."]

14. Etoundi M'Balla, *Lettre ouverte*, p. 97. [". . . le crime n'existe pas en soi. Ce qui crée le crime, c'est uniquement notre propre conscience ou, plus souvent, la conscience de la société dans laquelle nous vivons."]

15. Etoundi M'Balla, *Lettre ouverte*, p. 168. [". . . cruauté intransigeante de notre société décadente."]

16. For an account of this promotional campaign and its relation to governmental policies, see Ambroise Kom, "La Tentation de l'institué: *Une Vie à l'envers* de Patrice Etoundi M'Balla," *Peuples Noirs/Peuples Africains* 59–62 (1987–88): 227–39.

17. Patrice Etoundi M'Balla, *Une Vie à l'envers* (Yaounde: SOPECAM, 1987), p. 83. ["Il ne voulait pas mourir, même au prix d'une liberté et d'une vérité sans entraves."]

18. Etoundi M'Balla, *Une Vie à l'envers*, p. 137. ["Les hommes . . . n'acceptent de vivre véritablement dans l'harmonie et l'unité que sous une certaine contrainte, sous la férule d'une autorité persuasive."]

19. Etoundi M'Balla, *Une Vie à l'envers*, p. 192. [". . . afin que tout se passe conformément aux lois supérieures et imprescriptibles qui assurent l'ordre du monde."]

20. Etoundi M'Balla, *Une Vie à l'envers*, p. 199. ["La seule forme d'engagement que vous devez choisir est de vous taire et de laissez faire."]

21. Joseph Nkou, *Edima* (Dakar, Abidjan, Lomé: NEA, 1984), p. 51. [". . . un bonheur vrai ne se donne pas. Il se conquiert. Il se mérite."]

22. David Ndache Tagne, *La Reine captive* (Paris: L'Harmattan, 1986), p. 26. ["Pauvre de moi. On m'a gâché mon existence."]

23. Ndache Tagne, *La Reine captive*, p. 222. [". . . je ne sais plus qui je suis."]

24. Simo is a francophone Cameroonian who initially wrote *The Little Gringo* as a composition exercise when he was a student in the United States. It revolves around his own maturation as the result of reflecting on the meaning of his saintly younger brother's death. Asheri's little book is a straightforward account of her childhood in the Banso area of the Northwest Province.

25. Joseph Ngongwikuo, *Taboo Love* (New York: Exposition Press, 1980), p. 36.

19. THE CORRUPT SOCIETY AND THE SENSITIVE SELF

1. In addition to behind-the-scenes pressures from influential persons who felt themselves slandered by the book, the portrayal of a village that declared its independence from the country convinced the government to take action against *Les Chauves-souris*. Interview with Joseph Charles Doumba (Mar. 13, 1982). As often occurs with prohibited works, *Les Chauves-souris* circulated widely throughout the country, much to the annoyance of the authorities. Part of its popularity was due to the fact that Nanga's allusions to real people permitted it to be read as a roman à clef.

2. Interview with Bernard Nanga (Feb. 15, 1982).

3. Bernard Nanga, *Les Chauves-souris* (Paris: Présence Africaine, 1980), p. 119. ["Il lui sembla qu'il avait traversé la vie comme le vent, qui carressait et touchait tout sans se fixer. Et au moment où il avait voulu s'accrocher, il n'embrassait que le vide. Un vide à multiples facettes, qui n'était que son vide intérieur."]

4. In Bulu, *Vémélé* means that which is rejected or expelled, especially when it is disgusting or repugnant.

5. Evemba Njoku'a'vembe (François-Borgia Marie Evembe), "Propos de bistrot," *Les Morts . . . de demain* (Yaounde: CLE,1983), p. 152. [". . . une matière sécrétée par la société moderne et composée de viol de conscience, de viol de mineurs, de vol de biens publics, d'honneurs recherchés, de pouvoir recherché, d'argent amassé. . . . C'est la pollution de l'authenticité humaine."]

6. Marie-Thérèse Assiga-Ahanda, *Sociétés africaines et "High Society": Petite Ethnologie de l'arrivisme* (Libreville: Lion, 1978), p. 74. [". . . livrer une guerre sans merci à son homologue, de peur qu'il ne lui ravisse le poste qu'il occupe, ou simplement pour le plaisir de l'empêcher de jouir des mêmes biens que lui."]

7. Sévérin Cécil Abéga, *La Latrine* (Dakar, Abidjan, Lomé: NEA, 1988), p. 139. ["Autour de leurs corps souillés, les mouches chantaient des hymnes de victoire."]

8. Calixthe Beyala, *C'est le soleil qui m'a brûlée* (Paris: Stock, 1987), p. 125. ["J'ai épousé les étoiles."]

9. Beyala, *C'est le soleil qui m'a brûlée*, p. 109. [". . . prisonniers ambulants attachés à leurs crasses."]

10. Beyala, *C'est le soleil qui m'a brûlée*, p. 174. ["C'est Moi ton âme."]

11. Calixthe Beyala, *Tu t'appelleras Tanga* (Paris: Stock, 1988), p. 77. ["Le monde est brisé. Il faut le recoller."]

12. Fernando D'Almeida, "Avant-Dire," *Au Seuil de l'exil* (Paris: Pierre-Jean Oswald, 1976), p. 11. [". . . par une voix crystalline, cette étrange voix qui vous parle intérieurement, silencieusement."]

13. D'Almeida, "LXX," *Au Seuil*, p. 44. ["J'ignore mon identité vraie."]

14. D'Almeida, "DCCXLIV," *Au Seuil*, p. 50. ["La nuit est proche et j'ai peur des ombres qui barrissent."]

15. D'Almeida, *Traduit du je pluriel* (Dakar, Abidjan, Lomé: NEA, 1980), p. 9. ["La parole m'a été léguée / pour poser bas le masque du mensonge / La parole m'a été donné / pour participer au rut de mon peuple."]

16. D'Almeida, *Traduit*, p. 45. [". . . retrouver les débris épars de mon Moi."]

17. D'Almeida, *Traduit*, p. 19. ["Du particulier enfin je nais pour atteindre l'universel."]

18. D'Almeida, "Je dis toujours exile," *L'Espace de l'exil* (Paris: Silex, 1984), p. 23. ["Pour m'engager dans la vie / J'ai brûlé mes livres scolaires."]

19. D'Almeida, "Part trente-deuxième," *En Attendant le verdict* (Paris: Silex, 1984), p. 42. ["Je suis chez moi, je suis vraiment chez moi."]

20. Christophe Nguedam, "Le Poète à midi," *Chemin du monde* (Paris: Pierre-Jean Oswald, 1973), p. 11. ["Poète dans un monde en lambeaux / où le bien et le mal sont confondus."]

21. Nguedam, "Perdu en moi-même," *Chemin*, p. 48. ["Ciel! je me suis perdu en plein jour / Dans la forêt dense de mon être."]

22. Vincent Boujeka Fodieng, "L'Homme-Prodige et la victoire finale, mes frères" and "Pour le Comice agro-pastoral de Bafoussam," *Au Sommet du Mont-Cameroun* (Yaounde: CEPER, n.d.), pp. 68–69, 70–72. ["Homme-Nation," "notre grand parti national"]

23. Pierre Epato Nzodam, "L'Afrique des autres," *Soleil ensoleillé* (Yaounde: Pouksié-Youkeka, 1977), p. 60. ["Afrique des autres, redeviens nôtre."]

24. Jean-Marcel Meka d'Obam, "Cameroun, pays bien aimé," *Le Prisonnier nostal-*

gique (Yaounde: Saint Paul, 1976), p. 16. ["Tu es tout pour moi, tout pour tes enfants qui t'aiment / Tu es une perle dorée pour celui qui connaît ton histoire."]

25. Ayuk Tabe-Ebob, "Assertion," *Manyu Folklore* (Bamenda: New African Press, 1970), p. 48.

26. Mesack Takere, "My Country," *Kingfisher Poetry: Man and Nature* (Yaounde: CEPER, 1981), p. 27.

27. Kewai Nyamgha, "Mandating Spectres," *Spectres on Scale* (Calabar: Scholars Press, 1980), p. 32.

28. Claude Nana Sunji, "L'Etat de mon âme," in Paul Dakeyo, ed., *Poèmes de demain: Anthologie de la poésie camerounaise d'expression française* (Paris: Silex, 1982), p. 227. ["Le plus faible cri d'insecte m'inquiète / Je suis hanté par mille désirs superflus."]

29. Antoine Assoumou, *Poèmes* (Yaounde: private, 1982), pp. 54–55, ["Adieu, je m'en vais me démasquer / Sous l'ombre métallique du lac / . . . / Me reconnaître enfin sur son tain d'argent."]

30. Assoumou, *Poèmes*, p. 39. ["Le pouvoir est perdu de dire fièrement *Je*."]

20. NEW VOICES IN CAMEROONIAN THEATER

1. Hansel Ndumbe Eyoh, "Cameroon Theatre," in Bole Butake and Gilbert Doho, eds., *Théâtre camerounais/Cameroonian Theatre* (Yaounde: BET, 1988), p. 124. In *Répertoire du théâtre camerounais* (Paris: L'Harmattan, 1986), Wolfgang Zimmer lists 712 dramas written by Cameroonians, but his tabulation does not include many of the plays submitted to the French National Radio drama contest or circulated in manuscript form. Well over a thousand Cameroonian dramas have been submitted to the ORTF contest, more than from any other country. Interview with Françoise Ligier, *Cameroon Tribune* 1963 (Dec. 28–29, 1980): 11. See also *Cameroon Tribune* 1782 (May 27, 1980): 3. For subsequent years, statistics have been compiled by the ORTF.

2. Theater receipts reported to the government are far higher in Yaounde than in any other Cameroonian city—approximately 80% of the total according to official statistics. See Mathias Balla, "Théâtre et droit d'auteur," in Butake and Doho, *Théâtre camerounais/Cameroonian Theatre*, pp. 249–56.

3. For a discussion of this group, see Clément Mbom, "Le Théâtre camerounais ou les reflets d'une société en pleine mutation," in Butake and Doho, *Théâtre camerounais/Cameroonian Theatre*, pp. 181–201.

4. See Hansel Ndumbe Eyoh et al., *Hammocks to Bridges: An Experience in Theater for Development* (Yaounde: BET, 1986).

5. These plays did attract some attention, for *Assimilados*, *Les Asticots*, and *Nyia Bariba* all received prizes in the early years of the French National Radio drama competition.

6. Tsino (pseud. for Vincent de Paul Tsoungui-Ngono), *Nyia Bariba* (Paris: ORTF-DAEC, 1973), p. 12. ["Le poète moderne doit en effet faire oeuvre de création avec les matériaux que la tradition met à sa disposition, créer des oeuvres modernes dignes d'être versées dans la Culture de l'Universel."]

7. Jean-Baptiste Obama, *Assimilados* (Paris: ORTF, 1972), p. 80. [". . . aussi riches que le 'Blanc.'"]

8. Nearly twenty years after writing *Ngonrogo*, Oto delivered a lecture at the 1987 colloquium on Cameroonian drama. At this time, he reiterated his belief that the country's drama still must be decolonized so that it can contribute in an appropriate way to the construction of a truly national society. Such a program was already implicit in *Ngonrogo*, which could almost be read as a response to his later comment: "Nous devons inventer, à partir des formes théâtrales de notre passé, des formes théâtrales nouvelles pour dramatiser nos problèmes, les exposer de manière simplifiée ou militante afin de tenter de les resoudre." James Oto, "Le Théâtre traditionnel camerounais: Son

Existence chez les Fang/Ntumu," in Butake and Doho, eds., *Théâtre camerounais/ Cameroonian Theatre*, p. 15.

9. Adamou Ndam Njoya in Wolfgang Zimmer, "Dynamisme de mon peuple: Entretien avec Adamou Ndam Njoya sur son théâtre," *Recherche, Pédagogie et Culture* 68 (1984): 77. [". . . donner un reflet de cette perfection divine, vers laquelle nous tendons sans jamais l'atteindre. . . ."]

10. Joseph Tagne, "Théâtre englobant: Un Art dramatique en expérimentation," *Cameroon Tribune* 1445 (Apr. 8–9, 1979): 2. See also Abel Zomo Bem, "Le Théâtre englobant de nouveau sur la sellette," *Cameroon Tribune* 1970 (Jan. 7, 1981): 2.

11. Interview with Bassek ba Kobhio, March 27, 1982. ["Il faut courir des risques pour rester honnête envers soi-même."]

12. Bidoung Mkpatt, *Les Charognards* (Yaounde: private, n.d.), p. 52. ["Je suis l'homme utile, . . . je sers mes frères, . . . la nation, . . . le peuple. . . . Je suis de ceux qui ont sacrifié leur existence pour améliorer le sort des autres."]

13. Raymond Ekossono, *Le Soleil rouge* (Yaounde: private, n.d.), p. 49. ["l'incarnation du mal. . . . un des plus grands criminels qu'ait connu notre paisible nation."]

14. Ekossono, *Le Soleil rouge*, p. 49. ["La vérité ne s'énonce pas: elle se cherche, s'élabore, se construit."]

15. Bassek ba Kobhio, *Demain peut-être*, p. 26. ["Avoir un idéal, c'est déjà le réaliser en partie."]

16. Alexandre Kum'a Ndumbe III, undated letter to Hansel Ndumbe Eyoh, cited in Eyoh, "The Development of Drama in Cameroon: 1959–1979," unpublished thesis (Leeds, 1979), p. 173. ["L'influence essentielle . . . est pour moi la fête africaine, le spectacle du village, où tout le monde participe, où il n'y a pas vraiment deux camps, mais une communauté qui crée et improvise. Là les 'vrais' acteurs ont plutôt un rôle de détonateur, ils invitent les autres et déclenchent un spectacle dont toutes les représentations sont différentes, grâce à l'improvisation et à l'apport de 'spectateurs' (participants) différents selon les soirées."]

17. Kum'a Ndumbe, *Kafra-Biatanga* (Paris: Pierre Jean Oswald, 1973), p. 12. ["La pièce n'a un sens que si elle fait comprendre."]

18. Kum'a Ndumbe, *Cannibalisme* (Paris: Pierre Jean Oswald, 1973), p. 69. ["Dansez la négritude / Et laissez-vous exploiter . . . / Chantez la négritude / Et baisser vos têtes / Dansez / La négritude / oubliez / vos droits."]

19. Kum'a Ndumbe, *Lisa, la putain de* . . . (Paris: Pierre Jean Oswald, 1976), p. 72. ["Pourquoi nous arrêtent-ils / Au lieu de nous donner du pain / Pourquoi nous frappent-ils / au lieu de nous dire comment / gagner son pain dans cette ville."]

20. Werewere Liking and Manuna-Ma-Njock (Marie-José Hourantier), *A la rencontre de* . . . (Abidjan, Dakar, Lomé: NEA, 1980), p. 62. [". . . nous n'étions qu'un seul et même corps."]

21. Since that time, Liking has continued to live in Abidjan, where she founded an artists' commune that doubles as a cultural museum and a theater in which she stages plays with giant puppets.

22. Liking, *Vision de "Kaydara" d'Hamadou Hampaté Ba* (Abidjan, Dakar, Lomé: NEA, 1984).

23. Liking, "Orphée Dafric," in Liking and Manuna ma Njock (Hourantier), *Orphée Dafric/Orphée d'Afrique* (Paris: L'Harmattan, 1981), p. 45. ["Seul, je ne peux rien faire. J'ai besoin d'être habité par une force qui me maintienne en moi-même, qui m'empêche de fuir ce corps trouble qui m'inquiète tant."]

CONCLUSION

1. Interview with Patrice Ndedi Penda, January 27, 1982. ["Ça m'a libéré de savoir que j'ai été autorisé à écrire en quelque sorte."]

INDEX